Uganda

the Bradt Travel Guide

Philip Briggs

with Andrew Roberts

edition

7

www.bradtguides.com

Bradt Travel Guides Ltd, UK
The Globe Pequot Press Inc, USA

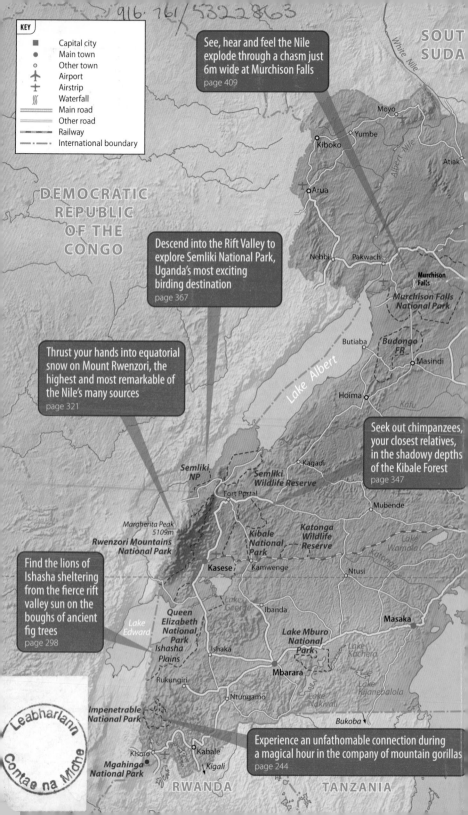

916.761/5322863

KEY

■	Capital city
●	Main town
○	Other town
✈	Airport
✈	Airstrip
≋	Waterfall
━━━	Main road
───	Other road
┣━┫	Railway
·─·─·	International boundary

See, hear and feel the Nile explode through a chasm just 6m wide at Murchison Falls
page 409

Descend into the Rift Valley to explore Semliki National Park, Uganda's most exciting birding destination
page 367

Thrust your hands into equatorial snow on Mount Rwenzori, the highest and most remarkable of the Nile's many sources
page 321

Seek out chimpanzees, your closest relatives, in the shadowy depths of the Kibale Forest
page 347

Find the lions of Ishasha sheltering from the fierce rift valley sun on the boughs of ancient fig trees
page 298

Experience an unfathomable connection during a magical hour in the company of mountain gorillas
page 244

SOUTH SUDAN

DEMOCRATIC REPUBLIC OF THE CONGO

White Nile

Moyo

Kiboko

Yumbe

Arua

Atiak

Albert Nile

Nebbi

Pakwach

Murchison Falls

Murchison Falls National Park

Butiaba

Budongo FR

Masindi

Lake Albert

Hoima

Kafu

Kagadi

Mubende

Semliki NP

Semliki Wildlife Reserve

Fort Portal

Margherita Peak 5109m
Rwenzori Mountains National Park

Kibale National Park

Katonga Wildlife Reserve

Lake Wamala

Kasese

Kamwenge

Ntusi

Katonga

Lake Edward

Lake George

Ibanda

Masaka

Queen Elizabeth National Park
Ishasha Plains

Ishaka

Lake Mburo National Park

Lake Kachera

Rukungiri

Mbarara

Lake Kijanebalola

Ntungamo

Lake Nakivali

Bukoba

Impenetrable National Park

Kisoro

Kabale

Kigali

Mgahinga National Park

RWANDA

TANZANIA

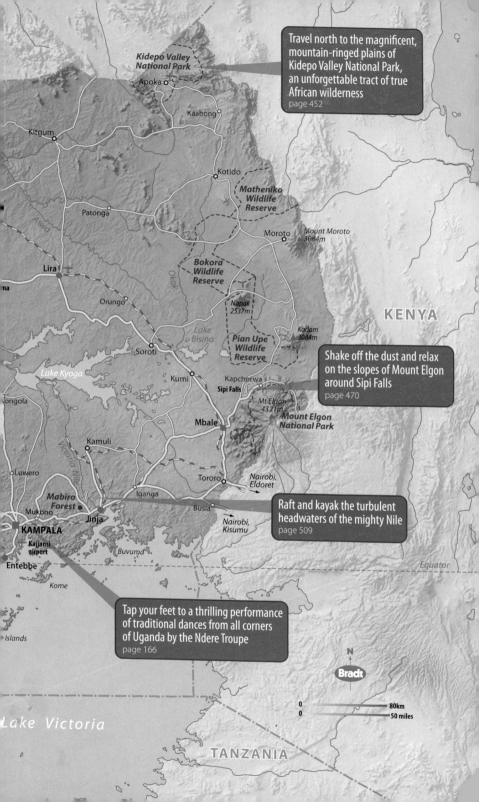

Travel north to the magnificent, mountain-ringed plains of Kidepo Valley National Park, an unforgettable tract of true African wilderness
page 452

Shake off the dust and relax on the slopes of Mount Elgon around Sipi Falls
page 470

Raft and kayak the turbulent headwaters of the mighty Nile
page 509

Tap your feet to a thrilling performance of traditional dances from all corners of Uganda by the Ndere Troupe
page 166

KENYA

TANZANIA

Kidepo Valley National Park
Apoka
Kaabong
Kitgum
Patonga
Assua
Kotido
Matheniko Wildlife Reserve
Moroto
Mount Moroto 3084m
Lira
Bokora Wildlife Reserve
Orungo
Napak 2537m
Lake Bisina
Pian Upe Wildlife Reserve
Kadam 3084m
Soroti
Kumi
Lake Kyoga
Kapchorwa
Sipi Falls
Mt Elgon 4321m
Mbale
Mount Elgon National Park
Kamuli
Kamuli
Victoria Nile
Tororo
Nairobi, Eldoret
Mabiro Forest
Mukono
Iganga
Busia
Nairobi, Kisumu
KAMPALA
Jinja
Kajjansi airport
Buvuma
Entebbe
Kome
Equator
Lake Victoria
Islands

N

Bradt

0   80km
0   50 miles

Uganda
Don't
miss...

White-water rafting
Every year, thousands of
adventure seekers enjoy
thrills and spills on the
turbulent headwaters of
the Nile near Jinja
(NR) pages 515–16

Fort Portal region
Between the Rwenzori and the
forest of Kibale National Park, the
landscape is pocked by dozens of
delightful volcanic crater lakes
(AVZ) pages 356–62

Tree-climbing lions

The unusual tree-climbing behaviour of Ishasha's lion prides makes these felines unusually easy to spot

(FLPA) page 299

Mountain-gorilla tracking

Few visitors are unmoved by the magical hour spent in the presence of a group of mountain gorillas

(AVZ) pages 242–3

Murchison Falls

At Murchison Falls, the Nile explodes through a 6m-wide gorge to form the most dramatic feature along its 6,650km course

(SS) pages 408–11

Uganda in colour

above left   Dugout canoes provide the simplest route to market for farmers living around Lake Bunyonyi (AVZ) pages 252–60

above right   Towering above the plains of eastern Uganda, Mount Kadam marks the gateway into the vast and undeveloped region of Karamoja (AVZ) pages 456–7

below   On the vast, semi-arid plains of Karamoja, hundreds of families still live in traditional *manyattas* (MT) pages 451–62

above Thanks to fertile soils, ample sunshine and abundant water, you'll see colourful displays of fresh market produce all year round (SS)

right Brightly coloured stools for sale at a stall along the Mbarara Road (AVZ) pages 216–17

below To travellers, the distinctive, long-horned cattle of Ankole are a traffic hazard; to the local pastoralists they are revered possessions (AVZ) page 226–7

above While Kampala's surburban sprawl extends along the western side of Lake Victoria's Murchison Bay, the eastern side remains distinctly rural (GC/A) pages 133–179

below Seen from surrounding hills, central Kampala still gives the appearance of a city arising from the rainforest (AVZ) pages 133–79

AUTHOR

Philip Briggs is a travel writer and tour leader specialising in east and southern Africa. Born in Britain and raised in South Africa, he started travelling in East Africa in 1986, and his first book *Guide to South Africa* was published by Bradt in 1991. Since then, Philip has divided his time between exploring and writing about the highways and byways of Africa. In addition to authoring or co-authoring 14 Bradt travel guides covering countries such as Tanzania, Rwanda, Uganda, Ghana, Ethiopia, Malawi, Somaliland and Mozambique, he has contributed to numerous other books, and to various travel and wildlife magazines.

MAJOR CONTRIBUTORS

Andrew Roberts has lived in Uganda since 1993. Born in Britain, he first visited the country with a backpack in 1990 and returned three years later to help the Ugandan Forest Department set up ecotourism projects. Twenty years later he's still there, now with a wife and two daughters. Andrew considers himself lucky to have worked in every national park in Uganda, settings which he greatly prefers to his office in Kampala. When not revising Bradt *Uganda* (this is his third update) he produces tourist maps.

Ariadne Van Zandbergen, who took most of the photographs for this book and contributed to the research, is a freelance photographer and tour guide. Born and raised in Belgium, she travelled through Africa from Morocco to South Africa in 1994/95 and is now resident in Johannesburg. She has visited 25 African countries and her photographs have appeared in numerous books, magazines, newspapers, maps, periodicals that pamphlets. She has recently established her own photo library (*www.africaimagelibrary.com*).

PUBLISHER'S FOREWORD   *Hilary Bradt*

Uganda is a fairy tale. You climb up a railway instead of a bean-stalk and at the top there is a wonderful new world. The scenery is different, and most of all the people are different from anywhere else in Africa.

Winston Churchill, 1908

On our trip north from Cape Town to Cairo in 1976, George and I liked Uganda more than any other country – and that despite being arrested during the aftermath of the Entebbe Raid. It wasn't necessarily the most interesting, but the people, landscape and wildlife were superb. For overlanders backpacking through Africa, the welcome (or otherwise) you get at the border post can colour your impressions for the rest of your stay. It took us three days to walk and hitch to the Ugandan border post from what was then Zaire, and, in the politically turbulent Amin era, we were afraid that we would be refused entry. George wrote: 'A Ugandan border guard walked towards us, starched khaki shorts, crisply ironed shirt, bright boots, and said, "Welcome to Uganda!" We were completely overwhelmed … After he'd finished stamping us in he said, "But there is one problem …" Our hearts sank. "… about transport. But some men are driving into Kasese tonight if you'd care to wait for them."'

I have not had the opportunity to return to Uganda since that memorable trip, but reading Andy's excellent update to Philip's ground-breaking Uganda guide convinces me that I must not leave it much longer.

Seventh edition published September 2013   First published in 1994

Bradt Travel Guides Ltd
IDC House, The Vale, Chalfont St Peter, Bucks SL9 9RZ, England
www.bradtguides.com

Print edition published in the USA by The Globe Pequot Press Inc, PO Box 480, Guilford, Connecticut 06437-0480

Text copyright © 2013 Philip Briggs
Maps copyright © 2013 Bradt Travel Guides Ltd
Illustrations/photographs copyright © 2013 Individual photographers and artists
Cover image research: Pepi Bluck
Project manager: Claire Strange

ISBN: 978 1 84162 467 9
e-ISBN: 978 1 84162 772 4 (e-pub)
e-ISBN: 978 1 84162 674 1 (mobi)

British Library Cataloguing in Publication Data
A catalogue record for this book is available from the British Library

Photographs and illustrations See page 560 for details.
Maps David McCutcheon FBCart.S
Colour map Relief map bases by Nick Rowland FRGS; additional map content supplied by Andrew Roberts/Uganda Maps

Typeset from the author's disc by Wakewing
Production managed by Jellyfish Print Solutions and manufactured in India

Acknowledgements

FROM PHILIP BRIGGS This seventh edition was updated almost single-handedly by Andrew Roberts, which leaves me little to say other than echo the acknowledgements below, and to thank Andrew for his abundant dedication to the task – may the travellers who use this edition come to appreciate the thoroughness of his efforts as much as I do!

FROM ANDREW ROBERTS Thanks are due to many people for helping this project to completion. First up is Nakajiri Maureen at Mweya Safari Lodge. Confused by a prolonged bout of research into how guests might expect to be wined and dined at Ndali Lodge, I left behind my copy of Bradt Uganda. On reaching Mweya, the following evening, Maureen kindly provided me with a replacement. Chapters six through nine might otherwise have turned out rather differently. Huge thanks also to Billy Reynell for driving me around the fabulous Kidepo-Karamoja circuit (page 453) in the White Baron and to John Hunwick for making a traverse of the Rwenzori a viable proposition.

Thanks also to the numerous people who provide up-to-date information both in person in Uganda and by emails to Phil's blog. These include Koen Sneyers, Dr Dick Stockley, Paula Robinson of VSO, Mary Ann Legan in Buhoma, Michael Reeve, Ian Baird-Smith, Anton Summerer, Gile and Heidi, Karen Treisman, Rolf Rabe, Fred Hodgson, Simon Turner of Malaika Honey and Dr Chris 'Rwenzori' Kidd.

Thanks also to Uganda Wildlife Authority staff around the country for responding to my reams of questions, notably Aggie Nakide in QENP, Fred Kizza and Christine Gumunya in Rwenzori, Balyesiima Godfrey and Geoffrey Twinomuhangi in Bwindi, Joshua Masereka at Murchison Falls, Steven Nyabru on Mount Elgon, Augustine in Kitgum, Johnson Masereka, Leslie Muhindo and Lotok Bernard in Kidepo, Florence in Kotido and Steven Masaba and Andrew Seguya in Kampala.

For assistance and hospitality whilst on the road I'm indebted to Aubrey and Clare Price, Chris Wilson, and Steve and Asha Williams in Fort Portal; Bingo Little, Cam Mcleay, Rainer Holst, Paul and Amina in the Jinja area; Chris and Georgie Higginson, Kara Blackmore and Nature Lodges at Murchison; Rukia Mwai, Anil Ghei, Richard Hodgson and Fred Andimilleh Makumbi at Marasa; Paul and Jane Goldring and their managers, Neil Tereszczak in Ishasha and Kenneth Mambo in Bwindi; Crystal Safaris in Bwindi; Jennifer Nyiramugisha in Kisoro; Grace Kooja in Hoima; Ivan Mbabazi at Lake Bunyonyi; Nelson in Mbarara; Sand Beach at Nabugabo; Masiga Wilson in Gulu; Priscilla Alowo in Kitgum; Patrick and Lynn Devy in Kidepo; George in Moroto; Lucy Chemtai in Mbale; and Neil and Teri at Sipi. I'm also grateful to my wife Sarah and my daughters Eleanor and Caitlin for their company along some of the roads travelled. I'm obliged too to Philip Briggs for having handed over his guidebook, nurtured by him for nigh on 20 years for me to update again.

Contents

LIST OF MAPS

ATTENTION WILDLIFE ENTHUSIASTS

For more on wildlife in Uganda why not check out Bradt's *East African Wildlife*. Go to www.bradtguides.com and key in UGANWILD40 at the checkout for your 40% discount.

NOTE ABOUT MAPS

Several maps use grid lines to allow easy location of sites. Map grid references are listed in square brackets after listings in the text, with page number followed by grid number, eg: [181 C3]. Accommodation and restaurants and their grid references are listed in key boxes next to maps of towns and cities.

Introduction

Nearly 20 years ago, in the introduction to the first edition of this guide, I wrote that Uganda's attractions 'tend towards the low-key'. Six editions later, when I re-read this assertion for the first time in years, my initial reaction was – well – bemusement, unease, even embarrassment.

Meeting the eyes of a mountain gorilla on the bamboo-clumped slopes of the Virungas? Rafting Grade 5 rapids on the Nile? Following a narrow rainforest trail awhirl with the heart-stopping pant-hoot chorusing of chimpanzees? Cruising the Kazinga Channel in the shadow of the Rwenzoris while elephants drink from the nearby shore? Watching a prehistoric shoebill swoop down on a lungfish in the brooding reed beds of Mabamba Swamp? The roaring, spraying sensory overload that is standing on the tall rocks above Murchison Falls ... Low-key? Goodness me – short of landing on the moon, what exactly would I have classified as a must-do or must-see attraction when I wrote that line?

But as I flicked through that yellowing first edition, all 150 pages of it, my unease slowly dissipated. It had not, I realised, been a reflection of any significant change in my own perceptions during the intervening decade, but rather of the remarkable strides made by Uganda in general, and its tourist industry specifically.

Uganda has changed. And how! When I first visited in 1988, Uganda's economy, infrastructure and human spirit – every aspect of the country, really – were still tangibly shattered in the aftermath of a 15-year cycle of dictatorship and civil conflict that had claimed an estimated one million human lives. Come 1992, when I researched the first edition of this guide, Uganda was visibly on the mend, but, a steady trickle of backpackers aside, its tourist industry remained in the doldrums. Incredible as it seems today, there was no facility to track gorillas within Uganda in 1992, no white-water rafting, no realistic opportunity to get close to chimpanzees, and the likes of Queen Elizabeth and Murchison Falls national parks were practically void of game. And many other tourist sites that today seem well established either didn't exist in their present form, were off-limits or unknown to travellers, or were far less accessible than they are now.

Uganda today does not lack for accessible travel highlights. There is the opportunity to trek within metres of one of the world's last few hundred mountain gorillas, arguably the most exciting wildlife encounter Africa has to offer – though observing chimps in the Kibale or Budongo runs it a damn close second. There is the staggering recovery made by Uganda's premier savanna reserves, where these days one can be almost certain of encountering lions, elephants and buffaloes, etc. There are the Rwenzoris and Mount Elgon, where one can explore East Africa's bizarre montane vegetation without the goal-oriented approach associated with ascents of mounts Kilimanjaro or Kenya. And there is Bujagali Falls, which – with its white-water rafting, kayaking and recently introduced bungee jump – is rapidly emerging as East Africa's answer to that more southerly 'adrenalin capital', Victoria Falls.

Nor does Uganda lack for tourist facilities. As recently as ten years ago, international-class hotels and restaurants were all but non-existent outside the capital. Today, by contrast, practically every major attraction along the main tourist circuits is serviced by one – or two, or three – luxury lodges and/or tented camps. Trunk roads have improved beyond recognition, as has the overall standard of local tour operators, public transport, budget accommodation, restaurants and service in general.

It should be noted, too, that the country's natural attractions far exceed the opportunity to see gorillas and lions and so on. Somebody once said that if you planted a walking stick overnight in the soil of Uganda, it would take root before the morning dawned. And it is certainly true that of all Africa's reasonably established safari destinations, Uganda is the most green, the most fertile – the most overwhelmingly tropical!

Uganda, in an ecological nutshell, is where the eastern savanna meets the west African jungle – and it really does offer visitors the best of both these fantastic worlds. In no other African destination can one see a comparable variety of primates with so little effort – not just the great apes, but also more than ten monkey species, as well as the tiny wide-eyed bushbaby and peculiar potto. And if Uganda will have primate enthusiasts wandering around with imbecile grins, it will have birdwatchers doing cartwheels. Uganda is by far the smallest of the four African countries in which more than 1,000 bird species have been recorded, and it is particularly rich in western rainforest specialists – in practical terms, undoubtedly the finest birdwatching destination in Africa.

And yet for all that, Uganda does feel like a more intimate, unspoilt and – dare I say it? – low-key destination than its obvious peers. For starters, it has no semblance of a package tourist industry: group tours seldom exceed eight in number, and even the most popular game-viewing circuits retain a relatively untrammelled atmosphere. The country's plethora of forested national parks and reserves remain highly accessible to independent travellers and relatively affordable to those on a limited budget, as do such off-the-beaten-track gems as the Ssese Islands, Katonga Wildlife Reserve, Sipi Falls and Ndali-Kasenda Crater Lakes.

Uganda has changed. More than 30 years after Idi Amin was booted into exile, and over two decades after President Museveni took power, the country bears few obvious scars of what came before. Today, Uganda enjoys one of the healthiest reputations of any African country when it comes to crime directed at tourists. The level of day-to-day hassle faced by independent travellers is negligible. And Ugandans as a whole – both those working within the tourist industry and the ordinary man or woman on the street – genuinely do come across as the most warm, friendly and relaxed hosts imaginable.

It's been with growing pleasure that I've documented Uganda's progress, as a country and as a tourist destination, over the course of six editions of this guidebook. And this progress is, I hope, reflected in the evolution of the book – from its backpacker-oriented earliest incarnation into this totally reworked and vastly expanded seventh edition, which provides thorough coverage of all aspects of the country for all tastes and budgets. But progress begets progress, and doubtless the next few years will see a host of new and exciting tourist developments in Uganda.

My first visit to Uganda, in late 1988, was decidedly lacking in premeditation. I'd flown from London to Nairobi with broad thoughts of travelling through Tanzania to South Africa over a few months. But on my first night in town, I had a couple of beers with an enthused Canadian who'd just bussed back from Uganda, and was persuaded to revise my plans.

My memories of that first trip to Uganda reflect the decades of war and deprivation that had culminated in the coup of 1986. Bananas, bananas everywhere and nothing else to eat. Buses that took a day to cover 100km of violently pot-holed road. Heaped toilet bowls whose flush mechanism was habitually disused after years without running water. Buildings scarred with bullet holes. The pitiful war orphans who accosted me at every turn.

But there was also much to enjoy. I was enchanted by the verdant landscapes of the west, thrilled by a semi-successful gorilla track in what was then the Impenetrable Forest Reserve (heard them, could see where they were, never actually saw them – all in all, a reasonable return for an investment of US$1), and felt a growing empathy with the guarded optimism, expressed by most of the Ugandans to whom I spoke, that the dark days just might be in the past.

And, with the notable exception of the civil war in the far north, so they were. By 1992, Uganda, once a byword for the worst malaises associated with post-independence Africa, was sufficiently stable for Bradt to commission me to research and write a guidebook to the country. Since then, it's been my privilege to watch and document Uganda as it embarked on one of the most staggering economic and political transformations of our time, to become, in the words of a recent Oxfam report, 'an inspirational economic success story, and a symbol of a more vibrant, successful Africa'.

For the latest travel news about Uganda, please visit the new interactive Bradt Uganda update website (*http://updates.bradtguides.com/uganda*).

Administered by *Uganda* author, Philip Briggs, this website supplements the printed Bradt guidebook, and provides a forum where the latest travel news can be publicised online with immediate effect.

This update website is a free service for readers of Bradt's *Uganda* – and for anybody else who cares to drop by and browse – but its success will depend greatly on the input of those selfsame readers, whose collective experience of Uganda's tourist attractions and facilities will always be more broad and divergent than those of any individual author.

So if you have any comments, queries, grumbles, insights, news or other feedback, you're invited to post them directly on the website, or to email them to Philip at e philipbriggs@bradtguides.com.

x

Part One

GENERAL INFORMATION

Area 235,796km² (91,041 square miles), similar to Great Britain or the state of Oregon

Location Equatorial Africa between latitudes 4°12′N and 1°29′S and longitudes 29°35′W and 25°E. Bordered by Rwanda (169km) and Tanzania (396km) to the south, Kenya (933km) to the east, South Sudan (435km) to the north and the Democratic Republic of Congo (DRC) for 765km to the west.

Altitude 85% of the country lies between 900m and 1,500m above sea level. The lowest region is the Lake Albert basin (612m) and the Albert Nile. The highest point is Mount Stanley (Rwenzoris) at 5,109m.

Population 34.5 million (2011), 13% urban. Previously 28 million (2002), 16.7 million (1991), 12.6 million (1980), 9.5 million (1969), 6.5 million (1959), 5 million (1940), 3.5 million (1931), 2.9 million (1921) and 2.5 million (1911).

Capital Kampala (estimated population 1.65 million in 2013)

Other major towns Gulu, Lira, Jinja. Other towns with populations of more than 50,000 are Mbale, Mbarara, Masaka, Entebbe, Kasese and Njeru in descending order.

Language English, the official language, is spoken by most reasonably educated Ugandans. Among the country's 33 indigenous languages, Luganda is the closest to being a lingua franca.

Religion Christian (85%), Islam (11%), also some Hindu and Jewish, while tribes such as the Karimojong adhere to a traditional animist faith.

Currency Uganda shilling; Ush2,600–2,200 = US$1 in 2013 (NB: A rate of Ush2,500/US$1 was used when updating this book)

Head of State President Yoweri Museveni (since 1986)

Time zone GMT+3

International dial code +256 (Kampala: 414)

Electricity 240 volts at 50Hz

Mineral resources Copper, cobalt, limestone, salt, alluvial gold, oil.

Major exports Coffee (55%), fish (7.5%), tea (5%), tobacco (4%)

Other crops Bananas, maize, millet, sorghum, cotton, rice, cassava, groundnuts, potatoes

GDP US$16.8 billion per annum (US$1,354 per capita, annual growth rate 6.7% in 2011).

Human development Average life expectancy 53.6 years; under-five mortality rate 9.9%; adult (age 15-49) HIV/AIDS prevalence 6.5% (estimate); primary school completion 56%; secondary school enrolment 22%; adult literacy 65%; access to safe water 66%; access to electricity 4%

Land use Arable land 25%; agriculture 9%; pasture 9%; forest and woodland 28%; open water 18%; marsh 4%; other 7%

National flag Two sets of black, yellow and red horizontal stripes, with a white central circle around the national bird, the grey crowned crane

National anthem

Oh! Uganda, May God uphold thee, We lay our future in thy hand,
United, free, for liberty, Together, We always stand.
Oh! Uganda the land of freedom, Our love and labour we give,
And with neighbours all at our country's call, In peace and friendship we'll live.
Oh! Uganda the land that feeds us, By sun and fertile soil grown,
For our own dear land we'll always stand, The Pearl of Africa's crown.

1

Background Information

GEOGRAPHY AND CLIMATE

Uganda lies on the elevated basin which rises between the eastern and western branches of the Great Rift Valley. Most of the country is over 1,000m in altitude, and the topography is generally quite flat. The most mountainous part of Uganda is the Kigezi region in the southwest. North of Kigezi, on the Congolese border, the 70km-long and 30km-wide Rwenzori Mountains form the highest mountain range in Africa; Margherita Peak (5,109m) on Mount Stanley, the highest point in the Rwenzori, is exceeded in altitude on the African continent only by the free-standing Mount Kenya and Mount Kilimanjaro. Other large mountains in Uganda include the volcanic Virunga range on the border with Rwanda and the DRC, and Mount Elgon, a vast extinct volcano straddling the Kenyan border. There are several smaller volcanic mountains in the north and east.

With the exception of the semi-desert in the extreme northeast, most of Uganda is well watered and fertile. Almost 25% of the country's surface area is covered by water. Lake Victoria, the largest lake in Africa and second-largest freshwater body in the world, is shared by Uganda with Tanzania and Kenya. Lakes Albert, Edward and George lie on or close to the Congolese border, while the marshy and ill-defined Lake Kyoga lies in the centre of Uganda. At Jinja, on the Lake Victoria shore, Owen Falls (now submerged by the Owen Falls Dam) is regarded as the official source of the Nile, the world's longest river. The Nile also passes through lakes Kyoga and Albert.

Uganda's equatorial **climate** is tempered by its elevated altitude. In most parts of the country, the daily maximum is between 20°C and 27°C and the minimum is between 12°C and 18°C. The highest temperatures in Uganda occur on the plains immediately east of Lake Albert, while the lowest have been recorded on the glacial peaks of the Rwenzori. Except in the dry north, where in some areas the average annual rainfall is as low as 100mm, most parts of Uganda receive an annual rainfall of between 1,000mm and 2,000mm. There is wide regional variation in rainfall patterns. In western Uganda and the Lake Victoria region it can rain at almost any time of year. As a rough guide, however, the wet seasons are from mid-September to November and from March to May (see the *Climate chart* box overleaf).

HISTORY

Africa is popularly portrayed as a continent without history. Strictly speaking, this is true, as history by definition relies upon written records, and there are no written records of events in central Africa prior to the mid 19th century. All the

3

CLIMATE CHART

KAMPALA (1,155m)

	Jan	Feb	Mar	Apr	May	Jun	Jul	Aug	Sep	Oct	Nov	Dec
Ave max (°C)	28	28	27	26	26	25	25	26	27	27	27	27
Ave min (°C)	18	18	18	18	17	17	17	16	17	17	17	17
Rainfall (mm)	45	60	125	170	135	75	50	85	90	100	125	105

ENTEBBE (1,145m)

	Jan	Feb	Mar	Apr	May	Jun	Jul	Aug	Sep	Oct	Nov	Dec
Ave max (°C)	27	26	26	25	25	25	25	25	26	26	26	26
Ave min (°C)	17	18	18	18	17	16	16	16	16	17	17	17
Rainfall (mm)	75	95	155	250	240	115	75	75	75	80	130	115

FORT PORTAL (1,540m)

	Jan	Feb	Mar	Apr	May	Jun	Jul	Aug	Sep	Oct	Nov	Dec
Ave max (°C)	27	27	26	26	25	25	25	25	25	25	25	26
Ave min (°C)	12	13	14	14	14	13	13	13	13	14	14	12
Rainfall (mm)	20	75	125	190	130	85	60	110	195	210	165	75

KABALE (1,950m)

	Jan	Feb	Mar	Apr	May	Jun	Jul	Aug	Sep	Oct	Nov	Dec
Ave max (°C)	24	24	23	22	22	23	23	24	24	24	23	23
Ave min (°C)	10	10	11	12	11	10	9	10	11	11	11	10
Rainfall (mm)	50	100	125	120	95	25	20	45	95	100	115	90

GULU (1,110m)

	Jan	Feb	Mar	Apr	May	Jun	Jul	Aug	Sep	Oct	Nov	Dec
Ave max (°C)	32	32	31	29	28	28	26	27	28	29	29	31
Ave min (°C)	17	18	18	18	18	17	17	17	17	17	17	16
Rainfall (mm)	10	35	85	160	200	140	155	215	165	140	95	30

MASINDI (1,145m)

	Jan	Feb	Mar	Apr	May	Jun	Jul	Aug	Sep	Oct	Nov	Dec
Ave max (°C)	31	31	30	29	29	28	27	27	28	29	30	30
Ave min (°C)	12	12	13	13	13	12	12	12	12	12	13	12
Rainfall (mm)	20	50	10	140	135	95	100	45	120	125	110	45

MBALE (1,150m)

	Jan	Feb	Mar	Apr	May	Jun	Jul	Aug	Sep	Oct	Nov	Dec
Ave max (°C)	32	32	31	29	28	28	27	28	28	29	30	3
Ave min (°C)	16	17	17	17	17	16	16	15	15	16	16	1
Rainfall (mm)	25	60	90	160	175	130	110	135	105	80	65	4

JINJA (1,145m)

	Jan	Feb	Mar	Apr	May	Jun	Jul	Aug	Sep	Oct	Nov	Dec
Ave max (°C)	29	30	29	28	27	27	27	28	28	29	30	29
Ave min (°C)	15	15	15	15	15	14	14	15	15	15	15	14
Rainfall (mm)	50	70	120	170	130	65	50	105	80	95	100	85

same, it would be foolish to mistake an absence of documentation for an absence of incident, as do those historical accounts of African countries which leap in the space of a paragraph from the Stone Age to the advent of colonialism.

Without written records to draw from, scholars of pre-colonial African history have to rely on two main resources: archaeological evidence and oral traditions. As a rule these resources are riddled with contradictions and open to a diversity of interpretations, making it impossible to say with any certainty what happened in any given region prior to the arrival of Europeans.

Events in Uganda between AD1100 and the present appear to be a happy exception to the above rule. As I read over various sources, I was struck by the remarkable degree of correlation between the oral traditions of the various kingdoms of Uganda and the more objective evidence unearthed by modern archaeologists. When stripped of the quasi-religious trappings and mythologising which are to be expected in any folk history, the oral traditions of Uganda seem to me to be a reasonably accurate and consistent account of actual events.

A NOTE ON TERMINOLOGY Most Bantu languages use a variety of prefixes to form words so that several similar words are made from a common root. When discussing the various peoples and kingdoms of Uganda, this can be somewhat confusing.

The most common prefixes are *mu-*, *ba-* and *bu-*, the first referring to an individual, the second to the people collectively, and the third to the land they occupy. In other words, a Muganda is a member of the Baganda, the people who live in Buganda. The language of the Baganda is Luganda and their religion and customs are Kiganda. To use another example, the Banyoro live in Bunyoro, where they speak Runyoro and follow Kinyoro customs.

There is not a great deal of consistency in the use of these terms in the English-language books. Some use the adjective *Ganda* to describe, for instance, the *Ganda kabaka* (King of Buganda). Others will call him the Muganda or Baganda kabaka. Standards are more flexible when dealing with ethnic groups other than the Baganda: the Ankole people are usually referred to as the Banyankole but I've never seen the kingdom referred to as Bunyankole; the people of Toro are often referred to as the Batoro but I've not come across the term Butoro. In this following historical account, I've generally stuck with what seems to be the most common usage: prefixes for -ganda, -nyoro and -soga; no prefixes for Ankole and Toro.

The name Uganda of course derives from the word Buganda. The most probable reason why the British protectorate came to be known by this abbreviated name is that most Europeans had their initial contact with Buganda through KiSwahili-speaking guides and translators. In KiSwahili, the prefix *u-* is the equivalent of the Luganda *bu-*, so that the Swahili speakers would almost certainly have referred to the Ganda kingdom as Uganda. Although many Baganda writers evidently find it annoying that their country has been misnamed in this way, it does simplify my task that there is a clear distinction between the name of Uganda the country and that of Buganda the kingdom.

When referring to the leaders of the various Ugandan groups, the title *kabaka* is bestowed on the Baganda king, the title *omakuma* on the Banyoro king, and *omugabe* on the Ankole king.

EARLY PREHISTORY It is widely agreed that the entire drama of human evolution was enacted in the Rift Valley and plains of East Africa. The details of this evolution are obscured by the patchy nature of the fossil record, but the combination of DNA evidence and two recent 'missing link' discoveries (the fossils of a 4.4-million-year-old hominid in the Ethiopian Rift Valley and a 5.6-million-year-old jawbone unearthed in the Turkana Basin in northern Kenya) suggests that the ancestors of modern humans and modern chimpanzees diverged roughly five to six million years ago.

Uganda has not thrown up hominid remains of comparable antiquity to those unearthed in Kenya, Tanzania and Ethiopia, largely because there are few places in the country where fossils of a suitable age might be sought. Nevertheless, it is reasonable to assume that Uganda has supported hominid life for as long as any other part of East Africa, an assumption supported by the discovery in Moroto district of fossils belonging to the semi-bipedal proto-hominid *Morotopithecus*, which is thought to have lived about 15 million years ago.

Stone Age implements dating to more than one million years ago have been discovered throughout East Africa, and it is highly probable that this earliest of human technologies arose in the region. For a quarter of a million years prior to around 8000BC, Stone Age technology was spread throughout Africa, Europe and Asia, and the design of common implements such as the stone axe was identical throughout this area. The oldest Stone Age sites in Uganda, Nsongezi on the Kigezi River and Sango Bay on Lake Victoria, were occupied between 150,000 and 50,000 years ago.

The absence of written records means that the origin and classification of the modern peoples of east and southern Africa are a subject of some academic debate. Broadly speaking, it is probable that East Africa has incurred two major human influxes since 1000BC, on both occasions, by people from west Africa.

IN THE BEGINNING ...

Ggulu, the creator, sent his daughter Nambi and her siblings on a day trip to earth, where they chanced upon its only human inhabitant: poor lonely Kintu, who lived in the vicinity of Lake Wamala, west of present-day Kampala, his sole companion a beloved cow. Nambi was at once attracted to Kintu and upset at his enforced solitude, and she determined there and then to marry and keep him company on earth. Nambi's brothers were appalled at her reckless decision, and attempted to dissuade her, eventually reaching the compromise that she and Kintu would return to heaven to ask Ggulu's permission to marry. Ggulu reluctantly blessed the union, but he did advise the couple to descend to earth lightly packed and in secret, to avoid being noticed and followed by Nambi's brother Walumbe, the spirit of disease and death.

The next morning, before dawn, the delighted newly weds set off for earth, carrying little other than Nambi's favourite chicken. When they arrived, however, Nambi realised that she had forgotten to bring millet to feed the chicken and decided to return to heaven to fetch it. Kintu implored Nambi to stay, fearing that she might encounter Walumbe, and suggesting that a substitute chicken feed would surely be available on earth. But Nambi ignored Kintu's pleadings and returned to heaven, where sure enough she bumped into Walumbe, who – curious as to where his sister might be headed so early in the morning – followed her all the way back to join Kintu.

A few years later, Kintu, by then the head of a happy family, received a visit from Walumbe, who insisted that he be given one of their children to help with his household chores. Heedful of his father-in-law's warning, Kintu refused Walumbe, who was deeply angered and avenged himself by killing Kintu's eldest son. When Kintu returned to heaven to ask for assistance, Ggulu chastised him for ignoring the warning, but he agreed nevertheless to send another son Kayikuzi to bring Walumbe back to heaven. Walumbe refused to leave earth, however, so that Kayikuzi was forced to try and evict him against his will. The brothers fought violently, but the moment Kayikuzi gained an upper hand, Walumbe vanished underground. Kayikuzi dug several large holes, found Walumbe's hiding place, and the two resumed their fight, but soon Walumbe fled into the ground once again, and so the pattern repeated itself.

The first of these influxes probably originated somewhere in modern-day DRC about 3,000 years ago. The descendants of these invaders, known locally as the Bambuti or Batwa, were slightly built hunter-gatherers similar in culture and physique to the Khoisan of southern Africa and the pygmoid people who still live in certain rainforests near the Congolese border. The rock paintings on several shelters near Mbale in eastern Uganda show strong affinities with Khoisan rock art, suggesting that at one time these people occupied most of Uganda, as did they most of east and southern Africa at the beginning of the 1st millennium AD.

The second human influx, which reached the Lake Victoria hinterland in roughly 200BC, apparently coincided with the spread of Iron Age technology in the region. There is good reason to suppose that the people who brought iron-working techniques into the region were the ancestors of the Bantu speakers who probably occupied most of sub-equatorial Africa by AD500. Few conclusive facts are known about the political and social structures of the early Bantu-speaking peoples who inhabited Uganda, but it is reasonable to assume that they lived in

After several days, Kayikuzi, now nearing exhaustion, told Kintu and Nambi he would try one last time to catch Walumbe, at the same time instructing them to ensure that their children stayed indoors and remained silent until his task was done. Kayikuzi chased Walumbe out of hiding, but some of Kintu's children, who had disobeyed the instruction, saw the sparring brothers emerge from underground and they started screaming, giving Walumbe the opportunity to duck back into his subterranean refuge. Kayikuzi, angry that his earthly charges had ignored his instructions, told them he was giving up the chase, and the embarrassed Kintu did not argue. He told Kayikuzi to return to heaven and said: 'If Walumbe wishes to kill my children, so be it. I will keep having more, and the more he kills, the more I will have. He will not be able remove them all from the face of the earth.'

And so ends the Kiganda creation myth, with its Old Testament association between human disobedience and the arrival of death and disease on earth. And one question raised by this story is the connection between Kintu the first man and Kintu the founding Kabaka of Buganda. It is often assumed that these two seminal Kintus of Kiganda lore are one and the same figure, a mythical embodiment of the creation of both mankind and Buganda. But certain Muganda traditionalists assert otherwise. Kintu, the first person on earth, they concede, is clearly an allegorical figure whose story has no basis in historical fact. But Kintu the founder of Baganda is a wholly separate person, and quite possibly a genuine historical figure.

The 'two Kintus' claim is legitimised by the contrast between the unambiguous absence of other humans in the creation myth, and the presence of humanity explicit in any foundation legend in which one king defeats another king and rules over his former subjects. There is a popular Kiganda saying, derived from the mythical Kintu's last words, that translates as 'Kintu's children will never be removed from the face of the earth.' And if this saying does pre-date the foundation of Buganda, then it is plausible – even likely – that the founder of Buganda would have adopted Kintu as his throne name, with the deliberate intention of legitimising his rule by association with the mythical father of mankind.

loosely assembled chiefdoms similar to the pre-colonial *ntemi* structures which existed in the Tanzanian interior until colonial times.

It has been established beyond doubt that relatively centralised political systems made an early appearance in Uganda. The origin of the first of these kingdoms, Bunyoro-Kitara, is shrouded in legend, and the rough date of its foundation has yet to be determined by scholars. Nevertheless, a number of archaeological sites in the Mubende and Ntusi districts of central Uganda suggest that Bunyoro-Kitara was established long before AD1500.

THE BATEMBUZI AND BACWEZI (AD1100–1500) Kinyoro and several other local oral traditions assert that the first dynasty to rule over Bunyoro-Kitara was the Batembuzi. These traditions place the Batembuzi as having ruled between 1100 and 1350, and there is ample physical evidence at Ntusi to confirm that a highly centralised society existed in this area as early as the 11th century.

The origin of the Batembuzi is obscured by legend and myth, but they must have ruled for several generations, as various local traditions list between ten and 22 dynastic kings. Oral traditions name Ruhanga, the King of the Underworld, as the founder of the dynasty (the Kinyoro Underworld is evidently closer to the Christian notion of heaven than to that of hell) and they consider the Batembuzi to have been deities with supernatural powers. Descriptions of the Batembuzi's physical appearance suggest that they may have migrated to the area from modern-day Sudan or Ethiopia. Whatever their origins, they evidently became culturally and linguistically integrated into the established Bantu-speaking culture of Bunyoro-Kitara.

Most traditions identify Isuza as the last Batembuzi ruler. Isuza is said to have fallen in love with a princess of the Underworld, and to have followed her into her homeland, from where he couldn't find his way back to Bunyoro-Kitara. Years later, Isuza's son Isimbwa visited Bunyoro-Kitara, and he impregnated the only daughter of the unpopular stand-in king, Bukuku. Their child, Ndahura, was thrown into a river shortly after his birth at the order of Bukuku, who had been told by diviners that he should fear any child born by his daughter; but his umbilical cord stuck in a tree, keeping him afloat, and he was rescued by a royal porter. Ndahura was raised by the porter and, after he reached adulthood, he drove Bukuku's cattle from his home, stabbed the king in the back, and claimed the throne as his own. His claim was supported by the people of Bunyoro-Kitara, who accepted that the true royal lineage was being restored because of Ndahura's striking physical resemblance to his grandfather Isuza.

Ndahura – 'the uprooter' – is remembered as the founder of the Bacwezi dynasty. The Bacwezi were most probably migrants from Ethiopia or Sudan (hence the physical resemblance between Ndahura and Isuza?), who, like the Batembuzi before them, adopted the language and culture of the local Bantu speakers over whom they assumed rule. Ndahura was almost certainly a genuine historical figure, and he probably came to power in the second half of the 14th century. In addition to having supernatural powers, Ndahura is traditionally credited with introducing Ankole cattle and coffee cultivation to Uganda.

The Mubende and Ntusi areas are identified by all traditional accounts as lying at the heart of Bunyoro-Kitara during the Bacwezi era, an assertion which is supported by a mass of archaeological evidence, notably the extensive earthworks at Bigo bya Mugyenyi and Munsa. This suggests that the Bacwezi Empire covered most of Uganda south and west of the Nile River. Traditional accounts claim that it covered a much larger area, and that Ndahura was a militant expansionist who led successful raids into parts of western Kenya, northern Tanzania and Rwanda.

Ndahura was captured during a raid into what is now northern Tanzania. He eventually escaped, but he refused to reclaim the throne, instead abdicating in favour of his son Wamala. Ndahura then disappeared, some claim to the Fort Portal region. He abandoned his capital at Mubende Hill to his senior wife, Nakayima, who founded a hereditary matriarchy that survived into the colonial era. Wamala moved his capital to an unidentified site before eventually relocating it to Bigo bya Mugyenyi.

Considering the immense Bacwezi influence over modern Uganda – almost all the royal dynasties in the region claim to be of direct or indirect Bacwezi descent – it is remarkable that they ruled for only two generations. Tradition has it that Wamala simply disappeared, just like his father before him, thereby reinforcing the claim that the Bacwezi were immortal. It is more likely that the collapse of the dynasty was linked to the arrival of the Luo in Bunyoro-Kitara towards the end of the 15th century. Whatever their fate, the Bacwezi remain the focus of several religious cults, and places like the Nakayima Tree on Mubende Hill and the vast earthworks at Bigo bya Mugyenyi near Ntusi are active sites of Bacwezi worship to this day.

BUNYORO, BUGANDA AND ANKOLE (1500–1650)

In the second half of the 15th century, the Nilotic-speaking Luo left their homeland on the plains of southeastern Sudan, and migrated southwards along the course of the Nile River into what is now Uganda. After settling for a period on the northern verge of Bunyoro-Kitara at a place remembered as Pubungu (probably near modern-day Pakwach), they evidently splintered into three groups. The first of these groups remained at Pubungu, the second colonised the part of Uganda west of the Nile, and the third continued southwards into the heart of Bunyoro-Kitara.

It was probably the Luo invasion which ended Bacwezi rule over Bunyoro-Kitara. The Bacwezi were succeeded by the Babiito dynasty, whose founder Rukidi came to Bunyoro from Bukidi (a Runyoro name for anywhere north of Bunyoro). The tradition is that Rukidi was the son of Ndahura and a Mukidi woman, and that he was invited to rule Bunyoro by the Bacwezi nobles before they disappeared. Many modern scholars feel that the Luo captured Bunyoro by force, and that they integrated themselves into the local culture by claiming a genetic link with the Bacwezi, adopting several Bacwezi customs and rapidly learning the local Runyoro tongue.

The arrival of the Luo coincided with the emergence of several other kingdoms to the south and east of Bunyoro, notably Buganda and Ankole in modern-day Uganda, as well as Rwanda, Burundi and the Karagwe kingdom in what is now northwest Tanzania. All these kingdoms share a common Bacwezi heritage. Kinyoro and Kiganda traditions agree that Buganda was founded by an offshoot of the Babiito dynasty, while Ankole traditions claim that Ruhinda, the founder of their kingdom, was yet another son of Ndahura. Ankole retained the strongest Bacwezi traditions, and its most important symbol of national unity was a royal drum or Bagyendwaza said to have been owned by Wamala.

Bunyoro was the largest and most influential of these kingdoms until the end of the 17th century. It had a mixed economy, a loose political structure, and a central trade position on account of its exclusive control of the region's salt mines. Bunyoro was presided over by an *omakuma*, who was advised by a group of special counsellors. The omakuma was supported at a local level by several grades of semi-autonomous chiefs, most of whom were royally appointed loyalists of aristocratic descent.

Prior to 1650, Buganda was a small kingdom ruled over by a *kabaka*. Unlike those in Bunyoro, the local chiefs in Buganda were hereditary clan leaders and not normally of aristocratic descent. Buganda was the most fertile of the Ugandan kingdoms, for which reason its economy was primarily agricultural. Ankole, by contrast, placed great importance on cattle, and its citizens were stratified into two classes: the cattle-owning Bahima, who claimed to be descendants of Ruhinda, and the agriculturist Bairu. Ankole was ruled by an *omugabe*. As with the Omakuma of Bunyoro and the Kabaka of Buganda, this was a hereditary title normally reserved for the eldest son of the previous ruler. Positions of local importance were generally reserved for Bahima aristocrats.

Another identifiable polity to take shape at around this time was the Busoga, which lies to the east of Buganda and is bordered by Lake Kyoga to the north and Lake Victoria to the south. The Basoga show strong linguistic and cultural affiliations to the Baganda, but their oral traditions suggest that their founder, remembered by the name of Mukama, came from the Mount Elgon region and had no Bacwezi or Babiito links. Busoga has apparently assimilated a large number of cultural influences over the centuries, and it seems to have remained curiously detached from the mainstream of Ugandan history, probably by allying itself to the dominant power of the time.

An indication of Bunyoro's regional dominance in the 16th century comes from the traditional accounts of the wars fought by Olimi I, the fifth omakuma. Olimi is said to have attacked Buganda and killed the kabaka in battle, but he declined to occupy the conquered territory, opting instead to attack Ankole (of the several explanations put forward for this superficially peculiar course of action, the only one that rings true is that Olimi was after cattle, which were scarce in Buganda but plentiful in Ankole). Olimi occupied Ankole for some years, and according to Kinyoro traditions he withdrew only because of a full solar eclipse, an event which Banyoro traditionalists still consider to be portentous. If this tradition is true (and there is no reason to doubt it), Olimi must have been ruling Bunyoro at the time of the solar eclipse of 1520. Assuming that the four Babiito rulers who preceded Olimi would together have ruled for at least 30 or 40 years, this suggests that the Babiito dynasty and the Buganda and Ankole kingdoms were founded between 1450 and 1500.

BUNYORO, BUGANDA AND ANKOLE (1650–1850) At its peak in the 17th century, Bunyoro covered an area of roughly 80,000km^2 south and west of the Nile and Lake Victoria. Buganda was at this time no more than 15,000km^2 in area, and Ankole covered a mere 2,500km^2 north of the Kagera River. Similar in size to Buganda, the relatively short-lived Kingdom of Mpororo, founded in about 1650, covered much of the Kigezi region of Uganda, as well as parts of what is now northern Rwanda, until its dissolution in the mid 17th century.

The period between 1650 and 1850 saw Bunyoro shrink to a fraction of its former area and relinquish its regional dominance to Buganda. The start of this decline can be traced to the rule of Omakuma Cwa I (or Cwamali) in the late 17th or early 18th century. During Cwa's reign, Bunyoro suffered an epidemic of cattle disease. Cwa ordered all the cattle in the kingdom to be killed, and he then raided Ankole to seize replacements. Cwa occupied Ankole for three years, after which he attempted to extend his kingdom into Rwanda. He was killed in Rwanda and his returning troops were evicted from Ankole by Omugabe Ntare IV, who thereby earned himself the nickname Kitabunyoro – 'the scourge of Bunyoro'. After chasing out the Banyoro, Ntare IV extended Ankole's territory north to the Karonga River.

Bunyoro descended into temporary disarray as the aristocracy tried to cover up the omakuma's death, and the empty throne was seized by one of his sisters, stimulating a succession war that lasted for several years. Buganda took advantage of Bunyoro's weakness by taking control of several of its allied territories, so that in the years following Cwa's death it doubled in area. It is unclear whether Buganda acquired these territories by conquest or merely by exploiting the faltering loyalty of chiefs who were traditionally allied with Bunyoro.

Also linked to the upheavals following Cwa's death was the migration of the Palwo, the name given to the Luo speakers who had settled in the north of Bunyoro two centuries earlier. Some of the Palwo settled in Acholi, the part of northern Uganda east of the Albert Nile, where they founded several small Luo-speaking kingdoms modelled along the traditions of Bunyoro. Others migrated through Busoga in eastern Uganda to the Kisumu region of what is now western Kenya, where they are still the dominant group. A few groups settled in Busoga, south of modern-day Tororo, to found a group of small kingdoms known collectively as Jopadhola.

In 1731, Omakuma Duhaga took the Banyoro throne. Kinyoro traditions remember him as being small, light-skinned, hairy and difficult, and as having had the second-greatest number of children of any omakuma (the third omakuma, Oyo I, reputedly had 2,000 children, a record which will take some beating). During Duhaga's 50-year reign, Buganda annexed the area around Lake Wamala, as well as the land immediately west of the Victoria Nile, from where it plundered large parts of Busoga. Duhaga died in battle along with 70 of his sons, attempting to protect Bunyoro from Baganda expansionists.

By the reign of Omakuma Kyebambe III (1786–1835), Buganda was firmly entrenched as the major regional power. During the late 17th century, Kabaka Mutebi consolidated his power by dismissing some traditional clan leaders and replacing them with confirmed loyalists; by the end of the 18th century, practically every local chief in Buganda was one of the so-called 'king's men'. Buganda forged loose allegiances with Busoga and Karagwe (in northern Tanzania), and they maintained a peaceful equilibrium with Ankole, which had in the meantime further expanded its territory by absorbing several parts of the former Mpororo kingdom. Towards the end of Kyebambe III's rule, Bunyoro was dealt a further blow as several local princes decided to rebel against the ageing omakuma. The most significant rebellion was in Toro, where a prince called Kaboyo declared autonomous rule in 1830, depriving Bunyoro of its important salt resources at Katwe.

By the mid 19th century, Buganda stretched west from the Victoria Nile almost as far as Mubende and over the entire Lake Victoria hinterland as far south as the Kagera River. Ankole covered an area of roughly 10,000km^2 between the Karonga and Kagera rivers, and the newly founded Toro kingdom occupied a similar area north of the Karonga. Bunyoro had been reduced to a quarter of its former size; although it had retained the Nile as its northern boundary, there was now no point at which it stretched further than 50km south of the Kafu River.

BUNYORO AND EGYPT (1850–89) The death of Omakuma Kyebambe III was followed by a period of internal instability in Bunyoro, during which two weak omakumas ruled in succession. In 1852, the throne was seized by Kamurasi, who did much to stop the rot, notably by killing a number of rebellious princes at the Battle of Kokoitwa. Kamurasi's rule coincided with the arrival of Arab traders from the north, who were admitted into Bunyoro in the recognition that their support could only strengthen the ailing kingdom. The Arabs based themselves at Gondoroko, from where they led many brutal raids into the small and relatively defenceless Luo kingdoms of Acholi.

In 1862, Kamurasi's court welcomed Speke and Grant, the first Europeans to reach Bunyoro. Two years later, Bunyoro was entered from the north by Samuel Baker, a wealthy big-game hunter and incidental explorer who travelled everywhere with his

In 1862, Speke spent weeks kicking his heels in the royal capital of Buganda, awaiting permission to travel to the river he suspected might be the source of the Nile. His sojourn is described in four long and fascinating chapters in *The Journal of the Discovery of the Source of the Nile*, the earliest and most copious document of courtly life in the kingdom.

The following extracts provide some idea of the everyday life of the subjects of Kabaka Mutesa – who is remembered as a more benevolent ruler than his predecessor Suuna or successor Mwanga. The quotes are edited to modernise spellings and cut extraneous detail.

A more theatrical sight I never saw. The king, a good-looking, well-figured, tall young man of 25, was sitting on a red blanket spread upon a platform of royal grass, scrupulously well dressed in a new *mbugu*. His hair was cut short, excepting on the top, where it was combed up into a high ridge, running from stem to stern like a cockscomb. On his neck was a large ring of beautifully worked small beads, forming elegant patterns by their various colours. On one arm was another bead ornament, prettily devised; and on the other a wooden charm, tied by a string covered with snakeskin. On every finger and every toe, he had alternate brass and copper rings; and above the ankles, halfway up to the calf, a stocking of very pretty beads. Everything was light, neat, and elegant in its way; not a fault could be found with the taste of his 'getting up'.

Both men, as is the custom in Uganda, thanked Mutesa in a very enthusiastic manner, kneeling on the ground – for no-one can stand in the presence of his majesty – in an attitude of prayer, and throwing out their hands as they repeated the words N'yanzig, N'yanzig, ai N'yanzig Mkahma wangi, etc, etc, for a considerable time; when, thinking they had done enough of this, and heated with the exertion, they threw themselves flat upon their stomachs, and, floundering about like fish on land, repeated the same words over again and again, and rose doing the same, with their faces covered with earth; for majesty in Uganda is never satisfied till subjects have grovelled before it like the most abject worms …

The king loaded one of the carbines I had given him with his own hands, and giving it full-cock to a page, told him to go out and shoot a man in the outer court; which was no sooner accomplished than the little urchin returned to announce his success, with a look of glee such as one would see in the face of a boy who had robbed a bird's nest, caught a trout, or done any other boyish trick. I never heard, and there appeared no curiosity to know, what individual human being the urchin had deprived of life …

The Namasole entered on a long explanation, to the following effect. There are no such things as marriages in Uganda; there are no ceremonies attached to it. If any man possessed of a pretty daughter committed an offence, he might give her to the king as a peace offering; if any neighbouring king had a pretty daughter, and the King of Uganda wanted her, she might be demanded as a fitting tribute. The men in Uganda are supplied with women by the king, according to their merits, from seizures in battle abroad, or seizures from refractory officers at home. The women are not regarded as property, though many exchange their daughters; and some women, for misdemeanours, are sold into slavery; whilst others are flogged, or are degraded to do all the menial services of the house ...

Congow was much delighted with my coming, produced *pombe*, and asked me what I thought of his women, stripping them to the waist. I asked him what use he had for so many women? To which he replied, 'None whatever; the king gives them to us to keep up our rank, sometimes as many as one hundred together, and we either turn them into wives, or make servants of them, as we please ...'

The king was giving appointments, plantations, and women, according to merit, to his officers. As one officer, to whom only one woman was given, asked for more, the king called him an ingrate, and ordered him to be cut to pieces on the spot; and the sentence was carried into effect – not with knives, for they are prohibited, but with strips of sharp-edged grass, after the executioners had first dislocated his neck by a blow delivered behind the head ...

Nearly every day, I have seen one, two, or three of the wretched palace women led away to execution, tied by the hand, and dragged along by one of the body-guard, crying out, as she went to premature death, at the top of her voice, in the utmost despair and lamentation; and yet there was not a soul who dared lift hand to save any of them, though many might be heard privately commenting on their beauty ... One day, one of the king's favourite women overtook us, walking, with her hands clasped at the back of her head, to execution, crying in the most pitiful manner. A man was preceding her, but did not touch her; for she loved to obey the orders of her king voluntarily, and in consequence of previous attachment, was permitted, as a mark of distinction, to walk free. Wondrous world! ...

A large body of officers came in with an old man, with his two ears shorn off for having been too handsome in his youth, and a young woman who had been discovered in his house. Nothing was listened to but the plaintiff's statement, who said he had lost the woman for four days, and, after considerable search, had found her concealed by the old man. Voices in defence were never heard. The king instantly sentenced both to death; and, to make the example more severe, decreed that, being fed to preserve life as long as possible, they were to be dismembered bit by bit, as rations for the vultures, every day, until life was extinct. The dismayed criminals, struggling to be heard, in utter despair, were dragged away boisterously in the most barbarous manner, to the drowning music of drums ...

A boy, finding the king alone, threatened to kill him, because he took the lives of men unjustly. The king showed us, holding the pistol to his cheek, how he had presented the muzzle to the boy, which so frightened him that he ran away ... The culprit, a good-looking young fellow of 16 or 17, brought in a goat, made his *n'yanzigs*, stroked the goat and his own face with his hands, *n'yanzigged* again with prostrations, and retired ... There must have been some special reason why, in a court where trifling breaches of etiquette were punished with a cruel death, so grave a crime should have been so leniently dealt with; but I could not get at the bottom of the affair.

wife. The Bakers spent a year in Bunyoro, during which time they became the first Europeans to see Lake Mwatanzige, which they renamed Lake Albert. Baker also developed an apparently irrational antipathy towards his royal host, which almost certainly clouded his judgement when he returned to the region eight years later.

The years following the Bakers' departure from Bunyoro saw radical changes in the kingdom. Omakuma Kamurasi died in 1869, prompting a six-month succession battle that resulted in the populist Kabalega ascending to the throne. Omakuma Kabalega is regarded by many as the greatest of all Banyoro rulers who, were it not for British intervention, would surely have achieved his goal of restoring the kingdom to its full former glory. Kabalega introduced a set of military and political reforms which have been compared to those of Shaka in Zululand: he divided the army into battalions of 1,500 men, each of which was led by a trained soldier chosen on merit as opposed to birth, and he minimised the influence of the eternally squabbling Banyoro aristocracy by deposing them as local chiefs in favour of capable commoners with a sound military background.

In 1871, the imperialist Khedive Ismail of Egypt appointed the recently knighted Sir Samuel Baker to the newly created post of Governor General of Equatoria, a loosely defined province in the south of Egyptian-ruled Sudan. When Baker assumed his post in 1872, he almost immediately overstepped his instructions by declaring Bunyoro to be an annexe of Equatoria. Kabalega responded to Baker's pettiness by attacking the Egyptian garrison at Masindi. Baker was forced to retreat to Patiko in Acholi, and he defended his humiliating defeat by characterising Kabalega as a treacherous coward, thereby poisoning the omakuma's name in Europe in a way that was to have deep repercussions on future events in Uganda.

The second Governor General of Equatoria, General Gordon, knew of Kabalega only what his biased predecessor had told him. Gordon further antagonised the omakuma by erecting several forts in northern Bunyoro without first asking permission. Kabalega refrained from attacking the forts, but relations between Bunyoro and the Egyptian representative became increasingly uneasy. Outright war was probably averted only by the appointment of Emin Pasha as governor general in 1878. Sensibly, Emin Pasha withdrew from Bunyoro; and, instead of using his position to enact a petty vendetta against Kabalega, he focused his energy on the altogether more significant task of wresting control of the West Nile and Acholi regions from Arab slave traders. In 1883, following the Mahdist rebellion in Sudan, Emin Pasha and his troops were stranded in Wadelai. In 1889, they withdrew to the East African coast, effectively ending foreign attempts to control Uganda from the north.

The combined efforts of Baker and Gordon did little to curb Kabalega's empire-building efforts. In 1875, the Banyoro army overthrew Nyaika, the King of Toro, and the breakaway kingdom was reunited with Bunyoro. Kabalega also reclaimed several former parts of Bunyoro which had been annexed to Buganda, so that Bunyoro doubled in area under the first 20 years of his rule. Even more remarkably, Kabalega's was the first lengthy reign in centuries during which Bunyoro was free of internal rebellions. Following the Emin Pasha's withdrawal from Equatoria in 1889, the continued expansion, stability and sovereignty of Bunyoro under Kabalega must have seemed assured.

Europeans in Buganda (1884–92)
In the mid 19th century, when the first Swahili slave traders arrived in central Africa from the east coast, the dominant regional power was Buganda, ruled over by Kabaka Mutesa from his capital at Kampala. Mutesa allowed the slave traders to operate from his capital, and he collaborated in slave-raiding parties into neighbouring territories. The Swahili

converted several Baganda clan chiefs to their Islamic faith, and later, when Kampala was descended upon by the rival French Catholics and British Protestants, even more chiefs were attracted away from traditional Kiganda beliefs. Mutesa's court rapidly descended into a hotbed of religious rivalry.

Mutesa died in 1884. His son and successor, Mwanga, was a volatile and headstrong teenager who took the throne as religious rivalries in Buganda were building to a climax. Mwanga attempted to play off the various factions; he succeeded in alienating them all. In 1885, under the influence of a Muslim adviser, Mwanga ordered the execution of Bishop Hannington and 50 Christian converts (many of whom were roasted to death on a spit). In 1887, Mwanga switched allegiance to the traditionalist Kiganda chiefs, who in return offered to help him expel converts of all persuasions from Buganda. Threatened with expulsion, Muslims and Christians combined forces to launch an attack on the throne. Mwanga was overthrown in 1888. His Muslim-backed replacement, Kiwewa, persecuted Christians with even greater fervour than Mwanga had in 1885–86, but when Kiwewa's Kiganda leanings became apparent the Muslims rebelled and installed yet another leader. Events came to a head in 1889, when a civil war erupted between the Christian and Muslim factions, the result of which was that all Muslims were driven from the capital, later to join forces with Kabalega in Bunyoro. Mwanga was re-installed as kabaka.

The rival European powers were all eager to get their hands on the well-watered and fertile kingdom of Buganda, where, with the Muslims safely out of the way, rivalry between Francophile Catholics and Anglophile Protestants was increasingly open. In February 1890, Carl Peters arrived at Mengo clutching a treaty with the German East Africa Company. Mwanga signed it readily, possibly in the hope that German involvement would put an end to the Anglo–French religious intrigues which had persistently undermined his throne. Unfortunately for Mwanga, German deliverance was not to be: a few months after Peters's arrival, Germany handed Buganda and several other African territories to Britain in exchange for Heligoland, a tiny but strategic North Sea island.

In December 1890, Captain Lugard, the representative of the British East Africa Company, arrived at Kampala hoping to sign a treaty with an unimpressed Mwanga. The ensuing religious and political tensions sparked a crisis in January 1892, when a Catholic accused of killing a Protestant was acquitted by Mwanga on a plea of self-defence. Lugard demanded that the freed man be handed to him for a retrial and possible execution. Mwanga refused, on the rightful grounds that he was still the kabaka. Lugard decided it was time for a show of strength, and with the support of the Protestants he drove Mwanga and his Catholic supporters to an island on Lake Victoria. He then sent troops to rout Mwanga from the island; the kabaka fled to Bukoba in Karagwe (northern Tanzania) before returning in March to his kingdom, which was by then on the verge of civil war. Mwanga was left with no real option but to sign a treaty recognising the Company's authority in Buganda.

Lugard returned to Britain in October 1892, where he rallied public support for the colonisation of Buganda, and was instrumental in swaying a Liberal government which under Gladstone was opposed to the acquisition of further territories. In November, the British government appointed Sir Gerald Portal as the commissioner to advise on future policy towards Buganda. Portal arrived in Kampala in March 1893, to be greeted by a flood of petitions from all quarters. Swayed by the fact that missionaries of both persuasions felt colonisation would further their goals in the kingdom, Portal raised the Union Jack over Kampala in April; a month later he signed a formal treaty with the unwilling but resigned Mwanga, offering British protectorateship over Buganda in exchange for the right to collect and spend taxes.

THE CREATION OF UGANDA (1892–99) The protectorate of Uganda initially had rather vague boundaries, mimicking those of the indigenous kingdom to which it nominally offered protection. It is not at all clear to what extent the early British administrators conceived of their protectorate extending beyond the boundaries of the kingdom, but all accounts suggest that Uganda was as chaotic an assemblage as can be imagined.

Captain Lugard had done a fair bit of tentative territorial expansion even before he signed a treaty with Buganda. It was evidently his intention to quell Bunyoro's rampant Omakuma Kabalega, against whom he had been prejudiced by the combination of Baker's poisonous reports, and the not entirely unpredictable antipathy held for the Banyoro in Buganda. In August 1891, Lugard signed a treaty with the Omugabe of Ankole in a vain attempt to block arms reaching Bunyoro from the south. Lugard drove the Banyoro army out of Toro and installed Kasagama, an exiled prince of Toro, to the throne. He then built a line of forts along the southern boundary of Bunyoro, effectively preventing Kabalega from invading Toro. The grateful Kasagama was happy enough to reward Lugard's efforts by signing a treaty of friendship between Britain and Toro.

Britain's predisposition to regard Kabalega as a villain became something close to a legal obligation following the treaty of protectorateship over Buganda, and it was certainly paralleled by the residual suspicion of foreigners held by Kabalega after the Equatoria debacle. Elements opposing British rule over Buganda fled to Kabalega's court at Mparo (near Hoima), notably a group of Muslim Baganda and Sudanese soldiers whose leader Selim Bey was deported in 1893 following a skirmish with the imperial authorities in Entebbe. With the assistance of the Baganda exiles, Kabalega re-invaded Toro in late 1893, driving Kasagama into the Rwenzori Mountains and the only British officer present back to Buganda.

In December 1893, Colonel Colville led a party of eight British officers, 450 Sudanese troops and at least 20,000 Baganda infantrymen on to Mparo. Kabalega was too crafty to risk confrontation with this impressive force: he burnt his capital and fled with his troops to the Budongo Forest. During 1894, Kabalega led several successful attacks on British forts, but as he lost more men and his supplies ran low, his guerrilla tactics became increasingly ineffective. In August 1894, on the very same day that the formal protectorateship of Uganda was announced by Colville, Kabalega launched his biggest assault yet on the fort at Hoima. The fort was razed, but Kabalega lost thousands of men. He was forced to leave Bunyoro to go into hiding in Acholi and Lango, from where he continued a sporadic and increasingly unsuccessful series of attacks on British targets. Kabalega's kingdom was unilaterally appended to the British protectorate on 30 June 1896; the first formal agreement between Britain and Bunyoro was signed only in 1933.

Meanwhile, back in Kampala, Kabaka Mwanga and his traditionalist chiefs were becoming frustrated at the power which the British had invested in Christian converts in general and Protestants in particular. In July 1897, Mwanga left Kampala and raised a few loyalist troops to launch a feeble attack on the British forces. Swiftly defeated, Mwanga fled to Bukoba where he was captured by the German authorities. The British administration officially deposed Mwanga and they installed his one-year-old son Chwa as kabaka under the regency of three Protestant chiefs led by Apollo Kaggwa. The administration adopted the same tactic in Bunyoro, where a blameless 12-year-old son of Kabalega was installed as omakuma in 1898 – only to be removed four years later for what the administration termed incompetence!

Mwanga escaped from his German captors in late 1897, after which he joined forces with his former rival Kabalega. After two years on the run, Mwanga and

Kabalega were cornered in a swamp in Lango. Following a long battle, Kabalega was shot (a wound which later necessitated the amputation of his arm) and the two former kings were captured and exiled to the Seychelles, where Mwanga died in 1903 and Kabalega died 20 years later. Kabalega remained the spiritual leader of Bunyoro until his death: it is widely held that the unpopular Omakuma Duhaga II, installed by Britain in place of his 'incompetent' teenage brother, was tolerated by the Banyoro only because he was Kabalega's son.

Ankole succumbed more easily to British rule. Weakened by smallpox and rinderpest epidemics in the 1870s, the kingdom then suffered epidemics of tetanus and jiggers in the early 1890s, and it only just managed to repel a Rwandan invasion in 1895. Omugabe Ntare died later in the same year, by which time all the natural heirs to the throne had died in one or other epidemic. Following a brief succession war, a youthful nephew of the Ntare was installed on the throne. In 1898, Britain occupied the Ankole capital at Mbarara; the battered kingdom offered no resistance.

The southeast also fell under British rule without great fuss, because of the lack of cohesive political systems in the region. Much of the area was brought into the protectorate through the efforts of a Muganda collaborator called Semei Kakungulu who, incidentally, had assisted in the capture of Kabalega and Mwanga in Lango. Kakungulu set up a fiefdom in the Lake Kyoga region, where he installed a rudimentary administrative system over much of the area west of what is now the Kenyan border and south of Mount Elgon. Characteristically, the British administration eventually demoted Kakungulu to a subordinate role in the very system which he had implemented for them. Kakungulu's life story, as recounted in Michael Twaddle's excellent biography (see page 540), is as illuminating an account as any of the formative days of the protectorate.

By the end of the 19th century, the Uganda protectorate formally included the kingdoms of Buganda, Bunyoro, Ankole and Toro. Three of them were ruled by juveniles, while Toro was under the rule of the British-installed Kasagama. Whether through incompetence or malicious intent, the British administration was in the process of creating a nation divided against itself: firstly by favouring Protestants over Baganda of Catholic, Muslim or traditionalist persuasion, and secondly by replacing traditional clan leaders in other kingdoms with Baganda officials.

It is often asked whether colonialism was a good or a bad thing for Africa. There is no straightforward answer to this question. When writing about Malawi in 1995, I was forced to the conclusion that British intervention was the best thing to happen to that country in the troubled 19th century. By contrast, the arrogant, myopic and partial British administrators who were imposed on Uganda in the late 19th century unwittingly but surely sowed the seeds of future tragedy.

BRITISH RULE (1900–52) Ironically, the first governor of Uganda was none other than Sir Harry Johnston, whose vigorous anti-slaving campaign in the 1890s was as much as anything responsible for Britain's largely positive influence over Malawi. Johnston's instructions were to place the administration of the haphazardly assembled Uganda protectorate under what the Marquis of Salisbury termed 'a permanently satisfactory footing'. In March 1900, the newly appointed governor of Uganda signed the so-called Buganda Agreement with the four-year-old kabaka. This document formally made Buganda a federal province of the protectorate, and it recognised the kabaka and his federal government conditional upon their loyalty to Britain. It divided Buganda into 20 counties, each of which had to pass the hut and gun taxes collected in their region to the central administration, and it forbade further attempts to extend the kingdom, a clause inserted mostly to protect neighbouring Busoga.

Alexander Calder and Dr Joseph Kivubiro

Since its foundation in 1937, the School of Fine Art at Kampala's Makerere University has been the nucleus for East Africa's most influential and widespread contemporary art movement. While indigenous arts have flourished and evolved for centuries throughout East Africa, Makerere provided the region's first formal instruction in modern fine-art techniques, including drawing, painting and modern sculpture. Over the years, many students and graduates of this school became recognised innovators of striking new techniques and original styles.

During the particularly active 1950s and 1960s, artists held solo and group exhibitions at numerous locations. Growing interest in exhibitions by local artists led to the establishment of sizeable art collections by public museums, corporations and government institutions throughout the country. Further stimulating Uganda's environment for advancing local art during this time, Esso and Caltex held widely publicised annual art competitions, publishing work by awarded artists on calendars distributed locally and abroad.

Until 1961, Makerere generally emphasised representative art, using drawing, perspective and shading in compositions inspired from local imagery. Following independence, however, a cadre of leading artists embraced a new role as visual cultural historians, producing interpretative works that document the early post-independence era – often using representative forms and figures to symbolise uncertainties and ideals within a rapidly changing society.

In 1966, artist Norbert Kaggwa underscored the importance of representational art in Uganda's rapidly evolving culture:'Wedged into a single generation, my own, is a double vision; we are the beginning of an industrialised, urban society and we are probably – to be realistic – the end of the nomadic and village ways of life. The two eras are usually separated by hundreds of years. Here they are separated by a few dozen miles. I am personally very moved by this phenomenon and feel some special responsibility towards it. This is at least one of the reasons why I am a realistic and not an abstract painter. In one way, I suppose, I consider myself as much a cultural historian as an artist … or rather, in my case, they are one and the same thing.'

Artists debated their perceived role and the purpose of their works against the backdrop of independence. Art of this period consequently benefited from rich cross-fertilisation: several artists embraced both idioms to find unique and expressive visual forms that drew from abstract as well as representational influences. The late Henry Lumu, Augustine Mugalula Mukiibi, Teresa Musoke and Elly Kyeyune were early leaders of Uganda's emerging Modernist school, spawning the distinctive semi-abstract styles that characterised much art of this era.

In 1968, Makerere graduate Henry Lumu was hired as art director by Uganda National Television, initiating regular broadcasts of televised art instruction classes. Exposure through this new medium further stimulated Kampala's burgeoning art community, which by that time extended well beyond the campus. The Uganda Art Club organised exhibitions throughout Kampala in the early to mid-1970s, prompting prominent hotels, banks and commercial buildings to amass and display collections of outstanding original works. During this period, artists attained unprecedented standing within Kampala's thriving cosmopolitan circles and among the country's élite.

By the late 1970s, political unrest had taken a dreadful toll among Uganda's artistic community. Professionals and intellectuals were targeted by the Obote and Amin regimes, and museums and galleries were looted or reoccupied – destroying numerous significant art collections. Forced to choose between seclusion, alternative occupations or self-imposed exile, many Ugandan artists emigrated to Kenya, South Africa, Europe or North America. The expatriate artists incorporated visual elements from their new surroundings into mediums, styles and colour palettes that still remained faithful to their Ugandan experience.

A large number of artists, including Henry Lumu, Joseph Mungaya, Dan Sekanwagi, Emmy Lubega, David Kibuuka, Jak Kitarikawe, David Wasswa Katongole and James Kitamirike, left for neighbouring Kenya. The colourful, innovative and uniquely stylised works of the Ugandan painters transformed Nairobi's art scene. Kenyan artist Nuwa Nnyanzi reflected recently: 'The impact of Ugandan artists in Kenya in the seventies and eighties was so great that it is still felt and highly visible today.'

Restored political stability in the late 1980s encouraged the homecoming or resurfacing of many Ugandan artists. Expressing rediscovered peacetime ideals through their art, many artists also reminded their audience of struggles and horrors endured during the troubled years. Exhibitions by Ugandan artists were held regularly at London's Commonwealth Institute, while other shows opened in Paris and Vienna. In 1992, President Museveni marked the opening of a Vienna show featuring Geoffrey Mukasa and Fabian Mpagi with these remarks:

> As those destructive years have regrettably shown, art cannot flourish in a situation plagued with terror and human indifference. Peace and security has returned to our country. We have gone a long way to encourage the revival of arts. The fine works exhibited are a vivid testimony that art has come to life again in Uganda. Certainly, both the public and the critics will recognise that Uganda has taken up her place in the world of modern art. It is an opportune moment for us to portray through these paintings a promising new picture of the 'New Uganda'.

Exhibitions by and for Ugandan artists have also been held in Stockholm, Amsterdam, Berlin, Frankfurt, Rome, Johannesburg and seven cities in the USA. In North America, expatriate artists such as James Kitamirike, David Kibuuka, Dan Sekanwagi and Fred Makubuya have united to spearhead renewed interest in their art through the Fine Arts Center for East Africa, which opened in San Francisco in 1998. Organising group exhibitions in the USA and Canada, this active contingent of artists continues to garner recognition for their innovative styles, mediums and potent individual voices within Uganda's art movement.

In Kampala today, Uganda's renewed art scene embodies a vibrant and vital country redefining its past yet also reaching for a hopeful future. Sharing their unique visual arts legacy, Uganda's fine-art pioneers have become the country's cultural ambassadors, creating global awareness of their homeland's unique colours, cultures, peoples and art.

Locations to view art in Kampala include the Uganda Museum, Nommo Gallery, AKA Gallery, AfriArt and Mish Mash. For contacts, see page 166.

Reprinted with minor edits from the website of the Fine Arts Center for East Africa in San Francisco, with permission from Alexander Calder (ก 415 333 9363; e gadart@aol. com; www.theartroom-sf.com).

The Buganda Agreement also formalised a deal which had been made in 1898, in recognition of Buganda's aid in quelling Kabalega. Six former counties of Bunyoro were transferred to Buganda and placed under the federal rule of the kabaka, a decision described by a later district commissioner of Bunyoro as 'one of the greatest blunders' ever made by the administration of the protectorate. For lying within the Lost Counties (as the six annexed territories came to be called) were the burial sites of several former omakumas, as well as Mubende, a town which is steeped in Kinyoro traditions and the normal coronation site of an incoming omakuma. In 1921, the Banyoro who lived in the Lost Counties formed the Mubende Bunyoro Committee to petition for their return to Bunyoro. This, and at least three subsequent petitions, as well as five petitions made by the omakuma between 1943 and 1955, were all refused by the British administration on the basis that 'the boundaries laid down in 1900 could not be changed in favour of Bunyoro'. The issue of the Lost Counties caused Banyoro resentment throughout the colonial era, and it is arguably the trigger which set in motion the tragic events which followed Uganda's independence.

When Johnston arrived in Kampala in 1900, Uganda's borders were ill-defined. The first 15 years of the 20th century saw the protectorate expand further to incorporate yet more disparate cultural and linguistic groups, a growth which was motivated as much as anything by the desire to prevent previously unclaimed territories from falling into the hands of other European powers. The Kigezi region, a mishmash of small kingdoms which bordered German and Belgian territories to the south and west, was formally appended to Uganda in 1911. Baganda chiefs were installed throughout Kigezi, causing several uprisings and riots until the traditional chiefs were restored in 1929.

In the first decade of protectorateship, Britain had an inconsistent and ambiguous policy towards the territories north of the Nile. In 1906, it was decided not to incorporate them into Uganda, since they were not considered to be appropriate for the Kiganda system of government which was being imposed on other appended territories. More probably the administration was daunted by the cost and effort that would be required to subdue the dispersed and decentralised northern societies on an individual basis. In any event, the policy on the north was reversed in 1911, when the acting governor extended the protectorate to include Lango, and again in 1913, when Acholi and Karamoja were placed under British administration. The final piece in the Ugandan jigsaw was West Nile province: leased to the Belgian Congo until 1910, after which it was placed under the administration of the Sudan, West Nile was found a permanent home as part of Uganda in 1914.

Obsessed with the idea of running the protectorate along what it termed a Kiganda system of indirect rule, the British administration insisted not only on exporting its bastardised Kiganda system throughout the country, but also on placing its implementation in the hands of Baganda officials. In effect, Britain ruled Uganda by deploying the Baganda in a sub-imperialistic role; as a reward for their doing the administration's dirty work, Buganda was run as a privileged state within a state, a status it enjoyed right through to independence, when it was the only former kingdom to be granted full federality.

This divisive arrangement worked only because the administration had the legal and military clout to enforce it – even then, following regular uprisings in Bunyoro and Kigezi, traditional chiefs were gradually reinstated in most parts of the country. The 1919 Native Authority Ordinance delineated the powers of local chiefs, which were wide-ranging but subject always to the intervention of British officials. The Kiganda system was inappropriate to anywhere but Buganda, and it was absolutely absurd in somewhere like Karamoja, where there were no traditional chiefs, and decisions were made on a consensual basis by committees of recognised elders.

For all its flaws, the administrative system which was imposed on Uganda probably gave indigenous Ugandans far greater autonomy than was found elsewhere in British-ruled Africa. The administration discouraged alien settlement and, with the introduction of cotton, it helped many regions attain a high degree of economic self-sufficiency. Remarkably, cotton growing was left almost entirely to indigenous farmers – in 1920, a mere 500km^2 of Uganda was covered in European-run plantations, most of which collapsed following the global economic slump of the 1920s and the resultant drop in cotton prices. Political decentralisation was increased by the Local Government Ordinance of 1949, which divided Uganda along largely ethnic lines into 18 districts, each of which had a district council with a high degree of federal autonomy. This ordinance gave even greater power to African administrators, but it also contributed to the climate of regional unity and national disunity which characterised the decades immediately preceding and following Uganda's independence.

The area that suffered most from this federalist policy was the 'backward' north. Neglected in terms of education, and never provided with reliable transport links whereby farmers could export their product to other parts of the country, the people of the north were forced to send their youngsters south to find work. There is some reason to suppose it was deliberate British policy to underdevelop an area which had become a reliable source of cheap labour and of recruits to the police and army. This impression is reinforced by the fact that when Africans were first admitted to the Central Legislative Council, only Buganda, the east and the west were allowed representation – the administrative systems which had been imposed on the north were 'not yet in all districts advanced to the stage requiring the creation of centralised native executives'. In other words, instead of trying to develop the north and bring it in line with other regions in Uganda, the British administration chose to neglect it.

Writing before Amin ascended to power, the Ugandan historian Samwiri Karugire commented that 'the full cost of this neglect has yet to be paid, not by the colonial officials, but by Ugandans themselves'. More recent writers have suggested that it is no coincidence that Milton Obote and Idi Amin both hailed from north of the Nile.

THE BUILD-UP TO INDEPENDENCE (1952–62) The cries for independence which prevailed in most African colonies following World War II were somewhat muted in Uganda. This can be attributed to several factors: the lack of widespread alien settlement, the high degree of African involvement in public affairs prior to independence, the strongly regional character of the protectorate's politics, and the strong probability that the status quo rather suited Uganda's Protestant Baganda élite. Remarkably, Uganda's first anti-colonial party, the Uganda National Congress (UNC), was founded as late as 1952, and it was some years before it gained any marked support, except, significantly, in parts of the underdeveloped north.

The first serious call for independence came from the most unlikely of sources. In 1953, the unpopular Kabaka Mutesa II defied the British administration by vociferously opposing the mooted federation of Uganda with Kenya and Tanzania. When the Governor of Uganda refused to give Mutesa any guarantees regarding federation, Mutesa demanded that Buganda – alone – be granted independence. The governor declared Mutesa to be disloyal to Britain, deposed him from the throne, and exiled him to Britain. This won Mutesa immense support, and not only in Buganda, so that when he was returned to his palace in 1955, it was as something of a national hero. Sadly, Mutesa chose not to use his popularity to help unify Uganda, but concentrated instead on parochial Kiganda affairs. A new Buganda Agreement was signed on 18 October 1955, giving the kabaka and his government even greater federal powers – and generating mild alarm among the non-Baganda.

Uganda's first indigenous party of consequence, the Democratic Party (DP), was founded in 1956 by Matayo Mugwanya after Mutesa had rejected him as a candidate for the Prime Minister of Buganda on the grounds of his Catholicism. The party formed a platform for the legitimate grievances of Catholics, who had always been treated as second-class citizens in Uganda, and it rose to some prominence after party leadership was handed to the lawyer Benedicto Kiwanuka in 1958. However, the DP was rightly or wrongly perceived by most Ugandans as an essentially Catholic party, which meant it was unlikely ever to win mass support.

The formation of the Uganda People's Union (UPU) came in the wake of the 1958 election, when for the first time a quota of Africans was elected to national government. The UPU was the first public alliance of non-Buganda leaders, and as such it represented an important step in the polarisation of Ugandan politics: in essence, the Baganda versus everybody else. In 1959, the UNC split along ethnic lines, with the non-Baganda faction combining with the UPU to form the Uganda People's Congress (UPC), led by Milton Obote. In 1961, the Baganda element of the UNC combined with members of the federal government of Buganda to form the overtly pro-Protestant and pro-Baganda Kabaka Yekka (KY) – which literally means 'The Kabaka Forever' (and was nicknamed 'Kill Yourselves' by opponents).

As the election of October 1961 approached, the DP, UPC and KY were clearly the main contenders. The DP won, largely through a Baganda boycott which gave them 19 of the seats within the kingdom – in East Kyaggwe, for instance, only 188 voters registered out of an estimated constituency of 90,000. The DP's Benedicto Kiwanuka thus became the first Prime Minister of Uganda when self-government was granted on 1 March 1962 – the first time ever that Catholics had any real say in public matters. Another general election was held in April of that year, in the build-up to the granting of full independence. As a result of the DP's success the year before, the UPC and KY formed an unlikely coalition, based on nothing but their mutual non-Catholicism. The UPC won 43 seats, the DP 24 seats, and the KY 24 (of which all but three were in Buganda), giving the UPC–KY alliance a clear majority and allowing Milton Obote to lead Uganda to independence on 9 October 1962.

THE FIRST OBOTE GOVERNMENT (1962–71) Obote, perhaps more than any other Commonwealth leader, inherited a nation fragmented along religious and ethnic lines to the point of ungovernability. He was also handed an Independence Constitution of singular peculiarity: Buganda was recognised as having full federal status, the other kingdoms were granted semi-federal status, and the remainder of the country was linked directly to central government. His parliamentary majority was dependent on a marriage of convenience based solely on religious grounds, and he was compelled to recognise Kabaka Mutesa II as head of state. Something, inevitably, was going to have to give.

The Lost Counties of Bunyoro became the pivotal issue almost immediately after independence. In April 1964, Obote decided to settle the question by holding a referendum in the relevant counties, thereby allowing their inhabitants to decide whether they wanted to remain part of Buganda or be reincorporated into Bunyoro. The result of the referendum, almost 80% in favour of the counties being reincorporated into Bunyoro, caused a serious rift between Obote and Mutesa. It also caused the fragile UPC–KY alliance to split; no great loss to Obote since enough DP and KY parliamentarians had already defected to the UPC for him to retain a clear majority.

Tensions between Obote and Mutesa culminated in the so-called Constitutional Crisis of 1966. On 22 February, Obote scrapped the Independence Constitution, thereby stripping Mutesa of his presidency. Mutesa appealed to the UN to intervene. Obote sent the army to the royal palace. Mutesa was forced to jump over the palace walls and into exile in London, where he died, impecunious, three years later. Ominously, an estimated 2,000 of the Baganda who had rallied around their king's palace were loaded on to trucks and driven away. Some were thrown over Murchison Falls. Others were buried in mass graves. Most of them had been alive when they were taken from the palace.

In April 1966, Obote unveiled a new constitution in which he abolished the role of prime minister and made himself 'Life President of Uganda'. In September 1967, he introduced another new constitution wherein he made Uganda a republic, abolished the kingdoms, divided Buganda into four new districts, and gave the army unlimited powers of detention without trial. In sole control of the country, but faced with smouldering Baganda resentment, Obote became increasingly reliant on force to maintain a semblance of stability. In September 1969, he banned the DP and other political parties. A spate of detentions followed: the DP leader Benedicto Kiwanuka, perceived dissidents within the UPC, the Baganda royal family, Muslim leaders, and any number of lawyers, students, journalists and doctors.

On 11 January 1971, Obote flew out of Entebbe for the Commonwealth Conference in Singapore. He left behind a memorandum to the commander of the Ugandan army, demanding an explanation not only for the disappearance of four million US dollars out of the military coffers, but also for the commander's alleged role in the murder of a brigadier and his wife in Gulu a year earlier, a dual murder for which he was due to be brought to trial. The commander decided his only option was to strike in Obote's absence. On 25 January 1971, Kampala was rocked by the news of a military coup, and Uganda had a new president – a killer with the demeanour of a buffoon, and charisma enough to ensure that he would become one of the handful of African presidents who have achieved household-name status in the West.

THE AMIN YEARS (1971–79) Idi Amin was born in January 1928 of a Muslim father and Christian mother at Koboko near the border with the DRC and Sudan. As a child, he moved with his mother to Lugazi in Buganda. Poorly educated and barely literate, Amin joined the King's African Rifles in 1946. He fought for Britain against the Mau-Mau in Kenya, after which he attended a training school in Nakuru. In 1958, he became one of the first two Africans in Uganda to be promoted to the rank of lieutenant. In 1962, he showed something of his true colours when he destroyed a village near Lake Turkana in Kenya, killing three people without provocation; a misdeed for which he only narrowly escaped trial, largely through the intervention of Obote.

By 1966, Amin was second in command of the Ugandan army, and, following the 1966 Constitution Crisis, Obote promoted him to the top spot. It was Amin who led the raid that forced Mutesa into exile, Amin who gave the orders when 2,000 of the kabaka's Baganda supporters were loaded into trucks and killed, and

1

Amin who co-ordinated the mass detentions that followed the banning of the DP in 1969. For years, Amin was the instrument with which Obote kept a grip on power, yet, for reasons that are unclear, by 1970 the two most powerful men in Uganda were barely talking to each other. It is a measure of Obote's arrogance that when he wrote that fateful memorandum before flying to Singapore, he failed to grasp not only that its recipient would be better equipped than anybody else to see the real message, but also that Amin was one of the few men in Uganda with the power to react.

Given the role that Amin had played under Obote, it is a little surprising that the reaction to his military takeover was incautious jubilation. Amin's praises were sung by everybody from the man in the street to the foreign press and the Baganda royals whose leader Amin had helped drive into exile. This, quite simply, was a reflection less of Amin's popularity than of Obote's singular unpopularity. Nevertheless, Amin certainly played out the role of a 'man of peace', promising a rapid return to civilian rule, and he sealed his popularity in Buganda by allowing the preserved body of Mutesa to be returned for burial.

On the face of it, the first 18 months of Amin's rule were innocuous enough. Arguably the first public omen of things to come occurred in mid-1972, when Amin expelled all Asians from the country, 'Africanised' their businesses, and commandeered their money and possessions for 'state' use. In the long term, this action proved to be an economic disaster, but the sad truth is that it won Amin further support from the majority of Ugandans, who had long resented Asian dominance in business circles.

Even as Amin consolidated his public popularity, behind the scenes he was reverting to type; this was, after all, a man who had escaped being tried for murder not once but twice. Amin quietly purged the army of its Acholi and Lango majority: by the end of 1973, 13 of the 23 officers who had held a rank of lieutenant colonel or higher at the time of Amin's coup had been murdered. By the end of 1972, eight of the 20 members of Obote's 1971 cabinet were dead, and four more were in exile. Public attention was drawn to Amin's actions in 1973, when the former prime minister, Benedicto Kiwanuka, was detained and murdered by Amin, as was the Vice Chancellor of Makerere University.

By 1974, Amin was fully engaged in a reign of terror. During the eight years he was in power, an estimated 300,000 Ugandans were killed by him or his agents (under the guise of the State Research Bureau), many of them tortured to death in horrific ways. His main targets were the northern tribes, intellectuals and rival politicians, but any person or group that he perceived as a threat was dealt with mercilessly. Despite this, African leaders united behind Uganda's despotic ruler: incredibly, Amin was made President of the Organisation of African Unity (OAU) in 1975. Practically the sole voice of dissent within Africa came from Tanzania's Julius Nyerere, who asserted that it was hypocritical for African leaders to criticise the white racist regimes of southern Africa while ignoring similarly cruel regimes in 'black' Africa. Nyerere granted exile to several of Amin's opponents, notably Milton Obote and Yoweri Museveni, and he refused to attend the 1975 OAU summit in Kampala.

As Amin's unpopularity with his own countrymen grew, he attempted to forge national unity by declaring war on Tanzania in 1978. Amin had finally overreached himself; after his troops entered northwest Tanzania, where they bombed the towns of Bukoba and Musoma, Tanzania and a number of Ugandan exiles retaliated by invading Uganda. In April 1979, Amin was driven out of Kampala into an exile from which he would never return prior to his death of multiple organ failure in a Saudi Arabian hospital in August 2003.

UGANDA AFTER AMIN (1979–86) When Amin departed from Ugandan politics in 1979, it was seen as a fresh start by a brutalised nation. As it transpired, it was Uganda's third false dawn in 17 years – most Ugandans now regard the seven years which followed Amin's exile to have been worse even than the years which preceded it.

In the climate of high political intrigue which followed Amin's exile, Uganda's affairs were stage managed by exiled UPC leaders in Arusha (Tanzania), most probably because the UPC's leader Milton Obote was understandably cautious about announcing his return to Ugandan politics. The semi-exiled UPC installed Professor Lule as a stand-in president, a position which he retained for 68 days. His successor, Godfrey Binaisa, fared little better, lasting eight months before he was bundled out of office in May 1980. The stand-in presidency was then assumed by two UPC loyalists, Paulo Muwanga and David Oyite-Ojik, who set an election date in December 1980.

The main rivals for the election were the DP, led by Paul Ssemogerere, and the UPC, still led by Milton Obote. A new party, the Uganda Patriotic Movement (UPM), led by Yoweri Museveni, was formed a few months prior to the election. Uganda's first election since 1962 took place in an atmosphere of corruption and intimidation. Muwanga and Oyite-Ojik used trumped-up charges to prevent several DP candidates from standing, so that the UPC went into the polling with 17 uncontested seats. On the morning of 11 December, it was announced that the DP were on the brink of victory with 63 seats certain, a surprising result that probably reflected a strong anti-Obote vote from the Baganda. In response, Muwanga and Oyite-Ojik quickly drafted a decree ensuring that all results had to be passed to them before they could be announced. The edited result of the election saw the DP take 51 seats, the UPM one seat, and the UPC a triumphant 74. After some debate, the DP decided to claim their seats, despite the overwhelming evidence that the election had been rigged.

Yoweri Museveni felt that people had been cheated by the election, and that under Obote's UPC the past was doomed to repeat itself. In 1982, Museveni formed the National Resistance Movement (NRM), an army largely made up of orphans left behind by the excesses of Amin and Obote. The NRM operated from the Luwero Triangle in Buganda north of Kampala, where they waged a guerrilla war against Obote's government. Obote's response was characteristically brutal: his troops waded into the Luwero Triangle killing civilians by their thousands, an ongoing massacre which exceeded even Amin's. The world turned a blind eye to the atrocities in Luwero, and so it was left to 'dissident' members of the UPC and the commander of the army, Tito Okello, to suggest that Obote might negotiate with the NRM in order to stop the slaughter. Obote refused. On 27 July 1985, he was deposed in a bloodless military coup led by Tito Okello. For the second time in his career, Obote was forced into exile by the commander of his own army.

Okello assumed the role of head of state and he appointed as his prime minister Paulo Muwanga, whose role in the 1980 election gave him little credibility. With some misgivings, the DP allied itself with Okello, largely because Ssemogerere hoped he might use his influence to stop the killing in Luwero. In a statement made in Nairobi in August 1985, Museveni announced that the NRM was prepared to co-operate with Okello, provided that the army and the other instruments of oppression used by previous regimes were brought under check. The NRM entered into negotiations with Okello, but after these broke down in December 1985, Museveni returned to the bush. On 26 January 1986, the NRM entered Kampala, Okello surrendered tamely, and Museveni was sworn in as president – Uganda's seventh head of state in as many years.

THE NRM GOVERNMENT (1986–2013) In 1986, Museveni took charge of a country that had been beaten and brutalised as have few others. There must have been many Ugandans who felt this was yet another false dawn, as they waited for the cycle of killings and detentions to start all over again. Certainly, to the outside world, Uganda's politics had become so confusing in all but their consistent brutality that the NRM takeover appeared to be merely another instalment in an apparently endless succession of coups and civil wars.

But Museveni was far from being another Amin or Obote. He shied away from the retributive actions which had destroyed the credibility of previous takeovers; he appointed a broad-based government which swept across party and ethnic lines, re-established the rule of law, appointed a much-needed Human Rights Commission, increased the freedom of the press, and encouraged the return of Asians and other exiles. On the economic front, he adopted pragmatic policies and encouraged foreign investment and tourism, the result of which was an average growth rate of 10% in his first decade of rule. Museveni has also tried to tackle corruption, albeit with limited success, by gradually cutting the civil service. Most significantly, Uganda under Museveni has visibly moved away from being a society obsessed with its ethnic and religious divisions. From the most unpromising material, Museveni has, miraculously, forged a real nation.

In 1993, Museveni greatly boosted his popularity (especially with the influential Baganda) by his decision to grant legal recognition to the old kingdoms of Uganda. In July 1993, the Cambridge-educated son of Mutesa II, Ronald Mutebi, returned to Uganda after having spent over 20 years in Britain; in a much-publicised coronation near Kampala, he was made the 36th Kabaka of Buganda. The traditional monarchies of Bunyoro and Toro have also been restored, but not that of Ankole.

In the 1990s, the most widespread criticism of Museveni and the NRM was their tardiness in moving towards a genuine multi-party democracy. At the time, Museveni argued rather convincingly that Uganda needed stability offered by a 'no party' system more than it needed a potentially divisive multi-party system that risked igniting the ethnic passions that had caused the country so much misery in its first two decades of independence. As a result, the NRM remained the only legal political party until as recently as 2005, though the country's first open presidential elections were held in 1996, slightly more than ten years after Museveni had first assumed power. Museveni won with an overwhelming 74% of the vote, as compared with the 23% polled by his main rival, Paul Ssemogerere, a former DP leader who once served as prime minister under Museveni. A similar pattern was registered in the 2001 presidential elections, which returned Museveni to power with 70% of the vote, as compared with the 20% registered by his main rival Kizza Besigye. At the time, and for several years afterwards, Museveni reiterated his commitment to stand down from the presidency in 2006, in accordance with the maximum of two presidential terms specified by a national constitution drawn up years earlier by the NRM constitution.

During the course of 2004, Museveni made two crucial political about-turn. Firstly, he advocated a return to multi-party system and in a national referendum on the subject, 92.5% of voters agreed with him. Just weeks after this political landmark, Museveni pushed a constitutional amendment to scrap presidential term limits through parliament, clearing the way for him to seek a third term in the looming elections. In November, barely three months before the election was due, the main opposition leader Kizza Besigye, having recently returned from exile, was imprisoned and charged with terrorism, only to be released on bail in January 2006. A month later, Uganda's first multi-party election in 25 years was largely held to be free and fair by international observers, though this verdict was loudly disputed by Besigye, who polled 37% of the vote as compared with Museveni's 59%. Once again, this result can be viewed as ambiguous – the gap between the two primary candidates, though by no means insubstantial, had halved since the 2001 presidential election, and it is difficult to say to what extent the vote for Museveni represented overt support for his presidency and to what extent it simply reflected a fear of change.

There is no doubt that under Museveni's rule, Uganda has made fantastic progress; Kampala in 2013 is unrecognisable from the shattered capital that the NRM took control of in 1986. The turnaround was showcased to the world in November 2007 when Uganda hosted Queen Elizabeth II and 57 heads of state for the Commonwealth Heads of Government Meeting (CHOGM). On the other hand, popular support for the NRM is continually damaged by regular corruption scandals; events that fuel a sense that those in senior government consider themselves above the law and accountable to themselves rather than their electorate. A growing resentment found an outlet during the Mabira Forest affair in 2007 when Museveni ordered the National Forest Authority to de-gazette the eastern part of central Uganda's largest remaining natural forest for an Asian industrialist to convert the land to a sugarcane plantation. This sparked an unprecedented and, it must be said, unexpectedly passionate, show of public opinion; a hitherto latent civil society united with NGOs, the press, and politicians from all parties to protest: modes of doing so ranged from reasoned letters to the newspapers to a nasty riot in the middle of Kampala. Eventually (possibly because the furore persisted uncomfortably close to the CHOGM) the proposal was dropped.

Museveni, predictably, won a fourth term in the 2011 elections. This coincided with a period of massive inflation – at times reaching 25% - which led to price rises and widespread hardship. Though in part due to instability in the global financial markets, the situation was made worse by a shortfall in hard currency as the NRM siphoned off a large chunk of the annual budget to bankroll its re-election. This led to the post-election, opposition-led 'Walk to Work' protests which were firmly quashed by the police. Scandals continue. As I write in early 2013, senior officials in the Office of the Prime Minister appear unable to account for billions of shillings of donor money meant to rebuild northern Uganda; as a result, a number of Western donor countries are withholding aid. Even within the NRM, a growing number of MPs seem to think it time for Museveni to call it a day and retire to his farm at Rwakitura. However he has expressed no interest in stepping aside, and there is no clear idea of who would step into the gap. No heir has been groomed to take up the reins of the NRM, while the opposition presents no obvious candidate either. In the absence of anyone better qualified for the job, it should be no surprise if Museveni stands for – and, if he does, presumably secures – a fifth term.

While the future remains open to speculation, the most important event in recent Ugandan history is an end to the civil war that caused so much suffering in northern Uganda between 1987 and 2005. Though protracted negotiations between representatives of the government and the rebel Lord's Resistance Army failed to result in a formal peace agreement, northern Uganda has been at peace now for eight years. The history of Joseph Kony and the Lord's Resistance Army is described in the box on pages 436–7.

ECONOMY

Uganda has, by and large, a free market economy. This suffered greatly under the presidencies of Amin and Obote, but since Museveni took power in 1986

Uganda's economy has maintained a growth rate of 4–6% per annum. Agriculture accounts for about 60% of the GDP, with major export crops including coffee, tea and tobacco. Over 90% of Ugandans are either subsistence farmers or work in agriculture-related fields.

PEOPLE

The 2002 census showed Uganda to have a population of 24.7 million, of which 87% live rurally. This represents an almost 50% increase on the 1991 figure of 16.7 million, an annual growth rate of more than 4% as compared with 2.5% per annum between 1980 and 1991. The majority of Uganda's people are concentrated in the south and west. The most populous ethnic group are the Bantu-speaking Baganda, who account for about 20% of the population and are centred on Kampala. Other significant Bantu-speaking groups are the Ankole, Toro, Banyoro and Busoga. The east and north of the country are populated by several groups of Nilotic or Cushitic origin, including the Teso, Karimojong, Acholi and Lango.

The table below shows data for Uganda's ten largest urban centres in Uganda in 2002 and in earlier censuses. Though long outdated (a 2012 census was postponed due to lack of funds), it remains a good indicator of the dramatic post-independence shifts in urban growth around the country. Kampala remains, obviously, the most populous city by far with 2012 estimates putting the figure at 1.6–1.8m. The most striking increases recorded by the 2002 census concern Gulu and Lira, both of which were experiencing huge rural–urban migration as a result of the LRA war and continued to do so until 2006.

LANGUAGE

The official language, English, is spoken as a second language by most educated Ugandans. More than 33 local languages are spoken in different parts of the country. Most of these belong to the Bantu language group: for instance, Luganda, Lusoga and Lutoro. Several Nilotic and Cushitic languages are spoken in the north and east, some of them by only a few thousand people. An unusual language of the extreme northeast is Karimojong, which has a vocabulary of only 180 words. Many Ugandans speak a limited amount of KiSwahili, a coastal language which spread into the east African interior via the 19th-century Arab slave traders. Few Ugandans speak any indigenous language other than their home language,

POPULATION TRENDS

	1959		1991		2002	
1	Kampala	46,000	Kampala	775,000	Kampala	1.2 million
2	Gulu	30,000	Jinja	65,000	Gulu	113,000
3	Lira	14,000	Mbale	54,000	Lira	89,500
4	Jinja	11,500	Masaka	49,500	Jinja	86,500
5	Mbale	11,000	Entebbe	42,700	Mbale	70,000
6	Mbarara	8,500	Mbarara	41,000	Mbarara	69,000
7	Masaka	8,000	Soroti	40,900	Masaka	61,000
8	Entebbe	7,000	Gulu	38,300	Entebbe	57,000
9	Kasese	6,000	Njeru	37,000	Kasese	53,000
10	Njeru	5,000	Fort Portal	32,800	Mukono	47,000

so KiSwahili and English are the most useful languages for tourists, and they are widely used between Ugandans of different linguistic backgrounds.

RELIGION

Some 85% of Ugandans are Christian, divided roughly equally between the Protestant Church of Uganda (an offshoot of the Church of England) and the Roman Catholic Church. In most rural areas, these exotic religions have not entirely replaced traditional beliefs, so that many people practise both concurrently. Roughly 11% of Uganda is Islamic, a legacy of the Arab trade with Buganda in the late 19th century. There is little or no friction between Christian and Muslim in modern Uganda, though post-independence political conflict did follow Catholic–Protestant lines. Although the country's Asian population was forced into exile by Amin in 1972, many individuals, both Islamic and Hindu, have been repatriated since 1986. The main centre of animism is the northeast, where the Karimojong – like the affiliated Maasai and other Rift Valley pastoralists – largely shun any exotic faith in favour of their own traditional beliefs.

Natural History

What most distinguishes Uganda from any other recognised African safari destination is quite simply its relatively high proportion of closed canopy forest. This embraces Afro-montane forest such as that found on Mount Elgon, which has strong affinities to similar habitats on mounts Kilimanjaro and Kenya, as well as the likes of Semliki National Park, effectively an easterly extension of the lowland rainforest that blankets the Congolese Basin and west Africa. Uganda thus harbours a wide variety of vertebrate and other species absent elsewhere in east and southern Africa, and the accessibility of its major forests by comparison to those in west Africa makes it an unbeatable destination for viewing African forest creatures – from gorillas and chimps to a colourful array of butterflies and birds – in their natural habitat.

When it comes to more conventional game viewing, Uganda is not a safari destination to bear comparison with Tanzania or Kenya, or for that matter the majority of countries in southern Africa. It is too small to have any reserves on the grand scale of Tanzania's Selous or Serengeti, or the Luangwa, Chobe, Hwange and Kruger national parks further south. Nevertheless, its savanna reserves are gradually recovering from the heavy poaching that took place during the years of civil war and political unrest. Today, Queen Elizabeth and Murchison Falls national parks offer as good a chance of encountering perennial safari favourites such as lion, elephant, buffalo, giraffe and even leopard as many more celebrated game reserves – with the added bonus of lying on a circuit that also offers some of the best forest primate viewing in Africa. For independent travellers on a limited budget, these two parks are also among the most accessible and affordable, comparably worthwhile savanna reserves anywhere in Africa.

A striking feature of the Ugandan landscape, with the exception of the semi-desert and dry acacia woodland of the far north, is its relatively moist climate. A high precipitation level makes the countryside far greener and more fertile than elsewhere in East Africa, while lakes, rivers and other wetland habitats account for almost 25% of the country's surface area. The most extensive freshwater bodies that lie within Uganda or along its borders are, in descending order, lakes Victoria, Albert, Kyoga, Edward, Kwania and George. Lesser expanses include Lake Wamala near Mityana, lakes Bunyonyi and Mutanda in Kigezi, lakes Bisina and Opeta in the east, and almost 100 small crater lakes dotted around the Rwenzori foothills. Of particular interest to birdwatchers are the half-dozen species associated exclusively with papyrus swamps – most notably the exquisite papyrus gonolek and eagerly sought-after shoebill, the latter seen more easily in Uganda than anywhere else.

Although most of Uganda is topographically relatively undramatic – essentially an undulating plateau perched at altitudes of 1,000–1,200m between the eastern and western arms of the Rift Valley – it is bordered by some of the continent's most impressive mountains. Foremost among these are the Rwenzori Mountains, which follow the Congolese border and are topped by the third-highest point in Africa, the 5,109m Margherita Peak on Mount Stanley. Other major mountains include Elgon (4,321m) on the Kenyan border, the Virungas on the Rwandan border (of which Muhabura is at 4,127m the highest of the Ugandan peaks), and Moroto (3,084m), Kadam (3,068m) and Morungole (2,750m) on the Kenyan border north of Elgon. Rising in solitude from the surrounding plains, these high mountains all support isolated microhabitats of forest and high grassland. The higher reaches of the Rwenzori, Elgon and to a lesser extent the Virungas, are covered in Afro-alpine moorland, a fascinating and somewhat other-worldly habitat noted for gigantism among plants such as lobelias, heather and groundsel, as well as habitat-specific creatures such as the dazzling scarlet-tufted malachite sunbird.

CONSERVATION AREAS

Uganda's list of gazetted conservation areas embraces ten national parks and several other wildlife reserves and forest reserves. National parks are accorded a higher status and conservation priority than other reserves, and from the visitor's point of view they are generally better developed for tourism.

Bureaucratic considerations aside, the most meaningful way to categorise Uganda's various national parks and reserves is on the basis of the type of habitat they protect. I will occasionally refer to some national parks as game or savanna reserves, forest reserves and montane reserves. In this sense, the term 'game reserve' applies to any reserve or national park that protects a savanna habitat and supports

NATIONAL PARK AND RESERVE FEES

The Uganda Wildlife Authority or UWA (pronounced ooh-er!) is the body responsible for Uganda's national parks and wildlife reserves. See page 168.

Visiting fees for UWA's protected areas fall into two categories. Murchison Falls, Queen Elizabeth, Bwindi Impenetrable, Mgahinga Gorilla, Lake Mburo, Kibale, Kidepo Valley and Rwenzori Mountains national parks are classed as Category A. Semliki and Mount Elgon national parks and Semliki, Katonga and Pian Upe wildlife reserves are classed as Category B.

Different prices apply to foreign non residents, essentially visiting tourists (FNR), foreign residents living in East Africa (FR) and Ugandan citizens. Under fives enter all protected areas for free. Children aged 5 to 15 years pay half price. The prices given below will apply until a new two-year tariff comes into operation on 1 January 2014. Expect entry fees to rise by US$5 with similarly modest increases for most park activities. Gorilla tracking fees may rise more sharply – though the rumoured US$600 (FR) remains considerably lower than the US$750 levied in Rwanda. For prevailing rates visit UWA's website, www.ugandawildlife.org and click on the About UWA header.

Entrance to **Category A** protected areas currently costs US$35/25 for foreign non-residents (FNR) and foreign residents/East African residents (FR). Entrance to **Category B** protected areas is US$25/US$15 FNR/FR. Permits are valid for 24 hours from time of entrance. In addition, Ugandan 4x4 vehicles pay an entrance fee of US$12/Ush30,000 while a rather stiffer US$150 applies to foreign vehicles. Ugandan saloon cars pay US$8/Ush20,000, and foreign ones US$50. Vehicle fees do not apply to forested parks such as Kibale and Mgahinga. Fees are currently

typical plains animals, whereas the term 'forest reserve' refers to any reserve or national park that protects a forest environment and associated animals. The three montane national parks can in some circumstances be bracketed with forest reserves, since they all support montane and bamboo forests up to around 3,000m above sea level, though this habitat gives way to Afro-montane moorland at higher altitudes. For Uganda's ten national parks see the box *National parks* overleaf.

Although several other wildlife reserves are gazetted in Uganda, most are merely adjuncts to one of the savanna national parks. The only ones that have any tourist facilities at present are Semliki, Katonga, Bugungu, Pian Upe, Kabwoya and Kyambura wildlife reserves. Also of interest to tourists are Uganda's forest reserves, of which the Budongo and Kanyiyo Pabidi forest reserves south of Murchison Falls National Park have well-established tourist sites offering camping facilities, *bandas* and guided forest walks. The Lake Victoria region supports large tracts of forest, the most accessible of which are protected in Mpanga Forest Reserve near Mpigi and the Mabira Forest Reserve near Jinja, both of which also now offer accommodation, camping and guided walks. Kalinzu Forest Reserve between Mbarara and Queen Elizabeth National Park is also developed for tourism. Chimp tracking in Budongo and Kalinzu forests is significantly cheaper than in the national parks.

Several other sites are also of interest for their natural history. These include Lake Nkuruba, Amabere Caves and Bigodi Wetland near Fort Portal, Lake Bunyonyi and the Echuya Forest in Kigezi, and the Sipi Falls near Mbale. For birders in particular, it is easy to view Uganda, with its lush natural vegetation and dense tropical cultivation, as nothing less than one giant nature sanctuary. There are

payable in shillings or dollars but an electronic system is planned whereby preloaded entry cards will be debited at entrypoints. News will be posted on the Bradt Uganda website; see page ix.

Additional rates apply for park activities. **Gorilla tracking** permits cost US$500/US$475 FNR/FR. Low season discounts may apply. **Chimpanzee tracking** in **Kibale** costs US$150/US$100 FNR/FR. The Kibale Chimpanzee Habituation Experience costs US$220/US$150 FNR/FR. The above activities include park entrance fees. Those below exclude entry unless specifically stated otherwise.

Chimpanzee tracking costs US$60/US$54 FNR/FR in **Kaniyo Pabidi** (Murchison Falls Conservation Area) and US$50 in **Kyambura Gorge**. **Golden monkey tracking** in Mgahinga costs US$50. The fee for **UWA launch trips** in **Queen Elizabeth** and **Murchison Falls** is US$25 and US$10 in **Lake Mburo**. Trips are subject to minimum numbers. Prices for boats run by private operators are given in the relevant chapters. Guides cost US$20 per vehicle for a **game drive** and US$15/US$10 per FNR/FR for a **guided walk**.

For mountaineering costs for the **Rwenzori** see Rwenzori Trekking Services and Rwenzori Mountaineering Services on page 325–6. The daily rate of US$90 for trekking on **Mount Elgon** includes entrance but not the camping fee. A day hike on the **Mgahinga** volcanoes costs US$60.

UWA also offers a range of basic accommodation (guesthouses, furnished tents and bandas) in Queen Elizabeth, Kidepo, Lake Mburo, Semliki and Mount Elgon national parks. Prices range from US$12/US$16 to US$24/US$28 sgl/dbl. DIY camping in all protected areas costs US$6pp (min US$18).

	Area	Habitat	Special attractions
Bwindi Impenetrable	310km²	forest	mountain gorillas, forest birds
Kibale Forest	766km²	forest	chimpanzees, monkeys, forest birds
Kidepo Valley	1,344km²	savanna	dry-country antelopes, predators & birds
Lake Mburo	256km²	savanna	wide variety of antelope & waterbirds
Mgahinga Gorilla	33km²	montane	mountain gorillas, hiking, volcanic peaks
Mount Elgon	1,145km²	montane	hiking, forest birds
Murchison Falls	3,900km²	savanna	Murchison Falls, big game, waterbirds
Queen Elizabeth	1,978km²	savanna	big game, chimps, 612 bird species
Rwenzori	996km²	montane	hiking, forest birds, Afro-montane plants
Semliki	220km²	forest	hot springs, Rift Valley setting, 45 birds found nowhere else in Uganda

extensive forests on Buggala and other islands in Lake Victoria's Ssese archipelago, while the small relict forest protected in the Entebbe Botanical Garden offers an excellent introduction to Uganda's forest birds and is a good place to get a close look at black-and-white colobus monkeys. Even the Backpackers' Hostel 2km from the heart of Kampala offers the opportunity to see such colourful species as Ross's turaco, woodland kingfisher, white-throated bee-eater and a variety of robin-chats and weavers.

MAMMALS

The official checklist of mammals found in Uganda numbers 342 species, with both west and east African mammals being well represented. Using the same distinction between small and large mammals as that of the checklist, 132 of the species recorded in Uganda can be classified as large mammals and the remainder are small mammals, the latter group comprising 94 bat species, 70 rats and mice, 33 shrews and otter shrews, eight gerbils, four elephant shrews and a solitary golden mole.

What follows is an overview of the large mammal species known to occur in Uganda. Several useful field guides to African mammals are available for the purpose of identification (see page 540), but they all lack specific distribution details for individual countries. The following notes thus place emphasis on distribution and habitat within Uganda: they are not intended to replace a regional or continental field guide, but to be a Uganda-specific supplement to such a book.

PRIMATES Primates are exceptionally well represented in Uganda. There is widespread disagreement about the taxonomic status of many primate species and subspecies, but the present checklist includes 13 diurnal and six nocturnal species. Six of the diurnal primates found in Uganda are guenon monkeys, members of the taxonomically controversial genus *Cercopithecus*. The vervet and blue guenon monkeys, for instance, are both widespread African species known by at least five different common names, and both have over 20 recognised races, some of which are considered by some authorities to be separate species. Having been forced to try to make sense of this taxonomic maze in order to work out what is what, I might as well save you the effort and provide details of local races where they are known to me.

Apes The great apes of the family Pongidae are so closely related to humans that a less partial observer might well place them in the same family as us (it is thought that the chimpanzee is more closely related to humans than it is to any other ape). There are four ape species, of which two are found in Uganda (for further details see pages 280–1 and pages 348–9).

Gorilla (*Gorilla gorilla*) This is the bulkiest member of the primate family: an adult gorilla may grow up to 1.8m high (although they seldom stand fully upright) and weigh up to 210kg. Three subspecies of gorilla are recognised. The most common race, the western lowland gorilla (*G. g. gorilla*), is not present in Uganda, but an estimated 40,000 live in the rainforests of west and central Africa. The endangered eastern lowland gorilla (*G. g. graueri*) is restricted to patches of forest in eastern DRC, where there are estimated to be 4,000 animals. The most threatened race of gorilla is the mountain gorilla (*G. g. beringei*). The total number is now estimated at 888 (a significant increase over the past few years): at least 480 in the Virunga Mountains (shared between Uganda, DRC and Rwanda) and 408 in Uganda, where mountain gorillas are resident in Bwindi Impenetrable National Park and Mgahinga Gorilla National Park. These reserves, along with the mountain gorilla reserves in Rwanda and DRC, are both covered in *Chapter 7*, and so I have included more detailed information on gorilla behaviour in that chapter.

Mountain gorilla

Common chimpanzee (*Pan troglodytes*) This distinctive black-coated ape, more closely related to man than to any other living creature, lives in large, loosely bonded communities based around a core of related males with an internal hierarchy topped by a benevolent alpha male. Females are generally less strongly bonded to their core group than are males; emigration between communities is not unusual. Mother–child bonds are strong. Daughters normally leave their mother only after they reach maturity, at which point relations between them may be severed. Mother–son relations have been known to survive for more than 40 years. A troop has a well-defined core territory which is fiercely defended by regular boundary patrols.

Chimpanzees are primarily frugivorous (fruit eating), but they do eat meat and even hunt on occasion – red colobus monkeys are regularly hunted in Tanzania's Gombe Stream and Mahale Mountains national parks, while researchers in Kalinzu Forest in Uganda have observed blue- and red-tailed monkeys being eaten by chimps, as well as unsuccessful attempts to hunt black-and-white colobus. The first recorded instance of chimps using tools was at Gombe Stream in Tanzania, where they regularly use modified sticks to 'fish' in termite mounds. In west Africa, they have been observed cracking nuts open using a stone and anvil. Chimpanzees are amongst the most intelligent of animals: in language studies in the USA they have been taught to communicate

Chimpanzee

in American sign language and have demonstrated their understanding, in some instances by even creating compound words for new objects (such as rock-berry to describe a nut).

Chimpanzees are typical animals of the rainforest and woodlands from Guinea to western Uganda. Their behaviour has been studied since 1960 by Jane Goodall and others at Gombe Stream and other sites across Africa, including the Budongo and Kibale forests in Uganda. Chimpanzees live in most of the forests of western Uganda, and they have been habituated to tourists in Kibale

ANIMAL TAXONOMY

In this chapter, I've made widespread use of taxonomic terms such as genus, species and race. Some readers may not be familiar with these terms, so a brief explanation follows.

Taxonomy is the branch of biology concerned with classifying living organisms. It uses a hierarchical system to represent the relationships between different animals. At the top of the hierarchy are kingdoms, phyla, subphyla and classes. All vertebrates belong to the animal kingdom, phylum Chordata, subphylum Vertebrata. There are five vertebrate classes: Mammalia (mammals), Aves (birds), Reptilia (reptiles), Amphibia (amphibians) and Pisces (fish). Within any class, several orders might be divided in turn into families and, depending on the complexity of the order and family, various suborders and subfamilies. All baboons, for instance, belong to the Primate order, suborder Catarrhini (monkeys and apes), family Cercopithecoidea (Old World Monkeys) and subfamily Cercopithecidae (cheek-pouch monkeys, ie: guenons, baboons and mangabeys).

Taxonomists accord to every living organism a Latin binomial (two-part name) indicating its genus (plural genera) and species. Thus the savanna baboon *Papio cyenephalus* and hamadrayas baboon *Papio hamadrayas* are different species of the genus *Papio*. Some species are further divided into races or subspecies. For instance, taxonomists recognise four races of savanna baboon: yellow baboon, olive baboon, chacma baboon and Guinea baboon. A race is indicated by a trinomial (three-part name), for instance *Papio cyenephalus cyenephalus* for the yellow baboon and *Papio cyenephalus anubis* for the olive baboon. The identical specific and racial designation of *cyenephalus* for the yellow baboon make it the nominate race – a label that has no significance other than that it would most probably have been the first race of that species to be described by taxonomists.

Taxonomic constructs are designed to approximate the real genetic and evolutionary relationships between various living creatures, and on the whole they succeed. But equally the science exists to help humans understand a reality that is likely to be more complex and less absolute than any conceptual structure used to contain it. This is particularly the case with speciation – the evolution of two or more distinct species from a common ancestor – which might occur over many thousands of generations, and like many gradual processes may lack for any absolute landmarks.

Simplistically, the process of speciation begins when a single population splits into two mutually exclusive breeding units. This can happen as a result of geographic isolation (for instance mountain and lowland gorillas), habitat differences (forest and savanna elephants) or varied migratory patterns (the six races of yellow wagtail intermingle as non-breeding migrants to Africa during the northern winter, but they all have a discrete Palaearctic breeding ground). Whatever the reason, the two

National Park, the Chambura Gorge in Queen Elizabeth National Park, Semliki Wildlife Reserve and the Budongo and Kanyiyo Pabidi forests near Murchison Falls National Park.

Monkeys All the monkeys found in Uganda are members of the family Cercopithecidae (Old World Monkeys). They fall into five genera: *Colobus* (closely related to the leaf-eating monkeys of Asia), *Cercopithecus* (guenons), *Papio* (baboons), *Erythrocebus* (patas) and *Cercocebus* (mangabeys).

breeding communities will share an identical gene pool when first they split, but as generations pass they will accumulate a number of small genetic differences and eventually marked racial characteristics. Given long enough, the two populations might even deviate to the point where they wouldn't or couldn't interbreed, even if the barrier that originally divided them was removed.

The taxonomic distinction between a full species and a subspecies or race of that species rests not on how similar the two taxa are in appearance or habit, but on the final point above. Should it be known that two distinct taxa freely interbreed and produce fertile hybrids where their ranges overlap, or it is believed that they would in the event that their ranges did overlap, then they are classified as races of the same species. If not, they are regarded as full species. The six races of yellow wagtail referred to above are all very different in appearance, far more so, for instance, than the several dozen warbler species of the genus *Cisticola*, but clearly they are able to interbreed, and they must thus be regarded as belonging to the same species. And while this may seem a strange distinction on the face of things, it does make sense when you recall that humans rely mostly on visual recognition, whereas many other creatures are more dependent on other senses. Those pesky cisticolas all look much the same to human observers, but each species has a highly distinctive call and in some cases a display flight that would preclude crossbreeding whether or not it is genetically possible.

The gradual nature of speciation creates grey areas that no arbitrary distinction can cover – at any given moment in time there might exist separate breeding populations of a certain species that have not yet evolved distinct racial characters, or distinct races that are on their way to becoming full species. Furthermore, where no conclusive evidence exists, some taxonomists tend to be habitual 'lumpers' and others eager 'splitters' – respectively inclined to designate any controversial taxa racial or full specific status. For this reason, various field guides often differ in their designation of controversial taxa.

Among African mammals, this is particularly the case with primates, where in some cases up to 20 described taxa are sometimes lumped together as one species and sometimes split into several specific clusters of similar races. The savanna baboon is a case in point. The four races are known to interbreed where their ranges overlap. But they are also all very distinctive in appearance, and several field guides now classify them as different species, so that the olive baboon, for instance, is designated *Papio anubis* as opposed to *Papio cyenephalus anubis*. Such ambiguities can be a source of genuine frustration, particularly for birdwatchers obsessed with ticking 'new' species, but they also serve as a valid reminder that the natural world is and will always be a more complex, mysterious and dynamic entity than any taxonomic construct designed to label it.

Baboons (*Papio spp*) Heavily built and mainly terrestrial, baboons can be distinguished from any other monkey found in Uganda by their larger size and distinctive dog-like head. They live in large troops with a complex and rigid social structure held together by matriarchal lineages. Males frequently move between troops in their search for social dominance. Baboons are omnivorous and highly adaptable, for which reason they are the most widespread primate in Africa. Four

DANGEROUS ANIMALS

The dangers associated with African wild animals are frequently overstated by hunters and others trying to glamorise their way of life. In reality, most wild animals fear us far more than we fear them, and their normal response to seeing a person is to leg it as quickly as possible. But while the risk posed to tourists by wild animals is very low, accidents do happen, and common sense should be exercised wherever they are around.

The need for caution is greatest near water, particularly around dusk and dawn, when hippos are out grazing. Responsible for more human fatalities than any other large mammal, hippos are not actively aggressive to humans, but they do panic easily and tend to mow down any person that comes between them and the safety of the water, usually with fatal consequences. Never cross deliberately between a hippo and water, and avoid well-vegetated riverbanks and lakeshores in overcast weather or low light unless you are certain no hippos are present. Be aware, too, that any path leading through thick vegetation to an aquatic hippo habitat was most probably created by grazing hippos, so there's a real risk of a heads-on confrontation in a confined channel at times of day when hippos might be on land.

Crocodiles are more dangerous to locals but represent less of a threat to travellers, since they are unlikely to attack outside of their aquatic hunting environment. That means you need to swim in crocodile-infested waters to be at appreciable risk, though it's wise to keep a berth of a metre or so from the shore, since a large and hungry individual might occasionally drag in an animal or person from the water's edge. In the vicinity of a human settlement, any crocodile large enough to attack an adult will most likely have been consigned to its maker by its potential prey. The risk is greater away from habitation, but the rule of thumb is simple: don't bathe in any potential crocodile habitat unless you have reliable local information that it is safe.

There are parts of Uganda where hikers might stumble across an elephant or a buffalo, the most dangerous of Africa's terrestrial herbivores. Elephants almost invariably mock charge and indulge in some hair-raising trumpeting before they attack in earnest. Provided that you back off at the first sign of unease, they seldom take further notice of you. If you see them before they see you, give them a wide berth, bearing in mind they are most likely to attack if surprised at close proximity. If an animal charges you, the safest course of action is to head for the nearest tree and climb it. And should an elephant or buffalo stray close to your campsite or lodge, do suppress any urge to wander closer on foot – it may well react aggressively if surprised!

An elephant is large enough to hurt the occupants of a vehicle, so if it doesn't want your vehicle to pass, back off and wait until it has crossed the road or moved off. Never switch off the engine around elephants until you're certain they are relaxed, and avoid allowing your car to be boxed in between an elephant and another vehicle (or boxing in another vehicle yourself). If an elephant does

types of baboon live in sub-Saharan Africa. The olive baboon, the only type found in Uganda, is accorded full species status (*P. anubis*) by some authorities and designated as a race of the yellow/savanna baboon (*P. cyanocephalus*) by others. Baboons are widespread and common in Uganda: they occur in all but the three montane national parks and are frequently seen on the fringes of forest reserves and even along the roadside elsewhere in the country.

threaten a vehicle in earnest and backing off isn't an option, then revving the engine hard will generally dissuade it from pursuing the contest.

Monkeys, especially vervets and baboons, can become aggressive where they associate people with food. For this reason, feeding monkeys is highly irresponsible, especially as it may ultimately lead to their being shot as vermin. If you join a guided tour where the driver or guide feeds any primate, tell him not to. Although most monkeys are too small to be more than a nuisance, baboons have killed children and maimed adults with their vicious teeth. Unless trapped, however, their interest will be food, not people, so in the event of a genuine confrontation, throw down the food before the baboon gets too close. If you leave food (especially fruit) in your tent, monkeys might well tear the tent down. Present only in a handful of African countries, chimps and gorillas are potentially dangerous, but only likely to be encountered on a guided forest walk, where you should obey your guide's instructions at all times.

Despite their fierce reputation, large predators generally avoid humans and are only likely to kill accidentally or in self-defence. Lions are arguably the exception, though they seldom attack unprovoked. Of the rest, cheetahs represent no threat to adults, leopards seldom attack unless cornered, and hyenas – though often associated with human settlements and potentially dangerous – are most likely to slink off into the shadows when disturbed. Should you encounter any other large predator on foot, the most important thing you need to know is that running away will almost certainly trigger its 'chase' instinct and it will win the race. Better to stand still and/or back off very slowly, preferably without making eye contact. If (and only if) the animal looks really menacing, then noisy confrontation is probably a better tactic than fleeing. In areas where large predators are still reasonably common, sleeping in a sealed tent practically guarantees your safety – but don't sleep with your head sticking out or you risk being decapitated through predatorial curiosity, and never store meat in the tent.

As for the smaller stuff, venomous snakes and scorpions are present but unobtrusive, though you should be wary when picking up the wood or stones under which they often hide. Snakes generally slither away when they sense the seismic vibrations made by footfall, though be aware that rocky slopes and cliffs are a favoured habitat of the slothful puff adder, which may not move off in such circumstances. Good walking boots protect against the 50% of snakebites that occur below the ankle, and long trousers help deflect bites higher on the leg. But lethal bites are a rarity – in South Africa, which boasts its fair share of venomous snakes, more people are killed by lightning! Some discussion of treatment is included on page 96.

When all's said and done, Africa's most dangerous non-bipedal creature, and exponentially so, is the malaria-carrying mosquito. Humans, particularly when behind a steering wheel, come in a close second!

Patas monkey (*Erythrocebus patas*)
Another terrestrial primate, restricted to the
dry savanna of north-central Africa, the patas
could be confused with the vervet monkey, but
it has a lankier build, a light reddish-brown
coat, and a black stripe above the eyes
(the vervet is greyer and has a black face
mask). In Uganda, the patas monkey is
restricted to the extreme north, where it can be
seen in Kidepo and Murchison Falls national parks, as well as the Pian Upe Wildlife
Reserve. It is also known as the hussar monkey. The race found in Uganda is the
Nile patas or nisras (*E. p. pyrrhonotus*).

*Patas
monkey*

Vervet monkey (*Cercopithecus aethiops*) This light-grey guenon is readily
identified by its black face and the male's distinctive blue genitals. Associated
with a wide variety of habitats, it's the only guenon you're likely to see outside of
forests and it is thought to be the most numerous monkey species in the world.
The vervet monkey is also known as the green, tantalus, savanna
and grivet monkey. More than 20 races are recognised, and some
authorities group these races into four distinct species. At least
four races are found in Uganda: the black-faced vervet (*C. a.
centralis*), Naivasha vervet (*C. a. callidus*), Jebel Mara tantalus
(*C. a. marrensis*) and Stuhlmann's green monkey (*C.
a. stuhlmanni*). Vervet monkeys are widespread
and common in Uganda, even outside of national
parks, but they are absent from forest interiors and
Afro-alpine habitats.

Vervet monkey

Blue monkey (*Cercopithecus mitis*) The blue monkey is the most widespread
forest guenon in East Africa – uniform dark blue-grey in colour except for its
white throat and chest patch, with thick fur and backward-projecting hair on its
forehead. The blue monkey is common in most Ugandan
forests, where it lives in troops of between four and 12
animals and frequently associates with other primates.
It is also known as the diademed guenon, samango
monkey, Sykes's monkey, gentle monkey and white-
throated guenon (the last regarded as a separate species by
some authorities). More than 20 races are identified, of
which three are found in Uganda, including the striking
and very localised golden monkey, which is more or less
restricted to bamboo forest in the Virunga Mountains. Blue monkeys occur in all
but two of Uganda's national parks (Murchison Falls and Lake Mburo being the
exceptions) and in practically every other forest in the country.

Blue monkey

Red-tailed monkey (*Cercopithecus ascinius*) Another widespread forest guenon,
the red-tailed monkey is brownish in appearance with white cheek whiskers, a
coppery tail and a distinctive white, heart-shaped patch on its nose, giving rise
to its more descriptive alternative name of black-cheeked white-nosed monkey. It
is normally seen singly, in pairs or in small family groups, but it also associates
with other monkeys and has been known to accumulate in groups of up to 200.
The race found in Uganda is *C. a. schmidti*. Red-tailed and blue monkeys regularly

interbreed in the Kibale Forest. Red-tailed monkeys occur in Kibale Forest, Bwindi, Semliki and Queen Elizabeth national parks, as well as in Budongo, Mpanga and several other forest reserves.

De Brazza's monkey (*Cercopithecus neglectus*) This spectacular thickset guenon has a relatively short tail, a hairy face with a reddish-brown patch around its eyes, a white band across its brow and a distinctive white moustache and beard. Primarily a west African species, De Brazza's monkey is very localised in East Africa, most likely to be seen in the vicinity of Mount Elgon and Semliki national parks.

L'Hoest's monkey (*Cercopithecus lhoesti*) This handsome guenon is less well known and more difficult to see than most of its relatives, largely because of its preference for dense secondary forest and its terrestrial habits. It has a black face and backward-projecting white whiskers that partially cover its ears, and is the only guenon which habitually carries its tail in an upright position. In Uganda, L'Hoest's monkey is most likely to be seen in Kibale Forest, Bwindi or Maramagambo Forest in Queen Elizabeth National Park.

Grey-cheeked mangabey (*Cercocebus algigena*) This greyish-black monkey has few distinguishing features. It has baboon-like mannerisms, a shaggier appearance than any guenon, light-grey cheeks and a slight mane. Grey-cheeked mangabeys live in lowland and mid-altitude forests. In Uganda, they are most likely to be seen in the Kibale Forest, where they are common, as well as in Semliki National Park. The race found in Uganda is also known as Johnston's mangabey (*C. a. johnstoni*).

Black-and-white colobus (*Colobus guereza*) This beautifully marked and distinctive monkey has a black body, white facial markings, long white tail and, in some races, a white side-stripe. It lives in small groups and is almost exclusively arboreal. An adult is capable of jumping up to 30m, a spectacular sight with its white tail streaming behind. This is probably the most common and widespread forest monkey in Uganda, occurring in most sizeable forest patches and even in well-developed riparian woodland. The Rwenzori race of the closely related **Angola colobus** (*Colobus angolensis*) occurs alongside the black-and-white colobus in forested parts of the Rwenzori National Park.

Black-and-white colobus

Red colobus (*Piliocolobus badius*) This relatively large red-grey monkey has few distinguishing features other than its slightly tufted crown. It is highly sociable and normally lives in scattered troops of 50 or more animals. About 15 races of red colobus are recognised, many of which are considered by some authorities to be distinct species. In Uganda, red colobus monkeys are largely restricted to Kibale Forest National Park and environs, where they are especially common in the Bigodi Wetland Sanctuary, though they do also occur in small numbers in Semliki National Park.

Nocturnal primates
Seldom observed on account of their nocturnal habits, the prosimians are a relict group of primitive primates more closely related to the lemurs of Madagascar than to the diurnal monkeys and apes of the African mainland.

Bushbabies Also called galagoes, these small, nocturnal primates are widespread in wooded habitats in sub-Saharan Africa. The bushbaby's piercing cry is one of the distinctive sounds of the African night. If you want to see a bushbaby, trace the cry to a tree, then shine a torch into it and you should easily pick out its large round eyes. Five galago species are found in Uganda, of which the lesser bushbaby (*Galago senegalensis*) is the most common. An insectivorous creature, only 17cm long excluding its tail, the lesser bushbaby is a creature of woodland as opposed to true forest, and it has been recorded in all of Uganda's savanna reserves. The eastern needle-clawed bushbaby (*G. inustus*), Thomas's bushbaby (*G. thomasi*) and dwarf bushbaby (*G. demidovii*) all occur in the Kibale and Bwindi forests, and the dwarf bushbaby has also been recorded in Lake Mburo and Queen Elizabeth national parks. I have no distribution information for Matschie's bushbaby (*G. matschiei*).

Lesser bushbaby

Potto (*Perodicticus potto*) This medium-sized sloth-like creature inhabits forest interiors, where it spends the nights foraging upside down from tree branches. It can sometimes be located at night by shining a spotlight into the canopy. The potto occurs in Kibale, Bwindi and Queen Elizabeth national parks, as well as most other major rainforests, and it is most likely to be seen in guided night walks in Kibale Forest.

CARNIVORES A total of 38 carnivores have been recorded in Uganda: five canid species, seven felines, three hyenas, ten mongooses, six mustelids (otters, badgers and weasels) and seven viverrids (civets and genets).

Felines

Lion (*Panthera leo*) The largest African carnivore, and the one animal that everybody wants to see on safari, the lion is the most sociable of the large cats, living in loosely structured prides of typically five to 15 animals. They normally hunt at night, and their favoured prey consists of buffalo and medium-to-large antelope such as Uganda kob. Females, working in teams of up to eight animals, are responsible for most hunts. Rivalry between male lions is intense: prides may have more than one dominant male working in collaboration to prevent a takeover and young males are forced out of their home pride at about three years of age. Pride takeovers are often fought to the death; after a successful one, it is not unusual for all the male cubs to be killed. Lions are not very active by day: they are most often seen lying in the shade looking the picture of regal indolence. They occur naturally in most woodland and grassland habitats, and are now fairly common in certain parts of Murchison Falls and Queen Elizabeth national parks. A healthy lion population survives in Kidepo National Park but they are no longer present in Lake Mburo.

Leopard

Leopard (*Panthera pardus*) The most common of Africa's large felines, the leopard often lives in close proximity to humans, but it is rarely seen because of its secretive, solitary nature. Leopards hunt using stealth and power, often getting to within 5m of their intended prey before pouncing, and they habitually store their kill in a tree to keep it from being poached by other large predators. They can be distinguished from cheetahs by their rosette-shaped spots and more powerful build, as well as by their preference for wooded or rocky habitats. Leopards are found in virtually all habitats which offer adequate cover, and are present in most Ugandan national parks and forest reserves. The only place in Uganda where they are seen with regularity is along the Channel Drive in Queen Elizabeth National Park.

Cheetah (*Acinonyx jubatus*) Superficially similar to the leopard, the cheetah is the most diurnal of Africa's cat species, and it hunts using speed as opposed to stealth. Cheetahs are the fastest land mammals, capable of running at up to 70km/h in short bursts. Male cheetahs are strongly territorial and in some areas they commonly defend their territory in pairs or trios. Cheetahs are the least powerful of the large predators: they are chased from a high percentage of their kills and 50% of cheetah cubs are killed by other predators before they reach three months of age. Like leopards, cheetahs are heavily spotted and solitary in their habits, but their greyhound-like build, distinctive black tear-marks and preference for grassland and savanna habitats preclude confusion. In Uganda, cheetahs are traditionally present only in the vicinity of Kidepo National Park, though several sightings in the north of Murchison Falls suggest that they might yet recolonise this park.

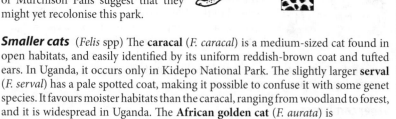
Cheetah

Smaller cats (*Felis* spp) The **caracal** (*F. caracal*) is a medium-sized cat found in open habitats, and easily identified by its uniform reddish-brown coat and tufted ears. In Uganda, it occurs only in Kidepo National Park. The slightly larger **serval** (*F. serval*) has a pale spotted coat, making it possible to confuse it with some genet species. It favours moister habitats than the caracal, ranging from woodland to forest, and it is widespread in Uganda. The **African golden cat** (*F. aurata*) is a rarely seen creature of the west African forest: it is widespread in western Uganda, where it has been recorded in every forested national park except Semliki. The **African wild cat** (*F. silvestris*) is reminiscent of the domestic tabby, with which it has been known to interbreed successfully, and it is found in most savanna habitats in Uganda.

Caracal

Canids The Canidae is a family of medium-sized carnivores of which the most familiar is the domestic dog. Five species – all recognisably dog-like in appearance and habits – are present in Uganda, though none is very common.

Black-backed jackal

Jackals (*Canis* spp) Jackals are small to medium-sized dogs associated with most savanna habitats. Although often portrayed as carrion-eaters, they are in fact opportunistic omnivores, hunting a variety of small mammals and birds with some regularity and also eating a substantial amount of fruit and bulbs. The most widespread canid in Uganda is the **side-striped jackal** (*C. adustus*), which occurs in all four savanna national parks as well as in Bwindi and Mgahinga, and is most likely to be seen in the north of Murchison Falls. Within Uganda, the similar **black-backed jackal** (*C. mesomelas*) is restricted to Kidepo National Park, Pian Upe and environs, while the **golden jackal** (*C. aureus*), though it appears on the national checklist, has been recorded in no national park and is presumably a vagrant.

Bat-eared fox (*Otocyon megalotis*) This small but striking silver-grey insectivore, rendered unmistakable by its huge ears and black eye-mask, is most often seen in pairs or small family groups during the cooler hours of the day. Associated with dry open country, the bat-eared fox is quite common in the Kidepo and Pian Upe, but absent elsewhere in Uganda.

Bat-eared fox

African hunting dog (*Lycaon pictus*) The largest African canid, and the most endangered after the rare Ethiopian wolf, the African hunting dog (also known as the wild or painted dog) lives in packs of five to 50 animals and is distinguished by its cryptic black, brown and cream coat. Hunting dogs are highly effective pack hunters and were once widely distributed and common throughout sub-Saharan Africa. Hunted as vermin and highly susceptible to epidemics spread by domestic dogs, hunting dogs today have a very localised and scattered distribution pattern, with perhaps 25% of the estimated wild population of 5,000 confined to the Selous ecosystem in southern Tanzania. The African hunting dog is locally extinct in roughly half the countries it once inhabited, Uganda included. Recolonisation, though unlikely, is not impossible, since hunting dogs are great wanderers and small populations do still survive in parts of western Tanzania and Kenya.

African hunting dog

Other carnivores

Spotted hyena (*Crocuta crocuta*) In Uganda, as elsewhere in Africa, the spotted hyena is by far the most common member of a family of large, hunchbacked carnivores whose somewhat canid appearance belies a closer evolutionary relationship to mongooses and cats. Often portrayed as an exclusive scavenger, the spotted hyena is an adept hunter capable of killing an animal as large as a wildebeest. In ancient times, the spotted hyena was thought to be hermaphroditic: the female's vagina is blocked by a false but remarkably realistic-looking scrotum and penis. Most hyena species live in loosely structured clans of around ten animals, and their social interaction is fascinating to observe. Clans are led by females, which are stronger and larger than males. The spotted hyena is bulky with a sloping back, a light-brown coat marked with dark-brown spots and an exceptionally powerful jaw which enables it to crack open bones and slice through the thickest hide. The spotted hyena is found in all of Uganda's savanna national parks, as well as in Mgahinga, but is only seen with great regularity in Queen Elizabeth. Note that the secretive **striped hyena** (*Hyaena hyaena*) and the insectivorous **aardwolf** (*Proteles cristatus*) are present but uncommon in Kidepo National Park and environs.

Spotted hyena

African civet

African civet (*Civetticus civetta*) This bulky, long-haired, cat-like viverrid has been kept in captivity for thousands of years (its anal secretions were used in making perfumes until a synthetic replacement was found). Surprisingly, little is known about their habits in the wild. Civets are widespread and common in most wooded habitats, and they have been recorded in most of Uganda's national parks, but they are seen very rarely on account of their secretive, nocturnal habits.

Genets (*Genetta* spp) Closely related to civets, but often referred to mistakenly as cats because of various superficial similarities in appearance, the genets are slender, low-slung viverrids characterised by beautiful spotted coats and extraordinarily long tails. Secretive except when habituated, and subject to some taxonomic debate, genets are attracted to human waste and are occasionally seen slinking around campsites and lodges after dark. The **servaline genet** (*G. servalina*), **large-spotted genet** (*G. tigrina*) and **small-spotted genet** (*G. genetta*) are all widespread in Uganda, with the latter two generally occurring in more lightly wooded areas than the former, and sometimes observed on night drives in the Semliki Wildlife Reserve. A west African species, the **giant forest genet** (*G. victiriae*), has been recorded in Maramagambo Forest in Queen Elizabeth National Park.

Otters Three species of these familiar aquatic predators occur in sub-Saharan Africa, and their ranges overlap in western Uganda, where all three have been recorded in certain areas such as Lake Mburo National Park. The **Cape clawless otter** (*Aonyx capensis*) and **DRC clawless otter** (*A. congica*), regarded to be conspecific by some authorities, are the largest African otters, growing up to 1.6m long, with a rich brown coat and pale chin and belly. Associated with most wetland habitats, the clawless otters are most active between dusk and dawn, and are hence less likely to be observed than the smaller and darker **spotted-necked otter** (*Lutra maculicollisi*), a diurnal species that is unusually common and visible on Lake Bunyonyi in Kigezi.

Ratel (honey badger) (*Mellivora capensis*) The ratel is a medium-sized mustelid with a puppy-like head, black sides and underparts and a grey-white back. It is an adaptable creature, eating whatever comes its way – it's said that they've been known to kill buffaloes by running underneath them and biting off their testicles which, if true, is certainly taking opportunism to a wasteful extreme. When not Bobbiting bovines, the ratel occasionally indulges in a symbiotic relationship with a bird called the greater honeyguide: the honeyguide takes the ratel to a beehive, which the ratel then tears open, allowing the honeyguide to feed on the scraps. Ratels are widespread in Uganda, but uncommon and rarely seen. Other mustelids found in Uganda include the **zorilla** (or striped polecat) and the **striped weasel**.

Mongooses Ten mongoose species have been recorded in Uganda, none of which – as is commonly assumed – feeds predominantly on snakes. Five species are widespread and common enough to have been recorded in at least half the national parks. They are the **marsh mongoose** (*Atilax paludinosus*), **Egyptian mongoose** (*Herpestes ichneumon*), **slender mongoose** (*Herpestes sanguineus*), **white-**

Banded mongoose

tailed mongoose (*Ichneumia albicauda*) and **banded mongoose** (*Mungos mungo*). Of these the banded mongoose is the most regularly observed, particularly on the Mweya Peninsula in Queen Elizabeth National Park.

ANTELOPE Some 29 antelope species – about one-third of the African total – are included on the checklist for Uganda, a figure that fails to acknowledge a recent rash of near or complete local extinctions. There are probably no more than ten roan antelope remaining in Uganda, for example, while no oryx are left at all. Of the species that do still occur, five fall into the category of large antelope, having a shoulder height of above 120cm (roughly the height of a zebra); eight are in the category of medium-sized antelope, having a shoulder height of between 75cm and 90cm; and the remainder are small antelope, with a shoulder height of between 30cm and 60cm.

Large antelope

Common eland (*Taurotragus oryx*) The world's largest antelope is the common or Cape eland which measures over 1.8m in height, and which can be bulkier than a buffalo. The eland has a rather bovine appearance: fawn-brown in colour, with a large dewlap and short, spiralled horns, and in some cases light-white stripes on its sides. The common eland occurs in open habitats throughout eastern and southern Africa. In Uganda, it is most likely to be seen in Lake Mburo National Park, but also occurs in Kidepo Valley and Pian Upe Wildlife Reserve.

Eland

Greater kudu

Greater kudu (*Tragelaphus strepsiceros*) This is another very large antelope, measuring up to 1.5m high, and it is also strikingly handsome, with a grey-brown coat marked by thin white side-stripes. The male has a small dewlap and large spiralling horns. The greater kudu live in small groups in woodland habitats. In Uganda, it occurs only in small numbers in Kidepo.

Hartebeest (*Alcelaphus buselaphus*) This large and ungainly looking, tan-coloured antelope – a relative of the wildebeest, which is absent from Uganda – has large shoulders, a sloping back and relatively small horns. It lives in small herds in lightly wooded and open savanna habitats. The typical hartebeest of Uganda is **Jackson's hartebeest** (*A. b. jacksoni*), though it is replaced by the **Lelwel hartebeest** (*A. b. lelweli*) west of the Nile. The closely related and similarly built **topi** (*Damaliscus lunatus*) has a much darker coat than the hartebeest, and distinctive blue-black markings above its knees. Jackson's hartebeest is most frequently seen in Murchison Falls, though it also occurs in Kidepo Valley.

Hartebeest

Defassa waterbuck (*Kobus ellipsyprymnus defassa*) Shaggy-looking, with a grey-brown coat, white rump and large curved horns, the Defassa waterbuck is considered by some authorities to be a distinct species, *K. defassa* (the common waterbuck found east of the Rift Valley has a white ring on its rump), but the two races interbreed where they overlap. Defassa waterbuck live in small herds and are most often seen grazing near water. They are found in suitable habitats in all four of Uganda's savanna national parks.

Defassa waterbuck

Roan antelope

Roan antelope (*Hippotragus equinus*) This handsome animal has a light red-brown coat, short backward-curving horns and a small mane on the back of the neck. It is present only in small numbers in Pian Upe having become locally extinct in Kidepo Valley and Lake Mburo national parks.

Medium-sized antelope

Uganda kob (*Kobus kob thomasi*) Uganda's national antelope is a race of the west African kob confined to grassy floodplains and open vegetation near water in Uganda and the southern Sudan. Although closely related to waterbuck and reedbuck, the kob is reddish-brown in colour and similar to the impala, but bulkier in appearance and lacking the impala's black side-stripe. Uganda kob live in herds of up to 100 animals in Queen Elizabeth and Murchison Falls and neighbouring conservation areas, as well as in Semliki and Katonga wildlife reserves.

Uganda kob

Bushbuck

Bushbuck (*Tragelaphus scriptus*) Probably the most widespread antelope in Uganda is the bushbuck, which lives in forest, riverine woodland and other thicketed habitats. The male bushbuck has a dark chestnut coat marked with white spots and stripes. The female is lighter in colour and vaguely resembles a large duiker. Although secretive and elusive, the bushbuck is very common in suitable habitats in most forests and national parks in Uganda.

Sitatunga (*Tragelaphus spekei*) This semi-aquatic antelope is similar in appearance to the closely related bushbuck, but the male is larger with a shaggier coat, both sexes are striped, and it has uniquely splayed hooves adapted to its favoured habitat of papyrus and other swamps. It is found in suitable habitats throughout Uganda, including six national parks, but is likely to be seen only in the Katonga Wildlife Reserve.

Sitatunga

Lesser kudu (*Tragelaphus imberbis*) This pretty, dry-country antelope is similar in appearance to the greater kudu, but much smaller and more heavily striped (greater kudu have between six and ten stripes; lesser kudu have 11 or more). Lesser kudu are present in Pian Upe and environs.

Grant's gazelle (*Gazella granti*) Yet another dry-country antelope which in Uganda has been reduced to 100 animals roaming the contiguous Pian Upe, Matheniko and Bokora wildlife reserves in Karamoja. This typical gazelle is lightly built, tan in colour, and lives in herds.

Reedbuck (*Redunca* spp) Also restricted to Kidepo is the **mountain reedbuck** (*R. fulvorufula*), a grey-brown antelope with small crescent-shaped horns. The very similar **Bohor reedbuck** (*R. redunca*) is more widespread, occurring in all four savanna national parks. Both reedbuck species are usually seen in pairs in open country near water, with the mountain reedbuck occurring at higher altitudes.

Reedbuck

Impala (*Aepyceros melampus*) This slender, handsome antelope, though superficially similar to the gazelles, belongs to a separate subfamily that is more closely related to hartebeest and oryx. The impala can be distinguished from any gazelle by its chestnut colouring, sleek appearance and the male's distinctive lyre-shaped horns. An adult impala can jump up to 3m high and has been known to broad-jump for over 10m. Impala live in herds of between 20 and a few hundred animals. They favour well-wooded savanna and woodland fringes, and are often abundant in such habitats. In Uganda, impalas are found only in Lake Mburo National Park and Katonga Wildlife Reserve.

Impala

Small antelope Nine of the small antelope species present in Uganda are **duikers**, a family of closely related antelopes which are generally characterised by their small size, sloping back, and preference for thickly forested habitats. Between 16 and 19 duiker species are recognised, many of them extremely localised in their distribution.

Grey duiker (*Sylvicapra grimmia*) Also known as the common or bush duiker, this is an atypical member of its family in that it generally occurs in woodland and savanna habitats. It has a grey-brown coat with a vaguely speckled appearance. The grey duiker is widespread in east and southern Africa, and it occurs in all four of Uganda's savanna national parks as well as in Mount Elgon.

Forest duiker (*Cephalophus* spp) The striking **yellow-backed duiker** (*C. sylviculter*) is also atypical of the family, owing to its relatively large size – heavier than a bushbuck – rather than any habitat preference. It is a west African species, but has been recorded in several forests in western Uganda, including those in Bwindi, Mgahinga, Rwenzori and Queen Elizabeth national parks; it's sometimes encountered fleetingly along the forest track leading uphill from the Buhoma headquarters at Bwindi. Of the more typical duiker species, **Harvey's red duiker** (*C. harveyi*) is a tiny chestnut-brown antelope found in forested parts of Queen Elizabeth National Park and in the Kibale Forest. The **blue duiker** (*C. monticola*), even smaller and with a grey-blue coat, is known to occur in Queen Elizabeth, Murchison Falls, Kibale and Bwindi national parks. **Peter's duiker** (*C.

Common duiker

callipygus) has been recorded in Bwindi, Kibale and Queen Elizabeth; the **black-fronted duiker** (*C. nigrifrons*) in Mgahinga and Bwindi; and there have been unconfirmed sightings of the **white-bellied duiker** (*C. leucogaster*) for Bwindi and Semliki. The **red-flanked duiker** (*C. rufilatus*) and **Weyn's duiker** (*C. weynsi*) have not been recorded in any national park, but they most probably occur in the Budongo Forest.

Bates's pygmy antelope (*Neofragus batesi*) Not a duiker, but similar both in size and its favoured habitat, this diminutive antelope – the second-smallest African ungulate – is a Congolese rainforest species that has been recorded in Semliki National Park and in forests within and bordering the southern half of Queen Elizabeth National Park.

Klipspringer (*Oreotragus oreotragus*) This distinctive antelope has a dark-grey bristly coat and an almost speckled appearance. It has goat-like habits and is invariably found in the vicinity of koppies or cliffs (the name *klipspringer* means 'rock-jumper' in Afrikaans). It lives in pairs in suitable habitats in Kidepo Valley and Lake Mburo national parks.

Oribi (*Ourebia ourebi*) This endearing gazelle-like antelope has a light red-brown back, white underparts, and a diagnostic black scent gland under its ears. It is one of the largest 'small' antelopes in Africa, not much smaller than a Thomson's gazelle. When disturbed, the oribi emits a high-pitched sneezing sound, then bounds off in a manner mildly reminiscent of a pronking springbok. The oribi favours tall grassland, and it occurs in all of the savanna national parks except for Queen Elizabeth. It is remarkably common in the Borassus grassland in the northern part of Murchison Falls National Park, most often seen in pairs or groups of up to five animals, consisting of one male and his 'harem', but also sometimes in larger groups.

Guenther's dik-dik (*Modoqua guentheri*) This pretty, small antelope has a dark red-brown coat and distinctive white eye markings. It is found in the dry savanna in and around Kidepo Valley.

OTHER HERBIVORES
African elephant (*Loxodonta africana*) The world's largest land animal is also one of the most intelligent and entertaining to watch. A fully grown elephant is about 3.5m high and weighs around 6,000kg. Female elephants live in closely knit clans in which the eldest female takes a matriarchal role over her sisters, daughters and granddaughters. Mother–daughter bonds are strong and may exist for up to 50 years. Males generally leave the family group at around 12 years, after which they either roam around on their own or form bachelor herds. Under normal circumstances, elephants range widely in search of food and water but, when concentrated populations are forced to live in conservation areas, their habit of uprooting trees can cause serious environmental damage. Two races of elephant are recognised: the **savanna elephant** of east and southern Africa (*L. a. africana*) and the smaller and slightly hairier **forest elephant** of the west African rainforest (*L. a. cyclotis*). The two races are thought to interbreed in parts of western Uganda. Despite severe poaching in the past, elephants occur in all national parks except for Lake Mburo. They are most likely to be seen in Murchison Falls, Queen Elizabeth and Kidepo national parks.

Black rhinoceros

Rhinoceros The **black rhinoceros** (*Diceros bicornis*) and **northern white rhinoceros** (*Ceratotherium simum cottoni*) both occur naturally in Uganda, but they have been poached to local extinction. The northern white rhino is a geographically isolated race of the white rhino of southern Africa: formerly common in Uganda west of the Albert Nile, and

ALBERTINE RIFT ENDEMICS

Most of Uganda's forest inhabitants have a wide distribution in the Democratic Republic of Congo (DRC) and/or west Africa, while a smaller proportion comprises eastern species that might as easily be observed in forested habitats in Kenya, Tanzania and in some instances Ethiopia. A significant number, however, are endemic to the Albertine Rift: in other words their range is more or less confined to montane habitats associated with the Rift Valley Escarpment running between Lake Albert and the north of Lake Tanganyika. The most celebrated of these regional endemics is of course the mountain gorilla, confined to the Virungas and Bwindi Mountains near the eastern Rift Valley Escarpment. Other primates endemic to the Albertine Rift include several taxa of smaller primates, for instance the golden monkey and Rwenzori colobus, while eight endemic butterflies are regarded as flagship species for the many hundreds of invertebrate taxa that occur nowhere else.

Of the remarkable tally of 37 range-restricted bird species listed as Albertine Rift endemics, roughly half are regarded to be of global conservation concern. All 37 of these species have been recorded in the DRC, and nine are endemic to that country, since their range is confined to the western escarpment forests. More than 20 Albertine Rift endemics are resident in each of Uganda, Rwanda and Burundi, while two extend their range southward into western Tanzania. All 24 of the Albertine Rift endemics recorded in Uganda occur in Bwindi National Park, including the highly sought African green broadbill, which is elsewhere known only from the Itombwe Mountains and Kahuzi-Biega National Park in the DRC. Other important sites in Uganda are the Rwenzori Mountains with 17 Albertine Rift endemics, the Virungas with 14, and the Echuya Forest with 12.

Outside Uganda, all but one of the 29 endemics that occur on the eastern escarpment have been recorded in Rwanda's Nyungwe Forest, a readily accessible site that is highly recommended for the opportunity to observe several species absent from, or not as easily located in, Uganda. Inaccessible to tourists at the time of writing, the Itombwe Mountains, which rise from the Congolese shore of northern Lake Tanganyika, support the largest contiguous block of montane forest in East Africa. This range is also regarded to be the most important site for montane forest birds in the region, with a checklist of 565 species including 31 Albertine Rift endemics, three of which are known from nowhere else in the world. The most elusive of these birds is the enigmatic Congo bay owl, first collected in 1952, and yet to be seen again, though its presence is suspected in Rwanda's Nyungwe Forest.

Several Albertine Rift forest endemics share stronger affinities with extant or extinct Asian genera than they do with any other living African species, affirming the great age of these forests, which are thought to have flourished during prehistoric climatic changes that caused temporary deforestation in lower-lying areas such as the Congo Basin. The Congo bay owl, African green broadbill and

at one time introduced into Murchison Falls National Park, its long-term future rests on the survival of one remaining breeding herd in eastern DRC.

Hippopotamus (*Hippopotamus amphibius*) This large, lumbering aquatic animal occurs naturally on most African lakes and waterways, where it spends most of the day submerged, but emerges from the water to graze at night. Hippos are strongly

Grauer's cuckoo-shrike, for instance, might all be classed as living fossils – isolated relics of a migrant Asian stock that has been superseded elsewhere on the continent by indigenous genera evolved from a common ancestor.

Among the mammals endemic to the Albertine Rift, the dwarf otter-shrew of the Rwenzoris is one of three highly localised African mainland species belonging to a family of aquatic insectivores that flourished some 50 million years ago and is elsewhere survived only by the related tenrecs of Madagascar. A relict horseshoe bat species restricted to the Rwenzoris and Lake Kivu is anatomically closer to extant Asian forms of horseshoe bat and to ancient migrant stock than it is to any of the 20-odd more modern and widespread African horseshoe bat species, while a shrew specimen collected only once in the Itombwe Mountains is probably the most primitive and ancient of all 150 described African species.

A full list of the Albertine Rift endemic birds that occur in Uganda follows, with species regarded to be of global conservation concern marked with an asterisk. All are present in Bwindi National Park; those present elsewhere are indicated as M (Mgahinga), E (Echuya), R (Rwenzori) and/or K (Kibale Forest).

Handsome francolin	*Francolinus nobilis*	M E R
Rwenzori turaco	*Tauraco johnstoni*	M E R
Rwenzori nightjar	*Caprimulgus rwenzori*	R
Dwarf honeyguide	*Indicator pumilio* *	
African green broadbill	*Pseudocalyptomena grauri* *	
Kivu ground thrush	*Zoothera tanganjicae* *	
Red-throated alethe	*Alethe poliophrys*	E R
Archer's robin-chat	*Cossypha archeri*	M E R
Collared apalis	*Apalis rwenzori*	M E R K
Mountain masked apalis	*Apalis personata*	M R
Grauer's scrub warbler	*Bradypterus grauri* *	M R
Grauer's warbler	*Graueria vittata*	
Neumann's warbler	*Hemetisia neumanni*	
Red-faced woodland warbler	*Phylloscopus laetus*	M E R K
Yellow-eyed black flycatcher	*Melaeornis ardesiascus*	
Chapin's flycatcher	*Musicapa lendu* *	
Rwenzori batis	*Batis diops*	M E R
Stripe-breasted tit	*Parus fasciiventer*	M R
Blue-headed sunbird	*Nectarinia alinae*	R K
Regal sunbird	*Nectarinia regia*	M E R
Purple-breasted sunbird	*Nectarinia purpureiventris*	R K
Dusky crimsonwing	*Cryptospiza jacksoni*	M E R K
Shelley's crimsonwing	*Cryptospiza shelleyi* *	M R
Strange weaver	*Ploceus alienus*	M E R

territorial, with herds of ten or more animals being presided over by a dominant male. The best places to see them are in Murchison Falls, Queen Elizabeth and Lake Mburo national parks, where they are abundant in suitable habitats. Hippos are still quite common outside of reserves, and they are responsible for killing more people than any other African mammal.

African buffalo (*Syncerus caffer*) Africa's only wild ox species is an adaptable and widespread creature that lives in large herds on the savanna and smaller herds in forested areas. Herds are mixed-sex and normally comprise several loosely related family clans and bachelor groups. Buffaloes can be seen in just about all of Uganda's national parks and large forests. In Queen Elizabeth and Murchison Falls national parks, you may see hybrids of the **savanna buffalo** (*S. c. caffer*) of East Africa and the **red buffalo** (*S. c. nanus*) of the west African forest.

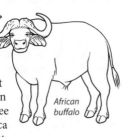

African buffalo

Giraffe (*Giraffa camelopardus*) The world's tallest animal (up to 5.5m) lives in loosely structured mixed-sex herds, typically numbering between five and 15 animals. As herd members may be dispersed over an area of up to 1km, they are frequently seen singly or in smaller groups, though unusually large aggregations are often seen in Uganda. The long neck of the giraffe gives it a slightly ungainly appearance when it ambles; giraffes look decidedly absurd when they adopt a semi-crouching position in order to drink. The race found in Uganda is **Rothschild's giraffe**, rare elsewhere in its former range but very common in the northern part of Murchison Falls National Park. A small herd is present in Kidepo Valley.

Burchell's zebra (*Equus burchelli*) This unmistakable striped horse is common and widespread throughout east and southern Africa. Zebras are often seen in large herds but their basic social unit is the small, relatively stable family group, which typically consists of a stallion, up to five mares, and their collective offspring. In Uganda, zebras are present only in Lake Mburo and Kidepo Valley national parks.

Swine The most visible pig species in Uganda is the **warthog** (*Phacochoerus africanus*), a common resident of the savanna national parks. Warthogs are uniform grey in colour and both sexes have impressive tusks. They are normally seen in family groups, trotting away briskly in the opposite direction with their tails raised stiffly and a determinedly nonchalant air. The bulkier and hairier **bushpig** (*Potamochoerus porcus*) is found mainly in thickets and dense woodland. Although bushpigs occur in all national parks except for Rwenzori, they are not often seen because of their nocturnal habits and the cover afforded by their favoured habitat. The **giant forest hog** (*Hylochoerus meinertzhageni*) is the largest African pig species. It is a nocturnal creature of the forest interior, and so very rarely seen, but it probably occurs in all national parks in western Uganda, and is often seen by day along Channel Drive in Queen Elizabeth National Park.

HYRAXES AND OTHER ODDITIES Uganda's five hyrax species are guinea pig-like animals, often associated with rocky habitats, and related more closely to elephants than to any other living creatures – difficult to credit until you've heard a tree hyrax shrieking with pachydermal abandon through the night. Four types of **pangolin** (similar in appearance to the South American scaly anteaters) occur in Uganda, as does the **aardvark**, a bizarre, long-snouted insectivore which is widespread in savanna habitats but very seldom seen because of its nocturnal habits. Also regarded as large mammals by the official checklist are 12 squirrel species, three flying squirrels (anomalures), three porcupines, three hares, two cane-rats, a hedgehog and the peculiar chevrotain.

Rock hyrax

BIRDS

Uganda is arguably the most attractive country in Africa to birdwatchers, not only because of the unusually high number of species recorded within its borders, but also because it offers easy access to several bird-rich habitats that are difficult to reach elsewhere. Uganda's remarkable avian diversity – 1,008 species recorded in an area similar to that of Great Britain – can be attributed to its location at a transitional point between the east African savanna, the west African rainforest and the semi-desert of the north.

Indicative of Uganda's transitional location is the fact that only one bird is endemic to the country, the somewhat nondescript Fox's weaver. However, if you take only East Africa into consideration, then approximately 150 bird species (more than 10% of the regional checklist) are found only in Uganda. This list includes seven of the 20 hornbill species recorded in the region, five out of 14 honeyguides, seven out of 21 woodpeckers, 11 out of 36 bulbuls and greenbuls, five out of 20 bush shrikes, as well as 13 members of the thrush family, 11 warblers, ten flycatchers, eight sunbirds, eight weavers, eight finches, four tinkerbirds, four pigeons or doves, three kingfishers, three sparrowhawks, three cuckoos and three nightjars.

Most of these 'Uganda specials' are west African and Congolese forest birds that would be very difficult to see elsewhere, for the simple reason that the other countries in which they occur are poorly developed for tourism. The rainforests of western Uganda must be seen as the country's most important bird habitat, and the one that is of greatest interest to birdwatchers, particularly if they are already reasonably familiar with typical east African birds. The most alluring forest in terms of localised species is probably Semliki, closely rivalled by Budongo, Kibale and Bwindi. However, in practical terms, Kibale Forest is probably Uganda's best single stop for forest birds, because of the proficiency of the guides who take tourists into the forest and the nearby Magombe Swamp. That said, just about any forest in Uganda will be rewarding; even the relatively tame botanical garden in Entebbe will throw up several interesting species.

Unfortunately, most forest birds are very secretive, and it can be difficult to get even a glimpse of them in the dense undergrowth, let alone a clear enough look to make a positive identification. You would probably identify more bird species in ten minutes at the Backpackers' Hostel in Kampala than you would in an afternoon walking through the Semliki Forest. For this reason, first-time visitors to Africa might do better concentrating on locations other than forests – if you want to see a wide range of Ugandan birds, try to visit Entebbe (water and forest birds), Lake Mburo (water- and acacia-associated birds), Queen Elizabeth (a wide variety of habitats; over 600 species recorded), Murchison Falls (a wide variety of habitats; the best place in East Africa to see the papyrus-associated shoebill) and Kidepo (northern semi-desert specials; over 50 raptors recorded).

Uganda's appeal as a birding destination has been enhanced in recent years by improving avian knowledge, and general guiding practices, on the part of local guides. The best of these are capable of identifying most species by call, and even calling up

BANANA REPUBLIC

With its distinctive tall green stem topped by a luxuriant clump of thick, wide leaves, the banana (or plantain) is such an integral feature of the Ugandan landscape that it may come as a surprise to learn that it is not indigenous to the country. Kiganda folklore claims that the first banana plant was brought to the kingdom by Kintu, whose shrine lies on a hill called Magonga (almost certainly a derivative of a local name for the banana) alongside a tree said to have grown from the root of the plant he originally imported. If this legend is true, it would place the banana's arrival in Uganda in perhaps the 13th–15th century, probably from the Ethiopian Highlands. Most botanists argue, however, that the immense number of distinct varieties grown in modern Uganda could not have been cultivated within so short a period – a time span of at least 1,000 years would be required.

Only one species of banana (*Musa ensete*) is indigenous to Africa, and it doesn't bear edible fruit. The more familiar cultivated varieties have all been propagated from two wild Asian species (*M. acuminata* and *M. balbisiana*), and hybrids thereof. Wild bananas are almost inedible and riddled with hard pits, and it is thought that the first edible variety was cultivated from a rare mutant of one of the above species about 10,000 years ago – making the banana one of the oldest cultivated plants in existence. Edible bananas were most likely cultivated in Egypt before the time of Christ, presumably having arrived there via Arabia or the Indian Ocean. The Greek sailor and explorer Cosmas Indicopleustes recorded that edible bananas grew around the port of Adulis, in present-day Eritrea, cAD525 – describing them as 'moza, the wild-date of India'.

The route via which the banana reached modern-day Uganda is open to conjecture. The most obvious point of origin is Ethiopia, the source of several southward migrations in the past two millennia. But it is intriguing that while the banana is known by a name approximating to the generic Latin *musa* throughout Asia, Arabia and northeast Africa – *moz* in Arabic and Persian, for instance, or *mus* or *musa* in various Ethiopian languages and Somali – no such linguistic resemblance occurs in East Africa, where it is known variously as *ndizi*, *gonja*, *matoke*, etc. This peculiarity has been cited to support a hypothesis that the banana first travelled between Asia and the east African coast either as a result of direct trade or else via Madagascar, and that it was entrenched there before regular trade was established with Arabia. A third possibility is that the banana reached Uganda via the Congolese Basin, possibly in association with the arrival of Bantu speakers from west Africa.

However it arrived in Uganda, the banana has certainly flourished there, forming the main subsistence crop for an estimated 40% of the population. Some 50 varieties are grown in the country, divided into four broad categories based on their primary use – *matoke* for boiling, *gonja* for roasting, *mbide* for distillation into banana beer (*mwenge*) or wine (*mubisi*), and the more familiar sweet *menvu* eaten raw for a snack or dessert. Within these broad categories, many subtleties of nomenclature and cultivation are applied to different varieties. And first-time visitors to Uganda might take note of the above names when they shop for the more responsive species. In the parks and reserves you'll meet some ranger guides whose knowledge compares favourably with their counterparts in any part of Africa. Birding capabilities do vary from one guide to the next, however, so specify your

bananas in the market – or sooner or later you'll bite into what looks to be a large, juicy sweet banana, but is in fact a foul and floury uncooked *matoke* or *gonja*!

The banana's uses are not restricted to feeding bellies. The juice from the stem is traditionally regarded to have several medicinal applications, for instance as a cure for snakebite and for childish behaviour. Pulped or scraped sections from the stem also form very effective cloths for cleaning. The outer stem can be plaited to make a strong rope known as *byai* in Luganda, while the cleaned central rib of the leaf is used to weave fish traps and other items of basketry. The leaf itself forms a useful makeshift umbrella, and was traditionally worn by young Buganda girls as an apron. The dried leaf is a popular bedding and roofing material, and also used to manufacture the head pads on which Ugandan women generally carry their loads.

The banana as we know it is a cultigen – modified by humans to their own ends and totally dependent on them for its propagation. The domestic fruit is the result of a freak mutation that gives the cells an extra copy of each chromosome, preventing the normal development of seeds, thereby rendering the plant edible, but also sterile. Every cultivated banana tree on the planet is effectively a clone, propagated by the planting of suckers or corms cut from 'parent' plants. This means that, unlike sexually reproductive crops, which experience new genetic configurations in every generation, the banana is unable to evolve mechanisms to fight off new diseases.

In early 2003, a report in the *New Scientist* warned that cultivated bananas could become extinct, because of their lack of defence against a pair of fungal diseases rampant in most of the world's banana-producing countries. These are black sigatoka, an airborne disease first identified in Fiji in 1963, and the soil-borne Panama disease, also known as fusarium wilt. Black sigatoka can be kept at bay by regular spraying – every ten days or so – but it is swiftly developing resistance to all known fungicides, which in any case are not affordable to the average subsistence farmers. There is no known cure for Panama disease.

So far as can be ascertained, Panama disease does not affect any banana variety indigenous to Uganda, but it has already resulted in the disappearance of several introduced varieties. Black sigatoka, by contrast, poses a threat to every banana variety in the world, and is present throughout Uganda. Buganda has been especially hard hit – a progressive reduction exceeding 50% has been experienced in the annual yield of the most seriously affected areas. In addition to reducing the yield of a single plant by up to 75%, black sigatoka can also cut its fruit-bearing life from more than 30 years to less than five.

International attempts to clone a banana tree resistant to both diseases have met with one limited success – agricultural researchers in Honduras have managed to produce one such variety, but it reputedly doesn't taste much like a banana. Another area of solution is genetic engineering – introducing a gene from a wild species to create a disease-resistant edible banana. Although ecologists are generally opposed to the genetic modification of crops, the domestic banana should perhaps be considered an exception, given its inability to spread its genes to related species – not to mention its pivotal importance to the subsistence economies of some of the world's poorest countries, Uganda among them.

interest when you ask for a guide. To secure the services of a guide for a nationwide tour of birding hotspots, contact the Uganda Bird Guides Club (m *077 518290;* e *ugandabirdguides@hotmail.com*), an organisation whose membership includes most of the country's best privately operating bird guides. Ibrahim Senfuma from Mabira Forest (see page 525) is one of Uganda's top bird guides and he's happy to take a break to conduct nationwide safaris (m *0712 920515*). Birders in Uganda are also better informed than ever before with the publication of Stevenson and Fanshawe's *Field Guide to the Birds of East Africa* in 2002. This superb book means that for the first time birdwatchers have access to accurate depictions, descriptions and distribution details for every species recorded in the country. Harder to obtain, but worth searching for, is the more specific *Where to Watch Birds in Uganda* by Russouw and Sacchi which contains excellent site descriptions.

Few visitors to Uganda will depart totally unmoved by its avian wealth, but they will tend to arrive in the country with a wide variety of expectations. Those European visitors for whom birdwatching ranks as a pursuit on a perversity level with stamp collecting might well revise that opinion when first confronted by a majestic fish eagle calling high from a riverine perch, or a flock of Abyssinian ground hornbills marching with comic intent through the savanna. First-time African visitors with a stated interest in birds are more likely to be blown away by their first sighting of a lilac-breasted roller or Goliath heron than by most of the country's long list of western forest specials. Birdwatchers based in Africa's savanna belt will generally want to focus more on forest birds, but mostly on such common and iconic species as great blue turaco or black-and-white casqued hornbill rather than on glimpsing a selection of more localised but duller forest greenbuls. The more experienced the individual birdwatcher in African conditions, the greater the priority they will place on the pursuit of Albertine Rift endemics and Semliki 'specials'. And at the extreme end of the scale there are those whose life's mission is to tick every bird species in the world, in which case dedicating several days to seeking out the endemic Fox's weaver might rank above all other considerations in planning a Ugandan itinerary.

At almost every level, the sheer variety of bird species in Uganda can be daunting, not only for first-timers to Africa, but also for bird enthusiasts familiar with other parts of the continent. Experienced South African birdwatchers, for instance, are likely to struggle with identification of the plethora of small warblers, forest greenbuls, Ploceus weavers, sunbirds and raptors that occur in Uganda (and one might argue that entering into serious battle with these difficult groups is best left for a repeat visit). Bearing the above in mind, two annotated lists follow, each containing concise details of 50 key birds resident in various parts of Uganda. The *Beginner's list* details some common and/or highly singular birds that are likely to make an impact on first-time visitors to Africa (or in some cases visitors from elsewhere in Africa), whether or not they have any great prior interest in ornithology. The *Twitcher's list* highlights a selection of species that are reasonably likely to be seen in the course of a normal birdwatching trip, and which for one reason or another (often relating to a specialised habitat or distribution) will feature high on the wish list of many experienced African birdwatchers visiting Uganda for the first time. Excluded from both of these lists in order to keep things manageable are the 30–40 species whose Ugandan range is restricted to Semliki National Park (discussed under the park itself on pages 367–70), the country's 24 Albertine Rift endemics (already listed in the box on pages 50–1), and the true weavers (see box, pages 60–1). Even allowing for these omissions, the *Twitcher's list* might easily run to more than 100 species, so preference is given to more common, striking and/or individualistic birds over the likes of greenbuls and cisticolas. For ease of reference, the plate number in Stevenson and Fanshawe is provided at the end of each entry.

BEGINNER'S LIST

Common ostrich (*Struthio camelus*) World's largest bird, a flightless savanna resident, in Uganda restricted to Kidepo and the far northeast. Plate 1

Pelicans (*Pelecanus* spp) Large, charismatic waterbirds often seen swimming in tight flotillas on open lakes and the Kazinga Channel, Queen Elizabeth National Park (QENP). Two species are present in Uganda. 7

African darter (*Anhinga rufa*) Also referred to as the snake-bird after its habit of swimming low with elongated rufous neck (longer than any cormorant) extended in serpentine fashion, fairly common in most freshwater habitats with fringing vegetation, perches openly, often with wings spread open to dry. 8

Goliath heron (*Ardea goliath*) As the name suggests, an immense heron – 1.5m tall – with lovely cryptic purple-grey and orange markings, commonly seen from launch trips in Murchison Falls. 12

Hamerkop (*Scopus umbretta*) Peculiar, medium-sized, brown waterbird with no close allies, a backward-pointing crest and long bill that combine to create the hammerhead effect for which it is named. Builds a vast scruffy nest, a good example of which can be seen on the Mweya Peninsula, QENP. 13

Saddle-billed stork (*Ephippiorhynchus senegalensis*) The largest and most handsome of several storks common in Uganda, up to 1.4m high, with black-and-white feathering and gaudy red, yellow and black bill, usually seen in pairs, regular on game drives north of Murchison Falls. 15

Marabou stork (*Leptoptilos crumeniferus*) Macabre carrion-eating stork, 1.5m tall, with large expandable air-sac below neck, and black-and-white feather pattern reminiscent of an undertaker's suit. Common in rural and urban environments – nowhere more so than in downtown Kampala. 15

Shoebill (*Balaeniceps rex*) Unmistakable large grey swamp-dweller, distantly related to pelicans, and the main motivating factor behind many an ornithological tour to Uganda. Most easily seen in Mabamba Swamp near Kampala, on the Nile below Murchison Falls, and Lake Albert in Semliki Wildlife Reserve. 15

Flamingos (*Phoenicopterus* spp) Stunning and gregarious pink-white algae-eaters, most likely to be seen in large concentrations in Katwe and Flamingo crater lakes in QENP and adjacent Chambura Wildlife Reserve. Two species in Uganda. 17

Secretary bird (*Sagittarius serpentarius*) Unique grey snake-eating raptor, with stork-like build, up to 1.5m tall, red face markings, black head quills, rare and localised in northern Uganda. 24

African fish eagle (*Haliaeetus vocifer*) Stunning fish-eating raptor, resident on most lakes and waterways, as notable for its high, eerie duetting as its bold black, white and chestnut feather pattern. 25

Palmnut vulture (*Gypohierax angolensis*) Superficially similar to the fish eagle, and also associated with palm-fringed waterways and lakes, but with more white than black, no chestnut, and a red rather than yellow cere. 25

Lappet-faced vulture (*Torgos tracheliotus*) Africa's largest vulture, dark black with a bare red head, often seen singly or in pairs alongside smaller vultures at kills in Uganda's savanna reserves. 27

Bateleur (*Terathopius ecaudatus*) Arguably the most striking of Uganda's large raptors, a predominantly black short-tailed eagle with unique red collar and face and bold white underwings seen clearly in flight. Common in savanna reserves, often seen soaring with a tilting motion reminiscent of the tightrope walkers from which its name derives. 39

Long-crested eagle (*Lophaetus occipitalis*) Handsome, medium-sized eagle, with diagnostic foppish long crest. Unlike many other large raptors it's common outside of game reserves, and often, though by no means exclusively, seen close to water. 39

Helmeted guineafowl (*Numida meleagris*) Gregarious and largely terrestrial wildfowl with striking white-speckled grey feathering and blue head with ivory casque. Panic-prone flocks common in savanna. The similar crested guineafowl is a forest resident with an unruly set of black head feathers. 46

African jacana (*Actophilornis africanus*) Unusual chestnut, white and black wader, also known as lily-trotter for its habit of walking across floating vegetation on its splayed feet, common in most wetlands in Uganda. 55

Grey crowned crane (*Balearica regulorum*) Uganda's national bird, 1.1m tall, grey and white feathering and a unique golden crest, common in swamp and associated moist grassland. North of the Nile, check carefully, since the northern black crowned crane has been recorded. 56

African green pigeon (*Treron calva*) Large, dove-like inhabitant of riparian woodland with cryptic green-grey feathering, often seen in fruiting fig trees. In north, check against Bruce's green pigeon, distinguished by yellow chest. 83

African grey parrot (*Psittacus erithacus*) Familiar caged bird – large, grey, with red tail feathers. Flocks are liable to be seen in any forested habitat; listen out for the loud squawking call emitted in flight. 89

Great blue turaco (*Corythaeola cristata*) Like a psychedelic turkey, this awesome blue-green forest dweller measures up to 75cm from the tip of its red-and-yellow bill to the end of its blue black-barred tail. Small flocks widespread in forested habitats countrywide, including Entebbe Botanical Gardens. 91

Ross's turaco (*Musophaga rossae*) Another stunner – deep purple with a bold yellow facemask and red crest and underwings. Widespread – but nowhere abundant – resident of forested habitats bordering wetlands or rivers. 91

Eastern grey plantain-eater (*Crinifer zonurus*) Large grey turaco-like bird with bold yellow bill and off-white crest, common in woodland and savanna countrywide, its loud chuckling call a characteristic sound of suburban Kampala and Entebbe. Check against black-faced go-away bird in acacia woodland of Lake Mburo. 93

African emerald cuckoo (*Chrysococcyx cupreus*) Brilliant green-and-yellow cuckoo associated with forest, where its deliberate, clear four-note call is as ubiquitous seasonally as the bird itself is impossible to locate in the high canopy. In breeding season, the three-note call of the red-chested cuckoo, variously rendered as 'it-will-rain' or 'Piet-my-vrou', also forms an unforgettable element in the Ugandan soundscape, but the bird itself is slightly less elusive. 97

Coucals (*Centropus* spp) Large, clumsy-looking relatives of the cuckoos, associated with rank grassland and swamp, with four species in Uganda of which the blue-headed and swamp-dwelling black coucal are the most enticing. 98

Verreaux's eagle-owl (*Bubo lacteus*) Largest of 13 owl species in Uganda, most of which might be seen by chance on night drives or roosting in large trees by day. 101

Pennant/Standard-winged nightjars (*Macrodipteryx* spp) Most spectacular of 11 nocturnal nightjars recorded in Uganda, the males of both species acquire wing streamers twice the length of their body during the breeding season. It might be seen in display flight in any savanna habitat, especially close to water, but there's no better place to seek them out than on the road to the top of Murchison Falls after dusk. 106

Pied kingfisher (*Ceryle rudis*) Boldly marked black-and-white kingfisher that hovers still above water for long periods and is ubiquitous in most wetland habitats. 111

Giant kingfisher (*Megaceryle maxima*) Like an overgrown pied kingfisher but with distinctive chestnut chest; widespread near water with tall fringing vegetation, but nowhere common. 111

Malachite kingfisher (*Alcedo cristata*) Exquisite African counterpart to European kingfisher, with blue back and wings and orange chest. Perches still on low reeds or twigs next to rivers and lakes; away from water, check against pink-cheeked but otherwise similar pygmy kingfisher. 113

Red-throated bee-eater (*Merops bulocki*) Stunning green, red and turquoise bee-eater, essentially west African though range extends into northwest Uganda. Breeds in tall sandbanks on Lake Albert and the Nile below Murchison Falls. 116

Northern carmine bee-eater (*Merops nubicus*) Bold red and blue bee-eater, not uncommon and perches openly north of the Nile in Murchison Falls. 117

Broad-billed roller (*Eurystomus glaucurus*) Dark chestnut and blue bird with bright-yellow bill, usually seen in pairs perched high but openly in woodland. Common countrywide including around Entebbe Golf Course. 117

Lilac-breasted roller (*Coracias caudata*) Dazzling pigeon-sized bird with chestnut back, lilac breast, blue chest and long tail streamers. Common in savanna habitats throughout East Africa, where it perches openly. A popular safari favourite, check it against the Abyssinian roller (no lilac) in Murchison Falls, where both species are present. 118

Hoopoe (*Upupa epops*) Distinctive orange, white and black bird with prominent crest, mainly terrestrial though it flies into trees when disturbed. Not uncommon in most wooded savanna habitats. 120

Black-and-white casqued hornbill (*Bycanistes brevis*) Characteristic Ugandan forest resident, a turkey-sized black-and-white bird with gross ivory bill, often first detected through its raucous braying and heavy wing flaps. 124

WEAVERS

Placed by some authorities in the same family as the closely related sparrows, the weavers of the family Ploceidae are a quintessential part of Africa's natural landscape, common and highly visible in virtually every habitat from rainforest to desert. The name of the family derives from the intricate and elaborate nests – typically but not always a roughly oval ball of dried grass, reeds and twigs – that are built by the dextrous males of most species.

It can be fascinating to watch a male weaver at work. First, a nest site is chosen, usually at the end of a thin hanging branch or frond, which is immediately stripped of leaves to protect against snakes. The weaver then flies back and forth to the site, carrying the building material blade by blade in its heavy beak, first using a few thick strands to hang a skeletal nest from the end of a branch, then gradually completing the structure by interweaving numerous thinner blades of grass into the main frame. Once completed, the nest is subjected to the attention of his chosen partner, who will tear it apart if the result is less than satisfactory, and so the process starts all over again.

All but 12 of the 113 described weaver species are resident on the African mainland or associated islands, with some 40 represented within Uganda alone. A full 25 of the Ugandan species are placed in the genus *Ploceus* (true weavers), which is surely the most characteristic of all African bird genera. Most of the *Ploceus* weavers are slightly larger than a sparrow, and display a strong sexual dimorphism. Females are with few exceptions drab buff or olive-brown birds, with some streaking on the back, and perhaps a hint of yellow on the belly.

Most male *Ploceus* weavers conform to the basic colour pattern of the 'masked weaver' – predominantly yellow, with streaky back and wings, and a distinct black facial mask, often bordered orange. Eight Ugandan weaver species fit this masked weaver prototype more or less absolutely, and a similar number approximate it rather less exactly, for instance by having a chestnut-brown mask, or a full black head, or a black back, or being more chestnut than yellow on the belly. Identification of the masked weavers can be tricky without experience – useful clues are the exact shape of the mask, the presence and extent of the fringing orange, and the colour of the eye and the back.

The golden weavers, of which only two species are present in Uganda, are also brilliant yellow and/or light orange with some light streaking on the back, but they lack a mask or any other strong distinguishing features. The handful of forest-associated *Ploceus* weavers, by contrast, tend to have quite different and very striking colour patterns, and although sexually dimorphic, the female is often as boldly marked as the male. The most aberrant among these are Vieillot's and Maxwell's black weavers, the males of which are totally black except for their eyes, while the black-billed weaver reverses the prototype by being all black with a yellow facemask.

Abyssinian ground hornbill (*Bucorvus abyssinicus*) Predominantly terrestrial hornbill, over 1m tall, very heavily built with black feathering with white underwings, blue and red face patches, and effete long eyelashes. A common savanna resident in Murchison Falls and Semliki Wildlife Reserve. 125

Double-toothed barbet (*Lybius bidentatus*) Colourful thrush-sized bird, black with bold red breast, chest and face, yellow eye-patch and heavy pale bill. Might be

Among the more conspicuous *Ploceus* species in Uganda are the black-headed, yellow-backed, slender-billed, northern brown-throated, orange and Vieillot's black weavers – for the most part gregarious breeders forming single or mixed species colonies of hundreds, sometimes thousands, of pairs. The most extensive weaver colonies are often found in reed beds and waterside vegetation – the mixed species colonies in Entebbe Botanical Garden or Ngamba Island are as impressive as any in Uganda. Most weavers don't have a distinctive song, but they compensate with a rowdy jumble of harsh swizzles, rattles and nasal notes that can reach deafening proportions near large colonies. One of the more cohesive songs you will often hear seasonally around weaver colonies is a cyclic 'dee-dee-dee-Diederik', often accelerating to a hysterical crescendo when several birds call at once. This is the call of the Diederik cuckoo, a handsome green-and-white cuckoo that lays its eggs in weaver nests.

Oddly, while most east African *Ploceus* weavers are common, even abundant, in suitable habitats, seven highly localised species are listed as range-restricted, and three of these – one Kenyan endemic and two Tanzanian endemics – are regarded to be of global conservation concern. Of the other four, Fox's weaver (*Ploceus spekeoides*) is the only bird species endemic to Uganda: a larger-than-average yellow-masked weaver with an olive back, yellow eyes and orange-fringed black facemask, confined to acacia woodland near swamps and lakes east of Lake Kyoga. The strange weaver (*Ploceus alienus*) – black head, plain olive back, yellow belly with chestnut bib – is an Albertine Rift endemic restricted to four sites in Uganda.

Most of the colonial weavers, perhaps relying on safety in numbers, build relatively plain nests with a roughly oval shape and an unadorned entrance hole. The nests of certain more solitary weavers, by contrast, are far more elaborate. Several weavers, for instance, protect their nests from egg-eating invaders by attaching tubular entrance tunnels to the base – in the case of the spectacled weaver, sometimes twice as long as the nest itself. The Grosbeak weaver (a peculiar, larger-than-average brown-and-white weaver of reed beds, distinguished by its outsized bill and placed in the monospecific genus *Amblyospiza*) constructs a large and distinctive domed nest, which is supported by a pair of reeds, and woven as precisely as the finest basketwork, with a neat raised entrance hole at the front. By contrast, the scruffiest nests are built by the various species of sparrow- and buffalo-weaver, relatively drab but highly gregarious dry-country birds, poorly represented in Uganda except for in the vicinity of Kidepo.

seen in any wooded habitat, especially near fruiting fig trees. In the north of Murchison Falls, check against rather similar but more localised black-breasted barbet. 130

White-browed robin-chat (*Cossypha heuglini*) The most common of seven similar thrush-sized species, most of which have orange-red chest, dark blue-black back and bold white eye-stripe. Associated with forest edge, well-developed gardens and other lush vegetation but not forest interiors. 166

Grey-capped warbler (*Eminia lepida*) Distinctive sparrow-sized resident of rank undergrowth, has green back, grey cap, black eye-stripe and red bib. Seldom comes out into the open, but very vocal and widespread, and especially common close to water. 198

Brown-throated wattle-eye (*Platysteira cyanea*) Delightful, highly vocal, common and widespread resident of woodland and forest edge, with neat black-and-white markings, bold red eye-wattle and (female only) chestnut-brown throat. 211

African paradise flycatcher (*Terpsiphone viridis*) Stunning and ubiquitous woodland and forest resident, usually blue-black on head and chest, rufous on back, male with extended tail up to twice the body length. A black-and-white morph is common in some parts of Uganda, and intermediate forms exist. In forested habitats, especially Kibale Forest, check against similar red-bellied paradise flycatcher. 212

Silverbird (*Empidornis semipartitus*) Striking silver-backed, orange-chested dry-country flycatcher, often seen perching openly in Murchison Falls. 212

Scarlet-chested sunbird (*Chalcomitra senegalensis*) Represented by more than 30 species in Uganda alone, sunbirds are small, colourful and often iridescent nectar-eaters, with long curved bills reminiscent of the unrelated hummingbirds which fill a similar niche in the New World. This is one of the more common species in Uganda, jet black with a bold scarlet chest patch and green head markings. 228

Black-headed gonolek (*Laniarius erythrogaster*) Brilliant black-and-red thrush-sized bird, common in most savanna habitats, especially riverine thickets. Secretive but not especially shy, its presence is often revealed by loud duetting, alternating loud liquid notes with a softer churring response. 234

Fork-tailed drongo (*Dicrurus absimilis*) Pugnacious all-black bird with deep forked tail, common in wooded savanna where it perches openly and often emits a series of harsh, nasal notes. Could be confused with similar but more lightly built northern black flycatcher. 241

Piacpiac (*Ptilostomus afer*) Smaller and more lightly built than other African crows, glossy black with a red eye, often seen in the vicinity of riverine palms and frequently associates with livestock or wild bovines, eating disturbed insects. Common in Jinja and Murchison Falls. 241

Black-winged red bishop (*Euplectes hordaecrus*) The most widespread of three red bishop species found in Uganda, all of which are small, bright, black-and-red birds, associated with reeds and rank grassland. 268

Red-cheeked cordon-bleu (*Uraeginthus bengalus*) Diminutive finch with blue underparts and (male only) bold red cheek-patch. Restless flocks regularly encountered in savanna habitats throughout Uganda. 274

Pin-tailed wydah (*Vidua macrouca*) Black-and-white male is small, but with a bright-red bill and tail streamers twice the length of the body. Often accompanied by harem of nondescript females, common in grassland and open savanna. 280

TWITCHER'S LIST

African finfoot (*Podica senegalensis*) Widespread but elusive red-billed resident of quiet lakes and rivers with overhanging vegetation. Ranks high on many African birdwatchers' wish list and seen very regularly from boat trips on Lake Mburo, and also on the crater lake at Jacana Lodge, QENP. 8

Nahan's francolin (*Francolinus nahan*) Small dark forest wildfowl with white-barred chest, and a red facemask and bill. In Uganda restricted to Bwindi and Mabira Forest, where it's most likely to be seen hurriedly crossing forest paths. 47

Jackson's francolin (*Francolinus jacksoni*) Large pale-headed wildfowl, localised on east African mountains, and in Uganda restricted to forest edge and open country on Mount Elgon, where it's common. 47

Denham's bustard (*Neotis denhami*) Localised ground bird, up to 1.2m tall and very heavily built. Open country north of the Nile in Murchison Falls is perhaps the most reliable site for it anywhere in Africa. 57

Black-headed lapwing (*Vanellus tectus*) Long black crest makes it arguably the most striking of seven Ugandan lapwing species; uncommon in East Africa generally, but seen very regularly on game drives in the north of Murchison Falls. 64

African skimmer (*Rynchops flavirostris*) Handsome tern-like build and black-and-white feathering complemented by long, bold red bill; often seen flocked on sandbanks or skimming above the water in Murchison Falls. 80

White-headed turaco (*Tauraco leocolophus*) Striking purple-green turaco with distinctive white crest/head. Widespread but secretive in woodland and riparian forest, and often seen along the Nile in Murchison Falls. 91

Black-billed turaco (*Tauraco schuetti*) Bright-green turaco with white markings above and below eye, white-tipped crest and small black bill. Resident and vocal in most forest interiors, but often difficult to see clearly. 92

Long-tailed nightjar (*Caprimulgus climacurus*) Unusually large nightjar, easily identified by long tail with narrow white outer feathers. Seasonally common in north, it's likely to be seen diving from the top of Murchison Falls after dark.103

Bar-tailed trogon (*Apaloderma vittatum*) Stunning forest bird, similar to more widespread Narina trogon but with blue breast band and barred (as opposed to white) tail. Secretive and often sits motionless for long periods, it's generally quite easy to locate along the road leading uphill from Buhoma (Bwindi) especially if you have a local guide who knows the call. 110

Blue-breasted kingfisher (*Halcyon malimbica*) Similar to the more widespread woodland kingfisher but with unique blue breast band. Common in several forests, especially Budongo and Chambura Gorge, where it often sits motionless, revealing its presence by a high scolding trill. 112

Chocolate-backed kingfisher (*Halcyon badia*) Localised forest kingfisher with unique chocolate-brown back and bold red bill; nowhere common, but fairly likely to be seen in Budongo Forest. 112

African dwarf kingfisher (*Ispidina lecontei*) Small forest kingfisher, differs from other blue-backed, rufous-fronted kingfishers in having red crown with a black frontal mark. Resident in most forests in Uganda, most common perhaps in Budongo. 113

Shining blue kingfisher (*Alcedo quadribrachys*) Considerably larger than other kingfishers, a blue-backed, rufous-fronted, localised denizen of rivers and pools within forest interiors. Sometimes seen at roadside pools and river crossings in Budongo and Kibale forests. 113

Black bee-eater (*Merops gularis*) The most eagerly sought of the 12 brightly coloured bee-eater species recorded in Uganda, with a distinctive blue-black colour and scarlet throat. Often found perched high on bare branches in forests such as Bwindi, or riparian woodland along the Chambura and Ishasha rivers. 115

Blue-throated roller (*Eurystomus gularis*) Similar to broad-billed roller but with clear blue throat patch, generally associated with forest interiors and regularly seen on the trail through Bigodi Wetland. 117

Forest/white-headed wood-hoopoe (*Phoeniculus castaneiceps/bolloi*) A pair of patchily distributed and generally scarce forest birds, similar in appearance (and noisy behaviour) to familiar green wood-hoopoe though *castaneiceps* has black bill and variable head colour (white, black or brown) and *bolloi* has white head and bright-red bill. The former is common only in Mabira Forest, while the latter is most likely to be seen in Bwindi or Kibale. 119

Black scimitarbill (*Rhinopomastus aterrimus*) In East Africa, confined to northwest of Uganda, the only scimitarbill present in Murchison Falls, where it's quite common in acacia woodland north of the Nile. 120

African pied hornbill (*Tockus fasciatus*) Medium-sized black-and-white hornbill with black-tipped ivory bill. The most common forest hornbill in Uganda after black-and-white casqued, it's resident in Entebbe Botanical Garden and also common in Kibale, Budongo and Mabira forests. 122

Piping hornbill (*Bycanistes fistulator*) Similar to but significantly larger than above, with heavier bill and more white in flight pattern. Common only in Semliki National Park but also regular in Budongo Forest. 123

White-thighed hornbill (*Bycanistes cylinddricus*) Large forest hornbill, distinguished from rather similar black-and-white casqued by diagnostic white tail with solitary black bar; present in several Ugandan forests, common in Budongo and forest patches along the Masindi–Hoima road to the south. 124

Grey-throated barbet (*Gymnobucco bonapartei*) Dull grey-brown forest barbet with diagnostic pale tufts standing erect on either side of the bill. Unique silhouette emphasised by habit of perching openly on dead trees, common in most Ugandan forests. 127

Hairy-breasted barbet (*Tricholaema hirsute*) Black, yellow and white forest barbet, not uncommon in Ugandan forests, often seen in Bigodi Wetland Sanctuary. 129

Yellow-spotted barbet (*Buccanodon duchaillui*) Black barbet with yellow streaking on breast and red forehead; common in most Ugandan forests, especially Kibale and Mabira. 129

Yellow-billed barbet (*Trachylaemus purpuratus*) Unique large barbet, glossy purple-black with yellow bill, face and chest. Widespread in forested and wooded habitats, regular in Bigodi Wetland Sanctuary. 131

Green-breasted pitta (*Pitta riechenowi*) Terrestrial forest bird with brilliant green breast, red vent, black-and-white face. Nowhere common, and unlikely to be seen unless accompanied by a knowledgeable guide, the best sites are Budongo and Kibale forests. 139

Petit's cuckoo-shrike (*Campephaga petiti*) Male all black with yellow gapes, female yellow with vertical bars on side of breast, fairly regular on the walk uphill from Buhoma in Bwindi. 154

Red-tailed bristlebill (*Bleda syndactyla*) Large yellow-breasted greenbul with diagnostic blue eye-wattle, fairly common in most Ugandan forests. 161

Blue-shouldered robin-chat (*Cossypha cyanocampter*) Similar in appearance to more common white-browed robin-chat, but significantly smaller and with distinctive light-blue shoulder patch, widespread but never common in forest interiors throughout southern Uganda. 166

Snowy-headed robin-chat (*Cossypha niveicapella*) Similar in appearance to more common white-browed robin-chat, but larger, white stripe through top of head replaces white eye-stripe. Widespread and generally fairly common in forest interiors throughout southern Uganda. 166

African thrush (*Turdus pelios*) Western counterpart to the ubiquitous olive thrush found elsewhere in eastern and southern Africa, very common and often quite tame in lodge gardens. 168

Spotted morning thrush (*Cichladusa guttata*) Lively streaky-breasted small thrush, attractively vociferous and common in lodges at Murchison Falls. 177

Papyrus yellow warbler (*Chloropeta gracilrostris*) Large yellow warbler restricted exclusively to papyrus swamps; very scarce in southwest of Uganda. 178

White-winged warbler (*Bradypterus carpalis*) Another papyrus endemic, large streaky warbler, widespread but secretive; resident in suitable habitats throughout Uganda. 180

Uganda's wealth of invertebrate life – more than 100,000 species have been identified countrywide – is largely overlooked by visitors, but is perhaps most easily appreciated in the form of butterflies and moths of the order **Lepidoptera**. An astonishing 1,200 butterfly species, including almost 50 endemics, have been recorded in Uganda, as compared with fewer than 1,000 in Kenya, roughly 650 in the whole of North America, and a mere 56 in the British Isles. Several forests in Uganda harbour 300 or more butterfly species, and one might easily see a greater selection in the course of a day than one could in a lifetime of exploring the English countryside. Indeed, I've often sat at one roadside pool in the like of Kibale or Budongo forests and watched ten to 20 clearly different species converge there over the space of 20 minutes.

The Lepidoptera are placed in the class Insecta, which includes ants, beetles and locusts among others. All insects are distinguished from other invertebrates, such as arachnids (spiders) and crustaceans, by their combination of six legs, a pair of frontal antennae, and a body divided into a distinct head, thorax and abdomen. Insects are the only winged invertebrates, though some primitive orders have never evolved them, and other more recently evolved orders have discarded them. Most flying insects have two pairs of wings, one of which, as in the case of flies, might have been modified beyond immediate recognition. The butterflies and moths of the order Lepidoptera have two sets of wings and are distinguished from all other insect orders by the tiny ridged wing scales that create their characteristic bright colours.

The most spectacular of all butterflies are the swallowtails of the family **Papilionidae**, of which roughly 100 species have been identified in Africa, and 32 in Uganda. Named for the streamers that trail from the base of their wings, swallowtails are typically large and colourful, and relatively easy to observe when they feed on mammal dung deposited on forest trails and roads. Sadly, this last generalisation doesn't apply to the African giant swallowtail (*Papilio antimachus*), a powerful flier that tends to stick at canopy levels and seldom alights on the ground, but the first two generalisations certainly do. With a wingspan known to exceed 20cm, this black, orange and green gem, an endangered west African species whose range extends into Bwindi, Kibale, Semliki, Budongo and Kalinzu forests, is certainly the largest butterfly on the continent, and possibly the largest in the world. One of the most common large swallowtails in Uganda is *Papilio nobilis*, which has golden or orange wings, and occurs in suburban gardens in Kampala, Entebbe, Jinja and elsewhere.

The **Pieridae** is a family of medium-sized butterflies, generally smaller than the swallowtails and with wider wings, of which almost 100 species are present in Uganda, several as seasonal intra-African migrants. Most species are predominantly white in colour, with some yellow, orange, black or even red and blue markings on the wings. One widespread member of this family is the oddly named angled grass yellow (*Eurema desjardini*), which has yellow wings marked by a broad black band, and is likely to be seen in any savanna or forest-fringe habitat in southern Uganda. The orange-and-lemon *Eronia leda* also has yellow wings, but with an orange upper tip, and it occurs in open grassland and savanna countrywide.

The most diverse family of butterflies within Uganda is the **Lycaenidae**, with almost 500 of the 1,500 African species recorded. Known also as gossamer wings, this varied family consists mostly of small to medium-sized butterflies, with a wingspan of 1–5cm, dull underwings, and brilliant violet blue, copper or rufous-orange upper wings. The larvae of many Lycaenidae species have a symbiotic relationship with ants – they secrete a fluid that is milked by the ants and are thus permitted to shelter in their nests. A striking member of this family is *Hypolycaena hatita*, a small bluish butterfly with long tail streamers, often seen on forest paths throughout Uganda.

Another well-represented family in Uganda, with 370 species present, is the **Nymphalidae**, a diversely coloured group of small to large butterflies, generally associated with forest edges or interiors. The Nymphalidae are also known as brush-footed butterflies, because their forelegs have evolved into non-functional brush-like structures. One of the more common and distinctive species is the African blue tiger (*Tirumala petiverana*), a large black butterfly with about two dozen blue-white wing spots, often observed in forest paths near puddles or feeding from animal droppings. Another large member of this family is the African queen (*Danaus chrysippus*), which has a slow, deliberate flight pattern, orange or brown wings, and is as common in forest-edge habitats as it is in cultivated fields or suburbia. Also often recorded in Kampala gardens is the African Mother of Pearl (*Salamis parhassus*), a lovely light-green butterfly with black wing dots and tips.

The family **Charaxidae**, regarded by some authorities to be a subfamily of the Nymphalidae, is represented in Uganda by 70 of the roughly 200 African species. Typically large, robust, strong fliers with one or two short tails on each wing, the butterflies in this family vary greatly in coloration, and several species appear to be scarce and localised since they inhabit forest canopies and are seldom observed. Bwindi is a particularly good site for this family, with almost 40 species recorded, ranging from the regal dark-blue charaxes (*Charaxes tiridates*) (black wings with deep-blue spots) to the rather leaf-like green-veined charaxes (*Charaxes candiope*).

Rather less spectacular are the 200 grass-skipper species of the family **Hersperiidae** recorded in Uganda, most of which are small and rather drably coloured, though some are more attractively marked in black, white and/or yellow. The grass-skippers are regarded as the evolutionary link between butterflies and the generally more nocturnal moths, represented in Uganda by several families of which the most impressive are the boldly patterned giant silk-moths of the family **Saturniidae**.

An obstacle to developing a serious interest in Uganda's butterflies has been the absence of useful literature and field guides to aid identification. The publication of Nanny Carter and Laura Tindimubona's *Butterflies of Uganda* (Uganda Society, 2002) goes a long way to rectifying this situation, illustrating and describing roughly 200 of the more common and striking species, with basic information about distribution and habitat. It's not quite the same as a comprehensive field guide, since many allied butterfly species are very similar to each other in appearance, while other species are highly localised or endemic to one specific forest. But certainly this book does pave the way for a greater appreciation of Uganda's most colourful invertebrate order, and as such it is highly recommended to anybody with even a passing interest in butterflies. If you can't find it in a bookshop, it can be bought at the Uganda Society shop at the National Museum in Kampala (e *ugsociety@bushnet.com*).

Black-faced rufous warbler (*Bathmocercus rufus*) Striking, secretive resident of forest undergrowth, most common at higher altitudes such as Bwindi and Mount Elgon. 189

Red-winged grey warbler (*Drymocichla incana*) Attractive, restless northern warbler whose range extends into Murchison Falls, where quite common in riverine scrub. 197

Black-throated apalis (*Apalis jacksoni*) Neat apalis with bright-yellow belly and black, grey and white head markings, resident in most Ugandan forests, also riverine woodland; commonest at higher altitudes. 203

Black-and-white shrike-flycatcher (*Bias musicus*) Patchily distributed and heavily built small flycatcher with long black crest, yellow eye, white belly, black back in male, chestnut back in female. Undertakes amazing circular display flights from treetops. Not uncommon garden bird in Entebbe and Kampala. 210

Chestnut-bellied wattle-eye (*Dyaphorophyia castanea*) The most likely to be seen of three blue- or yellow-wattled small forest birds in this genus, all reasonably common in suitable habitats in the southwest, but rather unobtrusive. 211

African blue flycatcher (*Elminia longicauda*) Pretty grey-blue flycatcher with distinct crest and long tail, common throughout Uganda, even in gardens in Entebbe and Kampala. 214

Chestnut-capped flycatcher (*Erythrocercus mccallii*) Diminutive and gregarious olive-grey flycatcher with streaked chestnut cap. In East Africa known only from Budongo Forest, where it's quite common. 214

Tit hylia (*Pholidornis rushae*) Tiny yellow-bellied, streaky-headed bird, moves around in small highly vocal parties, in East Africa known only from Budongo, Semliki and Mabira forests, most common in the last. 219

Green-headed sunbird (*Cyanomitra verticalis*) The wealth of sunbird diversity in Uganda is amazing, and several forest and highland species are likely to be seen in the course of a visit. This olive-bodied, green-headed resident of forest edge and wooded habitats is one of the more singular and common species. 222

Mackinnon's fiscal (*Lanius mackinnoni*) Boldly patterned grey, black and white shrike of forest edge and open woodland, most common at higher altitudes, especially around Buhoma in Bwindi. 232

Papyrus gonolek (*Laniarius mufumbiri*) Similar to black-headed gonolek but with bright-yellow cap complementing crimson breast, and white bar on the black wing. Endemic to papyrus habitats, where locally common and often heard but difficult to see. 234

Luhder's bush-shrike (*Laniarius luehderi*) Distinctive black-and-white gonolek-like shrike with unique orange crown and belly. Widespread but secretive forest resident most likely to be traced by call, and often observed around Buhoma in Bwindi. 234

Lagden's bush-shrike (*Malaconotus lagdeni*) Handsome yellow, green, grey and orange bird, similar in size and appearance to widespread grey-headed bush-shrike, within East Africa confined to forests of the Albertine Rift, where common and vocal but difficult to locate. 238

Red-billed helmetshrike (*Prionops caniceps*) Remarkably colourful helmetshrike, grey above, orange below, white on face, uncommon in western forests, but gregarious, noisy and highly active when present. 240

Grey-headed negro-finch (*Nigrita canicapilla*) Endearing finch with grey head separated from black body by thin white stripe. One of Uganda's more widespread and visible small forest birds. 269

Red-headed bluebill (*Spermophaga ruficapella*) Gobsmackingly pretty finch, with black back and chest (the latter spotted white in the female), red head and breast, and bright blue-and-red bill. Often seen in lodge grounds in Buhoma (Bwindi) and in Bigodi Wetland Sanctuary. 273

REPTILES

NILE CROCODILE The order Crocodilia dates back at least 150 million years, and fossil forms that lived contemporaneously with dinosaurs are remarkably unchanged from their modern ancestors. The largest species are the Australian saltwater and the African Nile crocodiles which regularly attain lengths of up to 6m. Widespread throughout Africa, the Nile crocodile was once common in most large rivers and lakes, but it has been exterminated in many areas in the past century – hunted professionally for its skin as well as by vengeful local villagers. Contrary to popular legend, Nile crocodiles generally feed mostly on fish, at least where densities are sufficient. They will also prey on drinking or swimming mammals where the opportunity presents itself, dragging their victim underwater until it drowns, then storing it under a submerged log or tree until it has decomposed sufficiently for them to eat. A large crocodile is capable of killing a lion or wildebeest, or an adult human for that matter, and in certain areas such as the Mara or Grumeti rivers in the Serengeti, large mammals do form their main prey. Today, large crocodiles are mostly confined to protected areas. The gargantuan specimens that lurk on the sandbanks along the Nile below Murchison Falls National Park are a truly primeval sight, silent and sinister, vanishing under the water when the launch approaches too closely. Other reliable sites for crocs are Lake Mburo and increasingly the Kazinga Channel in Queen Elizabeth National Park (QENP).

SNAKES A wide variety of snakes is found in Uganda, though – fortunately, most would agree – they are typically very shy and unlikely to be seen unless actively sought. One of the snakes most likely to be seen on safari is Africa's largest, the **rock python**, which has a gold-on-black mottled skin and regularly grows to lengths exceeding 5m. Non-venomous, pythons kill their prey by strangulation, wrapping their muscular bodies around it until it cannot breathe, then swallowing it whole and dozing off for a couple of months while it is digested. Pythons feed mainly on small antelopes, large rodents and similar. They are harmless to adult humans, but could conceivably kill a small child. A slumbering python might be encountered almost anywhere in East Africa, and one reasonably relaxed individual is often present at the bat cave near the visitors' centre in Maramagambo Forest, Queen Elizabeth National Park (QENP).

Of the venomous snakes, one of the most commonly encountered is the **puff adder**, a large, thick resident of savanna and rocky habitats. Although it feeds mainly on rodents, the puff adder will strike when threatened, and it is rightly considered the most dangerous of African snakes, not because it is especially venomous or aggressive, but because its notoriously sluggish disposition means it is more often disturbed than other snakes. The related **Gabon viper** is possibly the largest African viper, growing up to 2m long, very heavily built, and with a beautiful cryptic geometric gold, black-and-brown skin pattern that blends perfectly into the rainforest litter it inhabits. Although highly venomous, it is more placid and less likely to be encountered than the puff adder.

Several **cobra** species, including the spitting cobra, are present in Uganda, most with characteristic hoods that they raise when about to strike, though they are all very seldom seen. Another widespread family is the **mambas**, of which the black mamba – which will only attack when cornered, despite an unfounded reputation for unprovoked aggression – is the largest venomous snake in Africa, measuring up to 3.5m long. While the dangers from these snakes are well documented, those of two of Africa's most toxic species – the variably coloured, arboreal **boomslang** and its relative, the twig-coloured **twig snake** – were long underrated. In fact both were

CHAMELEONS

Common and widespread in Uganda, but not easily seen unless they are actively searched for, chameleons are arguably the most intriguing of African reptiles. True chameleons of the family Chamaeleontidae are confined to the Old World, with the most important centre of speciation being the island of Madagascar, to which about half of the world's 120 recognised species are endemic. Aside from two species of chameleon apiece in Asia and Europe, the remainder are distributed across mainland Africa.

Chameleons are best known for their capacity to change colour, a trait that has often been exaggerated in popular literature, and which is generally influenced by mood more than the colour of the background. Some chameleons are more adept at changing colour than others, with the most variable being the **common chameleon** (*Chamaeleo chamaeleon*) of the Mediterranean region, with more than 100 colour and pattern variations recorded. Many African chameleons are typically green in colour but will gradually take on a browner hue when they descend from the foliage in more exposed terrain, for instance while crossing a road. Several change colour and pattern far more dramatically when they feel threatened or are confronted by a rival of the same species. Different chameleon species also vary greatly in size, with the largest being **Oustalet's chameleon** of Madagascar, known to reach a length of almost 80cm.

A remarkable physiological feature common to all true chameleons is their protuberant round eyes, which offer a potential 180° degree vision on both sides and are able to swivel around independently of each other. Only when one of them isolates a suitably juicy-looking insect will the two eyes focus in the same direction as the chameleon stalks slowly forward until it is close enough to use the other unique weapon in its armoury. This is its sticky-tipped tongue, which is typically about the same length as its body and remains coiled up within its mouth most of the time, to be unleashed in a sudden, blink-and-you'll-miss-it

long considered harmless to humans, being back-fanged (meaning that they have to work at biting humans) and characteristically inoffensive. Nevertheless, their venom, if injected effectively, is deadly. Even so, African records contain just one confirmed fatality for each snake, both involving herpetologists subscribing to the 'harmless' theory.

Most snakes are in fact non-venomous and not even potentially harmful to any other living creature much bigger than a rat. One of the more non-venomous snakes in the region is the **green tree snake** (sometimes mistaken for a boomslang, though the latter is never as green and more often than not brown), which feeds mostly on amphibians. The **mole snake** is a common and widespread grey-brown savanna resident that grows up to 2m long, and feeds on moles and other rodents. Unusually, its fangs protrude as frontal spikes in order to spear prey in tunnels. The remarkable **egg-eating snakes** live exclusively on birds' eggs, dislocating their jaws to swallow the egg whole, then eventually regurgitating the crushed shell in a neat little package. Many snakes will take eggs opportunistically, for which reason large-scale agitation among birds in a tree is often a good indication that a snake (or small bird of prey) is around.

LIZARDS All African lizards are harmless to humans, with the arguable exception of the **giant monitor lizards**, which could in theory inflict a nasty bite if cornered.

lunge to zap a selected item of prey. In addition to their unique eyes and tongues, many chameleons are adorned with an array of facial casques, flaps, horns and crests that enhance their already somewhat fearsome prehistoric appearance.

In Uganda, you're most likely to come across a chameleon by chance when it is crossing a road, in which case it should be easy to take a closer look at it, since most chameleons move painfully slowly and deliberately. Chameleons are also often seen on night game drives, when their ghostly nocturnal colouring shows up clearly under a spotlight – as well as making it pretty clear why these strange creatures are regarded with both fear and awe in many local African cultures. More actively, you could ask your guide if they know where to find a chameleon – a few individuals will be resident in most lodge grounds.

The **flap-necked chameleon** (*Chamaeleo delepis*) is probably the most regularly observed species of savanna and woodland habitats in East Africa. Often observed crossing roads, the flap-necked chameleon is generally around 15cm long and bright green in colour with few distinctive markings, but individuals might be up to 30cm in length and will turn tan or brown under the right conditions. Another closely related and widespread savanna and woodland species is the similarly sized **graceful chameleon** (*Chamaeleo gracilis*), which is generally yellow-green in colour and often has a white horizontal stripe along its flanks.

Characteristic of east African montane forests, **three-horned chameleons** form a closely allied species cluster of some taxonomic uncertainty. Typically darker than the savanna chameleons and around 20cm in length, the males of all taxa within this cluster are distinguished by a trio of long nasal horns that project forward from their face. Perhaps the most alluring of East Africa's chameleons is the **giant chameleon** (*Chamaeleo melleri*), a bulky dark-green creature with yellow stripes and a small solitary horn, mainly associated with the Eastern Arc forests, where it feeds on small reptiles (including snakes) as well as insects.

Two species of monitor occur in East Africa, the **water** and the **savanna**, the latter growing up to 2.2m long and occasionally seen in the vicinity of termite mounds, the former slightly smaller but far more regularly observed by tourists, particularly along the Kazinga Channel in QENP. Their size alone might make it possible to fleetingly mistake a monitor for a small crocodile, but their more colourful yellow-dappled skin precludes sustained confusion. Both species are predatorial, feeding on anything from birds' eggs to smaller reptiles and mammals, but will also eat carrion opportunistically.

Visitors to East Africa will soon become familiar with the **common house gecko**, an endearing bug-eyed, translucent white lizard, which as its name suggests reliably inhabits most houses as well as lodge rooms, scampering up walls and upside down on the ceiling in pursuit of pesky insects attracted to the lights. Also very common in some lodge grounds are various **agama** species, distinguished from other common lizards by their relatively large size of around 20–25cm, basking habits, and almost plastic-looking scaling – depending on the species, a combination of blue, purple, orange or red, with the flattened head generally a different colour from the torso. Another common family are the **skinks**: small, long-tailed lizards, most of which are quite dark and have a few thin black stripes running from head to tail.

TORTOISES AND TERRAPINS These peculiar reptiles are unique in being protected by a prototypal suit of armour formed by their heavy exoskeleton. The most common of the terrestrial tortoises in the region is the **leopard tortoise**, which is named after its gold-and-black mottled shell, can weigh up to 30kg, and has been known to live for more than 50 years in captivity. It is often seen motoring along in the slow lane of game reserve roads in Uganda. Four species of terrapin – essentially the freshwater equivalent of turtles – are resident in East Africa, all somewhat flatter in shape than the tortoises, and generally with a plainer brown shell. They might be seen sunning on rocks close to water or peering out from roadside puddles. The largest is the **Nile soft-shelled terrapin**, which has a wide, flat shell and in rare instances might reach a length of almost 1m.

3

Practical Information

This chapter covers most practical aspects of planning a trip to Uganda, including overland crossings between Uganda and neighbouring countries. Practical advice relating to day-to-day travel in Uganda is also covered in this chapter, but in some instances it might bear on planning, so do at least skim through it before you travel. Aspects of trip planning relating to health – for instance organising vaccinations and putting together a medical kit – are covered in *Health*, pages 85–96.

WHEN AND WHERE TO VISIT

Uganda has a warm climate all year round and, because it lies on the Equator, seasonal temperature variations are insignificant. The main factor you should consider when planning a trip to Uganda is the rainfall pattern. The wettest months are April, May, October and November. Campers won't enjoy these months very much (you'll be packing up your tent in the rain as often as not) while hiking on the Rwenzori can be particularly miserable. Abundant rainfall also means that large wildlife tends not to congregate conveniently around water sources in the national parks. On the other hand, photographers seeking landscapes will revel in the haze-free atmosphere of the wetter months.

For many visitors, the highlight of a visit to Uganda is the opportunity to track mountain gorillas and consequently, most formal itineraries follow an established circuit between Kampala and the gorilla parks in the extreme southwest of the country. This is, fortunately, the area with the greatest density of natural attractions and associated infrastructure. A typical tour heads west from Kampala or the international airport at nearby Entebbe to the scenic Fort Portal area where the main attraction is chimpanzee tracking in the forested Kibale National Park, followed by a two- to three-night visit to Queen Elizabeth National Park (QENP) at the foot of the Rwenzori Mountains. South of QENP is Bwindi Impenetrable National Park which offers no fewer than four separate gorilla tracking locations. It's a long haul from Bwindi back to Kampala/Entebbe and many tour operators now offer their clients an overnight break at Lake Mburo National Park. It is possible to cover this itinerary in seven days (ten would be better) and many people do. However, those with time and flexibility to delay and detour will discover much more. Days can be spent exploring the Fort Portal and Rwenzori area, while Lake Bunyonyi and the Virunga volcanoes are worthwhile diversions near Bwindi. Visitors intent on reaching true East African wilderness (a rare commodity in the densely populated south of Uganda) will want to head north to the Murchison Falls and Kidepo Valley national parks. These experiences do, however, incur a cost of increased travel time and expenditure. Visitors with time for a day trip at the end of their visit invariably head east from Kampala to visit the famed Source of the Nile at Jinja. If this event represents a tick on a list rather than a life-affirming experience, the same cannot be said for Jinja's other main attraction: the menu of adventure sports offered along the Nile corridor north of the town. Activities such as white-water rafting, kayaking, bungee jumping and quad biking attract a steady flow of the young and young at heart.

TOURIST INFORMATION

Your best source of advance tourism information (other than this book of course) is the internet; Ugandan embassies and high commissions can only give limited advice. The best Uganda-operated websites are **Uganda Wildlife Authority** (*www. ugandawildlife.org*) and **Uganda Travel Planner** (*www.traveluganda.co.ug*). Be sure too, to check out the UK-based **Africa Travel Resource** (*www.africatravelresource. com/africa/uganda*). This excellent site contains hundreds of pictures illustrating primary destinations and the pick of the tourist accommodation available at each. The website for the car-hire company, **Roadtrip Uganda** (*www.roadtripuganda. com*) contains a selection of practical itineraries with an emphasis on camping which independent travellers may find useful. Lastly, don't leave home without visiting http://updates.bradtguides.com/uganda for updates compiled by the author from reader feedback. See also *Uganda online,* page 543.

Within Uganda, your main source of official information will be the Uganda Wildlife Authority (UWA) information and booking offices in Kampala, Masindi (for Murchison Falls), Kisoro (for Bwindi and Mgahinga) and Mbale (Mount Elgon). You'll find privately run information offices at Edirisa Hostel and the tourism information centre in Kabale, at Kabarole Tours in Fort Portal and Rwenzori Nature Adventures in Kasese (see listings for these towns for further details). Otherwise, it's down to the good old travellers' grapevine at popular backpacker hubs such as the Backpackers and Red Chilli hostels in Kampala, Explorers Backpackers and Nalubale Tea House in Jinja, and the Bunyonyi Overland Resort at Lake Bunyonyi near Kabale.

TOUR OPERATORS

An ever-growing number of local and international tour operators offer a range of standard and customised private safaris to Uganda. Two-week itineraries typically cover the full western circuit from Murchison Falls to Lake Mburo via Kibale Forest, Queen Elizabeth and Bwindi or Mgahinga national parks, sometimes nipping across the border to Rwanda to go gorilla tracking when no permits are available within Uganda. Shorter itineraries generally omit the long drive to and from Murchison Falls, and one-stop gorilla tours of three days' duration are also available out of Kampala. Several other variations are available, depending on the individual's interests and how much time they have available. The high cost of vehicle maintenance, fuel and upmarket accommodation in Uganda is reflected in the price of private safaris, but this can be reduced by using cheaper accommodation, such as the Red Chilli Rest Camp at Paraa at Murchison Falls or Mweya Hostel in QENP, or by camping.

Uganda, mercifully, shows no signs of trying to establish itself as a package destination, nor is it likely to for as long as its premier attraction remains the relatively exclusive experience of tracking mountain gorillas in Bwindi or the Virungas. The country is, however, well suited to small group tours that offer the same standard of accommodation and service as private safaris, but generally at a reduced individual price because transport and related costs are divided between several passengers. In addition to general group tours, packages are also available for special-interest groups such as birdwatchers, primate enthusiasts and photographers. The South African company Wild Frontiers runs regular general- and special-interest small group tours led by the highly regarded ornithologists Malcolm Wilson and Ian Davidson as well as – unabashed plug, I admit it! – the author of this guidebook.

The following locally based and international operators can all be recommended as experienced and reliable. Note that contacts for companies that operate offices in Uganda and abroad are combined in the *Uganda* section below.

UGANDA These six companies are reliable high-end companies.

Classic Africa Safaris Uganda: 0414 320121 m 0772 642527; e classic@classicafricasafaris. travel; www.classicuganda.com. US: PO Box 55, Shepherdstown, WV 25443; +1 304 876 1315; m + 1 304 268 0033; e phil@classicuganda.com. Fully escorted safaris. You'll probably never see Classic's superb vehicle workshop in Entebbe but it's reassuring to know it exists.

The Far Horizons 0312 264 894/5; e info@ thefarhorizons.com; www.thefarhorizons.com. Experienced operator specialising in tailor-made private & small-group tours with offices in Uganda & Rwanda (also trades in the UK under the name Journeys Discovering Africa – see page 78).

Premier Safaris 0312 260260/1 0414 255992; e gm@premiersafaris.com; www.premiersafaris. com. I'm assuming this brand-new outfit will deliver the goods, it being the safari arm of Marasa, owners of high-class national park lodges at Mweya, Paraa & Chobe.

Volcanoes Safaris (Kampala, London, USA) Kampala: 0414 346464/5; m 0772 741718; e salesug@volcanoessafaris.com; www. volcanoessafaris.com. London: 402 Linen Hall, 162–168 Regent St, London, W1B 5TE; +44 0870 870 8480; e salesuk@volcanoessafaris. com. USA +1 866 599 2737; e salesus@ volcanoessafaris.com. High-end company with 15 years' experience specialising in gorilla- & chimp-tracking safaris. Owns & operates luxury lodges in Bwindi, Mgahinga & Queen Elizabeth in Uganda & Parc National des Volcans (PNV) in Rwanda.

Wild Frontiers (Johannesburg & Entebbe) Uganda: 0414 321479; m 0772 502155; e info@wildfrontiers.co.ug; www.wildfrontiers. co.ug or www.wildfrontiers.com. South Africa: +27 11 702 2035; e reservations@wildfrontiers. com. Competitively priced tour operator with more than a decade of experience arranging safaris to all corners of East Africa. Wild Frontiers operates in Uganda through its own well-equipped ground operation in Entebbe, G&C Tours. In addition to creating customised private safaris, it offers a range of fixed-departure photographic, birdwatching, primate & other interest tours led by experts in their fields. G&C Tours operates Ishasha Wilderness Camp (Queen Elizabeth National Park), Buhoma Lodge (Bwindi), & Nile river boat trips in Murchison Falls National Park. See advert on page 415.

Wildplaces 0414 251182; m 0772 489497; e info@wildplacesafrica.com; www. wildplacesafrica.com. Guided safaris countrywide. Wildplaces operates lodges & camps in the Semliki Valley, Kidepo Valley & at Nkuringo adjacent to Bwindi Impenetrable National Park.

Reliable alternatives The following tour operators are also listed alphabetically but otherwise in no particular order. They are also considered reliable but easier on the pocket. I've only included addresses where a company is located in a particularly convenient location.

Abacus African Vacations 0414 232657; e info@abacusvacations.com; www. abacusvacations.com; www.gorillatours.co.ug
Acacia Safaris 0414 253597; m 0712 800004; e tours@acaciasafari.co.ug; www.acaciasafari.co.ug

Access Uganda e accessug@utonline.co.ug. Safari company run by Hassan Mutebi, one of Uganda's most experienced bird guides.
Adventure Trails 0312 261 930; m 0712 723191; e info@gorilla-safari.com

African Pearl Safaris ✆0414 233566; e aps@
africaonline.co.ug; www.africanpearlsafaris.com
Africa's Great Exploration (Munyonyo &
USA) (AGE) Safaris Uganda: Ground Fl, Speke
Commonwealth Resort, Munyonyo; ✆0414
662300; m 0776 723274; e info@agesafaris.com;
www.agesafaris.com. USA: Toll free ✆1 800 349
9930, ext 1122; e age@ugandatravelnetwork.com
Bird Uganda Safaris m 0777 912938; e info@
birduganda.com; www.birduganda.com. One for
the birders, BUS is run by Herbert Byarahanga, one
of Uganda's foremost bird guides.
Churchill Safaris (Kampala, USA, UK) Uganda:
✆+ 256 0414 341815; m 0772 671285; e ether@
churchillsafaris.com; www.churchillsafaris.com.
UK: ✆01844 290000; m 07906 137778;
e gcarr@churchillsafaris.com. US: ✆+ 1 909 509
2456; e henry@churchillsafaris.com
Crystal Safaris ✆0414 354712; e info@
crystalsafaris.com; www.crystalsafaris.com
Destination Jungle m 0712 385446;
e d.jungle@safaritoeastafrica.com; www.
safaritoeastafrica.com. See advert on page 132.
East African Safaris ✆0414 344332; m 0772
411232; e info@eastafricansafaris.net; www.
eastafricansafaris.net
Gorilla Tours Ltd ✆0414 200221; m 0777
820071; www.gorillatours.com. Office in Quality
Village Shopping Mall, Lubowa, 6km on Entebbe
Road. Reliable company that runs Kisoro's historic
Traveller's Rest Inn Hotel & the excellent Airport
Guesthouse in Entebbe.
Great Lakes Safaris Ltd ✆0414 267153;
m 0772 426 368; e info@safari-uganda.com;
www.safari-uganda.com. Mid-range company,
which runs Primate Lodge in Kibale Forest, Simba
Safari Camp close to Queen Elizabeth National Park
& Budongo Eco Lodge in Murchison Falls National
Park. See also advert on page 30.
Hog Safaris e hog@hogsafaris.co.ug; www.
hogsafaris.co.ug. Small company on Kampala's
Namirembe Hill recommended by readers.
Kazinga Tours Ltd 406 Makamba Rd, Lungujja
(behind Kampala Backpackers); ✆0414 274 457;
m 0772 552819; e mail@kazingatours.com;
www.kazingatours.com. Middle-market tour
company with offices in Kabale & Kampala.
Kombi Nation Tours m 0792 933773; e info@
komitours.com; www.kombitours.com. Instead of
the usual Land Cruiser safari vehicles, this friendly
bunch runs a fleet of vintage VW camper vans.

'Absolutely EPIC' emails a clearly delighted punter!
Let's Go Travel/BCD Travel ✆0414 346667;
e letsgo@bcdtravel.co.ug; www.bcdtravel.co.ug.
Conveniently located near the food hall in Garden
City Mall, BCD offers nationwide safaris & regional
package holidays.
Matoke Tours (Uganda, Germany & Netherlands)
Kampala: m 0751 057863; www.matoketours.
com. Netherlands: ✆+31 (0) 73 612 3364;
e info@matoketours.com or .nl or .de Reliable &
fast-growing mid-market Dutch outfit. See also
advert in fourth colour section.
Moses Uganda Tours & Taxis (Motours)
m 0772 422825/0752 422825;
e emotoursuganda@yahoo.com, moses.tours@
live.com; www.traveluganda.co.ug/motours.
Mbarara-based company.
NatureTrack Expeditions ✆0774 132967;
e safari@naturetrack-expeditions.com; www.
naturetrack-expeditions.com. See also advert in
fourth colour section.
Pearlafric ✆0414 232730; e info@pearlafric;
www.pearlafric.com. Another small, Kampala-
based outfit plugged by happy readers.
Pearl of Africa Tours & Travel Car park basement,
Oasis Mall, Kampala; ✆0312 260559/0414 340533;
m 0772 403 614; e info@pearlofafricatours.com;
www.pearlofafricatours.com
Primate Watch Safaris Ltd ✆0414 266 824;
www.primatewatchsafaris.com. See also advert on
page 188.
Safari Wildz www.safariwildz.com. New Jinja-
based budget outfit catering for large & small groups.
See also advert in fourth colour section.
Sharubu Safaris & Expeditions ✆0751
976325; www.discoveringuganda.com. Spanish-
owned company with divergent passions: the
gorillas of southwest Uganda & the wild & little-
visited region of Karamoja in the northeast.
Stebar Safaris ✆0414 323123; m 0785 754434;
e advice@stebar-safaris.com; www.stebar-safaris.
com. Entebbe-based company with Danish partners.
TIA m 0789 476328; e bookings@tia-
adventures.com; www.tia-adventures.com
Travelust African Safaris ✆0414 578209;
m 0772 419238; e travel@africaonline.co.ug;
www.travelust.com
Viva Safaris [149 H3] Airlines Hse, Colville St;
✆0312 100065; m 0755 465020; e info@
vivasafaris.net; www.vivasafaris.net. Expanding,
family-owned company with city centre office.

What's Wild 📞0784 461368; e safaris@ whatswildsafaris.com; www.whatswildsafaris. com. This small new safari outfit has just one vehicle but it's probably the finest in the country. See also advert in fourth colour section.

See also **Yebo Tours** in Masindi (page 386) and **Kabarole Tours** in Fort Portal (page 336). All of the above are (I believe) members of AUTO (Association of Ugandan Tour Operators; www.auto.or.ug), an accreditation that implies a certain standard of operation, experience and integrity. This is worth bearing in mind if you intend to make advance payments by credit card – one company, Volvo Tours, was blacklisted for making off with advances from clients. Visit the AUTO website (*www.auto.or.ug*) for a full list of members.

Local operators A growing choice of smaller operators is also emerging, often Ugandan safari guides setting up on their own with a vehicle. These are invariably not AUTO members and may not offer the same 'fully comprehensive' service as the operators listed above. Nevertheless, they may represent an affordable compromise between a fully fledged safari and the bus. Ask around or check noticeboards at the backpacker hangouts. If booking a freelance tour guide, check his (or her) status with the Uganda Safari Guides Association (USAGA) (*www.ugasaf.org*) or the Uganda Bird Guides Club (*www.ugandabirdguides.org*).

Eco-Specialists Tours m 0712 955671/0714 871145; e info@ecotoursuganda.com; www. ecotoursuganda.com. With 15 years' birding experience behind them, the Mabira Forest guides have formed their own company. Recommended to birders.
Emmy Gongo m 0772 853372; e emmygongo@ yahoo.com. Born on the edge of Bwindi Forest, Emmy is one of Uganda's best-known birding guides.

Farouk Busulwa 📞0392 813391; m 0701 858025; e moroukprod@yahoo.co.uk. Freelance safari/birding guide.
James Kiwanuka m 0772 465378. Loosely attached to Kampala Backpackers, James is a reliable fellow with a comfortable 6-seater minibus. Airport transfers or upcountry safaris.
Robert Ntale m 0772 413766/0752 413766. Reliable freelance driver.

All of the companies and individuals listed above can provide you with tailor-made itineraries. Another option is to sign up for a fixed-itinerary camping tour to a specific destination. Kampala Backpackers (see page 152) and Red Chilli (page 156) run trips from their Kampala hostels to Murchison Falls National Park. Another cost-saving strategy is to hire a car yourself and travel where and when the fancy takes you. The companies listed on page 144 typically offer self-drive or provide drivers if required. Worth singling out is the innovative car and camping gear service provided by Road Trip Uganda. Check their website for possible itineraries (*www.roadtripuganda.com*). Since you are most likely to need a private vehicle to visit a national park, the most economical strategy would be to take the bus to the closest town and engage a local tour or vehicle hire operator.

UK

Aardvark Safaris RBL Hse; 📞01980 849160; e mail@aardvarksafaris.com; www. aardvarksafaris.co.uk. Private & small-group tailored itineraries.
Africa Travel Resource 📞01306 880770; e info@africatravelresource.com; www. africatravelresource.com. Leading tailor-made safari company with a remarkably comprehensive website containing thousands of images of hotels & lodges across the region.
Bailey Robinson 📞01488 689 700; e travel@ baileyrobinson.com; www.baileyrobinson.com. Top-end safari specialists in in East & southern Africa.
Cox & Kings Travel 📞(brochure requests) 01235 824404, (reservations) 020 7873 5000; e cox.kings@

coxandkings.co.uk; www.coxandkings.co.uk. Group & individual tours.

Explore Worldwide 📞0845 291 4541; e hello@ explore.co.uk; www.explore.co.uk. Market leader in small-group, escorted trips worldwide.

Footloose 📞01943 604030; e info@footloose. co.uk; www.footlooseadventure.co.uk. Tailor-made tours, safaris & treks throughout Tanzania, including Zanzibar.

Gane & Marshall 📞01822 600 600; e info@ ganeandmarshall.com; www.ganeandmarshall. com. Long-established Africa specialist.

Hartley's Safaris 📞01673 861600; e info@ hartleys-safaris.co.uk; www.hartleys-safaris.co.uk. Reliable safaris to East & southern Africa, as well as diving & island holidays in the region.

Imagine Africa 📞020 7622 5114; USA 1 888 882 7121; e info@imagineafrica.co.uk; www. imagineafrica.co.uk. Award-winning luxury tours.

Journeys by Design 📞01273 623 790; e info@ journeysbydesign.com; www.journeysbydesign. com. Experienced operator offering stylish, tailor-made safaris across southern & East Africa including helicopter.

Journeys Discovering Africa 📞0208 144 4412; e enquiries@journeysdiscoveringafrica.com; www. journeysdiscoveringafrica.com. High-end company specialising in tailor-made private & small group tours with fully owned ground operations in Uganda & Rwanda. See also advert in third colour section.

Natural World Safaris 📞01273 691642; Toll free from US: 1866 357 6569 Toll Free from Australia: 1800 668 890; e sales@naturalworldsafaris.com; www.naturalworldsafaris.com. NWS specialise in tailor-made safaris to Uganda to track mountain gorillas. See advert on page 129.

Rainbow Tours 📞020 7666 1250; e info@ rainbowtours.co.uk; www.rainbowtours.co.uk. Independent Africa & Latin America specialists. See also advert on page 29.

Royle Safaris 📞0845 226 8259 e info@royle-safaris.co.uk; www.royle-safaris.co.uk. Small, specialist tours led by expert zoologists in search of rare & elusive wildlife.

Safari Consultants 📞01787 888590; info@ safariconsultantuk.com; www.safari-consultants. co.uk. Specialists in African safari holidays.

Steppes Travel 📞0845 075 6117; e enquiry@ steppestravel.co.uk; www.steppestravel.co.uk. Worldwide tailor-made specialists with a long Africa history. See also advert on page 130.

Theobald Barber 📞020 7723 5858; e info@ theobaldbarber.com; www.theobaldbarber.com. High-end operator specialising in highly individual holidays to East & southern Africa in remote wilderness areas far from any madding crowds.

Tribes Travel 📞01473 890499; e info@tribes. co.uk; www.tribes.co.uk. ATOL-protected tailor-made holidays in Uganda & elsewhere.

Wildlife & Wilderness 📞0845 00 44 599/01625 838 225; e info@wildlifewilderness.com; www. wildlifewilderness.com. Tailor-made & small group trips across Africa & worldwide.

Wildlife Worldwide 📞0845 130 6982; e sales@ wildlifeworldwide.com; www.wildlifeworldwide. com. Tailor-made & small group trips worldwide.

World Odyssey 📞01905 731373; e info@world-odyssey.com; www.world-odyssey.com. Tailor-made trips across the globe (a different company from Africa Odyssey).

US

Aardvark Safaris 12707 High Bluff Drive, Suite 200, San Diego, CA 92130; 📞Toll free (from USA) 1888 776 0888, (outside USA) +1858 794 1480; www.aardvarksafaris.com

eTrip Africa www.etripafrica.co.uk. Custom-built itineraries. See also advert in fourth colour section.

The African Adventure Company 5353 North Federal Highway, Suite 300, Fort Lauderdale, FL 33308; 📞+1 954 491 8877; e safari@ africanadventure.com; www.africanadventure.com

GERMANY

Abendsonneafrika www.abendsonneafrika.de. German safari company which engages some of Uganda's most experienced local guides.

Hauser Exkursionen International GmbH Spiegelstr 9, 81241 Munich; 📞+49 89 235 0060; e info@hauser-exkursionen.de; www.hauser-exkursionen.de

Safari Uganda KJ Sattler Weg 8, 69483 Wald Michelbach 📞+49 06 207 7378; e safariuganda@ yahoo.de; www.safariuganda.de. Reliable outfit run by the owners of Lagoon Resort near Kampala .

Wigwam 📞49 83 799 2060; e info@ wigwamtours.de; www.wigwamtour.de

ELSEWHERE

KK United Travel Service International KK Uti Hse, 4-5-5, Nakakasai, Edogawa-ku, Tokyo 134 0083; 📞+81 3 3675 6636; e waliangulu@aol.com

Oribi Tours & Safaris www.oribitours.com. Wildlife & activity tours led by local guides. See also advert on page 334.
Pulse Africa PO Box 2417, Parklands 2121, Johannesburg, South Africa; ☏+27 11 325

2290/+44 (0) 20 8995 5909 (UK); e info@ pulseafrica.com; www.pulseafrica.com
Ugandaresor ☏+46 706 152 007; e christer@ ugandaresor.se; www.ugandaresor.se. A Uganda–Sweden connection, this one.

RED TAPE

Check well in advance that you have a **passport** that is valid for a full year from the date on which you intend to enter Uganda. In the UK, you can have up to nine months validity on your current passport carried over onto a new passport. Should your passport be lost or stolen, it will generally be easier to get a replacement if you have a photocopy of the important pages.

If there is any possibility you'll want to drive or hire a vehicle in Uganda, bring a valid driving licence. You can use your domestic (home country) driving licence for up to three months; if you intend to drive in Uganda for longer, you're then supposed to obtain a Ugandan licence or (this is far cheaper and simpler) bring an international driving licence along with your domestic licence. Rather than carrying the originals, a photocopy will suffice. You may well be asked when entering Uganda for an **international health certificate** showing you've had a yellow fever shot. You will certainly need one if travelling onwards from Uganda to another country in the region (this virtually dormant requirement was revived following a short outbreak of yellow fever in northern Uganda in 2011).

For security reasons, it's advisable to detail all your important information on one sheet of paper, photocopy it, and distribute a few copies in your luggage, your moneybelt, and amongst relatives or friends at home. The sort of things you want to include are your travel insurance policy details, a 24-hour emergency contact number, passport number, details of relatives or friends to be contacted in an emergency, bank and credit card details, camera and lens serial numbers, etc.

VISAS Nationals of most countries require a visa in order to enter Uganda. This can be bought in advance at any Ugandan embassy or high commission abroad, either by applying in person or by post (obviously sending your passport by registered mail and in plenty of time). Alternatively, you can buy the visa upon arrival, a straightforward procedure that usually takes only a few minutes at Entebbe International Airport or any overland border. The only potential irritation is when a couple of major airlines arrive within an hour of each other making the visa queue a bit longer; you may want to check the likelihood of this with your local contacts. Visa rulings are prone to change, so all visitors are advised to check the current situation with their travel agent or a Ugandan diplomatic mission before they travel. A standard single-entry visa, valid for three months, costs US$50. Student visas cost US$20. Multiple-entry visas are only available at Ugandan consulates abroad (where they often cost more than two single-entry visas anyway) and not at entry points into the country. Travellers with a single-entry visa intending to leave and return to Uganda (eg: to track gorillas in Rwanda) must purchase another US$50 visa on re-entry. If, however, you intend to spend less than seven days in Uganda before leaving again, you may be able to purchase an inland transit visa for only US$15. There's talk, but as yet no action, of a single visa covering regional travel between Uganda, Kenya and Tanzania.

Important note Even though you hold a three-month visa, immigration authorities may only stamp your passport for a period of one month or less. This can be extended to three months at any immigration office in Kampala or upcountry. Irrespective of what they might tell you, there is no charge for this. In Kampala, you may be asked to provide an official letter from a sponsor or the hotel where you are staying. Don't overstay your visa or the date of the immigration stamp in your passport. If you do, you'll be liable of a fine of US$30/day.

CUSTOMS The following items may be imported into Uganda without incurring customs duty: 400 cigarettes or 500g of tobacco; one bottle of spirits and wine and 2.5 litres of beer; 1oz bottle of perfume. Souvenirs may be exported without restriction but game trophies such as tooth, bone, horn, shell, claw, skin, hair, feather or other durable items are subject to export permits.

UGANDAN DIPLOMATIC MISSIONS ABROAD

Belgium Av de Tervurn 317, 1150 Brussels; +32 2 762 58 25 (3 lines); e contactugandaembassy@gmail.com; www.ugandamission-benelux.org/embassy

Canada 231 Cobourg St, Ottawa KIN 8J2; +1 613 613 7797; www.ugandahighcommission.com

China 5 San Lt Tun Dong Jie, Beijing; +86 10 6532 1708; e info@ugandaembassycn.org; www.travelchinaguide.com

Denmark Sofievej 15, DK-2900, Heller up, Copenhagen; +45 39 620966; www.ugandaembassy.dk

Egypt 66 Rd, 10 Maadi, Cairo; +20 238 02514; e ugembco@link.net; www.uganda-embassy.com

Ethiopia Kirkos Kifle Ketema, Kebele 35, Addis Ababa; +251 11 551 3114; e uganda.emb@telecom.net.et

France 13 Av Raymond Poincaré, 75116, Paris; +33 1 4505 2122; e Uganda.embassy@club-internet.fr

Germany Dorenstrasse 14, 531 Bonn; +49 30 20 60 990; www.ugandaembassyberlin.de

India C-6/11 Vasant Vihar, New Delhi 110-05; +91 11 2614 4413; e ughcom@vsl.net.in

Italy Lungotevere dei Milani, 44 00193 Rome; +39 06 322 5220; e ugandaembassyrome@hotmail.com; www.ugandaembassy.it

Japan 23 Hachiyama-cho Shibuya-ku, Tokyo 150-0035; +81 3462 7107; e ugabassy@hpo.net; www.uganda-embassy.jp

Kenya Uganda Hse, 1st Fl, Kenyatta Av, Nairobi; +254 20 2217445; e info@ugahicom.co.ke; www.ugahicom.co.ke

Nigeria 28, Ontario Cres, Maitama, Abuja FCT; +234 9 413 8069; e ugandabuja@suritech.com

Russian Federation Mytnay Ulisa 3, Office 1, 119049 Moscow; +7 499 230 22 76; e info@uganda.ru; www.uganda.ry

Rwanda KG 205 St, Nyarukatama, Kigali; +250 72115; www.ugandaembassy.rw

South Africa 35B Trafalgar Court, 634 Park St, Pretoria; +27 12 344 4100; www.uganda.org.za

Tanzania Extelcom Bldg, 7th Fl Samora Av, Dar es Salaam; +253 22 266 7391; e ugadar@intafrica.com

UK Uganda Hse, 58–9 Trafalgar Sq, London WC2N 5DX; +44 20 7839 5783 e info@ugandahighcommission.co.uk; www.ugandahighcommission.co.uk; ⏰ 09.30–17.30.

UN (New York) Uganda Hse, 336 E 45th St, New York, NY 10017; +1 212 949 0110. Permanent representative +1 212 697 2918.

US 5911 16th St, NW, Washington, DC 20011; +1 202 726 7100; www.ugandaembassy.com

EMBASSIES AND HIGH COMMISSIONS IN UGANDA

Diplomatic missions, embassies and high commissions likely to be of interest to visitors to Uganda are listed below. The website, www.i-uganda.com/embassies.html, would seem a useful resource in the event that these contacts become redundant.

Algeria 14 Acacia Av, Kololo; 0414 423391

Austria 3 Portal Av; 0312 35104/5; kampala@ada.gv.at

Belgium 1 Lumumba Av, Rwenzori Hse, 3rd Fl; 0414 349559/69/70; e kampala@diplobel.org; www.diplomatie.be-kampala

Canada IPS Bldg, 14 Parliament Av; \0414 258141/348141/0312 260511; e canada. consulate@utlonline.co.ug

China 37 Malcolm X Av, Kololo; \0414 236895/259881; e chinaemb_ug@mfa.gov.cn

Denmark 3 Lumumba Av; \0312 263211/2; e kmtamb@um.dk; www.kmtamb@um.dk

Egypt 4, Lower Kololo Terrrace; \0414 254525/345152; e egyembug@utlonline.co.ug

Ethiopia Kitante Close; \0414 348340; e ethiokam@utlonline.co.ug

European Union 15th Fl, Crested Towers, Hannington Rd; \0414 701000/231226; www. deluga.ec.europa.eu

France 16 Lumumba Av, Nakasero; \0414 304500; e ambafrance.kampala@diplomatie.gouv.fr

Germany 15 Philip Rd; \0414 501111; e info@kampala.diplo.de; www. kampala.diplo.de

India 11 Kyadondo Rd; \0414 342994/344631; e hc@hicomindkampala.org

Ireland 25 Yusuf Lule Rd (aka Kitante Rd); \0414 713000; e kampalaembassy@dfa.ie; www. embassyofireland.ug

Italy 11 Lourdel Rd; \0414 250450; e segreteria.kampala@esteri.it; www. ambkampala.esteri.it

Japan 8 Kyadondo Rd; \0414 349542–5; e jambassy@jembassy.or.ug

Kenya 41 Nakasero Rd; \0414 258235; e kenhicom@africaonline.co.ug; www. kenyamission-uganda.com

Netherlands Rwenzori Courts, Lumumba Av; \0414 346000; e kam@minbuza.nl; www. netherlandsembassyuganda.org

Nigeria 33 Nakasero Rd; \0414 233691/2

South Sudan 2 Sezibwa Rd (off Nakasero); \0414 271625

Sudan 21, Nakasero Rd; \0414 230001

UK (British High Commission) Kira Rd, next to the Uganda Wildlife Authority; \0312 312000; e bhcinfo@starcom.co.ug; www. britishhighcommission.gov.uk/uganda

US Ggaba Rd; \0414 306001/306207/259791; e ambkampala@state.gov

Some other diplomatic missions accredited to Uganda are in Nairobi; for example Australia, Canada, Greece, Zambia and Zimbabwe. Australians and Canadians can contact the British High Commission in an emergency. Quite a number of backpackers pick up their Ethiopian visas in Kampala because the Ethiopian High Commission in Nairobi often refuses to issue visas to travellers who don't have an air ticket to Addis Ababa.

GETTING THERE AND AWAY

Since an outbreak of yellow fever in northern Uganda in 2011, neighbouring countries have revived the long-dormant requirement for visitors arriving from Uganda to show a valid yellow fever certificate. Since the alternative is to be vaccinated at immigration – at a cost - visitors should obtain a certificate in advance.

BY AIR For obvious reasons, the most convenient means of reaching Uganda from Europe and North America is by air. A full list of international airlines that fly to Uganda is included under the *Kampala* listings on page 139.

People flying from Europe or North America to Uganda might find it easier to get a cheap ticket to Nairobi, the capital of Kenya and East Africa's major entry point. You can normally get between Nairobi and Kampala overland in a day (see *To/from Kenya* below). If you are in Nairobi, or elsewhere in the region, **Air Uganda** (*www.air-uganda.com*) and **Kenya Airways** (*www.kenyaairways.com*) operate flights between Entebbe and regional destinations such as Nairobi, Dar es Salaam, Zanzibar and Juba. If choosing the latter, don't expect the same level of efficiency and customer care on a regional hop as on one of their international flights.

In Europe, the best place to find cheap tickets to Africa is London. Two London travel agents specialise in Africa: **African Travel Specialists** (*Glen Hse, Stag Pl,*

London SW1E 5AG; ✎ *020 7630 5434)* and **Africa Travel Centre** (*4 Medway Court, Leigh St, London WC1H 9QX;* ✎ *020 7387 1211*). The website www.cheapflights. co.uk has been recommended by a traveller who got 30% off the standard British Airways fare to Entebbe.

Trailfinders (*42–48 Earls Court Rd, London W8 6EJ;* ✎ *020 7938 3366*) and **STA** (*117 Euston Rd, London NW1 2SX;* ✎ *020 7465 0486*) are both respected agents who do cheap flights worldwide, and particularly worth speaking to for round-the-world-type tickets. There are STA branches in Bristol, Cambridge, Oxford, Leeds, Brighton, Glasgow, Newcastle, Aberdeen, Cardiff and Manchester.

The airport departure tax is now included in the final price of a return ticket to Uganda.

ARRIVING (AND LEAVING) The main entry point for flights into Uganda is **Entebbe International Airport** [190 C2], 40km from Kampala. International charter flights can also land, usually by arrangement with immigration, at some airstrips around the country such as Pakuba (Murchison Falls NP), Kakira (Jinja) and Apoka (Kidepo Valley NP).

Provided that you have a valid passport, a yellow fever certificate and a return ticket you should whizz through the entrance formalities at Entebbe with no hassle. The only reason why a fly-in visitor would be likely to arrive in Uganda without a return ticket is because they intend to travel more widely in Africa. Not many people start their African travels in Uganda, because from most parts of the world it's far cheaper to fly to Nairobi; but if for some reason you will be arriving with a one-way ticket, there is a small but real possibility that you will be given a rough time by immigration officials concerned that you won't have enough funds to buy a flight out of the country. Obviously, the more money you have, the less likely they are to query your finances. And a credit card will almost certainly convince them to let you in. Assuming that you do intend to travel to neighbouring countries, you can underline this intention by arranging a visa or visitor's pass for the next country you plan to visit before you land in Uganda. Finally, an onward ticket technically is an entry requirement for Uganda, so there is little point in arguing the toss or becoming needlessly aggressive with immigration officials who are only doing the job they are paid to do – patient diplomacy is a far better approach.

The very worst that will happen if you arrive without a return ticket is that you will have to buy a ticket back to your home country before being allowed entry. Assuming you intend to leave Uganda overland, it is important you check with the relevant airline that this ticket will be refundable once you have left Uganda, and also that you select a departure date that will give you time to get to a country where you can organise the refund. Once through customs and immigration at Entebbe, the first thing you will want to do is get some local currency. There are 24-hour foreign-exchange facilities at the airport, though the rates are lower than at private forex bureaux in town, so I wouldn't exchange any more money than I had to. A private taxi from the airport to Entebbe costs around US$8 and one to Kampala should cost no more than US$30. The alternative is to take a shared taxi between the airport and Entebbe, where you can pick up a minibus to the old taxi park in Kampala for roughly US$1.50 per person.

OVERLAND Uganda borders five countries: Kenya, Tanzania, Rwanda, DRC and South Sudan. A high proportion of visitors to Uganda enters and leaves the country overland at the borders with Kenya or Tanzania. Few people enter or leave Uganda ʼom Rwanda, though a fair number cross briefly from Uganda to see mountain gorillas. The DRC is still effectively off-limits to casual travel. International NGOs and other organisations are now active in South Sudan, the world's youngest nation, excised from the Republic of the Sudan in 2011. Plenty of Ugandan commercial traffic crosses the borders near Nimule, Oraba and Moyo and a growing number of foreign travellers are headed that way to explore. Uganda's land borders are generally very relaxed. Provided that your papers are in order, you should have no problem, nor is there a serious likelihood of being asked about onward tickets or funds. You should however have a valid yellow fever vaccination certificate. About the worst you can expect at Ugandan customs is a cursory search of your luggage. It may be necessary to exchange money at any overland border in or out of Uganda; take a look at the box *Changing money at borders*, page 108, for advice.

To/from Kenya Crossing between Kenya and Uganda couldn't be more straightforward, and there are several ways you can go about it. Though Akamba, the bus of choice for years, folded recently, there are several reputable alternatives. The **Crown** bus (m *0776 719944*) departs from Old Kampala Bus Terminal at 22.00 and costs Ush65,000. It reaches the old Akamba park on Nairobi's Lagos Road at 07.30. A ticket as far as Kisumu costs Ush35,000. The fare all the way to Mombasa is Ush100,000. **Easy Coach** (m *0776 727273; www.easycoach.com*) and **Queen's Coach** (m *0773 002010; www.queenscoach.com*) run comfortable buses between Kampala, Nairobi and towns in western Kenya. Both companies depart from Kampala's Oasis Mall (Easy at 07.00 and Queen's at 20.00) and have booking offices in the basement. Though these are not the only Nairobi-bound buses, in terms of comfort and, more importantly, safety, you get what you pay for and I'd hesitate to resort to Gateway or Busscar simply to save a few shillings. Whichever bus you take, they all dock at the rough (River Road) end of the Nairobi city centre from which, rather than walk, it's safer to take a taxi to your next destination.

There is of course no reason to dash straight between Kampala and Nairobi. You might detour north to visit Mount Elgon (on either side of the border) or dally in Kenya's lovely but little-visited Western Highlands. Queen's Coach will take you to Eldoret (Ush55,000) or Nakuru (Ush60,000) while Easy Coach will drop you in Kisumu (Ush40,000). Alternatively, rather than passing through the usual border crossings, you could travel around the northern slopes of Mount Elgon to cross over at Suam between Kapchorwa and Kitale (see page 476).

The direct rail service between Nairobi and Kampala foundered years ago, but it is possible to take the **train** from Nairobi as far as Kisumu. This leaves Nairobi every couple of days at 18.00 and reaches Kisumu the following day around noon. You might be lucky enough to find a **cargo boat** headed across Lake Victoria to Kampala, though I haven't heard of anyone doing so. There is, however, plenty of **public transport** running to the Ugandan border at Busia. If you overnight in Busia, be aware that the buses to Kampala pass through early in the day; after that you'll take your chances with some lunatic driving a *matatu*. If you are crossing from Kenya in your own vehicle, bear in mind that fuel prices in Uganda are higher than in Kenya, so stock up accordingly.

To/from Tanzania Following the suspension of the ferry service between Mwanza and Port Bell, the best way to cross between Uganda and Tanzania depends on which part of Tanzania you want to visit. The only direct road between the two countries connects Masaka to the port of Bukoba, crossing at the Mutukula border post. **Daily Link** buses run from Kampala to Mutukula, leaving the Qualicell Bus Terminal at 09.00 and return to Kampala from Mutukula at 14.00 daily (Ush15,000).

It is possible to travel between Kampala and Bukoba in hops, but far easier to take the direct **Friends Safaris** bus from their office on Rashid Khamis Street (opposite Mukwano Mall) in Old Kampala. This leaves at 10.00 and costs Ush25,000. The return from Bukoba departs at 18.00.

From Bukoba, overnight ferries continue to Mwanza thrice weekly. Beyond Mwanza, you're on your own unless you invest in another guidebook. Suffice to say that the roads heading south from Mwanza are poor and the train to Dar via Tabora no longer runs. Enjoy! A quicker, cheaper and more comfortable option if you simply want to travel from Kampala to Arusha or Moshi (or for that matter, Dar es Salaam), is to travel via Nairobi. Regular shuttle buses run between Nairobi and Arusha, taking around five hours and costing in the region of US$20, assuming that you're permitted to pay residents' rates (which you normally will be).

To/from South Sudan
The 'Nile Route' via Juba was very popular with travellers before it was closed for years by a long-running civil war in Sudan and northern Uganda. The conflict ended in 2005 and the insurgent area in the south of the country subsequently gained independence from the north in July 2011. It's now possible to travel between Uganda and Juba, the new capital of the Republic of South Sudan overland or by air with Air Uganda. You won't travel alone; since the 2005 peace accord a flood of NGOs and commercial opportunists has been pouring into the area. In principle, this development makes possible the alluring prospect of following the Nile between its Ugandan headwaters and its effluent into the Mediterranean. In reality, you will find it difficult to secure passage between South and northern Sudan; relations between the north and south remain strained while both countries are big on paperwork, requiring permits to go pretty much anywhere. Do obtain as much information as possible from embassies and NGO contacts before wandering around South Sudan. Though peaceful on paper, this is a country in which war has been the norm for decades and ongoing problems include widespread gun ownership, as well as landmines. For further information, refer to Sophie and Max Lovell-Hoare's new Bradt guide to South Sudan (*www.bradtguides.com*). Visas (US$50) can be obtained at Nimule border crossing or the South Sudan Embassy in Kampala. Don't arrive at Juba Airport hoping to get a visa unless you are certain that this is possible (and that doesn't mean asking at the South Sudan Embassy). You'll also need a valid yellow fever certificate to cross from Uganda to South Sudan.

Buses run to Juba, via Nimule from the Arua Stage in the middle of Kampala and the more accessible Old Kampala Bus Terminal. **LOL** buses depart the latter at 21.30, reaching Nimule at 08.00 and arriving Juba around noon.

To/from Rwanda
Two main border crossings connect Uganda and Rwanda. Cyanikia lies 15km south of Kisoro while Katuna is 21km south of Kabale. There's also a minor crossing at Mirama Hills, 30km from Ntungamo. It's perfectly straightforward to drive yourself so long as you remember that the Rwandan authorities expect vehicles to drive on the right, have appropriate insurance and carry breakdown warning triangles. **Jaguar** buses run from Kampala to Kigali from their stage on Namirembe Road, 500m uphill from the main cluster of bus and taxi parks around Nakivubu Stadium. Visas, if required, can be obtained on the border. See pages 79–80 for additional information.

To/from DRC
There are several routes between Uganda and the Democratic ˀepublic of Congo. From north to south, the main ones are Arua–Aru, Ntoroko–

Kasenyi (a boat crossing on Lake Albert), Bwera–Kasindi, Ishasha, and Bunagana. Of these, only the last sees much in the way of tourist traffic, this being the most convenient crossing for tracking mountain gorillas in the Virunga National Park, and visiting other locations such as Nyiragongo Volcano. Bunagana is 8km from Kisoro and served by daily buses from Kampala. However (and this happens every time I update this section), eastern Congo is currently embroiled in yet another civil war and travellers should seek reliable and up-to-date information before considering crossing into the DRC.

HEALTH with Dr Felicity Nicholson and thanks to Dr Vaughan Southgate of the Natural History Museum, London, and Dr Dick Stockley, The Surgery, Kampala

People new to exotic travel often worry about tropical diseases, but it is accidents that are most likely to carry you off. Road accidents are common in Uganda so be aware and do what you can to reduce risks: try to travel during daylight hours, always wear a seatbelt and refuse to be driven by anyone who has been drinking. Listen to local advice about areas where violent crime is rife too.

PREPARATIONS
Preparations to ensure a healthy trip to Uganda require checks on your immunisation status: it is wise to be up to date on **tetanus, polio, diphtheria** (now given as an all-in-one vaccine, Revaxis, that lasts for ten years), and hepatitis A. Immunisations against meningococcus, hepatitis B and rabies may also be recommended. Proof of vaccination against **yellow fever** is needed for entry into Uganda if you are coming from another yellow fever endemic area. The World Health Organization (WHO) recommends that this vaccine should be taken for Uganda by those over nine months of age for health reasons, although proof of entry is only officially required for those over one year of age. If the vaccine is not suitable for you, discuss your options with a travel health expert. If you intend to visit Uganda regardless, and there is a requirement for a yellow fever certificate on entry, then obtain an exemption certificate from your GP or a travel clinic and try to avoid the day-biting mosquitoes that spread the disease. Immunisation against cholera is no longer required for Uganda but may on occasion be recommended.

Hepatitis A vaccine (Havrix Monodose or Avaxim) comprises two injections given about a year apart. The course costs about £100, but may be available on the NHS; it protects for 25 years and can be administered even close to the time of departure. **Hepatitis B** vaccination should be considered for longer trips (two months or more) or for those working with children or in situations where contact with blood is likely. Three injections are needed for the best protection and can be given over a three-week period if time is short if you are aged 16 or over. Longer schedules give more sustained protection and are therefore preferred if time allows and must be used for those under 16. Hepatitis A vaccine can also be given as a combination with hepatitis B as 'Twinrix', though two doses are needed at least seven days apart to be effective for the hepatitis A component, and three doses are needed for the hepatitis B. Again, this faster schedule can only be used on those aged 16 or over.

The injectable typhoid vaccines (eg: Typhim Vi) last for three years and are about 75% effective. Oral capsules (Vivotif) are a viable alternative for those aged six and over who are not immunocompromised. Three capsules taken over five days will give protection for around three years but may be slightly less effective than the injectable forms as they may not always be absorbed as well. They should be encouraged unless the traveller is leaving within a few days for a trip of a week or less, when the vaccine would not be effective in time. **Meningitis** vaccine (containing strains A, C, W and Y), will usually be recommended for trips of more than four weeks or for any time if you are working and living with the local population, when the risk of exposure could be greater (see page 93). Vaccinations for **rabies** are ideally advised for everyone, but are especially important for travellers visiting more remote areas, especially if you are more than 24 hours from medical help and definitely if you will be working with animals (see pages 94).

Experts differ over whether a BCG vaccination against **tuberculosis** (TB) is useful in adults: discuss with your travel clinic.

In addition to the various vaccinations recommended above, it is important that travellers should be properly protected against **malaria**. For detailed advice, see below. Ideally you should visit your own doctor or a specialist travel clinic (see page 89) to discuss your requirements at least eight weeks before you plan to travel. Several travellers report that antimalarial drugs (and other medicines) in Kampala are far cheaper than in the UK, but you will still need to start the course of antimalarial tablets before you leave home.

Protection from the sun Give some thought to packing suncream. The incidence of skin cancer is rocketing as Caucasians are travelling more and spending more time exposing themselves to the sun. Keep out of the sun during the middle of the day and, if you must expose yourself to the sun, build up gradually from 20 minutes per day. Be especially careful of exposure in the middle of the day and of sun reflected off water, and wear a T-shirt and lots of waterproof suncream (at least SPF25) when swimming. Sun exposure ages the skin, makes people prematurely wrinkly and increases the risk of skin cancer. Cover up with long, loose clothes and wear a hat when you can. The glare and the dust can be hard on the eyes, too, so bring UV-protecting sunglasses and, perhaps, a soothing eyebath.

Malaria Along with road accidents, malaria poses the single biggest serious threat to the health of travellers in most parts of tropical Africa, Uganda included. It is unwise to travel in malarial parts of Africa whilst pregnant or with children: the risk of malaria in many parts is considerable and these travellers are likely to succumb rapidly to the disease. Pregnant women are twice as likely to be bitten by a malarial mosquito than a non-pregnant person. The risk of malaria above 1,800m above sea level is low.

Malaria in Uganda The *Anopheles* mosquito that transmits the parasite is commonly found near marshes and still water, and the parasite is most abundant at low altitudes. Parts of Uganda lying at an altitude of 2,000m or higher (a category that includes only high mountains such as the Rwenzoris and Elgon) are regarded to be free of malaria. In mid-altitude locations, malaria is largely but not entirely seasonal, with the highest risk of transmission occurring during the rainy season (March to May and October to December). Moist and low-lying areas such as the Nile at Murchison Falls are high risk throughout the year, but the risk is greatest during the rainy season. This localised breakdown might influence what foreigners living in Uganda do about malaria prevention, but all travellers to Uganda must assume that they will be exposed to malaria and should take precautions throughout their trip (see below).

Malaria prevention There is not yet a vaccine against malaria that gives enough protection to be useful for travellers, but there are other ways to avoid it; since most of Africa is very high risk for malaria, travellers must plan their malaria protection properly. Seek current advice on the best antimalarials to take: usually mefloquine, Malarone or doxycycline. If mefloquine (Lariam) is suggested, start this 2½ weeks (three doses) before departure to check that it suits you; stop it immediately if it seems to cause depression or anxiety, visual or hearing disturbances, severe headaches, fits or changes in heart rhythm. Side effects such as nightmares or dizziness are not medical reasons for stopping unless they are sufficiently debilitating or annoying. Anyone who has been treated for depression or psychiatric problems, has diabetes controlled by oral therapy or who is epileptic (or who has suffered fits in the past) or has a close blood relative who is epileptic, should probably avoid mefloquine.

In the past doctors were nervous about prescribing mefloquine to pregnant women, but experience has shown that it is relatively safe and certainly safer than the risk of malaria. It is now an option at some stages, but there are other issues and if you are travelling to Uganda whilst pregnant seek expert advice before departure.

Malarone (proguanil and atovaquone) is as effective as mefloquine. It has the advantage of having few side effects and need only be continued for one week after returning. However, it is expensive and because of this tends to be reserved for shorter trips. Malarone may not be suitable for everybody, so advice should be taken from a doctor. The licence in the UK has been extended for up to three months' use and in America can be used for up to a year. A paediatric form of tablet is also available, prescribed on a weight basis for children weighing 11kg or more.

Another very useful alternative is the antibiotic doxycycline (100mg daily). Like Malarone it can be started one day before arrival. Unlike mefloquine, it may also be used in travellers with epilepsy, although certain antiepileptic medication may make it less effective. In perhaps 1–3% of people there is the possibility of allergic skin reactions developing in sunlight; the drug should be stopped if this happens. It is also unsuitable in pregnancy or for children under 12 years.

Chloroquine and proguanil are no longer considered to be effective enough for Uganda but may be considered as a last resort if nothing else is deemed suitable.

All tablets should be taken with or after the evening meal, washed down with plenty of fluid and, with the exception of Malarone (see above), continued for four weeks after leaving.

Despite all these precautions, it is important to be aware that no antimalarial drug is 100% protective, although those on prophylactics who are unlucky enough to catch malaria are less likely to get rapidly into serious trouble. In addition to taking antimalarials, it is therefore important to avoid mosquito bites between dusk and dawn (see page 94).

There is unfortunately the occasional traveller who prefers to 'acquire resistance' to malaria rather than take preventive tablets, or who takes homeopathic prophylactics thinking these are effective. There is no scientific proof that homeopathic remedies are effective in either preventing or treating malaria. Furthermore, the Faculty of Homeopathy does not promote the use of homeopathic remedies to prevent malaria. Travellers to Africa should bear in mind that you cannot acquire any effective resistance to malaria until you have been in holoendemic areas for at least 18 months.

Malaria diagnosis and treatment Even those who take their malaria tablets meticulously and do everything possible to avoid mosquito bites may contract a strain of malaria that is resistant to prophylactic drugs. Untreated malaria is likely to be fatal, but even strains resistant to prophylaxis respond well to prompt treatment. Because of this, your immediate priority upon displaying possible malaria symptoms – including a rapid rise in temperature (over 38°C),

3

and any combination of a headache, flu-like aches and pains, a general sense of disorientation, and possibly even nausea and diarrhoea – is to establish whether you have malaria, ideally by visiting a clinic.

Diagnosing malaria is not easy, which is why consulting a doctor is sensible: there are other dangerous causes of fever in Africa, which require different treatments. Even if you test negative, it would be wise to stay within reach of a laboratory until the symptoms clear up, and to test again after a day or two if they don't. It's worth noting that if you have a fever and the malaria test is negative, you may have typhoid or paratyphoid, which should also receive immediate treatment.

Travellers to remote parts of Uganda – for instance in the game reserves and most of the popular hiking areas – would be wise to carry a course of treatment to cure malaria. Whilst some experts advocate using a rapid test kit, the evidence

LONG-HAUL FLIGHTS, CLOTS AND DVT

Any prolonged immobility including travel by land or air can result in deep vein thrombosis (DVT) with the risk of embolus to the lungs. Certain factors can increase the risk and these include:

* Previous clot or close relative with a history
* Being over 40 but an increased risk over 80 years of age
* Recent major operation or varicose veins surgery
* Cancer
* Stroke
* Heart disease
* Obesity
* Pregnancy
* Hormone therapy
* Heavy smoking
* Severe varicose veins
* Being very tall (over 6ft/1.8m) or short (under 5ft/1.5m)

A deep vein thrombosis (DVT) causes painful swelling and redness of the calf or sometimes the thigh. It is only dangerous if a clot travels to the lungs (pulmonary embolus).

Symptoms of a pulmonary embolus (PE) include chest pain, shortness of breath, and sometimes coughing up small amounts of blood and commonly start three to ten days after a long flight. Anyone who thinks that they might have a DVT needs to see a doctor immediately.

PREVENTION OF DVT
* Keep mobile before and during the flight; move around every couple of hours
* Drink plenty of fluids during the flight
* Avoid taking sleeping pills and excessive tea, coffee and alcohol
* Consider wearing flight socks or support stockings (see *www.legshealth.com*)

If you think you are at increased risk of a clot, ask your doctor if it is safe to travel.

shows that unless you are very used to using them they are not easy to use and lead to false results. With malaria, it is normal enough to go from feeling healthy to having a high fever in the space of a few hours (and it is possible to die from falciparum malaria within 24 hours of the first symptoms). In such circumstances, assume that you have malaria and act accordingly. Experts differ on the costs and benefits of self-treatment, but agree that it may lead to overtreatment and to many people taking drugs they do not need; yet treatment may save your life. There is also some division about the best treatment for malaria, but Malarone and Coarthemeter are the current treatments of choice. Discuss your trip with a specialist either at home or in Uganda.

Travel clinics and health information A full list of current travel clinic websites worldwide is available on www.istm.org. For other journey preparation information, consult www.nathnac.org/ds/map_world.aspx (UK) or http://wwwnc.cdc.gov/travel/ (US). Information about various medications may be found on www.netdoctor.co.uk/travel. All advice found online should be used in conjunction with expert advice received prior to or during travel.

Personal first-aid kit A minimal kit contains:
- A good drying antiseptic, eg: iodine or potassium permanganate (don't take antiseptic cream)
- A few small dressings (Band-Aids)
- Suncream
- Insect repellent; antimalarial tablets
- Impregnated bed-net or permethrin spray
- Aspirin or paracetamol
- Antifungal cream (eg: Canesten)
- Ciprofloxacin or norfloxacin, for severe diarrhoea
- Tinidazole for giardia or amoebic dysentery (see below for regime)
- Antibiotic eye drops, for sore, 'gritty', stuck-together eyes (conjunctivitis)
- A pair of fine-pointed tweezers (to remove hairy caterpillar hairs, thorns, splinters, coral, etc)
- Alcohol-based hand rub or a bar of soap in a plastic box
- Condoms or femidoms
- A digital thermometer (for those going to remote areas)

IN UGANDA
Medical facilities Private clinics, hospitals and pharmacies can be found in most large towns, and doctors generally speak fair to fluent English. The main private hospital is the International Hospital Kampala (*Namuwongo;* ☎ *0312 200400*). Private clinics include The Surgery in Kampala (☎ *0414 256003;* m *0752 756003; www.thesurgeryuganda.org*).

Consultation fees and laboratory tests are remarkably inexpensive when compared with most Western countries, so if you do fall sick it would be absurd to let financial considerations dissuade you from seeking medical help. Commonly required medicines such as broad-spectrum antibiotics, painkillers, asthma inhalers and various antimalarial treatments are widely available and cheap throughout the region. If you are on any short-term medication prior to departure, or you have specific needs relating to a less common medical condition (for instance if you are allergic to bee stings or nuts), then you are strongly advised to bring necessary treatment with you.

Water sterilisation You can fall ill from drinking contaminated water so try to drink from safe sources, eg: bottled water where available. If you are away from shops – such as halfway up the Rwenzori – and your bottled water runs out, make tea, pour the remaining boiled water into a clean container and use it for drinking. Alternatively, water should be passed through a good bacteriological filter or purified with chlorine dioxide tablets.

Common medical problems

Travellers' diarrhoea Travelling in Uganda carries a fairly high risk of getting a dose of travellers' diarrhoea; perhaps half of all visitors will suffer and the newer you are to exotic travel, the more likely you will be to suffer. By taking precautions against travellers' diarrhoea you will also avoid typhoid, paratyphoid, cholera, hepatitis, dysentery, worms, etc. Travellers' diarrhoea and the other faecal-oral diseases come from getting other people's faeces in your mouth. This most often happens from cooks not washing their hands after a trip to the toilet, but even if the restaurant cook does not understand basic hygiene you will be safe if your food has been properly cooked and arrives piping hot. The most important prevention strategy is to wash your hands before eating anything. You can pick up salmonella and shigella from toilet door handles and possibly banknotes. The maxim to remind you what you can safely eat is:

PEEL IT, BOIL IT, COOK IT OR FORGET IT.

TREATING TRAVELLERS' DIARRHOEA   Dr Jane Wilson-Howarth

It is dehydration that makes you feel awful during a bout of diarrhoea and the most important part of treatment is drinking lots of clear fluids. Sachets of oral rehydration salts give the perfect biochemical mix to replace all that is pouring out of your bottom but other recipes taste nicer. Any dilute mixture of sugar and salt in water will do you good: try Coke or orange squash with a three-finger pinch of salt added to each glass (if you are salt-depleted you won't taste the salt). Otherwise make a solution of a four-finger scoop of sugar with a three-finger pinch of salt in a 500ml glass. Or add eight level teaspoons of sugar (18g) and one level teaspoon of salt (3g) to one litre (five cups) of safe water. A squeeze of lemon or orange juice improves the taste and adds potassium, which is also lost in diarrhoea. Drink two large glasses after every bowel action, and more if you are thirsty. These solutions are still absorbed well if you are vomiting, but you will need to take sips at a time. If you are not eating you need to drink three litres a day plus whatever is pouring into the toilet. If you feel like eating, take a bland, high carbohydrate diet. Heavy greasy foods will probably give you cramps.

If the diarrhoea is bad, or you are passing blood or slime, or you have a fever, you will probably need antibiotics in addition to fluid replacement. A dose of norfloxacin or ciproflaxin repeated twice a day until better may be appropriate (if you are planning to take an antibiotic with you, note that both norfloxacin and ciprofloxacin are available only on prescription in the UK). If the diarrhoea is greasy and bulky and is accompanied by sulphurous (eggy) burps, one likely cause is giardia. This is best treated with tinidazole (four x 500mg in one dose, repeated three to seven days later if symptoms persist).

This means that fruit you have washed and peeled yourself, and hot foods, should be safe but raw foods, cold cooked foods, salads, fruit salads which have been prepared by others, ice cream and ice are all risky, and foods kept lukewarm in hotel buffets are often dangerous. That said, plenty of travellers and expatriates enjoy fruit and vegetables, so do keep a sense of perspective: food served in a fairly decent hotel in a large town or a place regularly frequented by expatriates is likely to be safe. If you are struck, see the box above for treatment.

Eye problems Bacterial conjunctivitis (pink eye) is a common infection in Africa; people who wear contact lenses are most open to this irritating problem. The eyes feel sore and gritty and they will often be stuck together in the mornings. They will need treatment with antibiotic drops or ointment. Lesser eye irritation should settle with bathing in salt water and keeping the eyes shaded. If an insect flies into your eye, extract it with great care, ensuring you do not crush or damage it otherwise you may get a nastily inflamed eye from toxins secreted by the creature. Small elongated red and black blister beetles carry warning colouration to tell you not to crush them anywhere against your skin.

Prickly heat A fine pimply rash on the trunk is likely to be heat rash; cool showers, dabbing dry, and talc will help. Treat the problem by slowing down to a relaxed schedule, wearing only loose, baggy, 100%-cotton clothes and sleeping naked under a fan; if it's bad you may need to check into an air-conditioned hotel room for a while.

Skin infections Any mosquito bite or small nick in the skin gives an opportunity for bacteria to foil the body's usually excellent defences; it will surprise many travellers how quickly skin infections start in warm humid climates and it is essential to clean and cover even the slightest wound. Creams are not as effective as a good drying antiseptic such as dilute iodine, potassium permanganate (a few crystals in half a cup of water), or crystal (or gentian) violet. One of these should be available in most towns. If the wound starts to throb, or becomes red and the redness starts to spread, or the wound oozes, and especially if you develop a fever, antibiotics will probably be needed: flucloxacillin (250mg four times a day) or cloxacillin (500mg four times a day). For those allergic to penicillin, erythromycin (500mg twice a day) for five days should help. See a doctor if the symptoms do not start to improve within 48 hours.

Fungal infections also get a hold easily in hot, moist climates so wear 100%-cotton socks and underwear and shower frequently. An itchy rash in the groin or flaking between the toes is likely to be a fungal infection. This needs treatment with an antifungal cream such as Canesten (clotrimazole); if this is not available try Whitfield's ointment (compound benzoic acid ointment) or crystal violet (although this will turn you purple!).

Insect-borne diseases Malaria (see pages 86–9) is by no means the only insect-borne disease to which the traveller may succumb. Others include sleeping sickness and river blindness (see box, page 94–5). Dengue fever is becoming more common in Uganda and there are many other similar arboviruses, which are equally unpleasant to get. These mosquito-borne diseases may mimic malaria but there is no prophylactic medication against them. The mosquitoes that carry dengue fever viruses bite during the daytime, so it is worth applying repellent if you see any mosquitoes around. Symptoms include strong headaches, rashes and excruciating joint and muscle pains and high fever. Viral fevers usually last about a week or so and are not usually fatal. Complete rest and paracetamol are the usual treatment; plenty of fluids also help. Some patients are given an intravenous drip to keep them from dehydrating. It is especially important to protect yourself if you have had dengue fever before, since a second infection with a different strain can result in the potentially fatal dengue haemorrhagic fever.

Sleeping sickness African trypanosomiasis, or sleeping sickness is a parasitic infection caused by *Trypanosoma brucei*. There are two subspecies; one predominates in East Africa and usually causes an acute infection, whereas the other predominates in Central and West Africa and causes a slower progressive, chronic infection. In the UK, travel-associated cases are rare, but those that have been reported have usually been associated with travel to the game parks of East Africa.

The parasite is transmitted by the bite of an infected tsetse fly. Tsetse flies are around the size of a honeybee. In East Africa, the main reservoirs for the parasites are domestic and wild animals such as antelope and cattle. The tsetse flies here tend to inhabit savanna and woodland areas. One bite from an infected tsetse fly is enough for a human to become infected. Trypanosomiasis cannot be spread directly from person to person.

For East African trypanosomiasis, first symptoms (skin lesion around the bite with lymph node enlargement) will occur five–15 days after the bite, with fever occurring after one to three weeks. For West African trypanosomiasis, symptoms may not present for some weeks after the infective bite. East African trypanosomiasis is a much faster progressing disease than the West African form which can progress over a number of years.

There is no vaccine or drug to prevent sleeping sickness. The only way to prevent it is to avoid tsetse fly bites and be aware of the risk. Tsetse flies are said to be attracted by movement and dark colours, particularly blue. They have been known to follow moving vehicles, therefore windows should remain closed when driving through endemic areas. Travellers are advised to wear insecticide-treated close-weave and loose-fitting clothing and use a good repellent containing N, N-diethylmetatoluamide (DEET) on exposed skin. Insect repellents are not as effective against tsetse flies as mosquitoes but are better than nothing. If sunscreen is also being used, repellent must be applied after sunscreen. More information about the disease is available from the NaTHNaC website (*www.nathnac.org*).

Bilharzia or schistosomiasis Bilharzia or schistosomiasis is a disease that commonly afflicts the rural poor of the tropics. Two types exist in sub-Saharan Africa – *Schistosoma mansoni* and *Schistosoma haematobium*. It is an unpleasant problem that is worth avoiding, though can be treated if you do get it. This parasite is common in almost all water sources in Uganda, even places advertised as 'bilharzia free'. Only lakes Bunyonyi and Nabugabo are widely held to be genuinely free of bilharzias (and there are plenty who dispute the claim of the former). The most risky shores will be close to places where infected people use water, wash clothes, etc.

It is easier to understand how to diagnose it, treat it and prevent it if you know a little about the life cycle. Contaminated faeces are washed into the lake, the eggs hatch and the larva infects certain species of snail. The snails then produce about 10,000 cercariae a day for the rest of their lives. The parasites can digest their way through your skin when you wade, or bathe in infested fresh water.

Winds disperse the snails and cercariae. The snails in particular can drift a long way, especially on windblown weed, so nowhere is really safe. However, deep water and running water are safer, while shallow water presents the greatest risk. The cercariae penetrate intact skin, and find their way to the liver. There male and female meet and spend the rest of their lives in permanent copulation. No wonder you feel tired! Most finish up in the wall of the lower bowel, but others can get lost and can cause damage to many different organs. *Schistosoma haematobium* goes mostly to the bladder.

Although the adults do not cause any harm in themselves, after about four–six weeks they start to lay eggs, which cause an intense but usually ineffective immune reaction, including fever, cough, abdominal pain, and a fleeting, itching rash called 'safari itch'. The absence of early symptoms does not necessarily mean there is no infection. Later symptoms can be more localised and more severe, but the general symptoms settle down fairly quickly and eventually you are just tired. 'Tired all the time' is one of the most common symptoms among expats in Africa, and bilharzia, giardia, amoeba and intestinal yeast are the most common culprits.

Although bilharzia is difficult to diagnose, it can be tested at specialist travel clinics. Ideally tests need to be done at least six weeks after likely exposure and will determine whether you need treatment. Fortunately it is easy to treat at present.

Avoiding bilharzia

- If you are bathing, swimming, paddling or wading in fresh water which you think may carry a bilharzia risk, try to get out of the water within ten minutes.
- Avoid bathing or paddling on shores within 200m of villages or places where people use the water a great deal, especially reedy shores or where there is lots of waterweed.
- Dry off thoroughly with a towel; rub vigorously.
- If your bathing water comes from a risky source, try to ensure that the water is taken from the lake in the early morning and stored snail-free, otherwise it should be filtered, or Dettol or Cresol added.
- Bathing early in the morning is safer than bathing in the last half of the day.
- Cover yourself with an insect repellent containing DEET before swimming: it may offer some protection.

HIV/AIDS The risks of sexually transmitted infection are extremely high in Uganda, whether you sleep with fellow travellers or locals. About 80% of HIV infections in British heterosexuals are acquired abroad. If you must indulge, use condoms or femidoms, which help reduce the risk of transmission. If you notice any genital ulcers or discharge, get treatment promptly since these increase the risk of acquiring HIV. If you do have unprotected sex, visit a clinic as soon as possible; this should be within 24 hours, or no later than 72 hours, for post-exposure prophylaxis. It costs US$15.

Meningitis This is a particularly nasty disease as it can kill within hours of the first symptoms appearing. The telltale symptoms are a combination of a blinding headache (light sensitivity), a blotchy rash and a high fever. Immunisation protects against the most serious bacterial form of meningitis and the tetravalent vaccine ACWY (preferably one of the conjugate vaccines Menveo or Nimenrix) is recommended for Uganda by British travel clinics.

Although other forms of meningitis exist (usually viral), there are no vaccines for these. Local papers normally report localised outbreaks. A severe headache and fever should make consult a doctor immediately. There are also other causes of headache and fever, one of which is typhoid, which occurs in travellers to Uganda. Seek medical help if you are ill for more than a few days.

Rabies Rabies is carried by all warm-blooded mammals (beware the village dogs and small monkeys that are used to being fed in the parks) and is passed on to man through a bite, scratch or a lick of an open wound. You must always assume any animal is rabid as they can often look well but can still be infectious. Have a low threshold for seeking medical help as soon as possible after any potential exposure. Meanwhile scrub the wound with soap under a running tap or while pouring water from a jug for a good ten–15 minutes. The source of the water is not important at this stage but if you do have antiseptic to hand then put this on afterwards. The soap helps stop the rabies virus entering the body and, along with the antiseptic, will guard against wound infections, including tetanus.

Pre-exposure vaccination for rabies is ideally advised for everyone, but is particularly important if you intend to have contact with animals and/or are likely to be more than 24 hours away from medical help. Ideally three doses should be taken over a minimum of 21 days. All three doses are needed in order to change the treatment necessary following an exposure.

If you are bitten, scratched or licked over an open wound by a sick animal, then post-exposure prophylaxis should be given as soon as possible, though it is never too late to seek help, as the incubation period for rabies can be very long. Those who have not been immunised before will need four to five doses of rabies vaccine given over 28–30 days and should also receive a blood product called Rabies Immunoglobulin (RIG), which should ideally be human, but horse (equine) will do. The RIG is injected round the wound to try and neutralise any rabies virus

AVOIDING INSECT BITES

As the sun is going down, don long clothes and apply repellent on any exposed flesh. Pack a DEET-based insect repellent (ideally containing 50–55% DEET). You also need either a permethrin-impregnated bed-net or a permethrin spray so that you can 'treat' bed-nets in hotels. Permethrin treatment makes even very tatty nets protective and prevents mosquitoes from biting through the impregnated net when you roll against it. Otherwise retire to an air-conditioned room if that is possible. Burning coils and overhead fans reduce rather than eliminate mosquitoes so nets should still be used. Putting on socks and long clothing (including long-sleeved shirts/blouses) at dusk reduces the risk of bites and the amount of repellent needed. Be aware that malaria mosquitoes usually hunt at ankle level and their bite can penetrate through socks, so apply repellent to your feet and ankles whether or not you wear socks. Travel clinics usually sell a good range of nets, treatment kits and repellents.

Aside from avoiding mosquito bites between dusk and dawn, which will protect you from elephantiasis and a range of nasty insect-borne viruses, as well as malaria (see pages 86–9), it is important to take precautions against other insect bites. During the day it is wise to wear long, loose (preferably 100% cotton) clothes if you are pushing through scrubby country; this will keep off ticks and also tsetse and day-biting *Aedes* mosquitoes which may spread viral fevers, including yellow fever.

Minute pestilential biting **blackflies** spread river blindness in some parts of Africa between 19°N and 17°S; the disease is caught close to fast-flowing rivers since flies breed there and the larvae live in rapids. The flies bite during the day but

present and is a pivotal part of the treatment if you have not had the pre-exposure vaccine. RIG is expensive and may not be readily available so it is important to insist on getting to a place that has it. Another reason for having good insurance.

Tell the doctor if you have had pre-exposure vaccine, as this will change the treatment you receive. You will no longer need RIG and will only need a couple of doses of vaccine, ideally given three days apart. And remember that, if you do contract rabies, mortality is 100% and death from rabies is probably one of the worst ways to go.

Tickbite fever African ticks are not the rampant disease transmitters they are in the Americas, but they may spread tickbite fever and a few dangerous rarities in Uganda. Tickbite fever is a flu-like illness that can easily be treated with doxycycline, but as there can be some serious complications it is important to visit a doctor.

Ticks should ideally be removed as soon as possible, as leaving them on the body increases the chance of infection. They should be removed with special tick tweezers that can be bought in good travel shops. Failing that you can use your fingernails by grasping the tick as close to your body as possible and pulling steadily and firmly away at right angles to your skin. The tick will then come away complete as long as you do not jerk or twist. If possible douse the wound with alcohol (any spirit will do) or iodine. Irritants (eg: Olbas oil) or lit cigarettes are to be discouraged since they can cause the ticks to regurgitate and therefore increase the risk of disease. It is best to get a travelling companion to check you for ticks and if you are travelling with small children remember to check their heads, and particularly behind the ears.

long trousers tucked into socks will help keep them off. Citronella-based natural repellents do not work against them.

Mosquitoes and many other insects are attracted to light. If you are camping, never put a lamp near the opening of your tent, or you will have a swarm of biters waiting to join you when you retire. In hotel rooms, be aware that the longer your light is on, the greater the number of insects will be sharing your accommodation.

TUMBU FLIES Often called mango flies in Uganda, tumbu flies (aka *putsi*) are a problem where the climate is hot and humid. The adult fly lays her eggs on the soil or on drying laundry and when the eggs come into contact with human flesh (when you put on clothes or lie on a bed) they hatch and bury themselves under the skin. Here they form a crop of 'boils' each with a maggot inside. Smear a little Vaseline over the hole, and they will push their noses out to breathe. It may be possible to squeeze them out but it depends if they are ready as the larvae have spines that help them to hold on.

In *putsi* areas either dry your clothes and sheets within a screened house, or dry them in direct sunshine until they are crisp, or iron them.

JIGGERS (SANDFLEAS) Another flesh-feaster, which can be best avoided by wearing shoes. They latch on if you walk barefoot in contaminated places, and set up home under the skin of the foot, usually at the side of a toenail where they cause a painful, boil-like swelling. They need picking out by a local expert.

Spreading redness around the bite and/or fever and/or aching joints after a tickbite imply that you have an infection that requires antibiotic treatment, so seek advice.

Snakebite Snakes rarely attack unless provoked, and bites in travellers are unusual. You are less likely to get bitten if you wear stout shoes and long trousers when in the bush. Most snakes are harmless and even venomous species will dispense venom in only about half of their bites. If bitten, then, you are unlikely to have received venom; keeping this fact in mind may help you to stay calm. Many so-called first-aid techniques do more harm than good: cutting into the wound is harmful; tourniquets are dangerous; suction and electrical inactivation devices do not work. The only treatment is antivenom. In case of a bite that you fear may have been from a venomous snake:

- Try to keep calm – it is likely that no venom has been dispensed
- Prevent movement of the bitten limb by applying a splint
- Keep the bitten limb BELOW heart height to slow the spread of any venom
- If you have a crêpe bandage, wrap it around the whole limb (eg: all the way from the toes to the thigh), as tight as you would for a sprained ankle or a muscle pull
- Evacuate to a hospital that has antivenom. At the time of writing this is only known to be available in Kampala. Many centres have an Indian antivenom that does not include the most common biting snakes in Uganda. The Surgery (see page 169) has South African antivenom that includes all the common biters. The best option is to phone for advice.

And remember:

- NEVER give aspirin; you may take paracetamol, which is safe
- NEVER cut or suck the wound
- DO NOT apply potassium permanganate

If the offending snake can be captured without risk of someone else being bitten, take this to show the doctor – but beware since even a decapitated head is able to bite.

SAFETY

Uganda has been an acceptably safe travel destination since Museveni took power in 1986, and the most significant threat to life and limb comes not from banditry or political instability, but rather from the malaria parasite and car or boat accidents. Nevertheless, as the fatal attack by Rwandan rebels on tourists staying at Bwindi in 1999 so brutally demonstrated, Uganda's location at the heart of a perennially unstable part of Africa does mean that its border areas in particular are bound to suffer intermittent security problems.

The only part of Uganda that has suffered from long-term internal instability lies north of Murchison Falls, in an area that traditionally sees few tourists and lacks for any compelling attractions. Due to the Lord's Resistance Army (LRA) rebellion (see box, pages 436–7) this region was off limits for almost 20 years. Despite the fact that a peace deal was never signed, the rebellion is considered to be over and northern Uganda has been safe for travel since 2007. This is reflected by expanded coverage of the area north of the Nile in this book. Murchison Falls is also considered safe, security advisory notices having been lifted by the British High Commission and the US embassy in Uganda. Security advisories still apply to the northeast because of banditry related to Karamojong cattle rustlers. In practice however, this region is now widely considered safe for travel, though still subject to certain precautions (page 452).

The problems afflicting the DRC and Rwanda have also frequently spilt over into neighbouring parts of Uganda. The most sustained instance of this overflow was the emergence of the Allied Democratic Forces (ADF) in the mid-1990s. This small and somewhat mysterious 'rebel' army – thought to consist solely of Congolese thugs – was responsible for several brutal attacks in the Rwenzori border area, including the massacre of 60 students at the Kichwamba Technical School near Fort Portal in June 1998. The activities of the ADF forced the closure of the Rwenzori and Semliki national parks in 1997 before Ugandan government troops managed to drive the ADF back into the DRC, and there have been no subsequent incidents of concern. Semliki National Park reopened in 1999, as did the Rwenzoris in July 2002, and it can be assumed that they would close again at the first hint of trouble.

In August 1998, four travellers were abducted in the DRC after crossing there from Uganda – one elderly woman was released but the other three are missing, presumed dead – an incident that at the time seemed to have little bearing on security in Uganda. Six months later, tragedy struck closer to home, when the park headquarters at Bwindi was attacked by an army of exiled Rwandan rebels, killing two rangers and eight tourists. If, as seems probable, the aim of the attack was to destabilise Uganda's tourist industry, then it could not have been better calculated, given that the mountain gorillas at Bwindi had done more than anything to help Uganda overcome a negative international image generated by the barbarities of the Amin and Obote regimes.

Prior to March 1999, Bwindi was considered to be safe by almost everybody involved in Uganda. The attack on the unprotected park headquarters came as a complete shock, but in hindsight it could so easily have been averted by a greater military presence. The lesson has been learned and security in Bwindi is high (soldiers accompany visitors on all walks) as indeed it is at all national park tourism sites close to Uganda's western border.

Fourteen years later, there seems little cause for serious concern regarding security along Uganda's established tourist circuits. Indeed, I would regard this country to be safer overall than Kenya or South Africa, both of which suffer from very high rates of armed crime. Equally, I'm a travel writer, not a political sage, and as such I'd regard it to be irresponsible to state categorically that the Bwindi incident was a one-off event, or that nothing of the sort could ever happen again. The decision to visit Uganda, and the responsibility, rests on the individual traveller. Assuming that you do, I would recommend you keep your ear to the ground, read the local newspaper, and avoid visiting known trouble spots – fortunately, the authorities are unlikely to allow tourists to visit reserves and national parks where there is a security problem.

BRIBERY AND BUREAUCRACY For all you read about the subject, bribery is not the problem to travellers in Africa it is often made out to be. The travellers who are most often asked for bribes are those with private transport, and even they only have a major problem at some borders and from traffic police in some countries (notably Mozambique and Kenya). If you are travelling on public transport or as part of a tour, or even if you are driving within Uganda, I don't think that you need to give the question of bribery serious thought.

3

There is a tendency to portray African bureaucrats as difficult and inefficient in their dealings with tourists. As a rule, this reputation says more about Western prejudices than it does about Uganda. Sure, you come across the odd unhelpful official, but then such is the nature of the beast everywhere in the world. The vast majority of officials in the African countries I've visited have been courteous and helpful in their dealings with tourists, often to a degree that is almost embarrassing. In Uganda, I encountered nothing but friendliness from almost every government official I had dealings with, whether they were border officials, policemen or national park staff. This, I can assure you, is far more than most African visitors to Europe will experience from officialdom.

A factor in determining the response you receive from African officials will be your own attitude. If you walk into every official encounter with an aggressive, paranoid approach, you are quite likely to kindle the feeling held by many Africans that Europeans are arrogant and offhand in their dealings with other races. Instead,

NOTES FOR DISABLED TRAVELLERS

Gordon Rattray (www.able-travel.com)
Uganda's highlights often involve trekking in rough terrain, and as a result do not lend themselves to people with mobility problems. On top of that, the country as a whole has a tourist industry that is relatively young by East African standards, meaning access for disabled people is rarely a consideration and never a priority. However, depending on your determination and ability, and aided by African resourcefulness, a rewarding trip is possible for most travellers.

ACCOMMODATION In general, it is not easy to find disabled-friendly accommodation in Uganda. Only top-of-the-range hotels and lodges have 'accessible' rooms. Occasionally (more by accident than through design), bathrooms are wheelchair accessible, but they usually contain standard fittings only. Budget disabled travellers will definitely need to compromise, as cheap guesthouses and lodgings are often small and campsites are basic and not ideal for wheelchairs.

The best advice is to research your options in advance. Tour operators will normally take time to listen to your needs, or if you prefer, many hotels can be found and contacted directly via the internet.

TRANSPORT
By air Entebbe International Airport has wheelchairs and a narrow aisle chair is also available.

By bus Buses and *matatus* (minibus-taxis) are cramped, with no facilities for wheelchairs, and getting off and on is often a hectic affair. You may need fellow passengers to help you to your seat, it will often be crowded and there will not be an accessible toilet. Therefore, unless you can walk at least to some degree then taxi is going to be your only easy way of getting around. If you can cope with these difficulties, then travelling by bus is feasible and is the most affordable method of transport.

By car Most tour companies use 4x4s and minibuses, which are higher than normal cars, making transfers more difficult. Drivers and guides are normally happy to try to be friendly and patient, and accept that the person to whom you are talking does not speak English as a first language and may thus have difficulty following everything you say. Treat people with respect rather than disdain, and they'll tend to treat you in the same way.

THEFT Uganda is widely and rightly regarded as one of the most crime-free countries in Africa, certainly as far as visitors need be concerned. Muggings are comparatively rare, even in Kampala, and I've never heard of the sort of con tricks that abound in places like Nairobi. Even petty theft such as pickpocketing and bag snatching is relatively unusual, though it does happen from time to time. Walking around large towns at night is also reputedly safe, though it would be tempting fate to wander alone along unlit streets. On the basis that it is preferable to err on the side of caution, I've decided to repeat a few tips that apply to travelling anywhere in East and southern Africa:

help, but they are not trained in this skill so you must thoroughly explain your needs and stay in control of the situation during any transfers.

Distances are great and roads are often bumpy, so if you are prone to skin damage you need to take extra care. If you use one, place your own pressure-relieving cushion on top of (or instead of) the original car seat and if necessary, pad around knees and elbows.

ACTIVITIES Gorilla tracking is literally a stumble in the jungle, even for able-bodied people. You don't need to be super-fit, but check with your tour operator if you think your disability may exclude you. Kibale Forest trails and other primate walks are generally less arduous, but are not designed with wheelchair users in mind. It is also worth remembering that Uganda has a fairly high rainfall and because most of these paths are not purpose built and rather hewn from continued use, they quickly become muddy in wet conditions. On the plus side, pleasant forest walks can be had following the main trails and, although you may need to be helped over obstacles and up steps, there will always be plenty of willing hands to do this.

HEALTH Ugandan hospitals and pharmacies are often basic so, if possible, take all essential medication and equipment with you. It is advisable to pack this in your hand luggage during flights in case your main luggage gets lost. Doctors will know about 'everyday' illnesses, but you must understand and be able to explain your own particular medical requirements.

SECURITY The usual security precautions apply (see page 96) but it is also worthwhile remembering that as a disabled person, you may be more vulnerable. Stay aware of where your bags are and who is around you, especially during car transfers and similar activities.

SPECIALIST OPERATORS I know of no operators in Uganda who specialise in disability. Having said that, most travel companies will listen to your needs and try to create an itinerary suitable for you. For the independent traveller, it is possible to limit potential surprises by contacting local operators and establishments by email in advance.

- Most casual thieves operate in busy markets and bus stations. Keep a close watch on your possessions in such places, and avoid having valuables or large amounts of money loose in your daypack or pocket.
- Keep all your valuables and the bulk of your money in a hidden moneybelt. Never show this moneybelt in public. Keep any spare cash you need elsewhere on your person; I feel that a button-up pocket on the front of your shirt is the most secure place as money cannot be snatched from it without the thief coming into your view. It is also advisable to keep a small amount of hard currency (ideally cash) hidden away in your luggage so that, should you lose your moneybelt, you have something to fall back on.
- Where the choice exists between carrying valuables on your person or leaving them in a locked room I would tend to favour the latter option (only one of the hundreds of thefts I've heard about in Africa happened from a locked hotel room, and that was in Nairobi where just about anything is possible). Obviously you should use your judgement on this and be sure the room is absolutely secure.
- Leave any jewellery of financial or sentimental value at home.

CARRYING MONEY AND VALUABLES It is advisable to carry all your hard currency as well as your passport and other important documentation in a moneybelt. The ideal moneybelt for Africa is one that can be hidden beneath your clothing. External moneybelts may be fashionable, but wearing one in Africa is as good as telling thieves that all your valuables are there for the taking. Use a belt made of cotton or another natural fabric, bearing in mind that such fabrics tend to soak up a lot of sweat, so you will need to wrap plastic around everything inside.

The best insurance against complete disaster should you be robbed is to keep things well documented. If you carry a photocopy of the main page of your passport, you will be issued with a new one more promptly. In addition, note down details of your bank, credit card (if you have one), travel insurance policy, electronic and camera equipment (including serial numbers). If all this information fits on one piece of paper, you can keep photocopies on you and with a friend at home.

TRAVELLING WITH CHILDREN

From a letter by Steve Lenartowicz
Ugandans are very interested in children and make them most welcome. On buses and *matatus*, the rule seems to be that you pay full fare for the seats you occupy, and so children sitting on a lap go free. Similarly, hotels are usually happy for children (and adults!) to share beds, and we usually negotiated to pay per bed rather than per person. Often, hotels were able to provide an extra bed or mattress on the floor. We travelled light, taking no camping gear or bedding, but we carried mosquito nets and often used them (although mosquitoes were never bad). Don't take white clothing, as the ubiquitous red dust and mud get everywhere. It was easier to order adult portions of meals and to share them rather than to try to negotiate children's portions. National park fees are significantly reduced for children.

If you are taking children to Uganda, you might like to get hold of the book *Your Child's Health Abroad: A Manual for Travelling Parents*, by Dr Jane Wilson-Howarth and Dr Matthew Ellis (Bradt, 2005).

WOMEN TRAVELLERS Women generally regard sub-equatorial Africa as one of the safest places in the world to travel alone. Uganda in particular poses few if any risks specific to female travellers. It is reasonable to expect a fair bit of flirting and the odd direct proposition, especially if you mingle with Ugandans in bars, but a firm 'no' should be enough to defuse any potential situation. And, to be fair to Ugandan men, you can expect the same sort of thing in any country, and for that matter from many male travellers. Ugandan women tend to dress conservatively. It will not increase the amount of hassle you receive if you avoid wearing clothes that, however unfairly, may be perceived to be provocative, and it may even go some way to decreasing it.

More mundanely, tampons are not readily available in smaller towns, though you can easily locate them in Kampala, Entebbe and Jinja, and in game lodge and hotel gift shops. When travelling in out-of-the-way places, carry enough tampons to see you through to the next time you'll be in a large city, bearing in mind that travelling in the tropics can sometimes cause heavier or more irregular periods than normal. Sanitary pads are available in most towns of any size.

WHAT TO TAKE

Two simple rules to bear in mind when you decide what to take with you to Uganda – particularly if you expect to use public transport – are to bring with you *everything* that might not be readily available when you need it, and to carry as little as possible. Somewhat contradictory rules, you might think, and you'd be right – so the key is finding the right balance, something that probably depends on personal experience as much as anything. Worth stressing is that most genuine necessities are surprisingly easy to get hold of in the main centres in Uganda, and that most of the ingenious gadgets you can buy in camping shops are unlikely to amount to much more than dead weight on the road. If it came to it, you could easily travel in Uganda with little more than a change of clothes, a few basic toiletries and a medical kit.

CARRYING YOUR LUGGAGE Visitors who are unlikely to be carrying their luggage for any significant distance will probably want to pack most of it in a conventional suitcase. Make sure the case is tough and durable, and that it seals well, so that the contents will survive bumpy drives to the game reserves. A lock is a good idea, not only for flights, but for when you leave your case in a hotel room – theft from upmarket hotels is unusual in Uganda, but it can happen anywhere in the world, and even a flimsy lock will act as a serious deterrent to casual finger-dipping. A daypack will be useful on safari, and you should be able to pack your luggage in such a manner that any breakable goods can be carried in the body of the vehicle, and on your lap when necessary – anything like an MP3 player or camera will suffer heavily from vibrations on rutted roads.

If you are likely to use public transport, then an internal frame backpack is the most practical way to carry your luggage. Once again, ensure your pack is durable, that the seams and zips are properly sewn, and that it has several pockets. If you intend doing a lot of hiking, you definitely want a backpack designed for this purpose. On the other hand, if you'll be staying at places where it might be a good idea to shake off the sometimes negative image attached to backpackers, then there would be obvious advantages in using a suitcase that converts into a backpack.

Before I started travelling with my wife Ariadne and her heavy camera equipment, my preference over either of the above was for a robust 35l daypack. The advantages of keeping luggage as light and compact as possible are manifold. For starters, you can rest it on your lap on bus trips, avoiding complications such as extra charges for luggage, arguments about where your bag should be stored, and the slight but real risk of theft if your luggage ends up on the roof. A compact bag also makes for greater mobility, whether you're hiking or looking for a hotel in town. The sacrifice? Leave behind camping equipment and a sleeping bag. Do this, and it's quite possible to fit everything you truly need into a 35l daypack, and possibly even a few luxuries – I refuse to travel without binoculars, a bird field guide and at least five novels, and am still able to keep my weight down to around 8kg. Frankly, it puzzles me what the many backpackers who wander around with an enormous pack and absolutely no camping equipment actually carry around with them!

If your luggage won't squeeze into a daypack, a sensible compromise is to carry a large daypack in your rucksack. That way, you can carry a tent and other camping equipment when you need it, but at other times reduce your luggage to fit into a daypack and leave what you're not using in storage. Travellers carrying a lot of valuable items should look for a pack that can easily be padlocked.

CAMPING EQUIPMENT There is a strong case for carrying a tent to Uganda, particularly if you are on a tight budget. Campsites exist in most Ugandan national parks, forest reserves and towns. Travellers who intend doing a fair bit of off-the-beaten-track hiking will find a tent a useful fallback where no other accommodation exists.

If you decide to carry camping equipment, the key is to look for the lightest available gear. It is now possible to buy a lightweight tent weighing little more than 2kg, but make sure that the one you buy is reasonably mosquito-proof. Usable sleeping bags weighing even less than 2kg can be bought, but, especially as many lightweight sleeping bags are not particularly warm, my own preference is for a sheet sleeping bag, supplemented by wearing heavy clothes in cold weather. Also essential is a roll-mat, which will serve as both insulation and padding. In Uganda, there is no real need to carry a stove, as firewood is available at most campsites where meals cannot be bought. If you do carry a stove, consider using one fuelled by methylated spirits which is far more easy to obtain than Camping Gaz cylinders. You'll only find the latter (if they're in stock) in Kampala at Oasis Mall (Nakumatt store) and Lugogo Mall (Game store). These stores represent Uganda's best selections of outdoor/camping equipment. If camping in the rainy season, bring a box of firelighter blocks: they will get a fire going in the most unpromising conditions. Cheap cutlery, plastic cups and plates and lightweight metal pans (*suferias*) suitable for camping are the norm for most Ugandans and are available everywhere.

CLOTHES Organising laundry along the way is a pain in the neck so you ought to carry at least one change of socks and underwear for every day you will spend on safari. A clean shirt each day would be ideal but if you opt for darker tones you could get away with fewer. It's a good idea to keep separate one or two shirts for evening use only.

Otherwise, and especially if you are travelling with everything on your back, try to keep your clothes to a minimum, bearing in mind that you can easily and cheaply replace worn items in markets. In my opinion, the minimum you need is one or possibly two pairs of trousers and/or skirts, one pair of shorts, three shirts or T-shirts, one light sweater, maybe a light waterproof windbreaker during the rainy season, enough socks and underwear to last five to seven days, one solid pair of shoes or boots for walking, and one pair of sandals, thongs or other light shoes.

Trousers It's widely held that jeans are not ideal for African travel, since they are bulky to carry, hot to wear and take ages to dry. I've repeated this advice in earlier editions of this guide, and seldom used to travel in jeans myself, but these days I almost always do, since they have the advantages of durability and comfort, and of hiding the dust and dirt that tends to accumulate on public transport. A good alternative is light cotton trousers, which dry more quickly and weigh less. Try to avoid light colours, as they show dirt more easily. If you intend spending a while in montane regions, instead of bringing a second pair of trousers, you might prefer to carry tracksuit bottoms. These can serve as thermal underwear and as extra cover on chilly nights, and they can also be worn over shorts on chilly mornings. Shorts on men are acceptable for travel and informal situations, though many Ugandans consider them inappropriate on grown men whose schooldays are clearly long past. Before travelling in shorts, it's worth considering whether you'll be able to don longer trousers before mosquitoes start snapping at your ankles.

Skirts Like trousers, these are best made of a light natural fabric such as cotton. For reasons of protocol, it is advisable to wear skirts that go below the knee: short skirts will cause needless offence to many Ugandans (especially Muslims) and, whether you like it or not, they may be perceived as provocative in some quarters. There are parts of Africa where it's still considered slightly off for women to wear trousers or jeans rather than a skirt, but this isn't a real issue in Uganda. In rural areas, women are probably best off not wearing shorts.

Shirts T-shirts are arguably better than button-up shirts, because they are lighter and less bulky. That said, I've found that the top pocket of a shirt (particularly if the pocket buttons up) is a good place to carry my spending money in markets and bus stations, as it's easier to keep an eye on than trouser pockets.

Sweaters Uganda is generally warm at night, though at higher altitudes (for instance in Fort Portal) it can cool down in the evening. For general purposes, one warm sweater, fleece jacket or sweatshirt should be adequate. If you intend hiking on Mount Elgon or the Rwenzoris, you will need very warm clothing. Western Uganda has a wet climate, and showers are normal even during the supposed dry seasons. A light waterproof jacket is close to essential. Alternatively, a lightweight umbrella can be useful against rain and sun (local ones are flimsy so bring this with you).

Socks and underwear These must be made from natural fabrics, and bear in mind that re-using them when sweaty will encourage fungal infections such as athlete's foot, as well as prickly heat in the groin region. Socks and underpants are light and compact enough for it to be worth bringing a week's supply.

Shoes Unless you're serious about off-road hiking, bulky hiking boots are probably over the top in Uganda. They're also very heavy, whether they are on your feet or in your pack. A good pair of walking shoes, preferably made of leather and with some ankle support, is a good compromise. It's also useful to carry sandals, thongs or other light shoes.

Rather than spending a fortune outfitting yourself for Africa before leaving home, you might follow the lead of informed travellers and volunteers who pack a minimum of clothes and buy the remainder in Kampala's superb Owino Market. This sells secondhand clothes from Europe and the US which have been bought by exporters in bulk from charity shops for export to the Third World where they are sorted, graded and priced accordingly for sale in markets and by hawkers. An American journalist once trailed a T-shirt from a US charity shop to eventual purchase in a remote village on Mount Elgon. You'll benefit a Ugandan when you purchase a nearly new pair of cotton chinos for around US$10, and you'll also have saved yourself US$30 on a new pair as well as saving luggage space and weight. Bargains include cotton clothing, lightweight fleece jackets, walking boots and brand-name frocks. Owino Market (officially renamed St Balikudembe Market in 2004) is conveniently located near the bus and taxi parks. Jinja and Fort Portal markets are also pretty good for secondhand clothes.

OTHER USEFUL ITEMS Most backpackers, even those with no intention of camping, carry a **sleeping bag**. A lightweight sleeping bag will be more than adequate in most parts of Uganda; better still in this climate would be to carry a sheet sleeping bag, something you can easily make yourself. The one time when you will definitely need an all-weather sleeping bag is on high mountains. You might meet travellers who, when they stay in local lodgings, habitually place their own sleeping bag on top of the bedding provided. Nutters, in my opinion, and I'd imagine that a sleeping bag placed on a flea-ridden bed would be unlikely to provide significant protection, and rather more likely to become flea-infested itself.

I wouldn't leave home without **binoculars**, which some might say makes *me* the nutter. Seriously though, if you're interested in natural history, it's difficult to imagine anything that will give you such value-for-weight entertainment as a pair of light compact binoculars, which these days needn't be much heavier or bulkier than a pack of cards. Binoculars are essential if you want to get a good look at birds (Africa boasts a remarkably colourful avifauna, even if you've no desire to put a name to everything that flaps) or to watch distant mammals in game reserves. For most purposes, 7x21 compact binoculars will be fine, though some might prefer 7x35 traditional binoculars for their larger field of vision. Serious birdwatchers will find a 10x magnification more useful.

Some travellers like to carry their own **padlock**. This would be useful if you have a pack that is lockable, and in remote parts of the country it might be necessary for rooms where no lock is provided. If you are uneasy about security in a particular guesthouse, you may like to use your own lock instead of or in addition to the one provided. Although combination locks are reputedly easier to pick than conventional padlocks, I think you'd be safer with a combination lock in Uganda, because potential thieves will have far more experience of breaking locks with keys.

Your **toilet bag** should at the very minimum include soap (secured in a plastic bag or soap holder unless you enjoy a soapy toothbrush!), shampoo, toothbrush and toothpaste. This sort of stuff is easy to replace as you go along, so there's no need to bring family-sized packs. Men will probably want a **razor**. Women should carry at least enough **tampons** and/or **sanitary pads** to see them through at least one heavy period, since these items may not always be immediately available. Nobody should forget to bring a **towel**, or to keep handy a roll of **loo paper** which, although widely available at shops and kiosks, cannot always be relied upon to be present where it's most urgently needed.

Other essentials include a **torch**, a **penknife** (or arguably more useful, a **Leatherman**-style tool) and a compact **alarm clock** for those early morning starts. As load shedding (a euphemism for scheduled power cuts) becomes an increasingly important factor of day-to-day life, so does a powerful **torch** rank as an increasingly important item of luggage. If you're interested in what's happening in the world, you might also think about carrying a **short-wave radio**. Some travellers carry **games** – most commonly a pack of cards, less often chess or draughts or Travel Scrabble. Many older hotels have baths but no bath plugs, so you might want to consider carrying your own **universal bath plug**.

You should carry a small **medical kit**, the contents of which are discussed on page 89, as are **mosquito nets**. If you wear **contact lenses**, bring all the fluids you need, since they are not available outside Kampala. You might also want to bring a pair of glasses to wear on long bus rides, and on safari – many lens wearers suffer badly in dusty conditions. In general, since many people find the intense sun and dry climate irritate their eyes, you might consider reverting to glasses. For those who wear **glasses**, it's worth bringing a spare pair, though a new pair can be made up cheaply and quickly in most towns, provided that you have your prescription available.

Novels are difficult to get hold of outside Kampala. Your best bet is to carry an e-book tablet loaded with reading material. If you prefer the real thing, bring a supply of books with you or visit Kampala's excellent Aristoc bookshop in Garden City Mall. This stocks a good range of literature, present bestsellers, Africana and local-interest material (including this guidebook). Books are competitively priced and sometimes cheaper than in the UK.

These days it seems to be standard practice to move around with either a **tablet** or **notebook computer**. If entertainment and internet access are your priorities, and your typing requirements are limited to the odd email, a tablet (fitted with a full-body protective casing) is ideal. If your surfing requirements can await the rare occasions you reach a Wi-Fi hotspot, then all well and good. If not, consider spending a bit more for a model with 3G capability. By fitting a local SIM card loaded with data credit, you can access the internet anywhere your chosen network provides a signal. If using a notebook computer, you can enjoy similar coverage by investing in a local USB stick (or 'dongle'). Orange and MTN provide the most comprehensive service.

MONEY

The local currency is the Uganda shilling, which traded at around Ush2,500 to the US dollar in early 2013. Notes are printed in denominations of Ush50,000, 20,000, 10,000, 5,000 and 1,000. Ush500, 200, 100, and 50 notes have been replaced by coins and are no longer legal tender. Ush1,000 notes are in the process of being phased out in favour of coins.

The most widely recognised currencies in Uganda are the US dollar, pound sterling and euro. The **euro** is now as widely accepted as the US dollar and is increasingly favoured by European travellers as a hard currency cash source (no need to change euros to dollars to Uganda shillings) with the added advantage that (besides its current strength) there are no problems with older notes being rejected. Other internationally recognised currencies will be fine in major cities, but they may cause some confusion at banks in smaller centres. As to what form you should carry your money in, it used be standard procedure to mix cash and travellers' cheques, the latter being refundable if lost or stolen. Unfortunately in Uganda, as in most African countries these days, travellers' cheques are no longer widely accepted. For more details, see page 106.

CASH You will in any case want to carry with you some **hard currency** in cash, ideally US dollars. Large-denomination bills (US$50/100) attract a better exchange rate than smaller denominations (US$20 and less). The latter attract a poor rate, but they can be useful in some situations, for instance direct hard-currency payments or when you want to exchange a small sum shortly before departure. I would advise bringing all the cash you intend to exchange directly in US$100 bills, but also carrying a few smaller-denomination notes just in case. Note that US dollar bills issued before 2000 are not accepted. To obtain additional funds once in Uganda, see below.

FOREIGN EXCHANGE Foreign exchange in Uganda is no longer the bureaucratic headache it used to be. Back in the early nineties, you needed to declare the hard currency money you were bringing into the country (some of it anyway) and, when exiting, produce a bank receipt to show you had been changing currency legitimately at the lousy government rate and not at the more realistic black market rate.

These days, one can simply walk into a bank or foreign exchange (forex) bureau and swap a fistful of dollars, pounds or what have you, for a wad of Uganda shillings in a couple of minutes. No ID is required and the receipt serves only as a souvenir. You'll receive a somewhat thicker pile than the one you handed over since Uganda's largest banknote is Ush50,000 (US$20); and also because you should ask for some of your money in lower denominations to avoid a lengthy search for 'balance' (change) whenever you purchase something. Before changing money, compare the rates offered by neighbouring forex or in the absence of any competitor, by perusing the selection of previous day's rates published between Tuesday and Saturday in the *Monitor* and *New Vision* newspapers. If you find you've exchanged more than you actually required in Uganda, it's perfectly straightforward to convert it back to foreign currency in a matter of minutes at any forex bureau, albeit at a slight loss.

So far, so good! But there are a few complications. In Uganda, as elsewhere in East Africa, US dollar banknotes printed before 2000 are not accepted, owing to a prevalence of forgeries dating from this period. Nor will banks or forex bureaux accept any torn or blemished notes, no matter how insignificant the damage. Also, significantly poorer rates – up to 20% lower – are offered for denominations of US$20 or less. Another, more significant complication is that the major banks stopped accepting travellers' cheques. The only place I know of that does so in Kampala is the forex in the Speke Hotel and that at poor rates.

Money can also be changed in banks though in Kampala this not so convenient as in a forex. The rates are slightly less favourable than those offered by the forex bureaux, a bit more paperwork is involved at a bank, you may need to show some ID and there will probably be a queue unless there is a designated forex counter. Beyond Kampala however, banks will be your main source of funds, either exchanged over the counter or drawn from ATMs using your credit or debit card (see opposite). Upcountry branches of the various banks all offer a standard rate set by the bank's head office in Kampala. Even so, keep your wits about you. Readers report being offered rates in Fort Portal Stanbic bank that were 20% lower than that set by Kampala headquarters.

Banks are open from 09.00 to 15.00 on weekdays (though some banks on Kampala Road do stay open later) and from 09.00 to 12.00 on Saturdays. Forex offices may open earlier and typically close at 17.00. Though you'll find forex open on Saturdays and public holidays, you'll struggle to find anywhere to change money on a Sunday. You may find a sympathetic hotel (with unsympathetic rates) but most restrict this service to guests. In Kampala, your best bet on Sunday is the private forex office within the Speke Hotel which is open seven days a week, as are forex bureaux at Entebbe International Airport which normally stay open late enough to serve passengers on major incoming and outgoing flights.

Do plan ahead if you intend to change money upcountry. Do check the list of public holidays on page 121 to avoid being inconvenienced or left short of funds, possibly over a long weekend. Stanbic branches are often very busy and as all transactions (including forex) are handled by the same counters, you'll probably find yourself in a long queue. Either get there early or leave yourself plenty of time. Barclays branches, on the other hand, have a specific forex counter. If your itinerary is tight, perhaps with one-night stopovers outside banking hours, plan accordingly.

If you're going to be in Uganda for a while, consider opening a bank account to hold your cash safely until you access with a local ATM cash. Barclays require a passport photo and copy of passport details. Stanbic has the additional requirement of a letter of recommendation.

CREDIT AND DEBIT CARDS Following the decline in the use of travellers' cheques, your main recourse to additional cash is though your credit/debit card. If you know your PIN, you can use these to withdraw a limited amount of funds each day in Uganda shillings using an ATM machine. Your Visa card is most widely accepted in Uganda, with MasterCard being a second choice. It would be prudent to contact your bank to check your card's compatibility with East African systems and find out what they will charge in addition to locally levied fees. It may also be a good idea to alert your bank to the dates you will be travelling so they will not be concerned about unusual foreign transactions.

Transactions with each of the main banks have their pros and cons. **Barclays** and **Standard Chartered** offer the best ATM deal, allowing you to draw up to US$700 in shillings (Barclays charge Ush10,000 for the service). So far so good, but Barclays ATMs can be choosy and may not 'like' your card for whatever reason. If you resort to an 'over the counter' transaction, you'll need ID and will incur a hefty charge of US$25. You'll find a Barclays in most regional centres, Kitgum, Moroto and Kisoro being notable exceptions. The problem with Standard Chartered is that their upcountry network is limited to Jinja, Mbale, Gulu and Mbarara. By far the most comprehensive network is provided by **Stanbic** bank which operates 138 machines nationwide, with at least one in every town. The downside is that each Stanbic ATM only allows Ush250,000 (US$100)/day while the charge is Ush12,500. You may however be able to obtain another Ush250,000 (and pay another Ush12,500) from a different Stanbic machine. Other banks with expanding upcountry networks with viable ATMs are Crane Bank and Kenya Commercial Bank.

Upcountry, you may encounter lengthy queues for ATMs so take advantage of any unused machines you happen to spot. Other than using ATM machines, there is little scope to use your credit card for direct payments and a levy of 5% will often be added to the bill. Don't forget your card in an ATM; one fellow who did so (again in Fort Portal Stanbic!) found his account being debited daily from Kampala ATMs!

MOBILE MONEY The reluctance on the part of ATMs to dispense useful sums of money is quite a nuisance. The solution, if you're going to be in Uganda for a while, is to sign up for an 'electronic wallet service' with a local mobile phone company. There are several options but MTN's mobile money service is the most widespread. You'll need an MTN SIM card for your mobile phone and a copy of your ID. After loading a maximum of Ush4,000,000 (US$1,600) onto your account, you can withdraw funds from any MTN office or agent nationwide (assuming that they have

3

sufficient cash to oblige). Visit www.mtn.co.ug/MTN-Services/Mobile-Banking for details of the registration process and deposit and withdrawal charges. This system will become less attractive if a transaction fee of 10% is implemented.

MONEY TRANSFERS Transferring funds between banks in Europe/North America and Uganda in this electronic age remains surprisingly slow, still taking several days. It's much quicker to have a friend or relative to send you money using Western Union or MoneyGram. You'll be able to collect Ugandan shillings converted from a sum paid to an agent in your home country as little as ten minutes earlier. It will take you at least this long to receive – by phone, email or text message – a codeword registered by your Good Samaritan which you must quote to obtain your money. The service is not cheap; the sender will pay about US$30 in commission. Branches are found in Kampala, Entebbe and most towns upcountry. Western Union operates out of Nile Bank branches. If you're the organised sort, you'll check the websites (*www.westernunion.com* or *www.moneygram.com*) before you travel to identify your likely benefactor's local agent in case the need arises.

PRICES QUOTED IN THIS BOOK Practically everything in Uganda can be paid for using the Uganda shilling, irrespective of the currency in which a price is quoted. For example, UWA tariffs for entrance fees and activities are quoted in US dollars, but can be paid either in US dollars or in Uganda shillings (except for gorilla-tracking permits which must be paid in dollars). I've therefore given UWA rates in

CHANGING MONEY AT BORDERS

Invariably, when crossing a land border into Uganda, you'll need to obtain some local currency, perhaps to pay for an onward bus ride to the next town and a room when you get there. Moreover, if you expect to reach this town after the banks have closed or over the weekend, you will need funds to see you through to the next banking day. One way to do this, assuming that the opportunity arises, is to ask travellers leaving Uganda whether they have any leftover cash to swap. The best option, and one that has only recently become available, is to head to the local branch of Stanbic bank – many border crossings and all major towns now have one. This is, however, not an infallible solution. You're quite likely to arrive outside business hours and even if you do find it open, your bus (if you're using public transport) will have sped onwards towards Kampala long before you get to the front of the queue. Your last resort is to change money on the street. This is the only situation in which you'll need to do so in Uganda today, since the once-thriving black market for hard currency was killed off by private forex bureaux years ago.

Changing money on the street is probably technically illegal, but it's done openly and represents no risk of running into trouble with the authorities. Any problems you encounter will certainly arise from the characters you deal with, many of whom are accomplished con artists. It will help your dealings with these guys if you've checked the approximate exchange rate in advance with a fellow passenger and calculated roughly what sum of local currency you should expect. I prefer to carry a small surplus of the currency of the country I am leaving (the equivalent of about US$10) to change into the currency of the country I am entering. Whether I exchange local or hard currency, I routinely stash whatever bill(s) I intend to change in a pocket discrete from my main stash of foreign

US dollars. A choice of currency with which to detail other expenditure is less clear-cut. US dollars will mean more to readers at the planning stage of the trip, while in country Uganda shillings are better suited for comparison of local prices. I've taken the view that consistency and ease of comparison are less important than the currency uses. Since all upmarket hotels and tourist lodges and many backpacker hostels quote in dollars, I've used this currency for all accommodation prices, where necessary converting the shilling rates used by local establishments at a rate of US$1 = Ush2,500. Conversions throughout are rounded upwards to the nearest dollar. Restaurant prices, by contrast, are uniformly given here in Uganda shillings, since very few establishments, even the most upmarket hotels, express the prices on their menus in any other currency.

As always, be assured that the prices given in this book will certainly change during the lifetime of this edition. These may be minor or they may be quite spectacular. During the lifespan of the sixth edition of this book, changes were even more significant than usual owing to the global economic squeeze, fluctuating fuel prices, highs and lows in the US dollar exchange rate and the considerable expense of a general election. This led to period of sudden inflation – up to 25% – during 2010–11 which rendered the restaurant prices I had accumulated a year before totally meaningless.

BUDGETING Independent travel in Uganda is inexpensive by most standards, but your budget will depend greatly on how and where you travel. The following guidelines may be useful to people trying to keep costs to a minimum.

currency before I arrive at the border. Personally, I'm not too worried about being offered a slightly lower rate than might be expected, since pushing too hard carries the risk of weeding out the honest guys and leaving only the con artists (and if I'm offered an exceptionally good rate, I know I'm being set up). I am wary of allowing a quick-talking moneychanger in a chaotic environment to exploit the decimal shifts involved in many African currency transactions.

Should you be surrounded by a mob of yelling moneychangers, pick any one of them and tell him that you will only discuss rates when his pals back off. Having agreed a rate, insist on taking the money and counting it before you hand over, or expose the location of, your own money. Should the amount that the moneychanger hands you be incorrect, it is almost certainly not a mistake, but phase one of an elaborate con trick, so it's safest to hand the wad of cash back and refuse to have anything further to do with him. Alternatively, if you do decide to continue, then recount the money after he hands it back to you and keep doing so until you have the correct amount counted in your hand. The reason for this is that some crooked moneychangers have such sleight of hand that they can seemingly add notes to a wad while actually removing a far greater number, all right in front of your eyes. Only when you are sure you have the right amount should you hand over your money.

Be aware too that you won't get the greatest rate of exchange on the street, which is fair enough, considering that moneychangers, like banks, need to make a cut on the deal. Thus there's no sense in exchanging more money than you'll require before you reach a bank or forex bureau. The only exception is when you have a surfeit of cash from the country you're leaving and no intention of returning there – the border may be the last place you can offload it.

In most parts of the country, it will be difficult to keep your basic travel expenses (food, transport and accommodation) to much below US$25 per day. You could spend as little as US$15 per day by camping everywhere and by staying put for a few days at somewhere cheap like the Ssese Islands or Lake Nkuruba. Typically a room in the most basic sort of local hotel will cost US$5, camping around US$3–5 per person, and a meal US$2–7 depending on whether you're content to stick to the predictable local fare or want to eat a more varied menu. A treat in one of Kampala's best restaurants won't cost more than US$10–12 for a main course. Bus fares cost around Ush15,000–25,000 so transport costs will probably work out at around US$6–10 daily, assuming that you're on the move every other day or thereabouts. If you don't want *always* to stay in the most basic room and *always* to go for the cheapest item on the menu, I would bank on spending around US$35–40 per day on basic travel costs. You could travel very comfortably for US$50–60 per day.

Unless you go on an organised safari, the only expenses over and above your basic travel costs will be incurred in national parks where you can expect to spend an extra US$60 per day for every 24-hour period. Entrance for foreign visitors in most parks is US$35 per day while food/accommodation is slightly more expensive than elsewhere, while activities such as launch trips and nature walks incur further expense. Gorilla tracking in Uganda will cost US$500.

If funds are tight, it is often a useful idea to separate your daily budget from one-off expenses. At current prices, a daily budget of around US$35–40 with US$300–500 set aside for expensive one-off activities (excluding gorilla tracking) would be comfortable for most travellers.

GETTING AROUND

BY AIR Since few major urban centres lie more than five to six hours' drive from the capital, flying has never been an option for most people. The only destination in Uganda which is reached by air more often than by road is Kidepo Valley National Park, since the drive up from Kampala takes two days (see page 455). Three operators, Fly Uganda, Aerolink and Eagle Air offer scheduled and charter flights to various tourist destinations. The scheduled flights are subject to minimum number of passengers and are often diversions to other destinations.

✈ **Eagle Air** Entebbe Airport; Kampala Office: 11 Portal Av; ✆ 0414 344292
✈ **Fly Uganda** Kajjansi Airfield, Gate 1; m 0772 712557; e bookings@flyuganda.com; www. flyuganda.com. See also advert in third colour section.

✈ **Kampala Aeroclub** Kajjansi Airfield; m 0772 706107
✈ **Ndege Juu Ya Africa** Kajjansi Airfield; m 0772 220132; www.ndegejuu.com

SELF-DRIVE By east African standards, Uganda's major roads are generally in good condition. Surfaced roads radiate out from Kampala, running east to Jinja, Busia, Malaba, Tororo, Mbale and Soroti, south to Entebbe, southwest to Masaka, Mbarara and Kabale, west to Fort Portal, northwest to Hoima, north to Gulu, northeast to Gayaza and Kayunga (and on to Jinja). Other surfaced roads connect Karuma Falls to Arua, Mbale to Sipi Falls, Masaka to the Tanzanian border, Mbarara to Ibanda, and Ntungamo to Rukungiri. Standards of highway maintenance are low and one or other of the major highways is usually in a serious state of disrepair pending a major roadworks programme (as I write, the Mbarara–Kabale road is being fixed while the Tororo–Mbale–Soroti road is a shocker).

Getting to the edge of Kampala from upcountry destinations is not difficult, though increased traffic volume, including trucks, inevitably slows speeds as the metropolis is approached. The long and bothersome process of getting from one side of the city to the other was eased in October 2008 with the opening of a 20km Northern Bypass, linking the Fort Portal and Mbarara roads in the west to Jinja road in the east.

Most other roads in Uganda – for instance from Fort Portal or Masindi to Hoima, and from Masindi to Murchison Falls – are unsurfaced. The condition of these and other more minor unsurfaced roads is discussed under the relevant section in the regional part of the guide. As a rule, however, unsurfaced roads tend to be very variable from one season to the next, with conditions likely to be most tricky during the rains and least so towards the end of the dry season. Even within this generalisation, an isolated downpour can do major damage to a road that was in perfectly good condition a day earlier, while the arrival of a grader can transform a pot-holed 4x4 track into a road navigable by any saloon car. The type of soil is also a big factor in how prone any given road is to deterioration, and in wet conditions one should always be conscious that firm soil or gravel can give way abruptly to a mushy depression or a black cotton-soil quagmire. Put simply, advice in this guide regarding road conditions is of necessity a snapshot of conditions in late 2012 and should not be taken as gospel. When in doubt, ask local advice – if minibus-taxis are getting through, then so should any 4x4, so the taxi station is always a good place to seek current information.

The main hazard on Ugandan roads, aside from unexpected pot-holes, is other drivers. Minibus-taxi drivers in particular have long been given to overtaking on blind corners, and speed limits are universally ignored except when enforced by road conditions. As big a threat as minibus-taxis these days are the spanking new coaches that bully their way along trunk routes at up to 120km/h – keep an eye in your rear-view mirror and if necessary pull off the road in advance to let the closing loony past. The coaches are in reality just a heavyweight manifestation of a more widespread road-hog mentality that characterises Ugandan drivers. Larger vehicles show little compunction when it comes to overtaking smaller ones so tightly that they are practically forced off the road, and vehicles passing in the opposite direction will often stray across the central white line forcing oncoming traffic to cut onto the verge. Bearing the above in mind, a coasting speed of 80km/h in the open road would be comfortable without being over cautious, and it's not a bad idea to slow down and cover the brake in the face of oncoming traffic. In urban situations, particularly downtown Kampala, right of way essentially belongs to he who is prepared to force the issue – a considered blend of defensive driving tempered by outright assertiveness is required to get through safely without becoming too bogged down in the traffic.

A peculiarly African road hazard – one frequently taken to unnecessary extremes in Uganda – is the giant sleeping policeman, or 'speed bump' as it's known locally. A lethal bump might be signposted in advance, it might be painted in black-and-white stripes, or it might simply rear like a macadamised wave a full 30cm or so above the road without warning. It's to be assumed that the odd stray bump will exist on any stretch of a major road that passes through a town or village, so slow down at any looming hint of urbanisation. Other regular obstacles include bicycles laden with banana clusters, which can often force traffic to leave its lane, as well as livestock and pedestrians wandering around blithely in the middle of the road. Piles of foliage placed in the road at a few metres interval warn of a broken-down vehicle. Though red warning triangles are mandatory items for vehicles in Rwanda and possibly Uganda, few drivers are foolish enough to use them for their intended

Most readers of Bradt guides live in countries where heavy traffic, congestion and ice and snow are almost the only problems encountered by drivers. They are therefore unaware of the hassles they are likely to meet once on the road in Uganda. Based on personal experience of over ten years of daily driving in the outback of Uganda, Kenya and Malawi I have compiled the following dos and don'ts readers should be advised to keep in mind in order to make their self-drive trip an enjoyable one:

1   Never travel without the following:
    • First-aid kit
    • Spare petrol to last for not less than 300km allowing for low-gear driving on rough roads (use jerrycans, as the caps of plastic spare tanks often leak)
    • Oil enough to refill the sump
    • Water of drinkable quality and for refilling the engine's cooling system if it bursts
    • Plastic bonding goo to fix sump, distributor cap, etc.
2   On corrugated roads, the most comfortable driving speed is about 60km/h. Always drive with anticipation and foresight and abstain from sudden steering movements, or steering and braking at the same time, both of which can result in skidding. Slowing down early and gentle breaking, alternating with cautiously dosed accelerator application, will prevent the car from going out of control.
3   Before negotiating flooded stretches of road, or rivers that aren't too deep for the car (wade through to find out!), remove the fan belt to stop water from spraying around, which could upset the electrical systems of the engine. Traverse the flooding in first gear with high revs to blow water from the exhaust. To remove water from electrical parts, use the hollow stem of tall-growing roadside grass as a pipette to drain less accessible areas of the engine compartment.
4   Stop well ahead of bush fires. The fire's front could well be 500m in length, and it doesn't always travel in a straight line as one might assume, making it difficult to judge the course and progress from a moving vehicle with bends, slopes, trees, anthills and other obstacles obscuring the view ahead. Traversing the fire in the belief that it can be negotiated without first checking the situation carefully is simply foolish: many a daring driver misjudging this type of scenario has found himself surrounded by choking smoke and intense heat in the middle of an inferno with no chance to retreat or get away. When in doubt, fire has the right of way!
5   When you have to change a right-hand wheel, park on the left side of the road, and vice versa. African roads are seldom level and are most likely to

purpose since these would obviously be stolen – leaving them nothing to show traffic police asking to see these items.

Indicator lights, according to local custom, are not there to signal an intent to turn. Instead, they are switched on when approaching oncoming traffic to suggest that following drivers should not overtake. Ugandans, like many Africans, display a strong and inexplicable aversion to switching on their headlights except in genuine

slope down towards the shoulders, leaving insufficient clearance for the jack if the punctured tyre is on the road edge. Do beware of passing traffic!

6 If the petrol tank leaks due to small holes caused by flying stones, try a cake of ordinary household soap to be rubbed on and around the holes in the same way an eraser is applied for removing pencil marks from paper.

7 During the dry season, patches of grass or savanna should be avoided when looking for a place to park, as there is a risk that the exhaust pipe or other hot engine parts will ignite the parched vegetation and spark off a fire, possibly damaging or destroying the car. If possible, leave the car in a field of young cotton, maize, groundnuts or other green vegetation. Provided the crops are small and the car is parked close to the perimeter of the field, with the wheels resting on empty furrows, the damage caused to the crops will be negligible. The owner of the field should, however, be informed. A dry riverbed would be an ideal alternative, but be aware that out of the blue it could become a raging stream – a slight risk during the dry season.

8 It's a good idea to have a fire extinguisher on board, of the professional type large enough to last for several minutes and also good for electrical fires. Drivers should be familiar with the technicalities of their extinguisher! Forget about fire-fighting sprays marketed like deodorants in little push-button spray-cans of a size fitting in the car's glove compartment – they run dry within seconds.

9 Petrol from remote filling stations or dubious pumps, drums or jerrycans might be dirty. To protect the engine, it may be prudent to use nylon stockings or some similar material to filter the petrol while filling up.

10 For elementary on-the-road maintenance and repair jobs, having a workshop manual in the car would be an excellent idea.

11 Beware of any snake crossing the road ahead, since it may rear up and (if not killed first) could strike at any arm, elbow or hand sticking out of a window. Should you accidentally run over the snake, look in your rear-view mirror or reverse to check it is dead. If it has vanished altogether, it could have lodged in your chassis or undercarriage, ready to attack when you alight, open the bonnet or boot, or change a wheel. A snake trapped in this manner will be very scared and aggressive, and I've witnessed several snakebites, some fatal, inflicted under such circumstances.

12 In the unfortunate event that you collide with a person or livestock, it's not advisable to stop. Assuming that the car still drives, it's safer to continue on to the next police station. This might sound harsh, but the reality is that an accident of this sort will often attract an angry *panga*- and stick-wielding crowd, possibly containing a drunken element, which will not hesitate to threaten and possibly attack the car's occupants.

darkness – switch them on at any other time and every passing vehicle will blink its lights back at you in bemusement. In rainy, misty or twilight conditions, it would be optimistic to think that you'll be alerted to oncoming traffic by headlights, or for that matter to expect the more demented element among Ugandan drivers to avoid overtaking or speeding simply because they cannot see more than 10m ahead. It's strongly recommended that you avoid driving at night on main highways outside towns since a significant proportion of vehicles either lack a full complement of functional headlights (never assume a single glow indicates a motorcycle) or keep their lights permanently on blinding full beam! Another very real danger is unlit trucks that, invariably overloaded, have broken down in the middle of the road.

If you decide to rent a self-drive vehicle, check it over carefully and ask to take it for a test drive. Even if you're not knowledgeable about the working of engines, a few minutes on the road should be sufficient to establish whether it has any seriously disturbing creaks, rattles or other noises. Check the condition of the tyres (bald is beautiful might be the national motto in this regard) and that there is at least one spare, better two, both in a condition to be used should the need present itself. If the tyres are tubeless, an inner tube of the correct size can be useful in the event of a repair being required upcountry. Ask to be shown the wheel spanner, jack and the thing for raising the jack. If the vehicle is a high-clearance 4x4 make sure that the jack is capable of raising the wheel high enough to change the wheel. Ask also to be shown filling points for oil, water and petrol and check that all the keys do what they are supposed to do – we've left Kampala before with a car we later discovered could not be locked! Once on the road, check oil and water regularly in the early stages of the trip to ensure that there are no existing leaks. See also the box *Self-drive in Uganda*, pages 112–13, for further survival tips.

Fuel is expensive in Uganda – the equivalent of around US$1.60 per litre for petrol and slightly less for diesel. If you are driving overland from Kenya it is worth stocking up before you enter the country. While driving in Uganda the following documentation is required at all times: the vehicle registration book (a photocopy is acceptable); the vehicle certificate of insurance and a driving licence. Your own domestic licence is acceptable for up to three months. Vehicle tax was abolished a few years ago. Ugandans follow, albeit somewhat loosely on occasions, the British custom of driving on the left side of the road. The general speed limit on the open road is 100km/h and 60km/h in built-up areas, unless otherwise indicated. For details of recommended car-rental agencies, see page 144.

Traffic police dressed in smart white uniforms are deployed along the main highways to ensure that road users obey the rules of the road. If you're nicked for speeding, not having a valid insurance sticker, having an empty reservoir for your windscreen wipers (this somehow qualifies as DMC; Dangerous Mechanical Condition), you'll be presented with a charge sheet to clear at a bank within 28 days. At police checks, show a photocopy of your licence or an expendable international licence in case the officer decides to retain it until you pay the fine; it could be quite a long way back to retrieve it. As often as not, after a few minutes or so of friendly back and forth (remain polite, Uganda is a wonderful country, admit guilt, plead stupidity), you'll be let on your way. If not, it'll teach you to forget to top up your windscreen wiper reservoir.

MOUNTAIN BIKING Uganda is relatively compact and flat, making it ideal for travel by mountain bike. New-quality bikes are not available in Uganda so you should try to bring one with you (some airlines are more flexible than others about carrying bicycles; you should discuss this with your airline in advance). However, if you are prepared to look around Kampala, some decent secondhand bikes can be bought from a few private importers for as little as US$75: check the shop opposite Old Kampala Police Station. Main roads in Uganda are generally in good condition and buses will allow you to take your bike on the roof, though you should expect to be charged extra for this. Minor roads are variable in condition, but in the dry season you're unlikely to encounter any problems. Several of the more far-flung destinations mentioned in this book would be within easy reach of cyclists.

Before you pack that bicycle, do consider that cyclists – far more than ~~1~~ – are exposed to an estimable set of hazards on African roads. The 'might-mentality referred to in the section about self-drive above is doubly concer~~n~~ cyclists, who must expect to be treated as second-class road users, and to ~~d~~ ~~y~~ constant vigilance against speeding buses, etc. It is routine for motorised vehicles to bear down on a bicycle as if it simply didn't exist, hooting at the very last minute, and enforcing the panicked cyclist to veer off the road abruptly, sometimes resulting in a nasty fall. Should this not put you off, do at least ensure that your bicycle is fitted with good rear-view mirrors, a loud horn and luminous strips, and that you bring a helmet and whatever protective gear might lessen the risks. Cycling at night is emphatically not recommended.

The **International Bicycle Fund (IBF)** (*4887 Columbia Drive South, Seattle, WA 98108-1919, USA; e intlbike@scn.org*) is an organisation promoting bicycle travel internationally. It produces a useful publication called *Bicycling in Africa* at a cost of US$14.95 plus US$5 post and packing, as well as several regional supplements including one about Malawi, Tanzania and Uganda.

ROAD TRANSPORT Following the permanent suspension of all passenger rail and ferry services over the past few years, public transport in Uganda essentially boils down to buses and other forms of motorised road transport. The only exceptions are the new passenger/vehicle ferry between Entebbe and the Ssese Islands and local boat services connecting fishing villages on lakes Victoria, Albert and Kyoga. Details of these services are given under the appropriate sections in the regional part of the guide, but it's worth noting here that overloading small passenger boats is customary in Uganda, and fatal accidents are commonplace, often linked to the violent storms that can sweep in from nowhere during the rainy season.

Buses Coach and bus services cover all major routes and, all things being relative, they are probably the safest form of public road transport in Uganda. On all trunk routes, the battered old buses of a few years back have been replaced or supplemented by large modern coaches that typically maintain a speed of 100km/h or faster, allowing them to travel between the capital and any of the main urban centres in western Uganda in less than five hours. According to Kampala Backpackers, which has carried out assessments of Ugandan public transport for visiting British school groups, Gaa Gaa Buses (West Nile) and Elgon Flyer (Mbale and the east) are the pick of the bunch. The best of the rest are Bismarken (southwest Uganda), Kalita (Fort Portal) and Annk (Gulu). Link operate seemingly well-maintained buses capable of terrifying speeds. Personally, I'd walk rather than board a Gateway bus, 40 of which were impounded by police (sadly all too briefly) following a spate of accidents in 2008/09, or a Nile Coach.

The Post Office's Post Bus service is considered the safest option. Five buses leave Kampala's main post office each morning terminating at Gulu, Lira, Kabale, Kisoro and Kasese. Along the way, they stop in numerous towns (22 in the case of the Gulu bus) to drop off and collect mail and passengers. Buses to Lira and Kisoro depart at 07.00 and cost Ush25,000. Other services depart at 08.00 to Kabale, Kasese, Kisoro and Gulu and also cost Ush25,000. Fares to towns along the way are cheaper; Mbale, Mbarara, Mubende cost Ush15,000, Masaka, Ush10,000 and Jinja, Ush5,000.

The better private bus services have reasonably fixed departure times, with one or other coach leaving in either direction between Kampala and the likes of Mbale, Mbarara, Kabale, Kasese, Fort Portal and Masindi every hour or so from around

07.00 to mid-afternoon. Coach and bus fares countrywide typically work out at around Ush4,000 per 50km.

Horizon buses run to Kabale (*5–6hrs; Ush25,000*) and Kisoro (*8–9hrs from their depot on Namirembe Rd; Ush30,000*). Kalita buses run to Mubende (*2hrs; Ush15,000*), Fort Portal (*4hrs; Ush20,000*) and Kasese (*5–6hrs; Ush25,000*) every two hours from the Kalita park at the front of the Nakivubu Stadium on Namirembe Road. Perfect buses run to Kihihi (between Bwindi and Ishasha) via Ntungamo at 05.30 (*7hrs; Ush25,000*) from the Kasenyi Bus Terminal (to the west of Nakivubu Stadium). Kasaba buses also run to Kihihi but from the Qualicell Bus Terminal. The Bismarken bus runs to Butogota (20km from Buhoma), leaving the Qualicell Bus Terminal at 19.30 (*8hrs*). The return to Kampala leaves Butogota at 05.00. The Ush30,000 fare can increase to Ush50,000 if a broken bridge or poor road imposes a longer route. Elgon Flyer runs to Mbale (*4hrs; Ush20,000*) from Qualicell Bus Park. Link buses also run several times a day to the following destinations from the Qualicell: Hoima (*3hrs; Ush13,000*); Masindi (*3hrs; Ush13,000*); Fort Portal (*Ush20,000*) and Kasese (*Ush25,000*); Masaka and Mbarara. Several companies run from the Qualicell park to Gulu and Lira (*4hrs; both Ush25,000*). Zawadi buses also run to Gulu from their office at the Bombo Road end of William Street (*Ush20,000*). The service continues north from Gulu to Ajumani (*Ush30,000*) and Moyo (*Ush35,000*), the latter stage including a memorable ferry crossing over the Nile at Laropi.

A word of warning: there have been a few incidents in East Africa in recent years whereby travellers have accepted drugged food from fellow passengers – and they awake much later to find themselves relieved of their belongings. Though 99 times out of 100 offers of refreshment will be made from genuine courtesy, a polite refusal may be the safest option.

Minibus-taxis In addition to buses, most major routes are covered by a regular stream of white minibuses, which have no set departure times, but simply leave when they are full – every ten to 30 minutes on busier routes. It is no longer the case that minibuses are significantly faster than buses, but the drivers tend to be more reckless. Fares are generally slightly higher than for buses, and it's customary on most routes to pay shortly before arriving rather than on departure, so there is little risk of being overcharged provided that you look and see what other passengers are paying. Minibuses are referred to as taxis in Uganda (though in this book I've called them minibus-taxis to preclude confusion with special hire taxis) and as *matatus* in Kenya, a term that is generally understood but not used by Ugandans. They are also sometimes called *kigatis*, in reference to their resemblance to a bread loaf. A law enforcing a maximum of three passengers per row is stringently enforced in most parts of Uganda, meaning that minibus travel is far more comfortable than in the majority of African countries where four bums per row is customary. Seat belts are now mandatory. All minibus-taxis by law now have to have a distinctive blue-and-white band round the middle, and special hire cars have to have a black-and-white band.

Shared taxis Shared taxis, generally light saloon cars that carry four to six passengers, come into their own on routes that attract insufficient human traffic for minibuses, for instance between Katunguru and Mweya in Queen Elizabeth National Park. They tend to be crowded and slow in comparison with minibuses, and on routes where no other public transport exists, fares are often highly inflated. The drivers habitually overcharge tourists, so establish the price in advance.

Special hire You won't spend long in Uganda before you come across the term *special hire* – which means hiring a vehicle privately to take you somewhere. There are situations where it is useful to go for a special hire, but beware of people at *matatu* stations who tell you there are no vehicles going to where you want, but that they can fix you up a special hire. Nine times out of ten they are trying their luck. If you organise a special hire vehicle, bargain hard. Urban taxis are also known locally as special hires.

Boda-boda One of the most popular ways of getting around in Uganda is the bicycle-taxi or *boda-boda*, so called because they originated as bicycles with large panniers, used for smuggling goods across borders by rural footpaths. Now fitted with pillions and powered by foot or by 50 to 100cc engines, they are a convenient form of suburban transport and also great for short side trips where no public transport exists. Fares are negotiable and affordable – Ush1,000 upwards in Kampala. If you're reliant on public transport it's inevitable that you'll use a *boda-boda* at some stage, but before hopping aboard you should be aware of a pretty poor urban safety record. *Boda-boda* riders are invariably lacking in formal training, road safety awareness and, it is frequently suggested, much between the ears. In December 2005, 1,383 vehicles were involved in accidents sufficiently serious to be reported. Of these, 22% (predictably enough) involved *matatu*-taxis and 15% *boda-bodas*. *Boda-bodas* and their passengers are of course far more vulnerable than the occupants of larger vehicles, and in the same month 15 *boda-boda* drivers were killed. By all means use *boda-bodas* but do try to identify a relatively sensible-looking operator. Older ones are generally better than 16-year-old kids straight from the village with no comprehension of traffic. Tell your driver to go slowly and carefully and don't be afraid to tell him to slow down (or even stop for you to get off) if you don't feel safe. Officially, helmets for *boda-boda* drivers and their passengers have been mandatory since 2005; however, the Regional Traffic Officer informs me that her officers are choosing to 'sensitise' *boda-boda* users before enforcing the law.

Hitching Although some guides to East Africa carry severe warnings against hitching, this strikes me as a knee-jerk reaction based on the type of risk associated with hitching in Western countries. Being picked up by a psychopath should be the least of your concerns when travelling around Uganda – there is a far greater risk of being injured or killed in a car accident, and since drivers of private vehicles are generally (but not always) less reckless than their professional counterparts, this is arguably reduced by hitching. An even greater risk attached to trying to hitch a lift is that you won't succeed. It is customary to pay for lifts in Uganda, so a free ride is likely only in the instance that you're picked up by a foreigner or a wealthy Ugandan with some exposure to Western ways. While waiting for a lift, you can expect to attract a stream of opportunists offering you a special hire. Hitching may be the only way to reach some reserves. Manic arm-flapping, as opposed to a gently raised thumb, is the standard way of signalling to passing traffic for a lift.

 ## ACCOMMODATION

The number of hotels in Uganda has grown enormously in recent years, and wherever you travel, and whatever your budget, you'll seldom have a problem finding suitable accommodation. Most towns have a good variety of moderately priced and budget hotels, and even the smallest villages will usually have somewhere you can stay for a couple of dollars. Upmarket accommodation, on the other hand, is available only in major towns and tourist centres such as national parks.

Travellers in Uganda have not always enjoyed such a wide choice and earlier editions of this book listed pretty much everything on offer in a town; a hotel had to be pretty ordinary indeed to escape inclusion. Times change, and to keep this book to portable proportions we now need to be selective. Some old, rotting wood (including some dismal fleapits first listed in the first edition in 1994) has been cut out and fresh new growth (with tiled rooms and hole-free mossie nets) grafted on.

All accommodation entries in this travel guide are placed in one of five categories: upmarket, moderate, budget, shoestring and camping. The purpose of this categorisation is twofold: to break up long hotel listings that span a wide price range, and to help readers isolate the range of hotels that will best suit their budget and taste. Any given hotel is categorised on its overall feel as much as its actual prices (rack rates are quoted anyway) and in the context of general accommodation standards in the town or reserve where it is situated. Comments relating to the value for money represented by any given hotel should also be read in the context of the individual town and of the stated category. In other words, a hotel that seems to be good value in one town might not be such a bargain were it situated in a place where rates are generally cheaper. Likewise, a hotel that I regard to be good value in the upmarket category will almost certainly seem to be madly expensive to a traveller using budget hotels.

Before going into further detail about the different accommodation categories, it's worth noting a few potentially misleading quirks in local hotel-speak. In Swahili, the word *hoteli* refers to a restaurant while what we call a hotel is generally called a lodging, guesthouse or *gesti* – so if you ask a Ugandan to show you to a hotel you might well be taken to an eatery (see page 530). Another local quirk is that most East African hotels in all price ranges refer to a room that has en-suite shower and toilet facilities as self-contained, a term that is also used widely in this guide. Several hotels offer accommodation in *bandas*, a term used widely in Africa to designate rooms or cottages that are detached from any other building.

Be aware, too, that Ugandan usage of the terms single, double and twin is somewhat inconsistent compared with Western conventions. Rather than automatically asking for a double room, couples might also check the size of a bed in a single room. Gay visitors should note that the internationally unacceptable but locally inflexible definition of 'a couple' means two people of opposite sex. Several hotels now provide oversize beds in which a couple may sleep at the single tariff. I've attempted to cover this with the notation '*sgl+*'. Where such places offer bed and breakfast, usually only one guest will be provided with breakfast. Some double rooms offer similar scope for triple occupancy, being furnished with a double and single bed.

UPMARKET This category embraces all hotels, lodges and resorts that cater primarily to the international leisure or business traveller, and would probably be accorded a two- to four-star ranking internationally. Most hotels in this category offer smart, modern accommodation with en-suite facilities, mosquito netting, air conditioning or fans (depending on the local climate) and in cities digital satellite television (DSTV) in all rooms. Outside Kampala, almost all upmarket listings consist of small lodges and tented camps of no more than ten double accommodation units, built and decorated in a style that complements the surrounding environment and which cater for the exclusive end of the safari market. Rates for a double room in this bracket exceed US$200 with a small handful chancing their arm at over US$700. Room rates for upmarket city hotels include breakfast but exclude all other meals, while at game lodges they normally also include lunch and dinner. This is the category to look at if cost is not a major consideration and you require hotel accommodation of a standard you'd expect at home.

MODERATE In Uganda, as in many African countries, there is often a huge gap between the price and quality of the very cheapest hotels that meet international standards, and that of the most expensive hotels that are geared primarily towards locals and budget travellers. For this reason, the moderate bracket is rather more nebulous than other accommodation categories. Essentially, it embraces those hotels which, for one or other reason, could not truly be classified as upmarket but are also too expensive or of a sufficiently high standard that they cannot be considered budget lodgings. Many places listed in this range are superior local hotels that suffice in lieu of any genuinely upmarket accommodation in a town that sees relatively few tourists. The category also embraces decent lodges or hotels in recognised tourist areas that charge considerably lower rates than their upmarket competitors, but are clearly a notch or two above the budget category. Hotels in this range normally offer comfortable accommodation in self-contained rooms with hot water, fan and possibly DSTV, and they will have a decent restaurant and employ a high ration of English-speaking staff. Most moderate hotels charge around US$100–200 for a double room inclusive of breakfast, but some are slightly more expensive or cheaper. This is the category to look at if you are travelling on a limited but not a low budget and expect a reasonably high but not luxurious standard of accommodation.

BUDGET The hotels in this category are generally aimed largely at the local market and they definitely don't approach international standards, but they will usually be reasonably clean and comfortable, and a definite cut above the basic guesthouses that proliferate in most towns. Hotels in this bracket will more often than not have a decent restaurant attached, English-speaking staff, and comfortable rooms with en-suite facilities, running cold or possibly hot water, fans (but not air conditioning) and good mosquito netting. Room rates are typically around US$20–100 for a double, including breakfast, which may or may not be very substantial. This is the category to look at if you are on a limited budget, but want to avoid total squalor!

SHOESTRING This category is dominated by the small local guesthouses that proliferate in most towns, catering almost exclusively to locals. These typically consist of around ten cell-like rooms forming three walls around a central courtyard, with a reception area or restaurant at the front. Guesthouse standards tend to vary widely both within towns and between them, far more so than do their prices. Note that while backpacker hostels do exist, their range of accommodation offered now extends far beyond cheap dorm beds and these are often more accurately classified in the budget category.

The places listed in this guide are the pick of what may be a much larger selection of basic guesthouses clustered together in the vicinity of the bus station or market, and often there is little to choose between them. If you're looking around, my experience is that guesthouses run by women or with a strong female presence are generally cleaner and more hospitable than those run by men, and that – standards of maintenance being low – the newest guesthouse will be the cleanest and the brightest. Shoestring accommodation typically costs around US$5–10 for a double, with some establishments costing a little more. In most cases, shared bathroom and toilets are provided rather than en-suite (or self-contained) facilities and breakfast will not be included in the room rate, or will be very insubstantial if it is. This category is the one to look at for travellers who want the cheapest possible accommodation irrespective of quality, though it does often include perfectly pleasant hotels that just happen to be cheap.

CAMPING There has been a great increase in the number of organised campsites in recent years, and there are now very few established tourist centres where you can't pitch a tent in a guarded site with good facilities. Camping typically costs around US$5 per person per night and US$10 in the national parks.

✖ EATING AND DRINKING

EATING OUT If you are not too fussy and don't mind a lack of variety, you can eat cheaply almost anywhere in Uganda. In most towns numerous local restaurants (often called *hoteli*s) serve unimaginative but filling meals for under US$2. Typically, local food is based around a meat or chicken stew eaten with one of four staples: rice, chapati, *ugali* or *matoke*. *Ugali* is a stiff maize porridge eaten throughout sub-Saharan Africa. *Matoke* is a cooked plantain dish, served boiled or in a mushy heap, and the staple diet in many parts of Uganda. Another Ugandan special is groundnut sauce. *Mandazi*, the local equivalent of doughnuts, are tasty when they are freshly cooked, but rather less appetising when they are a day old. *Mandazi* are served at *hoteli*s and sold at markets. You can often eat very cheaply at stalls around markets and bus stations.

Cheap it may be, but for most travellers the appeal of this sort of fare soon palls. In larger towns, you'll usually find a couple of better restaurants (sometimes attached to upmarket or moderate hotels) serving Western or Indian food for around US$5–8. There is considerably more variety in Kampala, where for US$10–12 per head you can eat very well indeed. Upmarket lodges and hotels generally serve high-quality food. Vegetarians are often poorly catered for in Uganda (the exception being Indian restaurants), and people on organised tours should ensure that the operator is informed in advance about this or any other dietary preference.

Note that Swahili names for various foods are used throughout Uganda (see page 530).

COOKING FOR YOURSELF The alternative to eating at restaurants is to put together your own meals at markets and supermarkets. The variety of foodstuffs you can buy varies from season to season and from town to town, but in most major centres, with the exception of Kisoro, you can rely on finding a supermarket that stocks frozen meat, a few tinned goods, biscuits, pasta, rice and chocolate bars.

Fruit and vegetables are best bought at markets, where they are very cheap. Potatoes, sweet potatoes, onions, tomatoes, bananas, sugarcane, avocados, paw-paws, mangoes, coconuts, oranges and pineapples are available in most towns.

For hikers, packet soups are about the only dehydrated meals that are available throughout Uganda. If you have specialised requirements, you're best off doing your shopping in Kampala, where a wider selection of goods is available in the supermarkets.

DRINKS Brand-name soft drinks such as Pepsi, Coca-Cola and Fanta are widely available in Uganda and cheap by international standards. If the fizzy stuff doesn't appeal, you can buy imported South African fruit juices at supermarkets in Kampala and other large towns. Tap water is reasonably safe to drink in larger towns, but bottled mineral water is widely available if you prefer not to take the risk.

Locally, the most widely drunk hot beverage is *chai*, a sweet tea where all ingredients are boiled together in a pot. In some parts of the country *chai* is often flavoured with spices such as ginger (an acquired taste, in my opinion). Coffee is one of Uganda's major cash crops, but you'll be lucky if you ever meet a Ugandan who knows how to brew a decent cup – coffee in Uganda almost invariably tastes insipid and watery except at upmarket hotels and quality restaurants.

The main alcoholic drink is lager beer. Jinja's Nile Breweries (a subsidiary of South African Breweries) brews Nile Special, Nile Gold and Club whilst Uganda Breweries at Port Bell near Kampala brews Bell, Pilsner, Tusker Export and Guinness. Moonberg is a new and popular beer produced by a small Kampala brewery. All local beers come in 500ml bottles, which cost US$1.50 in local bars and up to US$4 in some upmarket hotels. Nile Special is probably the most popular tipple with locals and travellers alike, though I must admit a preference for the milder Bell. Two of Africa's most pleasant lagers, Kenya Tusker and Congo Primus, are sometimes sold in towns near the respective borders. If you've never been to Africa before, you might want to try the local millet beer. It's not bad, though for most people once is enough.

A selection of superior plonk-quality South African wines is available in most tourist-class hotels and bars, as well as in some supermarkets, generally at around US$10–20 per bottle – outrageous to South Africans who know that exactly the same wine would cost 20% of that in a supermarket at home, but not unreasonable in international terms. Based on our experience, all wines – white or red – of more than two or three years' vintage are best avoided in preference for younger bottles, presumably because they are poorly stored. Local gins can be bought very cheaply in a variety of bottle sizes or in 60ml sachets – very convenient for hiking in remote areas or taking with you to upmarket hotels for an inexpensive nightcap in your room. These are known by the rather endearing term 'tot pack', though the African fondness for tacking an additional vowel to the end of a noun has actually resulted in 'totter pack'; you may appreciate this inadvertent irony if you overindulge.

PUBLIC HOLIDAYS

In addition to the following fixed public holidays, Uganda recognises as holidays the Christian Good Friday and Easter Monday and the Muslim Eid-el-Fitr and Eid-el-Adha, all of which generally fall in March or April. Expect any institutions that would be closed on a Sunday – banks and forex bureaux, for instance, or government and other offices – to also be closed on any public holiday, but most shops and other local services will function as normal. Public transport is typically more intermittent than normal on public holidays, but it still operates.

1 January	New Year's Day
26 January	NRM Anniversary Day
8 March	International Women's Day
1 May	Labour Day
3 June	Martyrs' Day
9 June	Heroes' Day
9 October	Independence Day
25 December	Christmas Day
26 December	Boxing Day

Until a few years ago it was difficult to buy anything much in Uganda, but things have improved greatly of late. A fair range of imported goods is available in Kampala, though prices are often inflated. If you have specific needs (unusual medications or slide film, for instance), then you'd be safest bringing what you need with you. Toilet rolls, soap, toothpaste, pens, batteries and locally produced foodstuffs are widely available. Normal shopping hours are between 08.30 and 18.00. Most upcountry

PHOTOGRAPHIC TIPS *Ariadne Van Zandbergen*

EQUIPMENT Although with some thought and an eye for composition you can take reasonable photos with a 'point-and-shoot' camera, you need an SLR camera if you are at all serious about photography. Modern SLRs tend to be very clever, with automatic programmes for almost every possible situation, but remember that these programmes are limited in the sense that the camera cannot think, but only makes calculations. Every starting amateur photographer should read a photographic manual for beginners and get to grips with such basics as the relationship between aperture and shutter speed.

Digital SLRs come in different formats, which refer to the size of the sensor. The format of the future is the full size sensor, but at present all full size sensor cameras are in the higher price bracket. Different lenses are designed to accommodate the camera sensor sizes.

Always buy the best lens you can afford. The lens determines the quality of your photo more than the camera body. Fixed fast lenses are ideal, but very costly. A zoom lens makes it easier to change composition without changing lenses the whole time. If you carry only one lens with a full size sensor camera, a 28–70mm or similar zoom should be ideal. This corresponds to a 17–55mm or similar for a camera with a smaller sensor. For a second lens, a lightweight telephoto zoom will be excellent for candid shots and varying your composition. Wildlife photography will be very frustrating if you don't have at least a 300mm lens. For a small loss of quality, tele-converters are a cheap and compact way to increase your focal length: a 300mm lens with a 1.4x converter becomes 420mm, and with a 2x it becomes 600mm. Note, however, that 1.4x and 2x tele-converters reduce the speed of your lens.

For wildlife photography from a safari vehicle, a solid beanbag, which you can make yourself very cheaply, will be necessary to avoid blurred images, and is more useful than a tripod. A clamp with a tripod head screwed onto it can be attached to the vehicle as well. Modern dedicated flash units are easy to use; aside from the obvious need to flash when you photograph at night, you can improve a lot of photos in difficult 'high contrast' or very dull light with some fill-in flash. It pays to have a proper flash unit as opposed to a built-in camera flash.

The resolution of digital cameras is improving the whole time and even the most basic digital SLRs are more than adequate for ordinary prints and enlargements. For professional reproduction cameras with a resolution up to 24 megapixels are available.

Memory space is important. The number of pictures you can fit on a memory card depends on the quality you choose. Calculate in advance how many pictures you can fit on a card and either take enough cards to last for your trip, or take a storage drive onto which you can download the content. A laptop gives the

towns, especially those with significant expatriate communities or tourist flow, have at least one well-stocked 'supermarket'– an overblown designation for what are essentially village stores.

CURIOS Items aimed specifically at tourists are available, but there is nothing like the variety you'll find in Kenya or Tanzania. Typical curios include carvings, batiks, musical instruments, wooden spoons and various soapstone and malachite knick-knacks. There are several curio shops in Kampala, and there's a good craft market

advantage that you can see your pictures properly at the end of each day and edit and delete rejects, but a storage device is lighter and less bulky.

Bear in mind that digital camera batteries, computers and other storage devices need charging, so make sure you have all the chargers, cables and converters with you. Most hotels have charging points, but do enquire about this in advance.

DUST AND HEAT Dust and heat are often a problem. Keep your equipment in a sealed bag and avoid excessive exposure to the sun. Digital cameras are prone to collecting dust particles on the sensor which results in spots on the image. The dirt mostly enters the camera when changing lenses, so be careful when doing this. To some extent photos can be 'cleaned' up afterwards in Photoshop, but this is time-consuming. You can have your camera sensor professionally cleaned, or you can do this yourself with special brushes and swabs made for the purpose, but note that touching the sensor might cause damage and should only be done with the greatest care.

LIGHT The most striking outdoor photographs are often taken during the hour or two of 'golden light', after dawn and before sunset. Shooting in low light may enforce the use of very low shutter speeds, in which case a tripod might be required to avoid camera shake. Some top digital SLR's now give good results with minimal grain when shooting at very high ISO settings which makes low light photography a lot easier and reduces the need of a tripod in many situations. With careful handling, side lighting and back lighting can produce stunning effects, especially in soft light and at sunrise or sunset. Generally, however, it is best to shoot with the sun behind you. When photographing animals or people in the harsh midday sun, images taken in light but even shade are likely to be more effective than those taken in direct sunlight or patchy shade, since the latter conditions create too much contrast.

PROTOCOL In some countries, it is unacceptable to photograph local people without permission, and many people will refuse to pose or will ask for a donation. In such circumstances, don't try to sneak photographs as you might get yourself into trouble. Even the most willing subject will often pose stiffly when a camera is pointed at them; relax them by making a joke, and take a few shots in quick succession to improve the odds of capturing a natural pose.

Ariadne Van Zandbergen is a professional travel and wildlife photographer specialising in Africa. She runs The Africa Image Library. For photo requests, visit www. africaimagelibrary.com or contact her by email at e info@africaimagelibrary.com.

next to the National Theatre. Antique shops are found in the Sheraton Hotel and in the city centre in Colline House.

MEDIA AND COMMUNICATIONS

NEWSPAPERS Uganda has a good English-language press, with the daily *New Vision* and *Monitor* offering the best international coverage as well as local news. The *East African*, a Kenyan weekly, has excellent regional coverage and comment. *Time* and *Newsweek* can be bought at street stalls in Kampala. The bi-weekly *Independent* magazine, produced by independent journalist Andrew Mwenda, provides insightful coverage of current controversies.

RADIO AND TELEVISION An increasingly varied selection of local and national radio stations service Uganda, most of them privately run, and offering listeners a lively mix of talk, hard and soft news, local and other current music – not to mention a litany of dodgy 1970s disco anthems you'd probably forgotten about! The national television channels aren't up to much, but most international hotels and many smaller ones subscribe to DSTV and GTV, multi-channel satellite services featuring the likes of CNN or Sky News as well as movie and sports channels. Bars and restaurants with DSTV and GTV tend to be packed solid on Saturday afternoons during the English football season, and for all other major football events.

TELEPHONE Uganda's land telephone system is reasonably efficient – from overseas, it's definitely one of the easiest African countries to get through to first time. The international code is +256, and area codes are as follows:

Entebbe	0414	Kampala	0414	Mbarara	04854
Fort Portal	04834	Kasese	04834	Mityana	0464
Jinja	0434	Masaka	04814	Mubende	046444
Kabale	04864	Mbale	04544	Tororo	04544

A major recent development in Uganda has been the upsurge of mobile satellite telephones, with services now provided by five companies: MTN, Uganda Telecom, Zain, Warid and Orange. It is rare to meet an employed Ugandan who doesn't own a mobile phone (rather more unusual, admittedly, to meet one who actually has any remaining airtime!). Peak-rate domestic calls between all phone networks cost around Ush250 per minute, depending on which tariff option you select. Calls to East Africa and the UK cost Ush360 per minute. In larger towns, stalls and booths on every block offer calls at slightly higher rates. The satellite networks are remarkably widespread and you'll be surprised to receive (or be able to make) calls from family and friends in the most unlikely places. If you bring your mobile from home, you'll enjoy international roaming – albeit at a significant cost – through a local network. If you intend to make extensive use of a mobile phone it'll be far cheaper to bring a compatible phone with you and insert a local SIM card for Ush3,000 or just buy a cheap phone, fully connected, for as little as US$25. Pay-as-you-go airtime cards are available everywhere. It's worth loading up with a Ush20,000 card in a town when you get the chance; out in the sticks you'll be offered peasant-friendly scratchcards in Ush1,000 denominations – or less!

All of the phone companies provide a good service in Kampala and the main urban centres, but to enjoy the reassurance of maximum possible network coverage out in the sticks, MTN is perhaps the best bet – for specific regions or itineraries, seek advice from your host or tour driver. Mobile numbers are included in this guidebook alongside conventional phone numbers, and generally you're more likely to get through to them more quickly than to land lines, though they also tend to change with greater frequency. If you're calling from outside the country, dial +256 then the full mobile number minus the leading zero. Note that many of the mobile numbers given here are actually the manager's personal line, so don't be surprised if a high proportion of those listed in this book become obsolete a couple of years down the line.

MTN 0772; 0782; 0774 & others
Uganda Telecom 0712
Airtel 0752

Warid 0702
Orange 0792

INTERNET AND EMAIL Email is by far the easiest way to keep in contact with people at home, much cheaper than the telephone, and almost as instantaneous. Assuming that you already have an email address, do check in advance whether your server offers the facility to browse email online through the internet (it will be both costly and complicated to dial your own server internationally to download messages). If not, it's probably worth setting up a temporary address with Hotmail, Yahoo! or any other similar free facility for the duration of your trip, and giving out that address to anybody who might want to contact you.

The number of internet cafés in Kampala seems to increase with every passing week, while browsing rates keep dropping. At the time of writing, there must be a dozen cafés on Kampala Road alone offering cheap internet facilities. Communication by email used to be extremely limited outside Kampala but this has changed. Jinja, Mbale, Masaka, Mbarara, Fort Portal, Kasese and Kabale all offer a choice of internet cafés, while internet facilities are even available by satellite link at such out-of-the-way locations as Lake Bunyonyi and Buhoma (Bwindi).

CULTURAL ETIQUETTE

Ugandans are generally relaxed, friendly and tolerant in their dealings with tourists, and you would have to do something pretty outrageous to commit a serious faux pas there. But, like any country, it does have its rules of etiquette, and while allowances will always be made for tourists, there is some value in ensuring that they are not made too frequently!

GENERAL CONDUCT Perhaps the single most important point of etiquette to be grasped by visitors to Africa is the social importance of formal greetings. Rural Africans tend to greet each other elaborately, and if you want to make a good impression on somebody who speaks English, whether they be a waiter or a shop assistant (and especially if they work in a government department), you would do well to follow suit. When you need to ask directions, it is rude to blunder straight into interrogative mode without first exchanging greetings. Most Ugandans speak some English, but for those who don't the Swahili greeting '*Jambo*' delivered with a smile and a nod of the head will be adequate.

Among Ugandans, it is considered to be in poor taste to display certain emotions publicly. Affection is one such emotion: it is frowned upon for members of the opposite sex to hold hands publicly, and kissing or embracing would be seriously offensive. Oddly, it is quite normal for friends of the same sex to walk around hand in hand. Male travellers who get into a long discussion with a male Ugandan shouldn't be surprised if that person clasps them by the hand and retains a firm grip on their hand for several minutes. This is a warm gesture, one particularly appropriate when the person wants to make a point with which you might disagree. On the subject of intra-gender relations, homosexuality is taboo in Uganda, to the extent that it would require some pretty overt behaviour for it to occur to anybody to take offence.

It is also considered bad form to show anger publicly. It is difficult to know where to draw the line here, because some minibus-taxi conductors in particular act in a manner that positively invites an aggressive response, and I doubt that many people who travel independently in Uganda will get by without the occasional display of impatience. Frankly, I doubt that many bystanders would take umbrage if you responded to a pushy tout with a display of anger, if only because the tout's behaviour itself goes against the grain. By contrast, losing your temper will almost certainly be counter-productive when dealing with obtuse officials, dopey waiters and hotel employees, or unco-operative safari drivers.

Visitors should be aware of the Islamic element in Ugandan society, particularly in Kampala. In Muslim society, it is insulting to use your left hand to pass or receive something or when shaking hands (a custom adhered to in many parts of Africa that aren't Muslim). If you eat with your fingers, it is also customary to use the right hand only. Even those of us who are naturally right-handed will occasionally need to remind ourselves of this (it may happen, for instance, that you are carrying something in your right hand and so hand money to a shopkeeper with your left). For left-handed travellers, it will require a constant effort.

TIPPING AND GUIDES The question of when and when not to tip can be difficult in a foreign country. In Uganda, it is customary to tip your driver/guide at the end of a safari or hike, as well as any cook or porter that accompanies you. A figure of roughly US$5–US$10 per day would be a fair benchmark, though do check this with your safari company in advance. It is not essential to tip the guides who take you around in national parks and other reserves, but it is recommended. A similar sum in shillings would be appreciated, especially if the guide has found you that lion, leopard or shoebill. In both cases, I see no reason why you shouldn't give a bigger or smaller tip based on the quality of service.

In some African countries, it is difficult to travel anywhere without being latched onto by a self-appointed guide, who will often expect a tip over and above any

STUFF YOUR RUCKSACK – AND MAKE A DIFFERENCE

www.stuffyourrucksack.com is a website set up by TV's Kate Humble which enables travellers to give direct help to small charities, schools or other organisations in the country they are visiting. Maybe a local school needs books, a map or pencils, or an orphanage needs children's clothes or toys – all things that can easily be 'stuffed in a rucksack' before departure. The charities get exactly what they need and travellers have the chance to meet local people and see how and where their gifts will be used.

The website describes organisations that need your help and lists the items they most need. Check what's needed in Uganda, contact the organisation to say you're coming and bring not only the much-needed goods but an extra dimension to your travels and the knowledge that in a small way you have made a difference.

agreed fee. This sort of thing is unusual in Uganda, but if you do take on a freelance guide, then it is advisable to clarify in advance that whatever price you agree is final and inclusive of a tip.

It is not customary to tip for service in local bars and *hotelis*, though you may sometimes *want* to leave a tip (in fact, given the difficulty of finding change in Uganda, you may practically be forced into doing this in some circumstances). A tip of 5% would be very acceptable and 10% generous. Generally any restaurant that caters primarily to tourists and to wealthy Ugandan residents will automatically add a service charge to the bill, but since there's no telling where that service charge ends up, it would still be reasonable to reward good service with a cash tip.

BARGAINING AND OVERCHARGING Tourists to Uganda will sometimes need to bargain over prices, but generally this need exists only in reasonably predictable circumstances, for instance when chartering a private taxi, organising a guide, or buying curios and to a lesser extent other market produce. Prices in hotels, restaurants and shops are generally fixed, and overcharging in such places is too unusual for it to be worth challenging a price unless it is blatantly ridiculous.

You may well be overcharged at some point in Uganda, but it is important to keep this in perspective. After a couple of bad experiences, some travellers start to haggle with everybody from hotel owners to old women selling fruit by the side of the road, often accompanying their negotiations with aggressive accusations of dishonesty. Unfortunately, it is sometimes necessary to fall back on aggressive posturing in order to determine a fair price, but such behaviour is also very unfair on those people who are forthright and honest in their dealings with tourists. It's a question of finding the right balance, or better still looking for other ways of dealing with the problem.

The main instance where bargaining is essential is when buying curios. What should be understood, however, is that the fact a curio seller is open to negotiation does not mean that you were initially being overcharged or ripped off. Curio sellers will generally quote a price knowing full well that you are going to bargain it down (they'd probably be startled if you didn't) and it is not necessary to respond aggressively or in an accusatory manner. It is impossible to say by how much you should bargain the initial price down. Some people say that you should offer half the asking price and be prepared to settle at around two-thirds, but my experience is that curio sellers are far more whimsical than such advice allows for. The sensible approach, if you want to get a feel for prices, is to ask the price of similar items at a few different stalls before you actually contemplate buying anything.

At markets and stalls, bargaining is the norm, even between locals, and the healthiest approach to this sort of haggling is to view it as an enjoyable part of the African experience. There will normally be an accepted price band for any particular commodity. To find out what it is, listen to what other people pay and try a few stalls. A ludicrously inflated price will always drop the moment you walk away. It's simpler when buying fruit and vegetables which are generally piled in heaps of Ush500 or Ush1,000. You'll elicit a smile and a few extra items thrown in if you ask 'Yongela ko' meaning 'addition'. Above all, bear in mind that when somebody is reluctant to bargain, it may be because they asked a fair price in the first place.

Minibus-taxi conductors often try to overcharge tourists. The best way to counter this is to check the correct ticket price in advance with an impartial party, and to book your ticket the day before you travel. Failing that, you will have to judge for yourself whether the price is right, and if you have reason to think it isn't, then question the conductor. In such circumstances, it can be difficult to find the right balance between standing up for your rights and becoming overtly obnoxious.

3

A final point to consider on the subject of overcharging and bargaining is that it is the fact of being overcharged that annoys; the amount itself is generally of little consequence in the wider context of a trip to Uganda. Without for a moment wanting to suggest that travellers should routinely allow themselves to be overcharged, I do feel there are occasions when we should pause to look at the bigger picture. Backpackers in particular tend to forget that, no matter how tight for cash they are, it was their choice to travel on a minimal budget, and most Ugandans are much poorer than they will ever be. If you find yourself quibbling over a pittance with an old lady selling a few piles of fruit by the roadside, you might perhaps bear in mind that the notion of a fixed price is a very Western one. When somebody is desperate enough for money, or afraid that their perishable goods might not last another day, it may well be possible to push them down to a price lower than they would normally accept. In such circumstances, I see nothing wrong with erring on the side of generosity.

TRAVELLING POSITIVELY

It goes without saying, or it ought to, that you'll observe a vast difference in Uganda between your standard of living and that of many local people, and many visitors are moved to help. To do so effectively and appropriately can, however, be difficult; there are plenty of tricksters looking to fleece well-meaning donors with school-fee scams, as well as the odd dodgy pastor using bogus community campsites/volunteer schemes to line their own pockets. Rather than handing out cash, a good way to be certain of making a difference is to stuff empty spaces in your rucksack with items that are hugely useful but which are costly or unavailable in Uganda. Check out www.sanyubabies.com before you travel. **Sanyu Babies Home** (see page 152) (℡ *0414 274032*; m *0712 370950*; e *barbara@sanyubabies.com*) is a charitable foundation that cares for orphaned, destitute and abandoned babies until they are adopted or graduate to orphanages. An annual needs list on the website includes 24 large tubs of Sudocrem, 21,900 disposable nappies and 2,160 tins of formula milk – all items easily bought in Europe or North America and stuffed into a empty corner in a suitcase or rucksack. Sanyu Babies Home also welcomes volunteers and paying guests; accommodation on site is provided in a pleasantly homely guesthouse (US$25 shared facilities). The home is found on the side of Namimembe Hill on Natete Road just before Mengo Hospital. It's a particularly convenient place to visit: many budget and independent travellers stay in this area, while tourists staying in central hotels will invariably pass the gate on their way to/from destinations in western Uganda.

If you're moved to support the Uganda Wildlife Authority's struggle to protect Uganda's wildlife, visit www.ugandacf.org to learn about the work of the **Uganda Conservation Foundation**. UCF supports UWA with much-needed infrastructure, equipment, training and support for research. Recent activities include the construction of ranger posts in Queen Elizabeth and Murchison Falls national parks, donation of bicycles and patrol boats, training of boat coxwains, a hippo survey in QENP and the refurbishment of a veterinary vehicle for MFNP. Administration costs are kept to a minimum (the directors, of which I am proud to be one, are unpaid) and 90% of funding is channelled directly into conservation action. If you would like to support UCF in the the US, a 501C facility can be accessed on the website. See also advert on page 129.

Part Two

THE GUIDE

4

Kampala and Around

Situated on rolling hills some 10km inland of the lake, Kampala, the economic and social hub of Uganda, is the archetypal African capital – more verdant than many of its counterparts, not quite so populous or chaotic as others – but essentially the familiar juxtaposition of a bustling compact high-rise city centre rising from a leafy suburban sprawl, increasingly organic in appearance as one reaches its rustic periphery.

As a city, Kampala's history dates back to the arrival of Captain Frederick Lugard, who established his camp on the stumpy Kampala Hill in 1890. However, the more prominent of the surrounding hills had already been used by the Bugandan *kabakas* for their *kibugas* (citadels). Kasubi Hill, only 2.5km northwest of the modern city centre, served briefly as the capital of Kabaka Suuna II in the 1850s, and it also housed the palace of Kabaka Mutesa I from 1882–84, while Mengo Hill formed the capital of Mutesa's successor Mwanga, as it has every subsequent kabaka. The name Kampala derives from the Luganda expression Kosozi Kampala – Hill of Antelope – a reference to the domestic impala that cropped the lawns of Mengo during Mutesa's reign.

In the first decade of the post-independence era, Kampala was widely regarded to be the showpiece of the East African community: a spacious garden city with a cosmopolitan atmosphere and bustling trade. It was also a cultural and educational centre of note, with Makerere University regarded as the academic heart of East Africa. Under Amin, however, Kampala's status started to deteriorate, especially after the Asian community was forced to leave Uganda. By 1986, when the civil war ended, Kampala was in complete chaos: skeletal buildings scarred with bullet holes dotted the city centre, shops and hotels were boarded up after widespread looting, and public services had ground to a halt, swamped by the huge influx of migrants from war-torn parts of the country.

These days, Kampala is practically unrecognisable from the dire incarnation of the mid-1980s. The main shopping area along **Kampala Road** might be that of any African capital, while the edge of the city centre has seen the development of a clutch of bright, modern supermarkets and shopping malls. The area immediately north of Kampala Road, where foreign embassies and government departments rub shoulders with renovated tourist hotels, is as smart as any part of Nairobi or Dar es Salaam. Admittedly it's a different story downhill of Kampala Road where overcrowded backstreets, congested with hooting minibus-taxis and swerving boda-boda drivers, reveal a more representative face of Kampala – the city as most of its residents see it.

Kampala is not only smarter than it used to be but considerably larger. These days it covers almost 200km² as the population has risen from 330,000 in 1969 to at least 1.65 million inhabitants today – a figure easily ten times greater than any other town in Uganda.

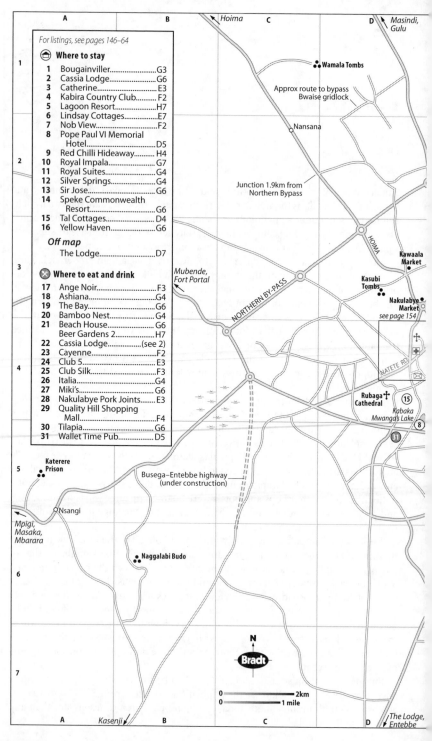

For listings, see pages 146–64

🛏 Where to stay

1 Bougainviller...................G3
2 Cassia Lodge..................G6
3 Catherine.......................E3
4 Kabira Country Club..........F2
5 Lagoon Resort.................H7
6 Lindsay Cottages................E7
7 Nob View.......................F2
8 Pope Paul VI Memorial
  Hotel............................D5
9 Red Chilli Hideaway..........H4
10 Royal Impala..................G7
11 Royal Suites...................G4
12 Silver Springs.................G4
13 Sir Jose........................G6
14 Speke Commonwealth
  Resort..........................G6
15 Tal Cottages..................D4
16 Yellow Haven..................G6

Off map
The Lodge........................D7

✕ Where to eat and drink

17 Ange Noir......................F3
18 Ashiana.........................G4
19 The Bay.........................G6
20 Bamboo Nest...................G4
21 Beach House...................G6
   Beer Gardens 2.................H7
22 Cassia Lodge..............(see 2)
23 Cayenne.........................F2
24 Club 5..........................E3
25 Club Silk.......................F3
26 Italia...........................G4
27 Miki's...........................G6
28 Nakulabye Pork Joints......E3
29 Quality Hill Shopping
   Mall.............................F4
30 Tilapia..........................G6
31 Wallet Time Pub...............D5

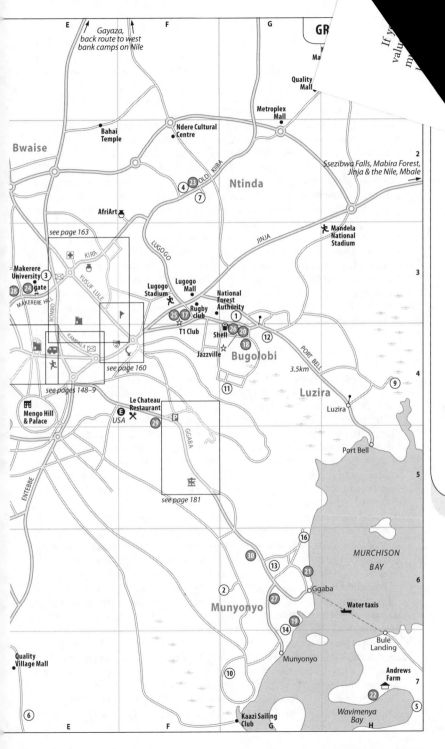

E ↗ *Gayaza,
back route to west
bank camps on Nile*

F

G

GR

Ma

**Quality
Mall**

**Metroplex
Mall**

**Bahai
Temple**

**Ndere Cultural
Centre**

Bwaise

OLD KIRA

④ ㉓

Ntinda

⑦

2

*Ssezibwa Falls, Mabira Forest,
Jinja & the Nile, Mbale* →

AfriArt ⚓

see page 163

KIRA

⚕

✡ **Mandela
National
Stadium**

JINJA

LUGOGO

**Makerere
University** ③
gate
㉘ ㉔

YUSUF LULE

MAKERERE HILL

BOMBO

KAMPALA

**Lugogo
Stadium**

**Lugogo
Mall**

**National
Forest
Authority**

🏃

㉕ ㉗
☆

**Rugby
club**

①

3

㉖ ㉚
Shell

㉘

⑫

T1 Club

see page 160

Jazzville
☆

Bugolobi

3.5km

PORT BELL

Luzira

⑨

4

see pages 148–9

⑪

Luzira

**Mengo Hill
& Palace**

**Le Chateau
Restaurant**

Ⓔ ✕
USA

P

㉙

GGABA

Port Bell

ENTEBBE

see page 181

🏛

5

**MURCHISON
BAY**

⑯

㉚

⑬

㉑

Ggaba

6

②

㉗

Munyonyo

Water taxis 🚤

⑲

⑭

**Bule
Landing**

Munyonyo

**Andrews
Farm** 🏠

⑩

**Quality
Village Mall**

⑥

E

F

**Kaazi Sailing
Club**

G

*Wavimenya
Bay*

㉒

⑤

H

7

ju're looking for a smart, international-standard hotel (or indeed a good
: budget hotel), a splendid choice of cuisine, shopping opportunities, live
isic and the latest movie – or just a taste of urban African life – you'll probably
ove Kampala. Compared with the likes of Nairobi or Dar es Salaam, it's a

BUGANDA: AN INTRODUCTION

Kampala lies at the political and geographical heart of the Kingdom of Buganda,
home to the Baganda (singular Muganda), who form the largest single ethnic group
in Uganda, comprising more than 20% of the national population. The kingdom
originally consisted of four counties: Kyadondo, Busiro, Busujju and Mawokota. It
expanded greatly during the early to mid 18th century, mainly at the expense of
Bunyoro, to extend over 20 counties, as well as the semi-autonomous Ssese Islands.
During the colonial era, Buganda remained a kingdom with unique privileges, but
it was relegated to provincial status after Obote abolished the monarchy in 1966.
Today, Buganda is divided across nine administrative districts: Kampala, Mpigi,
Mukono, Masaka, Kalangala, Kiboga, Rakai, Sembabule and Mubende.

Buganda is ruled by a kabaka, an autocratic monarch whose position, though
hereditary, is confined to no single clan. Traditionally, the kabaka would marry
into as many clans as possible – Stanley estimated Mutesa's female entourage to
number 5,000, of which at least one-tenth were members of the royal harem –
and his heir would take the clan of his mother, a custom that encouraged loyalty
to the throne insofar as each of the 52 clans could hope that it would one day
produce a king. Mutesa, who held the throne when Speke arrived in Buganda
in 1862, is listed by tradition as the 30th kabaka. Although the dates of Mutesa's
predecessors' reigns are a matter for conjecture, an average duration of a decade
would place the foundation of Buganda in the mid 16th century, while 20 years
would push it back into the 13th century.

The founding kabaka of Buganda was Kintu, who, it is widely agreed, came to
power after defeating a despotic local ruler called Bemba. Kintu is otherwise the
subject of several conflicting traditions. Some say that he descended from the
heavens via Bunyoro, others that he originated from the Ssese Islands, or was
indigenous to the area, or – most credible perhaps – that he arrived in Buganda
from beyond Mount Elgon, suggesting an origin in Sudan or Ethiopia. The identity
of Kintu is further confused by the Kiganda creation legend asserting that Kintu was
the name of the first man on earth (see box, pages 6–7). A common tradition holds
that Kintu, having defeated the unpopular Bemba, took over his house at Nagalabi
Buddo, about 20km west of present-day Kampala, as a spoil of victory. The house
was called Buganda, a name that was later transferred to all the territory ruled by
Kintu. Nagalabi Buddo remains the coronation site of the kabaka to this day.

Traditional Buganda society allowed for some upward and downward mobility
– any talented person could rise to social prominence – but it was nevertheless
strongly stratified, with three distinct classes recognised. The highest class was the
hereditary Balangira (aristocracy), which based its right to rule on royal blood. In
addition to the kabaka, several aristocratic figureheads were recognised, including
the *namasole* (queen mother), *lubuga* (king's sister) and *katikiro* (prime minister).
Other persons who occupied positions of political and social importance were the
gabunga and *mujasi*, the respective commanders of the royal navy and army.

The middle class in Baganda society consisted of chiefs or *baami*. Initially, the
status of the baami was hereditary, enjoyed solely by the *bataka* (clan heads). After

remarkably safe city to explore. If however, your main reason for visiting Uganda is its natural history, then you'll be much better off staying a night in Entebbe and then pushing on upcountry. Sightseeing options in and around Kampala are in any case pretty limited (see pages 170–9), but the main reason for giving

1750, however, *bakopi* men could be promoted by royal appointment to baami status, on the basis of distinguished service and/or ability. A hierarchic system of chieftaincy existed, corresponding with the importance of the political unit over which any given chief held sway. The most important administrative division was the Saza (county), each of which was ruled by a Saza chief. These were further subdivided into Gombolola (sub-counties), then into parishes and sub-parishes, and finally Bukungu, which were more or less village units. The kabaka had the power to appoint or dismiss any chief at will, and all levels of baami were directly responsible to him.

At the bottom of the social strata was the serf class known as the *bakopi*: literally, the people who don't matter. The bakopi were subsistence farmers, whose labour (as tends to be the case with those who matter not to their more socially elevated masters) formed the base of Buganda's agricultural economy. Many bakopi kept chickens and larger livestock, but they were primarily occupied with agriculture – the local staple of bananas, supplemented by sweet potatoes, cassava, beans and green vegetables. The bakopi were dependent on land to farm, but they had no right to it. All land in Buganda was the property of the kabaka, who could allocate (or rescind) the right of usage to any subsidiary chief at whim. The chiefs, in turn, allocated their designated quota of land as they deemed fit – a scenario that encouraged the bakopi to obedience. Peasant men and women were regularly sacrificed by the aristocracy – Kabaka Suuna, during one bout of illness, is said to have ordered 100 bakopi to be slaughtered daily until he was fully recovered.

Kiganda, the traditional religion of Buganda (discussed more fully in the box on pages 184–5) is essentially animist, in thrall not to a supreme being but rather a variety of ancestral and other spirits. Temples dedicated to the most powerful spirits were each served by a medium and a hereditary priest, who would liaise between the spirit and the people. The priests occupied a place of high religious and political importance – even the most powerful kabaka would consult with appropriate spirit mediums before making an important decision or going into battle. The kabaka appointed at least one female slave or relative to tend each shrine and provide food and drink to its priest and medium.

The traditions of Buganda are enormously complex, and the kingdom's history is packed with incident and anecdote. The above is intended as a basic overview, to be supplemented by more specific information on various places, events, characters and crafts elsewhere in this book. Readers whose interest is whetted rather than sated by this coverage are pointed to the informative website www.buganda.com, and to Richard Reid's excellent *Political Power in Pre-Colonial Buganda* (James Currey, 2002), a comprehensive source of information about most aspects of traditional Baganda society. Many old and out-of-print editions of the *Uganda Journal* also contain useful essays on pre-colonial Buganda – they can be viewed at the Uganda Society Library in the National Museum of Uganda in Kampala (see page 171).

the capital a wide berth is the horrendous traffic that results as the population, plus daily commuters from surrounding districts, attempt to move around in a motley assortment of private vehicles, buses, *matatus* and boda-bodas. If you *do* stay in Kampala, establish what you want to do and find lodgings in that part of town. Spending the evening sitting in 'the jam' instead of a selected restaurant or cinema is no fun at all. Of course, if you're at home on a boda-boda and happy for the lunatic of your choice to whizz you through the gridlock, then ignore this paragraph and have fun!

KAMPALA – GETTING ORIENTATED

Kampala might have long outgrown its initial seven hills but it remains a simple matter to remain orientated within the urban sprawl. Uganda's capital covers a landscape of distinct hills separated by swampy valleys draining into Lake Victoria. Many of these hills, both the historic seven (those included here are marked *) and others settled more recently, bear landmarks that mean that you need never get completely lost in Greater Kampala. This happy situation contrasts starkly with, say, Nairobi and Dar es Salaam, where geography is less helpful.

The city's most obvious reference point is the modern multi-storeyed city centre on Nakasero Hill. This is ringed by more discreet, but no less identifiable landmarks on neighbouring summits. These are described here moving clockwise around Nakasero, starting with **Old Kampala Hill***, just a few hundred metres southwest of the city centre. This stumpy knoll attained initial significance as the site of Lugard's 1899 encampment, but since the 1970s has provided central Kampala with its most dramatic reference point. Initially, this was the shell of an unfeasibly tall tower, noted for a distinct list halfway up, rising above an incomplete mosque initiated by Idi Amin. This well-loved folly was demolished around 2001 to make way for the magnificent new Old Kampala Mosque (see page 171) with its more practically proportioned tower. Due south of Old Kampala, the kabaka's palace stands on the broad, low hill of **Lubiri*** (see pages 174–5). This circular area, a full kilometre in diameter, remains mostly undeveloped and is conspicuous as a green expanse, enclosed within a crumbling brick wall in an area of low-rent housing and workshops. Lubiri is neighboured by **Namirembe*** and **Rubaga*** hills, topped by the Anglican and Catholic cathedrals respectively. St Paul's on Namirembe is identified by its dome (more modest than that of its London namesake but still striking) and Rubaga Cathedral by two bell towers. Moving northeast from Namirembe, the white bell tower of Uganda's oldest university is visible on the leafy ridge of Makerere. Looking north from Kisementi and Kiira Road, the striking Bahá'í temple is conspicuous on a grassy hill off the Gayaza road. Immediately behind Kisementi is leafy Kololo, the city's highest hill and the site of many embassies and diplomatic residences. South of Jinja Road, a cluster of white minarets and palm trees mark **Kibuli* Mosque**, where Uganda's first Islamic visitors settled in the mid 19th century. Just south of Kibuli is the upmarket Muyenga Hill, on which posh homes mushroomed during Kampala's 1990s renaissance. Popularly known as 'Tank Hill' after the conspicuous municipal water reservoirs on its summit, Muyenga is an effective beacon for the nightspots of Kabalagala and Ggaba Road at its base.

BY AIR Fly-in visitors will arrive in Uganda at **Entebbe International Airport**, which lies on the Lake Victoria shore about 3km from Entebbe Town. If you arrive outside banking hours, there are 24-hour foreign-exchange facilities at the airport. Historically, these used to offer dreadful rates compared with private forex bureaux in Kampala, and while their rates have improved of late, it's still worth waiting until you get into town for larger sums. Special **hire taxis** from the airport cost around US$5 to Entebbe and US$25 to Kampala. Airport collection can also be arranged in advance through most tour operators and upmarket hotels in Kampala and Entebbe. Several of the latter send their buses along to pick pre-booked clients and hopefully some additional trade.

The cheapest and simplest option is to take the regular **City Bus shuttle** (Ush1,200) to Kampala from the main public car park. Alternatively, take a **shared taxi** from the airport to Kitoro in Entebbe to hop on a **public minibus** to Kampala. This is safe enough during daylight hours, but probably not too sensible after dark. If you do arrive in Kampala (or any major African city) after dark with all your luggage, it's best to find a reasonable bed quickly and wait for the morning to locate more comfortable/affordable/quieter lodgings if this proves necessary.

If you're heading out to the airport from Kampala, minibuses to Entebbe leave from both the old and the new taxi park. Buses leave from the Entebbe Road end of Nasser Road.

Travel companies and airlines

✈ **Global Interlink Travel Services Ltd** [149 F3] Grand Imperial Hotel; ☎ 04142 35233; e global@global-interlink.org; www.global-interlink.org

✈ **Travelcare** [135 F3] Unit 16, Lugogo Mall; m 0754 222600; e declan@travelcare.co.ug; www.travelcare.co.ug

✈ **Uganda Travel Bureau** (UTB-2004 Ltd) [149 H3] ☎ 0312 223255/0414 335335; emergency 24hr line: m 0772 232555; e info@utb.co.ug; www.utb.co.ug

The following international airlines fly into/out of Entebbe:

✈ **Air Tanzania** [149 G4] Ground Fl, Workers Hse, Pilkington Rd; ☎ 0414 255501; www.airtanzania.com. Flights to & from Dar es Salaam on Tue, Thu, Fri & Sun.

✈ **Air Uganda** [160 B4] 14 Parliament Av; ☎ 0412 165555; www.air-uganda.com

✈ **British Airways** [149 H1] Centre Ct, 4 Ternan Av; ☎ 0414 257414–6; e contactba.1.uganda@britishairways.com; www.britishairways.com. Overnight flights from London Heathrow on Tue, Thu & Sun, returning daytime Mon, Wed & Fri.

✈ **Brussels Airlines** [149 F2] Rwenzori Hse, Lumumba Av; ☎ 0414 234200–2; http://uganda.brusselsairlines.com. Overnight flights from Entebbe to Brussels on Mon, Wed & Fri; daytime flights from Brussels to Entebbe on the same days.

✈ **EgyptAir** [149 F3] Grand Imperial Arcade, Speke Rd; ☎ 0414 233960; m 0772 200119; e egyptairuganda@africaonline.com; www.egyptair.com. Flights to & from Cairo on Sun only, with good connections to Europe.

✈ **Emirates** [149 H3] FNC Bldg, Kimathi Av; ☎ 0414 349941–4; www.emirates.com. Daily flights to Dubai with connections to Europe, the Far East & the US.

✈ **Ethiopian Airways** [149 H3] United Assurance Bldg, Kimathi Av; ☎ 0414 345577/8, 0414 254796/7; www.flyethiopian.com. 5 flights weekly to/from Addis Ababa, with connections to 2 dozen other African cities, several European capitals, as well as the US.

✈ **Kenya Airways** [160 B4] Jubilee Centre, 11 Parliament Av; ☎ 0312 236000/0414 233068; www.kenya-airways.com. Several flights daily

4

between Entebbe & Nairobi, with connecting flights most days to London Heathrow, Dar es Salaam & Johannesburg.

✈ **KLM Royal Dutch Airlines** [160 B4] 14 Parliament Av, Jubilee Insurance Bldg, 3rd Fl, ☏ 0414 338000/1; www.klm.com. Direct night flights to Amsterdam 3 times a week on Tue, Fri & Sat with connections to Europe, the US & Canada.

✈ **Precision Air** [160 B4] c/o Kenya Airways, Jubilee Centre, 11 Parliament Av; ☏ 0312 236000/0414 233068. Flights to Kilimanjaro & Mwanza on Mon & Sat.

EARLY DAYS IN KAMPALA

The original city centre – little more than a fort and a few mud houses – stood on the hill known today as Old Kampala. Its early expansion and urbanisation from 1897 onwards is best catalogued in the memoirs of two early settlers, the medical pioneer Sir Albert Cook (arrived 1897) and W E Hoyle (arrived 1903), both of which were published in early (and long out of print) editions of the *Uganda Journal*, the main sources of what follows. Unattributed quotes relating to before 1903 are from Cook.

Conditions for the few settlers in Kampala in 1897 were rudimentary. Imported provisions were scarce, and when available at the town's two English stores they were very expensive. Most settlers suffered ongoing health problems, often related to malaria, which had not yet been connected to mosquito bites. The settlers lived in simple abodes made of reeds, elephant grass and thatch, with a stamped mud floor 'cow-dunged once a week to keep out jiggers'. Cook, a doctor, performed his first operations 'on a camp bedstead, the instruments sterilised in our cooking saucepans, and laid out in vegetable dishes filled with antiseptics'. A 12-bed hospital, built in the local style, opened in May 1897, and a larger one was constructed three years later, only to be destroyed in a lightning strike in 1902. Still, Cook 'introduced the natives to the advantages of anaesthetics and antiseptics' and also started a programme of vaccinations after a chief warned him that a smallpox epidemic was approaching the capital.

The arrival of the telegraph line in April 1900 was a major boon to the remote community, allowing it regular contact with the coast and to keep abreast of world affairs. Cook notes that: 'this happy condition of affairs did not last long, however, for where the line passed through the Nandi country it was constantly being cut down. On one occasion no less than sixty miles [100km] of wire were removed and coiled into bracelets or cut into pieces and used as slugs for their muzzle-loading guns.' More significant still was the arrival of the Mombasa Railway at Kisumu, in December 1901, connected by a steamer service to Entebbe. Not only did this facilitate personal travel between Kampala and the coast, but it also allowed for the freight of imported goods on an unprecedented scale.

Prior to the arrival of the railway, most buildings in Kampala had been thatched firetraps, routinely destroyed by lightning strikes – not only Cook's hospital, but also the first cathedral at Namirembe, the telegraph office, a trading store and several private homesteads. Now, permanent brick buildings could be erected, with corrugated-iron roofing, proper guttering and cement floors, all of which made for more hygienic living, as well as reducing the risk of destruction by fire. The railway also improved the quality of life for the small European community by attracting 'a flood of Indian shopkeepers' and associated 'influx of European trade goods'.

The original European settlement, as already mentioned, stood atop Old Kampala Hill. To its east, an ever-growing local township sprawled downhill to where Nakivubo Stadium [148 B5] and Owino Market [148 B6] stand today.

✈ **Rwandair Express** [149 F2] Rwenzori Courts; ☎ 0414 344851; www.rwandair.com. Flights to Kigali (Rwanda) daily except Sat & daily to Nairobi.
✈ **South Africa Airways** [149 G4] Workers Hse, Pilkington Rd; ☎ 0414 255501/2; f 0414 255825;

www.saa.co.za. Flights to/from Johannesburg on Wed, Fri & Sun.
✈ **Turkish Airlines** [160 B2] Ruth Towers, Clement Hill Rd, Nakasero; m 0788 006296; www. turkishairlines.com. Flights to Europe & USA via Istanbul.

The present-day city centre took shape as an indirect result of the improved transportation to the coast via Kisumu. It was, Hoyle writes: 'realised by the government that the space below Kampala Fort was inadequate to meet growing trade, and they decided to start a new township on the more expansive hill named Nakasero, half a mile [0.8km] to the east. Already by 1903 a new fort had been built there [and] by 1905 practically all government offices and staff and traders' shops had been moved to Nakasero.' Over the next few years, writes Cook, the government had 'good roads cut and well laid out in the new town ... bordered with trees' – essentially the nascent modern city centre, which slopes across the valley dividing Old Kampala from Nakasero Hill.

The Mombasa Railway also facilitated the export trade out of Uganda, which until 1906 consisted primarily of wild animal produce such as hide, skins and ivory, controlled by an Italian and an American firm, as well as the Indian storekeeper Allidina Visram. Hoyle writes: 'It was a memorable sight to see frequent safaris laden with ivory tusks filing towards Kampala from the strip of country between the Congo Free State and Uganda Protectorate, which at that point was in dispute, a kind of no-man's-land and therefore the elephant-hunters' paradise.' Hoyle writes elsewhere of Allidina Visram's store that in 1903 it was 'to Europeans, the most important ... existence almost entirely depended on [it], for his firm not only supplied the necessities of life, but in the absence of any bank it provided ready money in exchange for a cheque'.

Oddly, perhaps, English money held no currency in Kampala's early days. The Indian rupee was effectively the official currency, equivalent to one English shilling and four pence. But Hoyle writes that: 'the most generally used currency among the Baganda was cowrie shells ... one thousand to the rupee ... through which a hole had been made for threading ... using banana fibre. The Baganda were very adept at counting shells, usually strung in hundreds ... It was amusing, having paid a porter ... five thousand shells, to see him sit down and count them ... report that he was one, two, or maybe up to five short, and it was easier to throw these to him from a quantity of loose shells kept in a bag for that purpose.' Cowries continued in general use until about 1905, and were still employed in petty trade until 1922, when the shilling was introduced.

Last word to Hoyle, and an improbable anecdote relating to Sir Hesketh Bell, Governor of Uganda from 1905–09: 'Bell conceived the idea that elephants might be trained to do the many useful jobs they do in India. The experiment was made of bringing a trained elephant from India. It was a great business getting the elephant aboard the [ferry] at Kisumu and landing it in Entebbe. [Bell] came to Kampala to make a triumphant entry riding the elephant, mounting it two miles outside the township. He was greeted by a large crowd of Europeans and Baganda. Some young elephants were caught, but the experiment of training them was not successful, and eventually the Indian elephant was sold to a menagerie in Europe.'

Kampala and Around   GETTING THERE AND AWAY

4

BY RAIL Travelling by train is not a viable option. There used to be two internal rail services in Uganda, one connecting Kampala to Kasese in the west, and the other connecting Kampala to Pakwach via Tororo and Gulu. Neither service was much used by travellers, because the trains were very slow and unreliable, and both were suspended in 1997 with little likelihood of resuming in the foreseeable future. The weekly overnight train service between Kampala and Nairobi, at one time the most attractive means of transport between these cities, has also been suspended on an indefinite basis.

BY BOAT It's been years since any official passenger boats ran out of Port Bell, Uganda's main ferry port, 10km southeast of Kampala. The ferry service between Port Bell and Mwanza (Tanzania) was aborted following the sinking of the MV *Bukoba* in 1996 (in which as many as 1,000 people are thought to have drowned) and there seem to be no plans to restore it. **Cargo boats** between Port Bell and Mwanza will sometimes take passengers, however, and many travellers crossing between Tanzania and Uganda use the thrice-weekly **overnight ferry** from Mwanza to Bukoba, which connects with a direct bus service to Kampala via Masaka. For further information, try ringing the Port Bell ferry office (℡ *0414 221336*).

BY BUS
Minibus-taxis Kampala's minibus-taxi station was once the most chaotic in East Africa: several hundred minibuses, identical in appearance bar the odd bit of panel-beating and with no indication as to their destination, all sardine-packed into a couple of acres of seething madness. To counter this, the city council built a second taxi station about 100m from the first – which means that Kampala now boasts the

BUGANDA'S FIRST FEMINIST?

The life of a *mumbeja* – a Muganda princess – wasn't quite as romantic as it might sound. The sisters of the kabaka generally lived a life close to bondage, as ladies-in-waiting to the king, at risk of being put to death for any perceived breach of conduct. Marriage was forbidden to the king's sisters and daughters, as was casual sex or becoming pregnant – and the punishment for transgressing any of these taboos was death by cremation.

The first princess to break the mould was Clara Nalumansi, a daughter of Mutesa I. Nalumansi angered Mwanga by converting to Islam during the first year of his reign, and further aggravated him by publicly reconverting to Catholicism in May 1886. Then, in early 1887, Princess Clara capitalised on her rights as a Christian – in the process scandalising the whole of Buganda – by tying the marital knot with another convert, a former page of Mwanga named Yosef Kadu.

The admirable princess didn't stop there. Shortly after her marriage, Clara was appointed to succeed the recently deceased *namasole* of Kabaka Junju, a charge that, traditionally, would have entailed her moving permanently to a house alongside Junju's tomb and tending the royal shrine in solitude for the rest of her days. Instead, Clara and Yosef arrived at the tomb, chased away the attendant spirit medium, then cleared the previous namasole's house of every last fetish and charm, and dumped the lot on a bonfire.

Clara's next move? Well, it's customary for the umbilical cord of a Muganda princess – and all other royals for that matter – to be removed with care and

two most chaotic taxi parks in East Africa. Minibuses to most destinations west of Kampala leave from the **new taxi park** [148 A3], while minibuses to Port Bell and destinations east of Kampala leave from the **old taxi park** [148 D5]. Local minibuses leave for Entebbe from both taxi parks every few minutes. Prices are generally slightly higher than bus fares, but departures are far more regular – before noon, you're unlikely to wait for more than 30 minutes for a minibus to leave for Jinja, Tororo, Mbale, Kabale, Kasese, Mityana, Mubende, Fort Portal, Masindi, Gulu or Hoima.

Note: As I write in early 2013, the taxi park is closed for renovation and taxis leave instead from an assortment of scattered parking yards and roadsides. Apparently, it should reopen by the end of 2013, but you never can tell in Kampala.

Buses Most bus services operate out of, or from sites close to, the central bus station. Officially titled the Qualicell bus terminal, it is more commonly known as the **Buganda bus park** [148 B4]. This lies between the two taxi parks, enhancing the general aura of chaos in this astonishingly congested part of town –even boda-bodas think twice before attempting the 200m section between Namirembe Road and Luwum Street. There are regular departures – every one to two hours from around 07.00 until noon – for most of the destinations listed above, though it's worth checking out departure times and booking a day ahead to save waiting around on the day. Note that public transport fares are hiked immediately before holiday periods such as Easter and Christmas when Kampala's multi-tribal society moves out *en masse* to their home areas. These increases are only partially due to opportunistic profiteering; they also compensate for vehicles returning almost empty to Kampala at these times.

4

preserved until they die, when it is buried with the rest of the body. So Clara dug out her umbilical cord from wherever it was stored, cut it into little pieces, and chucked it out – leading to further public outcry and a call for both her and her husband to be executed.

The general mood of unrest in Buganda in late 1887 diverted attention from the Christian couple and gave them temporary respite. But not for long. In December, Clara placed herself back in the spotlight when she arranged for an immense elephant tusk, placed by her grandfather Kabaka Suuna at a shrine dedicated to the water god Mukasa, to be removed from its sacred resting place.

The errant princess's luck ran out in August 1888, a month before Mwanga was forced into exile, when she was killed by a gunshot fired by a person or persons unknown. Not entirely incredibly, her relatives claimed that the assassination was arranged by Mwanga, who – characteristically paranoid – feared that the English Christians might follow the British example and name the princess as the new ruler of Buganda.

More than a century after her death, it's impossible to know what to make of Princess Clara Nalumansi's singular story. Quite possibly she was just a religious crank, recently converted to Christianity and set on a self-destructive collision course with martyrdom. But it's more tempting, and I think credible, to remember her as a true rebel: a proto-feminist whose adoption of Christianity was not a matter of blind faith, but rather a deliberately chosen escape route from the frigid birthright of a *mumbeja*.

Details of buses plying the route between Kampala and upcountry destinations are given in relevant chapters and on pages 115–16. The fastest means of travel is with private bus companies who have an obvious interest in getting from A to B as fast as possible. If safety is your priority however, it's generally accepted that the slower **Post Bus** [149 F4] (\ *0414 236436/256539*) is the best option (see page 115). Services to major towns run daily between 07.00 and 08.00 from the main post office on Kampala Road and tickets are booked from Counter 18 inside the building. For details of **international bus services** to and from Kampala, see pages 82–5.

GETTING AROUND

BY CAR

Car hire Poor roads make vehicle hire relatively costly in Uganda. Most expat/tourist-oriented safari companies charge well in excess of US$100 per day for a 4x4 with driver (but excluding fuel) but it's still possible to get some good deals.

🚗 **Alpha Rent A Car** [163 A5] \ 0414 344332; www.alpharentals.co.ug. This Kampala-based company offers excellent rates. A 4x4 for upcountry use with a driver excluding fuel costs US$95/day. A saloon used around Kampala costs US$50 with a driver & fuel, or US$35 without fuel. See also advert on page 132.

🚗 **Road Trip Uganda** m 0773 363012; e info@roadtripuganda.com; www. roadtripuganda.com. This new Dutch outfit provides Rav4 cars equipped with everything you need for a camping trip (tent, sleeping bags, mattresses, pillows, cooking utensils, BBQ roaster, cool box, storage box, chairs, headlights, maps – even a Bradt guide). How this all fits into a Rav4 I have no idea! Very attractive rates between US$50–70/day. See also advert in third colour section.

🚗 **Viva Safaris** [149 H3] m 0755 65020; e vivian@vivasafaris.net; www.vivasafaris.net. Another great deal – a 4x4 with driver costs US$70 while a saloon costs US$50, excluding fuel. Discounts available for long-term use.

The major international car-hire companies **Avis** (\ *0414 320516;* m *0752 694843; freephone* \ *0870 606 0100 (UK), +1 800 230 4898 (US); www.avis.com*) and **Hertz** (\ *0414 347191; freephone* \ *0870 848 4848 (UK), +1 800 654 3131 (US);* e *hertz-u@ africaonline.co.ug; www.hertz.com*) are both represented in Kampala, though you'll get better deals from local car-hire operators. It is advisable to make arrangements before you travel using their freephone central reservations services or websites.

Driving courses Courses are available at **On Course** [190 C1] (*5km off Entebbe Rd, just beyond Kajjansi;* m *0772 221107; www.OnCourse4wd.com; courses with your own vehicle cost US$240/day*). First-time drivers in Africa can learn how to cope with the hazards of dirt roads at On Course's training ground in a tract of remnant swamp forest (rich in birdlife). A network of tracks duplicates wet and dry conditions.

TAXIS (SHARED) A steady stream of minibus-taxis plies most trunk roads through Kampala, picking up and dropping off passengers more or less at whim, and charging around Ush1,000–3,000 per person depending on the routing. Unlike in many other African capitals, the minibuses are seldom overcrowded – police and passengers alike actively ensure that conductors adhere to the maximum of three passengers per row – and I've neither experienced nor heard of anything to suggest that pickpockets are a cause for concern.

It can be confusing coming to terms with minibus-taxi routes in Kampala, particularly as the routes are unnumbered and the minibuses seldom have their destination marked. Heading from the suburbs into central Kampala is pretty straightforward, however, since you can safely assume that any minibus pointed towards the city centre along a trunk route is going your way. Heading out from the city centre can be more daunting. At the time of writing the taxi park is closed for renovation until late 2013 but ordinarily, if you're heading to anywhere along the Natete and Hoima roads (for instance Kampala Backpackers, Namirembe Guesthouse, Kasubi Tombs) you're best off heading straight to the new taxi park to pick up a vehicle. Minibuses to most other parts of the city leave from the old taxi park, but in several instances it's easier to intercept them along Kampala Road – east of the junction with Entebbe Road for Red Chilli Hideaway and other places along Port Bell Road, northwest of the junction with Burton Street for Bombo Road, Makerere University, the National Museum, etc. When in doubt, the conductors are normally pretty helpful, assuming that they can speak English, or you can ask one of your fellow passengers.

TAXIS (SPECIAL HIRE) Conventional taxis – generally referred to as special hires – are usually easy to locate within the city centre and normally charge a negotiable Ush10,000 or so for short trips and up to Ush40,000 for longer rides or travel during congested hours. **Taxi stands** can be found outside most of the upmarket hotels, on Dastur Street close to the intersection with Kampala Road, on Ben Kiwanuka Street opposite the old taxi park, near the junction of Navibuko and Kyagwe streets behind the new taxi park, and at the roundabout at the junction of Bombo and Makerere Hill roads. Any hotel or decent restaurant will be able to call a special hire taxi for you.

BODA-BODA The easiest way to get around Kampala's increasingly congested traffic system is by boda-boda (moped taxi). However, you shouldn't hop aboard without reading about their poor road safety record on page 117. Fares start at Ush1,000.

TOURIST INFORMATION

The best sources of current practical information for budget travellers are the staff at the Kampala Backpackers' Hostel and Campsite, and Red Chilli Hideaway (see pages 152 and 156). The owners of these places keep their ears to the ground, particularly regarding the southwest of Uganda and Rwanda, and you're bound to meet plenty of travellers who've been in Uganda a while at either hostel and at other popular backpacker haunts such as Tuhende Safari Lodge in Old Kampala and the more central City Annex Hotel. Staff at the **Uganda Wildlife Authority** booking office (see page 168) are also generally well informed within their field.

You can ignore the offices of **Tourism Uganda** at the National Theatre, Garden City and Entebbe Airport. Supposedly the public face of the Uganda Tourist Board, these are invariably staffed by students whose information is derived from the internet and the locally produced *The Eye* magazine (✆ *0312 251117;* e *theeye@ theprinthouse.co.ug; www.theeye.co.ug*). Rather than have an intern riffle through an outdated copy of this free, monthly ad-mag on your behalf, you can do so yourself – you'll find current issues at most upmarket hotels, selected booksellers and tour agents. Essentially a privately run Yellow Pages, this A5 booklet contains useful and regularly updated nationwide listings for hotels, national park fees, buses, airlines, rafting companies, safari companies, etc plus a few general articles including lodge and restaurant reviews and plenty of ads.

TOURS AND TOUR OPERATORS

Full details of international and local tour operators servicing Uganda are listed on pages 74–9.

Ndege juu ya Africa m 0772 220132; e fly@ ndegejuu.com; www.ndegejuu.com. Sightseeing flights out of Kajjansi Airfield (12km out on Entebbe Road) over Kampala (*US$175 for 30mins*), the Ssese Islands (*US$375 for 90mins*) & Jinja/ source of the Nile (*US$375 for 90mins*). Prices are for a Cessna aeroplane which can carry 3 passengers. They'll also take you up to do acrobatics.

Walter's boda-boda tours m 0791 880106; www.kampalabodabodacitytours.com. Rather than crawling through traffic in a safari car, Walter Wandera & his mates can take you around the city sights by boda-boda. Walter is not only an extremely personable chap, he is also very knowledgeable. He & his team are exceedingly safety conscious & helmets are provided. Excursions cost US$10–30.

WHITE-WATER RAFTING The daily rafting excursions on the Nile below Bujagali Falls run by **Adrift** (m *0772 ADRIFT/237438 or 0782 BUNGEE/286433*), **Nile River Explorers** (\ *0434 120236;* m *0772 422373*) and **Nalubale** (m *0782 638938*) can be undertaken as a day trip out of Kampala inclusive of a free road transfer. Ring the various companies for details, or book through Kampala Backpackers, Red Chilli Hideaway, or any other upmarket hotel or tour operator. See also *Bujagali Falls*, pages 509–17.

WHERE TO STAY

The choice of accommodation in Kampala has come a long way since the early '90s when there were two established options; backpackers slept on the floor of the YMCA while NGO and business travellers stayed in the Sheraton. Also long gone are the days when we were able to list most reasonable facilities in the capital. With an abundance of hotels in every budget category, we're now forced to be selective. We've also split accommodation into geographical areas: city centre, western Kampala (Mengo, Namirembe and Rubaga), Ggaba Road and Muyenga Hill (southeastern Kampala) Ggaba and Munyono (Lake Victoria shore), eastern Kampala (mostly Bugolobi) and Kampala–Entebbe road. The Entebbe chapter lists developments out of town along the shores of Murchison Bay.

Historically, most of Kampala's smarter hotels have been comfortably bland places that one might encounter in any major city worldwide, with clues to their African setting being limited to a few crafts in a gift shop. This has changed, and a few hotels do enjoy genuine character (though not exclusively African) and sense of place. Check out the Speke and Emin Pasha in refurbished colonial buildings, the palatial excesses of the Serena in central Kampala, the safari-chic luxury of Le Petit Village on Ggaba Road, the panoramic setting of Cassia Lodge in Munyonyo and the Mediterranean-style Bougainviller in Bugolobi. The central shoestring listings are becoming rather depleted, as several classic dives have recently been demolished and replaced by downmarket shopping malls.

CITY CENTRE
Upmarket
🏠 **Kampala Serena** [160 B3] (150 rooms) Nile Av; \ 0414 309000; www.kampala@serena. co.ug. The former Nile Hotel, a facility remembered primarily for its gruesome associations with Idi Amin's secret service, was reborn as the Kampala Serena in 2006, courtesy of a US$12 million facelift funded by the Serena Hotel chain & the Aga Khan

Foundation. The doors reopened in Aug 2006 to mark a major quantum leap in Ugandan hotel standards. Outside are beautifully landscaped grounds, a 6ha site replete with cliffs, lakes & waterfalls while the interior of this once sterile 1960s 3-storey block reveals Moroccan influences complicated by a hint of Tomb Raider. Be warned, a journey of discovery through the Serena's revolving glass portal is only for adventurers of comfortable means. Be prepared to spend Ush8,000 for a beer in the Explorers Bar/Italian Restaurant, Ush60,000 for the superb lunch buffet in the Lakes Restaurant, Ush30,000–50,000 for dinner in the plush 1st-floor restaurant. *US$425/497 (plus 18% VAT) std/exec rooms B&B.*

⌂ **Emin Pasha Hotel** [163 B3] (20 rooms) 27 Akii Bua Rd, Nakasero; 0414 236977–9; e info@eminpasha.com; www.eminpasha.com. Located on leafy Nakasero Hill, 1km north of the city centre, the Emin Pasha is far & away the most attractive & atmospheric of central Kampala's hotels. Set in a carefully restored 2-storey 1930s town house, the place bristles with taste & character. Terraces, balconies & courtyards abound above a landscaped garden & swimming pool. The brasserie has gained a reputation for good food. Rooms contain large & comfortable beds, gorgeous antique-finish hardwood furniture & framed artwork. *US$250/270 sgl/dbl garden rooms & superior rooms, US$350/370 garden suites & superior suites B&B.*

⌂ **Kampala Sheraton** [160 A3] (200 rooms) Between Nile & Ternan avenues; 0414 420000/7; e reservation.kampala@sheraton.com. This 15-storey skyscraper stands in lush, manicured gardens bordering the city centre. During the 1980s & '90s, 'Sheraton' was a local synonym for 'smart, clean, luxurious & expensive' & today, despite being equalled or surpassed in these respects by newer developments, the Kampala Sheraton still delivers the goods. Though international & ubiquitous are keywords for the internal spaces & smallish bedrooms, the garden terrace is a delightful place to enjoy a drink, a meal & live music by local artists while the environs of the large, round, '70s-style pool provide a private setting for working on your tan. While the Sheraton has all the bells & whistles required by the business & NGO visitor travelling on expenses, it's perhaps less appealing to safari-goers seeking vernacular appeal & value for money. *US$267/326 sgl/dbl 'classic' rooms, US$291/350 'superior' rooms B&B.*

⌂ **Imperial Royale Hotel** [160 A3] (275 rooms) Shimoni Rd; 0414 311400 e information@irh.co.ug; www.imperialhotels.co.ug. Despite a grim, monolithic exterior, the s/c rooms in this modern, centrally located hotel are seriously smart, spacious, attractively furnished & with terrific views south across the city sprawl & north to the green & exclusive Kololo Hill. The site is too small to enjoy the luxury of a garden, but there's a 3rd-floor terrace with swimming pool. The rates seem excellent value. *US$170/200/200 deluxe sgl/db/twin; US$250/300 exec/exec suite. Rates excl 18% VAT.*

Moderate

⌂ **Golf Course Hotel** [160 C2] (100 rooms) Kitante Rd; 0414 563500; e reservation@golfcoursehotel.com; www.golfcoursehotel.com. At the upper end of the mid-market section, this attractive & luxurious hotel is conveniently located on the edge of the city centre next to Garden City Shopping Mall. There's a revolving restaurant, a serpentine swimming pool & Wi-Fi in the s/c rooms. Exercise machines are provided in the corridors for guests too lazy to walk to the gym. *US$150/176 deluxe sgl/dbl, US$176/193 exec. Rates excl 18% VAT.*

⌂ **Humura Resort** [163 C3] (18 rooms) Off Kitante Rd; 0414 700402; e reservations@humura.or.ug. Humura means 'peaceful' or 'calm' in the Lukiga language of southwest Uganda & this hotel near the golf course is certainly that. The rooms face a central garden area with a terraced restaurant, a gym & swimming pool. *US$135/160/165 sgl/dbl/twin B&B.*

⌂ **Hotel Africana** [160 D2] (115 rooms) Wampewo Av; 0414 348080/6; m 0772 748080/0752 748081; e africana@hotelafricana.com; www.hotelafricana.com. Situated opposite the golf course, immediately east of the city centre, this modern hotel offers similar facilities & standard of accommodation to its competitors, but in prettier surrounds & at a more realistic price. Facilities include a vast swimming pool, huge & very popular gym/health club, a forex bureau, shops & hair salons, 2 restaurants, business & internet services & 24hr room service. The garden can be noisy with parties at w/ends. *US$120/150 sgl/dbl B&B.*

⌂ **Speke Hotel** [149 G3] (50 rooms) Nile Av; 0414 235332/5; e spekehotel@spekehotel.com; www.spekehotel.com. The last of the city centre's older hotels to retain any suggestion of period character, the Speke enjoys a central location &

4

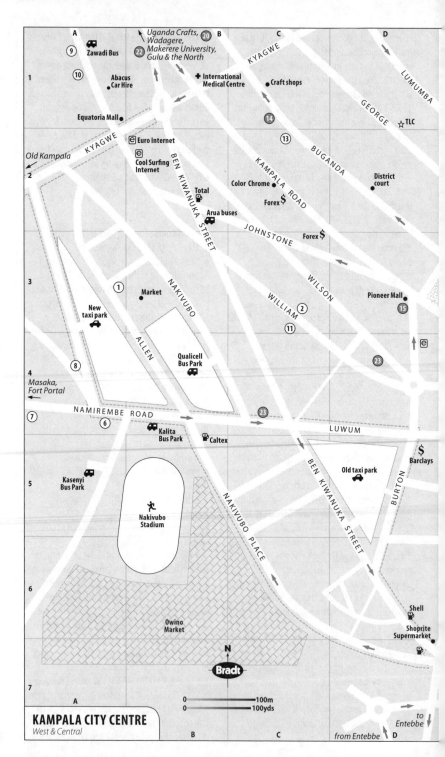

KAMPALA CITY CENTRE
West & Central

9 Zawadi Bus

10 Abacus Car Hire

Equatoria Mall

Old Kampala

Uganda Crafts, Wadagere, Makerere University, Gulu & the North

20

22

International Medical Centre

KYAGWE

Craft shops

14

George

LUMUMBA

TLC

13

BUGANDA

Euro Internet

Cool Surfing Internet

KYAGWE

BEN KIWANUKA STREET

KAMPALA ROAD

Color Chrome

Total

Forex $

Arua buses

JOHNSTONE

Forex $

District court

1 Market

NAKIVUBO

WILSON

WILLIAM

2

Pioneer Mall

15

New taxi park

ALLEN

Qualicell Bus Park

11

23

8

Masaka, Fort Portal

7 6 NAMIREMBE ROAD

23

LUWUM

Kalita Bus Park

Caltex

BEN KIWANUKA STREET

Old taxi park

BURTON

Barclays $

Kasenyi Bus Park

Nakivubo Stadium

NAKIVUBO PLACE

Shell

Shoprite Supermarket

Owino Market

N

Bradt

0   100m
0   100yds

to Entebbe

from Entebbe

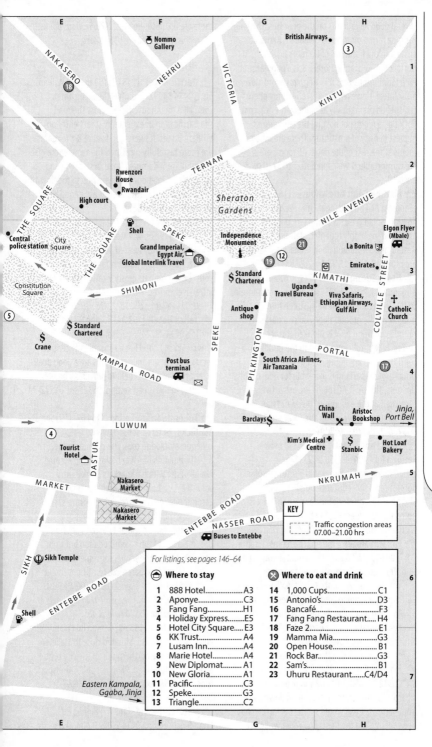

KEY

Traffic congestion areas
07.00–21.00 hrs

For listings, see pages 146–64

🏠 **Where to stay**

1	888 Hotel	A3
2	Aponye	C3
3	Fang Fang	H1
4	Holiday Express	E5
5	Hotel City Square	E3
6	KK Trust	A4
7	Lusam Inn	A4
8	Marie Hotel	A4
9	New Diplomat	A1
10	New Gloria	A1
11	Pacific	C3
12	Speke	G3
13	Triangle	C2

❌ **Where to eat and drink**

14	1,000 Cups	C1
15	Antonio's	D3
16	Bancafé	F3
17	Fang Fang Restaurant	H4
18	Faze 2	E1
19	Mamma Mia	G3
20	Open House	B1
21	Rock Bar	G3
22	Sam's	B1
23	Uhuru Restaurant	C4/D4

149

several good restaurants on the premises. The long veranda facing on to Speke Avenue is Kampala's answer to the frontages of Nairobi's historic Norfolk & New Stanley hotels, & is a popular spot for a reunion/business meeting/crossword/doze/drink/meal. However, the peaceful atmosphere is dispelled dramatically at night by the adjacent Rock Bar, a nightspot hosting the city centre's highest density of prostitutes. There are quieter rooms at the rear of the hotel. All rooms are s/c & are comfortable & well appointed. *US$110 sgl & dbl B&B.*

🛏 **Mamba Point Guesthouse** [163 B3] (6 rooms) Akii Bua Rd, near Emin Pasha; 📞 0312 563000. Small & exclusive modern guesthouse adjoining the highly regarded Mamba Point Restaurant. Swimming pool, sauna & a small gym are provided. *US$115/150 sgl/dbl B&B.*

🛏 **Hotel Triangle** [148 C2] (60 rooms) Buganda Rd; 📞 0414 231747; www.hoteltriangle.co.ug. The action in this new, street-front hotel is on the ground floor where a perfectly round swimming pool is plonked (rather curiously & hardly invitingly) in the middle of a central atrium adjoining the bar & restaurant. Underground parking is available for guests only. Upstairs, the s/c & AC rooms are attractively furnished at the expense of the Malaysian rainforests. Good value for the location. *US$100/120/140 sgl/dbl/twin.*

🛏 **Fang Fang Hotel** [149 H1] (30 rooms) Sezibwa Rd; 📞 0414 235828/233115; 📧 fangfang@gmail.com. Set in a restored colonial homestead a short distance uphill from the Sheraton, this comfortable, family-run hotel is noted for its Chinese cuisine & large gardens. Large s/c rooms with AC & DSTV. *$89/119 sgl/dbl B&B.*

🛏 **Fairway Hotel** [160 A1] (72 rooms) Kitante Rd; 📞 0414 259571/257171; www.fairwayhotel.com. This veteran Kampala hotel faces the golf course valley & is only a short walk from Garden City Shopping Centre. Facilities include a swimming pool, gym, business & conference centres, 2 restaurants & a garden bar. The refurbished rooms have AC & DSTV; those in Block A are superior. *US$95/115 sgl/dbl B&B.*

🛏 **Holiday Express** [149 E5] (60 rooms) Luwum St; 📞 0312 262858. This mid-range hotel is much smarter (& costlier) than its location downslope from Kampala Road would suggest. A fortune has been spent tiling the floors & corridor walls but

there are no mosquito nets. *US$65/90 sgl/dbl with AC, rooms without AC are US$10 cheaper.*

Budget

🛏 **Pacific Hotel** [148 C3] (53 rooms) William St; 📞 0414 340920; 📧 info@thepacifichotel.com. Like the Aponye Hotel across the road, the Pacific is an unexpectedly smart entry on William Street. It's very good value & the rooms are more tastefully furnished than anywhere else downhill from Kampala Road. A street-facing balcony of a 1st-floor bar keeps you in touch with the insalubrious setting. Prices are negotiable. *US$36/50 sgl/dbl B&B.*

🛏 **Aponye Hotel** [148 C3] (50 rooms) William St; 📞 0414 349239; www.aponyehotel.com. This hotel, conveniently located between Kampala Road & the bus/taxi parks, is far smarter than you'd expect from its grotty location, & it is very attractively priced. Tiled rooms have nets, fans & TV. Wi-Fi available. *US$16/22/18 sgl/dbl/twin.*

🛏 **Jeliza Hotel** [163 A4] Bombo Rd (city end); 📞 0414 232249; 📧 jelkam@utlonline.co.ug. This creaky old hotel has a conveniently central location & the spacious s/c rooms are a good deal. A terraced lawn & bar behind provides a bit of greenery in this urban setting. *US$26 sgl, US$32/34 dbl.*

🛏 **Tuhende Safari Lodge** [154 F2] (10 rooms) Martin Rd; 📱 0772 468360; www.tuhendesafarilodge.com. This popular lodge, in a 1940s building of Asian design in Old Kampala, is a favourite with backpackers & upcountry volunteers. A choice of basic but spacious accommodation is offered: 3-bed dorms, s/c suites & semi-s/c rooms (1 bathroom per 2 rooms). Tuhende's popularity derives not from the splendour of the accommodation but from the ambience, architecture, convenient location near the bus & taxi parks, & a terrific pavement restaurant (*3-course suppers Ush20,000, b/fasts Ush7,500*). *US$7 dorm bed with bedding & nets in large 3-bed room, US$30 twin & dbl.*

🛏 **College Inn** [163 A2] Bombo Rd (Wandegere end); 📞 0414 533835. Situated close to Makerere University on the northern side of the city centre & recently refurbished. Plenty of public transport runs past it. S/c rooms are comfortable & have DSTV. *US$24/28 sgl/dbl.*

🛏 **Hotel Catherine** [163 A2] Bombo Rd (Wandegere end); 📞 0414 530871. Almost directly

top Some chimpanzees use sticks to 'fish' for termites (AVZ) pages 35–6

above left The distinctive red-tailed monkey can be located by its cheerful, chirruping call and identified by its long, russet tail (AVZ) pages 40–1

above right Though it rarely comes to ground level, the black-and-white colobus is readily located thanks to a loud croaking call and distinctive coat (S/MR) page 41

left While most other Ugandan primates inhabit forest, the patas monkey is a creature of the open savanna (AVZ) page 40

above   The king of the jungle waits for his meal while the females in his pride do the hunting (AVZ) page 42

left   The side-striped jackal is the most widespread canid in Uganda (AVZ) pages 43–4

below   Elephants commonly roam the slopes of the Katwe volcanic craters in Queen Elizabeth National Park (S/MEH) page 49

above A crocodile basks on the banks of the Nile below the Murchison Falls (FLPA) page 69

right The hippo's characteristic gape may look like a yawn but it is a warning sign other creatures do well to heed (S/SU) pages 51–2

below Buffalo tolerate oxpeckers, which rid their hides of ticks (AVZ) page 52

<table>
<tbody>
<tr><td>above</td><td>Not the brightest of animals, the Jackson's hartebeest is said to run from lions before forgetting the reason for its flight and stopping — sometimes with dire consequences! (AVZ) page 46</td></tr>
<tr><td>above left</td><td>The graceful Uganda kob appears on the national coat of arms along with the crowned crane (AVZ) page 47</td></tr>
<tr><td>below left</td><td>Rothschild's giraffe are common in the Buligi grasslands of Murchison Falls National Park (AVZ) page 52</td></tr>
<tr><td>below</td><td>The handsome Defassa waterbuck inhabits grasslands close to reliable sources of water (AVZ) pages 46–7</td></tr>
</tbody>
</table>

above   Warthogs reverse into their burrows at night in order to present predators with a faceful of tusks rather than the desired rump of pork (AVZ) page 52

right   The gazelle-like oribi is usually seen in pairs or small groups in tall grassland (AVZ) page 49

below   Ankole pastoralists take great pride in their cattle's progeny and colouration, as well as the size and spread of the horns (AVZ) pages 226–7

above   The zig-zag outline of the Virunga volcanoes provides a dramatic backdrop to the placid waters of Lake Mutanda (CK) pages 268–9

below left   On its way downhill from Mount Elgon's central caldera, the Sipi River plunges over ochre basalt cliffs to create the massif's emblematic waterfall (S/P) pages 470–1

below right   The Bwindi Impenetrable Forest was not named lightly – as you'll appreciate as you traverse its steep, soggy and densely vegetated slopes in search of gorillas (S/KB) pages 273–93

above Ringed by distant mountains in Uganda,
Kenya and South Sudan, the plains of Kidepo
Valley National Park are one of Africa's great
wildernesses (CK) pages 452–9

right In the shadow of the Kijura Escarpment,
Uganda kob graze the Rift Valley plains in
Semliki Wildlife Reserve (AVZ) pages 364–6

below The trails to the snow peaks of the Rwenzori
Mountains follow the floors of glacier-carved
chasms inhabited by surreal groves of giant
groundsel (SS) pages 321–33

top	**Northern carmine bee-eater** (SS) page 59
above left	**Shoebill** (AVZ) page 57
above	**Yellow-backed weaver** (AVZ) page 61
left	**Verreaux's eagle-owl** (AVZ) page 59
below	**African fish eagle** (AVZ) page 57

opposite the College Inn, the newer Hotel Catherine is another good budget option. *US$12 sgl with shared facilities, US$28 sgl & 21/29 dbl B&B.*

🏠 **Hotel City Square** [149 E3] (23 rooms) Kampala Rd; ☎0414 256257/251451. Overlooking City Square, this is Kampala Road's best budget option. Only 200m from the post office, it's ideal for the 08.00 Post Buses to upcountry destinations. The balcony restaurant is nothing special but a good vantage point from which to watch city life go by. Good value! *US$25/32/32 sgl/dbl/twin B&B.*

🏠 **KK Trust** [148 A4] Namirembe Rd (40 rooms). Decent-looking hotel at the bottom of Namirembe Road, metres from Nakivubo Stadium, the new taxi park & the Kasenyi Bus Park. Restaurant attached. *US$20/24 sgl/dbl B&B.*

Shoestring

🏠 **City Annex** [160 C4] (31 rooms) De Winton Rd; ☎0414 254132; e ncahotel@gmail.com. This rambling & rather dated hotel is located opposite the National Theatre. It's a favourite with backpackers & volunteers due to its proximity to the Garden City & Oasis shopping malls, the Nairobi buses which run out of the latter, & evening events at the theatre. You'll find smarter & cheaper s/c accommodation in the suburbs but the rooms with shared facilities are a good deal. The thatched courtyard restaurant at the back is a bonus. Continental (Ush15.000–20,000) & local meals served. *US$7/10 sgl & 16 twin with spotless*

shared bathrooms, US$28/40 s/c dbl/twin. Rates excl b/fast.

🏠 **New Diplomat** [148 A1] (20 rooms) William St, behind Equatoria Mall; ☎0414 230165. A slightly inferior alternative to the nearby New Gloria. *US$13/16 s/c sgl/dbl.*

🏠 **888 Hotel** [148 A3] (23 rooms) Off Nakivuko Rd; ☎0414 346888; e chpalace888@yahoo. com. Backpackers appreciate the location of this labyrinthine Chinese-owned hotel rather more than its rooms. Close to the bus station & new taxi park it's a safe bet if you bus into town after dark or want an early start. A Chinese restaurant is attached. *US$10/12/14 sgl/dbl/twin with common showers, US$12/14/18 s/c sgl/dbl/twin.*

🏠 **Hotel New Gloria** [148 A1] (25 rooms) William St, behind Equatoria Mall; ☎0414 257790. This long-serving hotel at the western end of the city centre is near the Zawadi bus office serving northern Uganda. Secure parking. Rooms are clean & s/c. *US$12/20 sgl/dbl.*

🏠 **Lusam Inn Resthouse** [148 A4] (47 rooms) Namirembe Rd; m 0772 514773. This decent, no-frills lodge is conveniently located a few hundred metres uphill from the main bus & taxi parks & a short distance down from the Jaguar buses to Rwanda. *US$10/12/14 s/c sgl/dbl/twin.*

🏠 **Marie Hotel** [148 A4] (18 rooms) Corner of Martin Rd, just off Namirembe Rd; ☎0392 961139. This clean & surprisingly cheap hotel overlooking the new taxi park is rather better than its shoestring listing deserves. *US$12/16 s/c sgl/dbl.*

WESTERN KAMPALA See box, *Along the Natete Road*, page 154.

Moderate

🏠 **Sojovalo Hotel** [154 D4] (35 rooms) Rubaga Rd; ☎0414 271877. The interior of this smart new hotel contrasts sharply with its position on the least attractive part of Rubaga Road. You'll find a restaurant & spacious s/c rooms with TV, fridge, writing desk & AC. Secure parking. *US$55/70 sgl/dbl.*

🏠 **Kenron Hotel** [154 A4] (25 rooms) Natete Rd; ☎0414 272638. This surprisingly smart & modern hotel opened in 2013 on the busy road between the city centre & destinations west. Though the bar prices are steep (twice those of Harriet's bar/salon behind the Backpackers), the s/c rooms are very nice indeed, with AC & a bit of a view, too. *US$41/49 sgl & US$64 dbl B&B.*

Budget

🏠 **Namirembe Guesthouse** [154 C2] (40 rooms) ☎0414 237981/273778; e ngh@ utlonline.co.ug; www.namirembe-guesthouse. com. The Church of Uganda's sprawling guesthouse just below the Namirembe Cathedral has long provided a secure & convenient choice for visitors of a respectable & frequently church-oriented bent. Its reputation as such would seem sufficiently secure to justify the somewhat immodest rates (compare them with the Kenron Hotel above). Good view of the metropolis from the thatched Coffee & Juice Bar. *New block US$55/70/80/100 s/c sgl/dbl/twin/ exec dbl, old block US$25 per bed family rooms (4–9 people), US$30 sgl with shared facilities, US$45/56 s/c sgl/twin, US$72 3-bed rooms. All rates B&B.*

🏠 **Pope Paul VI Memorial Hotel** [134 D5] (over 60 rooms) Off Masaka Rd, Ndeeba; ☎ 0414 272456; e ppmh07@yahoo.com; www. popepaulhotel.co.ug. This large, long-serving establishment stands in spacious grounds near Kabaka Mwanga's lake. Though decidedly institutional in character, the PP-VI-MH is doing its best to shake things up by providing 'Garden Music every evening'. Good value. *US$24/48/48 s/c sgl/ dbl/twin B&B.*

🏠 **Tal Cottages** [134 D4] (60 rooms) Off Kabusu Rd, Rubaga; ☎ 0414 273330. A curious development on the eastern side of Rubaga Hill above Kabaka Mwanga's lake. Round, 2-storey cottages face a row of drab bungalows along a narrow private lane terminating at a 3-floor hotel/ conference centre block above a swimming pool. There are some nice touches: the hotel rooms have Zanzibar-style carved wooden doors while the cottages have some inspired names (Marie Antoinette, Princess Diana, Lewinsky, Venus de Milo, Black Eyed Susan …). Cottages are divided into 4 s/c rooms. *US$28 dbl in cottages, US$28/34 sgl/twin B&B in the main building.*

🏠 **Sanyu Babies Home** [154 C3] (12 rooms) Natete Rd, near Sam Sam Hotel & Mengo Hospital (see also *Chapter 3, Travelling positively*, page 128); ☎ 0414 274032; m 0712 370950; e barbara@ sanyubabies.com; www.sanyubabies.com. Pleasantly homely guesthouse. *US$25pp B&B, US$20 for volunteers helping in the home.*

🏠 **Manhatten Guesthouse** [154 C1] (10 rooms) Balintuma Rd; ☎ 0414 534824. Readers unimpressed by the Namirembe Guesthouse have praised alternative accommodation at this small & welcoming church-oriented guesthouse on the northern side of Namirembe Hill. Meals (*Ush15,000*) & beer are served. *US$21/29/29/43 s/c sgl/dbl/twin/suite B&B.*

🏠 **ICU Guesthouse** [154 A4] (10 rooms) m 0774 338 708/0701 100486; e sander@ icuganda.org; www.icuganda.org/guesthouse. This Dutch–Ugandan venture is located in a large residential house in a maze of roads behind Rubaga Cathedral. Dorms, rooms & a kitchen for guests' use are proving popular with students & volunteers seeking a slightly more homely base than the usual backpacker haunts. Safaris arranged (*www. grassrootzuganda.com*). *US$14/20/28 dorm/sgl/dbl.*

🏠 **Miraculen Grill** [154 E1] (3 rooms) Apollo Kagwe Rd; m 0772 337400. And now for

something completely different! This eccentrically decorated garden grill/bar near Old Kampala offers smallish s/c upstairs rooms. Evening 3-course grill menu Ush18,000. Convenient for the Old Kampala bus park. *US$20 sgl B&B.*

🏠 **G-One** [154 E3] (52 rooms) Rubaga Rd. Affordable new hotel at the city end of Rubaga Road. The amply proportioned, s/c tiled rooms have nets & fan. *US$16/20/24/28 sgl/dbl/twin/ exec B&B.*

🏠 **Kings Cross** [154 E3] (35 rooms) Rubaga Rd. Another new & affordable offering at the city end of Rubaga Road. Similar to the nearby G-One Hotel but perhaps slightly smarter. Tiled rooms with nets & fan. *US$16/18/20 sgl/dbl/twin. Rates excl b/fast.*

🏠 **Sam Sam Hotel** [154 C3] (25 rooms) Natete Rd; ☎ 0414 274211; m 0773 291351. This modern hotel stands on the side of Namirembe Hill close to the shops in Mengo. A sauna is provided. Steep driveway to the main road. Good value. *US$15 rather small sgls, US$16/24 more spacious dbls.*

🏠 **Kampala Backpackers' Hostel & Campsite** [154 A4] (15 rooms) On the main Kampala– Natete road, Lungujja, about 3km out of town on the Natete Rd minibus-taxi route; ☎ 0414 274767; m 0772 430587/502758; e backpackers@ infocom.co.ug; www.backpackers.co.ug. Almost 20 years old now, this is an excellent Australian-owned travellers' hangout. Facilities include gorilla-tracking information & permit bookings (US$50 commission), white-water rafting bookings & pick-up, an international MTN payphone, free luggage storage, free internet, clean ablution blocks with hot water, a good bar, craft shop & a restaurant serving filling pizzas (Ush20,000–25,000), burgers, salads, juices, smoothies, & daily 'specials' (main courses Ush12,000–22,000). Valuables, laptops, etc, can be left in secure lockers provided with individual keys & padlock fittings for additional security for Ush1,000/day. The green grounds are teeming with birds, & also host a resident troop of vervet monkeys & a ground squirrel colony. To get to the hostel, go to the new taxi park & ask for a minibus-taxi to 'Backpackers'. If headed for western Uganda in your own vehicle, Backpackers is ideally placed for a quick escape from the city. A wide range of accommodation spans budget & shoestring categories. There is camping in the lovely garden, as well as dormitory beds of which the most popular option is the open-fronted 4-bed 'Nature's dorm' on a 1st-floor balcony above the gardens. Twin-bed bandas & cottages in the garden share a smart new communal bathroom, & there's a new 1st-floor flat with 4

rooms that share a bathroom, lounge with TV & a veranda & is ideal for small groups. *US$4pp camping, US$7–9 dorm bed, US$20 bandas & cottages with shared bathroom, US$30 s/c sgl/dbl, US$22 twin/dbl in new flat.*

GGABA ROAD AND MUYENGA HILL
Upmarket

⌂ **Le Petit Village** [181 A3] (10 rooms) Quality Hill Mall, Ggaba Rd; ☎ 0312 265530–3; e info@ lepetitvillage.net; www.lepetitvillage.net. Why start/finish your safari sleeping under a concrete roof when you can do so under thatch? Beneath

massive grass & gumpole roof structures (works of art in themselves), cool & spacious s/c suites are furnished with understated elegance. All are provided with DSTV, complimentary Wi-Fi & minibar, AC, bathtub, & king-sized bed with net. There's a pool in which to swim off some pounds

NATETE ROAD

The Natete Road, which runs between the cathedral-capped hills of Mengo/ Namirembe and Rubaga, is Kampala's main focus for budget travellers: a broad category that in this case includes backpackers, budget safari clients, independently mobile travellers (ie: with own wheels) and church- and project-oriented groups. Part of the appeal lies in the easy escape from Kampala that the area offers. The main bus parks lie at the eastern, city end of this corridor, while travel in the opposite direction (towards Natete) leads out of town towards western Uganda. I'll therefore note a few useful locations which I'll describe in relation to the Backpackers' Hostel (see page 152).

Firstly, there's a 20m **swimming pool** [154 A4] 200m from the hostel opposite Lyna Day Care kindergarten on the steep road leading to Rubaga Cathedral. This gets very crowded at weekends but it's quiet enough during the week (Ush4,000). It's a stiff climb up the hill past the pool to the **Catholic cathedral** but worth it for the superb view across the city. A less precipitous route to this viewpoint turns right out of the Backpackers' gate, left at the nearby crossroads and then uphill at successive junctions. A less crowded pool (Ush5,000) and a gym/sauna and bar/restaurant can be found at the storeyed **Pacify Guesthouse**, 500m down the main road from Backpackers towards Natete. Along the way, you'll pass the new **Kenron Hotel** which provides Natete Road's smartest accommodation and bar/restaurant.

On the tarmac Lungujja road just behind the hostel, **Harriet's** [154 A4] bar/hairdresser's offers budget beer and beard trims while an adjacent row of shops sells basic provisions. The large green grounds of **Un Peu de Bali** [154 A4], 50m up the road, is perhaps Mengo's most pleasant spot for refreshments.

Back on the main road, heading from the hostel towards Kampala, market produce and cheap local food is available halfway up Mengo Hill in **Mengo Market** [154 B4]. Some small supermarkets and eateries (of the liver/sausage/ deep-fried object with chips ilk) can be found further up the hill in **Mengo trading centre**. **Mona Lisa** is Mengo's liveliest bar, with regular bands and dance troupes. From Mengo trading centre it's a pleasant stroll up to the **Anglican cathedral** on Namirembe Hill which has good city views. For those with an interest in history, the gravestones in the small, iron-fenced area and plaques inside the cathedral read like a Who's Who of early Kampala.

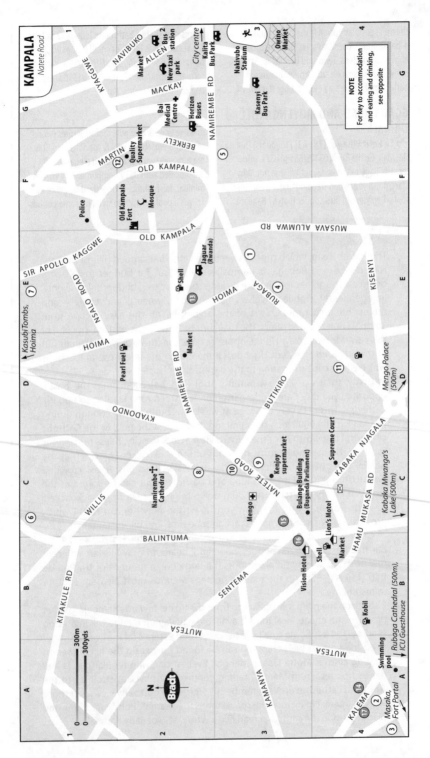

KAMPALA
Natete Road

NOTE
For key to accommodation
and eating and drinking,
see opposite

Where to stay

1 G-One...E3
2 Kampala Backpackers' Hostel.....A4
3 Kenron...A4
4 Kings Cross....................................E3
5 Lusam Inn Resthouse...................F3
6 Manhatten Guesthouse................C1
7 Miraculen Grill.............................E1
8 Namirembe Guesthouse...............C2
9 Sam Sam.......................................C3
10 Sanyu Babies Home.....................C3
11 Sojovalo.......................................D4
12 Tuhende Safari Lodge..................F2

Off map

ICU Guesthouse.............................A4

Where to eat and drink

13 Café Java......................................E2
14 Harriet's Bar/Apha Salon.............A4
15 Maggie's Bar.................................C3
     Miraculen Grill..........................(see 7)
16 Mona Lisa.....................................B3
     Tuhende Safari Lodge..........(see 12)
17 Un Peu du Bali..............................A4

before putting them back on in the adjacent Le Chateau Restaurant & La Patisserie. It's a decidedly

understated location – accessed through the rear of the Quality Hill Mall car park – but within, it's a different world. *US$177/188 sgl/dbl suites, US$194/218 junior suites & US$218/241 exec suites B&B.*

Budget

Hotel Diplomate [181 D4] (30 rooms) Tank Hill; 0414 267655/572828; e diplomatekampala@hotmail.com. Perched on the top of Tank Hill, this pleasantly low-key hotel is famous for the fabulous view north to the city centre. The restaurant serves grills, pizzas & other dishes at around Ush20,000. The s/c carpeted rooms with DSTV are good value. *US$28/36 sgl/dbl B&B.*

Hotel Olympia [181 D7] (30 rooms) Off Ggaba Rd; 0414 266743; m 0772 686300. Set along a quiet side road beyond the main cluster of pubs & restaurants on Ggaba Road, the Olympia is a smart & very reasonably priced 4-storey hotel. The tiled s/c rooms are comfortable. Excellent value. *US$15 sgl & 20/24 dbl B&B.*

GGABA AND MUNYONYO An extension of the Ggaba Road listings above, this section covers the lakeside suburbs of Ggaba and Munyonyo at the eastern end of Ggaba Road.

Upmarket

Speke Commonwealth Resort [135 G6] (449 rooms) Munyonyo; 0414 227111; e spekeresort@spekeresort.com; www.spekeresort.com. This top-quality resort offers sumptuous rooms & suites set in expansive & gorgeously landscaped grounds on the Lake Victoria waterfront. Those in the Commonwealth wing are furnished & decorated with impeccable taste in brown & copper tones, & fitted with everything you'd require; indeed the executive suites contain rather more (bathtub, shower cubicle, 2 hand basins, 2 loos, 2 flat-screen TVs …). The complex contains a large swimming pool, marina & stables. Horseriding, fishing & boat excursions are available. The restaurant serves continental meals for Ush25,000 upwards. Rates are extremely reasonable – even when you add a 5% service charge & 18% VAT on top. *US$120/130 sgl/dbl deluxe rooms, US$150 for 1-bedroom apt (sleeps 2) & US$200 for 2-bedroom apt (sleeps up to 4).*

Moderate

Cassia Lodge [135 G6] (30 rooms) Buziga Hill; m 0755 777004; e info@cassialodge.com; www.cassialodge.com. This deservedly popular lodge is found high on affluent Buziga Hill where it enjoys an improbably fabulous view of southern Kampala, the lake, & its adjoining wetlands. The main buildings are a curiosity, being a pair of 2-storey blocks softened by gumpole cladding in the fashion of an upcountry safari lodge. A swimming pool, an excellent 1st-floor restaurant (see page 164) & Wi-Fi are provided. The comfortable, tiled s/c rooms have fan, walk-in nets & a veranda or balcony, & are very reasonably priced. *US$95/120 sgl/dbl B&B.*

Yellow Haven [135 G6] (8 rooms) Off a back road behind Bunga trading centre, Ggaba Rd; 0782 900457; e kelly@coltalk.com; www.yellowhaven.com. Located beside a backwater of Lake Victoria, this lovely new guesthouse is a haven from the chaos of Kampala. Facilities include a swimming pool & sauna. *US$80/95/110 s/c sgl/dbl/trpl B&B.*

Budget

⌂ Royal Impala Hotel [135 G7] (31 rooms) Munyonyo; ☎0414 577413. This hotel is tucked away behind the Speke Resort in slightly eccentric but attractively landscaped grounds. Main courses on a varied menu cost around Ush22,000–25,000. The tiled & s/c rooms are pleasant enough, though some are more spacious than others. Outside the hotel is a shrine to St Andrew Kaggwa, a Baganda Christian who fell victim to the murderous 19th-century Kabaka Mwanga. *US$40/60/70 sgl/dbl/exec dbl B&B.*

⌂ Sir Jose [135 G6] (20 rooms) Ggaba Rd, Ggaba; ☎0414 667008; m 0772 500332; e care@sirjosehotel.com; www.sirjosehotel.com. This smart new hotel is definitely the pick of the budget hotels along Ggaba Road. Outside, a green garden is tucked away to the side of the hotel while upstairs the s/c tiled, glass-fronted rooms open on to balconies overlooking the lake & upmarket Buziga Hill. Watch out for functions at the w/ends but otherwise a terrific deal. *US$30/50 sgl/dbl B&B.*

EASTERN KAMPALA The areas of Ntinda and Bukoto are the stronghold of Uganda's emergent middle class. They are fast-growing suburbs and are conveniently located for the Northern Bypass and the Ndere Centre (see page 166). Meanwhile, Kololo is an affluent, 'embassyland' suburb that covers the hill immediately east of the city centre beyond the golf course.

Bugolobi & Luzira
Moderate

⌂ Royal Suites [135 G4] (80 rooms) Binayoba Rd, off Luthuli Av, Bugolobi; ☎0312 263816; m 0779 309556; e royal@royalsuites.co.ug; www.royalsuites.co.ug. Tucked away at the back of Bugolobi on the margins of the Nakivubo wetland, this sprawling apartment complex caters for everyone. Though mainly aimed at visiting consultants & business travellers (some stay for a year or more), the spacious s/c studio apartments are ideal for tourists. The green, landscaped grounds to the rear contain a swimming pool & a well-equipped gym. *US$130/150 sgl/dbl studio suite & US$200/300/325 1/2/3 bed apts B&B. Prices excl VAT.*

⌂ Tulip Tree Bugolobi [135 G4] (6 rooms) Luthuli Lane; m 0757 725555/7535555; e bbthetuliptree@gmail.com. Homely guesthouse in a quiet, residential lane with a mixture of s/c & non s/c rooms. *US$50/75 sg/dbl B&B.*

⌂ Hotel Bougainviller [135 G3] (24 rooms) Port Bell Rd opposite Shell Bugolobi; ☎0414 220966; e bougainviller@utlonline.co.ug; www.bougainviller.com. Inspired by classic Mediterranean villa architecture, this delightful French-owned hotel surrounds a terraced & landscaped courtyard with a small swimming pool. The airy, spacious rooms have stone-tiled floors & glass doors lead out to the patio & central garden. The suites are provided with a fitted kitchen & gas stove, & a large bed elevated on a small mezzanine floor. A restaurant for residents is provided. The target market is longer-stay consultants & business travellers, & tourist groups staying 1 night only are discouraged. *US$100/120 sgl/dbl standard, US$110/130 suites & 130/150 duplex rooms B&B.*

⌂ Silver Springs [135 G4] (92 rooms) Port Bell Rd, Bugolobi; ☎0414 505976; www.silverspringshotel.ug. Silver Springs Hotel was established in the 1930s to accommodate transit passengers using the flying-boat service to South Africa (planes landed on the lake at nearby Port Bell). The original structure has been long overlain by a series of renovations & it's currently a smart, modern hotel offering rooms & cottages, ample conference facilities, a swimming pool, & pizzeria. *US$100/120 sgl/dbl B&B.*

Budget

⌂ Red Chilli Hideaway [135 H4] (30 rooms) Butabika Rd, near Luzira; ☎0414 223903 (office); m 0772 509150; e reservations@redchillihideaway.com; www.redchillihideaway.com. In Sep 2013, the excellent Red Chilli backpackers' hostel shifts from its Mbuya site to new, purpose-built premises on a 2ha site in Butabika in southeast Kampala. It really is a hideaway now, situated as it is on the city's farthest extremity overlooking still-pristine wetland with Lake Victoria beyond. Not that the surroundings are undeveloped, there's an upmarket housing development nearby while a major shopping mall (currently under construction) will provide plenty of scope for shopping & entertainment. The main building contains both s/c & non-s/c rooms, & there are dorms & camping, plus an upstairs bar with a view. There's even a swimming pool. Cottages (1 & 2 bed) are to follow. It's a bit of a way out of town but once there, you'll realise just how little you miss the city centre. To get here, follow the Port Bell Road for 3.5km beyond its Bugolobi junction (see map on page 135) to Luzira. where you'll turn left in the market area & after 500m take the 2nd fork on your left. The hostel is 2km further along. *Matatus* & orange Pioneer buses run from central Kampala as far as Butabika Mental Hospital, 500m before the hostel (take a boda-boda from there), while a free Red Chilli shuttle will run regularly to/from town; check the website for details. Arrivals from Jinja can take a taxi from Nakawa at the Jinja Road/Port Bell Road junction. *US$5 camping, US$8 dorm bed, US$20/25/30 sgl/dbl/trpl with shared bathroom, US$25/30/35 s/c sgl/dbl/trpl.*

Ntinda & Bukoto
Upmarket
🏠 **Kabira Country Club** [135 F2] (95 rooms) Old Kiira Rd; ☎ 0312 227222; e info@kabiracountryclub. com; www.kabiracountryclub.com. Though the KCC, set in the ever-expanding surburbs of northeast Kampala, can hardly claim to be a 'country club' it is a calm & luxurious retreat from the busy commuter corridor of Kira Road. Amenities include a large, palm-fringed swimming pool, tennis courts, a well-equipped gym & a restaurant. *US$182 sgl/dbl, US$232/343 1-/2-bed suites.*

KAMPALA–ENTEBBE ROAD
These options lie to the south of Kampala and close to the Entebbe Road.

Moderate
🏠 **Lindsay Cottages** [135 E7] (10 rooms) Lubowa Hill; ☎ 0414 200457; e info@lindsay-cottages.com; www.lindsaycottage.co.ug. This attractive small hotel is located on the quiet Lubowa Hill, an upmarket estate 2km off the Entebbe Road & just south of Kampala. The use of wallpaper & heavy wooden furniture provides the communal areas & rooms (there are no cottages) with a rather formal, but stylish period feel. The gardens enjoy a (distant) lake view, & a swimming

Budget
🏠 **Nob View** [135 F2] (76 rooms) Kira Rd, Ntinda; ☎ 0414 286376; www.nobviewhotel. com. Should you need a decent budget hotel with a swimming pool & strange name in northeast Kampala, look no further. Upper rooms on the south side have balconies with a view. Turn off Kira Road between the Shell & Total fuel stations in Ntinda. *US$40/50/50 sgl/dbl/twin.*

Kololo
Upmarket
🏠 **Protea Hotel** [163 D3] (70 rooms) Acacia Av; ☎ 0312 550000; e res@proteakla.co.ug; www. proteahotels.com/kampala. This smart branch of the South African hotel chain lies in a large car park on the lower slopes of Kololo Hill where it caters primarily for business visitors & conference delegates. *US$160/190/240 standard/junior/exec suite B&B.*
🏠 **Metropole Hotel** [160 B1] (60 rooms) Acacia Av; ☎ 0414 391000; e metropole@ metropolekampala.com. This modern & attractively priced hotel has been shoe-horned into a small plot beside the golf course. Full marks to the architect who created a feeling of space using an open-plan central reception/café & 1st-floor balcony, taking full advantage of the views across the fairways. Facilities include Thai & grill restaurants, beauty spa & Wi-Fi. *US$118/143 exec sgl/dbl. US$143/168 business sgl/dbl. B&B.*

pool, gym & sauna are provided. *US$100/120 sgl/ dbl, US$170/190 suites B&B.*

Budget
🏠 **The Lodge** [off map, 134 D7] (14 rooms) Off Entebbe Rd, Lweza, 10km from Kampala; m 0772 367972/331332; e info@kampalalodge.com; www.kampalalodge.com. Guesthouse occupying adjoining modern villas. *US$50/60/70 sgl/dbl/ suite.*

✗ WHERE TO EAT AND DRINK

RESTAURANTS, CAFÉS AND BARS Over the past ten years, Kampala has transformed into a diner's paradise. Hundreds of new eateries have sprung up all over the city offering a variety of cuisine for all tastes and budgets. There are, of course, numerous small take-aways, pork joints, roadside chicken grills and market stalls which offer cheap and reasonable local food. It is impossible to recommend any particular one or to guarantee the standard of fare. This guide therefore concentrates on the larger and/or longer-established restaurants, whose quality and reputations are likely to ensure that they are around for some time to come.

During the troubled late 1970s and '80s, people headed directly out of the city before dark and drank (Ugandans like to drink) close to home in the suburbs. For many years after, the city centre was a dead zone while nightlife shifted to suburbs such as Kansanga and Kabalagala (3km down Ggaba Road), and Wandegeya. This trend has been reversed and many of Kampala's best restaurants and bars once again lie on or close to Kampala Road. However, Ggaba Road still boasts numerous lively bars and good eateries. Another popular peripheral location is Kisementi, 1.5km north of the city centre, and the nearby Acacia Avenue (recently put on the map by several exclusive restaurants).

In addition to the restaurants listed below, **Red Chilli Hideaway** (see page 152), **Kampala Backpackers** (see page 152) and most other hotels in the upmarket and moderate ranges have restaurants serving international cuisine to guests and outsiders. The list below is only a small selection of what's on offer. For a fuller picture (at least of Kampala's smarter eateries) get hold of the free monthly ad-mag *The Eye* or check www.theeye.co.ug. Each edition includes updated listings and a restaurant review.

City centre

These listings are presented as a geographical tour of the city's central restaurants. Starting with some budget options around the Nakivubo bus and taxi parks, we pop across to the excellent Tuhende Lodge in Old Kampala, before making an anticlockwise tour of a selection of the (mostly) smart restaurants mushrooming across the slopes of Nakasero Hill.

✗ **Uhuru Restaurant** [148 C4] Namirembe Rd. Sharp-eyed Australian readers might remember this popular lunchtime restaurant from a 2008 episode of the *Family Footsteps* series. Uhuru's solid reputation is built on pilau rice with meat & spicy sauce. The 2nd-floor location near the bus park offers great views over the gridlocked streets below. There's another branch on Wilson Road. *Meals Ush5,000.*

✗ **Tuhende Safari Lodge** [154 F2] Martin Rd; m 0772 468360. This excellent pavement restaurant in Old Kampala is one of the best deals in town, offering soup, an ample platter of grilled fillet/fish/goat kebab & a sweet. It's a favourite of local expats & travellers (it's conveniently located for Natete Road & city centre hotels), as well as upcountry volunteers looking to put some weight back on. Space is limited so booking is recommended. *Meals Ush19,000.*

🍽 **1,000 Cups** [148 C1] Buganda Rd; m 0772 505619/0782 544313. Drink in or takeaway – a wide selection of packaged Uganda coffees make novel presents to take home.

✗ **Antonio's** [148 D3] Pioneer Mall, Kampala Rd; ⏰ 06.30–late. Kampala Road's best budget eatery serves good b/fasts, lunch specials & juices at bargain prices. *B/fast Ush3,000–4,000, local food Ush7,000–8,000, burgers Ush5,000.*

🍽 **Bancafé** [149 F3] Grand Imperial Hotel; 🕿 0414 346834/0312 263003. Located in the Grand Imperial Hotel complex, this is a good spot for a cup of java & a muffin.

✗ **Nandos** [160 A4] Kampala Rd/Parliament Av; 🕿 0414 340840/3. This fast-food complex offers ice creams, pizzas, BBQ chicken, as well as good bread, pies & pastries baked by a Dutch company, Brood.

🍷 **Mateo's** [160 B4] Parliament Av; 🕿 0414 340840. Kampala's top cocktail bar (above Nandos) is a great place to kick off a night out.

✗ **Dominoes Pizza** [160 B4] Kampala Rd; 🕿 0414 251513. Dominoes, next to Nandos, offers excellent pizzas & burgers to eat in or take away. Food can also be delivered.

🍽 **Café Pap** [160 B4] 13 Parliament Av; 🕿 0414 254647; m 0772 652443. The place for coffee connoisseurs. Excellent coffee, good food & internet access make it a popular stop for laptop owners.

✗ **Haandi Restaurant** [160 B4] 1st Fl, Commercial Plaza, Kampala Rd; ☎ 0414 346283. Odd setting for the city centre's best Indian food. *Meals Ush30,000–40,000.*

✗ **Fang Fang Restaurant** [149 H4] 1st Fl, Communications Hse, Colville St; ☎ 0414 344806. Enjoy Kampala's best Chinese food either inside or on the airy roof terrace. *Meals Ush30,000.*

✗ **Kampala Casino** [160 A4] Pan Africa Hse, Kimathi Av; ☎ 0414 343628/30. This plush casino is worth visiting for the food even if you don't fancy a flutter – they have a range of good continental dishes. *Meals around Ush20,000.*

✗ **Mamma Mia** [149 G3] Speke Hotel; ☎ 0414 346340; m 0772 630211. The corner plot of Nile/ Kimathi avenues has served Italian food since the mid-1960s (with a few excusable interruptions in service). Handily located within the Speke Hotel complex this restaurant is popular for lunch & dinner alike. *Meals Ush20,000.*

✗ **Masala Chat House** [160 C4] De Winton Rd; ☎ 0414 236487. Popular with travellers as an informal, good-value Indian restaurant, this place is located just opposite the National Theatre. The food is reasonable – not as good as the more upmarket Indian restaurants, but significantly cheaper. *Main course Ush10,000–17,000.*

✗ **Centenary Park** [160 D3] Jinja Rd. This historic public green space has recently become controversially cluttered with a tacky cluster of bars & eating places – Turkish, Indian, *nyama choma* (roast meat) & Chinese.

✗ **Café Java** [154 E2] Oasis Mall. A branch of the Kenyan restaurant chain, this place serves pies, burgers, steaks (*Ush22,000*), wraps, quesadillas,

superb battered fish 'n' chips (*Ush23,000*) & a range of cakes for afters. It's not cheap but the portions are often enough for 2. Also branches in Kisementi & Namirembe.

✗ **Garden City Food Court** [160 C2] Options in the Garden City Shopping Centre food hall include quality Indian, Iranian & Chinese food as well as burgers & chicken & chips. Convenient for shoppers but predictably devoid of ambience. The same applies to the food hall in the next door **Oasis Mall.** *Meals Ush7,000–25,000.*

♀ **Alleygators** [160 C2] Garden City Complex. Karaoke bar & bowling alley.

✗ **Rancher's** [160 C2] 1st Fl, Garden City. The café outside Rancher's butchery has a more discreet setting than the expansive Food Court (see above), & serves good steaks, burgers & salads. *Meals Ush18,000–25,000.*

✗ **Nawab** [160 C2] Rooftop, Garden City; ☎ 0414 263333. Indian restaurant with sister branches in Dubai. Very good food, though it looks nothing like the pictures on the menu. *Main course with rice/ naan around Ush22,000.*

♀ **Boda boda** [160 C2] Rooftop, Garden City. A popular watering hole for smart Ugandans. Convenient for a drink after a trip to the cinema downstairs.

✗ **Silver City** [160 C2] Garden City. Smart South African chain serving American-style fast food. Popular for family outings. Kids' play area provided. *Meals Ush15,000–30,000.*

✗ **Golf Course Hotel** [160 C2] ☎ 0414 563500. Watch the world go by (once every 90mins) from Uganda's 1st revolving restaurant. *Main courses Ush25,000 & over.*

✗ **Soho Café & Grill** [160 C2] Course View Towers, Yusuf Lule Rd. Possibly the best 'spicy chips' in Kampala, in a very modern building with

4

THE HUMBLE ROLEX

A welcome, if humble, addition to Kampala's edible offerings is the 'rolex'. This is nothing more (or less) than a freshly cooked *chapati* enhanced by a fresh omelette, chopped onions, tomatoes, green peppers and finely sliced cabbage. The latter items are rolled up inside the former, hence the name, and popped into a polythene bag. You'll find rolex street vendors armed with metal hotplates, a charcoal stove and a chopping board in all popular nightspots of 'local' flavour. It's exactly the sort of street food your mother warned you against eating in Africa, so rolexes are obviously a firm favourite with backpackers, gap-year students, volunteers and this writer. Expect to pay around Ush1,500.

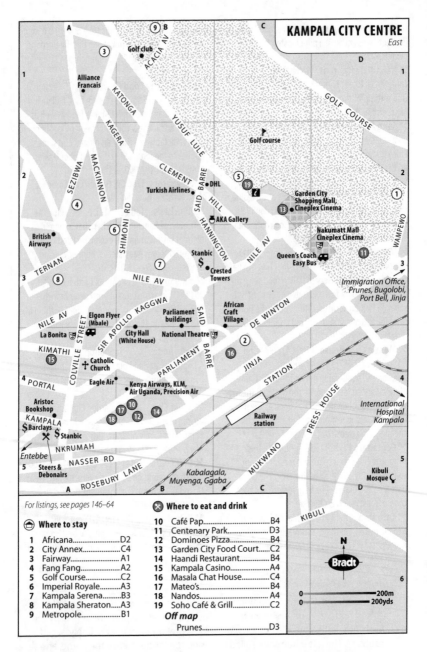

KAMPALA CITY CENTRE
East

For listings, see pages 146–64

🛏 **Where to stay**

1 Africana........................D2
2 City Annex....................C4
3 Fairway.........................A1
4 Fang Fang....................A2
5 Golf Course..................C2
6 Imperial Royale............A3
7 Kampala Serena...........B3
8 Kampala Sheraton.....A3
9 Metropole....................B1

✖ **Where to eat and drink**

10 Café Pap.......................B4
11 Centenary Park............D3
12 Dominoes Pizza...........B4
13 Garden City Food Court......C2
14 Haandi Restaurant.......B4
15 Kampala Casino...........A4
16 Masala Chat House.......C4
17 Mateo's........................B4
18 Nandos.........................A4
19 Soho Café & Grill..........C2
Off map
Prunes..........................D3

an open terrace area. Varied menu (with great vegetarian options) & free Wi-Fi.
✖ **Ekitoobero** [163 B3] Nakasero Rd; ☎0414 346834. *The* place to sample traditional Ugandan food in a restaurant rather than a market stall. *Meals Ush12,000–20,000.*

✖ **Yujo** [163 B3] Kyadondo Rd, Nakasero. Japanese food in pleasant garden setting.
✖ **Emin Pasha Hotel** [163 B3] Akii Bua Rd; ☎0414 236977. The terraced Brasserie restaurant at Kampala's 1st boutique hotel is a delightful setting for a special occasion, especially if someone

else is paying! *Starters Ush14,000–25,000, main course Ush35,000, desserts Ush15,000.*

✗ **Mamba Point** [163 B3] Akii Bua Rd, beyond the Emin Pasha Hotel; m 0772 243225. Excellent & sophisticated Italian food & wine list, on a leafy veranda. *Main courses Ush30,000.*

✗ **Open House** [148 B1] Buganda Rd. Located on the premises of the Uganda Institute, this (mostly) outdoor restaurant/bar serves brilliant Indian food at reasonable prices. *Main course excl rice /naan Ush16,000.*

✗ **Sam's Restaurant** [148 B1] 78 Kampala Rd; ☎ 0414 251694. A wide range of offerings include steaks, game meat, salads & some less inspiring Indian dishes. *Main courses Ush25,000 & over.*

Bugolobi

♀ **Jazzville** [135 G4] Bandari Rise. Popular & classy bar offering *muchomo* (roast meat) & with live music every evening until 2300.

♀ **Bamboo Nest** [135 G4] This popular bar occupies the rambling, storied thatched structure opposite Bugolobi Market. Roasted meat a speciality.

✗ **Italia** [135 G4] Behind Shell Bugolobi; m 0772 956882. Genuine Italian food in relaxed garden atmosphere.

✗ **Ashiana** [135 G4] Directly across the road from Bugolobi Market & the conspicuous Bamboo Nest. This Indian restaurant is worth seeking out for a top-quality curry. *Main course + naan Ush27,000.*

Western Kampala (Rubaga and Mengo)

✗ **Café Java** [154 E2] Namirembe Rd, near Bakuli crossroads. Eating out on the Mengo side of town is now an option with the opening of this Café Java outlet. Huge portions & free Wi-Fi. *Meals Ush15,000–27,000.*

✗ **Miraculean Grill BBQ Restaurant** [154 E1] Just 700m down Apollo Kagwe Rd from the big mosque. The 3-course menu offers a choice of chargrilled mains (steak, fish, kebab, beefburger). Eat upstairs with a city view or down in the small green garden surrounded by some funky concrete décor. *Ush18,000.*

✗ **Tuhende Safari Lodge** [154 F2] Martin Rd; m 0772 468360; www.tuhendesafarilodge.com. This popular veranda BBQ restaurant in Old Kampala, is within easy reach of Mengo's hotels & hostels. *Meals Ush20,000.*

✗ **Wallet Time Pub** [134 D5] Kabusu Rd, beyond Rubaga Cathedral. Excellent roast pork in

shady thatch shelters. A few similar setups are to be found in the vicinity.

♀ **Maggie's Bar** [154 C3] Natete Rd Mengo's oldest bar seems rather dingy these days but it's still a convenient stop-off after the walk up the hill from the Backpackers' Hostel.

✗ **Mona Lisa** [154 B3] On the corner of Natete & Sentema roads. Lively local bar in Mengo with music including live bands & dance troupes, & roast pork.

♀ **Harriet's Bar/Apha Salon** [154 A4] Kalema Rd, just behind the Backpackers' Hostel. Harriet, aka Mama Salooni, will provide you with a beer & a new hairdo.

✗ **Un Peu du Bali** [154 A4] Kalema Rd. Large thatched bar set in a expansive garden, 5mins' walk from Kampala Backpackers. Excellent performances of traditional music & dance some evenings.

Makerere area

✗ **Tipsy's Takeaway** [163 A3] Located near Wandegere crossroads, Tipsy's is a mandatory pilgrimage after a night's drinking for a late night snack.

✗ **Deep Blue & 2 stars** [163 A2] Next to Shell Wandegere. Pork feasts await! And also at Joys Joint next to Wandegeya Post Office.

✗ **Teachers Grill** [163 A2] Bombo Rd, Wandegere. Downstairs behind the College Inn, the 1970s interior must surely be in a scene in *The*

Last King of Scotland movie. A trendy hangout for university students.

✗ **Club 5** [135 E3] Makerere University. This café is worth a visit if you're on campus. Affordable local & international staples plus some good Indian specials are served in a semi-open setting. The complex includes a bar with DSTV, a gym, sauna, & an internet café. Take the 1st left inside the main gate.

✕ Nakulabye Pork Joints [135 E3] A kilometre west of the university, Makerere Hill Road is lined with pork joints/bars offering roast pork with 'accompaniments' (tomato, avocado, onion, cassava…). Strictly dining-with-fingers.

Kisementi and Kololo

The popular **Kisementi Plaza** hosts a selection of bars and restaurants, including **The Bistro** (burgers, steaks, wraps, etc), **Just Kicking** (a sports bar) and **Fat Boyz** (mostly Mexican; can you refuse their proud offer of 'warm beer and lousy food'?). Just down the road, leafy Acacia Avenue is becoming Kampala's main drag for smart restaurants and bars.

✕ Khana Khazana [163 D2] Acacia Av; 0414 233049/347346. The best setting of any of Kampala's restaurants, & serving creamy rich Indian food. Splash out! *Main + rice + naan Ush35,000.*

♀ Bubbles O' Leary [163 D2] Acacia Av. Authentic Irish pub (fittings imported from a bankrupt bar in Eire) but unfortunately without the Guinness. Popular expat pub, particularly on Fri & Sat when there's an entrance fee to keep out riff-raff like the author of this guide.

✕ Mish Mash [163 D3] Acacia Av; m 0794 010101; www.facebook.com/mishmash; ⊕ daily from 09.00 for b/fast, lunch, evening tapas & dinner. Vibrant gallery café with a kaleidoscopic programme of regular & one-off events, performances & exhibitions. The converted bungalow & pretty garden are Kampala's most popular location for food, drink, arts, crafts, live music, DJ events, cinema & more. If you can't get there, they'll deliver (m 0777 111214/111215). *Meals Ush18,000–30,000.*

✕ China Bowl [163 D1] Prince Charles Drive, Kololo. Excellent Chinese food served by Indians. In a bold break with convention, the 'authentically Chinese' dining arena draws on communist principles of scale & utilitarianism.

✕ The Barn Steakhouse & Terrace [163 D3] Windsor Crescent. Popular new spot for steaks

(*Ush25,000–30,000*) in a suitably barn-like, thatched building. Enjoy drinks on an adjacent 1st-floor rooftop terrace/bar.

✕ Tamarai Restaurant [163 D4] 14 Lower Kololo Terr, Kololo. Great Thai food in a pleasant environment.

✕ Iguana & Gusto [163 D1] Directly behind the new Acacia Mall facing Kisementi plaza. On the ground floor the new & already popular Gusto restaurant is decorated with cheerful blocks of primary colours softened by a dash of mauve. Burgers, salads, tapas, coffees, Dutch bread & pastries plus free Wi-Fi will keep you occupied throughout the day until an acceptable hour arrives to peruse the wine list & cocktail menu. Busy Iguana Bar is located on the 1st floor. *Meals Ush15,000–25,000.*

⌨ Prunes [off map, 160 D3] Wampewo Av, opposite IHK clinic. Stylish coffee shop & café in a garden setting between Kololo airstrip & Jinja Road. Ugandan Arabica coffee, juices, smoothies, sandwiches, salads …

✕ Cayenne [135 F2] Kira Rd, near Kabira Country Club. Restaurant complex with something for everyone: a wide-ranging menu to keep families happy, evening music, dancing til late at w/ends, a hairdresser's, a lovely poolside terrace, & a pool that for some reason you're not allowed to swim in. *Meals Ush18,000–25,000.*

Kabalagala

Kabalagala (or 'Kabs' to those in the know) contains Kampala's densest concentration of bars, restaurants and roadside grills. It's *the* place to enjoy a meal and party until late without moving too far. The traditional hotspot is the first few hundred metres of Muyenga Road above its junction with Ggaba Road. Evening parking here is all but impossible so take a *matatu* or a special hire taxi.

Two secondary hubs also exist. One is located 500m further down Ggaba Road and exploits its proximity to Kampala International University and the notorious Al's Bar. The second is centred on a new line of bars and cafés at the top of Muyenga Road near the landmark Reste Corner junction (named for a currently defunct hotel).

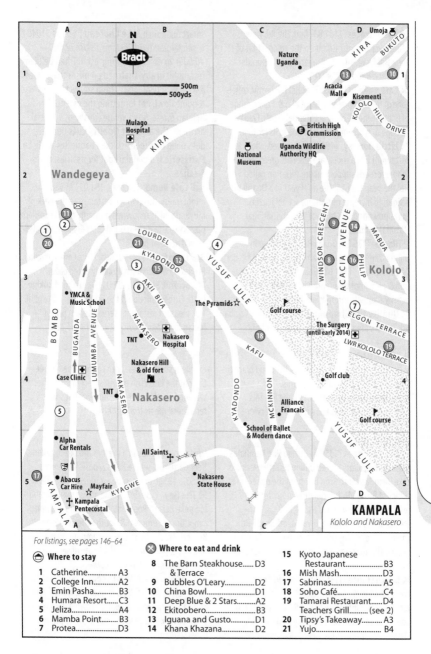

KAMPALA
Kololo and Nakasero

4

For listings, see pages 146–64

🏠 **Where to stay**

1 Catherine..................A3
2 College Inn..............A2
3 Emin Pasha.............B3
4 Humara Resort.......C3
5 Jeliza.........................A4
6 Mamba Point.........B3
7 Protea......................D3

😋 **Where to eat and drink**

8   The Barn Steakhouse......D3
    & Terrace
9   Bubbles O'Leary..............D2
10 China Bowl......................D1
11 Deep Blue & 2 Stars.......A2
12 Ekitoobero.......................B3
13 Iguana and Gusto...........D1
14 Khana Khazana...............D2

15 Kyoto Japanese
    Restaurant....................B3
16 Mish Mash.......................D3
17 Sabrinas...........................A5
18 Soho Café.........................C4
19 Tamarai Restaurant.......D4
    Teachers Grill.........(see 2)
20 Tipsy's Takeaway............A3
21 Yujo...................................B4

✖ **Fasika** [181 A3] Ggaba Rd opposite Tank Hill
Rd; ☎ 0414 510441. This good-value Ethiopian
restaurant next to Payless supermarket [181
B3] offers tasty & authentic Ethiopian dishes –
pancake-like *injera* with spicy *wat* sauces – in
a small garden. A good option for combining

eating with a night out at the nearby Al's Bar &
Capital Pub. *Meals Ush22,000.*
♀ **Fuego's** [181 C2] Turn left off Tank Hill Rd at
Reste Corner junction at the very top of Kabalagala.
Extremely popular bar in a converted storied
residential house & garden.

✕ **The Terraces** [181 B3] Tank Hill Rd. New hillside garden restaurant on the steepest bit of Tank Hill Road. The Mongolian BBQ is a popular speciality. *BBQ Ush25,000.*

✕ **Café Kawa** [181 D2] Tank Hill Rd. Terrific coffee (one of the best places in Kampala) & a good range of light lunches & more substantial meals. Free Wi-Fi. Popular with embassy staff due to its location.

✕ **Little Donkey** [181 D1] This raved-about restaurant has a cool atmosphere & great Mexican food. Proceeds support an organisation called S7 (ie: the year after S6, the final year in a Ugandan school) to increase options for school leavers. In Namuwongo, 100m from the International Hospital Kampala.

♀ **Tilapia** [135 G6] Ggaba Rd. Popular bar in Bunga, 2km beyond the main cluster around Al's Bar.

✕ **Punchline** [181 B3] Ggaba Rd. Popular local pub & pork joint frequented by students from nearby Kampala International University.

✕ **Quality Hill Shopping Mall** [181 A3] Ggaba Rd. There's plenty of choice at this small but

smart mall, such as **Le Chateau** (📞 *0414 510404; e sales@qualitycuts.net; meals Ush22,000–40,000)* an excellent & long-established Belgian restaurant in airy, thatched premises that serves a wide variety of food – from steaks to snails & guineafowl, not forgetting the essential Belgian *frites*– & is a venue worthy of a special occasion. The adjacent **Quality Cuts** butchery does good ham/beef/chicken baguettes while **La Patisserie** is a popular spot for pastries, cakes & coffee.

⬛ **Café Roma** [off map, 181 D2] As you might guess, this popular restarant at the back of Muyenga hill is renowned primarily for its excellent pizzas & pasta dishes. Good grills & salads are also served at expat prices.

⬛ **Palm Café** [181 C2] Near Reste Corner junction. Roadside joint serving reasonably priced pizza.

✕ **Coconut Shack** [181 D1] On the road linking Reste Corner junction & the International Hospital. This pleasant restaurant serves decent priced Indian food. *Main + rice + naan Ush25,000.*

Kansanga

♀ **Hunters' Bar** [181 C6] Ggaba Rd. Good place to relax with lively crowd & live bands.

✕ **Le Petit Bistro** [181 D6] Ggaba Rd. This long-serving eatery is known for slow service &

excellent steak dishes. I can confirm the former but not the latter: on our most recent visit, after waiting for 2½hrs, we left; not without some tetchiness. *Meals Ush24,000.*

Munyonyo

✕ **Cassia Lodge** [135 G6] Buziga Hill. Kampala's most spectacularly placed dining terrace overlooks Lake Victoria's Murchison Bay from the upper slopes of Buziga Hill. *1-course continental meals cost Ush25,000, 3-courses Ush50,000.*

♀ **Miki's** [135 G6] Munyonyo Rd, off Ggaba Rd. There's more to Munyonyo than the posh Speke Resort. This roadside bar is popular with locals & expats.

✕ **Beach House** [135 G6] 📞 *0392 964474; m 0772 448617.* A downsized & downmarket version of the sprawling Speke Resort, the Beach House is a pleasant spot to enjoy a lake view & platter of tilapia & chips. Beach House runs boat

trips across the bay to a pretty sand beach called Beer Gardens 2 where BBQs & basic s/c *bandas* (US$32/48 sgl/dbl) can be arranged.

✕ **The Bay** [135 G6] Off the access road leading to Speke Resort. Popular lakeside bistro offering a mixture of European & South African cuisine. Burgers, steaks, lamb curries, tempura prawns, salads, etc plus a lake view & boat cruises, too. *Main courses Ush16,000–35,000.*

✕ An additional option is **Lagoon Resort** [135 H7] on the other side of the bay from Munyonyo. It has quite a reputation as an out-of-town eatery (*tasty 3-course meals, cooked to German prescriptions, Ush50,000pp).*

NIGHTLIFE

NIGHTCLUBS It's perfectly possible to visit any of the places mentioned above for a meal and a couple of drinks and retire happily before midnight. If that doesn't appeal, try the locations listed below which exist to keep you entertained until very late. You can simplify things by taking a **Club Popping Tour** (e *clubpopping@*

gmail.com; Facebook: Kampala Club Popping). Tours cost Ush35,000 per person for a minimum six people. You're collected from Kampala Backpackers (on Friday nights) or Red Chilli (on Saturdays) at 21.30 to spend about 90 minutes at each of three clubs, before being returned at 03.30.

City centre

☆ **Rock Bar** [149 G3] Next to the Speke Hotel, see page 147. The city centre's liveliest hangout.

☆ **Sabrinas** [163 A5] Bombo Rd; ☎ 0414 250174. The original karaoke pub in Kampala with tasty buffet lunches & a good atmosphere.

☆ **Faze 2** [149 E1] Lumumba Av. Great bar/club with good music.

Kabalagala/Kansanga

☆ **Al's Bar** [181 B4] Ggaba Rd. Al's opened its doors in 1993 as a restaurant next to the famous (but now closed) Half London nightspot. But when the European crowd flocked in to rock to Alan's rather dated music collection, & the Kansanga girls followed them, he threw out the 3-course menu & cranked up the volume. The rest is all part of a lively 20-year history, though there's now so much competition along Gaba Road that Al's is no longer the standout venue that it was 'back in the day'.

☆ **Capital Pub** [181 B3] Kabalagala. This noisy, sprawling & crowded bar in the heart of the Kabalagala cluster of bars & restaurants still rocks

after all these years. Male visitors will be surprised at how many young ladies attempt to engage them in conversation. They might be attracted by your wit & good looks but your money is a more likely draw.

☆ **De Posh** [181 B2] Kabalagala. One of a couple of dozen nightspots lining the main drag in Kabalagala, De Posh can be distinguished by its multi-coloured illuminations.

☆ **Venom** [181 A2] Tirupatti Mall, Ggaba Rd. New nightclub containing Kampala's 1st microbrewery. Only sells its own beers (*Ush7,000*) plus the usual wines & spirits. Steep entrance fee.

Industrial area off Jinja Road

☆ **Club Silk** [135 F3] 15–17 1st St; ☎ 0414 250907. Cheap drinks & expensive admission.

☆ **Ange Noir** [135 F3] Off Jinja Rd, between 1 & 3 streets. Good DJs, cheap drinks, & a guaranteed lively crowd. Check out **Ange Mystique** upstairs for a more sophisticated crowd.

☆ **T1 Club** [135 F3] 2nd St near Ange Noir & Silk. Popular new offering.

ENTERTAINMENT

CINEMA You'll find brand-new international releases opening at Kampala's two **Cineplex** cinemas [160 C2] within a day or so of their premieres in London and New York (and at a fraction of the cost). Pick up a copy of the *New Vision* or *Monitor* to find out what's showing when you're in town. Cineplex operates a three screen cinema in both Garden City and the adjacent Oasis Malls.

THEATRES AND LIVE PERFORMANCES Kampala has an active English-language theatre community, which mainly stages locally written plays in English. The **National Theatre** [160 C4] (☎ 0414 254567), which opened in 1959 on the corner of Said Barre Avenue and De Winton Road, puts on productions most weekends. Tickets cost around Ush10,000–20,000. Regular events during the week include the Monday night jam session when local musicians gather for impromptu sessions. There's no charge and if you play an instrument, you'll be welcome to join in. On Tuesdays at 20.000 there's a cultural performance (*Ush10,000 entrance*), on Wednesdays youthful acrobats perform (⊕ *20.00; Ush5,000*) and on Thursdays there's comedy (⊕ *20.00; Ush10,000*). Performances take place inside the theatre, in the driveway just in front and in the bar/restaurant around the back.

Rather smarter than the National Theatre is the **La Bonita** [160 A4] theatre on Colville Street, home to The Ebonies, Kampala's most popular performing group. A plush restaurant is attached.

The **Ndere Centre** [135 F2] (✆ *0414 288123*), a purpose-built venue, set in large lawns on the outskirts of the city at Ntinda, is home to the well-known Ndere Troupe. Performances of traditional dance and music from all corners of Uganda are put on every Sunday between 18.00 and 21.00 (*Ush15,000*). Additional performances include an excellent Afro-jazz night each Thursday and a talent show on Fridays for up-and-coming artists (*free entrance*). Contact the centre for other one-off plays and performances. The Ndere Centre includes an outdoor auditorium, an indoor theatre, a restaurant and even some limited accommodation. To get there, head up Kiira Road to Ntinda trading centre in northeastern Kampala (see map, page 135), turn left at the crossroads and then head north for about 2km.

ART SCENE (*with thanks here to Rocca Gutteridge*) Kampala has a vibrant art scene with several good art galleries and other venues scattered around the city. Highly recommended locations are the **AfriArt Gallery** [135 F2] (*www.afriartgallery.org*) off Kiira Road in Kamwokya; **Mish Mash** [163 D3] (*www.mishmashuganda.com*) on Acacia Avenue in Kololo; **AKA Gallery** [160 B2] (*www.akagalleryuganda.com*) and **Umoja Art Gallery** [163 D1] (*www.umojaartgallery.com*) on Hannington Road and **Nommo Gallery** [149 F1] on Victoria Street, on the edge of the city centre in Nakasero. The Faculty of Fine Arts in **Makerere University** [135 E3] has some impressive resources and displays works by several of the country's leading or most promising talents. Down on the Ggaba Road opposite Al's Bar, **32° East: Ugandan Arts Trust** [181 B4] (*www.ugandanartstrust.org*) has studios, an art library, and supports new and upcoming talent through workshops and public art events.

SHOPPING

SHOPPING MALLS Several shopping malls have sprung up in Kampala in recent years. Probably the best of these (and that's not really saying much) is the centrally located **Garden City Shopping Centre** [160 C2] on Yusuf Lule Road overlooking the golf course. In addition to a cinema complex and Kampala's first bowling alley, it contains a good supermarket, half a dozen restaurants, an excellent bookshop, a casino, hairdresser, several banks, a forex bureau, and some trendy clothes shops. A brand-new mall next door is dominated by a two-floor branch of **Nakumatt** [160 D3], a Kenyan supermarket chain.

Lugogo Mall [135 F3] on the east side of the city contains two South African 'megastores', a Shoprite supermarket and an equally extensive 'Game' store. If you're using public transport, the rather limited **Shoprite Mall** [148 D7] by the old taxi park will be most convenient (avoid this if you're driving; this congested area is virtually impossible to reach in a vehicle). **Pioneer Mall** [148 D3] on Kampala Road contains the economical Antonio's Restaurant but an otherwise unremarkable selection of shops. Out of town, you'll find couple of malls at Naalya near the eastern end of the northern bypass; **Metroplex Mall** [135 G2] is beside the bypass while **Quality Mall** [181 A3] is 1km towards Namugongo. If you're on the southern, Entebbe side of town, the related **Quality Village** [135 E7] at Lubowa is the most convenient.

SUPERMARKETS You'll find most of your day-to-day requirements in small supermarkets in suburbs such as Mengo, Bugolobi, Kabalagala/Ggaba Road and Kisementi. Three major supermarket chains are present in Kampala. The best –

though not the cheapest – is the Kenyan megastore chain, **Nakumatt**. In addition to its flagship branch in Oasis Mall [160 D3], Nakumatt has smaller outlets in Bugolobi, Naguru and Katwe. **Uchumi,** another Kenyan chain, is represented at Garden City and Tirupati Mall [181 A2] on Ggaba Road. Otherwise the South African **Shoprite** [148 D6] (see above) is represented at Lugogo Mall, Metroplex Mall and the Shoprite Mall near the old taxi park. Better value than all the above is the local **Quality Supermarket** chain found in Old Kampala [181 A3] and inside the Quality Malls at Lubowa and Naalya (near Metroplex Mall).

If you're stocking up for a safari and hope to avoid the usual packaged foodstuffs from supermarket freezers, a few good delis/butcheries offer a variety of cold meats and cheeses as good as you'll find anywhere in East Africa. Try **Rancher's** (Garden City Mall) [160 C2] and **Quality Cuts** butchery [181 A3] (Ggaba Road near the US Embassy). The latter has additional branches in several Uchumi and Nakumatt supermarkets and also in Entebbe.

BAKERIES Salt bread, as well as the locally preferred sweet variety, is available from most supermarkets these days. For basic loaves, the **Shoprite** supermarkets will do nicely but for buns, baguettes, croissants, French sticks, etc, head down the Ggaba Road to **The Patisserie** in the tiny Quality Hill Mall [181 A3] or **Brood Bakery** in Tirupati Mall directly opposite. Brood also has a central outlet in Nandos on Kampala Road

BOOKSHOPS There are several bookshops in Kampala, though most focus exclusively on religious texts. The main exception is **Aristoc Bookshop** [149 H4] which has a branch on Kampala Road and another (considerably larger) in Garden City Shopping Mall. These stock an impressive selection of current novels, travel guides, field guides, tourist maps and publications about Ugandan history. The closest competition is **The Media Centre** in the neighbouring Oasis Mall.

HANDICRAFTS AND CURIOS Though home-produced crafts are increasing and improving, most local craft shops are still dominated by ubiquitous Kenyan carvings of animals and Maasai warriors. For the greatest choice of vendors (rather than choice of items), visit the **craft market** [160 C3] behind the National Theatre and the one in the **Exposure Africa** collective on Buganda Road [160 C3]. The small but long-established **Uganda Crafts** [148 B1] on Bombo Road, is pretty good and benefits disabled people. For less obvious items, try the lower section of **Nakasero Market** [149 F5].

The best outlets for quality crafts are the **'Banana Boat'** (0414 252190; e crafts@bananaboat.co.ug) shops at Kisementi, Garden City and Lugogo Mall. These contain an excellent variety of items produced by over 90 small Ugandan artisans and workshops, many of them exclusively for Banana Boat. Bespoke items include jewellery, leather trunks and boxes, tribal art, handmade paper products as well as guidebooks and maps. See also advert in third colour section.

PAPERCRAFT Located between Kampala and Entebbe (500m south of the conspicuous J&M Airport Hotel), **Papercraft** (www.papercraftafrica.com) is worth a visit. Products include handmade paper products, soap, and recycled-glass jewellery.

OTHER PRACTICALITIES

CLUBS AND SOCIETIES Travellers with special interests may want to contact the following clubs and societies. A fuller list is contained in Kampala's free monthly ad-mag, *The Eye*.

International Women's Organisation
e ugandaiwo@yahoo.com. Regular meetings on the 1st Thu of the month at the National Museum on Kiira Road. Special events.
Mountain Club of Uganda m 0772 200745/ 0757 107330; www.mcu.org. Meets at 17.30 on the penultimate (2nd last) Thu of each month at Mish Mash on Acacia Avenue (see page 162).

Nature Uganda 0414 540719. Ring for details of free monthly nature walks around Kampala.
Uganda Bird Guides Club m 0772 518290; e ugandabirdguides@hotmail.com. The country's top bird guides all belong to this club, which is well worth contacting if you're looking for a reliable freelance guide with local knowledge.

COMMUNICATIONS

Courier services Post into and out of Kampala is fairly reliable, but it is extremely slow and is best avoided for valuable or urgent dispatches. It is more expensive but safer to use a major international courier service such as **DHL** ([160 B2] Clement Hill Rd; *0312 210006*) or **TNT** ([163 A4] behind Clock Tower; *0414 343942*).

Internet and email It's scarcely possible to walk more than 100m in the city centre without tripping over an internet café. Standards are constantly improving and a fairly uniform rate of Ush25 per minute (around US$0.80 per hour) is charged.

Post The main **post office** [149 F4] on the corner of Kampala and Speke roads has a poste restante service as well as selling stamps etc.

Telephone Mobile phones have rendered the parastatal landline services all but obsolete when it comes to international calls. All over the city centre you'll see shops and kiosks offering domestic and international calls. Calls within Uganda cost around Ush300 per minute and Ush500 (a quarter US dollar) to most of the rest of the world. An international payphone is available at the Kampala Backpackers, and most upmarket hotels can book international calls at inflated rates.

Useful telephone numbers
Emergencies (ambulance, fire or police assistance) 999 or 0414 342222/3

Central Police Station 0414 254561/2

See page 169, for clinics with 24-hour emergency and ambulance services.

GORILLA-TRACKING PERMITS Permits for reserves in Uganda can be bought directly from the **Uganda Wildlife Authority (UWA) headquarters** on Kiira Road (*0414 355000*; e *info@ugandawildlife.org; www.ugandawildlife.org; information office* *08.00–13.00 & 14.00–17.00 Mon–Fri, 09.00–13.00 Sat*) between the Uganda Museum and the British High Commission or through any major tour operator. The **Kampala Backpackers' Hostel** can usually arrange permits for reserves in Uganda, Rwanda and the Democratic Republic of Congo (DRC). If in Jinja, contact Nile River Explorers (see page 501).

HAIR AND BEAUTY SALONS Recommended salons include the **Pearl Royale Beauty Parlour** on the ground floor of Rwenzori House on Lumumba Avenue (*0414 254534/342037*) and **Ashia** at Kisementi (*0414 344366*). Several of the upmarket hotels in the city centre have in-house salons.
  Gents can get a Ush2,000 crew cut with an electric shaver from any local barber (it's worth making sure your trip doesn't coincide with a scheduled power cut!).

If you expect the use of scissors, try **Aisha** (see above; *Ush20,000*) or the **Indian barber** (*Ush8,500*) in Old Kampala near Tuhende Safari Lodge [154 F2].

LIBRARIES The **Uganda Society** (☎ *0414 234964*; e *ugsociety@bushnet.net; www. africa.upenn.edu/ugandasoc/ugandasociety.htm;* ⊕ *08.00–12.30 Mon–Fri, closed public holidays; a nominal daily membership fee is charged to casual visitors*), in the National Museum Building on Kiira Road, houses what is probably the most comprehensive collection of current and out of print books about Uganda in existence.

MEDIA

Newspapers The main local English-language newspapers are *New Vision* and *Monitor*, both of which include reasonable coverage of African and international affairs and are widely available in Kampala, as is the excellent Nairobi-published weekly *East African*. Current and old issues of the American *Time* and *Newsweek* magazines can be bought from street vendors. You'll find UK and US newspapers in **Uchumi** in Garden City or the **Sheraton Bookshop**. **Media Hub** bookshop in Oasis Mall has a wide selection of regional magazines.

MEDICAL SERVICES Hospitals and medical services are not generally up to Western standards, and it's worth seeking current recommendations from your hotel before contacting any of the following private clinics.

✚ **Bai Medical Centre** [154 G2] Rashid Khamis Rd, Old Kampala; ☎ 0414 345326/34/0312 261551, emergency line: 0414 255700. This well-equipped hospital is conveniently located if you're staying in budget lodgings in the Natete Road area.
✚ **Case Medical Centre** [163 A4] 69–71 Buganda Rd; ☎ 0414 250362. Modern & expanding clinic. 24hr emergency line: ☎ 0312 250362.
✚ **International Hospital Kampala (IHK)** [181 D1] Namuwongo/Kisugu; ☎ 0312 200400; e ihk@africaonline.co.ug. This smart new hospital (allied to the IMC clinic) can be approached either from Kabalagala (off Ggaba Road), heading behind the Reste Corner junction (see Ggaba Road map, page 181) or from the junction just west of the 'Mukwano' roundabout railway crossing junction on Mukwano Road (see Kampala city centre: east map, page 160).

✚ **International Medical Centre (IMC)** [148 B1] KPC Bldg, Bombo Rd; ☎ 0312 200400, or Kitgum Hse, Jinja Rd; ☎ 0312 341291; 24hr emergency line: m 0772 741291; 24hr ambulance service: m 0772 200400/1. IMC also has several branches upcountry.
✚ **Kim's Medical Centre** [149 H5] 4 Entebbe Rd; ☎ 0414 341777; 24hr emergency & ambulance: m 0752 722000
✚ **The Surgery** [163 D4] 2 Acacia Av; ☎ 0414 256003, 24hr emergency & ambulance service: m 0752 756003. Previously the clinic in the British High Commission, this is the choice of many expats. Many travellers have also found the website a useful resource (*www.thesurgeryuganda.org*). During the lifetime of this book, The Surgery should move to a new site in Naguru in northeast Kampala so check the address in *The Eye* before heading there.

Dental services Dentists include **Jubilee Dental Practice** (☎ *0414 344647*) and **Doctors A & G Madan** (m *0772 433058/9*). **Mengo Hospital** [154 C3] has a smart, well-equipped and reasonably priced dental clinic.

MONEY

Credit cards Most upmarket hotels in Kampala accept major international credit and debit cards, as do some of the smarter restaurants, but you will need to pay cash for most services and purchases. Visa and MasterCard can be used to draw cash from ATM machines (see page 107).

4

Foreign exchange (cash) Private **forex bureaux** are dotted all over the city, with the main concentration along Kampala Road, and will readily exchange US dollars and other hard currencies into Uganda shillings. Most bureaux are open from 09.00 to 17.00 on weekdays and a few are also open on Saturday mornings – exchange rates at the major forex bureaux are pretty uniform, and better than at the banks, though you might want to shop around before you change large sums of money. If you need to change money on Sundays or outside normal office hours, try the forex in Speke Hotel. This will also exchange travellers' cheques but at an extremely poor rate. You could also try the upmarket hotels, but generally they change money only for hotel residents.

NATIONAL PARKS AND RESERVES The **UWA** (see page 168) is in charge of all of Uganda's national parks and game reserves. The main office is on Kiira Road between the Uganda Museum and the British High Commission. Gorilla-viewing permits for Bwindi and Mgahinga can be booked and paid for here (see also page 168), as can *banda* accommodation in the various national parks and game reserves, and you can also pick up some informative brochures. For information about Budongo, Mpanga, Mabira, Kalinzu and other forest reserves, contact the **National Forest Authority** (✆ *0414 230365*).

PHOTOGRAPHY Most visitors to Uganda now use digital cameras and are spared the disappointment that can result from poor-quality film and developing processes available in Uganda. If you are still using slide or photographic film, be sure to bring a sufficient supply with you and take it home to be developed. If you do need photographic services, Kampala's most professional are provided by **Colour Chrome**. There is a branch on Kampala Road [148 C2] (✆ *0414 230556*) and in Acacia Mall at Kisementi, off Kira Road [163 D1]. Photographic, digital photographic and slide-processing services are offered. See also the box on pages 122–3.

WHAT TO SEE AND DO

The National Museum, Kasubi Tombs and other sites of interest situated more-or-less within the city limits of Kampala are covered below. As with any city, however, just strolling around can be illuminating; the contrast between the posh part of town north of Kampala Road and the sleazier area near the bus and taxi parks is striking. It is also possible to take a boda-boda tour, see page 146. Sites of interest in Entebbe are covered in the next chapter, while those further afield from Kampala are covered under *Day trips out of Kampala*, pages 180–7.

CITY CENTRE Kampala's modern city centre – which sprawls across a valley about 2.5km east of Kabaka Mwanga's former capital on Kasubi Hill, immediately east of Lugard's original **fort** [154 F2] on Old Kampala Hill – boasts little in the way of compelling sightseeing. The most important cluster of architecturally noteworthy buildings is centred on the acacia-lined **Parliament Avenue** [160 B4] on the east side of the city centre. On Parliament Avenue itself, the imposing though not exactly inspiring **Parliament Building**, built during the colonial era and still the seat of national government today, is a vast white monolith entered via an angular and some might say rather ugly concrete arch, built to commemorate independence in 1962. On the same block lies the so-called **White House**, occupied by the Kampala City Council, while immediately to its east, on De Winton Road, stand the **National Theatre** [160 C4] and attached **African Crafts Village**. Arguably more attractive than any of the above is the **railway station** [160 C4], which lies on Jinja Road about 200m further south, and was built in the 1920s but has fallen into virtual disuse since passenger services out of Kampala were suspended a few years ago.

The **Independence Monument** [149 G3] on Nile Avenue, just outside the fenced gardens, is worth a minor diversion – a tall, attractively proportioned neo-traditional statue of a mother and child. The attractive gardens behind the statue were originally created to commemorate the jubilee of King George VI and now form the grounds of the Kampala Sheraton. Once a popular lunchtime space, today they are closed to the general public, security reasons being the rather lame excuse.

OLD KAMPALA MOSQUE [154 F2] Old Kampala Hill, which rises gently to the immediate west of the city centre, ten minutes' walk from the new taxi park, was the site of the original fort and capital founded by Captain Lugard in 1890. Enclosed within the oval Old Kampala Road, the hill is dotted with a few fine colonial-era buildings of Asian design, now generally rather rundown though some have been strikingly renovated. Old Kampala is most notable today as the focal point for Kampala's Islamic community and an imposing new **mosque** [154 F2]. It was initiated by Idi Amin in the 1970s, but the project stalled after the dictator's overthrow and was only completed in 2006 with funds provided by the late Libyan leader, Colonel Gadaffi. When work on the mosque restarted after a 25-year delay, Amin's concrete monolith was demolished to make way for today's magnificent copper-domed structure. A tour of the site is highly recommended (contact the mosque's Tourism Officer on m 0701 857922) to visit the main hall and ascend the minaret. The former is an imposing space which, carpeted but otherwise unfurnished, is dominated by a forest of massive columns that support the roof and copper dome. European, Arab and African influences meld with Italian stained-glass windows, Ugandan timber and an Arabian mosaic on the underside of the dome above a massive and magnificent metal chandelier. Inside the minaret, 306 steps spiral upwards to provide a superbly giddy 360° view over the city. Part of the complex, but accessed from Old Kampala Road, is a period building with a vaguely Arcadian frontage. This is an approximation of a historic building which was unfortunately demolished to make way for the mosque car park. Though widely known as the Old Fort, it was built some years after Lugard's occupation in 1908 and was actually Kampala's first museum.

MAKERERE UNIVERSITY [135 E3] The main campus of Uganda's respected Makerere University, which was founded in 1922, lies about 1km north of the city centre and can be entered via the main gate on Makerere Hill Road, some 200m west of Wandegeyre traffic lights on Bombo Road. The **university library** has an extensive Africana section, the **campus bookshop** stocks a wide selection of local-interest academic works, and the gallery in the **Faculty of Fine Arts** is highly regarded (see page 166). The spacious green grounds possess an aura of academic gentility at odds with the hustle and bustle of downtown Kampala, while the older buildings – in particular the whitewashed **Main Hall** with its handsome bell tower – will be of interest to students of colonial architecture. Students of contemporary architecture can also learn a thing or two (mainly the sort of thing they can expect to get away with these days) from recent additions to the campus.

NATIONAL MUSEUM OF UGANDA [163 C3] (*Kiira Rd, about 2km from the city centre;* ⊕ *08.00–17.00 daily; a small admission fee is charged*) The National Museum of Uganda is the oldest in East Africa, and perhaps the best, rooted in

JAWBONE SHRINES

The Baganda traditionally believe that the spirit of a dead man resides in his jawbone, for which reason it is customary for the jawbone of a deceased king to be removed and preserved in a separate shrine before the rest of the body is buried. The jawbone shrine is normally located at the last capital site used by the dead ruler, and is housed within a miniature reproduction of his palace. Jawbone shrines associated with almost all of the kabakas who preceded Mutesa I lie scattered across an area of less than 500km² northwest of present-day Kampala. Most are now untended, and have suffered from serious neglect over the past century, but their location remains well known to locals.

According to the historian Roland Oliver: 'after the dislocation of the jawbone, the body of the king was handed over to the chief executioner, Senkaba, who took it away … to the royal cemetery. There, the body was placed on a bed and certain friends and officials of the dead kabaka were killed and their bodies were thrown upon the heap. These sites did not, like the jawbone shrines, become places of pilgrimage. Nevertheless they were guarded by Senkaba and his representatives.' While jawbone shrines are associated with one specific king, the royal burial grounds are more centralised entities. At least ten tombs of the earlier kings are situated within a 1km² area at Gombe, 20km north of Kampala, while a similar number of more recent kings are buried at Merera along the Hoima Road.

The last ruler of Buganda to receive a traditional royal burial was Kabaka Suuna II, whose jawbone shrine is preserved in a large traditional structure at the site of his last *kibuga* (capital) at Wamala. Suuna's successors – influenced by Islam and Christianity – were buried at Kasubi with their jawbones intact. There is some ambiguity about where the rest of Suuna's remains are located: one tradition asserts that he was the last king to be buried at Merera, while others claim that he was buried at Wamala. The most likely explanation is that Suuna was originally buried at Merera, but his body was later exhumed by his son Mutesa I to be buried alongside the jawbone at Wamala.

an ethnographic collection first exhibited in 1905 in a small Greek temple near Lugard's fort on Old Kampala Hill. Formally established in 1908, the museum was initially known by the local Baganda as Enyumba ya Mayembe (House of Fetishes) and its exhibits were believed to bestow supernatural powers on the colonial administration. In 1954, the museum relocated to its present site on Kiira Road. For those with an interest in pre-colonial African history, there are stimulating displays on the Nakayima Tree, Ntusi and Bigo bya Mugenyi, as well as other aspects of Ugandan history. Of more general interest is a fantastic collection of traditional musical instruments from all over the continent, and the ethnographic gallery, which houses a variety of exhibits relating to traditional Ugandan lifestyles. On foot or in a private vehicle, follow Kampala/Bombo Road north out of the city centre, turning right at the traffic lights at Wandegeyre into Haji Kasule Road, crossing straight across another roundabout after 400m into Kiira Road. The museum is clearly signposted to the right, 600m past this roundabout. Minibuses between the new taxi park and Kamwokya will drop passengers roughly opposite the museum entrance, and can be picked up at taxi ranks along Kampala/Bombo road north of the junction with Burton Road. The

Uganda Society Library in the main museum building (🕐 *08.00–12.00 Mon–Fri*) has a comprehensive collection of published works relating to Uganda.

NATETE ROAD A number of minor historical sites lie within 1km of the Natete Road, which runs east out of central Kampala, past the popular Namirembe Guesthouse and Kampala Backpackers, in the direction of Masaka.

Namirembe Cathedral
[154 C2] The Anglican (now Church of Uganda) cathedral perched atop Namirembe Hill, roughly 1.5km west of the city centre off Natete Road, is one of the most impressive colonial-era constructions in Kampala, and it also offers superb views over the city centre and suburbs. The original cathedral, completed in 1903 and consecrated a year later (see box, page 176), was built entirely by Baganda artisans, albeit under the supervision of a British missionary, and could hold a congregation of 3,000 people. It was described contemporaneously by W E Hoyle as 'a remarkable building with walls of sun-dried bricks, and brick columns supporting the thatch roof, containing 120 tons of thatch [and a] ceiling covered with washed reeds of elephant grass'. This building was destroyed by lightning in 1910 and the present cathedral, a more conventional red-brick structure, built to vast dimensions and graced by some attractive stained-glass windows, was completed in 1919. The cemetery contains the grave of Bishop Hannington, murdered near Jinja in 1885, as well as that of Sir Albert Cook, a pioneering medical doctor who arrived in Kampala in 1896 and whose extensive writings about the early colonial era are quoted elsewhere in this guide. Brass memorial plaques on the wall testify to the often short lives of Europeans in those early days.

Bulange Building
[154 C3] Less than 500m past the turn-off to Namirembe, the Bulange Building – traditional seat of the Buganda Parliament – stands on the south side of Natete Road, directly opposite the junction with Sentema Road. It is one of the most impressive colonial-era buildings in Uganda. Though its high roof, capped with a trio of spires, is visible from the main road, to see the building properly you'll have to leave Natete Road to find the main entrance at the head of a straight, tree-lined avenue known as Kabaka Njagala ('the king is coming') which runs for a mile to Lubiri Palace (see below) on the facing hill. Entrance to the Bulange is allowed unless the building is in official use. About 100m downhill from the Bulange, two exotic giant tortoises dawdle around the gardens of an impressive old building, once the home of Stanley Kisingire, one of the regents of the infant king, Daudi Chwa. Local wisdom is that the tortoises are around 500 years old, but they apparently came to Mengo as recently as 1945.

A 'Buganda Tourism Center' [sic] stands beside the Bulange gate. It's early days for this new and worthy initiative, but as things stand, you'll be better informed by reading this book.

Kabaka Mwanga's Lake, Rubaga Cathedral and Mengo Palace
In 1885, Mwanga settled on the ultimately overambitious scheme of digging a large lake near his capital and linking it with Lake Victoria. The lake was completed in 1888, but the intended link was abandoned when Muslim dissenters drove the kabaka from his capital.

The lake was at one time more of a health hazard than it was a tourist attraction, but the surrounding area has been cleared and there are some interesting birds to be seen on its fringes – notably large colonies of cattle egrets and weavers. Follow the Natete Road out of the city centre for about 2km then turn left just beyond the spired Bulange Building. As you descend the hill, you'll see the lake. The shore can be reached about 1km further on, by taking a steep dirt road on your left towards the Miracle Church where the deep pockets of born-again Christians – or *savedees* as they are known – have funded a massive auditorium.

The lake can easily be visited in conjunction with the Catholic cathedral on Rubaga Hill, which lies about 500m south of Natete Road along Mutesa Road, but is neither as old nor as impressive as its Church of Uganda equivalent at Namirembe. Also close to the lake is the kabaka's Twekobe Palace on the low Lubiri Hill, the site chosen by Mwanga after his coronation in 1884. The ill-fated Kabaka Edward Mutesa was driven from this palace in 1966 by Idi Amin on Obote's orders. The army subsequently occupied the site until 1993, gaining a reputation for terror. Hundreds were taken through its gates by the agents of Amin and Obote, never to be seen again, while ill-paid and ill-disciplined troops

THE FUNERAL OF KABAKA MWANGA

Edited from the 'Uganda Notes' of September 1910

Mwanga was deported in the year 1899 [and] moved to the Seychelles, where he died in May 1903 ... Nothing can be more distressing to the Baganda mind than that a near relative should not be buried in his own Butaka [home] ... So the leading chiefs and the descendants of Mwanga have been agitating to exhume the body and have it transferred to Uganda, and at last permission was obtained.

2 August [1910] was a day of great excitement, and business, as far as natives was [sic] concerned, was suspended. A large crowd proceeded to meet the steamer at Kampala Port to bring up the large packing case in which was enclosed the leaden coffin containing the body of the deceased king [Mwanga], and at 15.00 an enormous concourse followed the body to Namirembe Cathedral ... The funeral cortège entered the church, filling it from end to end, and part of the Burial Service was read ... The body was then removed to Kasubi, the burial place of King Mutesa ... [where] a vault had been carefully prepared of brick and cement, and a double coffin was in readiness.

On the morning of Wednesday [3 August], everyone of any importance in or near Mengo was present at the tomb and the gruesome process of opening the leaden shell in order to examine the remains was gone through. Repugnant though it seems to open a coffin so many years after a death has taken place, it was insisted that as King Daudi had never seen his father in the flesh he must on no account miss seeing his corpse, and to the surprise of everyone concerned the features were quite recognisable ... Daudi took hold of a barkcloth together with Mugemo and Kago and covered up the corpse, this being the custom of a son whose father is dead, and then the body was buried ... In the afternoon the concluding part of the Burial Service was read; Bishop Tucker and a very large number of Europeans were present, together with a crowd of natives, to perform the last rites.

To follow old custom, Mwanga should really have been buried inside his own court [on Mengo Hill], and many of the natives were inclined to follow precedent; but it was finally decided that if he were to be buried in Mengo, the Kabaka Daudi would have to turn out [of his] comfortable and permanent residence, [which] seemed inadvisable, especially when there is the difficulty of securing a suitable site for the new court in the Capital. On the morning of Thursday 4 August, a very interesting ceremony took place, which had been deemed impossible until such time as Mwanga should be buried in his own country.

terrorised the leafy suburbs of Rubaga and Mengo. Tourist visits are not officially sanctioned but for a small consideration the caretaker will show you around the hill, on which the 'attractions' include Idi Amin's specially constructed underground cells and execution chambers, where there's some movingly defiant graffiti scrawled in charcoal by the doomed inmates (you'll need a translator). It's quite a relief to get out again under open skies into Mengo's picturesque environs and be thankful that those days are past.

HOIMA ROAD Two important sets of royal tombs, collectively housing the bodies of the four kabakas of Buganda to have died since the 1850s, lie within walking distance of the road running northwest from central Kampala towards Hoima. The Kasubi Tombs are the more publicised of the two sites, but the Wamala Tomb is no less worthwhile (its caretakers are less accustomed to tourist visits).

The following is a translation of an account of the ceremony, written by the Rev Henry Wright Duta:

[King Daudi] came and stood outside his court [on] the coronation chair ... Mugema opened proceedings by bringing a barkcloth and hanging it about the king from his shoulders ... He then put on a calfskin to remind [Daudi] that his first forefather was thus dressed ... Then came Kasuju, who brought a second barkcloth and also a leopard skin, with which he also proceeded to dress the king ... the meaning of the leopard skin is that it separates him from all other princes and makes him into the king ... The reason why he is dressed in two barkcloths is because he is called the 'father of twins', that is to say he gives birth to many people and he rules over many people.

[Kasuju] brought the king a sword ... saying 'take this sword and with it cut judgement in truth (distribute justice equally and fairly), anyone who rebels against you, you shall kill with this sword'. Then they brought before him the drum which is called Mujagazo which is very old indeed and which has carved on it a python (once sacred to the Baganda) ... this is supposed to be the drum which Kimera had with him when he came from Bunyoro ... A shield was then presented to the king and ... two spears ... [and] a bow and arrows ... the weapons with which Kimera first came to Uganda ... Then came a long string of people bringing offerings too numerous to mention.

After that the king was placed on the shoulders of Namutwe so that the crowd might all have a good look at him, saying 'This is your king' and the crowd set up a loud yell beating their hands with their mouths to produce a tremulant effect. Then the king together with the Lubuga (queen sister) and an old woman to represent the head of the king's wives were all carried on the shoulders of their attendants back into the [royal] Court ... Then came the whole of the visitors to the king to congratulate him on his accession, he sitting down on the seat called Mubanga, which resembles a drum, and old Prince Mbogo, the brother of [the late king] Mutesa, came and wrapped some cents around his wrist in place of the cowrie shells which used to obtain here. Every member of the king's tribe – princes, princesses and everyone else who could be present – brought him presents of money ... and for days afterwards all his relatives came in batches and went through the same ceremony.

4

Kasubi Tombs [134 D3] (m *0773 747319;* ⏲ *08.00–18.00 daily; admission Ush10,000, inc the services of a knowledgeable guide*) In 1882, Kabaka Mutesa relocated his *kibuga* (palace) to Nabulagala Hill, briefly the capital of his father Suuna II some 30 years earlier, and renamed it Kasubi Hill after his birthplace some 50km further east. Mutesa constructed a large hilltop palace called Muziba Azala Mpanga (roughly translating as 'a king is born of a king'), where he died in 1884 following a prolonged illness. As was the custom, Kasubi Hill was abandoned after the king's death – his successor Mwanga established a new capital at Mengo Hill – but rather less conventionally Mutesa was the first kabaka to be buried with his jawbone intact, in a casket built by the Anglican missionary Alexander Mackay. In a further break with tradition, Kasubi rather than Mengo was chosen as the burial place of Kabaka Mwanga in 1910, seven years after his death in exile (see box, page 174). It also houses the tombs of his successor Daudi Chwa II, who ruled from 1897 to 1939, and of Edward Mutesa II, whose body was returned to Uganda in 1971, two years after his death in exile.

Until 2010, the tombs were housed within the original palace built by Mutesa, a fantastic domed structure of poles, reeds and thatch, which – aside from the addition of a concrete base – seemed to have changed little in appearance over the intervening 130 years. Unfortunately on the night of 16 March 2010, the

---

THE CONSECRATION OF NAMIREMBE CATHEDRAL

The consecration of Namirembe Cathedral on 21 July 1904 was described vividly in the Mengo Notes *a month after the event:*

A great crowd began to assemble at 6am, and … the crush at the doors [was] so great that they had to be opened to prevent people being crushed to death. There was a considerable amount of struggling and good-natured fighting among the Baganda desirous of gaining admission, for not more than 3,000 could get in, and the crowd must have numbered nearly 10,000 … Numbers climbed through the windows and jumped down on to those seated inside … Mr Savile had a bone in the hand broken in trying to repress a rush. To while away the time of waiting Mr Hattersley gave half an hour's organ recital … The European and native clergy, over 40 in number, assembled at the west door, and all in procession marched up to the Church, repeating the opening sentences of the Consecration Service … in English and Luganda … Then came morning prayer … and the wonderful way in which the congregation responded, and joined in the hymns and chants, will long be remembered.

Instead of dispersing, the vast crowd unable to gain admission to the service had filled all the school rooms around the church, and still enough remained to nearly fill the yard. [They] contributed to the collection just as though they had taken part in the service. This considerably delayed matters, and it seemed as though the bringing in of offerings would never cease … The collection consisted of rupees, pice, and cowrie shells … in bundles more than enough to fill a whole collecting bag. Then came goats led up by ropes to the communion rails … fowls in a coop and singly; one, trussed feet and wings, was solemnly handed by the sideman to the Bishop along with his bag of shells … More than 30 head of cattle had been sent in by chiefs, but it was wisely decided that it would not be well to admit these to the church. The proceeds of the collection thus totalled up to over £80, the exact amount we cannot give, as the cattle have not all been sold at the time of writing.

building, for causes still unknown, burned down. The structure, reduced to an arching framework of hitherto unsuspected (or at least unmentioned) metal beams, remained under a patchwork of gaudy orange tarpaulins for almost three years before a Ush10 billion reconstruction programme started in January 2013. When complete, it should then be business as usual. Fifty-two giant reed rings in the roof of the new hut will once more represent each of the clans of Buganda while a giant veil – created from countless pieces of barkcloth – will screen the four tombs from the vulgar gaze of the public. In front of this curtain, you'll find a fascinating collection of irreplaceable royal artefacts ranging from portraits of the four monarchs, traditional musical instruments, weapons, shields and fetishes to exotic gifts donated by Queen Victoria – as well as a stuffed leopard once kept as a pet by Mutesa I. These were salvaged by brave custodians from the blazing building before it collapsed.

The tombs are maintained by the wives of the various kings – or more accurately by female descendants of their long-deceased wives – some of whom live on the property, while others do a one-month shift there twice every year. Many of the kings' wives, sisters and other female relations are also buried at Kasubi, not in the main palace but in the series of smaller buildings that flank the driveway. The complex is entered via a large traditional reception hut known as a *bujjabukula*. This is tended by the chief gateman, known as Mulamba (a hereditary title), who customarily dresses in a brilliant yellow barkcloth robe, as do his assistants.

An excellent booklet on the tombs is sometimes on sale at the site, and well worth buying for its background information on Baganda culture. To get there from the city centre, follow Namirembe/Natete Road east for about 1km until you reach a crossroads dominated by the **Kampala Regency Hotel** (currently closed). Turn right into Hoima Road. After nearly 2km you'll cross over Nakulabye roundabout and 2km further on you'll reach Kasubi Market at the junction with Kimera Road, from where the tombs – signposted to the left – lie about 500m uphill along Masiro Road. Plenty of minibus-taxis run from the city centre to Kasubi Market. Alternatively head out of town past Makerere University to Nakulabye roundabout and turn right.

Wamala Tomb

[134 C1] Situated on the crest of a low hill some 12km northwest of central Kampala, Wamala Tomb is housed in an attractive, traditional, thatched domed building, slightly smaller and older than its counterpart at Kasubi. The hill is the former palace and sacred resting place of Kabaka Mutesa I's father and predecessor Kabaka Suuna, who ascended the throne c1830 and died in 1856. Suuna is remembered as a despotic ruler and keen hunter. The menagerie he maintained at Wamala – said to have included lions, leopards, elephants and various smaller creatures – sufficiently impressed the first Arab traders to reach Buganda that word of it reached Sir Richard Burton at the Swahili Coast.

Wamala is neither as well known as Kasubi, nor as carefully tended, but it is just as interesting in its comparatively low-key way. A diverse array of royal artefacts – spears, shields, drums and other musical instruments – is displayed in front of the barkcloth drape that veils the tomb itself. Opposite the main building stands the former palace and tomb of Suuna's mother, Namasole Kanyange, according to tradition a very beautiful woman and also highly influential – it's said that Suuna insisted the namasole live alongside him so that he could keep an eye on her doings. In keeping with Kiganda royal custom, Kanyange appointed a successor as namasole before her death. The lineage survives to this day: the fourth namasole to Suuna is resident at Wamala and still performs traditional duties such as tending the royal tomb.

To reach Wamala, follow the Hoima Road out of Kampala, passing the junction for Kisubi, then after another 6km the trading centre of Nansana. Right at the end of the elongated sprawl of Nansana, a small faded purple signpost indicates a right turn to Wamala (200m before a swamp prevents Nansana's further extension). From this junction, a rough 1.5km dirt track marked with wooden signs leads to the hilltop tomb, which, though now surrounded by surburban growth, is still visible from some distance away.

GGABA AND MUNYONYO The twin ports of Ggaba and Munyonyo lie about 2km apart near the southwest of Murchison Bay on Lake Victoria, some 10km southeast of central Kampala. Both are worthwhile goals for a day's outing. Ggaba is a compact, bustling settlement with a busy market that spills down to a waterfront that used to consist of a grim and muddy littoral. This was tidied up a few years ago with the construction of a number of stone quays. While the vegetable market, fish auction, and fish smoking activities remain as sensory as ever, the quays have become a popular spot for residents and visitors to take the lake air and perhaps a drink at a makeshift bar. Folk do much the same, but in greener and more spacious surroundings, at the historically more significant port of Munyonyo, 2km south. This was (and technically still is), the royal port to which the Bagandan kabakas led their entourages in periodical exoduses from their Kampala palaces. During the 19th century it was home to a large canoe fleet reserved for the kabaka – mainly for pleasure cruises and hunting expeditions, but also on standby to evacuate the king in times of emergency.

Speke and Stanley both accompanied Kabaka Mutesa to the lakeshore where the former considered 'the royal yachting establishment' at Munyonyo to be 'the Cowes of Uganda'. Today however, the title would go the plush marina stocked with modern speedboats and cabin cruisers at the neighbouring **Speke Commonwealth Resort** (see page 155). This sprawling development is set in beautifully landscaped gardens with a magnificent tropical lakeshore setting opposite the forested Buliguwe Island. A Ush20,000 day entrance fee allows access to the swimming pool and restaurant – a great place to chill out should you have a spare day in the capital. For those using public transport, a steady stream of minibus-taxis connects the old taxi park in Kampala to Ggaba and Munyonyo.

NAMUGONGO MARTYRS' SHRINE Situated about 12km from central Kampala along the Jinja Road, Namugongo, an established place of execution in pre-colonial Buganda, is remembered today for the massacre that took place there on 3 June 1886 at the order of Kabaka Mwanga (see box, pages 182–3). In the last week of May, an unknown number of Baganda men and women, suspected or known to have been baptised, were detained near Mengo and forced to march, by some accounts naked, to Namugongo, where they were imprisoned for several days while a large pyre was prepared. On the morning of 3 June, those prisoners who had not already done so were given one final opportunity to renounce their recently adopted faith. Whether any of the neophyte Christians accepted this offer goes unrecorded, but 26 known individuals, divided evenly between Catholic and Protestant, declined. Charles Lwanga, the leader of the Catholic contingent, was hacked apart and burnt alive on the spot. Later in the day, the remaining individuals were bound in reed mats, thrown on to the pyre, and roasted alive. The 26 remembered victims of the massacre were all baptised, and thus known to one or other mission by name, but contemporary reports indicate that more than 30 people were thrown on to the fire.

In 1920, Pope Benedict XV paved the way for future canonisation by declaring blessed the 13 known Catholic martyrs at Namugongo, together with another nine

Catholic victims of separate killings in May 1886. The 22 Catholic martyrs were finally canonised by Pope Paul VI on 18 October 1964 during the Vatican II Conference. In July 1969, Pope Paul VI visited Uganda – the first reigning pope to set foot in sub-Saharan Africa – to make a pilgrimage to Namugongo, where he instructed that a shrine and church be built on the spot where Lwanga had been killed. The **Church of the Namugongo Martyrs**, dedicated in 1975 and subsequently named a basilica church, is an unusual and imposing structure, modernistic and metallic in appearance, but based on the traditional Kasiisira style (epitomised, ironically, by the tombs of Mwanga and two other kabakas at Kasubi). The site of the massacre was visited by Archbishop Robert Runcie of Canterbury in 1984, and by Pope John Paul II in 1993. The 3 June massacre remains a public holiday in Uganda and is marked worldwide on the church calendar in honour of the Uganda Martyrs.

BAHÁ'Í TEMPLE [135 E2] Opened on 15 January 1962, the Bahá'í Temple on Kikaya Hill, 6km from Kampala on the Gayaza Road, is the only place of worship of its kind in Africa. It is the spiritual home to the continent's Bahá'í, adherents to a rather obscure faith founded by the Persian mystic Bahá'u'lláh in the 1850s. Born in Tehran in 1812, Bahá'u'lláh was the privileged son of a wealthy government minister, but he declined to follow his father into the ministerial service, instead devoting his life to philanthropy.

In 1844, Bahá'u'lláh abandoned his Islamic roots to join the Bábí cult, whose short-lived popularity led to the execution of its founder and several other leading figures by the religious establishment – a fate escaped by Bahá'u'lláh only because of the high social status of his family. Bahá'u'lláh was nevertheless imprisoned, with his feet in stocks and a 50kg metal chain around his neck in Tehran's notoriously unsanitary and gloomy Black Pit. It was whilst imprisoned that Bahá'u'lláh received the Godly vision that led to the foundation of Bahá'í. Upon his release, Bahá'u'lláh dedicated the remaining 40 years of his life to writing the books, tracts and letters that collectively outlined the Bahá'í framework for the spiritual, moral, economic, political and philosophical reconstruction of human society.

Bahá'í teaches that heaven and hell are not places, but states of being defined by the presence or absence of spirituality. It is an inclusive faith, informed by all other religions – Hindu, Christian, Jewish, Zoroastrian, Buddhist and Islamic holy texts are displayed in the temple – which it regards to be stepping stones to a broader, less doctrinal spiritual and meditative awareness. It is also admirably egalitarian: it regards all humankind to be of equal worth, and any member of the congregation is free to lead prayers and meditations. Although not a didactic religion, Bahá'í does evidently equate spiritual well-being with asceticism: the consumption of alcohol and intoxicating drugs is discouraged in Bahá'í writings, and forbidden in the temple grounds, along with loud music, picking flowers and 'immoral behaviour'.

The Bahá'í Temple in Kampala, visible for miles around and open to all, is set in neatly manicured gardens extending over some 30ha atop Kikaya Hill. The lower part of the building consists of a white nonagon roughly 15m in diameter, with one door on each of its nine shaded faces. This is topped by an immense green dome, covered with glazed mosaic Italian tiles, and a turret that towers 40m above the ground. The interior, which can seat up to 800 people, is illuminated by ambient light filtered through coloured glass windows, and decorated with lush Persian carpets. Otherwise, it is plainly decorated, in keeping with the Bahá'í belief that it would belittle the glory of God to place pictures or statues inside His temple. A solitary line of Arabic text repeated on the wall at regular intervals approximately translates to the familiar Christian text Glory of Glories.

4

Further afield, the Mpanga Forest (see pages 215–18), Mabira Forest (see pages 524–6), Mabamba Swamp (see pages 201–2) and Entebbe Botanical Garden (see pages 198–9) make good day trips, particularly if you are interested in birds. The Nile corridor at Jinja offers a range of activities, including horseriding and white-water rafting trips, all of which are feasible as day trips from Kampala (see pages 493–526). Further options are described below, starting with an overview of the area. Potential day trips on the shores of Lake Victoria and along the Kampala–Entebbe road are described in the following chapter.

SSEZIBWA FALLS [off map, 135 H2] (*www.ssezibwafallsresort.com;* ⊕ *daily; admission Ush5,000 /2,000pp for foreign visitors/Ugandans, there's no charge for being shown around by 1 of the knowledgeable guides but it would be appropriate to tip them*) The Ssezibwa Falls, which lie 35km east of Kampala, are reputed to have been a favourite spot of Kabakas Mwanga and Mutesa II, both of whom planted trees there that still flourish today. The waterfall, and the Ssezibwa River on which it lies, are also steeped in Kiganda folklore. Many hundreds of years ago, the legend goes, a woman called Nakangu, of the Achibe (fox) clan, gave birth not to twin children, as expected, but to a twin river, split into two distinct streams by an island immediately below the waterfall. It is believed locally that the spirits of Nakangu's unborn children – Ssezibwa and Mobeya – still inhabit the river, and it was once customary for any Muganda passing its source at Namukono, some 20km further east, to throw a handful of grass or stones into it for good luck. Even today, a thanksgiving sacrifice of barkcloth, beer and a cock is made at the river's source every year, usually led by a Ssalongo (father of twins).

It is not surprising, given the supernatural significance attached to the birth of twins in many Ugandan societies, that a number of shrines are maintained among the colourful quartzite rocks over which the river tumbles for perhaps 15m before it divides into two. Specific gaps in the rock are dedicated to specific lubaale: including the river spirit Mukasa, the hunting spirit Ddunga and the rainbow spirit Musoke. There is also a fertility shrine in the rocks adjacent to the falls, associated with the thunder spirit Kiwanuka if I understand correctly, and generally used for individual rather than communal sacrifices. Women who have been blessed with twins, one of which is human, the other a benevolent spirit manifested in a python or leopard, often visit this shrine to leave eggs for their python spirit or a cock for its feline counterpart.

Communal sacrificial ceremonies, in which nine pieces of the meat most favoured by the individual spirit will be placed at the appropriate shrine, are still held at the waterfall, and sometimes even attended by the kabaka himself. Tourists are welcome to visit on such occasions, but unfortunately their timing is difficult to predict – ceremonies are not held every year, and the date is usually announced at short notice when a medium is consulted by a hungry spirit. Certain spirits, after having accepted a sacrifice and taken the requested action, appreciate having a live sheep or cock – white for Mukasa, brown for Kiwanuka – thrown over the waterfall itself, and they always ensure that the animal survives.

Ssezibwa is run as an ecotourism project, and although it is firstly a cultural attraction, the waterfall itself is very pretty, particularly during the rains, and the fringing trees harbour an interesting selection of birds. The falls can be reached by following the Jinja road out of Kampala to Kayanja trading centre (where a green, tea-covered hill comes into view), then turning right (southwards) for about 1.5km

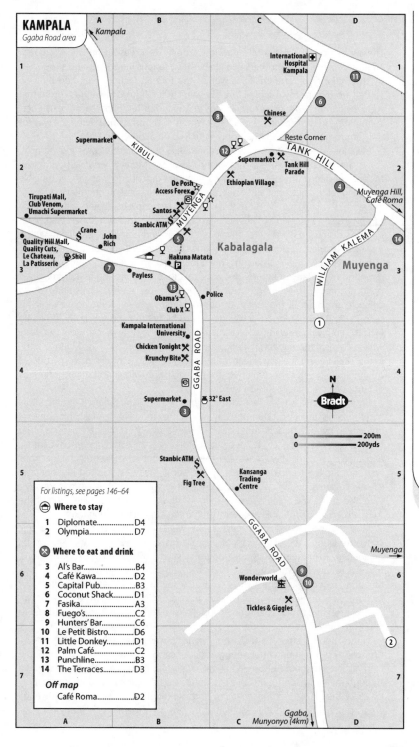

KAMPALA
Ggaba Road area

↖ *Kampala*

International Hospital Kampala ✚

Chinese ✗

Reste Corner

Supermarket ● KIBULI

TANK HILL

Tank Hill Parade

Supermarket ●

Ethiopian Village ✗

De Posh
Access Forex

Muyenga Hill, Café Roma →

Tirupati Mall, Club Venom, Umachi Supermarket ●

Santos

Stanbic ATM

Crane $
John Rich

Quality Hill Mall, Quality Cuts, Le Chateau, La Patisserie ●

Shell

Kabalagala

WILLIAM KALEMA

Muyenga

Hakuna Matata

Payless ●

Obama's

Police ●

Club X

Kampala International University ●

Chicken Tonight ✗
Krunchy Bite ✗

GGABA ROAD

Supermarket ● 32° East

N

Bradt

0 ————— 200m
0 ————— 200yds

Stanbic ATM $

Fig Tree ✗

Kansanga Trading Centre ●

GGABA ROAD

Muyenga →

Wonderworld

Tickles & Giggles ✗

For listings, see pages 146–64

🏠 **Where to stay**
| 1 | Diplomate.................D4 |
| 2 | Olympia.....................D7 |

✗ **Where to eat and drink**
3	Al's Bar.......................B4
4	Café Kawa..................D2
5	Capital Pub................B3
6	Coconut Shack..........D1
7	Fasika.........................A3
8	Fuego's......................C2
9	Hunters' Bar.............C6
10	Le Petit Bistro..........D6
11	Little Donkey............D1
12	Palm Café..................C2
13	Punchline..................B3
14	The Terraces.............D3

Off map
Café Roma..................D2

Ggaba, Munyonyo (4km) ↓

181

The succession of Kabaka Mwanga in October 1884 was an unusually smooth affair, accepted by his brothers and kin without serious infighting, and supported by the majority of Saza chiefs as well as the foreign factions that had by then settled around the royal capital. The five years that followed Mwanga's coronation were, by contrast, the most tumultuous in Buganda's 400-plus years of existence, culminating in three changes of kabaka within 12 months, and paving the way for the kingdom to relinquish its autonomy to a colonial power in 1890.

Mwanga's career comes across as the antithesis of the epithet 'come the moment, come the man'. In 1884, the missionary Alexander Mackay, who had witnessed Mwanga develop from 'a little boy … into manhood' described Mwanga as an 'amiable … young fellow' but 'fitful and fickle, and, I fear, revengeful', noting that 'under the influence of [marijuana] he is capable of the wildest unpremeditated actions'. These misgivings were echoed by other contemporary commentators: Robert Walker, for instance, dismissed Mwanga as 'frivolous … weak and easily led; passionate and if provoked petulant … possessed of very little courage or self-control'.

Whatever his personal failings, Mwanga was also forced to contend with a daunting miscellany of natural disasters, religious tensions and real or imagined political threats. Three months into his reign, he lost several wives and trusted chiefs to an epidemic that swept through his first capital at Nubulagala, while his second capital on Mengo Hill was destroyed by fire in February 1886 and again in 1887. Politically, Mwanga was threatened to the west by a resurgent Bunyoro, whose charismatic leader Kabalega inflicted several defeats on the Kiganda army in the 1880s. From the east, meanwhile, Buganda faced a more nebulous and less quantifiable threat, as news filtered through of the growing number and influence of European colonial agents on the coast.

Buganda c1884 was riddled with religious factionalism. Kiganda traditionalists had for some time co-existed uneasily with a growing volume of Islamic converts influenced by Arab traders. And both of these relatively established factions faced further rivalry from the late 1870s onwards, following the establishment of Catholic and Anglican missions near the capital. The divisions between these religious factions were not limited to matters purely ecclesiastical. Many established Kiganda and Islamic customs, notably polygamy, were anathema to the Christian missionaries, who also spoke out against participation in the slave trade – the lifeblood of the Arab settlers, and profitable to several prominent Kiganda traditionalists.

Mwanga's personal religious persuasions were evidently dictated by pragmatic concerns. During the early years of his rule, his views were strongly shaped by his *katikiro*, an influential Kiganda traditionalist who distrusted all exotic religions, but was relatively sympathetic to Islam as the lesser – or more tolerant towards Kiganda customs – of the two evils. It also seems likely that the traditionalist faction, not unreasonably, perceived a connection between the European missionaries and threat of European imperialism, and thus reckoned it had less to fear from the Arabs.

Three months after he took the throne, Mwanga signalled his hostility to Christianity by executing three young Anglican converts. Then, in October 1885, the king received news of Bishop Hannington's attempt to become the first European through the 'back door' of Busoga. In Kiganda tradition, the back door is used only by close friends or plotting enemies, and Hannington – a stranger to Mwanga – was clearly not the former. Motivated by fear more perhaps than any religious factor, Mwanga ordered the execution of Hannington (see box *The death of Bishop Hannington*, pages 502–3). Weeks after the bishop's death, Joseph Mukasa, a Catholic advisor to the king, criticised Mwanga for having Hannington killed without first giving him an opportunity to defend himself, and was also executed for his efforts. These two deaths led to an increasing estrangement between the kabaka and the missionaries – Mackay included – who resided around his court, fuelled partially by Mwanga's fear of a European reprisal for the attack on Hannington.

Mwanga's distrust of Christianity exploded into blind rage on 25 May 1886. The catalyst for this was probably the subversive actions of his sister Princess Clara Nalumansi (see box, pages 142–3), though it has been suggested by some writers that Mwanga was a homosexual paedophile whose temporary hatred of Christians stemmed from his rejection by a favoured page, recently baptised. Exactly how many Baganda Christians were speared, beheaded, cremated, castrated and/or bludgeoned to death over the next ten days is an open question – 45 deaths are recorded by name, but the actual tally was probably several hundred. The persecution culminated at Namugongo on 3 June 1886, when at least 26 Catholic and Anglican converts, having rejected the opportunity to renounce their new faith, were roasted alive (see box, pages 182–3).

His rage evidently spent, Mwanga set about repairing his relationship with the European missionaries, who had been not been directly victimised by the persecution, and who depended on the kabaka's tolerance to continue their work in the kingdom. Tensions resurfaced in June 1887 when, according to Mackay, Stanley's non-military expedition to Equatoria was described to Mwanga by an Arab trader as 'a Mazungu coming here with a thousand guns' – a ploy designed to reawaken the king's concern that Hannington's death would be avenged by his countrymen. In December 1887, Hannington's successor wrote Mwanga a letter, delivered by Rev E C Gordon, stating that: 'we do not desire to take vengeance for this action of yours, we are teachers of the religion of Christ, not soldiers … We believe that you must see now that you were deceived as to the object for which [Hannington] had come.' The increasingly paranoid Mwanga interpreted this as a declaration of war, and Gordon was imprisoned for two months.

During 1888, Mwanga's concerns about a foreign invasion were diverted by the domestic chaos induced by years of vacillation between the religious factions. On 10 September, Mwanga was forced to flee into exile. His successor, an Islamic convert called Kiwewa, enjoyed a six-week reign, marked by violence between the opposing converts, before he was ousted by another Islamic convert called Kalema. Under Kalema, Buganda descended into full civil war, with an unexpected reversal of alliances in which the Christian and traditionalist Baganda lent their support to Mwanga, who was restored to power in February 1890. Three months later, Captain Lugard arrived in Kampala waving a treaty of protectorateship with England.

E B Fletcher, who knew Mwanga in his later years, regarded him to be 'nervous, suspicious, fickle, passionate … with no idea whatever of self-discipline, without regard for life or property, as long as he achieved his own end'. Yet in 1936 Fletcher also wrote an essay exonerating many of the king's excesses and flaws as symptomatic of the troubled times through which he'd lived. 'To steer a straight course through a time when such radical changes were taking place', Fletcher concluded, 'needed a man of a strong character, a firm will and wide vision. Those characteristics Mwanga did not possess.'

KIGANDA RELIGION

The spirit of Kiganda, the traditional religion of Buganda, 'is not so much adoration of a being supreme and beneficent', wrote Speke, 'as a tax to certain malignant furies ... to prevent them bringing evil on the land, and to insure a fruitful harvest'. Certainly, like many traditional African religions, Kiganda does revolve largely around the appeasing and petitioning of ancestral and animist spirits both benign and malevolent. But Kiganda is unusual in that it has a core of monotheism. The supreme being of the Baganda is Katonda – literally, Creator – who is not of human form, and has neither parents nor children, but who brought into being the heavens, the earth, and all they contain. Katonda is the most powerful denizen of the spiritual world, but also the most detached from human affairs, and so requires little attention by comparison to more hands-on subordinate spirits.

Ranking below Katonda, the *balubaale* (singular *lubaale*) are semi-deities who play a central role in the day-to-day affairs affecting Buganda. At least 30 balubaale are recognised (some sources claim a total of 70), and many are strongly associated with specific aspects or attributes of life. The balubaale have no real equivalent in the Judaic branch of religions. Certainly not gods, they are more akin perhaps to a cross between a saint and a guardian angel – the spirits of real men (or more occasionally women) whose exceptional attributes in life have been carried over to death. Traditionally, the balubaale form the pivot of organised religion in Buganda: prior to the introduction of exotic religions they were universally venerated, even above the kabaka, who in all other respects was an absolute ruler.

The most popular lubaale is Mukasa, the spirit of Lake Victoria, honoured at many temples around Buganda, the most important of which is on Bubembe in the Ssese Islands, where the kabaka would send an annual offering of cows and a request for prosperity and good harvests. Mukasa is also associated with fertility: barren women would regularly visit an adjacent shrine on Bubembe, dedicated to his wife Nalwanga, to ask her to seek her husband's blessing. Another important lubaale is Wanga, guardian of the sun and moon, who also has no earthly shrine, and is the father of Muwanga, literally 'the most powerful'. Other prominent male balubaale with specific areas of interest include Musoke (rainbows), Kawumpuli (plagues), Ndahura (smallpox), Kitinda (prosperity), Musisi (earthquakes), Wamala (Lake Wamala) and Ddunga (hunting).

Female balubaale are fewer, and in most cases their elevated status is linked to kinship with a male lubaale, but they include Kiwanuka's wife Nakayage (fertility) and Kibuuka's mother Nagaddya (harvests). Nabuzaana, the female lubaale of obstetrics, is possibly unique in having no kin among the other balubaale, furthermore in that she is tended by priestesses of Banyoro rather than Baganda origin. The male lubaale Ggulu, guardian of the sky, is a confusing figure. Listed in some traditions as the creator, his existence, in common with that of Katonda, pre-dated that of humanity, and he has no earthly shrine, furthering the suggestion that unlike other balubaale he is not the spirit of a dead person. Ggulu's children include the lightning spirit Kiwanuka as well as Walumbe, the spirit of sickness and death.

The balubaale are expected to intercede favourably in national affairs related to their speciality when petitioned with sacrifices and praise. Sacrifices to the lake spirit Mukasa might be made during periods of drought, in case he has forgotten that the people need rain. The rainbow spirit Musoke, by contrast, might be placated with sacrifices after extended rains that prevent harvesting or ploughing, and he will signal his assent to stop the rain with a rainbow. In past times, all the major temples would be consulted and offerings made before any major national undertaking – a coronation, for instance, or a war – and any kabaka who ignored this custom was inviting disaster. One main shrine or *ekiggwa* is dedicated to each lubaale, though many are also venerated at a number of lesser shrines scattered around Buganda. Every shrine is tended by a *mandwa*: a priest or medium who is on occasion possessed by the shrine's spirit and acts as its oracle. The mandwa for any given temple might be male or female, but will usually come from a specific clan associated with that temple. The three main shrines dedicated to Katonda – all situated in Kyagwe, near the Mabira Forest – are, for instance, tended by priests of the Njovu (elephant) clan. Sacred drums, ceremonial objects and sometimes body parts of the deceased are stored in the temple, the upkeep of which is governed by elaborate customs.

While a relatively small cast of balubaale is concerned with national affairs, the day-to-day affairs of local communities and of individual Muganda are governed by innumerable lesser spirits. These are divided into two main categories: *mizimu* (singular *omuzimu*) are the spirits of departed ancestors, while *misambwa* (singular *omusambwa*) are spirits associated with specific physical objects such as mountains, rivers, forests or caves. Dealings with the ancestral spirits are a family matter, undertaken at a household shrine where small items, such as cowries or beans, are offered on a regular basis, while a living sacrifice of a chicken or goat might be offered before an important event or ceremony. Appeasing the misambwa, by contrast, is a community affair, with communal offerings made on a regular basis. Unlike balubaale or mizimu, misambwa are generally cantankerous spirits: one's main obligation to an omusambwa is to keep out of its way and uphold any taboos associated with it.

The place of Kiganda in modern Buganda is difficult to isolate. In the latter half of the 19th century, when the kingdom was first infiltrated by evangelical foreigners – initially just Arabs, later also Europeans – a significant number of Muganda, especially the elite, converted to an exotic religion. Thereafter, the converts tended to regard their indigenous spiritual traditions as backward and superstitious, a stance that caused considerable friction within the kingdom during the 1880s. The trend against traditionalism continued throughout the 20th century. Today, most if not all Baganda profess to be either Christian or Muslim, and certainly very few educated and urbanised Baganda take Kiganda traditions very seriously, if they consider them at all.

I'm not at all certain this is the case in rural Buganda. From Ashanti to Zululand, it is my experience that rural Africans frequently adhere partially or concurrently to two apparently contradictory religious doctrines. They might be dedicated Christians or Muslims, but in times of trouble they will as likely consult a traditional oracle or healer as they will a priest or imam or a Western doctor. This dualism in Buganda is perhaps less conspicuous to outsiders than it would be in many other parts of Africa. But that it exists, I have no doubt. Shrines such as those at Ssezibwa Falls are clearly still in active use, while – further afield – the likes of Bigo and the Nakayima Tree both remain a focal point for traditionalist cults. In the past 20 years, Christian cults have centred on the Acholi and Bakiga mediums Alice Lakwena and Credonia Mwerinde who, though very different, have both possessed undeniable traditionalist undertones. It is out of respect for Kiganda traditions, rather than any wish to offend the many Baganda who reject them, that this box has been written not in the past tense but in the present.

The centre of political power in Buganda for several centuries prior to the colonial era was the kibuga (capital) of the kabaka (king), generally situated on a hilltop for ease of defence. Based on the knowledge that at least ten different kibuga sites were used by three kabakas between 1854 and 1894, it would appear that the capital was regularly relocated, possibly for security reasons. It was also customary for a kibuga to be abandoned upon the death of its founder, at least until 1894, when Kabaka Mwanga founded a new capital on Mengo Hill, one that remained in use until the Baganda monarchy was abolished in 1966. Mengo Palace, damaged by the military during the Amin era, remains in poor shape, but following the reinstitution of the monarchy in 1993, a new kibuga was established 10km east of Kampala at Banda.

Banda was also the site of the first capital of Kabaka Mutesa, visited in 1862 by Speke, who wrote: 'the palace or entrance quite surprised me by its extraordinary dimensions, and the neatness with which it was kept. The whole brow and sides of the hill on which we stood were covered with gigantic grass huts, thatched as neatly as so many heads dressed by a London barber, and fenced all round with the tall yellow reeds of the common Uganda tiger-grass; whilst within the enclosure, the lines of huts were joined together, or partitioned off into courts, with walls of the same grass.' The next European visitor to Mutesa's capital – by then relocated to Rubaga – was Stanley, in 1875, who was equally impressed: 'Broad avenues [of] reddish clay, strongly mixed with the detritus of hematite ... led by a gradual ascent to the circular road which made the circuit of the hill outside the palace enclosure ... his house is an African palace, spacious and lofty.' Visitors to Kabaka Mwanga's kibuga some ten years later were less complimentary – Gedge, for instance, described it as a 'miserable collection of huts [where] dirt and filth reign supreme' – but this was probably a temporary decline linked to the instability that characterised Mwanga's early rule.

The most detailed description of a kibuga was published by the Rev John Roscoe in 1911:

> The king lived upon a hill situated in the neighbourhood of the lake. The summit of the hill was levelled, and the most commanding site overlooking the country was chosen for the king's dwelling houses, court houses, and shrine for fetishes, and for the special reception room ... The whole of the royal enclosure was divided up into small courtyards with groups of huts in them; each group was enclosed by a high fence and was under the supervision of a responsible wife. Wide paths between high fences connected each group of houses with the king's royal enclosure. In the reign of the famous King Mutesa, there were several thousand residents in the royal enclosure; he had five hundred wives, each of whom had her maids and female slaves; and in addition to the wives there were fully two hundred pages and hundreds of retainers and slaves. A high fence of elephant grass surrounded the royal residence, so that it was impossible for an enemy with the ordinary primitive weapons to enter ... There was one plan followed, which has been used by the kings for years without variation. The [royal] enclosure was oval shaped, a mile in length and half a mile wide, and the capital extended five or six miles in front and two miles on either side.

before turning right again on to a signposted track. This historically low-key site is now under private management and a restaurant and self-contained cottages are being developed (see the website for details). In the meantime, camping with your own equipment costs US$5 per tent. In addition to the standard tour covered by the entrance fee, longer cultural and nature walks are offered.

KATEREKE PRISON (◷ *daily; nominal entrance fee*) The extensive prison ditch at Katereke is a relic of the instability that characterised Buganda in the late 1880s (see box, pages 182–3). It was constructed by Kabaka Kalema, an Islamic sympathiser who was controversially placed on the throne in October 1888, less than two months after Kabaka Mwanga had been forced into exile. Kalema ordered that every potential or imagined rival to his throne be rounded up and sent to Katereke – which, given the fragility of his position in the divided kingdom, added up to an estimated 40 personages.

One of the first to be imprisoned at Katereke was Kiwewa, who had ruled Buganda for the brief period between Mwanga's exile and Kalema's ascent to the throne. Kiwewa was soon joined by a bevy of his wives, as well as the two infant sons of the exiled Mwanga, and the last two surviving sons of the late Kabaka Suuna. Kalema also feared a secession bid from his own brothers, and even his sisters – like Mwanga before him, Kalema was unsettled by the fact that a woman sat on the English throne – and most of them were imprisoned too.

Six months into his reign, sensing a growing threat from the budding alliance between the Christian faction in Buganda and its former persecutor Mwanga – the latter by this time openly resident on an island in Murchison Bay, only 10km from the capital – Kalema decided to wipe out the potential opposition once and for all. Most of the occupants of the prison were slaughtered without mercy. Other less significant figures, for instance some of the princesses and one elderly son of Kabaka Suuna, were spared when they agreed to embrace Islam. The massacre wasn't confined to the prison's occupants either: Mukasa, the traditionalist Katikiro who had served under Mwanga, was shot outside his house, which was then set on fire with the body inside. The wives of the former kabaka Kiwewa, according to Sir John Milner Gray, were 'put to death in circumstances of disgusting brutality'.

Ultimately, this massacre probably hastened Kalema's downfall by strengthening the alliance between Buganda's Christians, who suffered several casualties, and the island-bound Mwanga, left mourning several brothers and sisters as well as his two sons. And the lingering death that Kalema had reserved for his predecessor set many formerly neutral chiefs and other dignitaries against him. Kiwewa was starved of food and water for seven days, then a bullet was put through his weakened body, and finally his remains were burnt unceremoniously in his prison cell – not, in the words of Sir Apollo Kaggwa, 'a fit manner in which to kill a king'.

Katereke Prison lies to the west of Kampala, and can be reached by following the Masaka Road out of town for about 15km, passing through Nsangi trading centre, then about 2km later turning right at a left-hand bend in the road marked by a series a of speed bumps. The 2km track to Katereke is marked by a fading mauve signpost (ignore a similar but premature sign 1km back down the road towards Nsangi). It's a surprisingly peaceful and leafy spot, considering its bloody historical associations, and guides are available to show you around what remains of the prison trench. A visit to Katereke could be combined with a side trip to **Nagalabi Buddo**, which lies about 5km south of Nsangi trading centre and has reputedly served as the coronation site for the kabaka since Buganda was founded.

4

5

Entebbe and Lake Victoria

Almost a fifth of Uganda is covered by water in its various forms, from muddy trickles through swamps to glistening equatorial glaciers. Yet most visitors are only vaguely aware that three-quarters of this area is represented by a 31,000km² portion of Lake Victoria, almost half (45%) of Africa's largest lake. For though this vast aqueous expanse is larger than neighbouring Rwanda and its area exceeds (fourfold) that of Uganda's national park system, its appeal to visitors has long been remarkably underplayed. The lacustrine experience for most tourists is limited to an aerial descent over the lake into Entebbe Airport, followed by a few further glimpses along the road to Kampala. Granted, the appeal of Lake Victoria is less than comprehensive. Swimming is discouraged by the snail-borne scourge of bilharzia (see page 92) while only keen birdwatchers could honestly prefer its extensive tracts of swamp to the sandy beaches of the Kenyan and Tanzanian coasts. But despite these points, this vast inland sea, elevated a thousand metres above the sea coast, is imbued with its own tropical allure.

The northern lakeshore in Uganda, typically forest or swamp-fringed, is far more lush than the arid, stony landscapes to the south. These habitats are of immeasurable conservation significance; wetlands at Lutembe and Mabamba bays and the Sango Bay swamp forest are recognised internationally as Ramsar Sites (Wetlands of International Importance) and Important Bird Areas due to the presence of globally threatened papyrus species, vast numbers of seasonal migrants and the iconic shoebill. If you fail to locate the last in these locations, a face-saving sighting is guaranteed in the aviary at the lakeside Wildlife Education Centre in Entebbe. An equally contrived wildlife encounters is possible with chimpanzees at Ngamba Island Chimpanzee Sanctuary (see page 200) and Nile crocodile at Buwama crocodile farm (see page 216).

Those with even the slightest interest in history will be stirred by the lake's status as the explorer's holy grail: the answer to the age-old quest for the source of the Nile. Though John Speke resolved the matter back in 1862, there remains plenty of scope for modern-day exploration on either side of the river's famous exit from the lake at Jinja. The southern hinterland of the 80km Kampala to Jinja highway is virtually unvisited by tourists. Though I have explored this particular area extensively, I still have not the foggiest idea what lies on the offshore islands or along the stretch of shoreline further east between Jinja and the remote Majanji Beach Resort (see page 492) on the Uganda–Kenya border.

Happily, options for modern explorers extend beyond fishing villages, swamps and forests. If leaving the beaten track means watching the sun set from a sandy, tropical beach, head out to the Ssese archipelago. To do this, or indeed to explore any part of the lake properly, you'll need to take to the water and there are ample opportunities to do so. With crazily overloaded passenger canoes, booze cruises at

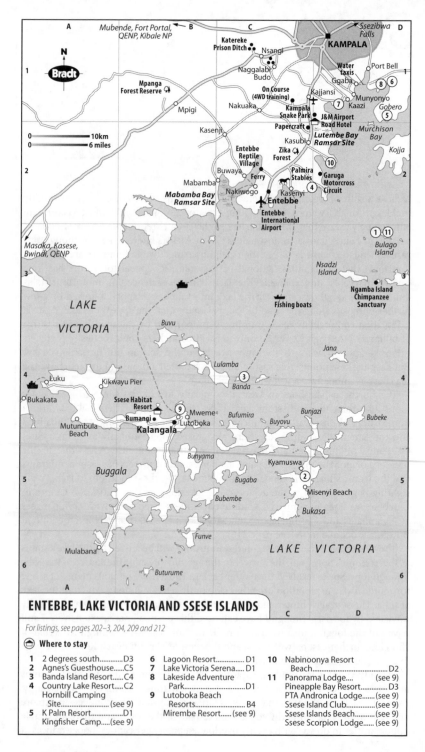

ENTEBBE, LAKE VICTORIA AND SSESE ISLANDS

For listings, see pages 202–3, 204, 209 and 212

Map labels:

Mubende, Fort Portal, QENP, Kibale NP — B
KAMPALA
Ssezibwa Falls
Katereke Prison Ditch
Nsangi
Naggalabi Budo
Mpanga Forest Reserve
Water taxis
Port Bell
Ggaba
On Course (4WD training)
Kajjansi
Munyonyo
Mpigi
Nakuaka
Kampala Snake Park
J&M Airport Road Hotel
Kaazi
Gobero
Kasenji
Papercraft
Kasubi
Lutembe Bay Ramsar Site
Murchison Bay
Entebbe Reptile Village
Zika Forest
Palmira Stables
Kojja
Buwaya
Ferry
Garuga Motorcross Circuit
Mabamba
Nakiwogo
Kasenyi
Mabamba Bay Ramsar Site
Entebbe
Entebbe International Airport
Masaka, Kasese, Bwindi, QENP
Bulago Island
Nsadzi Island
LAKE VICTORIA
Fishing boats
Ngamba Island Chimpanzee Sanctuary
Jana
Buvu
Lulamba
Banda
Luku
Kikwayu Pier
Bukakata
Ssese Habitat Resort
Mweme
Bufumira
Buyovu
Bunjazi
Bubeke
Mutumbula Beach
Bumangi
Lutoboka
Kalangala
Bunyama
Kyamuswa
Buggala
Bugaba
Misenyi Beach
Bubembe
Bukasa
Funve
LAKE VICTORIA
Mulabana
Buturume

0 ——— 10km
0 ——— 6 miles

N
Bradt

the Source of the Nile, fishing excursions, and scheduled ferry services running to the Ssese Islands, opportunities for messing around in boats on Lake Victoria are greater than ever before.

The choice of lakeside accommodation has also improved. While the earliest editions of this book offered an idiosyncratic list of rustic campsites and budget retreats (some so under-utilised it was best to take your own food) we now present an expanded menu of comfortable mid-range options topped by an upmarket retreat of sufficient opulence that one might be anywhere on earth.

ENTEBBE

Straddling the equator and sprawling along the Lake Victoria shore some 35km south of Kampala, Entebbe exudes an atmosphere of tropical languor, and – particularly for those with a strong interest in natural history (and who aren't looking for budget accommodation) – it offers an altogether more appealing introduction to Uganda than the capital. Even if you do stay in Kampala, this pretty lakeshore town is worth a visit if only for its excellent botanical garden, which teems with birds and practically guarantees close-up views of black-and-white colobus monkeys.

Unlike Jinja and Kampala, Entebbe has a remarkably unfocused urban centre; one carved haphazardly into lakeshore jungle in such a manner that one might reasonably wonder whether most of its 50,000-plus residents haven't packed up their tents and gone on holiday (most of them are in fact crammed into the discreetly located market suburb of Kitoro, 1km down the road). This must surely be the only African capital past or present to have entered the new millennium with a golf course more expansive than its nominal city centre, or whose tallest buildings are dwarfed by the antiquated trees of the botanical garden. In 1913, Sir Frederick Treves – coming fresh to Entebbe from the ports of Mwanza and Kisumu – described it as 'the prettiest and most charming town of the lake … a summer lake resort where no more business is undertaken than is absolutely necessary. The town spreads in a languid careless way to the lake … the golf links are more conspicuous than the capital.' A century later, it is difficult to take issue with Treves's assessment – indeed, it could almost have been written yesterday!

HISTORY Entebbe, the site of Uganda's only international airport, achieved instant immortality in June 1976 when an Air France airbus flying from Israel was hijacked by Palestinian terrorists and forced to land there. Non-Jewish passengers were released and the remainder held hostage against the demand that certain terrorists be freed from Israeli jails. In response, on 4 July 1976, a group of Israeli paratroopers stormed the airport in a daring surprise raid which resulted in all the hostages being freed. During the hijack, Amin pretended to play a mediating role between the Israeli government and the hijackers, but his complicity soon became apparent. A 75-year-old Israeli woman called Dora Bloch, rushed into a Ugandan hospital after choking on her food, was never seen again, presumably killed by Amin's soldiers. The raid also signalled the end of the already tenuous East African community when Amin broke off relations with Kenya (the Israeli raid was launched from Nairobi).

GETTING THERE AND AWAY Minibuses from Kampala to Entebbe leave from the old taxi park every ten minutes or so, and they take up to an hour. You'll find regular buses running to Entebbe from the junction of Entebbe and Nasser roads. If travelling in the opposite direction, you'll find Entebbe's **taxi park** [192 B6] tucked away in the warts-and-all suburb of Kitoro, 1km south out of the town centre, off the Airport Road.

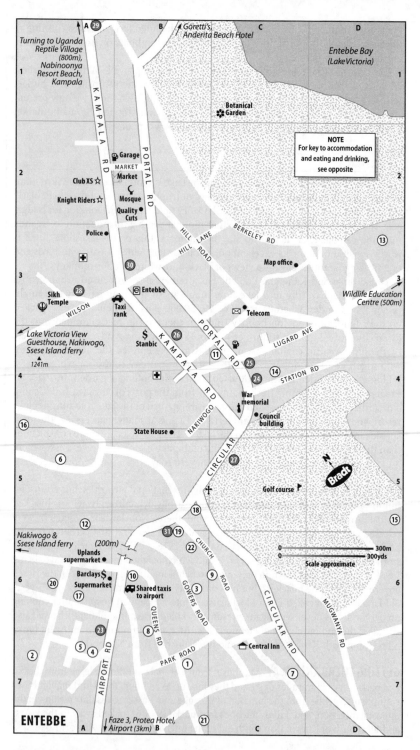

Entebbe Bay
(Lake Victoria)

Goretti's
Anderita Beach Hotel

Turning to Uganda
Reptile Village
(800m),
Nabinoonya
Resort Beach,
Kampala

Botanical
Garden

NOTE
For key to accommodation
and eating and drinking,
see opposite

Garage
Club XS ☆
MARKET
Market
Knight Riders ☆
Mosque
Quality
Cuts

Police ●

Map office ●

Wildlife Education
Centre (500m)

Sikh
Temple

Entebbe

Telecom

WILSON

Taxi
rank

LUGARD AVE

Lake Victoria View
Guesthouse, Nakiwogo,
Ssese Island ferry

1241m

Stanbic

STATION RD

War
memorial

Council
building

State House ●

Golf course

Nakiwogo &
Ssese Island ferry (200m)

Uplands
supermarket ●

Barclays $
Supermarket

Shared taxis
to airport

Central Inn

0   300m
0   300yds
Scale approximate

ENTEBBE

Faze 3, Protea Hotel,
Airport (3km)

KAMPALA RD · PORTAL RD · HILL LANE · HILL ROAD · BERKELEY RD · KAMPALA RD · NAKIWOGO · CIRCULAR · CHURCH ROAD · GOWERS ROAD · QUEENS RD · PARK ROAD · CIRCULAR RD · MUGWANYA RD · AIRPORT RD

ENTEBBE

For listings, see pages 193–7

🏠 **Where to stay**
1 Airport Guesthouse.........................B7
2 Airport View.....................................A7
3 The Boma..B6
4 Camp Entebbe..................................A7
5 Capital Cave Garden.......................A7
6 Carpe Diem.......................................A5
7 Christian Guesthouse.......................C7
8 Colonial Residence..........................B6
9 Entebbe Backpackers.......................C6
10 Entebbe Flight Motel.......................B6
11 Gately in Entebbe.............................C4
12 Glory Guesthouse.............................A5
13 Imperial Botanical Beach...............D3
14 Imperial Golf View..........................C4
15 Imperial Resort Beach....................D5
16 Karibu Guesthouse...........................A4
17 Kidepo Guesthouse..........................A6
18 Lake Victoria....................................B5
19 Oasis..B6
20 Shade Guesthouse............................A6
21 Skyway..B7
22 Sunset Motel.....................................B6

Off map
Anderita Beach Hotel.......................B1
Lake Victoria View Guesthouse....A4
Protea Hotel.......................................A7
Wildlife Education Centre.............D3

❌ **Where to eat and drink**
23 4 Point...A6
24 Anna's Corner..................................C4
25 China Garden....................................C4
26 Four Turkeys.....................................B4
27 Golf Club...C5
28 Malaika House Orphanage.............A3
29 Olubugo..A1
30 Rendezvous Club..............................B3
31 The Red Rooster................................B6

Off map
Faze 3...A7
Goretti's...B1

If you're using public transport to travel from Entebbe to southwestern Uganda (or vice versa), it's not necessary to go via Kampala's central taxi/bus parks. Take a *matatu* to Natete taxi park on the southern edge of the city and transfer to a vehicle headed to your destination. If driving, you can avoid the chaos of the capital entirely by heading to Entebbe's Nakiwogo port (behind Kitoro suburb) where a free **vehicle ferry** crosses Waiya Bay to Buwaya, 20km from Mpigi on the Kampala–Masaka–Mbarara road. The ferry shuttles across the bay throughout the day from around 07.30. This option is less convenient for pedestrians; you'll probably have to take a boda-boda to Mpigi where you'll be unlikely to find public transport going further west than Masaka. It is, however (if you're happy with a 16km boda-boda ride), a useful route from Entebbe to Mabamba Swamp (see page 201). If the ferry schedule doesn't match yours, you can hire a boat to cross the bay for about Ush15,000. Nakiwogo is also the site of the daily **passenger/vehicle ferry** departure (14.00) to Buggala Island in the Ssese archipelago (see page 208).

For details of **flights**, and getting between Kampala and the airport, see pages 139 & 191.

5

🏠 **WHERE TO STAY** Proximity to Uganda's primary airport – and primary international gateway – means that there is no shortage of accommodation in Entebbe for arriving and departing travellers. However, prices are considerably higher than Kampala and if you're on a budget, or looking for value for money, you'll be better off heading to the chaos of the capital. Most of the listings below range from bland internationalism to decidedly ordinary. If your criteria include character as well as comfort, the Lake Victoria Hotel, The Boma, Gately in Entebbe, Carpe Diem, Karibu Guesthouse, Airport Guesthouse, Oasis, Skyway and Entebbe Backpackers stand out from the crowds in their respective categories. When booking, check whether your hotel offers a complimentary airport transfer (usually one transfer per guest, either arriving or leaving). Entebbe's cheapest options are located in the town's unofficial centre, the scruffy but bustling suburb of Kitoro. This is found to the west of Airport Road, 1km beyond the official town centre.

For location of listings see maps on page 190 and page 192.

Upmarket

🏠 **Protea Hotel** (73 rooms); Airport Rd; 📞0312 217500; e res1@proteaebb.co.ug; www. protea.com/entebbe. The smartest thing in town is currently the brand-new, lakeshore Protea Hotel on the Airport Road. It's also the closest hotel to the airport – the end of Runway 2 is directly across the road! The rooms are every bit as smart & well appointed (Wi-Fi, AC, hairdryer, etc) as you'd expect from this established South African hotel chain. Private balconies attached to the south-facing suites view Lake Victoria beyond a neat garden & beach. The cheaper rooms on the northern side face the car park, a

EARLY DAYS IN ENTEBBE

The name Entebbe derives from the Luganda phrase Entebe za Mugala ('Headquarters of Mugala', head of the lungfish clan) and thus literally means 'Headquarters' – somewhat prescient, given that it would later serve as the British administrative capital of Uganda. Entebbe's prominence as a harbour is essentially a modern phenomenon: even into the 1890s, it was too remote from the centre of Baganda political activity to be of comparable significance to Munyonyo and Kaazi on Murchison Bay. But Entebbe's potential was hinted at as early as 1879 by the French missionaries Lourdel and Amans, who noted that 'the port ... is large and very well sheltered; on the shore there are no more than three or four houses for travellers'.

Entebbe's potential was first realised in 1896, with the arrival of a European steamship on Lake Victoria – shipped from Scotland to Mombasa, from where it was transported to Port Florence (Kisumu) in pieces by a caravan of porters! And it was sealed in 1901, when the railway line from Mombasa finally reached Port Florence, allowing travellers to and from the coast to reach Entebbe directly by the combination of train and ferry. Within two years, Entebbe had replaced Kampala as the colonial administrative capital – though Kampala would remain capital of the Buganda kingdom throughout the colonial era.

W E Hoyle, who arrived in Uganda in 1903, would later recall that Entebbe, not Kampala, 'was then regarded as the "metropolis" of Uganda'. This switch evidently occurred in 1901, judging by a lamentation published in the *Mengo Notes* late that year: 'The traders in Uganda are not very numerous ... we know of ... only two Germans [who] have both left Kampala and now appear to be doing chiefly wholesale business in Entebbe'. By 1903, certainly, Entebbe had a greater population of European residents than Kampala, most prominently the commissioner of Uganda and his administrative officers, who were 'mostly living in houses with thatched roofs'. By 1904, Entebbe even boasted a hotel, the Equatorial, evidently the precursor of the present-day Lake Victoria Hotel, owned by an Italian couple whose 'charming daughter', according to Hoyle, 'became engaged to the first English postmaster ...'. Neither knew the other's language, but both knew Swahili, so that little problem was solved.

Entebbe served as administrative capital of Uganda into the 1960s, and still houses a few government departments to this day, but its claims to outrank Kampala in the metropolitan stakes were rather more short-lived. Sir Frederick Treves wrote in 1913 that Entebbe 'is as unlike a capital as any place can well be, while as for administration it must be of that kind which is associated with a deck-chair, a shady veranda, the chink of ice on glass, and the curling smoke of a cigar'. Norma Lorimer, who visited 'gay little' Entebbe in the same year, paints a more pastoral picture: 'very tidy and clean and civilised ... its gardens by the lake, full of gorgeous flowering trees and ferns, its red roads with no dust, and its enchanting views of the islands ... Baganda moving about in their white *kanzus* on the red roads, silhouetted against a background of deep blue sky and tropical vegetation'.

dual carriageway & Runway 2. A swimming pool is under construction. *US$160/205 sgl/dbl for std rooms through to US$425/465 sgl/dbl for exec suites. B&B.*

⌂ **Imperial Resort Beach Hotel** (more than 100 rooms) 📞 0414 303000; e information@ irbhcom; www.imperialhotels.co.ug. Known locally as the 'Blue Hotel', the interior of this smart new hotel is dominated by an imposing central atrium, 6 floors high, capped by a glass roof. Glass-sided lifts scale the walls to access 4.5m-wide carpeted corridors & internal balconies that lead to the truly sumptuous rooms. Glazed entirely in blue & sinuous in plan, the building's lengthy façade has been designed to suggest a wave, which is unfortunate since waves don't have balconies & neither does this hotel, making it a bit of an AC prison. *US$150/180 deluxe sgl/dbl, US$200/250 club rooms, US$250/300 exec B&B.*

⌂ **Lake Victoria Hotel** 📞 0414 351600/0312 310100; e windsor@imul.com; www.laicohotels. com. The pick of Entebbe's large, upmarket hotels, this former government hotel exudes an atmosphere of tropical grandeur within smallish but immaculate grounds close to the golf course. A perennial favourite with safari-goers & other travellers, it offers AC & DSTV in all rooms, a swimming pool & health club, & secretarial & business services. There's a good b/fast buffet but other meals are rather ordinary (*Ush15,000–30,000*). It's a smashing location for a day visit but *US$180/230 sgl/dbl (B&B)* seems a bit steep.

Moderate

⌂ **Gately in Entebbe** (10 rooms) Portal Rd (the main road to the airport near the concrete rhino); 📞 0414 321313; e stay@gatelyinn.com; www. gatelyinn.com. The s/c rooms & cottages at this deservedly popular guesthouse are constructed & furnished using natural materials: stone, reed, wood, rough plaster & traditional fabrics. Though light sleepers may notice some traffic noise from the main road, the central dining/lounging terrace, sheltered from elements above & enclosed by foliage, is a delightful spot to spend time. Continental meals Ush25,000. An excellent gift shop is attached. See also advert in fourth colour section. *US$120/160 sgl/dbl B&B.*

⌂ **Imperial Botanical Beach Hotel** 📞 0414 320800; e ibbhotel@afsat.com. Back in '98, the sparkling new Botanical Beach was the obvious choice to accommodate President Bill Clinton when he brought his circus into town. These days it hosts conference delegates rather than heads of state, though the glory days may well return if internal fibreglass rock walls ever come back into vogue. A large, covered swimming pool & sandy lakeshore are redeeming features while the rooms are ordinary rather than actually bad. *US$120/140/ sgl/dbl B&B for new wing rooms (old wing US$20 cheaper). US$130/150 sgl/dbl exec room.*

⌂ **Airport View Hotel** Off Airport Rd, Kitoro; 📞 0312 261754; e byagaba@airportviewhotel. com; www.airportviewhotel.com. Despite an unpromising location behind the downmarket suburb of Kisoro, this smart hotel offers a friendly welcome & spacious, tiled rooms. A pleasant in-house restaurant serves good dinners for around Ush25,000. *US$120/150/150 sgl/dbl/suite B&B.*

⌂ **The Boma** (16 rooms) Plot 20a, Julia Ssebutinde Rd (aka Gowers Rd); m 0772 467929; e boma@infocom.co.ug; www.boma.co.ug. In the quiet suburb behind the Lake Victoria Hotel, this welcoming, family-run guesthouse is so popular with inbound/outbound tourists & expatriates that it's often full so be sure to book ahead. The Boma occupies a tastefully restored colonial homestead. Well placed for the airport. A swimming pool is welcome on hot equatorial afternoons. See also advert in third colour section. *US$120/140/180 sgl/dbl/trpl inc full English b/fast on a lovely veranda.*

⌂ **Carpe Diem** 📞 0793 396832; e carpediem. uganda@gmail.com; www.carpediemuganda. com. Smart new guesthouse overlooking Waiya Bay from the quiet Urungi Crescent on the hillside above Kitoro. The pristine lawn is a marvellous place to end the day with a drink as the sun sets over the lake. *US$95/105 sgl/dbl. B&B.*

⌂ **Karibu Guesthouse** (7 rooms) 84 Nsamizi Rd; m 0777 044984; e night@karibuguesthouse. com; www.karibuguesthouse.com. This new boutique guesthouse on the western side of town has quickly become a favourite with travellers using the airport. Inside, the s/c rooms are individually & distinctively furnished & colour-themed, while outside, a rooftop dining terrace (just about with a lake view beyond a verdant tropical garden) is a fine setting for the tasty & beautifully presented meals. See also advert on page 188. *US$85/110 sgl/dbl.*

Budget

⌂ **Christian Guesthouse** (3 rooms) 56 Church Rd; m 0772 421469. Small guesthouse with a pretty garden. S/c dbl & 2 sgls with shared b/rooms. *US$60 B&B.*

⌂ **Lake Victoria View Guesthouse** Plot 45, Urungi Crescent; m 0756 709560; e lakevictoriaguesthouse@gmail.com; www. victoriaviewguesthouse.com. This converted residential bungalow has a lake view, a friendly manageress & a choice of simple rooms, some s/c some not. *US$55/60. Non s/c rooms US$5 less. B&B.*

⌂ **African Roots Guesthouse** (7 rooms) m 0784 423207; e info@africanrootsgh.com. This small guesthouse offers a selection of s/c & non-s/c rooms in Manyago, a quiet residential area near the Sailing Club (1st road on the left coming from Kampala). *US$50/65/80 sgl/dbl/trpl B&B.*

⌂ **Airport Guesthouse** (8 rooms) Mugula Rd; ☎0414 370932; m 0772 445805; e postmaster@ gorillatours.com. This deservedly popular little guesthouse is perhaps the best deal in Entebbe. Located off Park Road in a quiet suburb, it offers smart & comfortable s/c rooms facing a pretty garden. Conveniently located for the airport & very reasonably priced indeed! *US$50/60/80 sgl/dbl/ trpl B&B.*

⌂ **Colonial Residence** (6 rooms) Queen's Rd; m 0772 829709. This small guesthouse occupies an old bungalow in a pretty garden. The rooms are comfortable & cheerfully decorated but share a bathroom so best suited to companionable groups. *US$45/55 sgl/dbl B&B. Day rooms for outgoing travellers on evening flights: US$25.*

⌂ **Sunset Motel** (13 rooms) Church Rd; ☎0414 323502; m 0776 323501; e enquiries@ sunsetentebbe.com; www.traveluganda.co.ug/ sunsetmotel. This new guesthouse offers rooms in a lovely colonial bungalow in pretty garden, as well as some small but adequate s/c rooms & a campground with smart showers at the back. *US$45/55/60 sgl/ dbl/twin standard rooms, US$80 trpl/family room, US$35 sgl+ budget rooms B&B. Camping US$5pp.*

⌂ **Anderita Beach Hotel** (40 rooms) ☎0414 322435/0312 271912; e anderitahotel@yahoo.com. Attractively located on the palm-lined Ntambi Road, rooms at the front of the hotel enjoy lake views. A restaurant is attached plus a bar on the beach across the road next to Goretti's pizzeria. Guests have a choice of rooms based on prices rather than occupancy needs. *US$45/50/60 s/c rooms.*

⌂ **Camp Entebbe** (8 rooms) m 0783 414877. Off Airport Rd, behind 4 Point (see page 197). A small site contains a tight cluster of tiled s/c 2-unit cottages surrounding a pleasant thatched dining shelter. *US$40/50 sgl/dbl B&B.*

⌂ **Oasis** (8 rooms) Church Rd (corner of Airport Road); m 0785 224475 e oasiscampsite@gmail. com; www.oasiscampsite.com. This appendage to the Red Rooster sports bar is great value. *US$40 sgl/dbl, US$15 for smaller twin/dbl rooms sharing a spotless communal bathroom.*

⌂ **Wildlife Education Centre** (5 cottages) ☎0414 322169; e info@uwec.ug; www.uweczoo. org. Ever wondered what happens in a zoo when the visitors go home? Try the basic but roomy s/c *bandas* at UWEC. Twin beds are provided downstairs & on a mezzanine platform. Meals are available in the UWEC café. The cottages are several hundred metres inside the zoo; hire a *boda-boda* if you've got luggage & no vehicle. *US$40/60 sgl/family occupancy inc the zoo entrance fee.*

⌂ **Entebbe Flight Motel** ☎0414 320812; www.entebbeflighthotel.com. This long-serving facility has been swallowed by a perennially incomplete multi-storeyed extension clad with gumpole scaffolding. The old-fashioned & rather threadbare s/c rooms are good value by Entebbe standards but it's all a little weird! *US$35/45 s/c sgl/dbl inc b/fast.*

⌂ **Capital Cave Garden** (10 rooms) Off Airport Rd behind 4 Point; m 0772 869774. You'll get better value for money in Kampala, but if you're in Entebbe for a night on a budget, this'll do fine. Eat snacks from the restaurant or wander up to 4 Point for greater choice. *US$30/35 sgl/dbl B&B.*

⌂ **Skyway Mugula Road** (24 rooms) m 0700 951317. A dash of style, imagination & expense could transform this superb, storied period building into Entebbe's most appealing hotel. As it is, the adequate rooms, pleasant upstairs bar/ restaurant, spacious lawns & fair prices make this a popular choice with budget travellers. *US$26/30 sgl/dbl s/c B&B.*

⌂ **Entebbe Backpackers** (c10 rooms) Church Rd; ☎0414 320432; m 0712 849973; e stay@entebbebackpackers.com; www. entebbebackpackers.com. This popular hostel fills a much-needed niche for affordable accommodation in Entebbe. Food is available & the lounge has DSTV. A selection of rooms including s/c dorm cottages, each with a bunk bed of 2 sgl+ units.

US$14/32 sgl/dbl s/c; US$8/10 sgl/dbl shared facilities. Garden Cottages s/c sgl US$16; Garden Cottage s/c 2x sgl & bunk beds US$24; camping US$4. Rates excl b/fast.

Shoestring

⌂ **Kidepo Guesthouse** (20 rooms) Kitoro; ☎0414 322722; www.kidepoguesthouse.com. Spruced up, tiled s/c rooms in a typical courtyard hotel. The prices must surely be negotiable! US$30/50/35 sgl/dbl/twin.

⌂ **Glory Guesthouse** (25 rooms) Fulu Rd, Kitoro; ☎0414 321563; e gloryhouse@yahoo.com. The s/c rooms (nets, TV & hot shower) would cost half the price in Kampala but this is Entebbe! Prices are, however, negotiable. US$20/30 sgl/dbl B&B.

⌂ **Shade Guesthouse** (8 rooms) Kitoro. This basic lodge offers reasonable rooms with nets. Snacks available on the premises or there are plenty of bars & BBQ joints close by. US$10/12 sgl/dbl with clean communal shower.

WHERE TO EAT AND DRINK   For location of listings see map on page 192.

✗ **4 Point** Airport Rd. This popular eating & drinking joint just past Barclays offers Indian & Chinese food. Meals Ush14,000–25,000.

✗ **Anna's Corner** Station Rd. This popular garden restaurant near the golf course serves delicious & reasonably priced pizzas (Ush16,000–25,000), as well as burgers (Ush15,000–20,000) & salads. The complex also contains crafts shops, a library & an internet café.

✗ **China Garden Restaurant** Corner of Lugard Av (which leads to the Wildlife Education Centre) & the main Airport Road. Long-serving Chinese restaurant with a large garden. You can't miss the turning – it's the only junction in Uganda marked by a life-size concrete rhino. The main courses are generously sized & reasonably priced. Meals Ush20,000.

✗ **Carpe Diem** 33 Urungi Crescent; m 0793 396832. New, hillside guesthouse with a pleasant lawn facing Waiya Bay & (around 19.00 daily) a panoramic sunset. Sandwiches, shakes, smoothies, 4-course dinners & reasonably priced daily specials (Ush16–20,000).

✗ **Faze 3** Circular Rd at Airport Road end. Best steaks in town, so I'm told. Meals Ush18,000–35,000.

⧉ **Four Turkeys** Kampala Rd. The town centre's liveliest hangout is an English-style pub full of prostitutes & UN operatives. Filling & inexpensive snacks such as burgers & toasted sandwiches are served. Meals Ush15,000–23,000.

✗ **Gately in Entebbe** [See page 195]. The covered terrace at this guesthouse is one of Entebbe's most pleasant settings for a meal. Gately offers grills, salads, Thai dishes & an impressive selection of smoothies, juices, teas & coffees. Main courses Ush25,000.

✗ **Golf Club** The veranda restaurant at the golf club offers grills, stews, burgers. Whole grilled tilapia is a speciality. Meals Ush15,000–25,000.

✗ **Goretti's** Nambi Rd. This lakeside pizzeria enjoys a smashing location beside a white-sand beach. Service can be slow so this is not the place to spend your last couple of hours before a flight. Don't leave your passports & tickets in the car either while you dine. Cheaper meals are available in the adjacent lakefront bar run by the **Anderita Beach Hotel**. Meals Ush15,000–50,000.

✗ **Malaika House Orphanage** m 0783 810728 for directions. The Tue & Thu pizza nights (⊕06.00–22.00) at this children's home are popular with Entebbe residents & others in the know. Head down Nakiwogo Road from the town centre towards Nakiwogo port but turn right at the sign for Entebbe Christian School. Pizzas Ush20,000, chocolate mousse Ush8000.

✗ **Olubugo** Kampala Rd. This new storied thatched restaurant is located on the northern edge of town next to My Choice supermarket. It's run by AidChild, an NGO with a self-explanatory cause, whose wide-ranging menu includes pasta, steaks, chicken dishes, burgers, sandwiches, pizzas & freshly caught fish. Meals Ush15,000–24,000.

⧉ **The Red Rooster** Church Rd, on corner of Airport Road. The place to watch live football events on DSTV. The pub's owner played for Watford during the Elton John era & the pub's large collection of sporting memorabilia includes a hilarious black & white picture of the be-wigged & bespectacled songster leading the team on to the pitch.

♀ **Rendezvous Club** Kampala Rd. One of a cluster of open-air bars in the town centre where you can drink inexpensive beer & nibble on meat grilled on roadside BBQs.

NIGHTLIFE The town's two main nightclubs, **Club XS** and **Knight Riders**, are located on Kampala Road, 500m downhill from the town centre.

SHOPPING The town's best supermarkets are found close to Barclays bank at the turning off Airport Road into Kitoro, the best being the cluttered **Uplands supermarket** [192 A6], aka 'John's shop'. The main market for fresh produce is also in Kitoro. Quality Cuts butchers/deli [192 B2] on Portal Road will provide you with the raw materials (or a ready-made sub sandwich) for a picnic in the botanical garden; gift shops are found at the Wildlife Education Centre, Anna's Corner (see page 197), Gately in Entebbbe guesthouse (see page 195), the Lake Victoria Hotel (see page 195) and on Lugard Avenue near Golf View Hotel.

OTHER PRACTICALITIES

Foreign exchange Stanbic [192 B4] (Kampala Road) and **Barclays** [192 A6] (Kitoro junction on Airport Road) will change money but expect long queues. Service at the forex next to Uplands supermarket (50m from Barclays) is quicker. Out of banking hours, hop on a minibus-taxi to the airport, where a number of private forex bureaux offer rates that are reasonable, though somewhat lower than you'd get in Kampala.

Internet Most guesthouses offer internet facilities. Otherwise, head for Anna's Corner (see page 197) on the main airport road, close to the golf course. There are also a couple of internet cafés on Kampala Road in the town centre.

Luggage storage Rather than risk sitting in Kampala traffic when you should be checking in for your outbound flight at Entebbe Airport, it's more relaxing to leave the city early to spend a relaxed afternoon in Entebbe town. Both the Lake Victoria and Imperial Botanical Beach hotels (see page 195) are happy to store luggage for day visitors using the swimming pool or taking lunch. The Lake Vic has the pleasanter setting but the Botanical is more convenient if you want to wander down to the botanical garden or Wildlife Education Centre.

Map sales office Entebbe was the administrative capital of Uganda in the colonial era and many government departments are still dotted around the residential area between the town centre and Imperial Botanical Beach Hotel. Most likely to be of interest to tourists is the **Department of Lands and Surveys** [192 C3], where a well-stocked map sales office sells 1:50,000 sheets covering most of the country for Ush10,000 apiece. Technically, you're supposed to go and pay in the town's Stanbic bank but staff now accept direct payment (and issue receipts).

Swimming pool The pool at the Windsor Lake Victoria Hotel is open to non-residents on payment of Ush10,000. The Imperial Botanical Beach Hotel has a huge covered pool which you can use, also for Ush10,000.

WHAT TO SEE

Entebbe Botanical Garden [192 C1] (⊕ *daily; admission Ush10,000, vehicle Ush2,000 & a camera Ush2,000*) Established in 1902, Entebbe's botanical garden is an attractively laid-out mix of indigenous forest, cultivation and horticulture, and a highly attractive destination to birdwatchers. The botanical garden offers an excellent introduction to Uganda's birds, ranging from Lake Victoria specials such as grey kestrel, yellow-throated leaflove, slender-billed weaver and Jackson's golden-backed weaver to the more widespread but nonetheless striking black-headed gonolek, red-chested sunbird, grey-capped warbler and common wattle-eye. In addition to various shorebirds, the impressive palmnut vulture and fish eagle are both common, and a pair of giant eagle owls is resident. Forest birds include the splendid Ross's and great blue turaco, as well as the noisy black-and-white casqued hornbill.

It is said that some of the early *Tarzan* films were shot on location in Entebbe – a thus-far unverifiable legend that gains some plausibility when you compare the giggling of the plantain-eaters that frequent the botanical garden with the chimp noises that punctuate the old movies. There are some mammals around – no chimps, of course, nor even the sitatunga and hippos that frequented the lakeshore swamps into the 1960s – but you can be confident of seeing vervet and black-and-white colobus monkeys, as well as tree squirrels.

On a less agreeable note, the botanical gardens are a popular haunt for young men lacking funds for college fees and/or with ambitions to visit your home country. If you engage in casual conversation with people matching this description, don't be surprised if these topics crop up.

Uganda Wildlife Education Centre [off map, 192 D3] (⊕ *daily; admission Ush15,000/20,000 foreign residents/non-residents*) The animal orphanage near the former Game Department headquarters was established as a sanctuary for animals which would be unable to fend for themselves in the wild, and it has played an important role in the protection of rare and threatened animals. Residents include a few lions (whose nocturnal vocalisations add a distinct sense of place to a night in any nearby hotel), a pair of recently reintroduced black rhinos, and a variety of smaller predators that are seldom seen in the wild. The aviary provides the most reliable opportunity in Uganda of getting a close-up shot of the renowned shoebill.

Golf [192 C5] The open expanse of the 18-hole golf course sloping towards Lake Victoria is Entebbe's most distinctive feature on the drive towards the airport. It's one of few clubs worldwide where a hooked drive on the 3rd might hit a rhino (in the neighbouring Wildlife Education Centre). Golfers should try for early morning or late afternoon starts to avoid the heat of the day. Non-members pay Ush30,000; club hire costs Ush20,000.

AROUND ENTEBBE

UGANDA REPTILES VILLAGE [190 C2] (m *0782 349583; www.reptiles.ug; tourists pay Ush15,000 & residents Ush10,000; A boda-boda from Entebbe costs about Ush4,000*) Established to encourage Ugandans to respect reptiles, rather than automatically banging them on the head, this worthwhile destination lies on the northwestern edge of Entebbe, 3km off the main road. You'll find a variety of snakes, chameleons, monitor lizards and a couple of crocodiles. It's a pretty site on the edge of the extensive Waiya Swamp; boat and birding voyages are available on a channel cut through to the open lake. Bottled refreshments but no food is available.

KAMPALA SNAKE PARK [190 D1] This low-key attraction is signposted off the east side of the main Kampala–Entebbe road, about 3km south of Kajjansi. It's then another 2km or so on dirt roads, also signed. It's not such a pretty site as that of Uganda Reptiles Village but there is a greater selection of snakes displayed in glass-windowed *bandas* dotted around the site. A reasonable entrance fee is charged for a guided tour.

ZIKA FOREST [190 C2] This small (40ha) patch of remnant forest lies a couple of hundred metres off the Kampala–Entebbe road at Kisubi, 23km from Kampala. If you've insufficient time to visit larger and better-known forests, or are short of money, a visit to Zika provides a cheap and convenient taste of a tropical forest. Owned by the Entebbe-based Uganda Virus Research Institute, it contains a unique (in Uganda) four-storey metal tower used to ascertain what sort of bugs inhabit which strata of forest vegetation. A forearm-burning ascent of a narrow metal ladder is rewarded when you emerge into open skies to enjoy a bird's- and monkey's-eye view of the forest canopy. A small trail network also explores the forest at ground level. From Kampala, turn right just beyond a 'Kampala 23km' sign (immediately before Mivule Primary School on the right and the Uganda Martyrs' University on the left) and then follow a left turn behind the school after 50m. A caretaker will have you sign a book and pay a quasi-official fee of Ush3,000.

NGAMBA ISLAND CHIMPANZEE SANCTUARY [190 D3] (*www.ngambaisland.com; standard day visits cost upwards of US$126pp depending on timing, group numbers, & whether you take the speedboat (45mins each way) or the traditional wooden boat (90mins each way); chimpanzee walks cost US$400pp. Visits can be arranged through most tour operators in Kampala.*)

Situated 23km southeast of Entebbe, the 50ha Ngamba Island forms part of the Kome archipelago, a group of about 15 islands and islets separated from the northern shore of Lake Victoria by the 10km-wide Damba Channel. Ngamba was established as a chimpanzee sanctuary in 1998, when 19 orphaned chimps were relocated there from the Uganda Wildlife Education Centre (UWEC) in Entebbe and the smaller Isinga Island in Queen Elizabeth National Park. These chimpanzees had all been saved from a life in captivity or a laboratory when they were confiscated by the Ugandan authorities and brought to UWEC for care and rehabilitation, with some being released on to Isinga in the mid-1990s.

The island is divided into two unequal parts, separated by an electric fence. On one side of the fence, the visitors' and staff centre extends over an area of about 1ha on a partially cleared stretch of northwestern shore notable for the immense weaver colonies it supports. The rest of the island is reserved more or less exclusively for the chimps and their attendants, the exception being tourists who opt to do the chimpanzee walk described below. There's also a small tented camp sleeping up to eight on the island.

Ngamba was chosen as a sanctuary because it was formerly uninhabited and its rainforest environment is almost identical to that of wild chimpanzees, with more than 50 plant species known to be utilised by free-ranging chimps in Uganda represented. There is plenty of room for the chimps to roam, but the forest isn't large enough to sustain the entire community – indeed its area corresponds roughly to the natural range of one chimpanzee – so the chimps are fed a porridge-like mixture for breakfast, and then fruits and vegetables twice during the day. The fruits are given to the chimps from a viewing platform, which provides an opportunity for visitors to observe and photograph the chimps through a fence. The chimps have the choice of staying in the forest overnight or returning to a holding facility built to enhance social integration and veterinary management, with sleeping platforms and hammocks as well as grass for nest building.

The sanctuary exists to provide the best facilities and care to captive chimpanzees, for which reason the management has elected not to allow the chimps to breed. All sexually mature females on the island are given a contraceptive implant, which doesn't disrupt the community's normal sexual behaviour, but does prevent pregnancy in the same way as the human contraceptive pill. The sanctuary may change this policy if it proves necessary or beneficial to allow breeding in the future.

Since 1998, UWEC has received an influx of orphaned chimpanzees, most of which were captured illegally in the forests of the DRC and smuggled across Uganda for trade. In 2013, 48 orphaned chimpanzees were resident on Ngamba Island. Workers on the island are constantly involved in helping the newly arrived orphans to integrate into the original community.

Ngamba Island is the flagship project of the Chimpanzee Sanctuary and Wildlife Conservation Trust, jointly established in 1997 by the Born Free Foundation, the International Fund for Animal Welfare, the Jane Goodall Institute, UWEC and the Zoological Board of New South Wales (Australia). It is part of an integrated chimpanzee conservation programme that also includes an ongoing census study of wild chimpanzee populations in Uganda, two snare-removal programmes, chimpanzee habituation for ecotourism, and education and outreach initiatives in local communities. Proceeds from tourist visits go directly back into the maintenance of the sanctuary and the organisation's other chimpanzee-related projects.

Day trips to the island are timed to coincide with the pre-arranged supplementary feeding times of 11.00 and 14.30, when the chimpanzees come to within metres of a raised walkway, offering an excellent opportunity to observe and photograph one of our closest animal relatives. Half-day trips by motorboat leave Entebbe at 09.30 and 13.00 daily by prior arrangement. Overnight accommodation in self-contained tented accommodation with solar lighting costs US$370/540 single/double (US$338/500 single/double off-peak), full board. Resident rates area available. These enable access to two daytime chimpanzee feedings from the visitors' platform, plus the early morning feeding in the holding facility. Kayaks are available to explore the island bays and go searching for monitor lizards, otters and some of the 154 recorded bird species, while other optional activities for overnight visitors include a visit to a local fishing village, a sunset cruise, and fishing.

Chimpanzee walks Also on offer are one-hour chimpanzee walks with a group of infant chimpanzees through their forest habitat, in the late afternoon or very early morning. A maximum of three visitors are allowed in the forest for each walk, always accompanied by trained staff. Even so, the chimpanzees are used to human contact and they will often play-bite visitors, climb on them, grab their glasses or pull their hair – or even just walk along holding their hand. This activity is limited to people aged between 18 and 65. Visitors are also required to be free of any flu-like disease or herpes (cold sores) outbreak at the time of their visit.

Anybody thinking of booking on the chimpanzee walk should check out the Ngamba website (*www.ngambaisland.com*) well in advance for current medical requirements, which at the time of writing included valid proof of a current vaccination against hepatitis A and B, measles, meningococcal meningitis, polio, tetanus and yellow fever. It also required visitors to have had a negative TB test within the past six months.

MABAMBA SWAMP [190 B2] Just 12km west of Entebbe as the crow flies, the Mabamba Swamp extends across more than 100km² from a shallow, marshy bay on the northern shore of Lake Victoria. Listed as a Ramsar Site and an Important Bird Area, Mabamba harbours an excellent selection of water-associated species, and is possibly now the most reliable place anywhere in the country for shoebill sightings. The villagers offer dugout trips into the swamp where they are usually capable of locating shoebills within a few minutes. Even if you're out of luck on that score, it's a lovely, mellow boat trip, and other localised birds likely to be seen include pygmy goose, lesser jacana, gull-billed tern, blue-breasted bee-eater and the papyrus-specific Carruthers's cisticola and white-winged warbler. A boat capable of carrying three visitors costs Ush100,000.

Getting there Despite their close geographical proximity, Entebbe and Mabamba lie at least 40km apart by road, and the trip there takes about one hour. The most direct route out of Entebbe involves following the surfaced Kampala Road north for about 12km north to Kisubi, then turning left along a dirt side road to Nakauka, where another left turn leads to the small town of Kasanje. Turn left again at an outsized roundabout and after 3.5km, you'll reach a minor road on the right by a large tree. Follow this for 9km to reach Mabamba.

Coming from Kampala, the best route is to follow the Masaka Road out of town for 30km, then to turn left along a side road signposted for Buyege, shortly before Mpigi Town. After 12km this road reaches Kasanje, where you go straight across the roundabout and turn right by the large tree. The route from Entebbe is a good place to look out for flocks of great blue turaco, while the route from Kampala passes through a large swamp about 6km before Kasanje, where papyrus gonolek is resident and could easily be combined with a visit to the Mpanga Forest Reserve near Mpigi (see pages 215–18). Mabamba can also be reached by public transport. You should have no problem getting from Kampala to Kasanje where you can hire a *boda-boda* or taxi to reach the swamp. If you're in Entebbe, take a boat from Nakiwogo port to Buwaya landing on the western side of Waiya Bay (see page 193). It's 5km from Buwaya to the large tree junction mentioned above (approaching from the opposite direction).

MURCHISON BAY

Murchison Bay extends south from Kampala's Port Bell, past the smart suburb and historic royal port of Munyonyo, before eventually opening out into the main lake near Entebbe. Though the Kampala–Entebbe road is essentially a ribbon of suburbia, side roads leading east towards Murchison Bay still access some unspoiled countryside – for the time being. The eastern side of the bay, though separated from Kampala's suburban sprawls of Ggaba and Munyonyo by just a kilometre or two of water, remains as undeveloped as anywhere you'll visit in southern Uganda. The recreational potential of this lovely area is only just starting to be exploited with the recent appearance of a few resorts and a smattering of weekend cottages.

 WHERE TO STAY AND EAT These listings include shoreline accommodation on both sides of Murchison Bay, extending south to Bulago Island. For lakeside facilities in Kampala, see the Ggaba and Munyonyo section, page 155). For location of listings see map on page 190.

Upmarket

🏠 **Pineapple Bay Resort** (10 rooms) Bulago Island; ☎ 0414 251182; e info@wildplacesafrica. com; www.wildplacesafrica.com. The long-serving Bulago Island Lodge (16km east of Entebbe & 2° south of the Equator) has been refurbished & rebranded by Wildplaces, which runs several luxurious lodges & camps nationwide. The new-

look Pineapple Bay Resort boasts a swimming pool & 10 typically sumptuous & spacious beachfront cottages. *US$300/400 FB, boat (up to 6 people) costs US$200 return.*

🏠 **2 degrees south** (6 rooms) Bulago Island; m 0776 709970; e stay@oneminutesouth.com; www.oneminutesouth.com. This gorgeous private house has a terrific clifftop location overlooking the lake. If the private sandy beach down below seems a little distant, worry not as the house has its own swimming pool. It's a self-catering setup, though a chef can be hired to take charge. Similarly, if opening your own booze seems a bit of a bother, wander over to the upmarket Pineapple Bay Resort (see above) & they'll open theirs for you (at a fee of course). *US$600 per night for up to 14 guests, US$43pp, US$50 discount for each further night. Rates inc boat transfer for up to 8 guests from Entebbe.*

🏠 **Lake Victoria Serena** (120 rooms) 5km off Entebbe Rd at Lweza; ☎0417 121000; e lakevictoria@serena.co.ug; www.serenahotels. com. This new & quite monumental development extends across a 100ha lakeshore site located 5km from Entebbe Road at Lweza. The interior of the main hotel building is inspired by Zanzibari architecture & surrounded by palatial, storeyed, Roman-style *insulae* distinguished by classical arches, pastel-toned walls & terracotta roofs. Each block contains 4 to 6 unashamedly luxurious rooms & suites. The beautiful swimming pool is operational while construction of a marina & 9-hole golf course is under way. B&B rates seem very reasonable. *US$200/260 sgl/dbl & US$250/300 exec suites B&B.*

🏠 **Lagoon Resort** (6 tented cottages) Wavimenya Bay; m 0775 787291; e lagoon. resort@yahoo.com; www.ug-lagoonresort.com. This offshore resort on the eastern side of Murchison Bay is popular with both tourists & Kampala residents (the wealthier ones anyway). A thatched lodge building & external viewing decks overlook a lovely garden sloping towards the sandy beach, while the accommodation is provided in elevated s/c tented cottages, discreetly positioned in a nearby patch of forest. A swimming pool is provided & mountain biking, kayaking & cultural walks are available. Also has a reputation as a good out-of-town eatery. Boats to Lagoon (*25mins*) run from Speke Commonwealth Resort at Munyonyo (see page 155). Advance booking is essential. *US$160/240 sgl/dbl FB inc boat transfers. Discounts for residents.*

Moderate
🏠 **Country Lake Resort** Garuga Rd; ☎0312 106482; www.countrylakeresort.com. Located beside the lake, this 2ha site represents by far the smartest & most attractive of the cheaper lakeside resorts on Murchison Bay. It's also more appealing than a few other lakeside hotels on the same road. Accommodation is in cottages. Turn off Entebbe Road, 23km from Kampala at Kitala Trading Centre. If you're out that way at a w/end, the nearby Garuga Motorcross circuit sees regular events. *US$80/100 B&B.*

Budget
🏠 **Beer Gardens 2** (see Beach House on page 164) & **Lakeside Adventure Park** (page 204). Simple accommodation on Wavimenya Bay.

Shoestring & camping
🏠 **Nabinoonya Resort Beach** (13 rooms, 5 dorm *bandas*) About 10km north of Entebbe; m 0774 972027; e ficnabinonya@yahoo.co.uk. A shady 30mins' walk from the Kampala Road at Kisubi, this secluded lakeshore resort is a peaceful w/day retreat, though w/ends are crowded & noisy. The accommodation, though ordinary, is a cheap alternative to budget accommodation in Entebbe. The large grounds are genuinely lovely, with remnant forest trees inhabited by red-tailed monkeys & plenty of birdlife. Also does food (*fish & chips Ush15,000–20,000*). *US$8/13/13 s/c sgl/dbl/ twin, US$15 twins using common showers, US$8 bed in a 4-berth banda, US$2.50pp camping.*

🏠 **K Palm Resort** Gobero Bay; m 0772 421444; e info@kpalmresort.com; http://kpalmresort.com. Popular with university students at w/ends, this pretty lakeshore on the east side of Murchison Bay is a delightful place to pitch a tent, chill out & hope for the best, foodwise. *Banda* accommodation is also available but for the time being, camping is the better option. K Palm is about 1hr by boat from Kampala's Ggaba Port. Booking essential.

Camping is also possible in Entebbe at the **Entebbe Backpackers** and **Sunset Motel**, both on Church Road (see pages 196–7).

WHAT TO SEE AND DO
East Murchison Bay With lake viewpoints, wetlands and numerous forest patches, the rural peninsulas of Kyagwe County on the eastern side of Murchison Bay, and separating the lateral Wavimenya and Gobero bays, are great to explore by pushbike, *boda-boda* or on foot. Attractive circuits are possible by heading down

Gobero Peninsula to one of several landing sites from where you can cross to the far side of either bay by boat to continue on your way. Of passing interest in Gobero are a couple of Bagandan shrines. If a day trip doesn't suffice, accommodation is available at Lagoon Resort and K Palm Resort (see page 203). The simplest way to reach Kyagwe is from Kampala's Ggaba Port where the 15-minute trip by 'special hire' boat to Bule or Kisinsi landings will cost around Ush7,000, or Ush2000 per person on a public boat. The latter are most numerous on Ggaba market days (Monday and Thursday). *Boda-bodas* are more numerous at Bule.

Far greater distances can of course be covered by motorbikes, which I've seen ferried across the bay from Ggaba by expats. Thus equipped, you could spend a delightful couple of days exploring lakeside bays, forests, ridges and peninsulas between Murchison Bay and Jinja. See (Uganda Maps) Sheet 3: *Beyond Kampala* for inspiration and location of shoestring lodgings.

Lakeside Adventure Park [190 D1] (m *0771 676880; www.lakeside.ug.info@ lakeside.ug; High Ropes course Ush60,000 pp. Dorm bed US$12; tents US$8. Costs exc boat transfers from KK Beach in Ggaba*) Located next to Lagoon Resort in an attractive lakeside garden site at the head of Wavimenya Bay, Kampala's first obstacle course offers the chance to test yourself on lofty rope walks, cable runways, climbing walls and the like.

Murchison Bay: west side
Lutembe Bay Ramsar Site [190 D2] This small (just 98ha) wetland on the eastern side of the Kampala–Entebbe road is notable for seasonal Palaearctic (26 species) and Afro-tropical (15) migrants. Regular surveys by Nature Uganda have recorded an average of 1,429,829 wetland birds. These include an average of 1,048,602 white-winged black terns, a figure representing more than half of the global population. The 108 species of waterbird recorded at the site include the globally vulnerable shoebill, Madagascar squacco heron, and the papyrus yellow warbler, the near-threatened papyrus gonolek, great snipe, African skimmer and pallid harrier, and 24 regionally threatened species such as the northern brown-throated weaver, greater cormorant, slender-billed gull and (as mentioned above) quite a lot of white-winged black terns. As far as getting there is concerned, contact one of the specialist bird guides (see page 77) and arrange an excursion to get the best out of your visit.

Garuga Motorcross circuit [190 D2] Uganda MotoX Club puts on regular, weekend events at its lakeside circuit, 10km off the Entebbe–Kampala road on Garuga peninsula. Competitions, which include club, national and regional-level events, make for a fun afternoon out. For details contact club director, Arthur Blick (m *0772 506380*; e *ablickjr@hotmail.com*).

Palmira Stables [190 C2] (m *0772 996889*; e *palmira.horses@gmail.com*) Located inside the Wagagai flower farm, the Peruvian-owned Palmira Stables offer 'natural horsemanship' on the shores of the lake. You'll find it just 5km along Kasenyi Road from Abaita town on the Entebbe–Kampala road. Booking essential.

THE SSESE ISLANDS
Situated in the northwest of Lake Victoria, the Ssese Islands form one of Uganda's prime destinations for casual rambling and off-the-beaten-track exploration.

During the 1990s, the islands were Uganda's most popular backpackers' chill-out destination until the ferry service from Port Bell (Kampala) was suspended in 1997. With access reduced to the less-than-comfortable 'lake-taxis' from Entebbe and a roundabout approach via Masaka to the Bukakata ferry, the islands surrendered their place in the hearts of independent travellers to the more accessible Lake Bunyonyi. However, the Ssese Islands are experiencing a renaissance in tourism activity with the introduction of a passenger ferry to Buggala Island from Entebbe.

The Ssese archipelago consists of 84 separate islands, some large and densely inhabited, others small and deserted, but all lushly forested thanks to an annual average rainfall in excess of 2,000mm. Only two islands regularly receive tourists. The more established of these is **Buggala**, the largest, and most accessible and most developed of the islands. A significant number of travellers also head to tiny **Banda Island**, which is popular with backpackers. Other islands that can be visited with varying degrees of ease are Bubeke, Bukasa and Bufumira.

Not least amongst the Ssese Islands' attractions are their rustic character and the sense of being well away from any established tourist circuit. But, as in other out-of-the-way places, it is suggested that you dress conservatively except in resort and campsite grounds.

BUGGALA ISLAND Extending over 200km² and measuring 43km from east to west, Buggala is the largest island set within the Ugandan waters of Lake Victoria, and the best developed for tourism. It is linked to the mainland by a regular motor ferry and dotted with accommodation to suit most tastes and budgets.

Kalangala, the administrative centre for the islands, is an unremarkable small town situated on a ridge at the eastern end of Buggala, while the nearby **Lutoboka Bay** hosts the island's main cluster of beach resorts. Be aware that Lutoboka can no longer be relied on as a quiet tropical island retreat. It may be peaceful enough during the week, but if one of the resorts hosts a weekend function, you'll know all about it – even if you're staying on Banda Island, 15km away!

This issue aside, Lutoboka Bay is a lovely setting that offers a variety of beach activities; building sandcastles, swimming (though bilharzia is certainly a risk; see pages 92–3 for more information) and building more sandcastles. Canoeing is available at some resorts. If you weary of the beach, Buggala Island offers great possibilities for walking. The road from the ferry to Mirembe Resort passes through grassland and a beautiful patch of forest that will interest birders. From Kalangala Town on the ridge above Lutoboka, strike out in any direction to find pleasing views over forests and grassy clearings to the lakeshore and more distant islands. To explore further afield, you can either hike or try to hire a bicycle from Andronica Lodge. A popular cycling excursion is to **Mutumbula swimming beach** – reputedly free of bilharzia – which lies off the road towards Luku. Travellers tend to concentrate on the Kalangala–Luku road, and justifiably so, since the road heading south from Kalangala is far more cultivated. One potentially interesting goal in this direction is the marshy southwestern shores, which harbour small numbers of hippo as well as a population of sitatunga antelope with larger horns than the mainland equivalent, regarded by some authorities to represent an endemic island race. Without a private vehicle, you would probably need to do an overnight walking or cycling trip to get to these swamps.

Another important landmark on Buggala is **Luku** itself, the small village on the western extreme of the island where the motor ferry from the mainland docks. A good dirt road connects Luku to Kalangala Town, while minor roads run to other villages lying further south on the island.

The most common large mammal on Buggala is the vervet monkey, often seen in the vicinity of Lutoboka and Kalangala. Bushbuck and black-and-white colobus are present, but seldom observed. Over the 12,000 years that the island has been separate from the mainland, one endemic creek rat and three endemic butterfly species have evolved. Water and forest birds are prolific. Expect to see a variety of hornbills, barbets, turacos, robin-chats, flycatchers and weavers from the roads around Kalangala. Particularly common are the jewel-like pygmy kingfisher, the brown-throated wattle-eye and a stunning morph of the paradise flycatcher intermediate to the orange and white phases illustrated in most east African field guides. African fish eagles and palmnut vultures are often seen near the lake, while immense breeding colonies of little egret and great cormorant occur on Lutoboka and other bays.

SSESE HISTORY

The Ssese Islands came into being about 12,000 years ago when a reduced Lake Victoria refilled at the end of the last Ice Age, forming the lake as we know it today. Little is known about the earliest inhabitants of Ssese, but some oral traditions associated with the creation of Buganda claim that its founder Kintu hailed from the islands, or at least arrived in Buganda via them. The Baganda traditionally revere Ssese as the Islands of the Gods. In pre-colonial times it was customary for the kings of Buganda to visit the islands and pay tribute to the several balubaale whose main shrines are situated there. These include shrines to Musisi (spirit of earthquakes) and Wanema (physical handicaps) on Bukasa Island, as well as the shrine to Mukasa, spirit of the lake, on Bubembe. Some Baganda historical sources romanticise this relationship, claiming that in pre-colonial times Ssese, because of its exalted status, was never attacked by Buganda, nor was it formally incorporated into the mainland kingdom. In reality, while Ssese probably did enjoy a degree of autonomy, it was clearly a vassal of Buganda for at least a century prior to the colonial era. Furthermore, while the Baganda revered the islands' spirits, Stanley recorded that they looked down on their human inhabitants for their 'coal-black colour, timidity, superstition, and generally uncleanly life'.

The most popular legend associated with a deity from the Ssese Islands dates from the mid-16th-century war, when Buganda, led by King Nakibinge, was being overwhelmed in a war against Bunyoro. Nakibinge visited the islands in search of support, and was offered the assistance of the local king's youngest son, Kibuuka, who leaped to the mainland in one mighty bound to join the war against Bunyoro. Tall and powerful though he was, Kibuuka – which means the flier – was also possessed of a somewhat more singular fighting skill. A deity in human form, he was able to fly high above the clouds and shower down spears on the enemy, who had no idea from where the deadly missiles emanated. Led by Kibuuka's aerial attacks, rout followed rout, and the tide of war reversed swiftly in Nakibinge's favour as the Baganda army proceeded deeper into Banyoro territory.

Although Buganda went on to win the war, Kibuuka didn't survive to enjoy the spoils of victory. After yet another successful battle, the Baganda soldiers captured several Banyoro maidens and gave one to Kibuuka as his mistress. Kibuuka told the Munyoro girl his secret, only to find that she had vanished overnight. The next day, Kibuuka sailed up into the sky as normal, and was greeted by a barrage of Banyoro spears and arrows projected up towards the clouds. Kibuuka fell wounded into a tall tree, where he was spotted the next morning by an elder, who attempted to rescue the wounded fighter, but instead accidentally let him drop to the ground,

OTHER ISLANDS The second-largest land mass in Ssese is **Bukasa Island**, which lies on the eastern end of the archipelago and is widely regarded by the few travellers who make it there to be even more attractive than Buggala. Extensively forested, the island supports a profusion of birds and monkeys, and can be explored on foot along a network of fair roads. Individual points of interest include an attractive beach at Misenyi Bay, 20 minutes' walk from Agnes's Guesthouse (see page 212), and a plunge-pool ringed by forest and a waterfall, about one hour's walk from the guesthouse. For monkeys and views, the road to Rwanabatya village has been recommended.

Also infrequently visited by travellers, **Bufumira Island** is readily accessible by fishing boat from Buggala, and there is a small guesthouse in its largest village

where he died on impact. The scrotum, testes, penis and certain other body parts of the great Ssese warrior – now regarded as the greatest lubaale of war – were preserved in a shrine, where his spirit could be called upon before important battles. The shrine, which lies close to the Mpanga Forest, can still be visited today, as can a nearby shrine to Nakibinge, also revered as a deity on account of his successful campaign against Bunyoro. The shrine to Kibuuka was desecrated by the British during the colonial era, and the contents, including his jawbone, are on display in a museum in Cambridge.

The people of Ssese played a more verifiable – albeit less overtly aggressive – role in Baganda expansionism during the second half of the 19th century, when Kabakas Suuna and Mutesa regularly dispatched fleets of 300-plus fighting canoes across Lake Victoria to present-day northwestern Tanzania. These military fleets comprised almost entirely canoes built on Ssese, which – in comparison with the simple dugouts used on the mainland – were highly sophisticated in design, constructed with several pieces of interlocking timber, and boasted an extended prow that could be used to batter other boats. Speke described one such fleet as follows: 'some fifty large [boats]… all painted with red clay, and averaged from ten to thirty paddles, with long prows standing out like the neck of a siphon or swan, decorated on the head with the horns of the Nsunnu [kob] antelope, between which was stuck upright a tuft of feathers exactly like a grenadier's plume'. The islanders were also more skilled as oarsmen and navigators than their landlubber Baganda neighbours, and although they played no role in the fighting, it was they who generally powered and directed the war fleets.

The demands of the Buganda military became a heavy drain on the Ssese economy in the late 19th century. In 1898, the islanders petitioned the British governor, complaining that they were 'regarded in Uganda as being inferior and subordinate to that country' and that the 'severe strain upon the island labour resources [was] so serious as to endanger the canoe service, now so essential with the increasing demands on the Victoria Nyanza lake transport'. In 1900, an agreement between Buganda and Britain placed Ssese and nine other formerly autonomous counties under the full jurisdiction of Buganda. Over the next ten years, Ssese was hit by a sleeping sickness epidemic that claimed thousands of lives annually, forcing the government to relocate 25,000 islanders to the mainland. Resettlement of Ssese was gradual, and it is largely due to the sleeping sickness epidemic that the islands' total population is today estimated at fewer than 20,000, and so much of the land remains uncultivated.

Semawundu, though you are advised to bring all food with you. Far more popular is the small **Banda Island**, site of a popular backpacker resort. Several other small, mostly uninhabited islands can be reached by fishing boat as day trips from Buggala.

Getting there and away The MV *Kalangala*, a **passenger/vehicle ferry**, travels daily between Entebbe and Lutoboka on Buggala Island. It leaves a small port at Nakiwogo at 14.00, reaching Lutoboka at 18.00 and returns next day at 08.00. Nakiwogo lies on the western side of Entebbe Peninsula, 3km from either the town centre or the scruffier market suburb of Kitoro. Parking is available in an adjacent fenced compound for a small fee. The supposed capacity is just 108 seated passengers (though I've heard reports of standing room only at busy times) and eight vehicles (fewer if a truck shows up) so foot passengers should turn up 30 minutes before departure and drivers at least an hour. Second-class passage on wooden benches costs Ush10,000 and first class (padded seats with tables) is Ush14,000. A car or 4x4 vehicle costs Ush50,000. Bottled drinks and snacks are available on board. The ferry overnights at Lutoboka, returning to Nakiwogo from 08.00 to 11.30. The return trip to Entebbe can be busy at the end of holiday weekends, and drivers should park on the jetty the night before and have a quiet word with the captain.

Before heading to Nakiwogo, call your intended hotel on Buggala Island to check that the ferry is operational. As I write, normal service has just resumed after a two-month interruption. If the ferry is suspended for whatever reason, you may have to resort to sitting on a **motorised lake-taxi** to Buggala Island for four to five hours from either Nakiwogo or Kasenyi ports. If you're intent on exploring other islands, you'll certainly need to take one. The busiest port is Kasenyi which is 7km off Entebbe Road from Abaita town (4km north of Entebbe). Boats run to Banda, Bufumira and Bukasa islands as well as Buggala. For Ush1,000, a bilharzia-infested porter will carry you out to the boat.

If headed to Banda Island (see page 209), you can either take a direct boat from Kasenyi (contact the resort managers for details) or take the Nakiwogo ferry to Lutoboka where you can charter a boat (Ush150,000) for the 80-minute trip across the strait. Should you wish, you can then complete a loop through the islands by returning to Kasenyi by lake-taxi.

The risk attached to using these lake-taxis should not be underestimated since overloaded boats have a tendency to capsize during stormy weather, and kill up to 100 people annually. Rather than relying on life jackets being provided (though they increasingly are), you might buy a plastic jerrycan (top screwed on tight!) and secure it to yourself with a piece of rope. Kasenyi is a pretty grotty place and since some time will usually elapse between booking your passage and your boat being considered full enough to leave, head for the Kasenyi Takeaway where the formidable Mama Grace will protect you from sunburn and hassle.

A more roundabout route to the islands is a **free vehicle ferry**, 40km east of Masaka, between Bukakata on the mainland and Luko on Buggala Island. To get there in a private vehicle, follow either of the Lake Nabugabo routes detailed on pages 212–13. In theory, the 50-minute ferry crossing leaves Bukakata at 08.00, 11.00, 14.00 and 17.00 and returns at 09.00, 12.00, 15.00 and 18.00 daily. On Sundays however, the earliest crossing in each direction is dropped. This timetable is somewhat flexible so try to be at the jetty a good hour in advance. The road between Luku and Kalangala is generally in good condition, and can usually be covered in less than one hour, though some stretches might be slippery after heavy rain. Note that the Luku ferry service occasionally stops for a few days while repairs are undertaken, in which case you would have to return on the Entebbe ferry.

A reliable **bus service** linking Kampala and Kalangala using the Bukakata ferry, leaves Kampala's new taxi park at 08.00 daily. The return from Kalangala (which leaves around 06.30 to 07.00 daily) is preferable to an endurance test in a pick-up taxi or *matatu*. Tickets cost Ush20,000.

The above options will get you as far as Buggala Island (and back again). To visit other islands, either from Buggala or Entebbe, prepare to experience the joys of lake taxis, or in other words, overloaded fishing boats with outboard engines (see page 208).

🏠 **Where to stay**   There are several budget resorts on Buggala Island, most of which are located around the sandy Lutoboka Bay Beach. If you visit at weekends, pray that the neighbours from hell, the notoriously inconsiderate Pearl Gardens Beach hotel next to the ferry landing and not listed below, is not hosting a transnight party. For location of listings, see map on page 190.

Buggala Island
Budget
🏠 **Ssese Islands Beach Hotel**   Lutoboka Beach; ☎0414 220065; m 0772 408244; e joyce@sseseislandsbeachhotel. This facility consists of a string of white, beachfront cottages set in the forest edge, 15mins' walk from the ferry landing. *US$40–60 cottages, US16 dorm, camping US$12pp. All rates B&B.*

🏠 **Ssese Island Club**   Lutoboka Beach; m 0772 641376; e islandsclub@hotmail.com. About 300m along the beach from the Beach Hotel, the Ssese Island Club provides s/c wooden chalets or standing tents between the lake & enclosing forest. *US$20/24 sgl/dbl B&B.*

🏠 **Mirembe Resort**   Lutoboka Beach; ☎0392 772703; e www.miremberesort.com; reservations@miremberesort.com. Set in a quiet location at the northern end of the beach, this resort provides s/c rooms with a lake view. *US$34/50 sgl/dbl B&B.*

🏠 **Panorama Lodge**   Near Lutoboka Beach; m 0773 015574; e arnoldinislands@yahoo.com. Situated in a forest clearing 500m inland from the ferry landing, this friendly lodge lacks a beachfront location, but has an attractive garden setting & a forest backdrop. A selection of spacious & recently renovated s/c chalets cost a negotiable *US$16/24; 24/32; 40/48 & 48/60 sgl/dbl B&B. Camping: tent hire US$4pp.*

Shoestring & camping
🏠 **Ssese Scorpion Lodge**   Situated at Luku, about 10mins' walk from the ferry jetty pier along the Kalangala Rd. Meals are served. *Rooms US$4, camping US$3pp.*

🏠 **PTA Andronica Lodge**   m 0772 375529. This long-established lodge in its ancient building is the only accommodation in Kalangala Town. PTA is certainly not lacking in character, with a dominant green-&-white colour scheme & abundance of potted plants but it remains a no-frills option. There's no food provided, but simple meals are served in an adjacent *hoteli*. Bicycles are available for hire. *Rooms US$4pp with shared facilities.*

⛺ **Hornbill Camping Site**   Lutoboka Beach. This German-run campsite has long been a favourite with budget travellers. It's a terrific spot to pitch a tent beneath shady trees with the sandy beach just metres away. Best, however, to give a wide berth to the wooden dormitory & tiny *bandas*. *US$15 dbl bandas, US$4pp dorm (no nets), camping US$3pp; for tent hire, add US$5 per night.*

⛺ **Kingfisher Camp**   near Lutoboka Beach; m 0754 157888. This simple & affordable campground lies close to the ferry landing. Rent a safari tent with bedding (shared facilities) or pitch your own tent.

Banda Island
🏠 **Banda Island Resort**   (4 cottages, 2 dorms) m 0772 222777; e banda.island@gmail.com. In 2011, the future of the marvellously idiosyncratic & laid-back Banda Island Resort hung in the balance with the untimely death of its creator, Dominic Symes, friend & hedonist extraordinaire. Happily though, his family & friends are making sure that

Known to the Baganda as Nalubaale – Home of the Spirit – Lake Victoria is the world's second-largest freshwater body, set in a shallow basin with a diameter of roughly 250km on an elevated plateau separating the eastern and western forks of the Great Rift Valley, and shared between Tanzania, Uganda and Kenya. The environmental degradation of the lake began in the early colonial era, when the indigenous lakeshore vegetation was cleared and swamps were drained to make way for plantations of tea, coffee and sugar. This increased the amount of topsoil washed into the lake, with the result that its water became progressively muddier and murkier. A more serious effect was the wash-off of toxic pesticides and other agricultural chemicals whose nutrients promote algae growth, and as a result a decrease in oxygenation. The foundation of several lakeshore cities and plantations also attracted migrant labourers from around the region, leading to a rapid increase in population and – exacerbated by more sophisticated trapping tools introduced by the colonials – heavy overfishing.

By the early 1950s, the above factors had conspired to create a noticeable drop in yields of popular indigenous fish, in particular the Lake Victoria tilapia (*ngege*), which had been fished close to extinction. The colonial authorities introduced the similar Nile tilapia, which restored the diminishing yield without seriously affecting the ecological balance of the lake. More disastrous, however, was the gradual infiltration of the Nile perch, a voracious predator that feeds almost exclusively on smaller fish, and frequently reaches a length of 2m and a weight exceeding 100kg. How the perch initially ended up in Lake Victoria is a matter of conjecture, but they regularly turned up in fishermen's nets from the late 1950s onwards. The authorities, who favoured large eating fish over the smaller tilapia and cichlids, decided to ensure the survival of the alien predators with an active programme of introductions in the early 1960s.

It would be 20 years before the full impact of this misguided policy hit home. In a UN survey undertaken in 1971, the indigenous haplochromine cichlids still constituted their traditional 80% of the lake's fish biomass, while the introduced perch and tilapia had effectively displaced the indigenous tilapia without otherwise altering the ecology of the lake. A similar survey undertaken ten years later revealed that the perch population had exploded to constitute 80% of the lake's fish biomass, while the haplochromine cichlids – the favoured prey of the perch – now accounted for a mere 1%. Lake Victoria's estimated 150–300 endemic cichlid species, all of which have evolved from a mere five ancestral species since the lake dried out 10,000–15,000 years ago, are regarded to represent the most recent comparable explosion of vertebrate-adaptive radiation in the world. In simple terms, this is when a large number of species evolve from a limited ancestral stock in a short space of time, in this instance owing to the lake having formed rapidly to create all sorts of new niches. Ironically, these fish also are currently undergoing what Boston University's Les Kauffman has described as 'the greatest vertebrate mass extinction in recorded history'.

For all this, the introduction of perch could be considered a superficial success within its own terms. The perch now form the basis of the lake's thriving fishing industry, with up to 500 metric tons of fish meat being exported from the lake annually, at a value of more than US$300 million, by commercial fishing concerns in the three lakeshore countries. The tanned perch hide is used as a substitute for leather to make shoes, belts and purses, and the dried swim bladders, used to filter beer and make fish stock, are exported at a rate of around US$10 per kg. The flip side of this is that as fish exports increase, local fishing communities are forced to compete against large commercial companies with better equipment and more economic clout. Furthermore, since the perch is too large to roast on a fire and too fatty to dry in the sun, it does not really meet local needs.

The introduction of perch is not the only damaging factor to have affected Lake Victoria's ecology. It is estimated that the amount of agricultural chemicals being washed into the lake has more than doubled since the 1950s. Tanzania alone is currently pumping two million litres of untreated sewage and industrial waste into the lake daily, and while legal controls on industrial dumping are tighter in Kenya and Uganda, they are not effectively enforced. The agricultural wash-off and industrial dumping has led to a further increase in the volume of chemical nutrients in the lake, promoting the growth of plankton and algae. At the same time, the cichlids that once fed on these microscopic organisms have been severely depleted in number by the predatorial perch.

The lake's algae levels have increased fivefold in the last four decades, with a corresponding decrease in oxygen levels. The lower level of the lake now consists of dead water – lacking any oxygenation or fish activity below about 30m – and the quality of the water closer to the surface has deteriorated markedly since the 1960s. Long-term residents of the Mwanza area say that the water was once so clear that you could see the lake floor from the surface to depths of 6m or more. Today visibility near the surface is more like 1m.

A clear indicator of this deterioration has been the rapid spread of water hyacinth, which thrives in polluted conditions leading to high phosphate and nitrogen levels, and then tends to further deplete oxygen levels by forming an impenetrable mat over the water's surface. An exotic South American species, unknown on the lake prior to 1989, the water hyacinth has subsequently colonised vast tracts of the lake surface, and clogged up several harbours. To complete this grim vicious circle, Nile perch, arguably the main cause of the problem, are known to be vulnerable to the conditions created by hyacinth matting, high algae levels and decreased oxygenation in the water. On a positive note, hyacinth infestation on the Ugandan waters of Lake Victoria has decreased markedly since 1998. But a new threat to the lake's welfare has emerged with the recent opening of a major Tanzanian gold mine less than 20km from the lakeshore, a location that carries a genuine risk of sodium cyanide, used in the processing of gold, finding its way into Lake Victoria.

As is so often the case with ecological issues, what might at first be dismissed by some as an esoteric concern for 'bunny-huggers' in fact has wider implications for the estimated 20–30 million people resident in the Lake Victoria basin. The infestation of hyacinth and rapid decrease in indigenous snail-eating fish has led to a rapid growth in the number of bilharzia-carrying snails. The deterioration in water quality, exacerbated by the pumping of sewage, has increased the risk of sanitary-related diseases such as cholera spreading around the lake. The change in the fish biomass has encouraged commercial fishing for export outside the region, in the process depressing the local semi-subsistence fishing economy, leading to an increase in unemployment and protein deficiency. And there is an ever-growing risk that Africa's largest lake will eventually be reduced to a vast expanse of dead water, with no fish in it at all – and ecological, economic and humanitarian ramifications that scarcely bear thinking about.

the legend lives on. While there will forever be a Dom-sized gap at the beachfront backgammon table, the camp is now a little cleaner & even enjoys some semblance of organisation. Whatever happens, Banda will remain on a different plane(t) to the beachfront resorts on Buggala Island. Indeed, a significant number of budget travellers forsake Lutoboka in search of a more authentic (a word covering all possible contingencies) experience on Banda. Bring your own tent or sleep in a dorm or a basic stone cottage. Rates include all (inevitably fish-oriented) meals (& other fresh local produce). For travel options, see pages 208 & 211. *US$40pp s/c beach cottage, US$30 dorm bed, lazy camping US$30pp. All accommodation uses shared facilities. FB.*

Bukasa Island

⌂ **Agnes's Guesthouse** A short walk from the ferry pier on Bukasa Island, this basic, rarely visited but friendly & relaxed guesthouse has a veranda overlooking the lake, which is spectacular at sunset. Meals are served, but it is a good idea to bring some food with you just in case.

✕ **Where to eat** Cooking is unspectacular at the Ssese Island resorts, due in part to the difficulty of obtaining fresh produce. Vegetables in local markets are limited and expensive compared with the mainland while overfishing renders our long-standing description of 'limited and inevitably fish-based menus' increasingly redundant. Still, the resorts at Lutoboka and Banda generally manage acceptable Ugandan and international meals if ordered well in advance.

LAKE NABUGABO

Lake Nabugabo, 20km east of Masaka, is quite distinct from Lake Victoria but there's a good reason why it's in this chapter. After all, it was only isolated from its larger neighbour 4,000 years ago when a narrow bar of sand drifted across a large, shallow bay of Lake Victoria to impound Lake Nabugabo as a separate satellite. Silt accumulation has subsequently reduced its original extent fourfold, so that today it covers about 25km², fringed on all but the western shore by the extensive Lwamunda Swamp. Despite its relatively recent formation, Nabugabo has a substantially different mineral composition from the main lake: its calcium content, for instance, is insufficient for molluscs to form shells (hence the absence of the freshwater snails that transmit bilharzia). Five of the lake's nine cichlid fish species are endemics that have evolved since it became separated from Lake Victoria, one of a handful of comparably recent incidents of speciation known from anywhere in the world.

Though more popular with Kampala weekenders than with foreign visitors, Nabugabo is an excellent place to rest up for a day or two, and its bilharzia-free beaches are serviced by three affordable and – on weekdays – tranquil resorts. The forest patches that line the lakeshore, interspersed with grassy clearings and cultivated smallholdings, are rustling with small animals such as tree squirrels, vervet monkeys and monitor lizards, and can easily be explored along several roads and footpaths. Birdlife is prolific, too – look out for broad-billed roller, Ross's turaco, black-and-white casqued hornbill, African fish eagle and a variety of sunbirds and weavers.

GETTING THERE AND AWAY Lake Nabugabo lies about 5km from the good dirt road that runs east from Nyendo (2km east of Masaka) to the Bukakata ferry jetty. The main turn-off out of Nyendo is clearly signposted, but after following it for about 300m you need to take an unmarked left turn at a crossroads beside a Petro filling station. Roughly 14km out of Nyendo, a side road to the right, which is signposted for Sand Beach Camp, runs for 5km to the lake and its three resorts. The road from Masaka is generally in good condition except perhaps for the last

5km, and the drive should take about 30–45 minutes in a private vehicle. Travellers driving themselves from Kampala can avoid Nyendo by taking a 6km short cut to the Bukakata road. About 16km, after Lukaya town (on the western end of a 10km-wide swamp), you'll pass though the second of two hilltop settlements distinguished only by television aerials elevated hopefully on eucalyptus poles. The shortcut turns left off a long, curving right-hand descent, 2.5km further on. If the road bends left into a broad swamp, you've missed it! When you reach the Nyendo–Bukakata road, turn left for 2.5km to find the signposted turning to Sand Beach Resort.

Using **public transport**, minibuses between Masaka and Nyendo run back and forth every few minutes throughout the day. Transport between Nyendo and Bukakata is rather erratic. You'll probably have to take a shared taxi, and can expect to wait around an hour for a lift. Another option is to catch a bus to Kalangala (on the Ssese Islands); these leave from the main bus station in Masaka at around 14.00 on Mondays, Wednesdays and Fridays, passing through Nyendo a few minutes later, then heading on towards Bukakata. Either way, you will need to be dropped at the last junction and – unless you get lucky with a lift – walk the last 5km to the resorts. Another option would be to organise a special hire from Masaka directly to the resort, which should cost around Ush60,000. A boda-boda would be significantly cheaper.

WHERE TO STAY
The three resorts listed below, from south to north, lie within a few hundred metres of each other on the Lake Nabugabo shore. For location of listings see map on page 214.

Church of Uganda Resort (4 twin-room cottages) m 0772 539000/433332; e info@ nabugabo.com; www.nabugabo.com. This long-serving – if now slightly rundown – resort has a friendly atmosphere & is set in a pretty lakeshore glade. The 2 dbl s/c cottages & 2 family cottages (4 beds apiece) are adequate but camping by the lake is the most appealing option. Firewood is available to cook your own meals, or fish & chips can be ordered. Soft drinks, tea & coffee are sold, but no alcohol (you can bring your own). Canoes can be hired. *US$18/32/40 sgl/dbl/twin. US$16pp family groups, US$4 dorm beds, camping US$5pp.*

Nabugabo Terrace View (6 rooms) m 0753 453911/0701 243361; e terraceviewbeach@yahoo.com. Whether the 'terrace' refers to the pleasant veranda of the thatched lodge building or the 3m wave-cut platform on which the resort stands depends on how clever you pertain to be. If the latter, impress your companions by suggesting that you seek out additional 12m & 18m platforms, carved before Nabugabo's isolation from Lake Victoria, a little

way inland. More practically, the 3m cliff means that this is not the best resort for swimming. Accommodation is in a row of spacious good-value s/c rooms served by a thatched lodge with bar, pool table & a restaurant. *US$24/32 sgl/dbl B&B.*

Sand Beach Resort (12 cottages) m 0702 416047. This extensive lake-level resort with its 200m lake frontage is a lovely, peaceful spot – assuming that you don't visit on Sun or public holidays. If you do, relax & enjoy Uganda's version of Brighton on a bank holiday. Busy days here are the local equivalent of the good old British migration to the seaside & this is reflected by a holiday camp-style row of mirror glass-fronted s/c chalets, boat rides on the lake, donkey rides on shore, loud music, cheap beer & a fish 'n' chips menu. If you're feeling posh, there's an exclusive & relatively smart bar/restaurant at the far end of the site. If that's not enough, the Forbe's plover was spotted in the adjacent wetland in 2010 (only the 4th sighting in Uganda). Something for everyone then! *US$20/30 sgl/dbl cottages. US$4pp camping.*

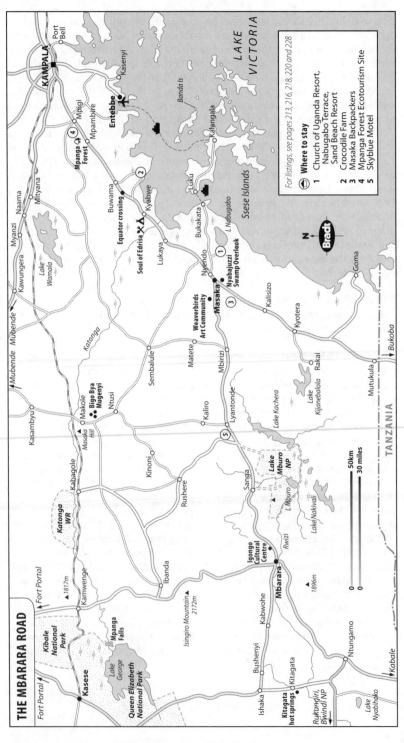

THE MBARARA ROAD

For listings, see pages 213, 216, 218, 220 and 228

ⓘ **Where to stay**
1 Church of Uganda Resort,
   Nabugabo Terrace,
   Sand Beach Resort
2 Crocodile Farm
3 Masaka Backpackers
4 Mpanga Forest Ecotourism Site
5 Skyblue Motel

6

The Mbarara Road

This chapter follows the 283km road running southwest from Kampala via Masaka to Mbarara, the bustling modern town located at the junction of the main roads southwest to Kisoro and north to Kasese and Fort Portal, as well as various sites of interest along the way. Many travellers, and organised tours in particular, rush along this smoothly surfaced road in their haste to reach the more lauded attractions of the Congolese border area, and certainly there is no reason to dally should you be pressed for time.

Equally, if there is no urgency to your travels, there are several places of interest between Kampala and Masaka, including the underrated **Mpanga Forest** and Lake Nabugabo (see pages 212–13). **Masaka** town is also a potential staging point for visiting the Ssese Islands (see pages 204–12). A little further along, in the direction of Mbarara, **Lake Mburo National Park** offers the only game viewing in the area – crocodiles and hippos in the lake, a surprising diversity of antelopes and other terrestrial herbivores, as well as a wealth of water- and acacia-associated birds.

MPANGA FOREST RESERVE

(The National Forest Authority (NFA) fee tariff quotes US$15/25/35 for foreign visitors & US$10/20/30 for foreign residents for 1/2/3 days, a guided walk is an additional US$15/10. In practice, all foreign visitors continue to pay an extremely reasonable Ush5,000 entrance & Ush5,000 for a forest walk) The 45km^2 Mpanga Forest Reserve, which lies near the small town of Mpigi, roughly 36km from Kampala along the Masaka road, makes for a rustic alternative to staying in the capital. The reserve protects an extensive patch of medium-altitude rainforest, characteristic of the vegetation that once extended over much of the northern Lake Victoria hinterland, but has largely been cleared over the past century due to human activity. The forest reserve was gazetted in the 1950s, and is criss-crossed by an extensive network of wide footpaths, initially made by researchers but now open to the public.

Mpanga harbours a less diverse fauna than the larger forests in the far west of Uganda, but there is still plenty to see, and its accessibility and proximity to Kampala more than justify a visit. The most readily observed mammal is the red-tailed monkey, though bushpig, bushbuck and flying squirrels are also present. Blue-breasted kingfisher, black-and-white casqued hornbill, African pied hornbill, African grey parrot and great blue turaco are among the more striking and conspicuous of the 180-plus bird species recorded. Resident birds with a rather localised distribution elsewhere in Uganda include shining blue kingfisher, spotted greenbul, Uganda woodland warbler, green crombec, Frazer's ant-thrush, grey-green bush shrike, pink-footed puffback and Weyn's weaver. Mpanga Forest is also noted for its butterflies, which are abundant wherever you walk.

A selection of forest walks run from the Mpanga Forest Ecotourism Centre. Though the site infrastructure is sadly dilapidated, the maintenance of the picnic/campground and forest trails still lie within the NFA's modest capabilities. You can wander alone if you wish or take a guide. Since this service is included in the modest cost, a decent tip would be appropriate, especially since NFA paydays can be irregular. The undemanding 3km **Base Line Trail** is the main route through the forest, crossing two streams before it emerges on the western margin at Nakyetema Swamp, where sitatunga and shoebill are resident, though seldom seen. The 5km **Hornbill Loop** covers more undulating terrain, and involves fording several streams along minor footpaths, passing a striking tree-root arch along the way. For those with limited time, the 1km **Butterfly Loop** offers a good chance of seeing monkeys and common forest birds, as well as myriad colourful butterflies, and can be completed in less than an hour.

In addition to forest walks, guided visits can also be arranged to two important Kiganda shrines that lie within walking distance of the forest. Less than 1km from the ecotourism centre, **Nakibinge Shrine**, dedicated to the eponymous 16th-

ALONG THE MBARARA ROAD

It's a long way down the Mbarara Road from Kampala especially if you're headed further west to Kabale and locations beyond. Though Mpanga Forest and Lake Mburo National Park are the only locations likely to detain travellers for any length of time along the 283km drive, several low-key sites lend themselves to a short break, some offering good refreshments and clean toilets. First up, about 1km beyond Mpanga Forest, the small village of **Mpambire**, traditional home of the Buganda royal drum-makers, is lined with stalls selling drums (Ush20,000 upwards, depending on size) and other musical instruments. Even if you're not interested in buying drums, it's interesting to watch the craftsmen at work, and there's no hassle attached to wandering around. Another 5km further towards Masaka, a row of stalls sells distinctive and colourful baskets and stools. Between these two locations, the road fords an extensive papyrus swamp – stretching all the way to Lake Victoria – in which the shoebill is resident and reportedly sometimes observed from the road.

At **Buwama**, about 70km from Kampala, you might make a 10km detour to **Camp Croc**, a commercial crocodile farm beside Lake Victoria (m *0712 844944*). You can see the farmed reptiles (up to three years old) as well as couple of man-eating monsters relocated here by UWA. Day visitors pay Ush5,000, and meals available include fish and chips (*Ush13,000*) and croc steak (*Ush15,000*). Basic cottages are also available (*US$24/40/16 sgl/dbl/dbl 'daytime resting'*).

The most popular stop on the Masaka road is found 75km from Kampala at **Nabusanke** (literally 'Small Parts'!), an unremarkable location shunted into the limelight by the fact that the **Equator** happens to cross the road here. A pair of much-photographed white concrete hoops attest to the fact, while a local entrepreneur has set up buckets and jugs between these unprepossessing landmarks. For a small fee he will demonstrate (or at least intimate) that water swirls in opposite directions in the northern and southern hemispheres. There's a long line of roadside craft stalls with the usual mundane offerings, as well as a few small cafés. The most professional setup is the large **Equation Café**. Run by an NGO, AidChild, this displays a variety of high-quality local crafts and artwork, and serves tasty coffee and muffins. There are flushing toilets,

century king, is housed in a small thatched building in the style of the Kasubi Tombs. The **Kibuuka Shrine** near Mpigi, 3–4km back along the Kampala Road, is dedicated to a god of war who hailed from the Ssese Islands (see box, pages 206–7). Beyond the forest, the **flat-topped hill** south of the main road is worth climbing for the attractive grassland environment and views over the forest and surrounding swamp valleys.

GETTING THERE AND AWAY Mpanga Forest can easily be visited as a day or overnight trip out of Kampala or as a stop-off *en route* to Masaka. Coming from Kampala, about 3km past the turn-off to Mpigi, the road passes through a dip flanked by the southernmost tip of the forest. Immediately past the dip, a signposted turn-off to the right leads to the ecotourism centre after about 500m. **Minibus-taxis** to Mpigi leave Kampala from the new taxi park and cost Ush6,000. From Mpigi, you can arrange a **boda-boda** to the forest. Alternatively, any minibus or bus heading between Kampala and Masaka can drop you at the turn-off 500m from the ecotourism centre.

too. It's not the cheapest option but money raised by AidChild goes to a self-explanatory good cause.

Next up is **Kyabwe** town and **The Soul of Edirisa** (m *0752 558558; www.edirisa. org/soul*) at Uganda Martyrs' University's Nkozi campus. Though the campus lies 2km north of Kyabwe, it's a worthwhile detour for an affordable snack or meal in an attractive, shady compound with distinctively designed and painted buildings. If you're moved to stay the night, rooms are available in a university guesthouse. It's an appealing location: the adjacent university campus is both pristine and pretty and set in pleasant scenery. Edirisa is a cultural NGO that also runs a backpacker hostel and volunteer programmes in the Kabale/Lake Bunyonyi area.

If you're travelling by bus, you'll miss these treats and will have to make do with barbecue snacks and bottled drinks thrust up to your window at **Lukaya**, 30km before Masaka. Lukaya Town lies on the western edge of a broad swamp, 14km across, close to the shore of Lake Victoria. Look out for colonies of pelicans and occasionally herons or storks roosting on roadside trees. Two hours' drive from the capital, the main road skirts Masaka Town by means of a bypass, at the eastern end of which the **Nyendo Takeaway** has become an obligatory pull-over for private drivers who want a cuppa and a snack. At the far end of the ring road is the small **Nyabajuzzi Ecotourism Project**. Developed with support from the UK's RSPB, a raised wooden viewing deck overlooks the Nyabajuzzi papyrus wetland at 'Sitatunga Corner', where the Masaka bypass meets the feeder road into town. Beyond an unlovely foreground – the Masaka Water Treatment Plant – the wetland is home to sitatunga, shoebill, rufous-bellied heron, papyrus yellow warbler and other rarities. A mounted telescope is provided and entrance costs Ush2,000 per person. Beyond Nyabajuzzi, other than **Lake Mburo National Park**, there is no reason whatsoever to delay along the 150km drive to Mbarara. Content yourself by watching the landscape change (surprisingly quickly) from the green farmland of the Lake Victoria hinterland to the drier Ankole grasslands. After two hours of this excitement, you'll be glad to reach the new **Igongo Cultural Centre**, 5km before Mbarara. where you can enjoy spotless toilets, a fine buffet lunch and worthy insights into traditional Ankole society.

WHERE TO STAY

⌂ **Mpanga Forest Ecotourism Site** (NFA Kampala) (3 rooms) ☏0414 230035. This pretty, forest-edge site centres on a grassy picnic area. Overnight options are limited to camping rooms in a newish Forest Department house. Other options listed in previous editions are now too dilapidated to use. With a few hours' notice, simple meals can be arranged. *US$12 sgl/dbl per bed in twin rooms, US$2 per tent camping on the picnic site.*

MASAKA

Masaka, the seventh-largest town in Uganda, is attractively situated among the undulating green hills of the Lake Victoria hinterland. Founded as an Indian trading post c1900, Masaka suffered more than any other town during the 1979 Tanzanian invasion (see box, page 221). Despite some rebuilding in recent years, the town centre still has a rather down-at-heel appearance and offers little to excite travellers. Nevertheless, Masaka is of interest as the springboard for the main overland route to Bukoba in Tanzania and for the rather closer Lake Nabugabo and Ssese Islands (see pages 204–12). The town centre is bypassed by the main Kampala–Mbarara road, and also by most traffic heading to locations further west. Perhaps as a lack of exposure to purposeful through traffic, you'll find Masaka's drivers bumbling around the streets at grandmotherly speeds, stopping and starting without warning and creating traffic chaos out of all proportion to their numbers.

GETTING THERE AND AWAY Masaka lies roughly 140km from Kampala along a good surfaced road. The **drive** should take about two hours depending on how easily the traffic around Kampala is cleared. Regular **minibus-taxis** to Masaka leave Kampala from the new taxi park, costing Ush9,000. There is also plenty of road transport from Masaka west to Mbarara, and tickets also cost about Ush9,000. The small town of Nyendo, which lies 2km from Masaka back along the Kampala Road, is an important road junction and the place to pick up light vehicles heading towards Ntusi, Lake Nabugabo and the Ssese Islands.

⌂ **WHERE TO STAY** In addition to those listed below, other reasonable options are the **Holiday Inn**, 50m up the road from the Vienna, and **Buddu Guesthouse**, downhill and around the corner. In the unlikely event that everywhere is full, or you're desperately skint, try the grim **Victoria End Rest House** on Elgin Road. For location of listings see map opposite.

Moderate

⌂ **Golf Lane Hotel** (95 rooms) Kinanina Rd; 📱 0700 868956; www.golflanehotel.com. This new, storied, hilltop development above the golf course is by far Masaka's largest hotel. Though smart & modern, it doesn't really do justice to the site, a single, ground floor terrace being expected

MASAKA
For listings, see pages 218–21

⌂ **Where to stay**

1	Buddu Guesthouse	C5
2	Golf Lane	B1
3	Holiday Inn	C5
4	Hotel Zebra	A3
5	La Nova	C7
6	Shabart Motel	C6
7	Terrace Club	B6
8	Tropic Inn	C3
9	Victoria End Rest House	B5
10	Vienna Guesthouse	C5

Off map

	Masaka Backpackers' Cottage & Campsite	A5
	The Weaverbird International Artist Village	A3

✖ **Where to eat and drink**

11	Ambience	D1
12	Dori's	D1
13	Elgon Inn Bar & Restaurant	B5
14	Plot 99	B2
15	Ten Tables	B6

Off map

	Café Frikadellen	B1

A   B   ↑ Bypass,   C   D
   ②   Café Frikadellen

NOTE
For key to accommodation
and eating and drinking,
see opposite

1

⑪ ⑫
1

Laston   Pentecostal ✝

Gapco

Nyendo,
Kampala,
Lake Nabugabu

2

CIRCULAR

KATWE

⑭

2

Fort

HILLTOP

KALUNGU

KAMPALA

Gapco   ⑧ $
Bank of
Uganda

GRANT

NALUBALE

HILL

3

Shell

3

Total

④

Weaverbird International
Artist Village, Mbarara

KOKI

Shell

Total

BROADWAY

AGIP

$

⊠

Stanbic $ e

MAWOGOLA

4

4

N

Bradt

0   200m
0   200yds

Minibuses/shared taxis

⑬
⑨

Government ●
buildings   ●

Supermarket ●

DFCU Forex
Bureau $

KABULA

BUDDU

5

BUKOBA

Masaka Backpackers'
Cottage & Campsite,
Tanzanian border

Police ●

MWANI

HOBART

③

⑩

Coca-Cola depot ●

5

Total

Shell

ELGIN

①

⑥

SSESE

Sports
ground

⑦
⑮

Ronell

VICTORIA

EDWARD

Market

Martyr's Shrine ♟

✝

GEORGE

Mosque ☾

JETHABHAI

6

6

BWALA

SPEKE

7

VANDRAVAN

Masaka
Secondary
School ●

⑤

7

MASAKA

A   B   C   D

219

to deal with a potential 360° panorama across the town & environs. The rooms do have balconies though, so if you moved to a different one each night ... *US$37/49 sgl/sbl B&B.*

🏠 **Tropic Inn Hotel** (70 rooms) Kampala Rd; 📞04814 32687; m 0774 517885. This large hotel stands in expansive grounds beside Kampala Road behind a lush frontage of barely controlled tropical vegetation. Inside, the plush, carpeted rooms are spacious with large beds, walk-in nets & sumptuous soft furnishings. The grounds contain a large swimming pool & a smart terrace restaurant. Very fairly priced. *US$32/50 sgl/dbl B&B.*

Budget

🏠 **Hotel Zebra** (30 rooms) 📞04814 20936; e hotelzebra2005@yahoo.com. This hotel occupies a pretty setting on the quieter side of the hill above Masaka town centre. The ground-floor terrace & 1st-floor balcony overlook suburbs extending towards the Nyabajuzzi Valley & green hills beyond. The conifer-lined ridge top just above the hotel is a fine place for a stroll past some restored colonial buildings. This appreciation does not quite extend to the rather ordinary but nonetheless fairly priced s/c rooms. *US$20/40 smallish sgl/dbl B&B.*

🏠 **Hotel La Nova** (10 rooms) 📞04814 21520. In the town's southern suburb, the Hotel La Nova is an unpretentious & rather old-fashioned favourite of expatriates & business travellers to Masaka. *US$10/16 s/c sgl+/dbl B&B.*

🏠 **Terrace Club** (8 rooms) Victoria St; m 0702 777751. Small, neatly furnished s/c rooms

conveniently located upstairs from the excellent Ten Tables restaurant (see opposite). *US$12/20 sgl/ dbl s/c B&B.*

Shoestring & camping

🏠 **Shabart Motel** (30 rooms) Hobart St. This brand-new hotel & restaurant looks to be the town centre's best bet in this category. *US$12/16 sgl/dbl s/c.*

🏠 **Masaka Backpackers' Cottage & Campsite** (10 rooms) 4km out of town, off the road towards Mutukula on the Tanzanian border; m 0752 619389; e masakabackpackers@yahoo.com; www. traveluganda/masakabackpackers. This excellent retreat is a great place to relax for a few days, especially if you've just slogged up overland from Tanzania. Tasty & inexpensive food is cooked to order, & there is a well-stocked drinks fridge. If you don't fancy walking out from Masaka, take a special hire taxi (*Ush10,000*) or boda-boda (*Ush1,500*). *US$11/17 s/c sgl/dbl, US$7 dorm bed, US$4pp camping.*

🏠 **Vienna Guesthouse** Hobart St; m 0782 457450. Like the Shabart Motel, directly opposite, this looks good value, though ask for a room with an external window rather than one facing into the corridor. Facilities include a restaurant/bar plus very hot sauna & steam. *US$7/9/13 sgl/dbl/twn.*

⛏ **The Weaverbird International Artist Village** Accessed from a turning 4km down the main road towards Mbarara; e info@weaverbirdartuganda. com; www.weaverbirdartuganda.com. This artist's co-operative has a campsite is located in an emergent sculpture park.

✕ **WHERE TO EAT AND DRINK** Life for local expats and volunteers is enhanced by the emergence of some excellent restaurants in Masaka. Otherwise, you'll find decent (albeit rather predictable) international cuisine at the **Tropic Inn**, **Hotel Zebra**, and **Hotel La Nova** (see page 218 and above). **Tuwereza Bakery** [219 C5] on Elgin Road sells good bread and pastries. For location of listings see map, page 219.

✕ **Café Frikadellen** Local expats rave about this Danish-run establishment. It's discreetly located down a bumpy side road at the northern end of town, somewhere below the new Golf Lane Hotel – so discreetly in fact that I failed to find it. The 'Every-other-Friday' BBQ seems to be a social & culinary highlight. Internet is available. Well worth searching for! The café is apparently in the same compound as Uganda Childcare which all the boda drivers know.

✕ **Elgon Inn Bar & Restaurant** Elgin Rd. Dropping down quite a few notches here, the Elgon Inn serves a variety of local dishes at affordable prices.

✕ **Plot 99** Hill Rd; m 0700 151649. This coffee house run by expats occupies a bungalow beyond the old fort & overlooking the area formerly known as the golf course. There's a lunch & dinner menu (*Ush5,000–30,000*), plus a gym, aerobics & massage.

✕ Ten Tables Victoria St; m 0782 700591. This great restaurant serves a themed 3-course set menu every evening (Mexican, continental, Chinese …). An offshoot of the AidChild gallery/café at the Equator (see box, page 216), the walls display work by Ugandan artists. Upstairs, a homely lounge, balcony & rooftop firepit are good spots for a drink. Football matches are shown on DSTV. *Meals Ush20,000.*

NIGHTLIFE The monumental, glass-fronted **Ambience** [219 D1] and the outwardly more modest **Dori's** [219 D1] discotheques, Masaka's two nightclubs, both lie on Kampala Road about 500m downhill from the town centre.

SHOPPING The **supermarket** [219 B5] opposite the Elgon Inn on Elgin Road sells a good range of imported foodstuffs, and there are a few other good supermarkets along the same road.

For **arts and crafts**, visit the Weaverbird International Artist Village in Ndegeya village, 4km from Masaka town centre and 2km off the Mbarara highway (see opposite).

OTHER PRACTICALITIES
Foreign exchange Cash can be exchanged at **Stanbic bank** [219 B4] next to the **post office** [219 B4] at the bank's national rates.

THE SACKING OF MASAKA

In October 1978, Amin ordered his Masaka-based Suicide Battalion and Mbarara-based Simba Battalion to invade Tanzania, under the pretext of pursuing 200 mutineers from his army. In the event, the Ugandan battalions occupied Tanzania's northwestern province of Kagera, and ravaged the countryside in an orgy of rape, theft and destruction that forced about 40,000 peasants to flee from the area.

In retaliation, Tanzania's Julius Nyerere ordered 45,000 Tanzanian troops, supported by the UNLA (a 1,000-strong army of exiled Ugandans), to drive Amin's army out of Kagera, then to create a military buffer zone by capturing the largest Ugandan towns close to the Tanzanian border, Masaka and Mbarara. Masaka was taken with little resistance on 24 February 1979. The outnumbered Suicide Battalion fled to a nearby hilltop, from where they watched helplessly as first the governor's mansion and several other government buildings collapsed under missile fire, and then shops and houses were ransacked as the Tanzanian soldiers poured into the town centre.

Two days later, Nyerere achieved his stated aims for the campaign with the capture of Mbarara. But in early March it was announced that Amin would be enlisting the help of 2,500 Libyan and PLO soldiers to recapture Masaka and Mbarara, and possibly launch a counterattack on Tanzanian territory. Nyerere decided to retain the offensive, ordering his troops to prepare to march northeast towards the capital. Meanwhile, Radio Tanzania broadcast details of the fall of Masaka and Mbarara across Uganda, demoralising the troops, and prompting several garrisons to mutiny or desert as it became clear their leader's rule was highly tenuous. On 10 April 1979, the combined Tanzanian and UNLA army marched into Kampala, meeting little resistance along the way. Amin, together with at least 8,000 of his soldiers, was forced into exile.

The Mbarara Road   MASAKA

6

Internet The new building [219 B4] just above Kampala Road near the Elgin Road junction is one of several central locations where Masakans surf for news of the world beyond the bypass. Internet is also available at **Café Frikadellen** and the **Ten Tables** restaurant (see page 220).

LAKE MBURO NATIONAL PARK

(*The visitation fees for a Class A protected area apply (see box, pages 32–3). An entrance permit is valid for 24hrs from time of entrance. The standard vehicle entry fees are levied*) One of Uganda's smaller national parks, Lake Mburo extends over 260km² of undulating territory with an altitude range from 1,220m to 1,828m above sea level. The annual rainfall figure of around 800mm is relatively low, but roughly 20% of the park's surface area nevertheless consists of wetland habitats. The most important of these is Lake Mburo itself, the largest of five lakes that lie within the park boundaries, and part of a cluster of 14 lakes that are fed by the Rwizi River and connected by several permanent and seasonal swamps. The remainder of the park mainly consists of open savanna and acacia woodland, with some of the more common trees being *Acacia hockii, Acacia gerrardii, Acacia sieberiana* and *Acacia polycantha*. In the western part of the park, the savanna is interspersed with rocky ridges and forested gorges, while patches of papyrus swamp and narrow bands of lush riparian woodland line the verges of the various lakes.

Lake Mburo is an underrated gem of a park, dominated by the eponymous lake, which – with its forest-fringed shores hemmed in by rolling green hills – is scenically reminiscent of the more celebrated Lake Naivasha in the Kenyan Rift Valley. That the park has historically been bypassed by the majority of safaris and independent travellers (despite its relative accessibility) is presumably down to the low 'big five' count, in particular the lack of elephant and infrequent presence of lion. Even in the absence of wildlife heavyweights, however, Lake Mburo offers some excellent game viewing, and you're likely to see as many different large mammal species over the course of a day as you would in any Ugandan national park.

The profile of the park has been raised by some recent developments. Lake Mburo has long been promoted, with some desperation, as an ideal overnight stop on the long drive between Kampala and the national parks that line the country's western border. The number of travellers actually accepting the invitation has risen sharply since the exemplary Mihingo Lodge opened in 2007. Lake Mburo is now also the only Ugandan protected area in which visitors can view game on foot, quad bike and horseback.

WILDLIFE Lake Mburo harbours several species not easily observed elsewhere in Uganda. It is the only reserve in the country to support a population of impala, the handsome antelope for which Kampala is named, and one of only three protected areas countrywide where Burchell's zebra occurs, the other two being the far less accessible Kidepo and Pian Upe. Other antelope species likely to be seen by casual visitors are topi, bushbuck, common duiker, oribi, Defassa waterbuck and Bohor reedbuck, while the lake and lush fringing vegetation support healthy populations of buffalo, warthog, bushpig and hippopotamus. Roan antelope, once common, are now locally extinct, but large herds of the majestic eland still move seasonally through parts of the park. The sitatunga antelope is confined to swamp interiors, and the klipspringer is occasionally observed in rocky areas. Only two diurnal primates occur at Lake Mburo: the vervet monkey and olive baboon. The

Masaka ← ↑ Sanga

Lyantonde

Kizimbi Swamp

Nshara gate

Mbarara

N

Bradt

0 ——— 5km
0 ——— 3 miles

Lake
Kachera

Sanga
gate

Zebra Track

Ruroko Track

Rwizi Track

Rwizi

Impala Track

Warukiri
Track

Ruroko Kopje
(picnic site)

Lake Mburo

Restaurant
& boat launch

Interpretation
Centre

Kazuma Track

Lakeside
Track

Kazuma
Lookout

Kigambira Loop

Lake
Kigambira

Mazinga Swamp

Lake Nakivali

For listings, see pages 227–9

Where to stay

1	Arcadia Cottages	5	Lake Mburo Safari Lodge
2	Eagle's Nest	6	Mihingo Lodge
3	Kimbla-Mantana Tented Camp	7	Rwaboko Rock
4	Lake Mburo Campsite	8	Rwonyo Rest Camp

eerie, rising, nocturnal call of the spotted hyena is often heard from the camps, and individuals are less frequently observed crossing the road shortly after dawn. Leopard, side-striped jackal and various smaller predators are also present, most visibly white-tailed mongoose (at dusk and dawn) and three otter species resident in the lakes. Lions, for which Lake Mburo was famed in the 1960s, were hunted to local extinction by the late 1970s, though the odd pride finds its way into the park, presumably from Akagera National Park in Rwanda. December 2008 saw the first confirmed lion sightings – of three adults and two cubs – for a decade.

Some 315 species of bird have been recorded in Lake Mburo National Park. It is probably the best place in Uganda to see acacia-associated birds, and Rwonyo Camp (see page 228) is as good a place as any to look for the likes of mosque swallow, black-bellied bustard, bare-faced go-away bird and Ruppell's long-tailed starling. A handful of birds recorded at Lake Mburo are essentially southern species at the very northern limit of their range, for instance the southern ground hornbill, black-collared and black-throated barbets, and green-capped eremomela. Of special interest to birders are the swamps, in which six papyrus endemics are resident, including the brilliantly coloured papyrus gonolek, the striking blue-headed coucal, and the highly localised white-winged and papyrus yellow warblers, the last recorded nowhere else in Uganda.

Many centuries ago, according to oral tradition, the valley in which Lake Mburo stands today was dry agricultural land, worked by a pair of brothers named Kigarama and Mburo. One night, Kigarama dreamed that he and his brother would be in danger unless they moved to higher land. The next morning, as Kigarama prepared to relocate to the surrounding hills, he shared the warning with Mburo, who shrugged it off and decided to stay put. Within days, the valley was submerged, and Kigarama watched on helplessly from the hills as his younger brother drowned. The lake was named for the unfortunate Mburo and the surrounding hills after Kigarama.

In pre-colonial times, the area around Lake Mburo, known as Nshara and referred to by Bahima pastoralists as Karo Karungyi (literally 'good grazing land'), was probably rather thinly populated. Pastoralist settlement would have been inhibited by the periodic prevalence of *Glossina morsitans*, a species of tsetse fly that transmits a strain of trypanosome harmless to wild animals and humans, but fatal to domestic cattle. Furthermore, the Omugabe of Ankole favoured Nshara as a royal hunting ground, and forbade the Bahima from grazing and watering their cattle there except during times of drought.

In the early 1890s, Mburo – like the rest of Ankole – was hit severely by the rinderpest epidemic that swept through East Africa, and the resultant depletion of livestock precipitated a famine that claimed thousands of human lives. The decreased grazing pressure also led to widespread bush regeneration, paving the way for a devastating tsetse fly outbreak c1910. Those pastoralists who had resettled the Mburo area were forced to relocate their herds to the more arid savanna of Nyabushozi, north of the present-day Kampala–Mbarara road.

In 1935, the colonial government set aside the vast tract of largely depopulated land centred on Mburo as a Controlled Hunting Area in which both regulated hunting and traditional human activities were permitted. Ten years later, another tsetse outbreak – this time not only *G. morsitans*, but also *G. palpalis*, which spreads sleeping sickness to humans – forced the pastoralists out of the Mburo area. As a result, the colonial authorities instituted a radical programme to eradicate the tsetse from Ankole in the 1950s – its premise being that if every last wild animal in the area were killed, then the bloodsucking tsetse would surely be starved to extinction.

Brian Herne includes a scathing account of this first phase of the anti-tsetse campaign in his book *African Safaris* (see page 539):

> They employed vast teams of African hunters with shot-bolt rifles ... with orders to shoot every single animal, irrespective of age or sex. Everything was to be exterminated. We watched in horror and anger. They did slaughter everything they could ... anything and everything that crossed their gunsights. The wildlife was decimated almost out of existence ... after the grass fires in July, the plains were richly scattered with bleached skeletons and gaunt sun-dried carcasses.

According to Herne, the 'wondrous final solution had proved a disastrous and expensive bloodbath ... It is of course almost possible to kill off entire populations but some stock always survives, especially of more elusive animals like duiker and bushbuck. Of course, some did survive – enough to ensure the survival of the tsetse fly!'

The authorities reasoned that if it was not possible to starve the tsetse to death, then the only solution was to eradicate the shady bushes and trees around which it lived. Hundreds of square kilometres of bush around Mburo were stripped, cut and/or burned, until barely any trees were left. After the first rains fell, however, a dense cover of secondary undergrowth quickly established itself, offering adequate cover for tsetse flies to survive, Herne wrote, 'voracious and hungry and as indiscriminate in their hunger as ever'. Over the next season, the authorities implemented a new campaign, aimed directly at the tsetse, employing teams of locals to spray every inch of Ankole with insecticide. This final phase did result in the virtual elimination of the tsetse, but at considerable ecological cost, since it also took its toll on almost every other insect species, as well as insectivorous birds and small mammals.

In the early 1960s, with tsetse-borne diseases all but eradicated, Bahima pastoralists flocked back to the controlled hunting area. It soon became clear that, were any wildlife to survive, the resettlement of Mburo would need to be regulated. In 1964, the first Obote government de-gazetted a large portion of the controlled hunting area to make way for subsistence farmers and herders, while the remainder was upgraded to become the Lake Mburo Game Reserve. Pastoralists were granted transit and dry-season watering rights to the newly gazetted reserve, but were forbidden from residing within it.

This stasis was undermined in the 1970s, after some 650km^2 of gazetted land were excised to become a state cattle ranch. Conservation activities in what remained of the game reserve practically ceased, allowing for considerable human encroachment along the borders. The volume of wildlife, largely recovered from the anti-tsetse slaughter 20 years earlier, was again severely depleted, this time as a result of subsistence poaching. The park's lions – unpopular with local herders not only because they occasionally hunted cattle, but also for their long-standing reputation as man-eaters (one particularly voracious male reputedly accounted for more than 80 human lives in the 1960s) – were hunted to local extinction.

In 1983, the second Obote government gazetted Lake Mburo as a national park, following the boundaries of the original game reserve and forcibly evicting some 4,500 families without compensation. As a result, local communities tended to view the park somewhat negatively – a waste of an important traditional resource from which they had been wrongly excluded. As the civil war reached its peak in 1986, Lake Mburo was almost wholly resettled, its facilities and infrastructure were destroyed, and subsistence poaching once again reached critical levels. In 1987, the Museveni government agreed to reduce the area of the national park by 60%, and it allowed a limited number of people to live within the park and fish on the lake, but still tensions between the park and surrounding communities remained high.

The turning point in Mburo's fractious history came in 1991, with the creation of a pioneering Mburo Community Conservation Unit, established with the assistance of the Africa Wildlife Foundation. A community representative was appointed for each of the neighbouring parishes, to be consulted with regard to decisions affecting the future of the park, and to air any local grievances directly with the park management. Between 1991 and 1997, the remaining inhabitants of the park were relocated outside its borders and awarded a negotiated sum as compensation. Since 1995, 20% of the revenue raised by park entrance fees has been used to fund the construction of local clinics and schools, and for other community projects.

FURTHER INFORMATION A 72-page *Lake Mburo National Park Guidebook*, published by the African Wildlife Foundation in 1994, contains complete bird and mammal checklists. Though outdated with regard to roads and infrastructure, it contains a wealth of detailed ecological information. Sheet 5 in the 'Uganda Maps' series covers Lake Mburo National Park and includes lists of wildlife and birding highlights.

GETTING THERE AND AWAY Two different roads connect Lake Mburo National Park to the main surfaced road between Masaka and Mbarara. Coming from the west, the better approach road branches south at Sanga, 37km east of Mbarara. Coming from Kampala, it's easier to use the road branching south from the 50km marker for Mbarara, about 20km past Lyantonde. The **drive** from Kampala should take about four to five hours, not allowing for breaks. The approach roads are both quite rough, so a 4x4 vehicle is recommended, though not essential during the dry season, and either way you're looking at about an hour's drive between the main road and the rest camp.

There is no public transport along either of the approach roads, but it is possible to charter a **special hire** from Sanga (expect to pay in excess of Ush50,000) or pick up a boda-boda (around Ush15,000). Another option is to ask the UWA headquarters in Kampala to radio through a day in advance to find out whether any park vehicle will be going to Mbarara, in which case you could wait for it at Sanga.

ANKOLE CATTLE

From mountain gorillas to lions, from elephants to shoebills, Uganda is blessed with more than its fair share of impressive wild beasties. But it is also the major stronghold for what is unquestionably the most imposing of Africa's domestic creatures: the remarkable long-horned breed of cattle associated with various pastoralist peoples of the Ugandan–Tanzanian–Rwandan border area, but most specifically with the Bahima of Ankole.

Ankole cattle come in several colours, ranging from uniform rusty-yellow to blotched black-and-white, but they always have a long head, short neck, deep dewlap and narrow chest, and the male often sports a large thoracic hump. What most distinguish the Ankole cattle from any familiar breed, however, are their preposterous, monstrous horns, which grow out from either side of the head like inverted elephant tusks and, in exceptional instances, reach dimensions unseen on any Ugandan tusker since the commercial ivory poaching outbreak of the 1980s.

The ancestry of the Ankole cattle has been traced back to Eurasia as early as 15,000BC, but the precursors of the modern long-horned variety were introduced to northern Uganda only in late medieval times. Hardy, and capable of subsisting on limited water and poor grazing, these introduced cattle were ideally suited to harsh African conditions, except that they had no immunity to tsetse-borne diseases, which forced the pastoralists who tended them to keep drifting southward. The outsized horns of the modern Ankole cattle are probably a result of selective breeding subsequent to their ancestors' arrival in southern Uganda about 500 years ago. The Bahima value cows less for their individual productivity than as status symbols: the wealth of a man would be measured by the size and quality of his herd, and the worth of an individual cow by her horn size and, to a lesser extent, her coloration.

Traditionally, Bahima culture was as deeply bound up with its almost mystical relationship to cattle as the lifestyle of the Maasai is today. Like Eskimos and their

WHERE TO STAY For location of listings see map, page 223.

Upmarket

⌂ **Mihingo Lodge** (12 tents) m 0752 410509; e safari@mihingolodge.com; www.mihingolodge.com. The superbly positioned Mihingo Lodge has become a safari highlight for many expatriates & foreign visitors, it's certainly one of the best (some say *the* best) lodges associated with any Ugandan park. In fact it's not actually in the park, but just outside Lake Mburo's eastern boundary in a private, 97ha wilderness on an extensive rock outcrop. Accommodation is provided in luxurious & privately positioned tents, all of which enjoy outward views from a veranda & spacious bathroom. 6 units are dramatically placed on the summit of the kopje while others are located along less giddy contours around the flanks of the outcrop. Attention to detail is evident throughout; from the loo handles to the organic thatched lounge/dining shelter supported by gnarled olive-wood branches. The setting for excellent 3-course dinners, this structure is perfectly positioned (as is an adjacent rock-sided swimming pool), to enjoy the breeze, sunsets & the wildlife visiting a salt lick in the valley below. Visitors with walking difficulties or small children should note that some tents are accessed by varying numbers of rough stone steps. Mihingo is the base for horseback safaris in & around the national park (see page 229). Guided walks, & rock climbing/abseiling on the kopje, are also possible. To reach the lodge, enter Lake Mburo National Park at the Nshara Gate & follow signposts off the Ruroko Track. See also advert in third colour section. *US$250pp FB non-residents, discounts available for East African residents.*

⌂ **Kimbla-Mantana Tented Camp** (8 tents) ☏0414 321552; m 0772 401391; e mantana@africaonline.co.ug; www.kimbla-mantanauganda.com. This classic luxury tented camp offers a genuine bush experience in secluded & fully

physical landscape, the abiding mental preoccupation of the Bahima is reflected in the 30 variations in hide coloration that are recognised linguistically – the most valued being the uniform dark-brown *bihogo* – along with at least a dozen peculiarities of horn shape and size. The Bahima day is traditionally divided up into 20 periods, of which all but one of the daylight phases is named after an associated cattle-related activity. And, like the Maasai, the Bahima traditionally regarded any activity other than cattle herding as beneath contempt. They also declined to hunt game for meat, with the exception of buffalo and eland, which were sufficiently bovine in appearance for acceptable eating.

In times past, the Bahima diet did not, as might be expected, centre on meat, but rather on blood tapped from the vein of a living cow, combined with the relatively meagre yield of milk from the small udders that characterise the Ankole breed. The Bahima viewed their cattle as something close to family, so that slaughtering a fertile cow for meat was regarded as akin to cannibalism. It was customary, however, for infertile cows and surplus bullocks to be killed for meat on special occasions, while the flesh of any cow that died of natural causes would be eaten or bartered with the agriculturist Bairu for millet beer and fresh produce. No part of the cow would go to waste: the hide would be used to make clothing, mats and drums, the dung used to plaster huts and dried to light fires, while the horns could be customised as musical instruments.

Ankole is not as defiantly traditionalist as, say, Ethiopia's Omo Valley or Maasailand, and most rural Bahima today supplement their herds of livestock by practising mixed agriculture of subsistence and cash crops. But the Ankole cattle and their extraordinary horns, common in several parts of Uganda but most prevalent in the vicinity of Mbarara and Lake Mburo, pay living tribute to the bovine preoccupations of Ankole past.

furnished s/c tents, all with solar lighting, eco-friendly toilet & private veranda. The camp runs along a lightly wooded ridge, which is rattling with birds, lizards & other small animals. If the views towards Lake Mburo are impressive from the new thatched dining/lounge shelter, they are even more memorable from the sundowner fireplace on the summit just above the camp. The tented camp lies off Impala Track along a 500m private road, clearly signposted about 7km from Sanga Entrance Gate & 4km from Rwonyo Rest Camp. *US$310/440 sgl/dbl FB, US$165/250 for East African residents.*

Moderate

🏠 **Rwaboko Rock** (8 cottages) 2km outside the Nshara Gate; m 0755 211771; e info@rwakoborock.com; www.rwakoborock.com. Like Mihingo, this attractive new setup is spread across a rock outcrop located outside, but looking into, the national park. The simple but comfortable & meticulously constructed s/c cottages are individually positioned in secluded sites across the kopje. Though each has a view, don't miss the 360° regional panorama from the top of the kopje. A python is a permanent resident below the main lodge, while zebra & impala are frequent visitors. See also advert in fourth colour section. *US$120/200 sgl/dbl FB, discounts for East African residents.*

🏠 **Arcadia Cottages** (8 cottages) About 2km south of Rwonyo, beyond the lakeshore campsite; m 0774 288773; e arcadiacottagesl.mburo@yahoo.com; www.arcadiacottages.net/mburo. The new setup is an improvement on the main Rwonyo site, there being a lake view of sorts beyond the car park & the Lakeside Track, made possible by extensive bush clearance. Comfortable accommodation is provided in s/c cottages, while meals (*Ush15,000*) & drinks are served in a small, open-sided restaurant/bar area. The concession was allocated by the UWA to fill the gap between upmarket & budget accommodation in Lake Mburo, & as a mid-range facility, Arcadia Cottages is difficult to fault (though if pressed, the cottage exteriors – cement plastered to resemble log cabins – are a trifle bizarre). However, the rates are anything but moderate. *US$160/250 sgl/dbl & US$450 family cottages FB.*

🏠 **Mburo Safari Lodge** (8 rooms) ☎0414 577997; m 0712 433744; e info@mburosafarilodge.com; www.mburosafarilodge.com. This new lodge is located just outside the eastern boundary of the park, 2km from Mihingo Lodge. Accommodation is provided in s/c wooden chalets with TV & king-sized beds. See also advert on page x. *US$120/180/240/270 sgl/dbl/twin/trpl FB.*

Budget

🏠 **Eagle's Nest** (8 rooms) Just outside the park's Western Gate at Sanga; www.gorillatours.com. This facility is so new I haven't seen it yet but it's run by Nature Lodges – which specialises in decent & very reasonably priced s/c accommodation close to national parks – so it should be excellent value. *US$67/104 sgl/dbl FB.*

🏠 **Skyblue Motel** (40 rooms) 25km east of Lake Mburo on the edge of Lyantonde town; m 0772 487559/0779 922991. This modern hotel is only 30–40mins' drive from the park's Nshara Gate so with an early start you'll miss little of the day's wildlife action. The motel is located beside the main road to Masaka so some traffic noise is likely, but the tiled s/c rooms look comfortable & there's a pleasant restaurant attached. *US$30/36/54 sgl/dbl/trpl B&B.*

🏠 **Rwonyo Rest Camp** (6 units) Book through UWA HQ; ☎0414 355000. Perched on a hillside no more than 1km from the lakeshore. The stalwart UWA rest camp offers a couple of rather basic *bandas* & some standing dbl tents, all with communal private showers, the latter being more discreetly placed in the bush uphill of the main camp. It's a pleasant enough site though a rather unimaginative choice given its proximity to the lovely Lake Mburo shoreline & the panoramic Rwonyo hilltop. You can cook for yourself, though most people eat at the open-air restaurant at the lakeshore campsite 1km away (travellers without transport will need to be walked there by a ranger). Rwonyo fills up at w/ends so book ahead through the UWA HQ in Kampala. At night, waterbuck, warthog & even the occasional bushpig wander through, & if you sit quietly they will often come very close. The tents (communal showers) provide a taste of a tented camp at a bargain price. *US$14/16 sgl/dbl bandas, US$12/16 sgl/dbl tents.*

Camping

🏕 **Lake Mburo Campsite** The lakeshore of Lake Mburo, 1km from Rwonyo, is an attractive place to pitch your own tent. Pods of hippos laze in the lake during the day, before coming ashore at night to keep your campground lawns cropped short. Cook your own food or order from the stilted restaurant/bar. If you have your own transport & provisions, lakeshore camping is also possible at Campsite 3, a few kilometres further south, while a little-used campsite on Rwonyo Hill offers good regional views. *US$8pp.*

WHAT TO SEE AND DO

Horseback safaris (*Prices vary – see below*) Mihingo Lodge (see page 227) has introduced horseback safaris in the east of the park – another first in a Ugandan protected area. The event is tailored to your experience and requirements. Kids can be led on good-natured ponies while (at the other extreme) experienced riders can help a couple of ex-racehorses burn off some calories. Day rates vary from Ush55,000 for a quick 30-minute taster (the grassy valley floor, 15 minutes' ride from the lodge, is habitually filled with game) to Ush460,000 for full-day hacks to hilltop viewpoints with a picnic breakfast and bush lunch. Overnight, two-day and three-day rides are also available.

Boat trips (*Fees (see pages 32–3) are for min 4 & max 8 people*) A motorboat trip on the lake leaves from the jetty at the main campsite 1km from Rwonyo Camp. In addition to the attractive scenery and simple pleasure attached to being out on the water, the boat trip reliably produces good sightings of hippo, crocodile, buffalo, waterbuck and bushbuck, and it's also worth looking out for the three species of resident otter. Among the more conspicuous waterbirds are African fish eagle, marabou stork, pied kingfisher and various egrets and herons, while Ross's turaco and Narina trogon are frequently seen in lakeside thickets. Lake Mburo is possibly the easiest place in Uganda to see the elusive African finfoot, which is generally associated with still water below overhanging branches.

Game drives The part of the national park to the east of Lake Mburo is traversed by a network of game tracks. The quality of game viewing in particular locations is influenced by the season as well as long-term vegetative changes. During the wet season, for example, you might hope for substantial concentrations of impala, zebra, waterbuck, topi and buffalo in the park-like savanna north of Rwonyo at the junction of Impala and Warukiri tracks. Historically, during the dry season, when animals tend to congregate around the swamps and lakes, you would have headed south from Rwonyo to explore the Lakeside Track and Kigambira Loop. However, increasingly dense bush cover has complicated game viewing in this area (unless you're searching specifically for bush-dwelling birds, or hoping to spot a leopard). A 360° panorama from the once-grassy summit of Kigambira Hill has been all but obscured by scrub. For this reason, head east from the Lakeside Track to find relatively open savanna along the Kazuma and Ruroko tracks. The landscape is interspersed with rocky hills where pairs of klipspringer are frequently observed. You should also park up and walk to the top of Kazuma Hill for the southern panorama over four of the park's lakes.

To the west of Rwonyo, starting near Sanga Gate, the Rwizi Track leads through an area of light acacia savanna. Impala, eland and Burchell's zebra are common in this area, and the western shore of Lake Mburo is visible at times. After 12km, the track approaches the Rwizi River and fringing swamps. It then veers to the west, following the wooded watercourse for 33km before reaching Bisheshe Gate, a stretch that is particularly rewarding for birds. It is possible to drive beyond the gate to the main Mbarara road, but the track is in appalling condition and is challenging even in a 4x4 vehicle.

Guided walks (*US$10pp*) One of the major attractions of Lake Mburo is that you are permitted to walk anywhere in the park in the company of an armed ranger. Near to the camp, the road to the jetty remains a good place to walk, rich in birds and regularly visited by hippos. An even better target is the viewing platform that overlooks a salt lick about 2km from the camp – this is an excellent place to see a wide variety of animals. Of particular interest to walkers and birders is the **Rubanga Forest**, which lies off the Rwizi Track and can only be visited with the permission of the warden, who will provide you with an armed ranger. Visitors used to be allowed to walk unaccompanied along the 1km stretch of road between Rwonyo and the main campsite, but this practice was discontinued a few years ago after a tour leader was mauled by a buffalo.

MBARARA AND AROUND

In 1955, when Alan Forward arrived in Mbarara to serve as its new district officer, he found himself 'choking in the dust' of what 'seemed to have the atmosphere of a one-horse town'. Indeed, in the dying years of the colonial era, Mbarara was too small to be ranked among 12 towns countrywide whose population exceeded 4,000. By 1991, however, the one-horse town had grown to become the sixth-largest in Uganda, with a population exceeding 40,000. The past 20 years have seen an even greater transformation. In the early 1990s, when I first visited Mbarara, it was a sleepy, nondescript junction town, still visibly scarred by the Tanzanian invasion during the Amin era. Subsequently, it has evolved into what is surely the only urban centre in western Uganda to which the adjectives 'modern' or 'vibrant' could be applied without a hint of facetiousness. Mbarara, in short, is the most rapidly expanding town in Uganda. Yet, paradoxically, while the town boasts perhaps the best selection of hotels and other tourist-related facilities anywhere in western Uganda – aimed mostly at local businessmen and the conference market – it lacks for any remotely scintillating sightseeing. Its bustling High Street almost qualifies, if only for the insight provided into the priorities of the modern Mbararan, for this contains what must be East Africa's highest upcountry concentration of shops dealing exclusively in mobile phones and their accessories. Of potential interest is the royal drum house at Kamukazi, the last Ankole capital, situated 2km out of town along the Fort Portal Road. Unfortunately, the royal drum, or *bagyendwaza*, an important symbol of Ankole national unity, said to have first belonged to the Bacwezi leader Wamala, was removed when the monarchy was banned in 1967, and Kamukazi is now occupied by the military and off-limits to travellers. The **Nkokonjeru Tombs**, about 3km from the town centre, are the burial place of the last two kings of Ankole.

GETTING THERE AND AWAY Mbarara is a major route focus, situated at the junction of the surfaced roads east to Kampala via Masaka, southwest to Kabale and Kisoro, and northwest to Fort Portal via Kasese. Using **public transport**, the best way to get to or from Mbarara is with the **Horizon Bus Company**, whose modern and generally not overloaded vehicles run out of a private tout-free stand in the town centre. The staff at the stand use mobile phones to keep in touch with the buses, so they usually know when the next one is due to pass through *en route* to Kampala or Kabale – you're unlikely to have to wait more than 30 minutes. If headed towards Queen Elizabeth National Park, a daily Kalita bus runs through Mbarara on the way to Kasese each day around 11.00.

All other buses run out of the old bus park, where travellers are likely to be swamped by bus touts the moment they enter. **Minibus-taxis** operate from the

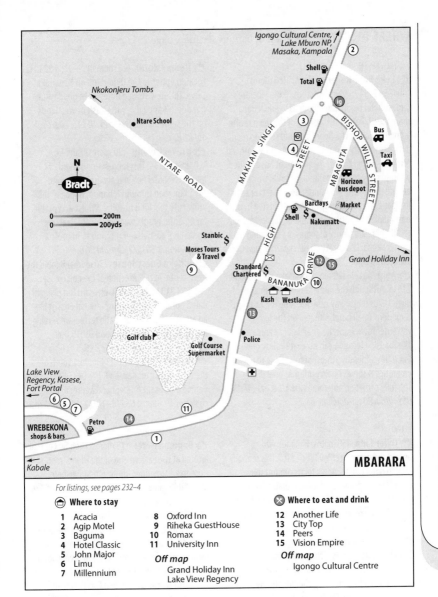

For listings, see pages 232–4

🛏 **Where to stay**

1 Acacia	**8** Oxford Inn
2 Agip Motel	**9** Riheka GuestHouse
3 Baguma	**10** Romax
4 Hotel Classic	**11** University Inn
5 John Major	*Off map*
6 Limu	Grand Holiday Inn
7 Millennium	Lake View Regency

✖ **Where to eat and drink**

12 Another Life
13 City Top
14 Peers
15 Vision Empire
Off map
Igongo Cultural Centre

new taxi park; they are efficient for shorter journeys but in general they are not as comfortable or as safe as the big buses. **Special-hire taxis** are available all over town, especially around the central roundabout near the Shell station. A **boda-boda** trip within the town centre should cost around Ush1,000.

TOUR OPERATORS

Moses Tours & Travel m 0772 422825/0752422825; e moses.tours@live. com; www.traveluganda.co.ug/motours. Moses Kyomukama seems to be Mbarara's 1st choice

for tours & vehicle hire. His 2nd-floor office is in the storied commercial building next to Stanbic bank.

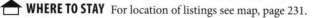

Moderate

🏠 **Lake View Regency Hotel** (80 rooms)
📞04854 22112; e ivh@infocom.co.ug. Mbarara's
largest hotel lies in large grounds overlooking a
manmade lake on the outskirts of the town centre
along the Fort Portal Road. It would seem to merit
a higher security status than Entebbe International
Airport – either that or management has attained
a comparable level of paranoia – since arrivals
are greeted by the only sniffer dogs I've ever seen
in Uganda! If you decline to be investigated by a
nasty looking Alsatian you don't get in. Inside, as I
recall, there are plenty of rooms, a swimming pool,
gym & sauna. *US$65/80/80 sgl/twin/dbl; superior
dbl US$120 B&B.*

🏠 **Agip Motel** (20 rooms) Masaka Rd; 📞04854
21615. Although the name conjures up images of a
dirty 1970s motorway café, the Agip is a luxurious
& modern small hotel, situated on the left as
you enter town from the direction of Kampala.
The roadside location can make it slightly noisy,
but it has a friendly atmosphere, is close to all
amenities & serves quality international dishes.
The fully carpeted, airy rooms are s/c & have DSTV.
US$40/60/80 sgl/dbl/suite B&B.

Budget

🏠 **Oxford Inn** (50 rooms) Bananuka Drive,
behind the post office; 📞0485 661167.This centrally
located hotel is best known for its comfortable
outside latticed area & indoor restaurant which are
popular places to meet & to eat. Nearby bars & the
Vision Empire nightclub make undisturbed Fri/Sat
nights unlikely. *US$31/38 sgl/dbl B&B.*

🏠 **Hotel Classic** (45 rooms) High St; 📞04854
21131; e hotclassic@swiftuganda.com. This
popular modern hotel is centrally located & as
a result it can be a bit noisy, though otherwise
it's very good value. The lively balcony bar is
a popular meeting place, & a good restaurant
serves international dishes for around Ush7,000.
US$30/34 s/c sgl/dbl B&B.

🏠 **Acacia Hotel** (35 rooms) 7 High St; 📞0392
916391; m 0779 494447; e acaciahotel@live.
com; www.skybluehotels.com. Going by the early
morning clatter of feet in the corridors, this smart
new hotel near the turning to Kasese seems to
be Mbarara's most popular budget option. Ample
secure parking & free Wi-Fi. *US$29/39 sgl/dbl B&B.*

🏠 **Romax Hotel** (28 rooms); m 0704 233233.
Located opposite the Oxford Inn on Bananuka
Drive, this new storied hotel looks good value.
If it doesn't appeal, try the Kash or Westlands
on the same side of the road. *US$16/20 s/c sgl/
dbl B&B.*

🏠 **University Inn** (20 rooms) High St;
📞04854 20334. This long-serving & rather
neglected hotel lies in leafy grounds along
the main road through Mbarara, opposite the
university teaching hospital. Whilst acceptable
for an unfussy sgl traveller, the dbl deal is less
appealing, costwise or if trying to impress a
companion. *US$15/25 sgl/dbl B&B.*

🏠 **Riheka GuestHouse** (30 rooms) Behind the
town centre in the direction of the golf course;
📞04854 21314. This small, pleasant but distinctly
dated hotel lies in a quiet residential area. It has
an attractive garden & a patio restaurant serving
international dishes for around Ush15,000.
US$14/24/24 sgl/dbl/twin s/c B&B.

🏠 **Grand Holiday Inn** (34 rooms) South of
the town centre off Kakoba Rd; 📞04854 433455.
Behind a pleasant timber bar & veranda, there is a
choice of s/c rooms. *US$10–18/24/28 sgl/dbl/twin.*

Shoestring

🏠 **Baguma Hotel** (23 rooms) High St. Centrally
located at the eastern end of the High Street,
close to all amenities, this multi-storey hotel is
acceptable value. *US$11/15 s/c sgl+/dbl, US$7/9
with shared facilities.*

🏠 **Millennium** (10 rooms) Fort Portal Rd. The
first of a long line of cheap lodgings in the old
market area of Wrebekona, this basic hotel has
secure parking & is located close to several local
bars & restaurants. *US$8/12 s/c sgl/dbl.*

🏠 **Limu Hotel** (14 rooms) Fort Portal Rd,
Wrebekona. An early morning cluster of NGO
vehicles outside this basic lodge, & the crowded
dining room within, would both seem to be
indicators of general approval. *US$8 sgl+.*

🏠 **John Major Hotel** (12 rooms) Fort Portal Rd,
Wrebekona. Drab, forgettable & budget oriented.
Ush10,000 sgl with shared bathrooms.

Camping

▲ **Agip Motel** Masaka Rd. This smart hotel has
the only custom-built camping site in Mbarara.

Mbarara lies at the heart of the former Ankole (or Nkore) kingdom, a centralised polity founded c1500 in the power vacuum created by the demise of the Bacwezi. Unlike the other pre-colonial kingdoms of Uganda, Ankole society was divided into two rigidly stratified but mutually inter-dependent castes: the pastoralist Bahima nobility and the agriculturist Bairu peasantry. Ankole was ruled by a king, called the *omugabe*, a hereditary title reserved for prominent members of the Bahinda clan of the Bahima, who was served by an appointed *enganzi* (prime minister) and a number of local chiefs.

Ankole rose to regional prominence in roughly 1700, after the 11th omugabe, Ntare IV Kiitabanyoro, defeated the Banyoro army (Kiitabanyoro means 'Killer of the Banyoro'). By the mid 19th century, the kingdom, bounded by the Katonga River in the north and the Kagera River in the south, extended from east of Lake Mburo to the shores of Lake Albert in the west. After 1875, however, Ankole went into decline, attributable partly to a combination of disease and drought, but primarily to the rejuvenation of Bunyoro under Kabalega, who might well have co-opted Ankole into his realm were it not for outside intervention.

In 1898, Omugabe Kahaya decided that the only way to safeguard his kingdom against Bunyoro advances was to enter into an alliance with the British administration in Buganda, and John Macallister, a former railway engineer, was dispatched to Nkore to establish a British government station and fort – the future Mbarara. In January 1899, Macallister settled on a site called Muti, which was eminently defendable and boasted a perennial water supply in the form of the Rwizi River. There was also a strong historical basis for Macallister's choice of location. When Captain Lugard had visited Ankole a few years earlier, Muti was the capital of Omugabe Ntare, though it had been abandoned in the interim, after a smallpox epidemic claimed the lives of several of its prominent citizens and one of Ntare's sons. That the station built at Muti was called Mbarara evidently stemmed from some confusion on the part of Macallister. Mbarara (or more correctly Mburara, after a type of grass that grows locally) was actually the name of the site of another of Ntare's short-lived capitals, situated a few kilometres from the abandoned Muti.

Whatever other merits it might have possessed, the site selected by Macallister had one serious drawback. 'The more one journeys about', wrote the missionary J J Willis, 'the more one is impressed with the fact that [Mbarara] is the one spot in all Ankole where you have to march a whole day or two days before you come on any cultivation worth the name.' The scarcity of food around Mbarara was rooted less in the area's geography than in local cultural attitudes – the Bahima, like so many other African pastoralists, had no tradition of cultivation. The British administration, supported by Enganzi Mbaguta, did much to encourage the growth of agriculture in Ankole during the early years of the 20th century. In 1905, Mbaguta remarked that, following the establishment of Mbarara, the annual famines were 'becoming yearly less severe'. Within a few years, the new capital of Ankole, accorded township status in 1906, would be practically self-sufficient in food, and its future role as the main centre of trade in Ankole secure.

The well-kept grassy site is enclosed within a secure wall, & the ablution block offers hot showers & flush toilets. The site is close to all town amenities, & the hotel has a pleasant outside bar & restaurant. *US$5 per tent.*

Camping is also permitted in the grounds of the **University Inn** (see page 232).

✖ **WHERE TO EAT AND DRINK** In addition to the restaurants listed below, several of the hotels recommended above have good restaurants attached. The **Lake View Regency Hotel** is good for a night out, especially on Fridays. The food at the **Agip Motel** is a few notches above the rest.

Numerous bars and *muchomo* (meat) joints come to life at night in the **Wrebekona** market area just up the Fort Portal Road. They serve cheap drinks and barbecue tilapia, pork, chicken and goat with *matoke*, cabbage and the like. For location of listings see map, page 231.

✖ **City Top** High St. According to local volunteers, this restaurant, on the west side of the Shell roundabout, serves good Indian food.

✖ **Igongo Cultural Centre** Masaka Rd, 6km east of Mbarara; www.igongomuseum.co.ug. At this excellent restaurant, a lunchtime buffet is served daily between 12.00 & 15.30 (*Ush20,000*), while a menu of traditional Ankole dishes & continental meals (*Ush15,000–12,000*) is also available. For more details about the centre, see pages 235–6.

✖ **Oxford Inn** Bananuka Drive (see page 232). The Oxford has a pleasant terrace screened from the street, & a restaurant inside.

♀ **Peers** Kabale Rd. This new establishment, set on a roadside terrace 200m before the turn-off to Kasese, seems to be the smart place for drinks & BBQ snacks.

☆ **Vision Empire & Another Life** Bananuka Drive. Mbarara's top 2 nightclubs. Vision Empire is dark & noisy but has a more exclusive upstairs area to which you can escape.

SHOPPING Lack of parking opportunities makes shopping in the busy town centre a frustrating experience. Nevertheless, it's worth a little hassle to visit the brand-new branch of **Nakumatt**, Kenya's smartest supermarket chain. Not only the best supermarket in Mbarara, it's the best you'll find outside Kampala. It's tucked away at the back of a small mall on Kakoba Road (turn off High Street at the Shell roundabout). There's limited street parking for customers and a private parking lot (*Ush2,000*) next door. Alternatively, head out down the Kabale Road to find the **Golf Course supermarket** opposite the Delta fuel station and the police station.

OTHER PRACTICALITIES
Foreign exchange The **Stanbic** bank, opposite the **post office**, changes cash at the bank's national rates. Out of banking hours, the Agip and Lake View hotels (see page 232) will also exchange money, but at a poorer rate.

Internet There are several **internet cafés** along High Street.

Swimming Day visitors can use the swimming pool at the **Lake View Regency Hotel** (see page 232) for a small fee.

WHAT TO SEE
Nkokonjeru Tombs The tombs of the last two kings of Ankole, Omugabe Edward Solomon Kahaya II, who died in 1944, and Omugabe Sir Charles Godfrey Rutahaba Gasyonga II, who ruled from 1944 until 1967 and died in 1982, can be visited at

Nkokonjeru, 3km from central Mbarara. To anybody who has seen the impressive and lovingly tended traditional royal tombs at Kasubi and Mparo, however, an excursion to Nkokonjeru is bound to prove anticlimactic. Protected within an isolated, rundown – almost derelict – colonial-style house, the royal graves at Nkokonjeru consist of two bland concrete slabs, overgrown with vegetation and layered in sickly sweet-smelling bat shit, on to which the names of the late kings are unceremoniously hand-scrawled. Several other graves of minor royalty lie outside the main building.

To reach Nkokonjeru, follow Ntare Road out of the town centre, passing the Ntare School after about 1km. After another 500m, turn right into the road signposted for Fort Coleb Rest House, ignoring a fork to the right after 200m. About 200m further, you reach a three-way junction, where the central fork leads after 500m to the tiled building housing the tombs.

Igongo Cultural Centre (*www.igongomuseum.co.ug; admission Ush20,000*) This smart new, multi-faceted development is set in large, neat lawns beside the Masaka Road, 6km west of Mbarara. Its primary purpose is to present, preserve and promote the history and culture of the dormant Ankole kingdom and so it's ironic that it's a hundred times better than the moribund efforts of any of the officially recognised kingdoms. That said, the most immediate attraction for tourists and

---

THE ANKOLE MONARCHY TODAY

The untended state of the Nkokonjeru Tombs is symptomatic of a popular ambivalence to the Ankole royalty that stretches back to the early years of independence. In 1967, the constitutional abolition of the monarchies under Obote was hotly protested in Buganda, Bunyoro and Toro. In Ankole, by contrast, the reaction was closer to muted indifference. In 1971, Idi Amin opened a short-lived debate with regard to reinstating all the ancient monarchies, a notion that garnered strong support in Buganda and elsewhere. Not so in Ankole, where a committee of elders signed a memorandum stating that the matter 'should not be raised or even discussed', since it would 'revive political divisions and factionalism' and stand in the way of the 'march forward to our stated goal of freedom and progress'.

The widespread anti-royalist sentiment in Ankole is so fundamentally at odds with popular attitudes in the other kingdoms of Uganda that it requires explanation. Two main factors can be cited. The first is that the traditional social structure of Ankole, like that of pre-colonial Rwanda but not of Buganda or Bunyoro, was informed by a rigid caste system. For the majority of Banyankole – who are of Bairu descent – reinstating the Bahima monarchy would smack of retrogression to that obsolete caste system. Secondly, Ankole, as it was delineated from the early colonial era until post-independence, was an artificial entity, one that encompassed several formerly independent kingdoms – Igara, Sheema, Bweju and parts of Mpororo – that had no prior historical affiliation or loyalty to the omugabe. Ankole is the only one of the ancient Ugandan kingdoms that was not officially restored by Museveni in 1993. And, despite ongoing lobbying from traditionalists (and the clandestine coronation of Prince Barigye, a ceremony that was immediately afterwards annulled by Museveni), it seems likely to remain that way for the foreseeable future.

6

Mbarara's moneyed elite is the **excellent restaurant** (see page 234). You'll also find clean toilets here and a decent craft shop. Nevertheless, the centrepiece is the museum which explores both Ankole and Bakiga histories and cultures. The conventional nature of the displays won't appeal to everyone but for those with the time and interest, it is a veritable treasure trove.

AROUND MBARARA

Ruhanga Uganda Lodge (*www.ugandalodge.com*) At Ruhanga, about 50km past Mbarara, just past Itojo Hospital, is a community guesthouse built to accommodate both passing visitors and long- or short-term volunteers. Located close to the eastern limit of the Kigezi Highlands, there is plenty of scope to explore the hills and visit markets, lakes and hot springs. Volunteer accommodation and projects are available. For details, visit www.volunteeringuganda.org.

Nshenyi Cultural Centre (*For more details contact Great Lakes Safaris;* ✆ *0414 267153/0312 78757;* e *info@safari-uganda.com; www.safari-uganda.com*) This secluded cultural centre is found in the village of Nshenyi, about 90km (two to three hours) from Mbarara Town and about 10km from the borders with Rwanda and Tanzania. Situated on a traditional Ankole farm, the centre offers basic accommodation in seven rooms with shared pit toilets and hot bucket showers, as well as traditional meals and a wide range of activities that encourage direct interaction with the local community. These include milking the long-horned Ankole cattle, joining the pastors as they graze the cattle, a market-day experience, nature walks and birdwatching on the undulating hills that overlook the village or along the Kagera River (the border with Tanzania), tribal encounters, visits to rock art and historical sites, traditional cooking, and cultural singing and dancing.

Ibanda Something of a minor route focus, the small town of Ibanda lies 67km north of Mbarara at the junction of the southern approach road to Katonga Wildlife Reserve and a little-used route north through Kamwenge to Kibale National Park and Fort Portal. Unless you're heading between these places,

MURDER IN IBANDA

On 19 May 1905, Harry St George Galt, stabbed to death on the veranda of the government resthouse outside Ibanda, achieved the unwanted distinction of becoming the only British administrative officer in Uganda ever to be murdered. The circumstances of Galt's death have never been satisfactorily explained. The killer was identified, somewhat tenuously, as a local man called Rutaraka, said to have been acting strangely prior to the murder, and found dead shortly afterwards in circumstances that may or may not have implicated suicide. If Rutaraka did kill Galt, it is widely believed somebody in authority enlisted his services, but nobody knows exactly who: a local Saza chief, tried and convicted for conspiracy in Galt's murder at a court in Kampala, later succeeded in having the ruling overturned on the basis of tainted evidence. Whatever else, as famous last words go, those uttered by the unfortunate Galt surely deserve greater recognition. According to an article by H F Morris in the *Uganda Journal* of 1960, the mortally wounded officer 'called for his cook, said "Look, cook, a savage has speared me", and thereupon fell down dead'.

Readers travelling directly between Kasese and Kabale should, instead of following the 125km surfaced road through Mbarara, think about using the short cut provided by the old Kabale Road which links Ishaka to Ntungamo. This route is unsurfaced, though usually in pretty good shape, for 31km before emerging on to the tarmac Rukungiri highway at Kagamaba. Turn left for Ntungamo (13km) or right for Rukungiri, Bwindi and Ishaka. If coming from Kabale, the Rukungiri Road is clearly signposted off to the left from the Mbarara Road 500m before Ntungamo, but the next turn-off to the right after 13km is less obvious. The main site of interest along the old Kabale Road is the **Kitagata Hot Springs**, which lie close to Kitagata trading centre, some 16km south of Ishaka. Kitagata is an oddly time-warped small town, dominated by a redundantly immense roundabout, and scattered with several colonial-era buildings including a rather pretty old church, all of which goes to suggest that urban development came to a standstill following the construction of the surfaced road via Mbarara. There are a few lodgings, should you be in the mood to linger, and the **Zanzibar Hotel** (*US$4*) on Liberation Road has been recommended. The hot springs lie about 1.5km south of Kitagata, and you're unlikely to miss them – their vaguely sulphuric whiff should draw your attention even if the prominent signposts don't. The name Kitagata holds few mysteries for linguists – it translates somewhat unimaginatively as 'boiling water' – and it could be argued that the actual springs, too, are of no more than passing interest, bubbling as they do into a clear, shallow, steaming pool about 200m from the main road. Kitagata has long been believed to possess therapeutic qualities (and so probably does, should you be suffering from creaky joints or aching muscles, though it's doubtful it would do much to cure malaria or several other ailments as it claims) and the surrounding rocks are generally draped in a couple of dozen half-naked bathers who, needless to say, will be less than enamoured of any passing tourist who pulls out a camera. The huge signpost announcing the presence of a rest camp at the springs flatters to deceive – you can pitch a tent, assuming you have one, for next to nothing, but facilities are limited to the communal hot bath created naturally by the springs. South of Kitagata, the road passes through some impressively scenic hills, a landscape characteristic of Kigezi, except that it is unusually grassy and lacking in cultivation. This stretch of road also follows a papyrus-fringed river for several kilometres, offering excellent views over patches of swamp that might potentially prove to be excellent for papyrus endemics.

however, it must be said that Ibanda is rather an out-of-the-way town, and – sprawling along one main road for about 1km – thoroughly unremarkable. But not so the surfaced road that connects Ibanda to Mbarara – possibly the smoothest drive in Uganda, and almost (but not quite) worth the diversion for that reason alone! This road winds through some lovely hilly scenery and passes the base of **Isingiro Mountain**. At 2,172m, this is the highest peak in Ankole, and reputedly climbable in a day from Lwesho trading centre. About 3km from Ibanda, a cairn-like memorial commemorates the murder of Harry St George Galt (see box, page 236).

Practicalities Ibanda is connected to Mbarara by regular **minibus-taxis**, and there is also a fair amount of transport on to Kamwenge and to a lesser extent Kabagole (for Katonga Wildlife Reserve). Should you need to overnight in Ibanda, there are a few local guesthouses to choose from. A short way out of town towards Mbarara, the **MK Resort Garden Hotel** is apparently a notch or two above the rest (*US$20/26 sgl/dbl s/c B&B*). The **Kanyiginya Guesthouse** (m *0788 234219;* e *mulinroger@yahoo.com*) is also highly recommended, albeit by an SMS from the proprietress, Mrs Rose Mulinde.

7

The Kigezi Highlands

Kigezi is perhaps the most fertile and scenic region of Uganda: a landscape of expansive blue lakes and steep terraced slopes tumbling southwest towards the rainforests of **Bwindi National Park** and the magnificent isolated peaks of the **Virunga volcanoes**. But for most visitors, whatever scenic qualities are attached to this hilly southwestern corner of Uganda will be secondary to the region's outstanding attraction, which is the opportunity to track the endangered mountain gorilla in its natural habitat – arguably the most exciting wildlife encounter to be had anywhere in Africa.

The global population of fewer than 900 wild mountain gorillas is restricted to, and divided between, the dense montane forest of Bwindi and the bamboo-clumped slopes of the Virungas. But, typical of the whimsical attitude to the carve-up of Africa in the 1880s, the Virungas were divided across three separate colonial territories, so that the mountain gorillas today are harboured within four independently managed national parks in three different countries. These are the Bwindi Impenetrable and Mgahinga Gorilla national parks in Uganda, and – contiguous to the latter – the Parc National des Volcans in Rwanda and Parc National des Virungas in the DRC. The most reliable locations in which to track gorillas are Uganda's Bwindi Impenetrable National Park, where 11 habituated groups now exist, and Rwanda's Parc National des Volcans (see box, pages 264–5). Tracking in Mgahinga is only sporadically possible since the park's habituated group took to wandering over the volcanic watershed into neighbouring Rwanda for weeks at a time. Tracking opportunities in the DRC are even rarer, owing to perennial insecurity in the east of this troubled country. Mountain gorilla tracking is inevitably the most popular tourist activity in **Kigezi**, but the area does have much else to offer. The slopes of Mgahinga harbour a rich faunal diversity, and it is possible to organise guided forest walks as well as day hikes to the three volcanic peaks within the reserve. Bwindi, too, offers some excellent day-walking possibilities, and it has possibly the richest faunal diversity of any forest in East Africa, including two dozen bird species endemic to the Albertine Rift. National parks aside, the lovely, island-strewn **Lake Bunyonyi** has supplanted the Ssese Islands as Uganda's most popular waterside chill-out venue, while a host of more obscure lakes and waterfalls form rewarding goals for more adventurous travellers.

The largest town in Kigezi, and main gateway to the region, is **Kabale**, which lies 430km from Kampala and 147km from Mbarara. The other important local urban centre is **Kisoro**, strategically situated at the base of the Virungas close to the borders with Rwanda and the DRC. Considerably smaller, but of potential significance to travellers moving between Queen Elizabeth National Park and Bwindi is Kihihi, the northern gateway to Kigezi (this is covered in the following chapter).

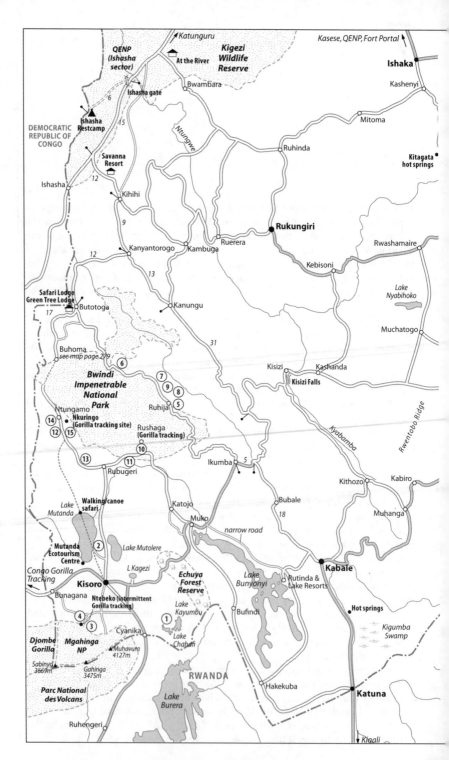

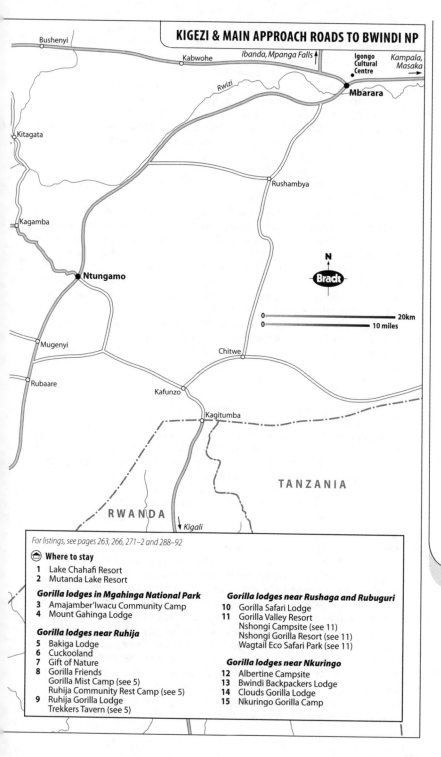

KIGEZI & MAIN APPROACH ROADS TO BWINDI NP

Bushenyi

Kabwohe

Ibanda, Mpanga Falls

Igongo Cultural Centre

Kampala, Masaka

Rwizi

Mbarara

Kitagata

Rushambya

Kagamba

N

Bradt

Ntungamo

0   20km
0   10 miles

Mugenyi

Chitwe

Rubaare

Kafunzo

Kagitumba

TANZANIA

RWANDA

↓ *Kigali*

The Kigezi Highlands

7

For listings, see pages 263, 266, 271–2 and 288–92

⊝ **Where to stay**

1   Lake Chahafi Resort
2   Mutanda Lake Resort

Gorilla lodges in Mgahinga National Park

3   Amajamber'Iwacu Community Camp
4   Mount Gahinga Lodge

Gorilla lodges near Ruhija

5   Bakiga Lodge
6   Cuckooland
7   Gift of Nature
8   Gorilla Friends
     Gorilla Mist Camp (see 5)
     Ruhija Community Rest Camp (see 5)
9   Ruhija Gorilla Lodge
     Trekkers Tavern (see 5)

Gorilla lodges near Rushaga and Rubuguri

10   Gorilla Safari Lodge
11   Gorilla Valley Resort
      Nshongi Campsite (see 11)
      Nshongi Gorilla Resort (see 11)
      Wagtail Eco Safari Park (see 11)

Gorilla lodges near Nkuringo

12   Albertine Campsite
13   Bwindi Backpackers Lodge
14   Clouds Gorilla Lodge
15   Nkuringo Gorilla Camp

Miha Logar, founder of the Kabale-based organisation, Edirisa, has produced a marvellously comprehensive e-book, *Gorilla Highlands: Travel Guide to Southwestern Uganda*. This beautifully presented publication is available from the Apple iTunes Store for £9.49. More conventionally, a couple of maps are available for the area. Sheet 5 in the 'Uganda Maps' series, *Bwindi and the Kigezi Highlands* (*Ush12,000*), illustrates the regional topography, main tourist routes and hotspots, viewpoints and gorilla ranges derived from the 2011–12 gorilla census. Outdated and increasingly rare but still useful is the larger scale, 1:125,000 *Kigezi Tourist Map* published in 1993. For more details on Uganda mapping see *Further Information*, page 543.

GORILLA TRACKING

Tracking the mountain gorillas in the Virungas or Bwindi ranks among the absolute highlights of African travel. The exhilaration attached to first setting eyes on a wild mountain gorilla is difficult to describe. These are enormous animals: up to three times as bulky as the average man, their size exaggerated by a shaggily luxuriant coat. Yet despite their fearsome appearance, gorillas are remarkably peaceable creatures – tracking them would be a considerably more dangerous pursuit were they possessed of the aggressive temperament of, say, vervet monkeys or baboons, or for that matter human beings.

More impressive even than the gorillas' size and bearing is their unfathomable attitude to people, which differs greatly from that of any other wild animal I've encountered. Anthropomorphic as it might sound, almost everybody who visits the gorillas experiences an almost mystical sense of recognition. Often, one of the gentle giants will break off from the business of chomping on bamboo to study a human visitor, soft brown eyes staring deeply into theirs as if seeking a connection – a spine-tingling wildlife experience without peer.

Gorilla tracking should not present a serious physical challenge to any reasonably fit adult whatever their age, but the hike can be tough going. Exactly how tough varies greatly, and the main determining factor is basically down to luck, specifically how close the gorillas are to the trailhead on the day you trek (one to two hours is typical, anything from 15 minutes to six hours possible). Another variable is how recently it has rained, which affects conditions underfoot – June to August are the driest months and March to May are the wettest.

The effects of altitude should not be underestimated. Tracking in Bwindi takes place at around 1,500m above sea level, but in the Virungas the gorillas are often encountered at almost 3,000m – sufficient to knock the breath out of anybody who just flew in from low altitude. For this reason, visitors to the Virungas in particular might want to leave gorilla tracking until they've been in the region for a week and are reasonably acclimatised – most of Uganda lies above 1,000m.

Take advantage when the guides offer you a walking staff before the walk; this will be invaluable to help you keep your balance on steep hillsides. Once on the trail, don't be afraid to ask to stop for a few minutes whenever you feel tired, or to ask the guides to create a makeshift walking stick from a branch. Drink plenty of water, and do carry some quick calories such as biscuits or chocolate. The good news is that in 99% of cases, whatever exhaustion you might feel on the way up will vanish with the adrenalin charge that follows the first sighting of a silverback gorilla!

Put on your sturdiest walking shoes for the trek, and wear thick trousers and long sleeves as protection against vicious nettles. It's often cold at the outset,

With a population of around 40,000, Kabale is one of the largest towns in western Uganda, as well as being an important transport hub and a useful base from which to visit mountain gorillas. It was founded in 1913, when the British government station at Ikumba was relocated to Makanga Hill – then known as Kabaare after a trough-like depression at its summit – above present-day Kabale town centre. The original hilltop site is dominated today by an expansive green golf course, a few old government buildings, and the venerable White Horse Hotel. Both the hill and the town centre below are studded with mature

so bring a sweatshirt or jersey. The gorillas are used to people, and it makes no difference whether you wear bright or muted colours. Whatever clothes you wear are likely to get very dirty, so if you have pre-muddied clothes, use them! During the rainy season, a poncho or raincoat might be a worthy addition to your daypack, while sunscreen, sunglasses and a hat are a good idea at any time of year, as are gloves to protect against nettles.

In all reserves, tourists are permitted to spend no longer than one hour with the gorillas, and may not eat or smoke in their presence. It is forbidden to approach the gorillas closer than 7m, a rule that is difficult to enforce with those curious youngsters (and some adults) who enjoy approaching human visitors. Gorillas are susceptible to many human diseases, and it has long been feared by researchers that one ill tourist might infect a gorilla, resulting in the possible death of the whole troop should no immunity exist. For this reason, you should not track gorillas when you have a potentially airborne infection such as a flu or cold, and should turn away from the gorillas if you need to sneeze in their presence.

As for photography, my advice, unless you're a professional or serious amateur, is to run off a few quick snapshots, then put the camera away, enjoy the moment, and buy a postcard or coffee-table book later. Gorillas are tricky photographic subjects, on account of their sunken eyes, the gloomy habitat in which they are often found, and a jet-black skin that tends to distort light readings. Flash photography is forbidden, so you're unlikely to get sharp results without a tripod or monopod. It might be worth carrying an ISO 800 or 1600 film (or programming your digital camera appropriately) in case you need the speed, but where light conditions permit, low-speed ISO 50 or 100 film will generally produce far better results. Make sure, too, that your camera gear is well protected – if your bag isn't waterproof, seal your camera and films in plastic bags.

Above all, do bear in mind that gorillas are still wild animals, despite the 'gentle giant' reputation that has superseded the old King Kong image. An adult gorilla is much stronger than a person and will act in accordance with its own social codes when provoked or surprised. The most serious incident to date occurred in Mgahinga in 1997 when a silverback took exception to a professional photographer who decided that he was the exception to the flash photography rule. The gorilla snatched the camera and charged, roughed up and then sat upon an innocent party who did/didn't break a limb depending on which version of the story you hear. The point, obviously, is to listen to your guide at all times regarding the correct protocol in the presence of gorillas.

eucalyptus trees, originally planted in the 1920s as part of a swamp-clearance and malaria-control programme.

Pretty though Kabale may be, the town itself doesn't offer much in the way of tourist attractions and, given the choice, most travellers opt to spend the night at nearby Lake Bunyonyi. However, Kabale is enjoying a new lease of life as an affordable overnight staging point for gorilla tracking tourists. Improved road access to the Rushaga and Ruhija sites means that trackers can avoid the expense of a trailhead lodge and still (with a 06.00 start) reach either site by 08.30.

GETTING THERE AND AWAY The 430km surfaced road that connects Kampala to Kabale via Mbarara should take six hours to cover in a private vehicle. **Buses** between Kampala and Kabale leave throughout the morning, cost Ush23,000, and generally take six to seven hours, stopping at Mbarara *en route*. The safest option seems to be the slow but reliable **Post Bus** that leaves Kampala from the rear of the main post office at 08.00 daily except for Sundays. Regular travellers recommend the **Bismarken bus** from the Buganda/Qualicell bus park. Another popular option is to take the Rwanda-bound **Jaguar bus** from their Namirembe Road premises.

GORILLA TRACKING IN UGANDA

Uganda is home to 12 habituated gorilla groups – a far cry from 1993 when gorilla tourism was limited to a single habituated group at Buhoma. One group – Nyakagezi – lives in Mgahinga Gorilla National Park, though it is prone to wandering off into Rwanda for long periods. The remaining 11 groups are all located in Bwindi National Park. Rushegura, Habinyanja and Mubare groups roam the forest around the primary tourism site at Buhoma; the Oruzogo and Bitukura groups are to be found at Ruhija. Five groups – Nshongi, Kahunge, Busingye, Mishaya and Bweza – are tracked at Rushaga, Uganda's newest trailhead which opened in 2009. These four groups have resulted from a series of divisions and sub-divisions within an (initially) unusually large Nshongi group since 2009. Lastly, the Nkuringo group inhabits the forest margins at Nkuringo. As eight permits are allocated daily to track each group, Uganda can now offer up to 96 gorilla tracking permits, though given the walkabout tendencies of the Mgahinga group, 88 is a more reliable total.

The magical hour spent with the gorillas does not come cheaply. The cost is currently US$500 per person in Uganda (and US$750 in Rwanda). The price includes park entrance, guides and trackers but not a porter. Even so, it is unusual to meet somebody who regretted the outlay. In addition to this cost, there are other financial considerations to take into account, one being the cost of transport, since mountain gorillas inhabit remote areas some way from tarmac highways and major bus routes. You'll either need to endure some basic forms of transport (foot, boda-boda, overladen pick-up truck …) on the way or be prepared to shell out to hire a vehicle from the nearest urban centre, or indeed all the way from Kampala. When you finally reach the trailhead, you'll find that the cost of accommodation is on the high side and you'll find plenty of opportunities to splash US$500–800 (dbl FB) on a self-contained tent or cottage in an upmarket lodge or camp. If your funds don't run to this, you'll find that each location has at least one budget option though it'll still be overpriced for what you get. You can either grin and bear it or stay in cheaper lodgings in the nearest town and drive up in the early morning (using the money saved to hire a vehicle if necessary).

You'll need to buy a full-price ticket to Kigali but you can jump off in Kabale. The once reliable Horizon buses, which run from their own Namirembe Road depot, seem to be out of favour. Regular transport also runs between Kabale and Kasese, Kisoro and the Rwandan border.

People **driving** between Kabale and Kasese might think about using a short cut avoiding Mbarara (see box, page 237). Another back route – that's longer and slower but more rewarding – takes in Bwindi National Park and the Ishasha sector of Queen Elizabeth National Park. The Kabale–Bwindi leg of this route is covered in the *Getting there and away* section under *Bwindi Impenetrable National Park* on page 274, while the Bwindi–Katunguru leg is included under the corresponding section in *Chapter 8, Ishasha*, page 299. Provided that you stick to the roads recommended in these sections (some other roads are in an appalling state), you could get between Kabale and Kasese in seven or eight hours, though you'd almost certainly want to stop at Bwindi and Ishasha along the way.

TOURIST INFORMATION The privately run **Kabale Tourist Information Centre** [246 B2] (m *0782 314190*), close to the Highland Hotel, provides current

If you're tracking gorillas as part of an organised tour, you can safely assume that your operator will make all the necessary arrangements to get you there and find you a bed, and will also have booked permits in advance. Independent travellers, on the other hand, will generally need to make their own booking, often at relatively short notice. Historically, when tracking was limited to Buhoma and Mgahinga, the coveted places were often booked up by tour operators months in advance and there was absolutely no point in heading to southwest Uganda hoping to see gorillas unless clutching a valid permit. Things are a bit more flexible now since, with five gorilla-tracking locations in Bwindi, securing a permit is far easier than it used to be. Firstly, the itinerant nature of the Mgahinga gorillas (see page 271) means that permits are available at short notice at the Kisoro UWA office rather than Kampala. It is also possible to obtain unsold permits at the Bwindi trailheads on the day of tracking (the full rate applies). However, due to the effort involved in reaching the trailheads and the cost of accommodation in the vicinity, you'd be very unwise to travel in the hope of a standby permit without enquiring about the likelihood of availability from a UWA office.

OBTAINING A PERMIT To book a Ugandan gorilla permit, visit the UWA headquarters on Kiira Road in Kampala (\ *0414 355000*). If booking privately from abroad, write to UWA at e info@ugandawildlife.org. Payment is currently made by bank transfer, though UWA plans to establish a credit card payment mechanism. Alternatively, most tour agents and backpackers' hostels can sort you out. By way of example, Kampala Backpackers charge a US$50 commission. You might also check out the Kampala-based online gorilla booking website, www.gorilla-permits.com (also US$50 commission). During the last couple of years, UWA has offered discounted permits (US$350) during low tourist seasons but it remains to be seen whether this becomes a regular event. However you get your permit, do check whether this is a discounted period, as I've heard of some intermediaries charging their clients the full price plus commission during these times, which is naughty of them.

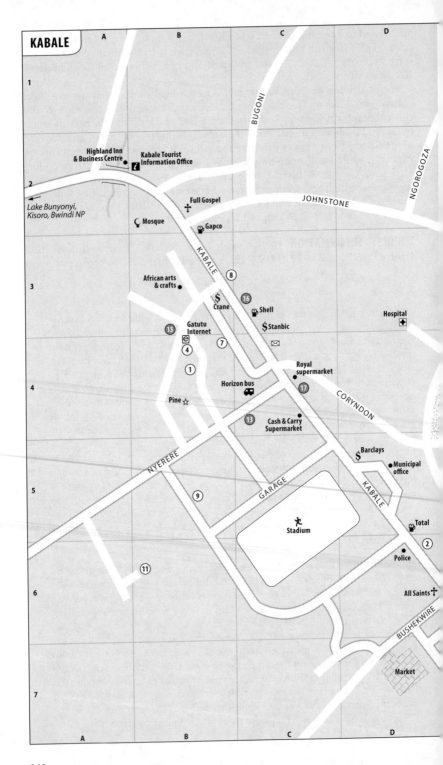

KABALE

A B C D

1

Highland Inn & Business Centre ●

Kabale Tourist Information Office *i*

2

Lake Bunyonyi, Kisoro, Bwindi NP ←

BUGONI

JOHNSTONE

NGOROGOZA

Full Gospel †

ç **Mosque**

🏠 **Gapco**

KABALE

3

African arts & crafts ●

⑧

Crane $

⑯

🏠 **Shell**

$ **Stanbic**

Hospital ✚

⑮

Gatutu Internet

ⓔ

④

⑦

✉

①

Royal supermarket ●

⑰

CORYNDON

4

Horizon bus 🚐

Pine ☆

⑬ **Cash & Carry Supermarket** ●

Barclays $

Municipal office ●

NYERERE

⑨

GARAGE

KABALE

5

Stadium 🏃

🏠 **Total**

②

Police ●

⑪

All Saints †

6

BUSHEKWIRE

Market

7

A B C D

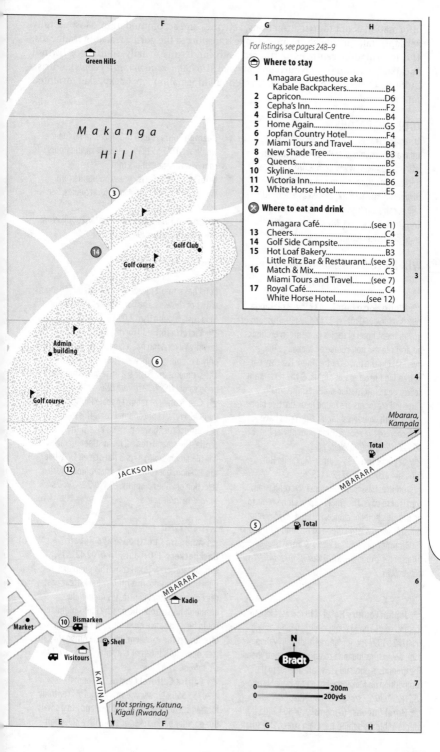

For listings, see pages 248–9

Where to stay

1 Amagara Guesthouse aka
  Kabale Backpackers.....................B4
2 Capricon...D6
3 Cepha's Inn.....................................F2
4 Edirisa Cultural Centre................B4
5 Home Again.....................................G5
6 Jopfan Country Hotel...................F4
7 Miami Tours and Travel...............B4
8 New Shade Tree...............................B3
9 Queens..B5
10 Skyline..E6
11 Victoria Inn.....................................B6
12 White Horse Hotel........................E5

Where to eat and drink

   Amagara Café...........................(see 1)
13 Cheers...C4
14 Golf Side Campsite.......................E3
15 Hot Loaf Bakery.............................B3
   Little Ritz Bar & Restaurant...(see 5)
16 Match & Mix....................................C3
   Miami Tours and Travel..........(see 7)
17 Royal Café..C4
   White Horse Hotel...................(see 12)

Green Hills

M a k a n g a

H i l l

③

⑭

Golf Club

Golf course

Admin
building

⑥

Golf course

⑫

JACKSON

Mbarara,
Kampala

Total

MBARARA

⑤ Total

MBARARA

Kadio

N

Bradt

0 _____ 200m
0 _____ 200yds

Market

⑩ Bismarken

Shell

Visitours

KATUNA

Hot springs, Katuna,
Kigali (Rwanda)

information about tourist attractions, activities and accommodation. Most usefully perhaps, staff can advise on and arrange transport to the gorilla tracking trailheads. The information centre is partnered with, and runs a daily shuttle to, Bwindi Backpackers, 4km from Nkuringo trailhead (*US$30pp return, min 2 people*). Edirisa Cultural Centre (see page 250) has good information on backpacker oriented activities and transport.

TOUR OPERATORS

Amagara Travel m 0752 296197; e info@ amagaratours.com; www.trekkerstours.com
Edirisa [246 B4] www.edirisa.org. This local cultural organisation offers tours to Queen Elizabeth National Park, as well as extended canoe/camping trips on Lake Bunyonyi.
Engagi Safaris m 0782 421519; www. engagiexperience.com

Kazinga Tours Plot 91–5, Mbarara Rd (near Total); m 0772 552819; e felex@ kazingatours. com; www.kazingatours.com
OribiTours & Safaris www.oribitours.com. Wildlife & activity tours led by local guides. See advert on page 334.
Safari 2 Gorilla Tours www.safari2gorilla.com. See advert on page 294.

 WHERE TO STAY For location of listings see map, pages 246–7.

Moderate

⌂ **White Horse Hotel** (48 rooms) Makanga Hill; ☎04864 26010; m 0772 459859. This former government hotel occupies large green grounds adjacent to the golf course on Makanga Hill, overlooking the town centre. There is a cosy bar, lit by a log fire on cooler nights, & the restaurant serves good international dishes. The small, carpeted s/c rooms are found in distinctive blocks roofed with wooden shingles. The rates have yet to recognise the competition from newer hotels. *US$37/49/81 sgl/dbl/suite B&B.*

⌂ **Cepha's Inn** (33 rooms) Makanga Hill; ☎04864 22097; m 0772 444536; e birungicephas@yahoo.com; www.cephasinn. com. These days, the smart Cepha's Inn seems to be Kabale's hotel of choice. Located on Makanga Hill, it is set in a large green compound with sauna & swimming pool. Good views & attractively furnished s/c rooms. *US$20/40/30/60 sgl/dbl/twin/deluxe B&B.*

Budget

⌂ **Jopfan Country Hotel** (18 rooms) Close to the golf course on Makanga Hill; ☎04864 26055; m 0772 510973; e jopfancountryhotel@yahoo. com; www.traveluganda.co.ug/jopfancountryhotel. The grounds & outward views are inferior to the competition on Makanga, but it is reasonably priced. *US$18/30/30/37 s/c sgl/dbl/twin/exec B&B.*

⌂ **Hotel Queens** (8 rooms) ☎04864 24054. A couple of blocks behind the main street, this small

hotel has a smart façade & offers clean tiled rooms with hot showers. The bar provides DSTV, & tasty food costs around Ush12,000. *US$20 dbl.*

⌂ **Victoria Inn** (30 rooms) ☎04864 22154. The friendly Victoria Inn has a quiet back-road location only a couple of mins' walk from the town centre. The s/c rooms are basic & a little dated but are good value. *US$9/12 sgl/dbl B&B.*

⌂ **Capricon** (24 rooms) Kabale Rd; ☎0392 944996; www.capriconhotel.com. This new hotel is a distinct cut above anything else in the town centre. The smart, storied, main street premises has tiled rooms with nets & flat-screen TV, while the 1st-floor bar contains an uncommonly varied selection of wines & spirits. *US$20/28/40/60 s/c sgl/dbl/twin/deluxe.*

Shoestring

⌂ **Amagara Guesthouse aka Kabale Backpackers** (10 rooms) m 0702 421519; e basimarobert@gmail.com. This popular guesthouse lies down a grubby backstreet past the Edirisa Cultural Centre. It's great value, although noise from the nearby Pines nightclub could be a nuisance on some nights. A major incentive is the excellent, in-house Amagara Café (see opposite). Internet is available. *US$10/14 s/c sgl/dbl.*

⌂ **Edirisa Cultural Centre** (6 rooms) m 0752 558222; www.edirisa.org. This centrally located set-up (see page 250) extends to a small but popular backpacker hostel with a selection of individually sized rooms. Facilities include a lounge with book & DVD library, & an excellent menu of affordable meals served on a rather cool elevated deck. Proceeds support community development activities beside Lake Bunyonyi. *US$7/10/4 sgl/dbl/dorm bed with shared facilities, US$12 dbl to toilet.*

🏠 **Miami Tours & Travel** (8 rooms)The courtyard behind this popular lunchtime eatery contains decent rooms & spotless shared ablutions. *US$6/10/12 sgl/twin/dbl.*

🏠 **Skyline** (8 rooms) Katuna Rd junction. The pick of the town's conventional, courtyard-style shoestring guesthouses, this decent lodge has been hosting travellers for at least 20 years now &

is convenient for buses & taxis. Cheap & satisfying food is served on the premises. *US$6/10 s/c sgl+/dbl, US$6 twin with shared bathroom.*

🏠 **Hotel Home Again** (30 rooms) Kampala Rd One of the better storied shoestring lodges on Kampala Road on its way out of town. Home Again offers tiled rooms using common showers. A sauna/aerobics club at the rear is a popular spot for an evening beer & BBQ chicken. *US$6/8 sgl/dbl.*

🏠 **New Shade Tree** (8 rooms) Kabale Rd, opposite the turning to Hot Loaf & Edirisa. Provides decent-sized rooms with sgl beds & shared bathrooms. *US$4 sgl.*

✗ **WHERE TO EAT AND DRINK** For location of listings see map, pages 246–7.

✗ **Amagara Café** 📱 0772 959667. This excellent café attached to the Amagara Guesthouse (see opposite) offers daily specials taken from a diverse menu created by a long defunct expat-run restaurant. With a bit of notice, guests can order whatever they fancy from the full menu. The servings (of meat anyway) seem constrained by the bargain prices (*steak in wine Ush11,000*). Try offering a little more for a fuller portion.

✗ **Hot Loaf Bakery** Fresh bread & a variety of filling cakes, pies & pastries are baked daily.

✗ **Golf Side Campsite** Overlooking the golf course on the hill above the town centre, this attractive spot doesn't actually permit camping, but the wooden bar is a good spot for a drink. Local expats recommend the Indian menu highly.

✗ **Little Ritz Bar & Restaurant** Above Hot Loaf Bakery. This excellent restaurant serves a variety of Indian & continental dishes, & a good bar with DSTV is attached. Dine outside on the

breezy balcony or, if it's chilly, enjoy a drink by the warming log fire. *Meals Ush8,000–15,000.*

🍷 **Match & Mix** Kabale Rd. This large, multi-roomed bar on the main street is a lively place to drink & watch Premier League football on large, flat-screen TVs. Open until late.

✗ **Miami Tours & Travel** Kabale Rd, opposite the post office. The filling lunchtime buffet (*Ush15,000*) is clearly popular. See also, *Where to stay*, above.

✗ **Royal Café** Kabale Rd. I think the local volunteers who rave about this newish caff next to Royal supermarket appreciate the Indian dishes on the evening menu rather than the brownish, carpeted interior & the lunchtime fish 'n' cold chips. *Meals Ush10,000–20,000.*

✗ **White Horse Hotel** See opposite. This hilltop hotel serves acceptable grub & is a lovely spot to take lunch or an early dinner on the terrace & enjoy the large & immaculate gardens & views of the surrounding hills. *Main courses around Ush20,000.*

NIGHTLIFE Kabale's most popular nightclub is **Cheers Discoteque** [246 C4] on Nyerere Road. In its previous incarnation as Club Earthquake, I vaguely remember some rather bizarre murals suggesting a fascination amongst local youth for outrageously busty females and hinting at activities that suggest that the traditional Bakiga taboo concerning pre-marital relations is a thing of the past.

SHOPPING There are a couple of good supermarkets in Kabale, notably the **Royal supermarket** [246 C4] near the post office and the newer **Cash and Carry** [246 C4] just across the street. Don't miss the affordable blocks of excellent, locally made Belgian cheese. **Handicrafts** can be bought from the Edirisa Cultural Centre; see page 250.

OTHER PRACTICALITIES
Culture The **Edirisa Cultural Centre** ([246 B4] m *0752 558222; www.edirisa. org*), located opposite the Hot Loaf Bakery, is a non-profit organisation that strives to promote and preserve Bakiga culture. It was started several years ago by a Bakiga elder concerned at the erosion of his local culture and has developed with the help of young European volunteers into a community development project. Richard Curley writes that 'The operation offers four high-value features: (1) a serviceable fast-food take-away (the giant vegetable samosas are a real triumph); (2) guided tours of an authentic fully furnished old Bakiga roundhouse; (3)

FISHY TALES

According to the late Paul Ngologoza, an eminent Kigezi politician and historian, Lake Bunyonyi harboured 'no fish at all, just *encere*, which are edible frogs' prior to 1919. While this claim seems rather unlikely, several other sources do imply that Bunyonyi naturally harbours very low fish densities. Presumably, this is because the lake slopes underwater too sharply and deeply from the shoreline to provide suitable habitat for shallow-water species such as tilapia and Nile perch, which would have lived in the river before Bunyonyi became a lake.

Whatever the situation before 1919, great efforts were made to stock Lake Bunyonyi during the colonial era. The most valiant of these was initiated in 1927 by District Commissioner Trewin, who arranged for a volume of fish to be relayed manually from Lake Edward to Lake Bunyonyi. 'This was a very involved task,' writes Ngologoza,

'because of the difficulty created by fish dying in transit. Many people [were] divided into groups … The first group brought fish from a place called Katwe … This group raced at great speed to hand over the fish to the second group, who raced to hand over to the third group, and so on, putting in fresh water, pouring out the old water, and finally bringing them to Lake Bunyonyi. It took a day and a night to cover the distance of about 80 miles [120km].'

Initially, the introduced fish flourished, as did commercial fishing, and the rapidly multiplying schools were used to restock several other lakes in the region. Then, in the early 1950s, for reasons that remain unclear, they died out *en masse*, so that 'one might see the whole lake full of floating bodies of dead fish'. Following this disaster, Ngologoza himself experimented with digging a shallow pool next to the lake and stocking it with 50 fish, which rapidly reproduced, allowing him to distribute 4,500 fish to local fishermen, to be bred in the same way.

The only fish to thrive in the lake today is *Claria mozambicus*, known locally as *evale*, which forms an important component of the local subsistence diet. Bunyonyi is also well known for its small freshwater crayfish, a delicacy served in curries at most of the tourist resorts along the shore.

Quotes extracted from the late Paul Ngologoza's excellent and often amusing introduction to the history and culture of Kigezi entitled Kigezi and its People, *first published in 1967, reprinted by Fountain Publishers in 1998 and still widely available.*

honest, friendly advice about tourist activities and accommodation in the district, including field trips to Batwa villages; and most importantly (4), they now serve the best cup of coffee in Uganda outside of Kampala. In addition, there's a good gift shop, a library and sitting room.' It's a good place to park yourself for a few hours if you need to'. Edirisa supports community development activities beside Lake Bunyonyi.

Foreign exchange Stanbic [246 C3], **Crane** [246 B3] and **Barclays** [246 D5] will all change cash. Outside banking hours, try the **Highland Business Centre** [246 B2] (next to the Highland Inn), but expect poorer rates.

Internet Internet is available at the **Amagara Café** (see page 249; Ush1,000 for 30 minutes) and at **Gatatu Internet** opposite Hot Loaf.

WHAT TO SEE The most popular tourist attractions around Kabale are the nearby Lake Bunyonyi (see page 252) and more remote Bwindi and Mgahinga national parks (see pages 273 and 270), all covered under separate headings later in this chapter. The following more obscure sites might be of interest to those wanting to get away from the beaten track.

Hot springs There are some hot springs south of Kabale towards Katuna on the Rwandan border. Set in a eucalyptus stand, immediately to the left of the road from Kabale, the disappointing springs are no more than a muddy, lukewarm pool. To get there, either board a Katuna-bound pick-up truck and ask to be dropped at the springs, or else walk or cycle the 8km from Kabale. You can swim in the pool if you like – it's supposed to have therapeutic qualities, and you're bound to provide a few Ugandan bathers with some company and/or amusement.

Kisizi Waterfall This 30m-high waterfall lies on the Kyabamba River a few hundred metres from the Church of Uganda's Kisizi Hospital, some 65km from Kabale by road. It is a very pretty, peaceful spot, serviced by an excellent small guesthouse, and the surrounding forests and quiet roads offer pleasant rambling possibilities. The waterfall is used to provide hydro-electric power to the hospital – in Uganda's darker days, Kisizi was one of the few places countrywide that had a reliable 24-hour electricity supply and functional street lamps.

The tranquil atmosphere around the waterfall belies its macabre historical association with the local custom described somewhat euphemistically by one Ugandan source as 'damping'. In traditional Bakiga society, virginity was a highly prized asset and an unmarried girl who fell pregnant could, at best, hope to be a social outcast for the rest of her days. More often, however, the offender would be mortally punished: tied to a tree and left at the mercy of wild animals, thrown from a cliff, or abandoned to starve on an island. And many disgraced girls were 'damped' at Kisizi: tossed over the waterfall, arms and legs tightly bound, to drown in the pool below.

Getting there and away To reach Kisizi, follow the surfaced Kampala Road out of Kabale for 32km as far as Muhanga, from where a 33km dirt road leads north to the hospital and waterfall. The drive should take less than two hours in a **private vehicle**. Using public transport, regular **minibus-taxis** connect Kabale to Muhanga, from where a more erratic trickle of **pick-up trucks** bump their way to Kisizi.

7

Lake Bunyonyi, as its serpentine shape suggests, is essentially a flooded valley system, extending northwards from the Rwandan border over a distance of 25km through the contours of the steep hills that separate Kabale from Kisoro. It is thought to have formed about 8,000 years ago, as a result of a lava flow from local craters which blocked off the Ndego River at present-day Muko to create a natural dam. The lake has a total surface area of around 60km², but it forms the core of a 180km² wetland ecosystem, also incorporating the Ruvuma Swamp and several other permanent marshes. It lies at an altitude of 1,840m, but several of the enclosing hills rise up to 2,500m, and although reported estimates of its depth vary wildly, it is probably nowhere greater than 45m deep.

Dotted with at least 20 small islands and encircled by steep terraced hills, Bunyonyi is a magical spot, and it has been a popular day trip out of Kabale for decades. Over the past few years, the lake has further gained in popularity thanks to a proliferation of campsites and resorts around the small fishing village of Rutinda (also known as Kyabahinga) and nearby islands. Also in its favour is the

VISITING THE BATWA IN KIGEZI   *Derek Schuurman*

Of all Uganda's peoples, the one group visitors most wish to visit is the Batwa, the Pygmies indigenous to the dense rainforests of the southwest. But, while meeting a Batwa community is easily achievable, visitors should be aware of the current situation of this tiny, ostracised minority, which has no land rights or legal forest access, and remains subject to discrimination on local and institutional levels (see box, pages 258–9).

Arguably the best places in which to meet Batwa are the Mgahinga Gorilla and Bwindi national parks, where attendance at a Batwa music and dance performance is a reputable activity. One organisation currently working hard to address the plight of the Batwa is the **Forest Peoples Project (FPP)** (01608 652893; e info@fppwrm.gn.apc.org; www.forestpeoples.org), a UK-based charity that supports forest peoples' rights to determine their own future, to control the use of their lands, and to carry out sustainable use of the forest resources.

The five main goals of the FPP, aimed broadly at providing a voice for forest people, are as follows:

* To help establish an effective global movement of forest peoples.
* To promote the rights and interests of forest peoples in environmental and human rights circles.
* To co-ordinate support among environmental organisations for forest peoples'visions.
* To counter top-down projects which deprive local peoples of resources.
* To support community-based, sustainable forest management.

Presently, the FPP is working with the Batwa in southwest Uganda to help them support and defend themselves against the problems and injustices they face. Should you happen to witness any incident where Batwa are exploited or victimised, please contact the FPP and speak to your tour operator, who will follow up through the appropriate channels.

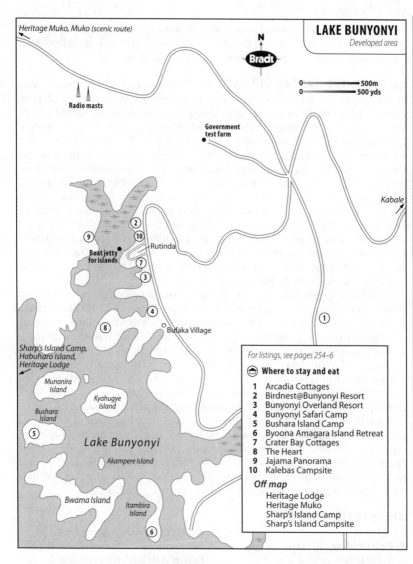

LAKE BUNYONYI
Developed area

Heritage Muko, Muko (scenic route)

Radio masts

Government test farm

Kabale

Rutinda

Boat jetty for islands

Bufaka Village

Sharp's Island Camp, Habuharo Island, Heritage Lodge

Munanira Island

Kyahugye Island

Bushara Island

Lake Bunyonyi

Akampere Island

Bwama Island

Itambira Island

0 ——————— 500m
0 ——————— 500 yds

For listings, see pages 254–6

Where to stay and eat

1   Arcadia Cottages
2   Birdnest@Bunyonyi Resort
3   Bunyonyi Overland Resort
4   Bunyonyi Safari Camp
5   Bushara Island Camp
6   Byoona Amagara Island Retreat
7   Crater Bay Cottages
8   The Heart
9   Jajama Panorama
10 Kalebas Campsite

Off map
Heritage Lodge
Heritage Muko
Sharp's Island Camp
Sharp's Island Campsite

high-altitude location, which ensures a moderate climate (often becoming quite chilly at night) and a relatively low incidence of malaria. Active travellers are catered for, with canoes, kayaks and mountain bikes available for hire, and enough potential excursions to keep busy for days. Swimming is also a pleasure, particularly since hippos and crocodiles are absent and the lake is widely held to be bilharzia free. That said, we've been contacted by parasite-ridden readers who are adamant that they contracted the disease at Lake Bunyonyi.

Bunyonyi translates as 'place of little birds', which is possibly a reference to the prolific weaver colonies along its shore, but larger birds are also represented by the likes of grey-crowned crane and a variety of herons and egrets. It is also probably the best place in Africa to see otters – the diurnal spotted-necked otter in particular – with several pairs resident around Rutinda and the nearby islands. It is difficult to say just why otters are so much more visible here than anywhere else I've visited in Africa, but it must be related to the absence of crocodiles, which would normally prey on and compete for prey with smaller aquatic carnivores.

GETTING THERE, AROUND AND AWAY An all-weather dirt road connects Kabale to Rutinda, the focal point of tourist activity on Lake Bunyonyi. If you're **driving** yourself, follow the Kisoro Road out of Kabale for 500m then, just beyond a filling station, turn left at a junction distinguished by several signposts to the various lakeshore resorts. After about 5km, the road reaches a five-way junction at the summit of the hill overlooking Lake Bunyonyi. The track on the left leads to Arcadia Cottages, while the road on the right takes a lovely (but narrow) 20km route along the lakeshore to Muko on the main Kabale–Kisoro road. Otherwise, keep going straight on for the 2km descent to Rutinda on the lakeshore. Motorists bound for island resorts will find safe overland parking here, either in compounds provided by their intended destination or for a small charge at Lake Bunyonyi Overland Camp.

For those without private transport, regular **minibus-taxis** and **pick-up trucks** run between Kabale and Rutinda on market days (Monday and Friday) but the service is somewhat more erratic on other days. A special hire to Rutinda should cost Ush20,000 and a **boda-boda** about half that.

It's also possible to **walk** to the lake along the road described above, with a slight chance of hitching a lift. A quieter, more scenic route involves following Butambuka Road west out of the town centre then following local footpaths – there are plenty of villagers around to point you in the right direction. Either way, the walk out is worthwhile in its own right, passing by traditional homesteads and patches of forest rustling with birdlife, and it should take the best part of two hours, involving a very stiff ascent as you approach the summit above the lake. One thing you don't want to do is hire a pushbike to get to Bunyonyi – unless you are exceptionally fit, you'll probably spend as much time pushing the bike up steep hills as you will cycling.

If you want to go out on the lake, or to spend a night or two at one of the islands, you can hire a **dugout** or **motorboat** from Rutinda jetty. Prices are negotiable, but expect to pay about Ush20,000 each way for the 15-minute motorboat trip to either Byoona Amagara or Bushara Island, or Ush6,000 per person for a 30- to 45-minute ride in a dugout canoe. Bushara Island is closer than Byoona Amagara, but it's a more expensive place. For location of listings see map, page 253.

WHERE TO STAY AND EAT
Upmarket

Birdnest@Bunyonyi Resort (14 rooms) m 0779 229870/0776 252560; e info@birdnestatbunyonyi.com; www.birdnestatbunyonyi.com. This once long-derelict 1970s hotel set in a quiet bay 1km before Rutindo village has been tastefully restored & expanded by Belgian investors. A lot of thought has gone into creating the lovely 1st- & 2nd-floor s/c rooms, though a higher power must take credit for the lake prospect visible through the sliding doors & from the private balconies. My notes say 'meticulously colour-themed, crisp modernist lines with a nod to the safari setting' – the sort of thing I'm capable of with a cold sundowner beer on a delightful terrace with a terrific view. Less cryptically I've also got 'wide ranging menu with equally diverse wine list'. For more on the hotel's history, see pages 256–7. *US$120/130 sgl/dbl B&B.*

Heritage Lodge (7 tents, 1 family cottage) 0312 265454; e reservations@heritagelodgesuganda.com; www.heritagelodgesuganda.com. Over on the secluded Habuharo Island, on the western side of the lake, this comfortable tented camp enjoys a lovely garden setting. Lawns & flowering plants, laid out beneath mature trees, slope down to the lake from an open-sided lounge & dining area; the latter are well laid out & tastefully decorated with local artefacts. In such an idyllic setting you'll be disposed to overlook any managerial shortcomings. Free motorboat transfer for guests. *US$100/160 sgl/dbl s/c tents, US$350 family cottage FB.*

Moderate

⌂ **Arcadia Cottages** (11 cottages) ✆04864 26231; m 0772 981155/0782 424232; e arcadiacottages@yahoo.com; www. arcadiacottages.net. The outlook from this pleasant ridgetop lodge, high above Lake Bunyonyi, must surely appear in some Top 50 list of panoramas to see before you die or are otherwise incapacitated. Arcadia enjoys a truly sensational, indeed surreal, almost map-like view of the lake & its myriad islands. From Kabale, turn left at the 5-way junction at the ridgetop viewpoint for about 2km. *US$60/73 sgl/dbl B&B.*

⌂ **Jajama Panorama** (10 rooms) m 0772 361434; e www.jajamapanorama. com. Conveniently sited directly across the bay from Rutinda, a couple of mins by motorboat or 5mins' paddle. Brick-floored s/c *bandas* & a large, open-sided dining/lounge building face the lake. *US$50pp B&B.*

Budget

⌂ **Byoona Amagara Island Retreat** m 0752 652788; e bookings@lakebunyonyi.net; www. lakebunyonyi.net. A popular getaway for budget travellers, the most southerly of the Lake Bunyonyi resorts is distanced from the relative bustle of Rutinda. A range of accommodation is available, the most popular option being the 'geodomes', fresh-air arrangements consisting of a round thatched roof & a rear wall over twin or dbl beds (nets provided). Byoona Amagara has a private compound for guests' parking at Rutinda. *US$70 s/c Family Cottage (sleeps 5), US$28pp for s/c Wood Cabin (sleeps 5), US$24/48 sgl/dbl basic geodome, US$32/64 s/c sgl/dbl deluxe geodome, US$6–8 dorm beds, US$4 camping. High season rates stated.*

⌂ **Bunyonyi Safari Camp** (36 rooms) ✆0486 23100; m 0772 507311; e info@bunyonyisafaris. com; www.bunyonyi.com. This large, 3-storied development lies in the next bay along from Overland Resort. The large, open-plan public area & the spacious, s/c parquet-floored rooms cater for those who prefer conventional hotels to rustic tents & cottages. There are, however, 6 cottages in the grounds. *US$64 B&B sgl/dbl for rooms & cottages.*

⌂ **Crater Bay Cottages** ✆04864 26255; m 0772 643996/671458; e craterbay@yahoo.com; www.craterbaycottagelakebunyonyi.com. Situated within Rutinda on the opposite side of the same small bay as the Overland Resort, this lodge offers a row of clean & comfortably furnished round s/c cottages set in compact flowering grounds that drop down to the lake. Rather lacks the ambience of the Overland Resort, but it's friendly, quiet & uncrowded. *US$50 old cottages, US$60, US$10/20 sgl/dbl using common shower, US$4pp camping.*

⌂ **Bunyonyi Overland Resort** ✆04864 26016; m 0772 409510; e highland@imul.com, resort@ bunyonyioverland.com; www.bunyonyioverland. com. Overland Resort, on the edge of Rutinda village, represents the heart of Lake Bunyonyi tourism, insofar as everything else is compared (for better or worse) with this justifiably popular set-up. The resort sprawls down a terraced green slope to a lovely papyrus-fringed bay. Facilities include an open-sided restaurant/bar that serves affordable meals & has DSTV & a small curio shop, & inexpensive canoe (*US$5/day*) & mountain-bike (*US$10/day*) hire. Away from the main camping area is a row of comfortable s/c twin chalets & smaller twin rooms using common showers as well as furnished tents. It's a truly excellent setup for which the only criticism is a function of its high quality – up to 5 overland trucks might congregate on a busy night, a scenario that can be off-putting to independent travellers. *US$30/40/100 sgl/ dbl/family unit chalets, US$23/40 sgl/dbl rooms, US$20/25 sgl/dbl furnished tents, US$6/8/10pp own tent/rented tent/tent with bedding.*

⌂ **Sharp's Island Camp** (8 units) m 0773 149752/0772 524139; e kdwd@infocom.co.ug. This pleasant, low-key retreat occupies the island home of Dr Leonard Sharp, who established the leper colony on nearby Bwama Island in 1929. Though the interior of the refurbished house – not the original, but pretty old all the same – lacks warmth, it stands in a pretty garden containing aged flowering trees & young ones planted in 2008 by the doctor's grandson. An interesting history is displayed, with a terrific map of the lake drawn in *Swallows & Amazons* style: the work of the doctor's children who roamed Bunyonyi in the manner of Arthur Ransome's characters in the English Lake District. *US$22/40/50 sgl/dbl/trpl for ordinary s/c rooms & furnished s/c tents, US$6pp per tent camping.*

⌂ **Bushara Island Camp** (10 units)
m 0772 464585; e busharaisland@africaonline.
co.ug; www.acts.ca/lbdc. The medium-sized
island of Bushara, which lies about 10mins from
Rutinda by motorboat, has been developed as
a community-run resort with the assistance of
Canadian missionaries. It's come a long way since
its 1st incarnation in 1993 when a few cramped
standing tents were crammed with rickety beds to
create a 'furnished tented camp'. Today, a selection
of s/c furnished tents, cottages & a 'tree house'
(a slightly elevated wooden cabin) are offered.
Accommodation set in secondary vegetation
along the southern side of the island is preferable
to that located within the eucalyptus forest on
the northern slopes. A bird list is available for
the 100-plus bird species recorded on the island.
Day visitors are also welcome. The camp's own
motorboat provides free transfers for overnight
guests from Rutinda jetty. Internet is available to
keep you in touch with the world beyond. *US$60pp
cottages & tents FB, US$6pp camping.*

Shoestring

⌂ **The Heart** (4 rooms) m 0752 558222;
e volunteer@edirisa.org. Run by Edirisa, a
Bunyonyi-based cultural NGO, The Heart provides
lakeshore accommodation in clean but decidedly
traditional cottages for short- & long-term
volunteers helping at 2 nearby schools, 1 of which
involves an attractive commute by dugout canoe.
For more on Edirisa, visit www.gorillahighlands.
com/trail & www.canoetrekking.com. *US$7pp
excl food.*

Camping

⋏ **Heritage Muko** ☎ 0312 265454;
e reservations@heritagelodgesuganda.com;
www.heritagelodgesuganda.com. This campsite
enjoys a beautiful location at the Lake Bunyonyi
outflow close to the Kabale–Kisoro highway.
Though a couple of furnished s/c tents are
provided, they are placed unappealing, just
metres from the main road & cost *US$80/100 B&B.
camping US$5 per tent*

The most popular place to pitch a tent at Rutinda is the **Lake Bunyonyi Overland Resort** (see above), & in most respects this is also probably the best option, though nearby **Kalebas** and **Crater Bay** (see above) might be quieter. Campers are also welcomed out on the lake at Bushara Island, Sharp's Island & Byoona Amagara.

WHAT TO SEE AND DO Lake Bunyonyi and surrounds offer numerous opportunities for organised excursions and casual exploration. Visits to most of the places of interest described below can be arranged through the lakeshore resorts and hotels, and it's also possible to reach some sites using public transport and/or dugout canoes chartered at a negotiable rate from the jetty at Rutinda.

Canoe safaris The Kabale-/Bunyonyi-based cultural organisation **Edirisa** (m *0752 558084; www.edirisa.org; see page 250*) runs combined paddling and hiking excursions on and around Lake Bunyonyi. Options range from five-hour trips to one-, two- or three-night expeditions with nights spent at pretty lakeshore and island campsites. Edirisa also offers the chance to experience a day in the life of local craftswomen.

The lakeshore near Rutinda Rutinda itself, though rather small and humdrum, is considerably enlivened on Mondays and Fridays, when dozens of canoes arrive in the early morning from all around the lake, carrying local farmers and their produce to a colourful **market** on the main jetty.

A pleasant short stroll from Rutinda leads north along the lakeshore, following the Kabale Road for roughly 1km before it begins the steep ascent to the summit above the lake. The smart **Birdnest Hotel** (see page 254), shortly before this ascent, has had a chequered history. Back in 1965 it opened as the Bunyonyi Lake View Resort, owned by Frank Kalimuzo, a Kigezi-born politician who served as the permanent secretary to the prime minister in the first Obote government and was appointed Vice Chancellor of Makerere University in Kampala in 1969. It closed in 1972, after Amin's soldiers (or, as the official explanation had it at the time, 'men masquerading as security officers') abducted and permanently silenced Kalimuzo on suspicion of being a Rwandan spy. The building, which is still owned by Kalimuzo's family, stood empty for many years before being restored and extended by Belgian investors to create the splendid hotel you see today. Just beyond the hotel, the road skirts a patch of papyrus swamp where various colourful bishop- and widow-birds breed and a few pairs of the peculiar thick-billed weaver construct their distinctive neat nests. From here, more energetic travellers could ascend to the top of the steep hills, via a series of switchbacks, to the five-way junction at the summit. Turn right here, and after about 2km you'll reach **Arcadia Cottages** (see page 255), with its stunning view over the lake and islands. Using local footpaths, it's possible to descend directly from here to Bufuka, on the lakeshore about 1km south of Rutinda, but the paths are very steep and probably best avoided after rain.

The islands Several of the 20-plus islands on Bunyonyi are worth a visit, with the most accessible being the half-dozen or so situated in the central part of the lake close to Rutinda. Aside from Bushara Island, which uses its own motorboat for transfers, the best way to reach most of the islands is by dugout canoe, easily arranged with local fishermen at Rutinda jetty.

Bwama Island is the largest on Lake Bunyonyi and the site of a well-known mission, school and handicraft centre for the disabled. Most of the buildings on Bwama date to 1929, when Leonard Sharp, a British doctor with several years' medical experience in southwest Uganda, established a leper colony on the island. Leprosy was a serious problem in Kigezi at that time, and for longer than three decades the island provided refuge to up to 100 victims of the disease. Leprosy was eradicated from Kigezi in the 1960s and the colony ceased operating in 1969. The island remains of interest for its scenery, architecture and handicraft shop, and it's possible to camp or rent a room at Byoona Amagara on neighbouring **Itambira Island**. The trip from Rutinda takes about 30 minutes in a local canoe.

Immediately north of Bwama, **Bushara Island** is well developed for tourism, and although the accommodation is highly recommended, day trips are also encouraged. The ideal would be to go to the island for a lingering lunch, then either arrange to take a dugout canoe around its circumference or else to walk the self-guided trail along the shore – both options cost day visitors US$2–3.

Shaded by a solitary tree, the tiny **Akampene Island** – Island of Punishment – is visible both from the north shore of Bwama and the east shore of Bushara. Like Kisizi Falls, this island is traditionally associated with the Bakiga taboo against pre-marital sex. In times gone by, unmarried girls who became pregnant would be exiled to Akampene, where they faced one of two possible fates. Any man who did not own sufficient cows to pay for an untainted bride was permitted to fetch the disgraced girl from the island and make her his wife. Failing that, the girl would usually starve to death.

A somewhat more fanciful legend is attached to the nearby island of **Akabucuranuka**, the name of which literally means 'upside down'. Many years ago, it is said, a group of male revellers on Akabucuranuka refused to share their abundant stock of beer with an old lady who had disembarked from her canoe to join them. Unfortunately for the drinking party, the woman was a sorceress. She returned to her canoe, paddled a safe distance away, and then used her magical powers to overturn the island – drowning everybody in the party – and then flip it back the right way up as if nothing had happened.

We have always lived in the forest. Like my father and grandfathers, I lived from hunting and collecting in this mountain. Then the Bahutu came. They cut the forest to cultivate the land. They carried on cutting and planting until they had encircled our forest with their fields. Today, they come right up to our huts. Instead of forest, now we are surrounded by Irish potatoes!

Gahut Gahuliro, a Mutwa born 100 years earlier on the slopes of the Virungas,
talking in 1999

The Batwa (singular Mutwa) Pygmies are the most ancient inhabitants of interlacustrine Africa, and easily distinguished from other Ugandans by their unusually short stature – an adult male seldom exceeds 1.5m in height – and paler, more bronzed complexion. Semi-nomadic by inclination, small egalitarian communities of Batwa kin traditionally live in impermanent encampments of flimsy leaf huts, set in a forest clearing, which they will up and leave when food becomes scarce locally, upon the death of a community member, or when the whim takes them. In times past, the Batwa wore only a drape of animal hide or barkcloth, and had little desire to accumulate possessions – a few cooking pots, some hunting gear, and that's about it.

The Batwa lifestyle is based around hunting, undertaken as a team effort by the male members of a community. In some areas, the favoured *modus operandi* involves part of the hunting party stringing a long net between a few trees, while the remainder advances noisily to herd small game into the net to be speared. In other areas, poisoned arrows are favoured: the hunting party will move silently along the forest floor looking for prey, which is shot from a distance; then they wait until it drops and if necessary deliver the final blow with a spear. Batwa men also gather wild honey, while the women gather edible plants to supplement the meat.

According to a survey undertaken in 1996, fewer than 2,000 Batwa reside permanently in Uganda, mostly concentrated in Kigezi. Only 2,000 years ago, however, East and southern Africa were populated almost solely by Batwa and related hunter-gatherers, whose lifestyle differed little from that of our earliest common human ancestors. Since then, agriculturist and pastoralist settlers, through persecution or assimilation, have marginalised the region's hunter-gatherers to a few small, and today mostly degraded, communities living in habitats unsuitable to agriculture or pasture, such as rainforest interiors and deserts.

The initial incursions into Batwa territory were made when the Bantu-speaking farmers settled in Kigezi, sometime before the 16th century, and set about clearing small tracts of forest for subsistence agriculture and pasture. This process of deforestation was greatly accelerated in the early 20th century: by 1930 the last three substantial tracts of forest remaining in Kigezi were gazetted as the Impenetrable and Echuya forest reserves and Gorilla Game Sanctuary by the colonial authorities. In one sense, this move to protect the forests was of direct benefit to the Batwa, since it ensured that what little remained of them would not be lost to agriculture. But the legal status of the Batwa was altered to their detriment – true, they were still permitted to hunt and forage within the reserves, but where formerly these forests had been recognised as Batwa communal land, they were now government property.

Only some three generations later would the Batwa be faced with the full ramifications of having lost all legal entitlement to their ancestral lands. In 1991, the Gorilla Game Sanctuary and Impenetrable Forest Reserve were re-gazetted to become Mgahinga and Bwindi national parks, a move backed by international donors who stipulated that all persons resident within the national parks were to be evicted, and that hunting and other forest harvesting should cease. Good news for gorillas, perhaps, but what about those Batwa communities that had dwelt within the forest reserves for centuries? Overnight, they were reduced in status to illegal squatters whose traditional subsistence lifestyle had been criminalised. Adding insult to injury, while some compensation was awarded to non-Batwa farmers who had settled within the forest since the 1930s and illegally cleared forest for cultivation, the evicted Batwa received compensation only if they had destroyed part of the forest reserve in a similar manner.

Today, more than 80% of Uganda's Batwa are officially landless, and none has legal access to the forest on which their traditional livelihood depends. Locally, the Batwa are viewed not with sympathy, but rather as objects of ridicule, subject to regular unprovoked attacks that occasionally lead to fatalities. The extent of local prejudice against the Batwa can be garnered from a set of interviews posted on the website www.edirisa.org. The Batwa, report some of their Bakiga neighbours, 'smoke marijuana … like alcohol … drink too much … make noise all night long … eat too much food … cannot grow their own food and crops … depend on hunting and begging … don't care about their children … the man makes love to his wife while the children sleep on their side' – a collection of circumstantially induced half-truths and outright fallacies that make the Batwa come across as the debauched survivors of a dysfunctional hippie commune!

Prejudice against the Batwa is not confined to their immediate neighbours. The 1997 edition of Richard Nzita's otherwise commendable *Peoples and Cultures of Uganda* contrives, in the space of two pages, to characterise the pygmoid peoples of Uganda as beggars, crop raiders and pottery thieves – even cannibals! Conservationists and the Western media, meanwhile, persistently stigmatise the Batwa as gorilla hunters and poachers – this despite the strong taboo against killing or eating gorillas that informs every known Batwa community. Almost certainly, any gorilla hunting that might be undertaken by the Batwa today will have been instigated by outsiders.

This much is incontestable: the Batwa and their hunter-gatherer ancestors have in all probability inhabited the forests of Kigezi for some half-a-million years. Their traditional lifestyle, which places no rigorous demands on the forest, could be cited as a model of that professed holy grail of modern conservationists: the sustainable use of natural resources. The Batwa were not major participants in the deforestation of Kigezi, but they have certainly been the main human victims of this loss. And Batwa and gorillas cohabited in the same forests for many millennia prior to their futures both being imperilled by identical external causes in the 20th century. As Jerome Lewis writes: 'They and their way of life are entitled to as much consideration and respect as other ways of life. There was and is nothing to be condemned in forest nomadism … The Batwa … used the environment without destroying or seriously damaging it. It is only through their long-term custody of the area that later comers have good land to use'.

Quotes from Lewis and Gahuliro are sourced from Jerome Lewis's report Batwa Pygmies of the Great Lakes Region, *downloadable at www.minorityrights. org/ admin/Download/Pdf/Batwa%2520Report.pdf. See also box, page 252.*

Muko Forest Reserve and Ruvuma Swamp (*Bushara Island Camp charges US$25 for a motorboat plus US$4pp for a 6hr guided excursion; the same trip can be done over a full day, more cheaply, by chartering a dugout canoe from Rutinda*) The small trading centre of Muko, on the northern tip of Bunyonyi, is the site of the vast papyrus expanses of Ruvuma Swamp, formed as the Ndego River flows out of the lake. Prior to the 1940s, the area around Muko was densely forested, and harboured a large population of elephants and other wildlife, but much of the indigenous vegetation was cleared in 1941 to make way for plantations of cypress and other conifers, and the large animals are long gone too. The neat plantations, which still dominate the scenery today, are of limited interest. Not so Ruvuma Swamp, which is one of the best places in Uganda to see a good variety of birds endemic to this habitat, including papyrus gonolek, papyrus canary and papyrus yellow warbler.

Muko lies along the main 80km road between Kabale and Kisoro, roughly equidistant from either town, and one elevated stretch of road affords good views over the swamps. A slightly rougher but shorter back road, roughly 20km long, runs north from the five-way junction on the hills above Rutinda to connect with the Kabale–Kisoro road at Muko, offering some fantastic views over the northern part of the lake. There is a fair amount of public transport along the main Kabale–Kisoro road, but little or none along the back route. It is also possible to visit Muko from Rutinda by boat. There is no accommodation at Muko and the campsite that formerly operated within the forest reserve has closed.

Batwa Pygmies In the pre-colonial era, Kigezi – and in particular the present-day Echuya Forest Reserve and Bwindi National Park – supported a significant population of Batwa hunter-gatherers, an ancient pygmoid people who traditionally foraged mainly within the interior of forests (see box, pages 258–9). The lifestyle of Kigezi's Batwa has subsequently been compromised by several factors, ranging from forest clearance to intermarriage with neighbouring tribes to misplaced missionary zeal. Most significant, perhaps, was the forced resettlement of Batwa living in forest reserves and national parks, coupled with tight restrictions on their utilisation of traditional resources within these protected areas, which occurred during the colonial and post-independence eras. Today, an estimated 1,700 Batwa eke out a peripheral existence in Kigezi, many of them living in artificial villages outside their preferred forest home.

If you want to visit the Batwa, I'd get in touch with **Edirisa** (*www.edirisa.org; see page 250*) for details. You'll at least be sure that Batwa will benefit from any visit and won't be ripped off by a local middle man. Batwa visits usually occur at Rubanga on the other side of the lake from Rutinda. It is pointless making your own way there (via a southerly road from Muko) hoping to meet Batwa. They live on the higher slopes on the edge of Echuya Forest Reserve and only descend to Ruhanga by arrangement.

KISORO AND AROUND

The amorphous and scruffy town of Kisoro, situated at the base of the Virunga Mountains, appears to have grown significantly in recent years, presumably as a result of its proximity to the borders with Rwanda and the DRC, and sporadic influxes of refugees from both of these countries. As with so many towns in Uganda, Kisoro is a pleasant enough place with good facilities, but it is of little inherent interest to travellers. Should you be passing through at the right time of week, the enormous Monday and Thursday markets along the Kabale Road are emphatically worth a look. Whenever you visit Kisoro, you may be approached about whether you want to visit a local Pygmy (Batwa) community, who have been evicted from the forest to eke out an existence in a block of stable-like rooms supplemented by bivouacs of plastic sheeting behind the district offices. Your answer to this query should be no. This filthy and insanitary setting is no place to gain an even faintly accurate impression of the rich culture of Uganda's oldest extant ethnic group. Instead, visit Kisoro's UWA office for details of more mutually rewarding activities, such as the Batwa Trail in Mgahinga Gorilla National Park (see pages 270–3) and Buniga Forest Trail at Bwindi's Nkuringo trailhead.

What Kisoro lacks in intrinsic appeal is made up for by the utterly stupendous backdrops formed by the tall volcanic peaks of the Virungas to the south, and green hills rolling out of town in every other direction. The town is also an important travel hub, passed through by all travellers who intend to visit Mgahinga National Park, and a popular springboard for cross-border gorilla tracking excursions in Rwanda's Parc National des Volcans and (when security permits) the Congolese gorilla sanctuary at Djombe. Even if you have no intention of tracking gorillas, the undulating countryside is studded with lakes, caves and craters that make ideal goals for off-the-beaten-track day walks.

The prospect of a night in Kisoro is gaining popularity as an economical option before tracking gorillas from Bwindi's Nkuringo or Rushaga trailheads, both of which are only a little over an hour's drive away. Kisoro has hosted plenty of Mgahinga-bound gorilla trackers over the years though for less obvious reasons, given that a cheap and beautifully located community campground lies just outside the park gate.

LAKE KAGEZI

In 1910, Captain Coote was dispatched to the far southwest of Uganda to establish the first British government station in the region. He built the station next to a lake called Kagezi, a site that would be abandoned two years later in favour of Ikumba (near the present-day junction to Ruhija along the main Kabale–Kisoro road). But the name of Coote's short-lived station stuck and – bastardised to Kigezi – it would eventually be applied formally to the southwestern administrative district of Uganda. During the Amin era, the original Kigezi District was divided into two administrative components and in 1980 it was further subdivided and renamed to become the present-day districts of Kabale, Kisoro, Kanungu and Rukungiri. The name Kigezi thus has little historical validity, and it has also fallen into official disuse. Nevertheless, most locals still refer to the above four districts collectively as Kigezi.

On our 2002 trip to Uganda, we couldn't resist the temptation to seek out the lake for which Kigezi is named. For those who are interested, it's easy enough to reach, situated only 800m from the Kisoro–Kabale road along a rough track leading north from alongside a conspicuous church. Whether the short diversion is worth the effort is another question. Lake Kagezi – or the lake we were shown, anyway – is little more than a grassy seasonal swamp, set in an approximately circular small depression, possibly an extinct crater, and no more than 200m in diameter. And no trace of any former government building remains either. Bizarrely, when we asked one passing local for confirmation that we were indeed looking at the legendary Kagezi, he nodded in proud agreement and expansively proclaimed the vegetated puddle to be the deepest lake in the whole of Uganda.

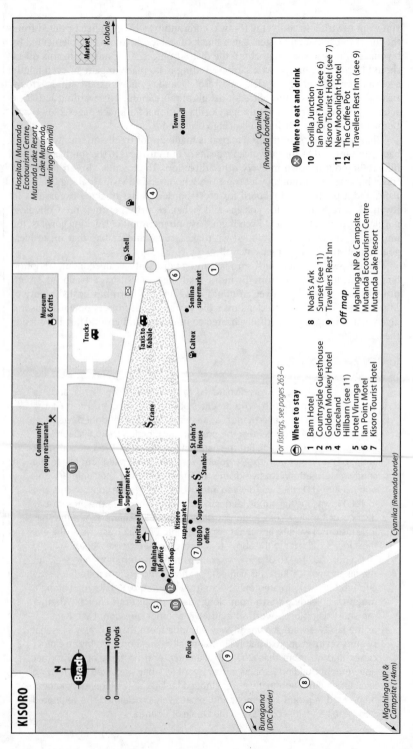

KISORO

N

0   100m
0   100yds

Bradt

Kabale ↑

Market

Hospital, Mutanda
Ecotourism Centre,
Mutanda Lake Resort,
Lake Mutanda,
Nkuringo (Bwindi)

Shell

Town
council

Cyanika
(Rwanda border)

Museum
& Crafts

Community
group restaurant

Imperial
Supermarket

Heritage Inn

Mgahinga
NP office
Craft shop

Trucks

Taxis to
Kabale

$ Crane

Caltex

Senlina
supermarket

St John's
House
Stanbic

Kisoro
supermarket
$ Supermarket
UOBDO
office

Police

Bunagana
(DRC border)

Mgahinga NP &
Campsite (14km)

Cyanika (Rwanda border)

For listings, see pages 263–6

GETTING THERE AND AWAY Kisoro lies little more than 30km west of Kabale as the crow flies, but the distance by road is more than 80km, thanks to the obstacle presented by Lake Bunyonyi. The road has recently been tarmacked, making the journey infinitely more comfortable and enjoyable. However, the route remains extremely windy and the journey will still take the sensible driver the best part of two hours. Nor is there any reason to hurry for the Kabale–Kisoro highway is arguably the most scenic in the whole country. Highlights include the drive through the bamboo and montane forest of the Echuya Forest Reserve, elevated views over Lake Bunyonyi and the Virunga panorama from the lofty Kanaba Gap.

From Kabale, follow the main road through town out past the Highland Inn and the turn-off to Lake Bunyonyi. After roughly 20km, the turn-off to Bwindi's Buhoma Gate is signposted on your right and after another 5km or so, the turn-off to Ruhija. Roughly 40km past Kabale, the road skirts the northern tip of Lake Bunyonyi, and then crosses the Ndego River, shortly before reaching Muko trading centre. An alternative – and more scenic – but narrow route to Muko branches north from the five-way junction on the summit above Rutinda on Lake Bunyonyi.

Several **buses** run daily between Kampala and Kisoro. The conservative choice is the **Post Bus**, though with numerous stops along the way, it is far from being the fastest. Of the private options, the **Bismarken bus** seems to be the current choice of foreign residents and volunteers in Kisoro. These leave the capital around 08.00 and Kisoro at 05.00. Tickets cost Ush30,000. More locally, a few **minibus-taxis** and overcrowded **pick-up trucks** run between Kabale and Kisoro every day, leaving when they are full.

TOURIST INFORMATION The **Mgahinga National Park office** at the western end of town provides information about the national park as well as other tourist attractions in the region. You can obtain a Mgahinga gorilla tracking permit here, as well as contacts for reliable local guides, and advice concerning transport to Mgahinga, and the Nkuringo and Rushaga gorilla tracking trailheads in Bwindi.

WHERE TO STAY When using water in your hotel or lodge, be aware that Kisoro suffers from a chronic water shortage. The plains at the base of the Virungas overlie porous volcanic rock with the result that streams flowing down from the volcanoes soon vanish underground, as does rainfall.

For an upmarket accommodation option, you will have to head out towards Mgahinga National Park and the **Mount Gahinga Lodge** (see page 271). For location of listings see map, page 248.

Moderate

⌂ **Mutanda Lake Resort** (13 cottages) m 078 9951943 (lodge); ☏ 075 1057863 (Matoke Tours); e mutandalakeresort@gmail.com; www.lake-mutanda.com. Located on the shore of Lake Mutanda between Kisoro & the southern Bwindi gorilla tracking trailheads, this lodge enjoys a stupendous southerly outlook so be sure to insist on a cottage facing in this direction. You could cross continents without finding a panorama to compare with the view across these peaceful, island-studded waters towards the Virunga volcanoes. In contrast, the interiors of the s/c lakeside cottages seemed rather

ordinary but expect this issue to be resolved by the time you read this following the 2013 takeover of NSL by Kampala-based & Dutch-owned safari company, Matoke Tours. Camping facilities are also planned. See also advert on page 238. *US$100/140/200 sgl/dbl/trp B&B. Discounts for East Africa residents.*
⌂ **Travellers Rest Inn** (11 rooms) m 0772 533029; e postmaster@gorillatours.com; www.gorillatours.com. Kisoro's oldest old hotel was built & managed in the 1950s by gorilla enthusiast Walter Baumgartel, & formed the 1st hub of gorilla-tracking activities in the Virungas – hosting such eminent personages as George Schaller

& Dian Fossey – until it was taken over by the government during the Amin era. Restored in the late 1990s, Travellers Rest is located in pretty gardens at the turn-off to Mgahinga National Park. A good 4-course dinner costs Ush30,000. *US$70/80 sgl/dbl/suite inc a good b/fast.*

🏠 **Kisoro Tourist Hotel** (16 rooms) 📞04864 30135. This smart & centrally located multi-storey hotel can be found close to the national park office. The grounds & public areas lack the individuality of the Travellers Rest, but the s/c rooms are large & airy with tiled floors, DSTV & hot showers. *US$60/80 sgl/dbl.*

Budget

🏠 **Golden Monkey Hotel** (12 rooms) m 0772 435148; e amajamcamp@yahoo.com. Located behind the UWA offices, this small lodge offers rather more atmosphere & warmth than the competition. Decorated with murals, providing a tourist information point & curio shop, & quoting over-the-odds rates in dollars, Golden Monkey is clearly set up for the local backpacker market. Food is best ordered in advance. Local excursions arranged. *US$28/35/25 sgl/dbl/twin s/c, US$20 twin, US$10 dorm bed.*

🏠 **Hotel Virunga** (15 rooms) 📞04864 30109; m 0782 360820; e snakeafrica@yahoo.co.uk. A long-established favourite with budget travellers, the Virunga can provide information & arrange local excursions. A pleasant restaurant serving Ugandan dishes is attached. Secure compound parking. *US$16 dbl with common showers, US$20 s/c dbl, US$3pp camping.*

🏠 **Countryside Guesthouse** (12 rooms) m 0781 570884. On the western edge of town, & with clean rooms & a restaurant. *US$14/20/22 s/c sgl+/dbl/twin, US$7.50 sgl+ with shared showers, US$2.50 camping.*

🏠 **Mutanda Ecotourism Centre** m 0772 435148/0712 435148; e amajamcamp@yahoo. com. This development, a partnership between a

GORILLA TRACKING IN RWANDA

Volcanoes National Park (VNP), which protects the Rwandan section of the Virungas, is a popular goal for fly-in and cross-border gorilla-tracking tourists. Coming from Uganda, tracking in VNP necessitates a stop of at least one night in Rwanda, either at the gateway town of Musanze (formerly known as Ruhengeri) or at one of the lodges near the Kinigi Park headquarters, 20 minutes' drive further north.

VNP harbours at least half of the Virunga's estimated 480 mountain gorillas, and each of eight habituated groups can be visited by eight tourists every morning, meaning that 64 permits are available daily. These gorilla tracking permits cost US$750 each, and advance booking is usually necessary, particularly during the peak season of June to September, and over holiday periods. Booking can be made through any tour operator, or directly through the **Rwanda Development Board (RDB)** office on Boulevard de l'Umuganda in the capital Kigali (📞 *0252 576514/573396*; e *reservation@rwandatourism.com; www.rwandatourism.com*). If you're prepared to risk non-availability, it is also possible to pitch up at the park headquarters at Kinigi the day before you want to track, and to buy a permit on the spot.

Trackers assemble at Kinigi at 07.00 (or 08.00 coming from Uganda, which is an hour behind). Kinigi lies about 20 minutes' drive from Musanze, which is situated 40km from Kisoro via the Cyanika border post. The road between Cyanika and Musanze is covered by plenty of public transport, though you may need to change vehicles at the border. Bilateral agreements currently allow nationals of Burundi, Canada, DR Congo, Germany, Hong Kong, Kenya, Mauritius, Singapore, South Africa, Sweden, Tanzania, Uganda, UK and USA to visit Rwanda without a visa for a period of up to 90 days. Visas must be obtained in advance by all other nationals, either through the nearest Rwandan consulate, or online at www.migration.gov.rw (click on 'public forms' then 'single entry visa'). Independent travellers will need to charter transport from Musanze

local tourism entrepreneur & a Swede, occupies a stunning location on the southern shores of Lake Mutanda. *US$20 log cottage, US$15 walk-in tents, US$3 camping.*

🏠 **Bam Hotel** (28 rooms) m 0756 565665; e bamkisoro@gmail.com. This new storied hotel stands a little way behind the main road, conveniently located for the early morning buses & the mosque. Simon Turner, roaming apiarist for Malaika Honey, informs us that neither of these are particularly intrusive. Perhaps Simon's as deaf as he is budget-conscious but he rates the Bam as the best deal in town. Secure compound parking. *US$10/18/12 sgl/dbl/twin.*

Shoestring Several courtyard-style lodges are located on Mutanda Road, around the corner from the Golden Monkey and Virunga hotels. Local in style, rather than tweaked and priced for tourists, the most acceptable seem to be the **Sunset** and **Hillbarn** near the New Moonlight Hotel. **Graceland** on the main road on the Kabale side of town is also recommended. Another possibility is **Ian Point Motel** (m *0772 412509; US$14 s/c dbl rooms with nets & TV, US$8 twin with shared showers*), which is centrally located with a good restaurant attached.

Camping Camping is possible at **Countryside Guesthouse**, **Mutanda Ecotourism Centre** and the **Community Campground** at the Mgahinga National Park gate.

✖ **WHERE TO EAT** Historically, it was unwise to expect too much from Kisoro's eateries but this has suddenly changed. The best (and costliest) hotel fare is found

to whichever trailhead they will be using, which will cost at least US$100 per group for the round trip.

The closest accommodation option to Kinigi, a few minutes' walk from the park headquarters, is the **Kinigi Guest House** (↘ *0252 547156;* m *078 8433606/8461913;* e *kinigi2020@yahoo.fr; www.rwanda-kinigi-guesthouse.com; US$22/26 sgl/dbl or US$8 for a bed in a 4-berth dorm*). A more luxurious out-of-town option is **Virunga Lodge** (↘ *0252 502452; www.volcanoessafaris. com*), which boasts one of the most stunning locations in Africa, on a hilltop overlooking lakes Burera and Ruhondo. There are also several lodges in Musanze, including the upmarket **Hotel Gorillas Musanze** (↘ *0252 546700;* m *078 8425653;* e *reservation@gorillashotels.com; www.gorillashotels.com; US$90/110 sgl/dbl*), the moderate **Hotel Muhabura** (↘ *0252 546296;* m *078 8364774;* e *info@hotelmuhabura.com; www.hotelmuhabura.com; US$40/50 sgl/dbl*) and the inexpensive **Centre Pastoral Notre Dame de Fatima** (↘ *0252 546780/4;* m *078 8324033;* e *info@fatimamusanze.com; www.fatimamusanze.com; from US$16/20 sgl/dbl, US$8 dorm bed, US$5pp camping*).

Gorillas aside, there is plenty to see in Rwanda, a scenic and remarkably welcoming country that has made great progress since the tragic events of 1994. Other attractions in VNP include golden monkey tracking and day hikes to Dian Fossey's tomb and the summit of several volcanoes. Rubavu (formerly Gisenyi), 60km further west, is a seductively faded tropical port on the shore of Lake Kivu. Further afield, the rolling green hills of Nyungwe Forest National Park – swathed in East Africa's largest montane forest – is home to 13 species of primate, including chimpanzee, L'Hoest's monkey and troops of 400 Angola colobus, along with more than 275 bird species. For more detailed information, get hold of the *Bradt Rwanda* (5th edition, 2012) by Philip Briggs.

at the **Travellers Rest**, where buffets (at busy times) or four-course dinners cost Ush30,000. The **Kisoro Tourist Hotel** is the only other hotel to offer continental food. See page 263, for contact details.

On the corner plot next to the UWA office you'll find the **Coffee Pot Café** (*www. coffee-pot-café.com*) and its excellent selection of sandwiches, hamburgers, stews, teas and coffees. Directly across the road, the **Gorilla Junction** provides more of the same. Elsewhere, it's traditional dishes or chips 'n' stuff menus. The **Ian Point Motel** (see above) has the pleasantest restaurant, while the Mgahinga park rangers appreciate the good local food at the **community group restaurant**, a block or two behind the main street. The nearby **New Moonlight Hotel** is good for beer and roast pork. You'll get the best results if you can give a couple of hours' advance notice; go for the 'lean' pork option and insist on 'roasted' rather than 'fried-with-cabbage'.

NIGHTLIFE Local volunteers tell me that **Club Volcano** is the place to stay up late, while **New Kisoro View** is a lively place for a drink and to watch European football.

SHOPPING **Senlina supermarket** is next to the Ian Point Motel and there's another shop on the same road close to Stanbic. However, you're best stocking up in Kabale. The **main market** – busiest on Mondays and Thursdays – is a short distance along the Kabale Road opposite the California Inn.

Crafts The **Coffee Pot** and **Gorilla Junction** (see above) both sell good selections of crafts, while a wide selection of Congolese 'antique' carvings and masks decorate the foyer of the **Travellers Rest**. Do seek out Jean Mugisha's decidedly eccentric museum and craft shop on Muhubura Street behind the taxi park. It's worth a detour to meet the self-appointed custodian of Kisoro's cultural heritage and tour the dusty room in which it is piled (Ush5,000 for the entertaining ten-minute tour).

OTHER PRACTICALITIES Branches of **Crane** and **Stanbic** banks offer the usual forex services.

WHAT TO SEE AND DO The most popular destinations from Kisoro are **Mgahinga National Park**, **Parc National des Virungas** in the DRC and the **Parc National des Volcans** in Rwanda for hiking and gorilla tracking (covered elsewhere in this chapter). However, tracking on the Virungas is only a reliable option in Rwanda since the Mgahinga gorillas took to wandering into the neighbouring parks for weeks at a time, while tracking in the DRC is regularly prevented by insecurity. The area around Kisoro is also great **walking** country, and there are several worthwhile goals for day hikes even if you never set foot in any of the gorilla reserves. You'll find your way around more easily with a guide but be wary of engaging a self-styled tourist guide off the street. Instead, ask for a recommendation at your hotel or the Coffee Pot Café. The UWA office, incidentally, will suggest the same chaps who accosted you in the street.

Lake Chahafi This pretty lake to the southeast of Kisoro, is a realistic destination for an excursion, particularly as you'll find an eponymous and recently opened resort there with pleasant gardens, a swimming pier and a bar and restaurant (m *0782 754496/0775 664594; US$20pp dbl safari tent & US$17pp 5-bed dorm B&B*). To reach the lake, head out of Kisoro for 5km towards the Rwandan border at Cyanika. At Muganza village, turn left and continue for 7km to the lake.

The setting
will tell you tha
outpost positioned

GORILLA TRACKING

Running along the DRC
the 7,900km² Virunga Nat
conservation areas, protecting
Volcanoes, Ruwenzori Mountain
national park in terms of avian div
while a checklist of 208 mammals in
endemics such as the eastern lowland go
savanna dwellers such as lion, elephant and

The park was established in 1925 and inscri
Site in 1979, but remained largely ungovernable
war. The long years of neglect ended in 2010, how
Congolais pour la Conservation de la Nature (ICCN) ove
of several tourist activities, as well as the construction o
lodge and tented camp. Unfortunately, a new bout of military
Goma forced the park to close to tourism in late 2012. It has yet
the time of writing, though the structures are all in place for touri
resume as and when things settle down.

Virunga National Park offers a mountain gorilla tracking experi
comparable in quality to Uganda and Rwanda, but is significantly cheaper a
US$400 per permit. Six gorilla groups are habituated, and a total of 30 permits
are issued daily. Ten of these permits apply to gorilla groups based around
Djomba, which is only 40 minutes' drive from the Bunagana border post with
Uganda, and can easily be visited as a day trip from Kisoro (assuming the park
has reopened to tourists). Regular updates on the situation are posted on the
website www.visitvirunga.org.

Deeper into the park, two to three hours' drive from Bunagana, the upmarket
Mikeno Lodge lies in the heart of the forest, while the less expensive but
beautifully located **Bukima Tented Camp** is the best base for gorilla tracking
at Bukima (20 permits available daily). The key attraction here, however, is
the hike up Nyiragongo (the volcano responsible for the killer lava flows that
devastated Goma in 2002), where the nested caldera contains a spectacular
live lava lake. The ascent takes four to six hours and you can overnight in a basic
hut on the rim before descending the next day. Up to 16 overnight volcano
permits are issued daily, corresponding to the number of beds at the rim, and
these cost US$200 for foreign adults. Porters are also available.

All accommodation, activities and transport within the park can be
booked through the website www.visitvirunga.org, which also operates an
office in Goma (the Congolese town bordering Rwanda's Rubavu/Gisenyi
on the shores of Lake Kivu). The park website is also the best place to buy a
Congolese visa, but you must allow at least one week for it to be processed
and delivered to your email address. It should be stressed that even if the
park reopens, government travel advisories will most likely still warn against
all non-essential travel to anywhere in the eastern DRC for some time to
come. See advert on page 428.

was not always so tranquil; Nelson Mugisha, the resort owner,
on 1 January 1915, German forces attacked an Anglo–Belgian
on nearby Murora Hill (he might also show you the remnants

IN VIRUNGA NATIONAL PARK (DRC)

border with Rwanda and Uganda for 300km,
onal Park is one of Africa's most biodiverse
the entire Congolese portion of the Virunga
and Lake Edward. It is Africa's richest
rsity, with 706 bird species recorded,
ludes mountain gorilla, Congolese
illa and bizarre okapi, and typical
buffalo.
bed as a UN World Heritage
due to the ongoing civil
ever, when the Institut
saw the resumption
a new upmarket
action around
to reopen at
t visits to
ence

The Kigezi Highlan

med *gahingas*. Of Uganda, Karisimbi – which occasionally sports a small cap of snow – is named for the colour of a cowrie shell, while Visoke simply means 'watering hole', in reference to the crater lake near its peak.

The vegetation zones of the Virungas correspond closely with those of other large East African mountains, albeit that much of the Afro-montane forest below the 2,500m contour has been sacrificed to cultivation. Between 2,500m and 3,500m, where an average annual rainfall of 2,000mm is typical, bamboo forest is interspersed with stands of tall *hagenia* woodland. At higher altitudes, the cover of Afro-alpine moorland, grassland and marsh is studded with giant lobelia and other outsized plants similar to those found on Kilimanjaro and the Rwenzori.

The most famous denizen of the Virungas is the mountain gorilla, which inhabits all six of the extinct or dormant volcanoes, but not – for obvious reasons – the more active ones. The Virungas also form the main stronghold for the endangered golden monkey, and support relic populations of elephant and buffalo along with typical highland forest species such as yellow-backed duiker and giant forest hog. The mountains' avifauna is comparatively poorly known, but some 150 species are recorded including about 20 Albertine Rift endemics.

Still in their geological infancy, none of the present Virunga Mountains is more than two million years old, and two of the cones remain highly active. However, eruptions of earlier Virunga volcanoes ten to 12 million years ago marked the start of the tectonic processes that have formed the western Rift Valley. The most

leading in the direction of the lake. There's a cave near the lake where a 10m python is regularly encountered. Lakeside accommodation is provided by the **Mutanda Ecotourism Centre** (see page 264).

Lake Mutolere lies a little further afield in the direction of Bwindi. You'll find a couple of basic tourism sites where the road reaches the lake.

The insular and distinctively terraced hill, just south of Kisoro on the Mgahinga Road, contains a dry crater and offers terrific regional views. Just beyond town, turn left down a motorable track until an obvious path leads to the right. This climbs steeply up the terraced hillside for a circular walk around the crater rim.

dramatic volcanic explosion of historical times was the 1977 eruption of the 3,465m Mount Nyiragongo in the DRC, about 20km north of the Lake Kivu port of Goma. During this eruption, a lava lake that had formed in the volcano's main crater back in 1894 drained in less than one hour, emitting streams of molten lava that flowed at a rate of up to 60km/h, killing an estimated 2,000 people and terminating only 500m from Goma Airport.

In 1994, a new lake of lava started to accumulate within the main crater of Nyiragongo, leading to another highly destructive eruption on 17 January 2002. Lava flowed down the southern and eastern flanks of the volcano into Goma itself, killing at least 50 people. Goma was evacuated, and an estimated 450,000 people crossed into the nearby Rwandan towns of Gisenyi and Musanze for temporary refuge. Three days later, when the first evacuees returned, it transpired that about a quarter of the town – including large parts of the commercial and residential centre – had been engulfed by the lava, leaving 12,000 families homeless. The lava lake in Nyiragongo's crater remains active, with a diameter of around 50m, and although there has been no subsequent eruption, red and white plumes reaching a height of up to 3km were regularly observed above the crater in late 2002.

Only 15km northwest of Nyiragongo stands the 3,058m Mount Nyamuragira, which also erupted in January 2002. Nyamuragira is probably the most active volcano on the African mainland, with 34 eruptions recorded since 1882, though only the 1912–13 incident resulted in any fatalities. Nyamuragira most recently blew its top on 26 July 2002, spewing lava high into the air, along with a large plume of ash and sulphur dioxide, and destroying large tracts of cultivated land and forest.

It is perhaps worth noting that these temperamental Congolese volcanoes pose no threat to visitors to Uganda. The three cones shared by Uganda are all dormant or extinct and while the plumes from the Congolese volcanoes might well be seen at night from around Kisoro, no active lava flow has touched Ugandan soil in recorded history. That might change one day: there is a tradition among the Bafumbira people of the Ugandan Virungas that the fiery sprits inhabiting the crater of Nyamuragira will eventually relocate to Muhavura, reducing both the mountain and its surrounds to ash.

Another Bafumbira custom has it that the crater lake atop Mount Muhavura is inhabited by a powerful snake spirit called Indyoka, which only needs to raise its head to bring rain to the surrounding countryside. It is said that Indyoka lives on a bed of gold and protects various other artefacts made of precious metal, and that it can extend itself as far as Lake Mutanda to a lakeshore sacrificial shrine at Mushungero. An indication of its presence at the lake and associated shrine is the inundation of the seasonal Gitundwe Swamp near Lake Mutanda.

Shozi Crater and caves Shozi Crater, reaching an altitude of 2,000m, is a relic of the volcanic activity that shaped this mountainous corner of Uganda. Close by is a 400m-long cave, formed by a petrified lava flow, which houses a colony of thousands upon thousands of bats. The crater and cave are located near Mutolere trading centre, about 5km outside Kisoro.

Echuya Forest Reserve Extending over 340km² of hilly terrain between Lake Bunyonyi and Kisoro, Echuya is one of the least-visited and most under-researched reserves in Uganda, yet it still ranks among the top six sites in the country in terms of forest biodiversity. With an altitude span of 2,200m to 2,600m, the reserve protects a range of montane habitats including evergreen and bamboo forest, while the adjacent Muchuya Swamp is one of the most extensive perennial high-altitude wetlands in East Africa, harbouring the largest-known population of the globally endangered Grauer's swamp warbler. Little information is available about the reserve's non-avian fauna, but it is likely to be similar to the forest belt of nearby Mgahinga National Park and includes at least four small mammal species endemic to the Albertine Rift. Until recent times, Echuya was permanently inhabited by Batwa Pygmies (see box, pages 258–9). Several Pygmy communities living on the verge of the forest still derive their livelihood from bamboo and other resources extracted from within the reserve.

A surprisingly low bird checklist of 100 species suggests that scientific knowledge of Echuya is far from complete, but even so 12 Albertine Rift endemics have been recorded, and it is the only locality outside the national park system where a comparable selection of these sought-after specialities is resident. How to find them is now unclear since the main birding corridor – which was a slow, bumpy, 6km section of the Kisoro road which crossed the forest – has been surfaced and traffic speeds are faster. For this reason, Echuya can't ready be recommended as a safe birding destination until trails deeper into the forest are created.

MGAHINGA GORILLA NATIONAL PARK

(The standard UWA entrance fees apply (see pages 32–3). These fees are included in the prices for volcano climbing & caving, & are not applicable to overnight stays at the community campsite at the park gate) Mgahinga National Park protects the Ugandan part of the Virunga Mountains (see box, pages 268–9) and its three main peaks: Muhavura, Gahinga and Sabinyo. Established in 1930 as the Gorilla Game Sanctuary, the national park was gazetted in 1991, when more than 2,000 people were relocated from within its boundaries. Covering less than 34km², Mgahinga is the smallest national park in Uganda, but it forms part of a cross-border system of contiguous reserves in Rwanda and the DRC extending over some 430km² of the higher Virungas. Small it might be, but Mgahinga is also arguably the most scenic park in Uganda, offering panoramic views that stretch northward to Bwindi, and a southern skyline dominated by the steep volcanic cones of the Virungas, surely one of the most memorable and stirring sights in East Africa.

Mgahinga protects 76 mammal species, including the golden monkey (a localised and distinctive race of the blue monkey), black-and-white colobus, mountain gorilla, leopard, elephant, giant forest hog, bushpig, buffalo, bushbuck, black-fronted duiker and several varieties of rodents, bats and small predators. Bafflingly, only 115 bird species have been recorded here, possibly a reflection of the park's small size but also suggesting that no serious study of its avifauna has ever been undertaken. However, the park is still of great interest to birdwatchers, as several of the species recorded are localised forest birds, and 12 are considered to be endemic to the Albert Rift region.

Mgahinga is best known to tourists for gorilla tracking. Oddly enough, no gorillas live permanently within the park, but a fair number move freely between Uganda and the neighbouring Parc National des Volcans in Rwanda, and one habituated troop frequently spends months at a time within Mgahinga. Unfortunately, in 2004 the park's habituated group was subjected to attacks from a belligerent lone silverback and has since spent most of its time across the border in Rwanda. The group returned to Uganda in November 2012, however, and gorilla tracking has recommenced. For how long this will be possible, it is impossible to say. Check the Bradt website/email newsletter for updates (see page ix for details).

Gorilla tracking is not the only reason to visit Mgahinga though; it also offers a far broader range of activities than any of the other 'mountain gorilla reserves', including golden monkey tracking, a cultural trail, caving, forest walks, and day hikes to the three volcanic peaks. Anybody who enjoys challenging day hikes or who has an interest in natural history could happily spend a week based at Mgahinga without going near a gorilla.

The national park's office in Kisoro (see page 263) always has current information regarding Mgahinga, as well as sometimes stocking maps and pamphlets. The best source of background information is the 96-page booklet *Mgahinga Gorilla & Bwindi Impenetrable National Parks*, written by David Bygott and Jeannette Hanby, and published by the UWA in 1998. Payments, bookings and enquiries are handled in a new **visitors' centre** 100m beyond the entrance gate.

GETTING THERE AND AWAY Ntebeko Entrance Gate lies roughly 14km from Kisoro along a dirt road. Pending improvements, the second half of this route is slow and bumpy and, until improvements are made, you should expect the journey to take about an hour. A **4x4** may be necessary after heavy rain. To get to Mgahinga from the national park's office in Kisoro, follow the main road towards the DRC for about 100m, turn left at the first main junction, immediately before the Travellers Rest Inn, then turn right about 100m further on. Follow the stone cairns up to Ntebeko.

If you don't have a vehicle, the national park's office in town will know whether any **official vehicles** are heading out to the entrance gate. You can also normally hire a **private vehicle** to take you there – this costs around 50,000, which is not too expensive for a group. The other option is to **walk**: it's quite a hilly road, but it shouldn't take you much longer than three hours to get there. You might be able to pick up a lift some or all of the way. If you do walk, fork right at Nturo trading centre, roughly 1km out of Kisoro, for a shorter and prettier route. This is just about motorable, but it's a tooth-rattling ride with plenty of rocks.

WHERE TO STAY AND EAT It's perfectly possible to visit Mgahinga on a day trip from Kisoro, but it's more atmospheric to stay in accommodation at the Ntebeko Entrance Gate. For location of listings see map, pages 240–1.

Upmarket

⌂ **Mount Gahinga Lodge** (6 cottages) \0414 346464/5; m 0752 741718; e sales@ volcanoessafaris.com; www.volcanoessafaris.com. This pleasant little lodge, situated a few hundred metres from the entrance gate, offers s/c cottages

& tents. *High season rates US$350/700 sgl/twin inc drinks FB.*

Budget & camping

✗ **Amajamber'Iwacu Community Camp** (aka Mgahinga Community Campground) m 0772

954956; e amcamp@yahoo.com. The community campsite just outside the entrance gate to Mgahinga has a truly spectacular setting, with Muhavura, Gahinga & Sabinyo peaks forming an arc to the south, & a grandstand view over Lake Mutanda & the rolling hills of Bwindi to the north. Very simple meals such as potatoes & other, mixed vegetables can be prepared with plenty of notice

& cost about Ush10,000. You'll eat far better at the nearby Mount Gahinga Lodge (see above), but expect to pay US$30 for a 3-course meal. Simple but reasonably priced accommodation is available. *US$26 s/c dbl banda, US$18 sgl/dbl banda with shared bathroom, US$6 dorm (up to 6 people), US$4 camping.*

WHAT TO SEE AND DO

Gorilla tracking Gorilla tracking is a less reliable option in Mgahinga than Bwindi since its gorilla population – including the habituated Nyakagazi group – is free to roam across the international borders into Rwanda and Congo. Indeed, since an altercation with a rogue silverback back in 2005, the Nyakagezi group has spent much of its time in Rwanda – much to the delight of the Rwandese gorilla tracking industry. However, in November 2012, the Nyakagezi gorillas returned 'home' and tracking permits are once again available. These are sold from the UWA office in Kisoro (⋏ *0486 430098; see page 263*) rather than the central booking office in Kampala. Since long-term bookings cannot be guaranteed, organised tour groups tend to favour Bwindi so (should the gorillas stick around in Uganda), Mgahinga permits are relatively easy to obtain at short notice.

Mountain hikes (*See pages 32–3 for current fees*) Guided day hikes are available to each of the three volcanic peaks in Mgahinga. A reasonable level of fitness and an early start are required for any of the mountain hikes, and good boots, raingear and warm clothes are recommended. The least-demanding mountain hike, the 1,100m climb from Ntebeko up Mount Gahinga, offers a good chance of seeing various forest birds in the bamboo zone, while duikers and bushbuck inhabit the marshy crater at the peak. Expect the round trip to take six to seven hours. The tougher, 1,300m ascent from Ntebeko to Sabinyo, which takes at least eight hours there and back, passes through montane forest and moorland, and culminates in three challenging climbs up rock faces using ladders.

The most challenging hike is to the peak of Muhavura, the highest peak. This starts at a base camp a few kilometres from the entrance gate (it is advisable to camp here the night before the hike) and the round trip will take at least nine hours. The open moorland that characterises Muhavura offers great views in all directions though unless you're lucky this will be reduced by haze by the time you reach the top. A campsite is planned in the saddle between Mgahinga and Muhuvura peaks to enable climbers to summit Muhuvura rather earlier. Look out for Afro-alpine endemics such as the beautiful scarlet-tufted malachite sunbird. A small crater lake at the top of Muhavura is encircled by giant lobelias. Note that hikers may well feel altitude-related symptoms near the peak, due to the rapidity of the 1,793m ascent.

Golden monkey tracking (*See pages 32–3 for fees*) The next-best thing to seeing the mountain gorilla is the chance to track the golden monkey *Cercopithecus kandti* (sometimes treated as a distinctive race of the more widespread blue monkey *C. mitis*), a little-known bamboo-associated taxa primate listed as 'endangered' by the World Conservation Union. Endemic to the Albertine Rift, the golden monkey is characterised by a bright orange-gold body, cheeks and tail, contrasting with its black limbs, crown and tail end. Until a few years ago, this pretty monkey was common in Rwanda's Gishwati Forest Reserve, most of which was chopped down by returned refugees in the aftermath of the 1994 genocide, and unconfirmed sources indicate that a small population might occur further south in the same country's Nyungwe National Park. More likely, however, is that the Virunga Volcanoes harbour the only remaining viable breeding population of this localised monkey. Fortunately, the golden monkey is the numerically dominant primate within this restricted range – a 2003 survey estimated a population of 3,000–4,000 in Mgahinga National Park, but no figures are available for neighbouring parks in Rwanda and DRC. Golden monkey tracking can be undertaken at Mgahinga daily.

Nature walks (*US$15pp; up to 4hrs*) Half-day nature trails concentrating on the forest zone run out of Ntebeko. Of particular interest to birders, the **Sabinyo Gorge Trail** ascends through the heath around Ntebeko into a stand of bamboo forest before following a small stream through a lushly forested gorge. The bamboo forest is a good place to see the pretty golden monkey, as well as handsome francolin, Kivu ground thrush and regal sunbird. The evergreen forest harbours such localised birds as Rwenzori turaco, western green tinkerbird, olive woodpecker, African hill babbler, Archer's ground robin, Rwenzori batis, montane sooty boubou, Lagden's bush-shrike and strange weaver, several of which are Albertine Rift endemics.

Another day trail leads to **Rugezi Swamp**, where, in addition to the usual forest animals and birds, you stand a fair chance of seeing elephants and, in the late afternoon, giant forest hog.

Yet another excursion leads to **Garama Cave**, 4km from Ntebeko, which was occupied by humans during the late Iron Age and later used by the Batwa as a hiding place after raiding neighbouring Bantu-speaking tribes. The main passage leads only 100m to the Batwa's subterranean council chamber but the cave is rumoured to cut right through the mountain to Rwanda. Bring a good torch with batteries (don't rely on these being available at the park headquarters). The round trip takes about three hours and the terrain is reasonably flat.

The Batwa Trail (*Book through UWA;* ☎ *0141 355000;* e *info@thebatwatrail.com; www.the batwatrail.com*) A welcome diversion from the usual tawdry visits to impoverished Batwa/Pygmy communities, this initiative provides a genuine opportunity to experience something of traditional Batwa forest culture. The event follows a trail along the lower slopes of Mgahinga Volcano to Garama Cave and involves visitors and their Batwa guides in a range of practical (rather than verbal) interactions such as firelighting, bivouac building, target practice with a bow and arrow (meat must have been a rare dish indeed!) and food gathering. The trail culminates with a memorable performance of Batwa song and music in the Batwa's council chamber in Garama Cave, a dramatic setting with powerful acoustics. Importantly, the Batwa Trail is no 'pretty Pygmy' celebration; the day should include a discussion of the Batwa's current plight, living as squatters in bivouacs on Bakiga-owned farmland along the forest margins. The Batwa Trail is a partnership between UWA and the worthy United Organisation for Batwa Development in Uganda. The activity is US$80 per person (including park entrance) split approximately 50–50 between UWA and the Batwa. A half-day version is also available at the same price.

BWINDI IMPENETRABLE NATIONAL PARK

(The standard rates for a Class A protected area apply; see pages 32–3. Note that these are included in the prices for gorilla tracking (again see pages 32–3) & are not applicable to staying in accommodation inside the park gate at the Buhoma Lodge,

Gorilla Forest Camp & Community Campground) The Bwindi Impenetrable Forest is regarded to be one of the most biologically diverse forests in Africa, largely owing to its antiquity (it dates to before the Pleistocene Ice Age, making it over 25,000 years old) and a broad altitude range between 1,160m and 2,607m above sea level. Bwindi is a true rainforest, spread over a series of steep ridges and valleys that form the eastern edge of the Albertine Rift Valley. The national park has an average annual rainfall of almost 1,500mm, and it is a vital catchment area, the source of five major rivers, which flow into Lake Edward. Until about 500 years ago, when agriculturists started planting crops in the Kisoro area, Bwindi was part of a much larger belt of forest stretching south to the slopes of the Virunga Mountains.

Tourism to Bwindi focuses on gorilla tracking at four locations: **Buhoma** in the northwest of the park, **Ruhija** in the east, **Nkuringo** in the southwest and **Rushaga** in the south. Slightly more than half the world's mountain gorilla population is resident in Bwindi: an estimated 408 individuals living in 15 troops. Given the focus on gorillas, it may come as a surprise to learn that Bwindi harbours at least 120 mammal species, more than any national park except Queen Elizabeth. This list consists mainly of small mammals such as rodents and bats, but it does include 11 types of primate, including a healthy chimpanzee population and substantial numbers of L'Hoest's, red-tailed and blue monkeys, as well as black-and-white colobus and olive baboon. Of the so-called 'big five', only elephants are present, though the herd of 30 animals in the southeast of the park – assigned to the forest race – is very seldom seen by tourists. Buffaloes and leopards were present until recent times, but they are thought to have been hunted to extinction. Six antelope species occur in the park: bushbuck and five types of forest duiker.

A total of 350 bird species have been recorded in Bwindi, a remarkably high figure when you consider that, unlike most other national park checklists, it includes very few water-associated birds. Of particular interest to birders are 23 species endemic to the Albertine Rift, and at least 14 species recorded nowhere else in Uganda, among them the African green broadbill, white-tailed blue flycatcher, brown-necked parrot, white-bellied robin chat and Frazer's eagle owl. In addition to its extensive bird checklist, Bwindi is also home to at least 200 butterfly species, including eight Albertine Rift endemics, and dedicated butterfly watchers might hope to identify more than 50 varieties in one day.

The UWA offices in Kampala (see page 168) and Kisoro (see page 263) can give up-to-date information on gorilla tracking and other travel practicalities in Bwindi and Mgahinga. The best source of background information is the 96-page booklet *Mgahinga Gorilla & Bwindi Impenetrable National Parks*, written by David Bygott and Jeannette Hanby and published by UWA in 1998. A full checklist of the birds recorded in Bwindi can be bought for a nominal price at the park headquarters. The 'Uganda Maps' sheet for Bwindi shows the ranges of the habituated gorillas as established by the 2010–11 census.

BUHOMA
Getting there and away Buhoma – site of Bwindi's park headquarters, a range of tourist accommodation, and the primary gorilla tracking trailhead – can be approached using several different routes, converging near the town of Butogota 17km before the park entrance. All of the approach routes involve some **driving** along dirt roads that may become slippery after rain, so an early start is recommended to be certain of reaching the park before dark. It's advisable to carry all the fuel you need but, if you run short, there are two filling stations in Kihihi, roughly 10km north of Kanyantorogo on the road towards Ishasha.

From Kabale The 108km drive from Kabale to Buhoma follows dirt roads the whole way, and it typically takes about three hours, a bit longer after rain. The usual route is to follow the Kisoro Road out of Kabale for 18km to Hamurwa, then turn right at the turn-off signposted for Buhoma. This route runs for 45km to Kanungu, then 15km to Kanyantorogo where you turn left to Butogota, which is 17km from Buhoma, with all forks signposted. Alternatively, you could travel through the Ruhija sector of the park to Buhoma (see page 287). Approaching from this direction, a signposted left turn 5km before Butogota cuts through to the Buhoma Road. Though the historically lousy Ruhija Road has recently been greatly improved, it still takes at least three hours to drive between Buhoma and Kabale. Though a few **pick-ups** run between Kabale and Butogota via Ruhija, if you're using public transport from Kampala, you'll be more comfortable passing via Rukungiri.

From Kampala Coming directly from Kampala, the best route to Buhoma entails following the surfaced road towards Kabale as far as Ntungamo, roughly 60km past Mbarara. At Ntungamo, you need to turn right to zip up a newly surfaced road for 45km to Rukungiri. From here, you will need to follow dirt roads in a roughly westerly direction through Kambuga (see box, page 282) to Kanungu, where you converge with the route from Kabale described above.

From Kasese/Fort Portal Travellers coming from northern destinations such as Kasese, Fort Portal or Queen Elizabeth National Park can use two routes to Buhoma. The more interesting route, via Katunguru, Ishasha and Kihihi, takes three to five hours, and is discussed in some detail in *Chapter 8*, page 299. The alternative route entails following the surfaced Mbarara road as far south as Ishaka, where a right turn on to the unsurfaced old main road to Kabale leads for 33km to Kagamba at the junction with the newly surfaced Ntungamo–Rukungiri road. From

BWINDI IMPENETRABLE

The name Bwindi derives from the local phrase 'Mubwindi bwa Nyinamukari', which most probably originally referred to the Mubwindi Swamp in the southeast of the park rather than the forest itself. The story behind this name goes back to about a century ago, when, it is said, a family migrating northwards from the Kisoro area found themselves standing at the southern end of a seemingly impenetrable swamp. The parents asked the swamp spirits for guidance, and were told that only if they sacrificed their most beautiful daughter, Nyinamukari, would the rest of the family cross without mishap. After two days of deliberation, the family decided that they could not turn back south, and so they threw the girl into the water to drown, and went on their way safely to the other side. When news of the sacrifice spread, people began to avoid the swamp, calling it 'Mubwindi bwa Nyinamukari' – 'Dark Place of Nyinamukari'.

The forest was proclaimed as the Impenetrable Forest Reserve in 1932, its official name until 1991 when it was gazetted as a national park and named Bwindi. Realising that this local name has less allure to tourists than the colonial name (though the two words are close in meaning), UWA expanded it to be the Bwindi Impenetrable National Park. Today, most people refer to the park as plain Bwindi, though the murderous swamp is still known by the more correct name of Mubwindi.

Over the two decades following the European discovery of mountain gorillas, at least 50 individuals were captured or killed in the Virungas, prompting the Belgian government to create the Albert National Park in 1925. This protected what are now the Congolese and Rwandan portions of the Virunga Mountains, and was managed as a cohesive conservation unit.

The gorilla population of the Virungas is thought to have been reasonably stable in 1960, when a census undertaken by George Schaller indicated that some 450 individuals lived in the range. By 1971–73, however, the population had plummeted to an estimated 250. This decline was caused by several factors, including the post-colonial division of the Albert National Park into its Rwandan and Congolese components, the ongoing fighting between the Hutu and Tutsi of Rwanda, and a grisly tourist trade in poached gorilla heads and hands – the latter used by some sad individuals as ashtrays! Most devastating of all perhaps was the irreversible loss of almost half of the gorillas' habitat between 1957 and 1968 to local farmers and a European-funded agricultural scheme.

In 1979, Amy Vedder and Bill Webber initiated the first gorilla tourism project in Rwanda's Parc National des Volcans, integrating tourism, local education and anti-poaching measures with remarkable success. Initially, the project was aimed mainly at overland trucks, who paid a paltry – by today's standards – US$20 per person to track gorillas. Even so, gorilla tourism was raising up to ten million US dollars annually by the mid-1980s, making it Rwanda's third-highest earner of foreign revenue. The mountain gorilla had practically become the national emblem, and was officially regarded to be the country's most important renewable natural resource. To ordinary Rwandans, gorillas became a source of great national pride: living gorillas ultimately created far more work and money than poaching them had ever done. As a result, a census undertaken in 1989 indicated that the local mountain gorilla population had increased by almost 30% to 320 animals.

Despite the success of ecotourism, there are still several threats to the ongoing survival of mountain gorillas in the wild. For the Virunga population, the major threat is undoubtedly political. In 1991, the long-standing ethnic tension between Rwanda's Hutu and Tutsi populations erupted into a civil war that culminated in the genocide of 1994. In context, the fate of a few gorillas does seem a rather trivial concern, even if you take into account the important role that gorilla tourism is playing in rebuilding Rwanda's post-war economy, and the fact that the integrated conservation of their habitat will also protect a watershed that supplies 10% of the country with water.

Nevertheless, the Rwandan conflict had several repercussions in the Virungas. Researchers and park rangers were twice forced to evacuate the Parc National des Volcans, leaving the gorillas unguarded. Tourism to Rwanda practically ceased in 1991, and although gorilla tracking has been available since 1999, tourist arrivals have yet to approach the level of the 1980s. Remarkably, however, when researchers were finally able to return to the Parc National des Volcans in the late 1990s, only four gorillas could not be accounted for. Two of the missing gorillas were old females who had most probably died of natural causes. The other two might have been shot, but might just as easily have succumbed to disease.

But in this most unstable part of Africa little can be taken for granted. Just as Rwanda started to stabilise politically, the DRC descended into anarchy. For years, eastern Congolese officials, who lived far from the capital, received no formal salary and were forced to devise their own ways of securing a living, leading to a level of corruption second to none in the region. At least 20 gorillas were killed in the DRC between 1995 and 2007, during most of which time the Congolese part of the Virungas was effectively closed to tourists and researchers alike. Under the circumstances, it is remarkable to learn that the latest gorilla count – undertaken in 2003 – showed a continued increase to at least 480 individuals in the Virungas – almost double the number recorded in the early 1970s. The Bwindi population has also increased by around 20% since 1997, the 2010–11 census returning an estimate of around 408 individuals.

The Bwindi population is more immediately secure than the gorillas in the Virungas. Bwindi is not divided by arbitrary political borders, which means that the entire population can be protected within one well-managed and carefully monitored national park. Nevertheless, the habituation of the Bwindi gorillas has increased their vulnerability to poachers, who, during 1995, killed a total of seven habituated mountain gorillas. These incidents were linked to one dealer's attempts to acquire an infant gorilla, so it would perhaps be an overreaction to view them as a trend. Nevertheless, the very fact that habituated gorillas were targeted does highlight an area of vulnerability linked directly to tourism and research.

Less critical perhaps, but something that directly affects readers, is that humans and gorillas are genetically close enough for there to be a real risk of a tourist passing a viral or bacterial infection to a gorilla. To reduce this risk, there is a restriction on the number of people allowed to visit a troop on any given day, and visitors are asked to keep a few metres' distance between themselves and the animals. It is up to individual tourists to forgo their gorilla tracking permit if they are unwell – easier said than done when you've already spent a small fortune to get all the way to Uganda, but perhaps not if you imagine the consequences if even one individual were to be infected by a contagious disease to which gorillas have no acquired resistance.

Given the above, a reasonable response might be to query the wisdom of habituating gorillas in the first place. The problem facing conservationists is that gorillas cannot be conserved in a vacuum. For instance, roughly 2,000 farmers were evacuated from Mgahinga when it was gazetted as a national park in 1993, a situation that created some local resentment of gorillas. However, against this immediate deprivation can be balanced the long-term consideration that 10% of revenue raised by gorilla tourism in Uganda is handed to local communities, in addition to which community campsites outside the national parks can generate funds at a grassroots level. So long as gorilla tourism can generate revenue and create employment opportunities locally, there is a strong incentive for neighbouring communities to perceive the gorillas' survival to be in their long-term interest. Without tourism, why should they give a damn?

The benefits of gorilla tourism also extend much further afield, for the activity now forms the foundation of Uganda's national tourist industry: the majority of people who come to Uganda to see gorillas will also spend money in other parts of the country, thereby generating foreign revenue and creating employment well beyond the immediate vicinities of the mountain gorilla reserves. The result is a symbiotic situation whereby a far greater number of people, nationally and internationally, are motivated to take an active interest in the protection of the gorillas than would otherwise be the case.

continued overleaf

FRIEND-A-GORILLA *(www.Friendagorilla.org)* It's now possible to get involved in gorilla conservation and have fun (a word that doesn't really describe the rewards of tracking them). In 2009, UWA launched the Friend-a-Gorilla initiative which, for a consideration of US$1, enables interested individuals to befriend a mountain gorilla and, through regular online updates, learn more about this animal, its character, family group and interactions. A Geo-Trek link on the website enables you to establish your friend's whereabouts in Bwindi using GPS technology. You can also apply your gorilla friend's thumbnail photo to your Facebook profile (and similar sites).

here, directions are as for the route from Kampala (see above). Public transport along this route is limited – instead of trying to travel directly, I would recommend heading to Mbarara to pick up the bus from Kampala.

By public transport If you're driving yourself or travelling with a tour company, reaching Buhoma is a long but simple enough process. It is, however, rather more challenging using public transport. That said, and assuming that the arrangements below go according to plan, you could leave Kampala at 05.00 one morning and be tracking gorillas at 08.00 the next day. Though with a US$500 tracking permit at stake, I'd suggest that you give yourself a day to spare just in case. Do be sure to pre-book your bus ticket and check the exact departure time as well.

Travelling from Kampala, the **Bismarken** and **Muhubura** bus services will get you as far as Butogota town, 17km from Buhoma. These leave Kampala's Qualicell bus park around 05.30–6.00 and reach Butogota in the late afternoon or early evening. Tickets cost Ush30,000 but may increase due to poor road conditions, a broken bridge imposing a longer route, etc. The return from Butogota leaves at 05.00. There are other, overnight buses which I wouldn't recommend. Depending on what time you arrive in Butogota, you'll need to decide whether to head straight up to Buhoma or find lodgings and go up the following day. If the latter, the preferred choice seems to be **Green Tree Lodge** (*US$6/8 sgl/dbl s/c or US$5 with a grim shared bathroom*) right next to the bus stage. A new hotel seems to be under construction at the Buhoma end of town.

To reach Buhoma from Butogota, you could take the **Green Bus** which passes through Butogota, *en route* between Kihihi and Buhoma around 08.00. This reaches Buhoma at 09.00 and starts the return trip at 14.00. A more flexible strategy, and not expensive if you are in a group, is to engage a **special hire taxi** for around Ush50,000 each way. UWA suggest Ivan in Butogota (m *0772 560853*) and Paul (m *0712 837702*). Alternatively, hire a **boda-boda** for a bumpy 17km ride (*Ush10,000*). Otherwise, try to find a **pick-up** truck heading to Buhoma or try to hitch a lift with private tourists. As a last resort, you could always **walk**; the terrain is fairly hilly, but the gradients are reasonably gentle and it shouldn't take more than five hours.

Another option, useful perhaps if you're exploring the region north of Bwindi is to head to Buhoma from Kihihi, a small town with basic lodgings (see page 299) between the Ishasha sector of Queen Elizabeth National Park and Butogota. The Green Bus described above will take you all the way, while local public transport can drop you at Kanyantorogo junction, 9km from Kihihi, where you can take a boda-boda to Butogota (*Ush10,000*) or Buhoma (*Ush20,000*).

Rwakobo Rock

Natural – Comfortable – Friendly

Accommodation and Restaurant
Lake Mburo National Park

www.rwakoborock.com   info@rwakoborock.com   +256 (0) 755 211 771

Safari Wildz
East African Adventures
+256 (0)775 201 119

Budget - Midrange - Lodge
Private Safaris & Scheduled small group departures
www.safariwildz.com   info@safariwildz.com

UGANDA CONSERVATION FOUNDATION

Atta

Gately Uganda Boutique Hotels

TWO LODGES - ONE CONCEPT

Two Lodges-One Concept Entebbe airport and Jinja town Uganda.

Elegantly decorated, modern African, eclectic accommodation catering to discerning style conscious business and independent travelers alike.

If you are looking for a Hotel or Lodge that is both casual & rustic yet has the attention to elegant finish, then look no further.

Relax in our oasis of tropical gardens that surround every room.

ENTEBBE
(m) +256 (0) 777 555 966
(t) +256 (0) 414 321 313
(e) stay@gatelyinn.com
(w) www.gatelyinn.com

Gately Inn promises to indulge your senses to ensure your utmost relaxation and delight...

JINJA
(t) +256 (0) 434 122 400
(m) +256 (0) 772 469 638
(e) stay@gatelyonnile.com
(w) www.gately-on-nile.com

At Gately on the Nile we have created an oasis of peace and tranquillity set amongst acres of tropical gardens...

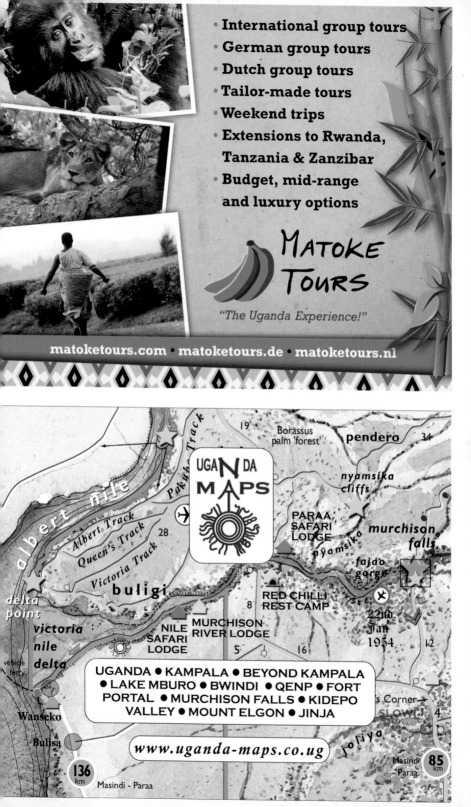
UGANDA • KAMPALA • BEYOND KAMPALA • LAKE MBURO • BWINDI • QENP • FORT PORTAL • MURCHISON FALLS • KIDEPO VALLEY • MOUNT ELGON • JINJA

www.uganda-maps.co.ug

Relax and unwind in this extraordinary lodge, nestled into luxuriant rainforest on a private island between thundering NIle rapids. Enjoy the magic of a bygone era, steaming up the Nile in Humphrey Bogart and Katharine Hepburn's original African Queen (1951).

Wildwaters Lodge contact details:
tel: +256 (0)3 9277 6669 or 0772 237 400
www.wild-uganda.com

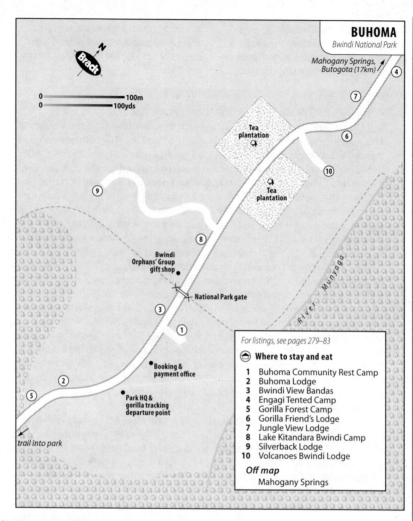

Bwindi National Park

Mahogany Springs,
Butogota (17km)

100m
100yds

Tea
plantation

Tea
plantation

River Munyaga

Bwindi
Orphans' Group
gift shop

National Park gate

For listings, see pages 279–83

Where to stay and eat

1 Buhoma Community Rest Camp
2 Buhoma Lodge
3 Bwindi View Bandas
4 Engagi Tented Camp
5 Gorilla Forest Camp
6 Gorilla Friend's Lodge
7 Jungle View Lodge
8 Lake Kitandara Bwindi Camp
9 Silverback Lodge
10 Volcanoes Bwindi Lodge

Off map
   Mahogany Springs

Booking &
payment office

Park HQ &
gorilla tracking
departure point

trail into park

7

Where to stay You'll quickly appreciate a few things about the accommodation at Buhoma. Most obviously, it costs considerably more than comparable facilities elsewhere. Note that the rates given below are rack rates and most lodges offer discounts for East African residents. Secondly, the camps and lodges are spread along the steeply sloping side of the Munyaga river valley. Consequently, you'll negotiate an inordinate number of steps as you move around each site; it also means that most sites enjoy a memorable view of the wall of misty forest covering the valley side beyond the river. Finally, the accommodation, which is invariably set within secondary vegetation on the edge of this misty rainforest, can feel pretty damp, which is why most lodges are replacing canvas tents with more solid constructions. For location of listings see map, above.

Upmarket

Volcanoes Bwindi Lodge (8 cottages)
0414 346464/5; e sales@volcanoessafaris.

com; www.volcanoessafaris.com. 70 steps below the parking area, you'll find one of Buhoma's most attractive lodges – as indeed it should be given the prices. The spacious half-timbered lodge & cottages, all recently overhauled by an Australian architect, are quite delightful with an eclectic – indeed eccentric – range of fabrics, furnishings, colours & framed botanical prints within, & the usual forest view without. High season rates. *US$480/800 sgl/dbl FB inc drinks & a massage.*

MOUNTAIN GORILLAS: ECOLOGY AND TAXONOMY

The largest living primates, gorillas are widespread residents of the equatorial African rainforest, with a global population of perhaps 100,000 concentrated mainly in the Congo Basin. Until 2001, all gorillas were assigned to the species *Gorilla gorilla*, split into three races: the **western lowland gorilla** G. g. *gorilla* of the western Congo Basin, the **eastern lowland gorilla** G. g. *graueri* in the eastern DRC, and the **mountain gorilla** G. g. *beringei*, which lives in highland forest on the eastern side of the Albertine Rift. The western race was formally described in 1847, but the eastern races were only described in the early 20th century – the mountain gorilla in 1903, a year after two individuals were shot on Mount Sabinyo by Oscar van Beringe, and the eastern lowland gorilla in 1914.

The conventional taxonomic classification of gorillas has been challenged by recent advances in DNA testing and fresh morphological studies suggesting that the western and eastern gorilla populations, whose ranges lie more than 1,000km apart, diverged some two million years ago. For this reason, they are now treated as discrete species G. *gorilla* (western) and G. *beringei* (eastern). One distinct western race – the Cross River gorilla G. g. *dielhi* of the Cameroon–Nigeria border region – fulfils the IUCN criteria for 'Critically Endangered', since it lives in five fragmented populations, only one of which is protected, with a combined total of fewer than 200 individuals. In 2000, the Cross River gorilla and mountain gorilla shared the dubious distinction of being placed on a shortlist of the world's 25 most endangered primate taxa.

The status of the western gorilla is relatively secure, since it is far more numerous in the wild than its eastern counterpart, and has a more extensive range spanning half a dozen countries. Recent estimates place the total population of western gorillas at around 80,000, but numbers are in rapid decline, largely due to hunting for bushmeat and the lethal Ebola virus. The fate of the eastern gorilla – still split into a lowland and mountain race – is far less certain. In the mid-1990s, an estimated 17,000 eastern lowland gorillas remained in the wild, but it is widely thought that the population has halved – or worse – since the outbreak of the ongoing civil war in the DRC. Rarer still, but more stable, is the mountain gorilla, with just 700 individuals confined to two ranges: the border-straddling Virunga Volcanoes and Bwindi National Park in Uganda.

The first study of mountain gorilla behaviour was undertaken in the 1950s by George Schaller, whose pioneering work formed the starting point for the more recent research initiated by Dian Fossey in the 1960s. The brutal – and still unsolved – murder of Fossey at her research centre in December 1985 is generally thought to have been the handiwork of one of the many poachers with whom she crossed swords in the Virungas. Fossey's acclaimed book *Gorillas in the Mist* remains perhaps the best starting point for anybody who wants to know more about mountain gorilla behaviour, while the epnonymous movie, a posthumous account of Fossey's life, drew global attention to the plight of the mountain gorilla.

The mountain gorilla is distinguished from its lowland counterparts by several adaptations to its high-altitude home, most visibly a longer and more luxuriant

340290; e kenya@sanctuaryretreats; www.
sanctuaryretreats. This long-serving tented
camp is 500m inside the park entrance at
Buhoma where it's cut into a forest glade at the
top of 91 steps. It's worth the climb to sleep in
a large individually secluded s/c twin-bed tent,
enjoy a hot soak in a bathtub looking out into

coat. It is on average bulkier than other races, with the heaviest individual gorilla
on record (of any race) being the 220kg dominant silverback of Rwanda's Sabinyo
group. Like other gorillas, it is a highly sociable creature, moving in defined troops
of anything from five to 50 animals. A troop typically consists of a dominant
silverback male (the male's back turns silver when he reaches sexual maturity at
about 13 years old) and sometimes a subordinate silverback, as well as a harem of
three or four mature females, and several young animals. Unusually for mammals,
it is the male who forms the focal point of gorilla society; when a silverback dies,
his troop normally disintegrates. A silverback will start to acquire his harem at
about 15 years of age, most normally by attracting a young sexually mature
female from another troop. He may continue to lead a troop well into his 40s.

A female gorilla reaches sexual maturity at the age of eight, after which she will
often move between different troops several times. Once a female has successfully
given birth, however, she normally stays loyal to the same silverback until he dies,
and she will even help defend him against other males. (When a male takes over a
troop, he generally kills all nursing infants to bring the mothers into oestrus more
quickly, a strong motive for a female to help preserve the status quo.) A female
gorilla has a gestation period similar to that of a human, and if she reaches old
age she will typically have raised up to six offspring to sexual maturity. A female's
status within a troop is based on the length of time she has been with a silverback:
the alpha female is normally the longest-serving member of the harem.

The mountain gorilla is primarily vegetarian, with bamboo shoots being the
favoured diet, though they are known to eat 58 different plant species in the
Virungas. They may also eat insects, with ants being a particularly popular protein
supplement. A gorilla troop will spend most of its waking hours on the ground,
but it will generally move into the trees at night, when each member of the
troop builds itself a temporary nest. Gorillas are surprisingly sedentary creatures,
typically moving less than 1km in a day, which makes tracking them on a day-to-
day basis relatively easy for experienced guides. A troop will generally only move a
long distance after a stressful incident, for instance an aggressive encounter with
another troop. Gorillas are peaceable animals with few natural enemies and they
often live for up to 50 years in the wild, but their long-term survival is critically
threatened by poaching, deforestation and exposure to human-borne diseases.

It was previously thought that the Virunga and Bwindi gorilla populations
were racially identical, not an unreasonable assumption given that a corridor of
mid-altitude forest linked the two mountain ranges until about 500 years ago.
But recent DNA tests indicate the Bwindi and Virunga gorillas show sufficient
genetic differences to suggest that they have formed mutually isolated breeding
populations for many millennia, in which case the 'mountain gorilla' should
possibly be split into two discrete races, one – the Bwindi gorilla – endemic to
Uganda, the other unique to the Virunga Mountains. Neither race numbers more
than 500 in the wild and neither has ever bred successfully in captivity, while both
meet several of the criteria for an IUCN classification of 'Critically Endangered'.

forest vegetation & eat a 1st-class meal in the organically decorated open-sided common area. *US$450/600 sgl/dbl FB.*

⌂ **Buhoma Lodge** (8 cottages) ✆ 0414 321479; m 0772 502155/721155; e reservations@ugandaexclusivecamps.com; www.ugandaexclusivecamps.com; www. wildfrontiers.co.ug. This terrific lodge has a particularly atmospheric 1st-floor lounge-dining room & comfortable s/c cottages facing the forest. These are accessed by flights of wooden stairs that provide useful practice for tracking gorillas. With mesh windows & gumpole 'n' plaster walls (a lightweight version of a half-timbered medieval building), they avoid the clinging dampness common to tropical forest accommodation. See advert on page 334. *US$390/580 s/c cottages sgl/ dbl FB, East African resident rates available.*

⌂ **Mahogany Springs** (8 cottages) e barrie@ mahoganysprings.com; www.mahoganysprings. com. This popular new lodge faces farmland & forest on the northern edge of Buhoma village. The lodge & cottages present a rather modernistic take on the usual safari style & if this results in some austere interiors, the scales are tipped the other way by the warmth of the service & the excellence of the food. *US$325/490/645 sgl/dbl/trpl FB.*

Moderate

⌂ **Engagi Tented Camp** (8 cottages) ✆ 0414 321552; e mantana@africaonline.co.ug; www. kimbla-mantana.com. Upmarket in execution, moderate (for Buhoma anyway) in price, this recently overhauled camp on the edge of Buhoma is the best value in town. The open-fronted, wooden-floored lodge is provided with lounge chairs & fireplace, historical prints you'd give any number of eye teeth to own, a library, bar, veranda

& the usual great forest view. These priorities within a structure of local stone, timber & thatch brings to mind the home of a colonial-era settler (a successful one anyway). The improvements extend to the accommodation with the damp canvas tents being replaced by comfortably furnished timber & plaster s/c cottages. *US$215/325 sgl/dbl FB, generous discounts for East African residents.*

⌂ **Silverback Lodge** (10 rooms) ✆ 0312 60260; e reservations@marasa.com; www. silverbacklodge.com. This small lodge has just been taken over by Marasa, a company responsible for a string of luxury lodges in Uganda & Kenya. An imminent makeover will doubtless transform the décor & dimensions of the rather cramped rooms & presumably, the prices. One aspect needs no tinkering with: Silverback is located high above the competition in Buhoma village & enjoys the best forest view of the lot. See advert in third colour section. *US$200/280 sgl/dbl FB (high season), US$170/230 (low season).*

Budget

⌂ **Lake Kitandara Bwindi Camp** (19 tents) ✆ 0312 277304; www.kitandarabwindicamp. Located just outside the park gate, this long serving camp offers basic s/c furnished tents. *US$180/250 sgl/dbl FB, US$10pp camping.*

⌂ **Buhoma Community Rest Camp (BCRC)** (6 tents, 5 *bandas* & a dorm) ✆ 0312 100060; m 0772 384965; e buhomacommunitycampground@yahoo. com; www.buhomacommunity.com. Located just inside the park gate, BCRC is Buhoma's most popular 'budget' option. The rates are considerably lower than almost everything else in the vicinity while over the years, profits have done much for local community development. It's an entirely

IHIMBO HOT SPRING

If you're driving through Kambuga on the way between Rukungiri and Bwindi, you might want to ask about the location of the hot spring known locally as Ihimbo. Discovered by a Bakiga settler in the 1950s, the boiling water that bubbled from the spring rapidly acquired national fame for its therapeutic powers. One legend tells of a flat-chested girl who bathed there and emerged with an enviably voluptuous bosom, another of a man who lost his leg in an accident and regained it after swimming in the hot water. At its peak of popularity, Ihimbo attracted up to 1,000 invalids annually from all around the county, but whether it still receives visitors today, I cannot say.

frill-free set-up but there may be some tweaks forthcoming; a Peace Corps volunteer has been installed at the BCRC to introduce concepts such as 'value for money' & 'conveniently placed ablutions'. *US$96/120 s/c sgl/dbl tents FB, US$78/96 non-s/c sgl/dbl tents, US$48pp dorm bed FB, US$10 camping.*

⌂ **Bwindi View Bandas** (10 *bandas*) m 0772 399224; e bwindiview@yahoo.com; www.gorilladestination.com. This privately run, backpacker-oriented facility beside the park gate enjoys a fine forest view from a wonderfully rustic, covered, 1st-floor restaurant/bar deck. The basic s/c rooms are 10x the price of comparable accommodation in Butogota but, as the manager points out, 'This is Buhoma.' Cynical stuff! *US$80/100/100/160 basic s/c sgl/dbl/twin/trpl FB,*

US$50 using communal facilities, US$90 furnished s/c tent FB.

Shoestring
⌂ **Gorilla Friend's Lodge** (14 rooms) m 0782 822043/0791 761987; e gorillafriendslodge@ yahoo.com. Known locally as 'Magezi's place' this simple roadside guesthouse, 2km before the park gate, is far & away the best value in the area. This is where the safari drivers stay, so be sure to book in advance. Acceptable s/c rooms. *US$10/12 s/c sgl/ dbl B&B, US$8/12 sgl/dbl with shared facilities.*
⌂ **Jungle View Lodge** (15 rooms) m 0772 549088 (phone or SMS). Shoestring lodge in Buhoma village. Acceptable rooms, expect rates to rise when renovations are completed. *US$12/20 sgl/dbl with shared showers.*

Other practicalities
Internet Internet access is available at the **Bwindi Community Hospital**, 4km from Buhoma.

What to see and do
Gorilla tracking (*A permit costs US$500 for foreign visitors, US$475 for residents, low season discounts may apply*) Three habituated gorilla groups – Mubare, Rushegura and Habinyanja – live in the vicinity of Buhoma. Eight permits are available for each of these groups, bringing the daily total to 24.

Gorilla tracking excursions leave from Buhoma at 08.00 and the round trip might take anything from three to ten hours, depending on the proximity of the gorillas and how easily they are located. The success rate is as good as 100% – one Kampala operator who has sent hundreds of clients to Bwindi annually reckons that they have failed to see gorillas only twice in the past six years.

See box, pages 244–5.

Guided day walks from Buhoma (*US$15pp for a half-day's walk*) Bwindi is widely thought to support the greatest biodiversity of any East African forest, and the Buhoma area has more to offer than just gorilla tracking. Five different day trails, ranging from 30 minutes to eight hours in duration, lead from Buhoma, offering the opportunity to enjoy the tranquillity of the forest and to see several different monkey species. For birders, roughly 190 bird species have been recorded in the Buhoma area, ten of which are either listed in the *Red Data Book* or else are endemic to the Albertine Rift.

Guided trails are well worth it, since most of the guides are very knowledgeable and good at finding animals that you'd probably miss. A tip is not mandatory but it is more or less customary, bearing in mind that the rangers are very poorly paid. For monkeys and general scenery, the best of the guided walks is probably the three-hour **Waterfall Trail**. This leads for 2km along an abandoned road before heading into what I consider one of the most beautiful areas of forest in Uganda, and following the Munyaga River on the ascent to the 33m-high waterfall. Other trails are the **Mazubijiro Loop Trail** and **Rushara Hill Trail**, which both take about three hours and offer good views across to the Virunga

7

On the morning of 17 March 2000, a larger than normal congregation gathered in the church of Kanungu's Movement for the Restoration of the Ten Commandments of God (MRTCG). The assembled cultists had been promised that today, finally, after long years of waiting, the apocalypse of fire spoken of by the Virgin Mary would sweep the earth. The Blessed Virgin had also asserted, or so the congregation was told, that the only survivors of the terrible inferno would be the select few assembled within the church, which should be sealed to ensure that nobody wandered outside at the wrong moment.

While the congregation sang their praises, a person or persons unknown locked the church doors for the last time, boarded and nailed closed the windows, and then doused the wooden building with 40 litres of sulphuric acid purchased illegally four days earlier by one of the cult leaders, Dominic Kataribabo. A match was struck, and the building exploded in a fireball of such intensity that many of its occupants' skulls exploded. Later, the remains of 330 charred bodies would eventually be identified, but church records indicate that more than 500 people must have died in the blaze. The only certain survivor was a teenage boy who had slipped out to buy some food shortly before the building was boarded up.

Initial police investigations indicated that the cremated cultists had been participants in a mass suicide pact. But then six more bodies were found buried in the Nyabugoto compound, and over the next six weeks a further 450 corpses were unearthed in mass graves at four other cult-associated properties. The buried victims had clearly not been acquiescent suicides, but had instead been strangled, clubbed or poisoned to death by the cult leadership. The police duly changed their verdict to mass murder – the largest cult killing in world history.

Years later, the circumstances surrounding the MRTCG massacre remain shrouded in mystery, as does the origin of the doomsday cult itself. Its chief apostle was a 68-year-old retired schoolteacher and civil servant called Joseph Kibwetere, deeply religious despite having fathered several illegitimate children, and once diagnosed as manic depressive after he claimed to have died and been resurrected. Kibwetere reputedly founded the cult after he overheard a conversation in which Jesus and the Virgin Mary complained about the world's departure from the Ten Commandments, and then decided to set the apocalypse for the turn of the millennium.

Subsequent investigations suggest that the MRTCG's true leader was not Kibwetere but Credonia Mwerinde, a 48-year-old school dropout who passed through four unsuccessful marriages, and produced a similar number of offspring, before she ended up a bar-girl and prostitute in Kanungu's Independence Bar. While working there, she became the seventh wife of a local Mukiga man – polygamy is still widely practised in the area – but the relationship fell apart when she was unable to conceive. One day, probably in early 1989, Mwerinde visited the Nyabugoto Caves, formerly associated with a fertility cult and more recently with visitations by the Virgin Mary, who duly appeared to say that the baby had been withheld so that Mwerinde could serve as Mary's medium. Over the months that followed, Mwerinde established a cult not dissimilar to that of Nyabingi, curing infertile and ill women as the oracle of the Blessed Virgin.

In mid-1989, Mwerinde met Kibwetere and his wife Teresa, and was invited to relocate her spiritual practice to their home in Ntungamo. A year later, the MRTCG was officially launched, and by 1991 some 200 followers were living at the house, and Mwerinde and Kibwetere had become lovers. In 1993, Teresa and her children bade Kibwetere and his growing cult – the membership eventually reached 5,000 – a less than fond farewell when it relocated to a 5ha hillside plot near Kanungu. Here, the cult was joined by a disgraced priest called Dominic Kataribabo, who would effectively become third in command to Mwerinde and Kibwetere.

In 2002, a Uganda Human Rights Commission team report on the MRTCG indicated that its leaders had violated 'all human rights' even before the killing started. The rank and file were forbidden from talking, worked long hours of hard manual labour, were given limited food, could not wear shoes, and were forced to sleep on the floor of the compound's unsanitary and overcrowded dormitories. Children were separated from their parents, sex was forbidden even between married couples, and contact with neighbouring communities was banned. Upon joining the cult, members were expected to sell all their property and other possessions, the proceeds of which were to be donated to the cult, whose increasingly wealthy leaders suffered no such deprivations in their large modern house.

The MRTCG was centred on the Virgin Mary's announcement, relayed via Mwerinde and Kibwetere, that the world would end at midnight on 31 December 1999, and that the only survivors would be those cult members who had shed all their money and possessions and were gathered at the Nyabugoto camp when the moment came. And inevitably, once that long-awaited moment did come, and then went, without event, the mood of the dispossessed and formerly compliant cultists changed. Some left and never returned. Those who took up the leaders' invitation to submit a written complaint ended up in the mass graves later discovered by the police. And about 500 followers were appeased by a statement to the effect that the Virgin had contacted the leaders to say that Armageddon had not been cancelled, only rescheduled. It would take place on 17 March.

Who actually started the blaze and whether they survived remain open questions. International arrest warrants have been issued against Mwerinde, Kibwetere, Kataribabo and other prominent cult leaders, and a handsome police reward is at stake for information leading to their detainment. Some say that all the main leaders died in the inferno, but of them Kataribabo alone has been identified among the bodies, and then only tentatively. Another hypothesis is that Kibwetere had been diagnosed with AIDS in 1999 and died sometime before 17 March, either of natural causes, or at the hand of his angry lover Mwerinde – some surviving cultists say he had not been seen since October. Contradicting this are reports of Mwerinde and Kataribabo having been observed together shortly after the massacre, headed in the direction of the nearest border – only 25km distant – and presumably across to the DRC. Kibwetere's car, though present in the compound on the morning of the fire, has not been sighted since. Clearly, somebody escaped.

The promised judicial inquiry into the cult killings never materialised owing to lack of funding. Several other doomsday cults as potentially deluded and/or murderous as the MRTCG still operate in Uganda, though the more prominent ones have been disbanded by the authorities. In January 2003, journalist Kalungi Kabuye visited the site of the massacre and wrote in the New Vision: 'There is nothing left but empty, rotting buildings and overgrown bush ... no plaque commemorating their passage ... Where was the church that was burnt down? Where are the mass graves? ... Shouldn't there be something to warn coming generations of just how bad man can be?'

Mountains. The eight-hour **Ivo River Walk**, which leads to the Ivo River on the southern boundary of the park, offers a good opportunity for seeing monkeys, duikers and a variety of birds.

Visitors with a particular interest in birds should ask for UWA guides, Medi and Silva. Birders with specific boxes to tick could engage private bird guides possessed of birdsong-playing gadgetry, namely Alfred Twinomujuni (**e** *twinoalf555@ hotmail.com*) and his protégé, Fred Tugaruriwe (**m** *0775 204131*).

Birdwatchers with a limited amount of time in Buhoma are strongly urged to stick to the **Mungaya River Trail** on the edge of the park (behind the gorilla tracking trailhead) and the old road that runs through the forest south of Buhoma. Both provide better birding opportunities than a narrow forest path and on a good morning you could hope to see around 40–50 species over a slow 2km walk, a high proportion of them more easily seen here than in any other similarly accessible part of Uganda. Among the great many remarkable birds that are commonly seen along this road, some of the more readily identifiable include the great blue and black-billed turacos; dusky and barred long-tailed cuckoos; bar-tailed trogon; black bee-eater; grey-throated barbet; Petit's cuckoo-shrike; Elliot's woodpecker; red-tailed bulbul; mountain, icterine and yellow-whiskered greenbuls; white-bellied robin-chat; white-tailed ant-thrush; rusty-faced warbler; white-browed crombec; yellow-eyed black flycatcher; white-tailed blue flycatcher; white-tailed crested monarch; narrow-tailed starling; McKinnon's grey shrike; Luhder's and Doherty's bush-shrikes; and black-headed waxbill. Indulgent as the above list may sound to non-birders, it is really no more than a taster! In addition to the outstanding birding, this road supports a dazzling array of colourful butterflies, and the lovely L'Hoest's monkey is often encountered.

Village walk (*US$15pp*) This three-hour stroll through Buhoma and its margins immerses visitors in the customs and practices of the Bakiga and Batwa people. The tour takes in varied activities such as farming, brewing local beer, dispensing traditional medicines and concludes with dancing displays by members of the Batwa community. The walk is organised through the Buhoma Community Rest Camp (see pages 282–3).

Batwa Experience (*www.batwaexperience.com*; *US$70pp*) Organised by the Batwa Development Programme, this new cultural encounter takes place in a patch of private forest contiguous with the national park. The day-long event provides a fascinating insight into the traditional forest life and lore of the Batwa people.

Shopping and dance performances While most lodges contain some sort of sales area, take the time to browse through the roadside craft shops in **Buhoma village**. At the risk of ignoring private enterprise, I'll single out the **Batwa Women's Organisation** shop (50m village-side of the park gate) as a worthy cause. Next door is a stage outside the **Bwindi Orphan's Group** premises where members assemble daily at 18.00 to put on song and dance performances. There is no charge but donations are welcomed.

RUHIJA Uganda's highest gorilla-tracking trailhead is sited at 2,340m in the hills of eastern Bwindi. Ruhija is one of the most beautiful places I've ever seen, with fabulous southerly views over forested ridge after forested ridge to the Virunga Volcanoes. Equally panoramic views towards the western Rift Valley are afforded from sections of the road leading beyond Ruhija towards Buhoma, as well as from the hill a short distance beyond the lodges (see below). Prior to the opening of the Bitakura gorilla group for tracking, activity at Ruhija was limited to the odd visiting birdwatcher and research carried out by the International Trust for Forest Conservation (ITFC) which runs a field station there. Though a motorable road passed through Ruhija linking the Kisoro Road to Buhoma, its condition was so poor that traffic was more or less limited to hardened UWA and ITFC staff. Recently, however, this backwater status has changed. Road improvements mean that the route is now negotiable by saloon cars, while half a dozen new facilities have appeared in nearby Ruhija village to feed and water (up to) 16 gorilla tracking tourists daily.

Two habituated gorilla groups can be tracked from Ruhija. The Bitakura group range across the steep mountainside between the roadside trailhead on Ruhija Ridge and the Mubwindi Swamp several hundred metres below while the Oruzogo clan inhabits the section of forest between Ruhija and the Bwindi 'neck'. Gorilla tracking apart, Ruhija merits further exploration. The 'main' road offers good monkey viewing, with black-and-white colobus particularly common. It's also the only part of the park in which elephant are resident, so caution is required – Ruhija's elephants have been known to rock vehicles. Because it lies at a higher altitude than Buhoma, the tree composition is more characteristic of Afro-montane than lowland forest, and it supports a significantly different avifauna, making it an essential destination for enthusiasts. It is one of the few places where you stand a chance of seeing all four crimson-wings recorded in Uganda, and other specialities include a variety of apalis species, Lagden's bush-shrike, African green broadbill, and the handsome francolin. The only Ugandan record for the uncommon yellow-crested helmet-shrike is an unconfirmed sighting at Ruhija.

The six-hour **Bamboo Trail** leads to Rwamunyoni Peak, at 2,607m the highest point in the park, and also notable for good birding. Also of interest is the three-hour trail descending to Mubwindi Swamp, several hundred metres below Ruhija. This is one of the most alluring bird walks in Uganda, with the possibility of ticking off some 20 bird species listed in the *Red Data Book* and/or endemic to the Albertine Rift, notably the extremely local African green broadbill and Grauer's rush warbler.

Getting there and away To get to Ruhija from Kabale, follow the surfaced Kisoro Road for roughly 25km, then turn right at a clearly signposted junction. Though this road is currently well maintained (the drive should take between 90 minutes and two hours) there are rocky sections and the route can deteriorate during rainy seasons, so ask for an update before you set off in a **saloon car**. Though there is now plenty of accommodation at Ruhija, many visitors still stay in cheaper lodgings in Kabale and head up to the trailhead early in the morning. Staff at the **Kabale Tourist Information Office** in Kabale (m *0782 314190; see page 245*) can help you find arrange a saloon car (carries 4) for about Ush200,000 or a 4x4 safari vehicle Ush250,000. Alternatively, contact the Kabale-based safari companies listed on page 248. If you're content to perch on the back of a **pick-up**, these leave Kabale market between 12.00 and 14.00, returning from Ruhija around 06.00 (*Ush10,000*). For the record, a boda boda from Kabale to Ruhija costs Ush60,000; do please let us know how you get on!

Where to stay With the exception of Cuckooland and Gift of Nature guesthouse, the accommodation listed below is accessed from a track running through Ruhija village, beyond the International Trust for Forest Conservation research station. The turning off the main road is 1km east of the gorilla tracking trailhead and is easily identifiable by the cluster of signposts. Though there's nothing here to match Buhoma's genuinely high-end lodges, you'll find a wider choice of reasonably priced lodgings.

There are three consistent similarities. Firstly, most lodges enjoy terrific northeasterly views of the forest and adjacent terraced hills. Secondly, the evenings can be pretty chilly at 2,300m above sea level, so the better-planned lodges are provided with a fireplace. Thirdly, Ruhija has a serious water shortage. If it doesn't fall from the sky, it has to be fetched from a valley stream spring located a parachute-worthy distance below Ruhija ridge. Consequently, in place of the usual grass thatch, you'll find roofs covered by tile or corrugated sheets to maximise the potential for rainwater harvesting.

In addition to those listed below, here are a couple more locations to look out for, both of which I found under construction. Just east of the Bwindi 'neck', the hilltop **Hachikorwe Campsite** is putting up some pretty basic cottages and an elevated platform bar with a fantastic 360° view. Meanwhile, at **Bwindi Panorama**, some simple wooden cottages are nearing completion in a private patch of montane woodland just west of Ruhija. For location of listings see map, pages 240–1.

Moderate

⌂ **Ruhija Gorilla Lodge** (8 rooms) m 0712 187411; e reservations@gorillasafari.travel; www. asyanutours-safaris.com. This smart facility on a hillside behind Ruhija village enjoys a terrific view across the forest towards the Virungas & the Rift Valley. The spacious rooms are in semi-detached cottages, some of which have a welcome fireplace – it gets pretty chilly at 2,340m above sea level. *US$240/400 sgl/dbl 'deluxe' cabins & US$270/470 'superior' cabins FB.*

⌂ **Gorilla Mist Camp** (8 units) m 0754 315151; e info@gorillamistcamp.com; www. gorillamistcamp.com. At the end of the road behind Ruhija village, the staff seem committed to the success of this new venture. Half-timbered cottages & furnished tents (all s/c) are offered. Prices are negotiable. *US$130/212 sgl/dbl FB.*

⌂ **Bakiga Lodge** (2 tents) m 0774 518421; e info@bakigalodge.com; www.bakigalodge. com. Run by the Bakiga Community Project, which funds local water projects, this small lodge provides attractively furnished s/c tents & a simple open-plan lodge building with fireplace & view. *US$100pp FB.*

⌂ **Cuckooland** (4 tents) m 0793/0757 399046; e info@cuckooland.com; www.bwindicuckooland. com. This small tented camp 30mins' drive east of Ruhija offers spacious s/c tents set in 4ha of regenerating farmland looking directly into the part of Bwindi Forest roamed by the Oruzogo gorilla group. Though there's nothing particularly cuckoo about this, the lodge does lie halfway down a steep hillside, a considerable way below

the hilltop car park. Since this is mountain gorilla-tracking country, think of the stiff, 10–15min climb back up to the parking area as a small test. If you can't manage, you'll stand no chance of finding gorillas. Cuckooland is also the only gorilla lodge to counter the cool Kigezi climate with a swimming pool (a 'natural' pool with aquatic marginal plants) & to provide a gym of sorts (the heavy things are engine blocks, differential housings, etc). The prices are refreshingly sane. *US$100/130 sgl/twin B&B, US$125/180 sgl/twin FB.*

⌂ **Trekkers Tavern** (5 cottages) m 0772455423/0777 117101; e accessug@ utlonline.co.ug; www.trekkerstavern.com. Set in a patch of woodland beyond Ruhija village, this small lodge offers inferior copies of the upmarket cottages at Ndali Lodge. They are, nevertheless, fair value while the pedigree of the chef suggests that you won't lack for culinary enjoyment. *US$100/150 sgl/dbl FB.*

Budget

⌂ **Gift of Nature** (5 rooms) m 0755 216333; www.giftofnaturelodge.com. Modern residential house with rising damp in Mburamuzi village 3km from the Ruhija trailhead. *US$90/160/100 s/c sgl/ dbl/ twin FB.*

Shoestring

⌂ **Ruhija Community Rest Camp** (6 rooms) m 0771 846635; e ruhijacommunityrestcamp@ yahoo.com. Very basic, clean s/c rooms accessed through a pretty flowering garden in Ruhija village. Profits (which must presumably be fairly minimal) fund community projects. *US$25/50 sgl/ dbl B&B.*

Å Gorilla Friends (4 twin-bed tents) m 0785 106591. This low-key campsite occupies a compact

site behind the Ruhija trading centre. Simple furnished tents & rooms have shared facilities & enjoy the usual fabulous views. *US$30pp tents. US$20pp rooms B&B*

RUSHAGA Rushaga, on the southern edge of Bwindi, became Uganda's newest gorilla tracking site in October 2009. An unusually high-profile launch saw a bratpack of young American film stars jet in to track gorillas at Rushaga and make positive statements about their experience. At the time, Nshongi, the group they tracked, was by far the largest of Uganda's habituated gorilla groups (with 34 members) and included three silverbacks, six blackbacks and eight infants. Today, however, since the addition of another habituated group and a number of subsequent divisions and subdivisions within both of these, the Rushaga sector is home to no fewer than five (rather smaller) habituated gorilla groups – Nshongi (seven animals), Mishaya (seven animals), Kahungye (18 animals), Busingye (nine animals) and Bweza (seven animals).

With 40 daily gorilla permits now on offer, Rushaga is set to have major implications for regional tourism. Though I imagine tour companies will continue to favour Buhoma (thanks to plenty of quality accommodation and easy accessibility from Ishasha and destinations north), Rushaga will be an obvious Plan B for large groups during the high season and, by dragging the established safari circuit southwards, bring little-visited gems such as Lake Bunyonyi into the picture. Another consideration is that Rushaga is just 90 minutes from the Rwandese border at Cyanika meaning that flying to Kigali to track gorillas in Uganda is perfectly feasible. Also, at the time of writing anyway, Rushaga permits can be bought on site at the time of tracking (contact the Kisoro UWA office, see page 263, or a local tour company for availability). This will appeal to independent travellers, backpackers, overland truck groups, and regional expatriates, especially those approaching from Rwanda, and others with no wish to go to Kampala.

An abundance of independent, flexible visitors is a good thing because there's no reason to rush off after tracking gorillas. There's plenty to attract birders including the localised Rwenzori turaco and Shelley's crimson wing. The scenery is also terrific and unlike some parts of Bwindi, where you can't see the wood for the trees, Rushaga has great views across deep, forested valleys and offers southern glimpses of the Virunga Volcanoes. A particular highspot is the self-explanatory destination of the three- to four-hour (round trip) **Waterfall Trail**: after descending into a steep valley dripping with giant tree ferns, you'll clamber upwards through a narrow, stream-filled fissure in the cliff face to reach a towering, rock-walled atrium containing a cascade of more than 30m. The usual UWA guided walk fees apply. Outside the park, one candidate for further exploration would seem to be the dramatic and deeply incised **Ruhezanyenda river valley**.

Getting there and away Located on the southern edge of the national park, Rushaga is straightforward to reach in a **private vehicle**. From Kabale, head along the Kisoro Road to Muko (40km), just beyond the northern tip of Lake Bunyonyi. At the foot of the hill beyond Muko, turn right off the tarmac on to a *murram* road. At Katojo village, atop the following hill, turn right. Rushaga lies 25km further on, the drive culminating in a long, winding descent into the Ruhezanyenda Valley. Just beyond a bridge over the pretty river, a 1.5km track at Nyamasinda village runs to the trailhead at Rushaga ranger post.

If approaching from Kisoro, head north along the signposted route for 25km as far as the Nkuringo–Rubugeri junction. Turn right here, pass through Rubugeri town (1km) and then follow a mountainous 7km road over a lofty pass before descending towards Nyamasinda village. Turn left just before the brige to Rushaga.

A **special hire** from Kabale will cost Ush150,000 and Ush100,000 from Kisoro; rather more if you go through a tour company (see listings, page 248). The tourist information office in Kabale (see page 245) and the Kisoro UWA office (see page 263) can help arrange a vehicle. Public transport (trucks) runs from Kabale (from Ki-kollegi behind the taxi park) and Kisoro early on Saturday and Tuesday mornings for Rubuguri market. The Kabale **trucks** will pass Rushaga and cost Ush6,000 if you're perched in the back, Ush10,000 up front with the driver. Ask to be dropped at a signpost indicating a steep-looking short cut, about 1km beyond Nyamasinda towards Rubuguri. Trucks from Kisoro will leave you in Rubugeri, from where a **boda-boda** to Rushaga costs around Ush9,000.

 Where to stay The listings below cover lodges at Rushaga and Rubuguri town. If you're prepared to make an earlier start, it's also possible to stay in Kabale, Lake Bunyonyi or Kisoro, and travel to Rushaga on the day of tracking. At present, telephone reception is extremely poor in the Rubuguri–Rushaga area (locals will show you the single spot to get a signal in Rushaga village). If you can't get through to a lodge on a mobile line, send a text message. For location of listings see map, page 240.

Moderate

Gorilla Safari Lodge (8 rooms) 0414 345742; m 0772 470260; e info@crystalsafaris. com; www.gorillasafarilodge.com, www. crystalsafaris.com. The Kampala-based Crystal Safaris have created a little gem of a lodge at Rushaga on a hillside facing the forest. 1km from the trailhead, 8 attractive s/c cottages (& a spa) are spread across a pretty garden site surrounded by scattered homesteads & facing the forest. *US$250/350 sgl/dbl FB.*

Budget

Nshongi Gorilla Resort (18 rooms) m 0785 003091; e nshongiresort@yahoo.com; www.nshongigorillaresort.com. On the northern edge of Rubuguri town, this church-built set-up has undergone a rather slipshod conversion to accommodate gorilla trackers. The dorm block now contains s/c rooms, & a couple of s/c cottages have been added. There's nothing to admire in the way of artisanship but the prices are not ridiculous. *US$70/100 sgl/dbl rooms & US$100/160 sgl/dbl cottages FB, US$10pp camping.*

Gorilla Valley Resort (6 cottages) www. naturelodges.biz. Due to open in mid 2013, this is the latest offering from Nature Lodges, a company that specialises in decent & very reasonably priced s/c accommodation adjoining the national parks. Offering 2-room cottages. The rates seem reasonable for any park but for Bwindi they are a bargain! *US$92/124 sgl/dbl FB.*

Wagtail Eco Safari Park (8 rooms) m 0775 208775; e kanyamuny@yahoo.com; www.nkuringo. com. This facility offers s/c cottages & furnished tents in a rather shady compound just off the main road in Rubugeri, 7km from Rushaga. *US$80pp FB.*

Shoestring

Nshongi Campsite (5 cottages) e nshongicamp@gmail.com; http://nshongicamp. altervista.org. Occupying a lush garden site by a stream, right on the edge of the forest behind Rushaga village, this simple set-up offers basic cottages & camping. There's no vehicle access; the site lies 5mins' walk down a long but gentle path & is 15mins' walk from the trailhead. *US$41/68 sgl/ dbl FB, US$4pp or US$24 FB camping.*

NKURINGO The Nkuringo sector of Bwindi opened for gorilla tracking in 2004. Covering the southwestern part of the forest, it's just 40km north of Kisoro, but feels far more remote and, although densely settled by farming communities, is very undeveloped on account of its location on a dead-end road ending at the nearby DRC border.

Nkuringo is an extremely beautiful area with good potential for hiking. The approach along the Nteko Ridge provides grandstand views across the Kashasha river valley to the Bwindi Forest which cloaks its northern slopes. 'Nkuringo' means 'round stone' and refers to a knoll-like forested hill beside the river, dwarfed by loftier ridges above it. To the south and west, superb panoramas include the western Rift Valley and the entire length of the Virunga volcanic range.

One group of gorillas has been habituated at Nkuringo. This consists of 21 individuals: two silverbacks, four blackbacked males, four adult females, six sub-adults and juveniles and five infants, including twins born in 2009. The group ranges over a 10km section of the Kashasha river valley which forms the boundary of the national park. They are usually encountered in the forest but do also range along the public lands to eat crops on the southern slopes of the valley. The International Gorilla Conservation Programme has purchased a 10km-long by 400m-wide strip of public land along the river as a buffer zone. Land-use practices such as pasture and tea are planned for this area since these are not appealing to gorillas and will encourage them to remain in the park.

Getting there and away
The trailhead for tracking in Nkuringo is in Ntungamo village on the Nteko Ridge, which can be reached **by vehicle** from either Kabale or Kisoro. From Kabale, you have a choice of two routes, both of which take about three hours. The shorter option (91km) runs via Rubuguri and is about an hour on tarmac and two on winding dirt roads. Follow the directions for Rushaga (see page 289) but pass through Nyamasinda (ignoring the Rushaha turn-off) and continue for 7km to Rubuguri. A kilometre beyond the town, turn right at a junction signposted for Nkuringo junction (1km). Ntumgamo village lies 10km along this road. The other option (115km) is to follow the tarmac to Kisoro – a short two hours – followed by a long hour on dirt roads to Nkuringo. From Kisoro, head north for 25km to the signposted junction for Nkuringo where you turn left.

The dirt sections of the routes described are generally in reasonable condition, although the hilly section can be narrow and windy with steep drops. Heavy rain and steep terrain also mean that landslides can occasionally block the road and a **4x4 vehicle** driven at a sensible speed is recommended in wet conditions.

There's no regular public transport to Ntungamo village from Kisoro. Most vehicles from Kabale and Kisoro come mostly on market days (Mondays and Thursdays) to Rubugeri Town, 11km away. You can then find a **boda** either in Rubuguri or the Nkuringo junction, 1km from town. Alternatively, the 10km ridge-top road offers marvellous views and with time and energy you might consider **walking**. Indeed, you could eschew vehicular transport altogether, following local paths from Kisoro and crossing Lake Mutanda by **canoe** (see *Nkuringo walking safaris*, below). If you really enjoy walking, you can continue from Nkuringo through the forest to Buhoma (UWA fees apply)

To **hire a vehicle** to reach Nkuringo, ask at the UWA office in Kisoro (see page 263) or the tourist information centre in Kabale (see page 245) for advice. The latter also runs a **shuttle** to its Nkuringo hostel, Bwindi Backpackers (*US$30pp return*). A **taxi** from Kisoro costs Ush100,000–150,000, and Ush200,000–250,000 from Kabale, rates depending on the season and the state of the roads.

Where to stay
Though accommodation in the vicinity of Nkuringo is limited, you'll find additional lodgings in Rubuguri (30 minutes distant) or Kisoro (an hour

or so away). It's feasible to spend the night in either location and then travel up to Ntungamo in the early morning. Like Ruhija, Ntungamo is located on a lofty ridge and water must be collected as rain or transported from streams in distant valleys. Do bear this in mind when you open a tap or flush a loo. For location of listings see map, pages 240–1.

Upmarket

🏠 **Clouds Gorilla Lodge** (8 cottages) 📞0414 251182/0312 261658; m 0772 489497; e info@ wildplacesafrica.com; www.wildplacesafrica.com. This luxurious lodge stands on the Nkuringo Ridge where it enjoys unparalleled views of the Virunga chain & the western Rift Valley by day & the glowing cone of the active Nyirangongo Volcano by night. Spacious (80m²) cottages incorporate a 2-sofa lounge & bedroom with interconnected fireplace, & bathroom with piping-hot shower. Each is decorated with work by a Ugandan artist. The comfort of guests in the main lodge building, a large & airy stone building with massive timber roof beams, is also assured, not least through a generous ratio of 1.8 armchair/sofa spaces per guest. Clouds has been built through a partnership between Wildplaces safari company, African Wildlife Foundation & the local community. *US$470/940 sgl/dbl.*

Moderate

🏠 **Nkuringo Gorilla Camp** (2 *bandas,* 6 rooms) m 0774 805580/0702 805580; www.nkuringocampsite.com, www. nkuringowalkingsafaris.com. The old Nkuringo community campground is unrecognisable in its new incarnation as a boutique backpackers. Now privately run, the site offers accommodation (s/c, non-s/c & camping) priced for a variety of budgets but none of which, you'll note, are traditionally associated with backpackers. With

meticulous construction, generous dimensions, suitable furnishings & vibrant décor, the result is an upmarket lodge with (mostly) shared bathrooms & the homely atmosphere of a budget hostel. You'll see what I mean. It's also a stunning site with views north across Bwindi towards Buhoma village, Lake Edward & the Rwenzori, & the Virungas to the south. Worth visiting for the views; forget the gorillas! *US$210/290 sgl/dbl s/c cottages (2 units), US$100/150 sgl/dbl rooms with shared bathroom, US$63/110 sgl/dbl dome tents. All rates FB.*

Budget

🏠 **Bwindi Backpackers Lodge** m 0772 661854/661854; e info@ bwindibackpackerslodge.com; www. bwindibackpackerslodge.com. This new, roadside set-up 5km before Nkuringo has a storied, half-timbered structure with rooms at the bottom, & a restaurant & forest view above. It's an offshoot of the Kabale Information Centre (see page 245), which provides a shuttle to/from the hostel (*US$30pp return*). *US$65/120 s/c sgl/dbl, US$50/90 sgl/dbl with shared bathrooms, US$33 dorm bed, US$30 camping. All rates FB.*

Shoestring

🏠 **Albertine Campsite** (3 rooms) Small, basic rooms just across the road from the gorilla tracking trailhead. *US$30/50 sgl/dbl FB.*

What to see and do

Gorilla tracking The staging point for gorilla tracking is the small UWA office 500m beyond the Ntungamo trading centre on the Nteko Ridge above the park boundary. You need to check in at 08.00. Nkuringo is the most physically challenging of all gorilla-tracking locations. Unlike existing tracking sites at Buhoma and Mgahinga, there is no vehicle access from the Nteko Ridge to the park boundary which follows the Kashasha River. The closest road is the Rubugiri–Ntungamo–Nteko road on the ridge 600m above the river. Trackers face a steep one-hour descent simply in order to cross the river and enter the forest. That said, the gorillas are as often as not found in a strip of regenerating, former farmland purchased as a buffer zone on the non-park side of the river. After the arduous but rewarding business of gorilla tracking, you'll face a one- to two-hour climb back up to the ridge. This is not a problem for the fit, but Nkuringo is definitely not for the unfit or faint-hearted, though a number of routes have been improved by the addition of steps and gentler switchback turns. The gorillas range along the Kashasha Valley so you can walk or drive (if you have a vehicle) to the most convenient descent. It's hotter on the open hillside than in the forest so do take plenty of water with you. Porters can be hired to carry your bag to and from the forest if required for Ush10,000.

Buniga Forest walk (*www.bunigaforestwalk.com; US$25pp, no park fees or UWA guide fees are involved*) With the tagline, 'Meet the Batwa, then and now', this new activity gives you the chance to see a forest through the eyes of Batwa guides before visiting them in a contemporary settlement. In a patch of ridgetop forest near the gorilla tracking trailhead, Batwa guides from the settlement of Sanuriio demonstrate aspects of their traditional forest life – creating shelter, firing bows and arrows, making fire, identifying medicinal herbs, etc. The event concludes with a visit to Sanuriio, 5km distant, certainly one of the better Batwa settlements, to see how the forest people exist today (for background information, see box *Batwa Pygmies* on pages 258–9).

Hiking Nkuringo is a superbly scenic area with great potential for hiking outside the forest. I would suggest, however, that this is not an area for haphazard exploration, though in all probability the available options are pretty limited. The steep nature of Nteko Ridge means that the main alternatives for a pleasant stroll are either west along the ridge-top road towards DRC or east towards Rubugeri. Bear in mind that Ntungamo lies about 8km from the Congolese border and it is a sensitive area. Tourism development has been subject to all manner of evaluations to ensure visitor safety and it's most unlikely that you'd wander off into the DRC, or indeed be allowed to.

Nkuringo Community walk (*US$30pp*) This community-run activity provides insights into Bakiga life and culture, with visits to a traditional healer, blacksmith, brewer and homestead in the vicinity of Ntungamo village. The walk can be arranged through Clouds Lodge or Nkuringo Gorilla Camp (see opposite).

Nkuringo walking safaris (m *0774 805580/0702 805580;* e *info@ nkuringowalkingsafaris.com; www.nkuringowalkingsafaris.com*) This ridiculously scenic excursion connects Kisoro Town and Ntungamo village by means of a dugout-canoe voyage across Lake Mutanda and footpaths leading through the Kigezi Hills to Nkuringo Gorilla Camp. The option of continuing through a lovely section of Bwindi Forest to Buhoma is also highly recommended. A two-day excursion with overnight accommodation at Nkuringo Gorilla Camp (see opposite; lazy camping on full-board arrangement) costs from US$151 for one person and drops to US$90 per person for groups of six. Prices exclude Bwindi park fees if applicable.

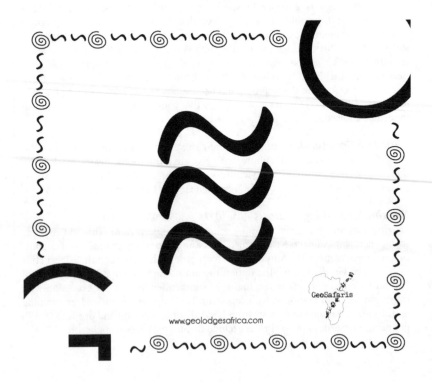

www.geolodgesafrica.com

GeoSafaris

8

Kasese and Environs

The most populous centre in western Uganda after Mbarara – and ninth-largest in the country according to the 2002 census – Kasese is of little interest to travellers, lacking even the urban cohesion and scattering of quaint colonial structures that redeem the likes of Kabale and Fort Portal from small-town tedium. It is, however, rescued from anonymity by a smattering of acceptable budget accommodation and a convenient location between two superb and strongly contrasting national parks.

Immediately west of Kasese, the Rwenzori foothills rise to a string of glacial peaks – topped by Africa's third-highest mountain – the upper slopes of which are protected within the **Rwenzori Mountains National Park**, one of the most popular hiking destinations in East Africa. On the Rift Valley floor in the shadow of the Rwenzori, and immediately south of Kasese, the **Queen Elizabeth National Park** is, along with Murchison Falls, the oldest in the country. Established in 1952, it protects a fabulously varied expanse of moist savanna, tropical rainforest, acacia woodland, wetland, numerous small crater lakes, and the 40km-long Kazinga Channel which links lakes Edward and George.

KALINZU FOREST RESERVE

Flanking the Kasese–Mbarara road southeast of Queen Elizabeth National Park, the 137km² Kalinzu Forest Reserve is essentially an eastern extension of the better-known Maramagambo Forest (within Queen Elizabeth National Park), and it supports a similar range of forest species. In addition to an alluring variety of forest birds, Kalinzu protects six diurnal primate species: chimpanzee, olive baboon, black-and-white colobus and red-tailed, blue and L'Hoest's monkeys, as well as the rare pygmy antelope. Nocturnal primates such as potto and two varieties of galago can be sought on night walks, when you're also likely to hear the eerie shrieking of the tree hyrax. An ecotourism site within the reserve is currently being revamped to offer improved facilities and a wider range of activities, including **chimpanzee tracking**. The latter should provide an affordable alternative to Maramagambo for budget-conscious travellers, since entrance fees are low compared with national park fees and access is relatively straightforward on public transport. You could call the National Forest Authority Kampala Headquarters (✆ *0414 360400*) for information; ask for Levi, the tourism officer.

GETTING THERE AND AWAY The office and campsite lie at Nkombe Forest Station about 20km north of Ishaka, beside the main Mbarara–Kasese road as it climbs towards the Rubare pass. Any **public transport** heading along the main road can drop you there.

WHERE TO STAY Campers need to be self-sufficient, though water and firewood are available and basic supplies can be purchased at a nearby trading centre. Visitors not wishing to camp can find budget lodgings in Ishaka Town.

QUEEN ELIZABETH NATIONAL PARK

(The standard entrance fees for a Category A national park apply; see pages 32–3 for the cost of these & core QENP activities. No visiting fee is charged merely for driving along the public roads that run through the park, such as the surfaced Mbarara–Kasese road, the dirt road to Katwe & the dirt road between Katunguru & the Ishasha border post) Uganda's most popular and accessible savanna reserve, the 1,978km² Queen Elizabeth National Park (QENP) is bounded to the west by the Ishasha River and Lake Edward along the Congolese border, to the north by Kasese and the Rwenzori foothills, to the east by Lake George, the Kyambura (pronounced 'Chambura') Gorge and Kalinzu Forest Reserve, and to the south by the Kigezi Wildlife Reserve. QENP is primarily associated with open savanna, studded in some areas with a dense cover of acacia and euphorbia trees, but it also embraces large areas of swamp around Lake George, the extensive Maramagambo Forest in the southeast, and the forested Kyambura Gorge along the border with the Kyambura Game Reserve. At least ten crater lakes lie within the park, including a highly accessible cluster immediately north of the main road to Mweya Lodge, as does the entire Ugandan shore of Lake Edward, the northern and western shores of Lake George, and the connecting Kazinga Channel.

A total of 95 mammal species has been recorded in QENP, the highest for any Ugandan national park. Ten primate species are present, including chimpanzee, vervet, blue, red-tailed and L'Hoest's monkeys, black-and-white colobus and olive baboon. Around 20 predators are found in the park, including side-striped jackal, spotted hyena, lion and leopard. The most common antelope species are Uganda kob, bushbuck, topi and Defassa waterbuck. The elusive semi-aquatic sitatunga antelope occurs in papyrus swamps around Lake George, while four duiker species are primarily confined to the Maramagambo Forest. Buffaloes are common and often reddish in colour due to interbreeding with the redder forest buffalo of the Congolese rainforest. The park's elephants display affinities with the smaller and slightly hairier forest-dwelling race of elephant found in the DRC.

Protected as the Lake George and Lake Edward game reserves since the late 1920s, the present-day QENP was gazetted as the Kazinga National Park in 1952, to protect the varied landscapes and prolific wildlife on the Rift Valley floor between Lake Edward and the Rwenzori. It was renamed QENP in 1954 to commemorate a visit by the British monarch (it was also temporarily called Rwenzori National Park during the Amin era, and might still be shown under that name on older maps of Uganda; potentially confusing as the higher slopes of the Rwenzori Mountains were gazetted as the Rwenzori Mountains National Park in 1991). QENP's once-prolific wildlife declined greatly during the years of

QUEEN ELIZABETH NP

For listings, see pages 301–2, 304–5, 310–11 and 325

🍴 **Where to stay and eat**
1 Abbey Guesthouse
2 At the River
3 Ishasha campsites and bandas
4 Ishasha Jungle Lodge
5 Ishasha Ntungwe River Camp
6 Ishasha Wilderness Camp
7 Jacana Safari Lodge
8 Katara Lodge
9 Kingfisher Kichwamba Lodge
10 Maramagambo Campsite
11 Mbara Safari Lodge
12 Pan-Afrique Hippo Resort
13 Rwenzori Trekkers
14 Savanna Resort Hotel
15 Twin Lakes

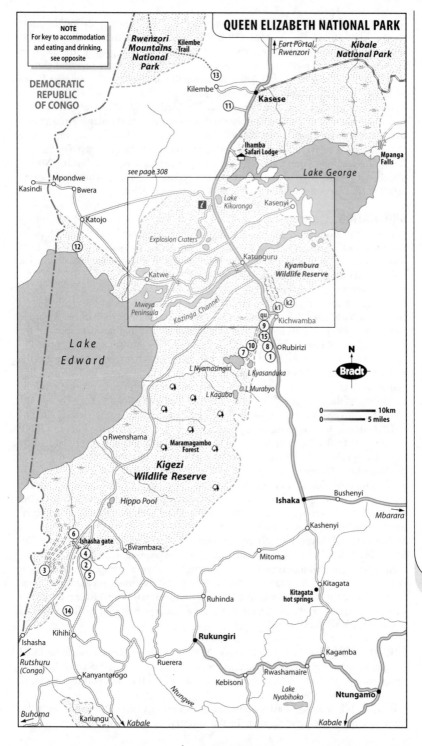

NOTE
For key to accommodation
and eating and drinking,
see opposite

QUEEN ELIZABETH NATIONAL PARK

Rwenzori
Mountains
National
Park

Kilembe
Trail

Kibale
National
Park

↑ Fort Portal,
Rwenzori

DEMOCRATIC
REPUBLIC
OF CONGO

(13)

Kilembe

(11)   Kasese

Ihamba
Safari Lodge

Mpanga
Falls

Mpondwe

Kasindi   Bwera

see page 308

Lake George

Lake
Kikorongo

Kasenyi

Katojo

Explosion Craters

(12)

Katunguru

Kyambura
Wildlife Reserve

Katwe

Mweya
Peninsula

Kazinga Channel

(k2)

(k1)

(qu)

Kichwamba

Lake
Edward

(9)

(15) (8)
(10)   (1)
(7)

Rubirizi

N

Bradt

L Nyamasingiri

L Kyasanduka

L Murabyo

L Kaguba

0   10km
0   5 miles

Rwenshama

Maramagambo
Forest

Kigezi
Wildlife Reserve

Hippo Pool

Ishaka

Bushenyi

Mbarara →

Kashenyi

(6)
Ishasha gate

(4)

Bwambara

Mitoma

Kitagata

(2)
(5)
(3)

Kitagata
hot springs

(14)

Ruhinda

Kihihi

Rukungiri

Ishasha

Ruerera

Kagamba

Rutshuru
(Congo)

Kanyantorogo

Kebisoni

Rwashamaire

Lake
Nyabihoko

Ntungamo

Buhoma

Kanungu

Kabale

Ntungwe

Kabale ↓

instability that followed Amin's 1971 coup, with the elephant population dropping from a high of 4,000 to perhaps 150 in 1980, and buffalo from 18,000 to 8,000. Over the past 25 years, however, the situation has improved greatly. The elephant population is today estimated at around 2,500, while lions, once rare and elusive, are thought to number at least 200 and are readily observed in the Kasenyi Plains and to a lesser extent around Ishasha and Mweya.

Some 610 bird species have now been recorded in QENP, a truly remarkable figure for a reserve that is relatively small by continental standards. In addition to 54 raptors, the checklist includes virtually every waterbird species resident in Uganda, and a variety of woodland and forest birds, the latter largely confined to the Maramagambo Forest. Birding anywhere in the park is good, but the Mweya stands out for the myriad waterbirds on the Kazinga Channel, while the riparian forest at Ishasha is a good place to see more unusual species.

ORIENTATION A variety of natural and artificial barriers cut QENP into a patchwork of discrete sectors. The most important of these barriers is formed by the Kazinga Channel and Lake Edward, which divide the park into its northern and southern components, linked only by an artificial bridge across the channel at Katunguru on the main Mbarara–Kasese road.

The main tourist focus in QENP is the **Mweya Peninsula** – site of a luxury lodge, budget hostel and campsite – which lies on the northern bank of the channel at its confluence with Lake Edward. For years, Mweya was also home to the park headquarters and a tatty village of staff housing, but these have shifted to a new site south of the Kazinga Channel near Katunguru Bridge. This northern tourist circuit is chopped in two by the surfaced Kasese Road which runs north–south between the bridge and the Equator junction at Kikorongo. Mweya, the small town of Katwe and surrounding crater lakes, and a network of game-viewing roads through dense riverine scrub lie to the west of the main road. Running east from the Kasese Road to Lake George, the Kasenyi Plains provide the park's prime, or at least most visited, game-viewing circuit.

Little developed for tourism in comparison with the north, the bulk of QENP actually lies to the south of the Kazinga Channel, where it is further bisected by the Mbarara Road. The small area of the park to the east of this road is the site of the **Kyambura Gorge** – an important site for chimp tracking – while the fantastic **Maramagambo Forest**, immediately west of the Mbarara Road, is the site of one small upmarket lodge and an underrated forest campsite. Further southwest, on the route to Bwindi National Park, lie the remote **Ishasha Plains**, an area best known for its population of tree-climbing lions.

The sectional nature of QENP makes it unrealistic to cover the park as one entity below. Instead, each sector is covered under its own heading, with details of getting there and accommodation provided as though it were a destination in its own right. Also included on pages 304 and 295 respectively, under separate headings, is coverage of the **Kyambura Game Reserve** and **Kalinzu Forest Reserve**, both of which abut QENP and can be visited from the 20km stretch of the Mbarara Road south of the Kazinga Channel.

FURTHER READING Andrew Roberts's QENP guidebook describes the national park and contains checklists for mammals and birds. Sheet 6 in the 'Uganda Maps' series covers QENP (*Ush12,500*). Both are available at the park entrance gates.

ISHASHA The remote Ishasha Plains in the southwest of QENP ranks with the most alluring game-viewing areas in the country, as much for its untrammelled mood as its varied wildlife. This compelling pocket of wilderness is, however, easily accessible, assuming you have private transport and are in any case travelling between QENP and Bwindi National Park.

Ishasha is well known for its tree-climbing lion population, which currently consists of around 40 individuals split across three prides. Unusual elsewhere in Africa, the tree-climbing behaviour at Ishasha might be observed throughout the year but is most frequently encountered during the rainy seasons. The explanation for this localised behaviour is open to conjecture. Limited studies undertaken in Tanzania's Lake Manyara National Park, also noted for its tree-climbing lions, indicate that the custom of ascending trees is culturally ingrained rather than a response to any immediate external stimuli, though it may well have been initiated to escape the attention of biting flies during an epidemic of these irksome creatures. In Ishasha, the sycamore fig and to a lesser extent Albezia trees are favoured over other trees, and the lions are most likely to be seen in arboreal action in the heat of the day, descending back to the ground before dusk.

Rather surprisingly, given its superb wilderness character, the Ishasha sector is actually nowhere more than 5km wide. Its seemingly boundless horizons extend west across the Congo's Virunga National Park and east over QENP and the Kigezi Wildlife Reserve (the last lies to the east of the main road bordering Ishasha). Effectively a buffer between QENP and the densely populated public lands beyond, Kigezi Wildlife Reserve contains the same species as the national park but no tourism facilities.

Getting there and away
By air, **Fly Uganda** (*www.flyuganda.com*) and **Aerolink** (*www.aerolinkuganda.com*) both fly daily to Kihihi (subject to demand), the former from Kajjansi Airfield near Kampala, the latter from Entebbe.

By **road**, Ishasha can be approached from three directions: Kabale and Bwindi National Park in the south, from Rukungiri to the east, or from the north via Katunguru on the main Mbarara–Kasese road. It is thus easily visited *en route* between Bwindi and Mweya in the north of QENP, though road conditions are such that it would be difficult to explore the game-viewing tracks thoroughly without spending a night there.

From Kabale/Bwindi via Kihihi
Ishasha can be approached from Kabale or Bwindi National Park via Kihihi. Coming directly from Kabale, take the road towards Bwindi for roughly 75km (see page 275), but instead of turning left at Kanyantorogo for Bwindi's main tourism site at Buhoma, continue straight on to Kihihi. Coming from Bwindi, you must retrace the 30km to Kanyantorogo, and then turn left towards Kihihi. The dirt road between Kanyantorogo and Ishasha is generally in good condition; you can get through in an hour or so in a private vehicle, though it might take longer after heavy rain.

The small town of Kihihi, 9km north of Kanyantorogo and 22km from the Ishasha entrance gate, is quite a jacked-up little place. There's a **Stanbic** bank providing the usual financial services and an excellent little supermarket (Kihihi Modern supermarket where the road to Rukungiri leaves town). Across the road, the **filling station** is a good place to top up your vehicle; other than Kanungu town (22km towards Kabale) Kihihi is the only reliable source of fuel between Kasese, 120km north, and Kabale, 70km south. On the other side of the diminutive town centre, the **Meeting Point** is a popular lunch stop for travellers while the nearby **Embassy Guesthouse** and **Westland Inn** are the best bets for an overnight stay. The daily Kihihi coach runs from Kampala to Kihihi.

8

Heading north from Kihihi, it's 22km to the Ishasha entrance gate. About 6km out of town, you'll enter the Kigezi Wildlife Reserve (no fees apply) and after 10km, the road will join the Kihihi–Katunguru road. The Ishasha sector of QENP lies on the opposite/western side of this road. Turn left in the unlikely event that you want to visit Ishasha Town on the Congo border (5km) or right for Ishasha Gate (12km). This section of road can get pretty bad during the rains and it's not unusual for it to be blocked by trucks. In this case, take a back road to Ishasha via Kameme, turning right 1km outside Kihihi. This joins the main road near the Ntungwe river bridge, 500m north of the Ishasha gate.

If you don't have your own vehicle, the Kihihi and Savanna **bus services** run daily from Kampala to Kihihi. From Kihihi, the established means of reaching the Ishasha sector is to head up to the Congo–Katunguru road junction described above. Plenty of **trucks** come up from the border and you should have no problem finding a lift to the park gate. That said, the junction is a lonely spot inside the Queen Elizabeth Protected Area and is within sight of trees visited by lions. Do also check the border isn't closed because of the latest rebellion in Congo or you could have a very long wait! The conservative option would be to head directly down to Ishasha Town (a short cut leads out of town behind the Westlands Inn) to find a lift; if you fail, you can at least sleep at the grubby **Kaduma Lodge**, the least foul of some grotty truckers' haunts. Once you reach the gate, you can wait for a lift from obliging tourists or ask the clerk to phone for a **boda-boda** from Kameme village to take you to the River Camp (8km).

Perhaps a better bet is to take a **pick-up** or **special hire** to Kameme village (about 10km from Kihihi). From there, take a boda-boda through the park gate (about 6km) to the Ishasha River Camp. Alternatively, base yourself at the budget **At the River** camp near Kameme (see pages 301–2) and ask for a special hire to tour the park.

From Kampala via Rukungiri If coming directly from Kampala, the best option is to turn off the main Mbarara–Kabale road at Ntungamo and follow the new 45km tarmac road to Rukungiri. Beyond Rukungiri, 70km of *murram* road leads to Ishasha via Kihihi (see above). However, a right turn about 4km out of Rukungiri (signposted to Rwenshama, a Lake Edward fishing village) provides a slightly shorter route, stepping down on to the Rift Valley floor before crossing the grasslands of the Kigezi Wildlife Reserve to join the Katunguru–Ishasha road. Turn left to reach the sector gate (15km).

From Kasese via Katunguru Ishasha Entrance Gate lies 70km southwest of the Kasese–Mbarara road, and is reached via a dirt track that starts 4km south of Katunguru Bridge and continues to the Congolese border at Ishasha Town. Ishasha Entrance Gate is clearly signposted about 1km beyond the Ntungwe River bridge,

RIVER OF THE BLIND

Local tradition maintains that the Kyambura River had no name until one day, without warning, it flooded, surprising the locals who lived along its banks or washed their clothing there. As the waters subsided, the locals one by one waded upriver to Lake George in search of the possessions that had been washed away in the flood. Invariably, they would return empty-handed and announce 'Kyambura' – a local phrase meaning 'I cannot see it'. This eventually became the river's name.

and about 17km before the border post. The full length of the Katunguru–Ishasha road passes through the Queen Elizabeth Protected Area with QENP in the latter part of the drive. QENP lies west of the road/Kigezi Wildlife Reserve and it is considered public – in other words no entrance fee is charged for driving along it. This is fair enough, for surprisingly little game is seen along the way.

A few years ago, the Katunguru–Ishasha road was a legendary mudbath strewn with pot-holes, and trucks might be bogged down for days after heavy rain. Today, the road is generally well maintained, and under normal conditions the drive between Katunguru and Ishasha Entrance Gate shouldn't take more than two hours. The road still tends to deteriorate quickly during the wet season, however, and it has been subject to sporadic outbreaks of bandit attacks, so do ask local advice before using it. A 4x4 is recommended, though any robust saloon car should get through with ease in normal conditions.

If you don't have private transport, the only way to get to Ishasha is to try to **hitch a lift** from the junction 4km south of Katunguru. A steady stream of trucks passes this way, so the chances of picking up a lift as far as the entrance gate (see above) are reasonably good. For location of listings see map, page 297.

Where to stay and eat

Upmarket

⌂ **Ishasha Wilderness Camp** (8 tents) \0414 321479; m 0772 502155/721155; e reservations@ugandaexclusivecamps.com; www.ugandaexclusivecamps.com, www.wildfrontiers.co.uk. Uganda's only true wilderness facility is this excellent (though costly) camp on the banks of the Ntungwe River. It's located in the thick of the wildlife action; elephant regularly cross the river, lion & leopard are heard close to (& are occasionally seem within) the camp, while colobus croak in the trees beyond the channel. The place is alive with sights & sounds of birds & notable residents include the African finfoot & Pell's fishing owl. The s/c canvas-sided cottages are comfortable & beautifully appointed while the large mesh windows bring the river views right inside. The tasty, ample & beautifully presented 4-course dinners demonstrate that isolation is no excuse for mediocre catering. With all comforts assured & a convenient location, this is a place to leave with genuine regret. See also advert on page 334. *US$420/640 sgl/dbl, discounts available for East African residents.*

Moderate

A Ishasha Ntungwe River Camp (4 tents, 2 cottages) m 0772 602205 (reservation), 0772 993177 (camp); wwwtreelionsafarilodge.com. This small camp lies between the Kameme Road & the Ntungwe River. Though the Kigezi Wildlife Reserve lies directly across the channel, the s/c furnished tents & cottages are set back from the meandering Ntungwe & consequently lack a sense of place. Don't turn up on spec; give the kitchen & bar plenty of prior notice. *US$130/260 sgl/dbl 'River Edge cottages & US$110/220 sgl/dbl tents FB.*

⌂ **Savanna Resort Hotel** (46 rooms) m 0772 777317/0753 932987; e info@savannaresorthotel.com. Set in large, park-like grounds 4km from Kihihi Town, & with an attractive 'country club' façade, this hotel represents a lone oasis of comfort between Bwindi (Buhoma, 1hr) & Ishasha Gate (30mins). Facilities include a swimming pool, golf course, steam/sauna & an airstrip (to which Aerolink flies daily). Though far more affordable than the alternatives listed above, & infinitely smarter than anything in Kihihi, the cottage accommodation is still unremarkable. It'a popular lunch spot for travellers (*meals cost Ush17,000–25,000*). *US$75/115 sgl/dbl B&B.*

⌂ **Ishasha Jungle Lodge** (4 cottages) \0782 385446; www.ugandajunglelodges.com. This smart-looking Italian-owned lodge is currently under construction beside the Ntungwe River where the large, thatched s/c cottages face an oxbow lake. Accessed from Kameme Road, the lodge is 10mins from the Ishasha gate. *US$65/80/80 sgl/twin/dbl; superior dbl US$120 B&B.*

Budget & camping

⌂ **At The River** m 0772 722688; e bookings@attheriverishasha.com; www.attheriverishasha.com.

8

com. This new camp lies off the Kameme Road beside the Ntungwe River in the wedge of public land between Ishasha/QENP & the Kigezi Wildlife Reserve (directly across the river). Assuming they haven't yet fallen into the wildly meandering river (which changes course regularly) or been flattened by visiting elephants, you'll find lazy camping & a selection of rustic shacks. A raised thatch bar looks out over the river & the birdlife & monkeys in the riparian forest beyond. S/c cabins are planned. *US$50pp shacks with shared bathrooms & US$40pp tents HB.*

Å Ishasha campsites & *bandas* 2 lovely UWA-run campsites lie by the Ishasha River, a few hundred metres north of the UWA offices. Set in riverine forest, these provide guaranteed views of (& sometimes encounters with) hippos. There are showers & flush toilets, & bottled drinks & simple meals are available in a canteen at the park offices. Occasionally, these campsites are closed due to the civil war across the river in DRC; when this happens, campers are directed to a pleasant hillside within the South Circuit provided with water (fit for washing but not drinking) & a basic pit toilet & shower (placed to provide foreground detail to the wilderness panorama beyond). A couple of simple *bandas* are also available close to the park offices. *US$14/16 sgl/dbl bandas, US$8pp camping.*

What to see and do

Game viewing Two main game circuits run out of Ishasha, the northern and southern loops, both of which are roughly 20km in length. The southern circuit is the more productive for lion sightings, since it passes through the main kob breeding grounds – as in Kasenyi, the predators often stick close to their prey, and their presence is often revealed by the antelope's alarm calls. This area is also better provided with the trees favoured by lions. Navigating the **South Circuit** is a tricky task, being confused by side tracks leading to lion trees and diversions to bypass boggy sections Though the 'Uganda Maps' QENP sheet makes a good stab at making sense of all this, it's a good idea to take a guide. The simpler **North Circuit** is better for general game viewing while the open landscape and boundless horizons on the northwestern part of the loop represents, to my mind, the finest wilderness in southwestern Uganda. Or as I should say, 'sense of wilderness'; you're actually only 4km from the main road linking Katunguru and Ishasha town. This section of the North Circuit also overlooks a long, low trough punctuated by pools and wallows enjoyed by buffalo; look out here for redder animals related to the forest buffalo of the Congo.

At the northern part of the loop, the boggy wallows described above develop into a full-blown wetland where birdwatchers might look out for black coucal, compact weaver, fan-tailed widow and other water-associated birds. A cairn in this area marks an 8km track extending north towards the marshy shore of Lake Edward, another good site for waterbirds, including various herons, storks and plovers. This area often harbours decent concentrations of elephant, buffalo, kob, topi and waterbuck, and it currently ranks as one of the most reliable spots in Uganda for shoebill (we had two good sightings in three visits in mid-2006). Road conditions around Lake Edward are particularly erratic so do seek advice from the rangers before striking out alone, particularly after rain. Getting stuck or lost here is a very real risk!

The Ishasha River, which can be explored on foot from the campsites along its bank, supports a healthy hippo population, most easily observed from Campsite Two. The fringing riparian forest harbours good numbers of bushbuck and black-and-white colobus monkey, and an interesting variety of birds including black bee-eater, broad-billed roller and the localised Cassin's grey flycatcher. Away from the river, light acacia woodland and savanna support large herds of Uganda kob, topi and buffalo, while elephants are seasonally common.

Ishasha Community Uplift Group (e *reservations@ugandaexclusivehomes. com, ishashacommunityupliftgroup@gmail.com*) Ishasha's wildlife might be popular with tourists but it has few fans when it strays into the farming communities that live along the protected area boundary at Bukorwe village. This fascinating community tour shows how Deo, a typical local farmer, copes. This really is life on the front line – Deo and Co even use a 20km-long trench in their daily battle to defend their crops. Dug with support from the Uganda Conservation Foundation, this is one of various strategies employed by park-edge communities to keep hungry elephants out of the crops. Bukorwe is 1km off the road to Kihihi, just outside the Kigezi Wildlife Reserve boundary. A second visit, to Agartha in nearby Kazinga trading centre, 2km along the main road towards Kihihi, demonstrates the day-to-day life of Bakiga women.

MARAMAGAMBO FOREST AND KYAMBURA GORGE The southeastern section of QENP is strikingly different in character from the southwest and the north, dominated as it is by the extensive Maramagambo Forest, which possibly harbours a greater biodiversity and faunal affinity with central Africa than any East African forest bar Semliki and Budongo. Relatively undeveloped for tourism, Maramagambo is nevertheless very accessible, especially following the construction of a superb, exclusive lodge and lovely low-key campsite overlooking Nyamasingiri and Kyasanduka crater lakes. Several worthwhile guided walks can be undertaken, offering the opportunity to observe a selection of the rich forest avifauna, as well as elusive mammals such as chimpanzee, red-tailed and L'Hoest's monkeys, potto, giant forest hog, yellow-backed duiker, pygmy antelope and giant elephant shrew.

The most popular tourist draw in this part of QENP, however, is the Kyambura Gorge, where a community of chimpanzees – unlike those in Maramagambo, fully habituated – can be tracked within the confines of a forested river gorge carved into the surrounding flat savanna. The gorge forms the border between QENP and the Kyambura Wildlife Reserve, a little-visited tract of savanna notable less for its wildlife viewing than the waterbirds – in particular flamingo – attracted to its lovely crater lakes.

Getting there and away All the sites described under this heading can be accessed from the surfaced Mbarara Road running south from the Katunguru Bridge across the Kazinga Channel.

Fig Tree Camp, on the rim of the Kyambura Gorge, lies 2.5km east of the main road along a turn-off that is clearly signposted some 9km south of the bridge. Travellers without private transport can ask any **bus** or **shared taxi** to drop them at this junction. You're permitted to walk along the 2.5km track to Fig Tree Gorge unguided, despite some risk of encountering elephant, buffalo or other potentially dangerous animals. Alternatively, charter a **taxi** from Katunguru, or from the village of Kyambura, about 4km south of Kyambura junction

The dirt turn-off to Maramagambo Forest lies 2.5km further south, on the west side of the Mbarara road, where it is clearly signposted for Jacana Safari Lodge. The visitors' centre and campsite lies 14km along this dirt road, and Jacana Safari Lodge is situated another 1km past the visitors' centre. There's no public transport along this road, and private vehicles aren't sufficiently regular for hitching to be a realistic proposition. Travellers without private transport will either have to **walk**, or must arrange a taxi or **boda-boda** from Kichwamba trading centre, 1km along the main road on the escarpment. The turn-off to Kyambura Wildlife Reserve runs east from Kichwamba village, 13km south of the Katunguru Bridge, where it is clearly signposted. The reserve entrance lies 4km past the turn-off, and it's another

8

9km from there to Flamingo Lake. Although this road isn't in great condition, you'll have no problems in a **4x4**, and it is traversed by a fairly steady trickle of shared taxis terminating at Kashaka fishing village on the southern shore of Lake George.

Where to stay and eat
To avoid repeating myself, all these lodges (unless stated) enjoy a terrific view north across the Rift Valley plains of QENP. The vast bulk of the Rwenzori provides the backdrop while in the middle ground, the Kazinga Channel zigzags across the plain between lakes George and Edward. These lodges lie outside the park, but are conveniently placed for visits to Maramagambo Forest and Kyambura Gorge. Mweya is about 50 minutes' drive away. For location of listings see map, pages 297 and 308.

Upmarket

Kyambura Gorge Lodge (6 cottages) 0414 346 464; m 0772 741 718; www.volcanoessafaris. com. This remarkable new lodge, the latest offering from the high-end Volcanoes safari company, lies in a private tract of savanna facing the QENP plains & the Kyambura River. It is a facility born of humble & unpromising beginnings, Prior to a remarkable makeover by Australian architects, it comprised a derelict coffee shed & outbuildings. The shed is now a spacious, airy lodge building adjacent to a swimming pool & there are newly constructed cottages scattered though the savanna. The latter are strongly influenced by local building styles, with carefully selected rusted roofing sheets & unplastered internal brick walls (reflecting, apparently, the utilitarian nature of the traditional rural sleeping space). Inside these individually colour-themed bedsits, the marginal furnishings owe everything to the rarely encountered 'African bric-a-brac chic' school of interior design. Some of these perform, more or less, their original purposes: your bedside table might be a ramshackle stand created for a village payphone (still crudely painted with networks & rates). Other items enjoy new uses, for example an old cable drum has become a coffee table. It's eclectic, eccentric & great fun! Reassuringly, the vernacular influences extend only far enough to create the theme: the large beds, cosy sofa areas, bathrooms, communal lodge areas, swimming pool, etc are all unashamedly luxurious – as you would expect from the rates. *US$480/800 sgl/ dbl FB inc drinks.*

Kyambura Game Lodge www. kyamburalodge.com. Though the names of the 2 new Kyambura lodges seem likely to cause endless confusion, they are easily distinguished right now. Kyambura *Game* Lodge is the one that burned down, just months after opening. Prior to this

event, some fabulous cottages were characterised by imaginative use of natural materials – banana fibres, bamboo, twisted acacia trunks, carved wooden hand basins, etc. The view & wilderness feel are compromised by trucks rattling down the nearby Kasese Road but it's well worth checking the website to see how rebuilding is coming along.

Jacana Safari Lodge (12 cottages) 0414 258273; e geolodges@africa.com; www.geolodgesafrica.com. This wooden construction stands beside the jungle-fringed Lake Nyamasingiri, which comprises 5 interlocking craters at the northern end of the Maramagambo Forest. Accommodation is in s/c wooden, dbl suites with a private veranda overlooking the lake. The open-sided bar & restaurant are suspended over the shore. Enjoy the lakeshore swimming pool, watch for primates & birds, & take a boat trips on the lake. *US$200/320 sgl/dbl FB.*

Katara Lodge (8 cottages) m 0773 011648; e info@kataralodge.com; www.kataralodge.com. A lodge, swimming pool & cottages perch on the edge of the escarpment above QENP. The canvas-sided, timber-floored cottages each contain 2 large beds, 1 of them wheeled to allow guests to sleep outside under the stars on a small balcony. The cottages are big enough for a family & extra beds can be provided. There's a good wine list & cocktail menu. If the lodge is full, try its new neighbour, **Engazi Lodge** (*www.engazilodge.com*). It's such a blatant copy of Katara, it doesn't deserve its own listing! *US$180/300 sgl/dbl FB with 3-course dinner, 30% discount for East African residents, family-friendly rates for kids are offered: US$40 children 13+, US$20 for 8–12 year olds, younger kids free.*

Moderate

Twin Lakes (4 units) m 0777 567152; e info@twinlakessafari.com; www.

twinlakessafari.com. Signposted off the Mbarara road between Kingfisher & Katara, this new lodge offers a couple of canvas-sided cottages on the lip of the escarpment & a couple of rooms in a modern bungalow. The lodge building is a wooden chalet that was erected by the same engineers who built the Katunguru Bridge across the Kazinga Channel back in 1948. Little wonder they chose this glorious spot over Katunguru village. The name refers to a couple of lakes, 1km distant on the other side of the main road. *US$140 2-bed family cottage B&B, US$70/170 sgl/ dbl cottages.*

Budget

🏠 **Kingfisher Kichwamba Lodge** (15 rooms) ✆0753 367980/0774 159579; e kingfisher-kichwamba@ gmx.net; www.kingfisher-uganda. net. Kichwamba's oldest lodge comprises a cluster of s/c cottages on the edge of the escarpment. Round, whitewashed & with crenulated, battlement-like verandas, these are suggestive of a fortified mountain village (with the thoughtful addition of a swimming pool). *US$55/100/125 sgl/*

dbl/trpl cottages, US$120 family rooms sleeping 2 adults & 2 kids B&B.

🏠 **Queen Elizabeth Safari Camp** (3 rooms) ✆0414 597257; e tours@adventure-travellers. com; www.adventure-travellers.com/content. This new camp just beyond Kichwamba village is a miniature & cheaper version of nearby Kingfisher (without the swimming pool). *US$50 sgl/dbl cottage B&B, US$8pp camping with tents provided.*

Shoestring & camping

🏠 **Abbey Guesthouse** Rugazi; m 0772 367588. Small courtyard-style hotel a couple of kilometres behind the escarpment just north of Rugazi village. The rates reflect the convenient location between QENP & Kalinzu. *US$20 small s/c dbl, $10 sgl shared facilities.*

⚐ **Maramagambo Campsite** Rustic campsite cut into a forest glade close to (but not in sight of) Lake Kyasanduka. Facilities are limited to cold showers & firewood but it's possible (at a price) to eat at Jacana Lodge, 1km away (see above). The birdlife around the campsite is superb, & monkeys are everywhere. *US$8pp to pitch a tent.*

What to see and do

Chimp tracking (*Kyambura Gorge; see rates opposite*) The Maramagambo Forest and abutting forest reserves collectively protect one of the largest chimpanzee populations in East Africa, but the only habituated community is resident in the gorge carved by the Kyambura River along the eastern boundary of QENP. Some 16km long and 100m deep, the gorge contains an isolated strip of riparian forest, surrounded by open savanna, which means that the resident chimpanzee community has a restricted territory and is normally quite easy to locate by sound. In addition to chimps, black-and-white colobus, vervet monkey and olive baboon are regularly observed in the gorge, while less visible residents include red-tailed monkey and giant forest hog. For birdwatchers, Kyambura is one of the best places in Uganda for black bee-eater and blue-bellied kingfisher, and a good range of other forest birds is present.

Guided chimp-tracking excursions depart at 08.00 and 13.00 daily from Fig Tree Camp, which lies on the rim of the gorge 2.5km east of the Mbarara Road. A maximum of eight permits (two groups of four people) is issued for each morning or evening session (*US$50/40 for residents/non-residents*), and no additional visitation fee is charged as it's assumed you've already paid this elsewhere in QENP. The success rate currently stands at around 85%, probably the highest in Uganda after Kibale Forest, and once the chimps have been located it is often possible to get within 5m of them. Permit availability can be checked, and bookings made, by radio from the park office at Mweya or the visitors' centre at Maramagambo.

Maramagambo Forest walks The 1km stretch of road between the visitors' centre and Jacana Lodge passes through lush primary forest and can be walked unguided at no charge other than the standard visitation fees. Plenty of monkeys are likely to be seen – most commonly black-and-white colobus, red-tailed and vervet – and there's a slimmer chance of encountering the lovely L'Hoest's monkey, chimpanzees and even leopard. Birdwatchers could pace up and down here several times without exhausting the opportunities to identify a confusing assembly of forest greenbuls, sunbirds, woodpeckers and other more elusive species.

Three different guided walks can be undertaken from the visitors' centre at Maramagambo. A half-day's walk costs US$15 per person. The most straightforward walk loops around the forested shore of Lake Kyasanduka, and shouldn't take much longer than an hour, depending on how interested you are in the prolific birdlife. A more popular walk, of roughly 90 minutes' duration, leads to a large cave where significant concentrations of bats are resident, as well as a rock python. The cave is viewed from a platform 15m away, a precaution imposed after a visitor died of Marburg fever thought to have been contracted through contact with a bat when inside the cave. For dedicated birdwatchers, the most rewarding walk is likely to be the longer loop around the back of Lake Nyamasingiri, which typically takes half a day to complete, and offers the opportunity to seek out rarities such as scaly-breasted illadopsis, snowy-headed robin-chat and chestnut wattle-eye.

Kyambura Wildlife Reserve Characterised by wooded savanna, this small and little-visited wildlife reserve is divided from QENP by the Kyambura Gorge and the Kazinga Channel. Though home to the same species as the Kasenyi sector beyond the channel, it cannot be regarded as prime game-viewing territory perhaps only because of a lack of game tracks exploring the reserve. The main point of interest is a series of scenic crater lakes, of which two are readily accessible from the public road track that runs through the reserve, between Kyambura trading centre on the tarred Mbarara Road and Kashaka fishing village on Lake George. This bumpy track runs along the rim of the first of these lakes some 10km out of Kyambura village, offering the opportunity to alight from the car and scan its surface for waterbirds such as little grebe and various ducks. About 3km further on, the road offers distant views over the aptly entitled **Flamingo Lake**, where impressive concentrations of thousands upon thousands of greater and lesser flamingo gather when conditions are conducive. The lake lies within a crater, and although the roughly 1km track leading down from the outer crater rim to the inner wall is just about motorable, it would probably be a safer bet to head down on foot. The main road continues past this lake, skirting Lake Bagusa after another 6km or so and passing a breached crater connected to Lake George immediately before Kashaka village. A small side turning along the southern edge of this breached crater leads to Lake Maseche where flamingos are also sometimes seen. Assuming that you've paid the visitation fee for QENP, no additional fee is charged to enter the Kyambura Wildlife Reserve.

Game drives Lodges on the Kichwamba Escarpment should be able to arrange for ranger guides to meet guests at Katunguru Gate for game drives (rather than going all the way to Mweya to collect them). Alternatively, contact **Jimmy Ochungu** (m *0782 383739*), an ex-UWA ranger living at Kichwamba.

MWEYA AND THE NORTHERN CIRCUIT Flanked by Lake Edward to the northwest and the Kazinga Channel to the southwest, the Mweya Peninsula is a triangular plateau roughly 10km² connected to the mainland by a narrow natural isthmus little wider than the road that traverses it. The main tourist focus within QENP, Mweya is also the site of housing for rangers and lodge staff which results in an oddly village-like atmosphere subverted by the prolific and exceptionally habituated resident game. The peninsula also has a magnificent location, with spectacular views across the channel to the glacial peaks of the Rwenzori Mountains on the rare occasions when they're not blanketed in cloud. A good network of game-viewing roads runs between the peninsula and the main Kasese Road north of the channel, and the game-viewing circuit on the Kasenyi Plains is only 45 minutes' drive away, while the launch trip on the Kazinga Channel below the lodge is for most visitors a highlight of QENP.

Although most tourists on the peninsula are resident at Mweya Safari Lodge, the combination of affordable accommodation and relatively easy access makes it a realistic goal for backpackers, especially as it has plenty of game that can be seen without moving outside the village. Herds of buffalo and elephant often amass on the channel shore facing the lodge, while Defassa waterbuck, hippo and warthog are certain to be seen from the roads on the peninsula – there is no restriction on walking within the village, but do be cautious of hippos in particular. Giant forest hogs sometimes emerge on to the airstrip towards dusk, a family of habituated banded mongooses lives in the lodge grounds, and lion and spotted hyena are heard – and seen – with a frequency that might unnerve solitary campers! Birdlife is prolific, too. Marabou storks regularly roost on a bare tree between the lodge and canteen – a hamerkop pair has built one of their vast nests in the wooded dip just before the campsite – while the exquisite red-throated sunbird, black-headed gonolek and a variety of weavers are among the more common residents of the lodge grounds. It's also well worth taking a bottle of beer down to the end of the peninsula airstrip to watch the sun set behind the DRC mountains – but ask which track to use, as driving down the airstrip itself is prohibited for obvious reasons.

Getting there and away
By road Mweya lies roughly 20km west of the surfaced Mbarara–Kasese road. There are two main approach routes. Coming from the direction of Mbarara, the most direct route is to turn left from the main road at the signpost for Katunguru Gate, just beyond Katunguru trading centre at the Kazinga Channel bridge. From Katunguru Gate, the 20km **Channel Track** runs straight to Mweya. It is quicker (though longer) to follow the main road north from Katunguru for 4km to Kasenyi crossroads and then turn left down the Katwe Road and follow it for 14km to enter the park through the main gate at Kabatoro, 8km from Mweya. This is also the most direct approach from the north (in which case, Kasenyi crossroads is about 7km south of the Equator junction at Kikorongo).

Mweya Camp is easy to reach without your own transport. The cheapest option is to ask around in Kasese for transport to Katwe. Ask to be dropped off on the way at the Kabatoro Entrance Gate. It's customary for park and lodge staff to **hitch** along the 8km stretch of road between the gate and Mweya, and the rangers are generally helpful when it comes to finding lifts for backpackers, too. If you fail, the shoestring Kabatoro Guesthouse is just 200m away.

Alternatively, you can engage a **special hire** taxi at Katunguru which should cost you between Ush30,000 and Ush40,000 one-way. Try Pascal (m 0772 668851), Moses (m 0782 767495) or Mustapha (m 0772 608614). This option is particularly cheap if you're in a group (the park and lodge staff also often use taxis for this trip) and the UWA vehicle entry fee does not apply. It would also be possible to charter a taxi out of Kasese, which saves some hassle but is obviously costlier on account of the greater distance – expect to pay Ush100,000 one-way. When you're ready to leave Mweya, wait for a lift with outgoing lodge and park staff at the barrier guarding the entrance to the peninsula.

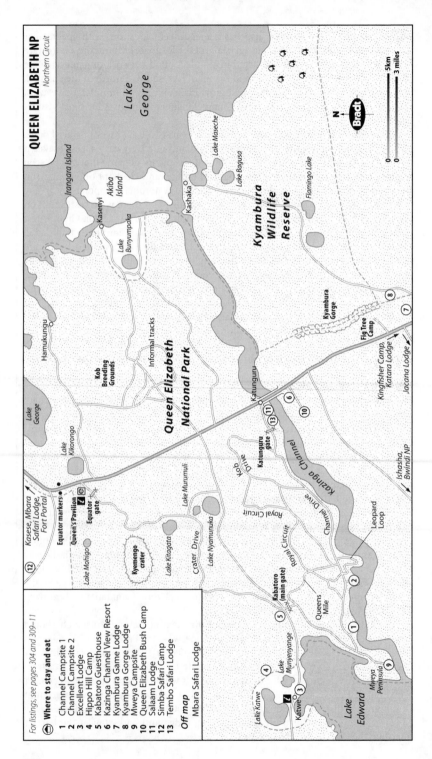

QUEEN ELIZABETH NP
Northern Circuit

For listings, see pages 304 and 309–11

Where to stay and eat

1 Channel Campsite 1
2 Channel Campsite 2
3 Excellent Lodge
4 Hippo Hill Camp
5 Kabatoro Guesthouse
6 Kazinga Channel View Resort
7 Kyambura Game Lodge
8 Kyambura Gorge Lodge
9 Mweya Campsite
10 Queen Elizabeth Bush Camp
11 Salaam Lodge
12 Simba Safari Camp
13 Tembo Safari Lodge

Off map
Mbara Safari Lodge

Lake George

Lake George

Irangara Island

Akiba Island

Hamukungu

Kasenyi

Lake Bunyumpoka

Lake Maseche

Kashaka

Lake Bagusa

Kyambura Wildlife Reserve

Flamingo Lake

Kob Breeding Grounds

Informal tracks

Kyambura Gorge

Fig Tree Camp

Queen Elizabeth National Park

Katunguru

Kingfisher Camp, Katara Lodge

Jacana Lodge

Lake Kikorongo

Kasese, Mbara Safari Lodge, Fort Portal

Equator markers
Queen's Pavilion
Equator gate

Lake Mohigo

Kyemengo crater

Lake Kitagata

Crater Drive

Lake Murumuli

Lake Nyamunuka

Katunguru gate

Kazinga Channel

Channel Drive

Royal Circuit

Kob Drive

Leopard Loop

Ishasha, Bwindi NP

Kabatoro (main gate)

Queens Mile

Lake Munyenyange

Lake Katwe

Katwe

Mweya Peninsula

Lake Edward

By air Fly Uganda (*www.flyuganda.com*) fly daily from Kajjansi airfield (between Kampala and Entebbe) to Kasese, while **Aerolink** (*www.aerolinkuganda.com*) fly daily from Entebbe to Kihihi. All flights are subject to demand, and both companies can divert to Mweya Airstrip on request.

Tourist information Information and bookings are handled in the purpose-built Mweya Visitor Information Centre near Kabatoro Guesthouse. This well-planned facility contains clear and concise (if now a little weathered) interpretive exhibits. The centrepiece is a topographic model which, complete with buttons and flashing lights to identify landscape features, illustrates QENP's setting within the dramatic Albertine Rift Valley. Outside, a covered timber deck faces the dramatic panorama across Lake Edward towards the Semliki Valley and the Rwenzori.

The **Katwe Tourism Information Centre** (KTIC; m *0751 933806/0752 618265; www.pearlsofuganda.org*) is located on the right just beyond what passes for downtown Katwe. KTIC staff will arrange a variety of activities including a visit to the salt lake to see the various mining processes (*US$10pp*). This enables a hassle-free visit conducted by well-informed and articulate guides, and freedom to take photographs. Revenue from tourism is intended to improve the lives of the wretched people who toil in the salt works (safety clothing for men working in the corrosive water is a condom, for heaven's sake!).

 Where to stay For location of listings see map, pages 297 and 308.

Upmarket

⌂ **Mweya Safari Lodge** (49 rooms) ✆0312 260260/1/0414 255992; e mweyaparaa@ africaonline.co.ug; www.mweyalodge.com. To contact the lodge directly: ✆0414 340054/04834 44266. One of Uganda's plushest offerings outside Kampala, Mweya Safari Lodge has aptly been described – by both admirers & detractors – as a 'Sheraton in the Bush'. Certainly this sprawling facility lacks the intimate, wilderness feel that some may expect within a national park but it is difficult to fault the fabulous location, proximity to QENP's main attractions, good food & the excellence of the service. To my mind, on an extended safari (a progress typically punctuated by some idiosyncrasy) Mweya provides an island of relative normality with knock-the-dirt-off pressure showers. On a clear day, the Rwenzori Mountains provide an incomparable backdrop while the dining veranda enjoys a grandstand view of the opposite bank of the Kazinga Channel, which routinely attracts large herds of buffalo & elephant. The lodge gardens rustle with animal life, ranging from warthogs & banded mongoose to a variety of lizards & slender-billed weavers & marsh flycatchers that approach the veranda so closely you can practically touch them. The s/c rooms are decent enough (insist on a room facing the channel & not the entrance road)

but pale in comparison with the palatial new safari tents. Facilities & activities include daily game drives, a discreet TV lounge with DSTV, a good curio shop & a foreign-exchange facility. See also advert in third colour section. *US$180/320/345 sgl/dbl/deluxe dbl rooms FB, US$360/395 dbl/deluxe dbl tents.*

Moderate

⌂ **Queen Elizabeth Bush Camp** (6 cottages) ✆0312 294894; m 0774 636410; e booking@ naturelodges.biz; www.naturelodges.biz. This excellent & reasonably priced camp is located on the south bank of the Kazinga Channel in the Katunguru enclave (surrounded by, but technically outside, the park). The dining tent faces the channel while the simple s/c chalets on timber platforms overlook a swamp-filled tributary valley bristling with chattering birdlife & honking hippos. Convenient for Kasenyi game drives & Kyambura Gorge. *US$90/110 sgl/dbl B&B, US$115/160 sgl/dbl FB.*

⌂ **Simba Safari Camp** (12 rooms) ✆0414 267153; m 0772 426368; e info@ugandalodges. com; www.ugandalodges.com. This affordable facility 2km along the Bwera/Congo road from the Equator junction is well placed for early morning visits to the Kasenyi lion area, & late arrivals from Kibale or Fort Portal. I got egg on my face last time around by suggesting that the wooden

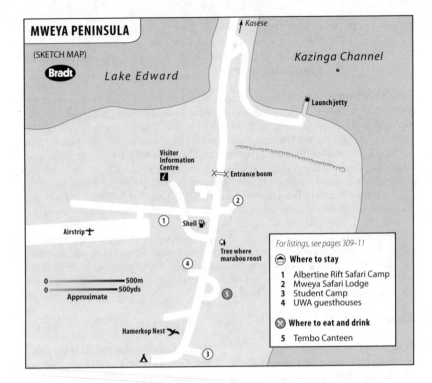

For listings, see pages 309–11

MWEYA PENINSULA

(SKETCH MAP)

Bradt

Lake Edward

↑ Kasese

Kazinga Channel

● Launch jetty

Visitor
Information
Centre
ℹ

✕ Entrance boom

②

① Shell ⛽

Airstrip ✈

Tree where
marabou roost

④

0 ———— 500m
0 ———— 500yds
Approximate

⑤

Hamerkop Nest ✈

⛺ ③

For listings, see pages 309–11

🛏 **Where to stay**
1 Albertine Rift Safari Camp
2 Mweya Safari Lodge
3 Student Camp
4 UWA guesthouses

✕ **Where to eat and drink**
5 Tembo Canteen

---

accommodation blocks occupy a rather exposed site. Within months, Simba was concealed behind a forest of fast-growing cassia trees! A couple of rooms at the top of the site enjoy outward views towards Lake Kikorongo. *US$50/70/70/135 s/c sgl/dbl/twin/family (sleeps 5) B&B, US$20/25 sgl/ dbl furnished tents B&B, US$12 dorm bed, US$6pp camping.*

Budget

🛏 **Albertine Rift Safari Camp** aka Mweya Hostel (22 rooms) ✆ 0414 373050 (Kampala Office); 📱 0772 609969/0782 802650/802650/381576; ✉ rift_hostelmweya@ yahoo.co.uk. The attraction of the long-serving Mweya Hotel lies in its convenient location rather than the spartan accommodation. 12 rooms use shared facilities, while 2 nearby guesthouses contain bedrooms provided with nets & fans & a lounge, kitchen (useful if you have your own provisions, stove & utensils), bathroom & veranda. The hostel is frequently booked solid, so do try to make a reservation. A restaurant is also attached. *US$27/41/50 sgl/dbl/trpl, US$83/124 4-/6-bed guesthouses B&B.*

🛏 **UWA guesthouses** (20 rooms) ✆ 0414 35000. Following the relocation of park staff to a new HQ near Katunguru, UWA offers former staff housing to tourists. There are 3 guesthouses (former wardens housing) & some 'Lower Camp Cottages', which means renovated rooms in the dilapidated ranger camp. Houses have 1 s/c room & a shared bathroom for the other rooms, as well as a gas cooker & tea, coffee & sugar. Meals can be obtained at the nearby Tembo Canteen. *US$120 4-bed guesthouse, US$100 3-bed units, US$12/20 sgl/dbl in 'Lower Camp'.*

🛏 **Pan-Afrique Hippo Resort** Kayanja fishing village. I spotted the 'Hippo Resort 12km' sign at a junction on the tarmac Kikorongo–Bwera road but not, apparently, a small but significant dirt side track close by. So I was more than a little taken aback, after driving 22km, to find myself in Katwe. Thus I can only borrow from a couple of volunteer blogs & tell you that it is a beautiful spot, fish & chips cost Ush7,000, basic accommodation is available, & the hippos show up for the Peace Corps but not for medical volunteers from Kagando Hospital.

🛏 **Hippo Hill Camp** (15+ tents) ✆ 0312 277304; ✉ kitanda@infocom.co.ug; www.lkttsafaris.co.ug.

This grid of s/c tented cottages lies above Katwe town, 1km from QENP's Kabatoro Gate. The site enjoys good views over Lake Edward &, with a short stroll, Lake Munyenyange. While the official rates are on the high side, I gather that there's scope for negotiation. *US$150/200 sgl/dbl FB*.

🏠 **Kazinga Channel View Resort** (16 rooms) Built by the folks who run the Mweya Hostel, this new development in the Katunguru enclave on the south side of the Kazinga Channel is a smarter version of ... Mweya Hostel. If a room with a shared bathroom & a distant view of the channel doesn't appeal, there's cluster of s/c cottages 500m down the track in a clearing with no view at all. A nice-looking thatched lodge is under construction just up the road. *US$55/100/100 sgl/dbl/twin*.

🏠 **Mbara Safari Lodge** (5 rooms) 200m off the main road, 2km outside Kasese & 500m beyond the Kasese Cobalt plant; m 0772 382204/0703 301650; e mbarasafarilodge@ymail.com. Ignore the unprepossessing directions for, in spirit at least, this new set-up with its pretty grounds & rural setting belongs in the QENP listings & not those for Kasese. Accommodation is provided in s/c thatch-roofed & stone-floored cottages of varying sizes & appeal while a viewing deck looks towards the national park beyond the main road. *US$32/40/48 sgl/dbl/family B&B*.

Shoestring

🏠 **Kabatoro Guesthouse** m 0783 604860; www.kabatorocampsite.com. This new guesthouse provides basic s/c rooms in a restored shop building in the strange setting of the (otherwise) abandoned Kabatoro trading centre. Standing right by the main Katwe Road & 100m from the Kabatoro park entrance gate, it's an ideal base for hitching into the park (& elsewhere). *US$20/24 sgl/dbl B&B*.

🏠 **Salaam Lodge** (8 rooms) Basic lodge in Katunguru village, just north of the Kazinga Channel. Management has cottoned on to the potential of its location & provided some upgraded s/c rooms. *US$12/20 sc sgl+/dbl, US$6 for grubbier sgl+ with shared bathroom*.

🏠 **Tembo Safari Lodge** (5 rooms) A grand name for a block of distinctly ordinary rooms at the back of Katunguru fishing village. Rooms are basic, with nets & fans. The attached bar/canteen overlooks the Kazinga Channel & you can watch the fishing boats, see the kids jumping off the road bridge, & scan the shoreline for wildlife. With a vehicle, follow the dirt road towards Katunguru park gate for 500m. *US$21/26 s/c sgl/dbl*.

🏠 **Excellent Lodge** (12 rooms) Katwe. The most acceptable of a few small basic lodges in Katwe, & better than the flaking frontage suggests. *US$12/16 small s/c sgl+/dbl, US$8/12 for basic sgl/ dbls with shared bathrooms*.

🏠 **Student Camp** Mweya Peninsula. Technically this hostel is for students only, & it is often full with them. However, UWA has permitted tourists to sleep there as 'a last resort'. The rooms are very basic & I've heard reports of theft, so be careful. *US$8*.

Camping

⋏ **Channel Campsites 1 & 2** If you have your own vehicle & are self-sufficient in food & water, you might prefer to camp at 1 of the secluded exclusive campsites which lie along Channel Drive about 5km from Mweya. Camping here is relatively expensive, but nocturnal encounters with large mammals are thrown in for free. Campsite No 2 has a good reputation for leopard sightings, but do ask advice about security in advance. *US$8pp*.

⋏ **Mweya Campsite** This fabulously located campsite on the southern end of the peninsula has few facilities, & is rattling with wildlife – potentially dangerous after dark if you don't have a vehicle, as hippo pass through *en masse* nightly & lions are also frequent visitors. Beware also the termites that 'chewed millions of holes in the groundsheet' of one reader's tent. If you intend cooking for yourself, bring your own food. Alternatively, you could brave the hippos & wander up to the Tembo Canteen for a meal, but be careful after dark, & don't even think about it without a good torch. *US$8pp*.

A new campsite is being developed beside Katwe town's **tourism office** (*www. pearlsofafrica.org*). Though a smart ablution block is provided, the site is neither private nor particularly pretty.

✗ **Where to eat** There can be few more attractive places to dine than the patio of **Mweya Safari Lodge** (see page 309). Dinner is a choice of set three-course meals

Connected by the 40km Kazinga Channel, lakes Edward (known locally as Ruisamba) and George lie on the Albertine Rift floor at an identical surface altitude of 913m above sea level, and both are regarded to be relics of a much larger lake that extended across the region during the most recent Ice Age. In other respects, however, these linked lakes could not be more different in character. Lake Edward, extending over almost 2,000km^2, is the smallest of a quartet of major freshwater bodies – starting with Lake Albert in the north and terminating with Lake Tanganyika in the south – that arc through the base of the Albertine Rift floor along the border with the DRC and Uganda, Rwanda, Burundi and Tanzania. In common with the rest of these lakes, Lake Edward, roughly three-quarters of which falls in the DRC, is elongated in shape with a broadly north–south orientation following the contours of the Rift Valley, and it is relatively deep – up to 120m in parts. The 250km^2 Lake George, by contrast, is essentially an extension of Lake Edward fed by the Kazinga Channel: roughly circular in shape, it is nowhere more than 3.5m deep, and is bordered by extensive marshes, especially to the north.

Although geologically calm in recent millennia, the area around lakes Edward and George has been subject to massive volcanic upheaval over the past half-million years, as evidenced by a total of at least 35 crater lakes and numerous dry volcanic calderas clustered in the area 10km north and 20km south of the Kazinga Channel. The geological and archaeological records indicate that a particularly violent bout of volcanic activity occurred perhaps 7,000 years ago, temporarily denuding the area of practically its entire fauna and flora.

The most enduring casualty of this episode was the crocodile, which subsequently vanished from the archaeological record and was not known to occur around the lakes or channel until recent historical times. The lack of crocodiles was a subject of considerable debate during the colonial era. Some biologists attributed their absence to a physical or chemical factor, a theory that had little grounding in fact, since crocodiles are elsewhere tolerant of far more extreme water temperatures and levels of alkalinity and other chemical dilutes than are presented by either of the lakes in question. As a Cambridge scientific expedition to Uganda in 1931 noted, 'Lake Edward seems to be an ideal habitat for crocodiles; there are plenty of quiet beaches and swamps and an abundance of fish and other food.'

The other prevalent notion was that crocodiles had been unable to re-colonise the lake on account of their inability to navigate a series of rapids and gorges on the Semliki River, the only major waterway connected to the lake that is inhabited by crocodiles. Implausible as this theory may sound, it would appear to be at least halfway correct. It was probably not the rapids or gorges per se that inhibited the crocodiles, but rather the obstacle they presented in tandem with the surrounding rainforest, a habitat that would be likely to impede their movement. Following widespread deforestation along the relevant stretch of the Semliki in the 1980s, crocodiles made an unexpected reappearance on Lake Edward towards the end of that decade. Today, large crocodiles are quite often seen during launch trips along the Kazinga Channel, and their numbers have proliferated in the reedy shallows of Lake George to the extent that they're regarded as a hazard by local fishermen.

(*Ush50,000*), or a buffet at busy times (*Ush60,000*), while a cheaper, daytime snack menu offers excellent burgers, steak sandwiches and the like for around Ush25,000. Mweya's cheapest eatery, the **Tembo Canteen** overlooks the Channel and serves inexpensive beers and other drinks, and the Albertine Rift Safari Camp aka **Mweya Hostel** (see page 310) offers acceptable meals (*Ush10,000–18,000 from the menu & Ush30,000 for a buffet*).

Other practicalities

Foreign exchange The only place to change money is the forex desk in the **Mweya Safari Lodge**, where fair rates are offered for cash. Travellers' cheques attract lousy rates and the service is limited to guests.

Fuel Diesel and petrol are available from the filling station at Mweya, which charges the same prices as in Kasese. You need to pay at the lodge and take the receipt while you go looking for the attendant.

Ranger/guides Although it is not mandatory to take a ranger/guide on private game drives, it is strongly recommended, at least until you get to know your way around the park, and it will greatly improve your odds of seeing lions and leopards. The fee for a guide is US$20 per party. Guided nature walks on the peninsula can also be arranged for US$10 per person. Guides can be booked through the visitor information centre (see page 309).

What to see and do

The activities and game-viewing circuits described below all lie on the north side of the Kazinga Channel. For those without private transport, organised **game drives** along Channel Drive to the Kasenyi Plains are offered by Mweya Safari Lodge (see page 309). Residents pay US$200 for one to three people and US$220/240/280 for four/five/six. Non-residents are charged more (eg: US$290 for four people). A cheaper option is to engage a Katunguru taxi driver. Mustapha (m *0772 608614;* e *kcsafari@yahoo.com*) has been highly recommended to us by Ineke at Fort Portal's Rwenzori View Guesthouse; alternatively call Pascal (m *0772 668851*) or Moses (m *0782 767495*). They will take you from Katunguru to Kasenyi for a morning game drive then to Mweya for the boat trip, then back to Katunguru. All for Ush150,000.

Maramagambo Forest and the Kyambura Gorge and Wildlife Reserve

Although they lie to the south of the channel and are described under the separate heading *Maramagambo Forest and Kyambura Gorge*, pages 303–6, these destinations can easily be visited as a day trip out of Mweya. Chimp tracking excursions in the Kyambura Gorge can be booked at the tourist office on the peninsula. The drive from Mweya to either Kyambura or Maramagambo shouldn't take significantly longer than one hour. A UWA ranger guide costs US$20 for a full day, and night game drives (19.00–23.00) have recently been introduced, accompanied by a guide, at a cost of US$15 per person.

Kazinga Channel launch

The most popular activity at Mweya is the launch trip to the mouth of the Kazinga Channel. Subject to demand, UWA and Mweya Lodge boats leave daily at 09.00, 11.00, 15.00 and 17.00; the trip lasts for roughly two hours. Although not perhaps as spectacular as the equivalent in Murchison Falls, it's a great trip, with elephant, buffalo, waterbuck, Uganda kob and large hippo pods seen on a daily basis, and giant forest hog, leopard and lion also observed from time to time. Keep an eye open for the enormous water monitor lizard, which is common in the riverine scrub, as well as crocodiles, seen with increasing regularity since first colonising the area in the early 1990s.

Waterbirds are plentiful, in particular water thickknee, yellow-billed stork and various plovers, while pink-backed pelicans and white-bellied cormorants often flock on a sandbank near the channel mouth. One smaller bird to look out for is

SALT PRODUCTION AT KATWE

The highly saline Lake Katwe, separated from the northern shore of Lake Edward by a narrow sliver of dry land, lies in the base of an extinct volcanic cone that last erupted between 6,000 and 10,000 years ago. In pre-colonial times, salt was regarded to be as valuable as any precious metal, and control of the lake regularly shifted between the rulers of the various kingdoms of western Uganda. When Speke travelled through Uganda in 1862, he recorded several local references to a legendarily wealthy salt lake near the base of the Mountains of the Moon, almost certainly Lake Katwe. For much of the 19th century, Katwe was part of the Toro kingdom, an offshoot of Bunyoro, but in the late 1870s it was recaptured by the Banyoro king, Kabalega, setting the scene for the first military confrontation between Bunyoro and a combined British–Toro expedition led by Captain Lugard.

Lugard arrived at Katwe in 1890 and recorded that: 'Everywhere were piles of salt, in heaps covered with grass, some beautifully white and clean. On our right was the Salt Lake, about three-quarters of a mile [1.2km] in diameter, at the bottom of a deep crater-like depression with banks some 200ft [61m] high. The water was of a claret red, with a white fringe of crystallised salt about its margin. A narrow neck, only some 40 yards [36m] across at the top, and perhaps 300 yards [274m] at its base, divided the Salt Lake from [Lake] Edward.' Lugard and his Toro entourage had little difficulty claiming the site – the resident Banyoro were not soldiers but miners and businessmen, and evidently they subscribed to the view that discretion forms the better part of valour – and built there a small fort, of which little trace remains today, before continuing northwards to Fort Portal.

You'll be fortunate to encounter Lake Katwe in the rich claret incarnation encountered by Lugard and other early European visitors. This seems to happen only when the level of salt in the water approaches a certain concentration. However, this phenomenon is frequently seen in individual salt pans when they are almost ready to be 'harvested'. Particularly in the harsh midday light, however, Lake Katwe still retains the vaguely foreboding atmosphere described by E J Wayland: 'stifling and malodorous … a fiend-made meeting place for the Devil and his friends'. Commercial salt extraction from the lake peaked in the early 1970s when the faded plant that dominates Katwe village briefly pumped out an annual 2,000 tons before breaking down owing to corrosion of the pipework. Extraction of the lake's characteristic pink-hued coarse salt remains the main source of local income – judging by the state of the village, not quite so lucrative an activity as it was in Katwe's heyday.

Even if you don't formally enter QENP from Katwe, the road there is as reliable as any in the park for elephant, while the likes of warthog and waterbuck stroll around the outskirts of town, together with an abundance of waterbirds and hippos, which frequent the Lake Edward shoreline.

the black-headed gonolek, a member of the shrike family with a dazzling red chest – and look closely, as the localised papyrus gonolek, similar in appearance but with a yellow crown, has also been recorded in the area.

The 15.00 departure is most likely to yield good elephant sightings, particularly on a hot day, when these thirsty creatures generally gravitate towards water from midday onwards, sometimes bathing in the channel. The 08.00 and 17.00 departures should be more rewarding photographically, as the light will be softer, though this might be countered by the increased probability of camera shake on a rocking boat in low light. The odds of seeing predators and other nocturnal creatures coming to drink are highest in the late afternoon. In practice, however, the departure time chosen by independent travellers is likely to depend on additional considerations, most notably when other groups are doing the launch trip. In early 2013, the 40-seater UWA craft cost US$25 per person subject to a minimum of ten people. The boat would also run if a smaller group got together a kitty of US$250, eg: if two people paid US$125 or five people chipped in US$50 each. Bookings are made at the visitor centre (see page 309). Alternatively, the smaller Mweya Lodge boats require a minimum of only four passengers. A ten-seater boat costs US$24 per person, while a 12-seater costs US$34 per person including refreshments.

Channel Drive circuit A compact network of game-viewing tracks emanates from Channel Drive – the road running roughly parallel to the northern shore of the Kazinga Channel between Mweya and Katunguru. The vegetation along these roads is generally quite dense and scrubby, and notable for the cactus-like euphorbia trees that protrude above the tangled thickets. The most common large mammals here are warthog, bushbuck and waterbuck, while elephant often cross the tracks from midday onwards, heading to or from the water. Leopard Track and the short side road to Campsite No 2 (see page 311) are the best places to look for the unusually habituated leopards that frequent the area, while lions are seen fairly regularly. Because it lies so close to Mweya and consists of several interconnecting tracks, this network can easily be explored over two hours from the lodge.

Katwe and the Katwe lakes This sprawling and unfocused settlement occupies an odd urban enclave enclosed by the park boundaries on three sides: monumentally rundown but also, perversely, rather charming, with the aura of a recently resettled ghost town. It has a superb situation, on a grassy rise flanked to the south by Lake Edward and to the north by two saline crater lakes, both of which also lie outside the park boundaries, and have formed one of the most important sources of coarse salt in Uganda for centuries (see box opposite). Hippos and warthogs are common in the area, and elephants can sometimes be seen on the opposite shore. The birdlife can be spectacular: most notably the large flocks of flamingo that amass seasonally on the crater lakes, together with a wide selection of waders. For those who cannot afford a full-scale safari into QENP, the shoreline on the edge of Katwe is as reliable as any location in the park to sight elephant, hippo, warthog and waterbuck, as well as an abundance of waterbirds. Enjoy a shoreline stroll but keep your eyes open – it has been necessary to fence off a small area of lake to allow townsfolk to collect water without being taken by crocodiles or attacked by hippos. Katwe is readily accessible by public transport – with a good chance of encountering elephant on the way – and shoestring accommodation is available.

Nearby **Lake Munyenyange** is known for large numbers of lesser (and a few greater) flamingos when conditions are right. You can watch the birds from the road that skirts the lake but step off it and you'll be charged US$10 per person for visiting this bird sanctuary. With prior arrangement, however, the fee includes an informative escort in the form of Richardson, Katwe's resident flamingo expert. A trip in a fishing boat on Lake Edward's Katwe Bay also costs US$10 per person and you'll certainly spot hippos and other wildlife along the shoreline. Vehicle hire is available for game drives, call Kasim (m 0752 397354).

Between Katwe and the Kasese Road, the landscape is studded by several dozen volcanic explosion craters, variously filled with water, grassland, acacia woodland and forest. Visible from the Katwe Road, 5km from its junction with the Kasese highway, is the impressive **Lake Nyamunuka**, its green and odorous waters often attended by herds of buffalo. With a solid 4x4 and at least two hours to spare, it's also worth exploring the rough, rocky and occasionally vertiginous **Katwe Explosion Craters Track**, which runs for 27km between the Kabatoro Entrance Gate (6km from Mweya) and the Queen's Pavilion (built to receive the Queen Mother and George Rukidi III of Toro in 1958) which overlooks the circular Lake Kikorongo from a low ridge above the Kasese Road. The **Crater Drive** offers some splendid views over Lake Kyemengo as well as a number of other deep craters, each with its own microhabitat – some lushly forested from rim to rim, others supporting a floor of practically treeless savanna. Although more notable for its scenic qualities than its game viewing, the hilly country traversed by this road is frequently haunted by large elephant herds in the dry season, and the thick woodland is the best place in QENP for acacia-associated birds (and tsetse flies). If starting/ending the Crater Drive drive at the **Queen's Pavilion**, or simply passing on the main road, you can stop for refreshments in a UWA information centre provided with a coffee/internet café. This was constructed prior to the 2007 Commonwealth Summit so that the Duke of Edinburgh could open something after scoffing lunch in a specially restored Queen's Pavilion. The site is located off Kasese Road, 1km south of Kikorongo junction and the Equator markers.

Immediately west of Katwe, the **Pelican Point** sector of QENP was suggested as the location for the park's first lodge in the 1950s, but Mweya was selected owing to its more central location. Despite its proximity to Katwe, this sector has a remote, unspoiled flavour, and although wildlife volumes are relatively low, buffalo, kob, warthog, hippo and lion are all present. The main attractions are excellent views across Lake Edward and the opportunity to explore off-road. There are currently no facilities in the area, not even tracks, but the QENP management plan proposes that a basic campsite be cleared in the near future.

Kasenyi Plains and Lake George

Stretching east from Kasese Road towards Lake George, the Kasenyi Plains probably support the largest concentrations of game anywhere in QENP, and a very different selection of species from those most frequently observed around Mweya. It's also perhaps the most reliable place in Uganda for lion sightings, assuming that you know where and how to locate them, and get there as soon after sunrise as possible. The drive from Mweya takes 45–60 minutes, so aim to head out at 06.30 when the gates open. The fastest route is to drive 6km from the peninsula to Kabatoro Gate, turning right on to the Katwe Road (in the opposite direction to Katwe itself) until after about 15km you reach the junction with the Kasese Road, where you'll see the Kasenyi track opposite. An alternative route from Mweya entails following Channel Drive through Katunguru Gate. A left turn on to the Kasese Road will bring you to the Kasenyi crossroads after 5km.

About 5km from the junction with the Kasese Road, a series of unofficial but clear tracks run north and south from the Kasenyi Road through an extensive area of short-grass savanna interspersed with solitary euphorbia trees and small clumps of thicket. This plain is one of the most important breeding grounds for Uganda kob – thousands congregate here at times and it is also frequented by numerous buffalo and more skittish pairs of bushbuck. The Kasenyi Plains also support an interesting selection of grassland birds, including grey-crowned crane, red-throated spurfowl and yellow-throated longclaw.

Kasenyi's main attractions are the prides of lions that shadow the area's resident herbivores. Thanks to the open habitat, these can be located and observed far more readily than in the bushier environment closer to Mweya. Even so, scanning beige horizons for beige animals can be a tiresome and possibly fruitless task, so do what you can to maximise the probability of success. Firstly, be on the plains at first light to give you time before the sun drives the prides into the shade of thicker bush. If you can't locate them directly by sight or sound, pay attention to the male kobs, whose high whistling alarm call may warn of a lion lurking in a nearby thicket. Vultures – most commonly white-backed and white-headed – either circling or perched purposefully in a tree may indicate a kill, perhaps with predators still in attendance. Such bushcraft is thrilling when it works but it isn't half as effective as watching where safari vehicles are congregating and tagging along. Hiring a UWA guide – they generally have a good idea where to look – could provide you with a more exclusive sighting; unless of course, some cheapskates decide to follow you. The failsafe method is to spend the morning with the **Queen Elizabeth Predator Project** as they monitor the activities of lion prides north of the Kazinga Channel. Since members of the research prides have been fitted with radio collars, finding them is a piece of cake. Thus, five minutes after we watched the 06.00 safari vehicles stream out of Mweya towards Kasenyi (30km distant), Dr Ludwig Siefert and James Kaliewa, his antennae-wielding assistant, showed me a pair of mating lions beside the airstrip. Then we drove to Kasenyi to watch three separate prides and a leopard! Contact UWA for details.

Lake Kikorongo and Lake George Ramsar Site

Following the informal tracks that lead north from the Kasenyi Road for about 10km, you'll eventually reach a proper dirt road linking the tarmac highway and the Lake George fishing villages of Hamukungu. North of this road, between lakes Kikorongo and George, lies a tract of swamp. This is part of a larger wetland area which extends across the expansive but inaccessible northern sector of QENP and which constitutes Uganda's first Ramsar Wetland Site. It is possible to approach the southern tip of the Kikorongo Swamp in a 4x4 vehicle, though only in the company of an official ranger/guide and access may be difficult during the rains. The main attraction here is one of the country's most substantial breeding populations of shoebill. Other swamp inhabitants include the elusive sitatunga antelope, various papyrus endemics such as white-winged warbler, papyrus gonolek and papyrus warbler, and during the northern winter large concentrations of migrant waders and waterfowl. Alternatively, a guided walk from the Queen's Pavilion/Crate Drive Gate crosses the main road to circle around the lake.

Rwenzori foothills

If you've had your fill of lakes and savannas and have a vehicle and time on your hands, you might strike north from the tarmac Kikorongo–Congo/Bwera road for a lovely loop though some beautiful Rwenzori foothills via the village of Kyarumba. If you fancy delaying, there's a guesthouse at Kagando Hospital. The new **Farmland Guesthouse** (3km north of the main road from Kiburara) is notable for a fine mountain backdrop and a commendably frank approach to tourism. 'Rates for the whites' are US$30–40 single and US$40–60 double bed and breakfast 'though sometimes we are lenient on them'. Right at the end of the tarmac road, a colourful market takes place on Tuesdays and Fridays at Mpondwe border town, 2km beyond Bwera.

KASESE

Hot, dusty and rundown, Kasese is not the most prepossessing of Ugandan towns, and its poky atmosphere contrasts oddly with its attractive setting at the base of one of Africa's largest mountain ranges. As the terminus of the railway line from Kampala, Kasese was once a popular springboard for independent travel in western Uganda, but following the suspension of passenger-train services in 1995, it has fallen off the travel map somewhat. Improved supermarkets make it a convenient place to shop prior to a Rwenzori hike, and it could be used as a cheap base for visits to Queen Elizabeth National Park, but otherwise it offers little to travellers and has far less going for it than Fort Portal, only 75km to the north.

GETTING THERE AND AWAY Plenty of road transport connects Kasese to Mbarara, Kabale and Fort Portal – just go to any local bus station and wait for the next vehicle to leave. Link and Kalita **buses** run between Kampala and Kasese in both directions throughout the day, and they take around six hours (*Ush25,000*). You could also reach Kasese on the Horizon buses from Kampala or Kabale, though you'll need to change in Mbarara.

Driving yourself, the road from Kampala to Kasese via Fort Portal is surfaced in its entirety and is in excellent condition. The stretch of road between Katunguru and Kasese passes through the Queen Elizabeth National Park – Uganda kobs are abundant and you might even see an elephant or buffalo in the distance.

The simplest route if driving or taking public transport between Kasese/QENP and Kabale, passes via Mbarara. Though the drive takes four or five hours, travellers using public means will need to change buses in Mbarara. With your own vehicle, you might strike south from Ishaka via Kitagata Hot Springs to pick up the Mbarara–Kabale road at Ntungamo (see page 237). The most appealing route, though not for a day trip, passes the Ishasha sector of Queen Elizabeth National Park before heading to Kabale via Kanungu or the Ruhija sector of Bwindi Impenetrable National Park. Both decant you (rather unexpectedly) on to the marvellous new tarmac Kisoro road, a few kilometres west of Kabale.

TOURIST INFORMATION AND TOUR OPERATORS The **Rwenzori Tourist Information Centre** (m *0700 604279; www.rwenzoriinfo.com*) can be found outside Virina Gardens Hotel.

An uncommon amount of positive feedback suggests that Robert, the owner of Kasese-based **Rwefuma Safaris** (m *0772 573399; www.rwefumasafaris.com*), should be your first choice of driver-guide for a safari around Kasese or further afield.

WHERE TO STAY Though Kasese town offers a decent selection of budget accommodation, its appeal as an overnight stop compares poorly with that of the Rwenzori trailheads, Ndali Craters, QENP or Fort Portal. Nevertheless, the information below may well be useful should you wish to save money, find yourself inconvenienced by a vehicle breakdown or experience a sudden, debilitating illness. The Saad Hotel, a perennial backpackers' haunt, has now permanently closed. For the record, the hilltop Spring Hotel is too ghastly, and Rwenzori The Gardens too mouldy to contemplate, though the implied garden in the latter is a pleasant escape from the heat of the town centre. For location of listings see map, page 319.

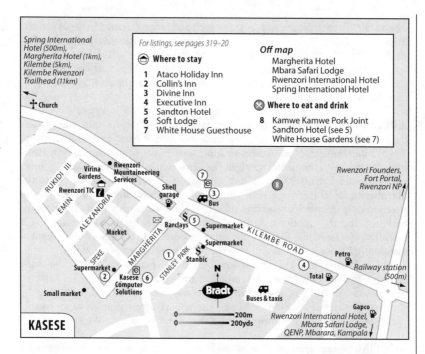

For listings, see pages 319–20

Where to stay

1 Ataco Holiday Inn
2 Collin's Inn
3 Divine Inn
4 Executive Inn
5 Sandton Hotel
6 Soft Lodge
7 White House Guesthouse

Off map

Margherita Hotel
Mbara Safari Lodge
Rwenzori International Hotel
Spring International Hotel

Where to eat and drink

8 Kamwe Kamwe Pork Joint
Sandton Hotel (see 5)
White House Gardens (see 7)

KASESE

Spring International
Hotel (500m),
Margherita Hotel (1km),
Kilembe (5km),
Kilembe Rwenzori
Trailhead (11km)

Church

Moderate

⌂ **Margherita Hotel** (50 rooms+)
☎ 04834 44015; m 0772 695808; e info@hotel-margherita.com; www.hotel-margherita.com. Situated 3km from the town centre along the Kilembe Road, this large & now privatised hotel has spacious & comfortable rooms, as well as a commanding view of the Rwenzori at the front & some birdlife in a garden to the rear. Even so, the rather institutional public areas could do with livening up (some comfortable chairs would be a start). If you have the funds (& there is a bit of leeway for negotiation) this really is the only reasonable place in town, especially if you're seeking a hot, post-Rwenzori bath. *US$70/95 standard sgl/dbl, US95/107 with TV/AC.*

Budget

⌂ **Sandton Hotel** (43 rooms) ☎ 0483 445307; e www.sandtonhotelkasese.net. This new & centrally located hotel is the best in the town centre, as is the restaurant. Even so, I'm really struggling with the idea of spending US$40 or more *of my own money* to stay in downtown Kasese. Rooms have AC & Wi-Fi. *US$40/50/60 sgl/dbl/twin.*

⌂ **Rwenzori International Hotel** (30 rooms)
☎ 04834 44148. Acceptable hotel in a quiet,

suburban location west of the town centre. The hotel is signposted off the Mbarara–QENP road about 2km from the roundabout. *US$22/26 s/c sgl/dbl B&B.*

⌂ **Collin's Inn** (30 rooms) Margherita St; m 0777 094197. Hotel with distinctive frontage at the far end of the main street. Small but clean s/c rooms with fans. *US$16/20 sgl/dbl B&B.*

⌂ **Executive Inn** (25 rooms) m 0772 586394/0775 642406. This smart budget hotel with attached restaurant is plonked beside Kilembe Road, 200m from the main highway. Tiled s/c rooms with nets & (a useful item in this hot town) fan. Good value. *US$11/16 s/c sgl/dbl.*

Shoestring

⌂ **White House Guesthouse** (23 rooms)
☎ 04834 44706. The popular White House stands off Kilembe Road, roughly opposite the Shell garage. Small but clean rooms, & a reasonable restaurant with DSTV. The nearby bus park is noisy in the early morning but guesthouse is good value. *US$8/13 sgl/twin with common showers & US$15 s/c dbl with hot water B&B.*

⌂ **Ataco Holiday Inn** (8 rooms) Stanley Rd. Tiled floors & bathrooms have been added to

Kasese and Environs KASESE

8

319

the rooms in this long-serving shoestring lodge. *US$12/15 s/c dbl/twin.*

🏠 **Divine Inn** (25 rooms) Though not quite on a par with the adjacent White House, this new guesthouse is still good value. *US$6/8 sgl/twin shared facilities, US$10 s/c dbl B&B.*

🏠 **Soft Lodge** (12 rooms) Stanley Rd. At the far (& presumably quieter) end of the line of cheapies on Stanley Road, the Soft Lodge represents astonishing value for perfectly clean rooms with nets using common showers. *US$4/5 sgl/twin.*

✗ WHERE TO EAT AND DRINK Some preparation is advisable to enjoy your Kasese dining experience to the full, ideally a week-long diet of noodles on the Rwenzori. The **White House** does an acceptable lunchtime buffet while the **Sandton Hotel** provides the best continental menu in the town centre (see above). Main courses go for around Ush14,000. For a pre- or post-Rwenzori dinner, head out to the **Margherita Hotel** (see page 319). Though the food isn't fantastic, it will seem so after ten days of noodles. The real attraction is the fabulously daunting montane backdrop and the emotions stirred by the knowledge that you will soon be (or recently were) far higher than the highest visible peak. On the first Tuesday night of the month, Kasese Rotary assembles to provide unwitting entertainment.

The open-air **White House Gardens** beside the eponymous guesthouse is the greenest spot in town for a drink, which is not saying a lot. For local character, head downtown and downmarket to the bars and roadside barbecues fronting the shoestring lodges along **Stanley Road**. Alternatively, treat yourself to an equally 'authentic' evening at the **Kamwe Kamwe Pork Joint** behind the White House.

SHOPPING Shopping opportunities in Kasese, according to the A J Roberts index of international development (ie: can you buy a tube of Pringles?) have recently improved greatly thanks to two small but well-stocked **supermarkets** close to Stanbic bank. Even so, buy any specialist items such as fresh deli, dairy or bakery produce in Kampala or Fort Portal, or do without.

OTHER PRACTICALITIES

Foreign exchange The usual services are provided by **Stanbic** bank at the eastern end of Stanley Road and **Barclays**, opposite the Shell garage on Margherita Road.

Internet Internet facilities are available at **Kasese Computer Solutions** on Margherita Road, at the **White House Guesthouse** and upstairs at the **Rwenzori Tourism Information Centre**.

Mechanic **Bagambe's workshop** (behind the Delta fuel station on the Fort Portal Road) is considered the town's best (📞 *0392 842298;* m *0772 551701*). Taxi services are also available.

WHAT TO SEE AND DO The most popular tourism activity in Kasese is a visit to the new **Rwenzori Tourism Information Centre** (see page 318), where Noeline, the informed manageress, will lead you rapidly to the conclusion that there really is nothing else to do in Kasese Town. Nevertheless, she can advise you on accommodation options for miles around and dispatch you on a **community walk** into the Rwenzori foothills (*Ush15,000–50,000 depending on group size*), or send you to discover a few minor diversions further up the Kilembe Road.

The first of these is the strange and sprawling hilltop **Spring International Hotel** (2km from town) where you can swim (*Ush5,000*) and ask to hear a cautionary tale concerning the controversially acquisitive career and bizarre demise of its late owner, Major James Kazini. You could then play the recently revived **golf course** (3km), marvel at a roadside colony of thousands of **fruit bats**, or continue for another 8km to the strangely time-warped **Kilembe** copper-mining town. You can visit the mine, which closed in 1982, with the underemployed safety officer, Vincent Kalisa (m *0752 262007*), for a negotiable Ush20,000 per person.

Rwenzori Founders [off map page 319] (m *0782 238036;* e *rfkasese@yahoo.com; www.rwenzorifounders.com*) As you well know, 'founders' are folk who 'found' for a living in a 'foundry'. And 10km out of Kasese, just before the turning to Rwenzori Mountains National Park, you can meet a team of artists who do just that. Rwenzori Founders comprises a team of UK-trained Ugandan sculptors, locally recruited staff and visiting artists-in-residence. Their bronze artwork, created using the lengthy lost-wax casting process, is displayed for sale in a gallery. Though I doubt everything will be to your taste, you'll long to own one of Isaac Okwir's magnificent wildlife pieces. The prices, by UK standards, are extremely reasonable. Visits are by appointment only.

RWENZORI MOUNTAINS NATIONAL PARK

This 996km² national park protects the upper slopes of the Rwenzori Mountains, which run for almost 120km along the Congolese border west of Kasese and Fort Portal. The Rwenzori Mountains are thought to have been the source of the legend of the Mountains of the Moon, the snow-capped range cited as the source of the Nile by the Alexandrine geographer Ptolemy around AD150. The first Europeans to see these legendary mountains were Arthur Jephson and Thomas Parke, members of Stanley's cross-continental 1888–89 expedition to rescue the Emin Pasha. The range was first comprehensively explored by Europeans in 1906, when an expedition led by Luigi da Savoia conquered all the major peaks.

The Rwenzori is the highest mountain range in Africa. Its loftiest peaks, Margherita (5,109m) and Alexandra (5,083m) on Mount Stanley, are exceeded in altitude elsewhere in Africa only by Kilimanjaro and Mount Kenya, both of which are extinct volcanoes standing in isolation above the surrounding plains. The Rwenzori Mountains are unique among East Africa's major peaks in that they are not volcanic in origin, but they do rise directly from the Rift Valley floor and their formation, like that of Kilimanjaro and Kenya, was linked to the geological upheaval that created the Rift. In addition to Mount Stanley, there are four other glacial peaks in the Rwenzori: Mount Speke (4,890m), Mount Emin (4,791m), Mount Gessi (4,715m) and Mount Luigi da Savoia (4,627m).

The Rwenzori is known primarily for its challenging hiking and climbing possibilities, but the range also supports a diversity of animals, including 70 mammal and 177 bird species, several of the latter being Albertine Rift endemics. It is the only national park in Uganda where the Angola colobus has been recorded, though identification of this localised monkey will require careful examination as the similar and more widespread black-and-white colobus also occurs on the mountain.

Like other large East African mountains, the Rwenzori range can be divided into several altitude zones, each with its own distinct microclimate and flora and fauna. The forest zone, which starts at around 1,800m, has the most varied fauna. The only mammals you are likely to see in the forest are the aforementioned colobus and blue monkeys, though several other large mammals are present, including elephant, golden cat, servalline genet, chimpanzee, yellow-backed duiker and giant forest hog. At night, listen out for the distinctive and eerie call of the southern tree hyrax.

The forest zone is home to a diversity of birds, including Rwenzori turaco, barred long-tailed cuckoo, long-eared owl, handsome francolin, cinnamon-chested bee-eater, Archer's ground robin, white-starred forest robin, Rwenzori batis, montane sooty boubou, Lagden's bush shrike, slender-billed starling, blue-headed sunbird, golden-winged sunbird, strange weaver, and several varieties of barbet, greenbul, apalis, illadopsis, flycatcher and crimsonwing.

Above an altitude of roughly 2,500m, true forest gives way to dense bamboo forest stands. Higher still, spanning an altitude of roughly 3,000m to 4,500m, the open vegetation of the heather and alpine zones is renowned for its otherworldly quality: forests of giant heather plants, and giant lobelias and groundsel up to 10m high. The striking *Lobelia wollanstonii* and *Senecio admiralis* are most common above 3,800m. Mammals are scarce above the forest zone, but there are a few birds worth looking out for: the lammergeyer (bearded vulture) and black eagle are occasionally seen soaring overhead, while the alpine and scarce swifts and scarlet-tufted malachite sunbird are practically restricted to high-altitude habitats in East Africa.

There is a good network of trails and huts on the mountains. The snow peaks are generally only tackled by experienced climbers. Expeditions take eight to ten days. Most people stick to circuits that wind between these peaks through magnificent montane scenery (see boxes on pages 326–7 and 328–9). These routes typically take six to nine days and reach a maximum altitude of 4,372m. It is possible to do shorter hikes through the forested foothills into the moorland zone, and also to detour from the main routes to scale the lesser peaks. It should be stressed that hiking in the Rwenzori requires above-average fitness and stamina, largely owing to the muddy condition of the trails (in parts, you might literally have to walk through waist-high mud). Most people regard the Rwenzori to be a tougher hike than the ascents of either Mount Kilimanjaro or Mount Kenya.

HIKING ARRANGEMENTS Two routes lead into the high Rwenzori. The more established and, until recently, the only, option ascends the Mubuku and Bujuku valleys from Nyakalengija to the Central Circuit that winds between the main peaks. The other route, long closed to hikers and now being reopened, runs up the Nyamwamba Valley above Kilembe near Kasese. The organisation of expeditions on the Rwenzori is currently in a state of change – a welcome development since many, indeed perhaps most, hikers and mountaineers have been far from happy with their montane experience in recent years. Invariably, problems boil down to the organisation mandated to manage expeditions on the Nyakalengija route. On the face of it, **Rwenzori Mountaineering Services (RMS)** is a worthy entity: a local community tourism group established to provide local Bazonzo people with the wherewithal to benefit from tourism on the mountain that has for centuries been central to their existence and cosmology. Local men are employed as guides and porters and profits are supposed to be invested in community projects. Though expected to be a model of its type, and for a while the darling of donor organisations, the reality of RMS has proved otherwise. The closure of the park owing to the Allied Democratic Front (ADF) war in the late 1990s didn't help, but then neither has an even longer history of creative accountancy and other duplicitous and obstructive practices which have seen the organisation shunned by its erstwhile sponsors. More relevant to you is a veritable pile of reader feedback complaining of opportunistic tariffs, the poor condition of some of the mountain huts and latrines, inadequate equipment provided to the unfortunate porters, lack of first-aid training, poor environmental practices, inadequate rescue procedures, and dangerously poor technical mountaineering skills on the part of the guides.

RWENZORI MOUNTAINS NATIONAL PARK
Central Circuit

For listings, see pages 325, 328–9

⊕ **Where to stay**
1 Bujuku Hut
2 Guy Yeoman Hut
3 John Matte Hut
4 Kitandara Hut
5 Nyabitaba Hut

Off map
Rwenzori Trekkers Hostel

Portal Peaks

Lake Rutara

Kihuma ▲4321m

Portal ▲4370m

Skull Cave △3810m

Lake Bukurungu West

3 3505m

Central Circuit

Bujuku

Mubuku

Rwenzori Trekkers Hostel, Nyakalengija

5 2651m

Lake Mahoma

△

approximate route
Mahoma Trail

N

Bradt

0   3km
0   2 miles

⊕ Kichuchu

2 3505m

Kinyangoma ▲4361m

Nyamwamba

Kabamba 3450m

Bujongolo 3720m

Nakyamabuli

Freshfield Pass 4282m

Stairs ▲4544m

Baker ▲4843m

Mt Luigi da Savoia

4627m ▲

4 4023m

Kitandara Lakes

4547m Weissman ▲

ascent from Kilembe

Scott Elliott Pass 4372m

Lake Bujuku

Speke ▲4890m

Irene Lakes ▲4900m

1 3962m

Elena ▲4541m

Moebius ▲4925m

Savoia 4977m

Elena Glacier

Bavoia Glacier

Margherita 5109m▲
Alexandra 5083m▲

Albert 5101m ▲

Mt Stanley

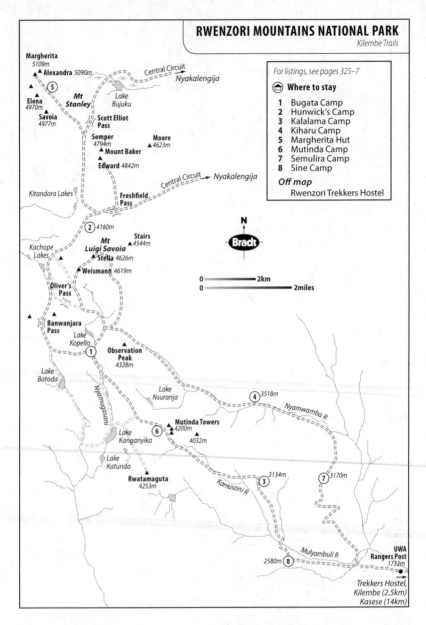

Margherita
5109m
▲ Alexandra 5090m

Central Circuit
Nyakalengija

⑤

Elena
4970m

Mt
Stanley

Lake
Bujuku

Savoia
4977m

Scott Elliot
Pass

Semper
4794m
▲ Mount Baker

Moore
▲ 4623m

Edward 4842m

Kitandara Lakes

Central Circuit → Nyakalengija

Freshfield
Pass

② 4160m

Stairs
▲ 4544m

Mt
Luigi Savoia
▲ Stella 4626m

Kachope
Lakes

▲ Weismann 4619m

Oliver's
Pass

Banwanjara
Pass

Lake
Kopello

①

Observation
Peak
4328m

Lake
Batoda

Lake
Nsuranja

④ 3518m

Nyamwamba R

Nyamugasani

Mutinda Towers
⑥ ▲ 4200m
▲ 4032m

Lake
Kanganyika

Lake
Katunda

Rwatamaguta
4253m

Kamusoni R

③ 3134m

⑦ 3170m

2580m ⑧

Mulyambuli R

UWA
Rangers Post
1732m

Trekkers Hostel,
Kilembe (2.5km)
Kasese (14km)

N

Bradt

| 0 | 2km |
| 0 | 2miles |

For listings, see pages 325–7

Where to stay

1 Bugata Camp
2 Hunwick's Camp
3 Kalalama Camp
4 Kiharu Camp
5 Margherita Hut
6 Mutinda Camp
7 Semulira Camp
8 Sine Camp

Off map
Rwenzori Trekkers Hostel

I recently met a professional South African mountain guide who was amazed by his guides' lack of risk-assessment skills, primarily a failure to belay on an exposed 40m slab on Mount Speke. (See also box, page 333.) Everything will be fine, until something happens, was his assessment.

Happily, there is now an alternative, the recently reopened Kilembe route run by **Rwenzori Trekking Services (RTS)**. Allied to the Kampala Backpackers, RTS has redefined standards for trekking and mountaineering on the Rwenzori with such novel concepts as guide training, safety procedures, rescue plans and a functioning satellite phone with a charged battery (RMS have the other sort). I'm in a rare position to directly compare the two organisations, having been part of a 2012 expedition that ascended the mountain with RTS and descended with RMS (an unprecedented and unlikely to be repeated event). RTS impressed in all areas, notably when, after visiting a remote lake on Mount Savoia, a seasonal rivulet prevented our descent of a slippery gully. Our guides, Enoch and Edson, identified an alternative route, used belaying ropes competently in the twilight, and brought us safely off the mountain in darkness. They even radioed ahead to the camp to send down torches and restorative flasks of coffee before a long, tiresome ascent over moraine boulders to the camp. RTS also keep two stretchers in each hut, while each team leader carries a comprehensive first-aid kit and a satellite phone. In hilarious contrast (retrospectively anyway), RMS sent three porters to meet us at the Bujuku Hut rendezvous, one of whom was carrying their own provisions. There was no guide, and no food for us. I suggest that if you have technical climbing experience, are prepared to insist (or advise) on good mountaineering practice, and won't ask for assistance if you break a limb, then it doesn't really matter which organisation you sign up with. Members of both groups are, for the record, equally adept at locating the magnificent forest chameleons that you and I would be oblivious to.

THE KILEMBE TRAIL The operator for routes on the south Rwenzori, **Rwenzori Trekking Services (RTS)** (m *0776 114441–3/0774 114499;* e *rwenzoritrekking@ gmail.com; www.rwenzoritrekkers.com*) offers a variety of mountain treks and climbs using a combination of trails along (and between) the Nyamugasani, Kamusoni and Nyamwamba river valleys. The distance to the peaks is greater than on the established Central Circuit, and an ascent of Margherita will require nine to ten days rather than eight or nine. The routes do, however, run though pristine landscapes – unvisited by hikers for decades – of astonishing beauty. Even though part of this southern route was burned by fire in early 2012, the stark beauty of the scorched heather branches and the re-emergent groundsels represent part of the Rwenzori's amazing story. Incidentally, as a tourist trail, the Kilembe route is rather older than the established Nyakalengija Trail. The Nyamwamba Valley was first ascended in 1895 by Professor Scott Elliot, 11 years before the Italian duke of Abruzzi pioneered the more direct route along the Bujuku Valley.

Getting there and away
The base camp for the Kilembe Trail is the Rwenzori Trekkers hostel at the upper end of Kilembe Town, 14km from Kasese, and 2km beyond the market and the bridge. A **boda-boda** from Kasese costs Ush5,000 (Ush7,000 with a big backpack!). A **special hire** costs Ush25,000.

Where to stay
Alternative accommodation is available, 14km away in Kasese Town (see pages 318–21). For location of listings see map, page 297.

Rwenzori Trekkers (30 beds) m 0774 199022; e rwenzoribackpackers@gmail.com; www.rwenzoritrekking.com. Run by Rwenzori Trekking Services, this hostel is sited in the deep Nyamwamba river valley in structures occupied long ago by miners working at the long-closed Kilembe Copper Mine. The hostel, located 3km before the Kilembe Trail enters the national park, enjoys enticing (or daunting!) views of the high Rwenzori. Flushing toilets & hot showers are provided. *US$8/13 sgl/dbl rooms, US$6 dorm bed, US$4 camping.*

THE KILEMBE ROUTE The Kilembe Trail, described in the box on pages 326–7, is run by Rwenzori Trekking Services. The cost of an eight-day hike with RTS to the summit of Mount Stanley is US$1,050 for one to two people. Larger groups pay US$950. This covers a guide, one porter for personal effects, hut accommodation, climbing gear, wellingtons and food but excludes park entrance and your own high-energy snacks. Sleeping bags and raingear can be hired if needed. An extra day on the mountain costs about US$122 (excluding park entrance). A shorter, six-day trek descending from Bugata Camp after climbing Mount Savoia costs US$760 for one to two hikers and US$680 for larger groups.

THE CENTRAL CIRCUIT The Central Circuit route ascending from Nyakalengija trailhead, and described in the box on page 328, is run by Rwenzori Mountaineering Services (✆ *0414 237497; www.rwenzorimountaineeringservices.com*). The seven-day, six-night hike along the Central Circuit loop trail costs US$780/705 for foreigners/foreign residents and US$990/870 for the seven-night/eight-day trip to the top of Mount Stanley. Additional days on the mountain cost US$120 per day and additional peaks may be climbed at US$150 per peak. Rates include one porter carrying a maximum of 25kg, hut accommodation and park entrance, but exclude food and mountaineering equipment. RMS has booking offices in Kasese and at UWA headquarters in Kampala (see page 168).

WALKING THE KILEMBE TRAIL

An exciting variety of mountain treks and climbs are possible using the Kilembe Trail. This text describes the route from Rwenzori Trekkers in Kilembe to Mount Baker. Visit the Rwenzori Trekking Services website for more options (*www.rwenzoritrekking.com*).

DAY ONE: Rwenzori Trekkers hostel (Kilembe) (1,450m) to Sine (2,580m) (altitude gain: 1,130m) This day involves the greatest altitude gain. The route first runs along the side of the Nyamwamba river valley for 3km before entering the park for a long, steady climb through montane forest , followed by a stiff ascent through bamboo to reach the campsite at Kalalama in the heather zone. Note: the first 2km from the hostel can be covered by vehicle as far as a roadhead at Kyambogho. Strong climbers can push on to Kalalama Camp.

DAY TWO: Sine (2,580m) to Mutinda (3,810m) (altitude gain: 654m) After a stiff climb through bamboo to Kalalama Camp, the route follows the Kamusoni river valley up to Mutinda. The overnight camp enjoys a particularly pretty setting among giant groundsels and moss-draped *Erica* at the foot of the 4,200m multi-pronged Mutinda Towers.

DAY THREE: Mutinda (3,810m) to Bugata Camp (4,060m) (altitude gain: 250m) From Mutinda, the landscape becomes bleaker and more dramatic as the trail traverses open moorland between the Kamusoni and Nyamugasani valleys. The third night's campsite, set on a high rocky bluff above the Nyamugasani enjoys a terrific, map-like view of Lake Bugata far below (one of eight glacial lakes in this valley) and north towards Mount Luigi da Savoia. Most hikers (as opposed to peak-driven mountaineers) will probably consider this superbly scenic area sufficient reward for their exertions. But, if you do descend from Bugata Camp, I'd strongly suggest you spend two nights there in order to ascend Mount Savoia. This day hike through superb Afro-montane vegetation provides the possibility (weather

You can book through most local tour operators, though it is simpler to book directly with RMS or RTS. If you plan to climb the mountain as part of a longer safari to QENP and elsewhere, RTS can provide a vehicle and driver.

LAKE MAHOMA TRAIL This new route was opened in late 2012 as a shorter alternative to the full Central Circuit. The route climbs from the Nyakalengija trailhead to Lake Mahoma, a glacial lake above Nyabitaba hut. The lake lies within the bamboo zone with fine views towards the high peaks (weather permitting of course). It's an excellent idea but I'm not convinced that the rewards justify the exertion. The ascent to Nyabitaba ridge is about the stiffest bit of legwork on the whole Central Circuit and having willed yourself thus far, it's a shame not to see some Afro-montane vegetation. I'd be inclined to do a three-day round trip on the Kilembe trail; the first day is equally tough but day two is easier going and gets you up there with the giant heathers, lobelias and groundsels. The second stage of the Central Circuit leading to John Matte Hut provides similar rewards (with the superb, lobelia-studded Bigo Bog just beyond the hut) but the trail to John Matte is a boulder-strewn pig to walk. Contact UWA for details of prices and how to book.

permitting of course) of viewing the high peaks to the north and encountering patches of equatorial snow.

DAY FOUR: Bugata Camp (4,060m) to Hunwick's Camp (3,974m) (altitude loss: 15m) Though this day ends with a net descent of 86m, it involves several ups and downs through magnificent scenery. The trail starts with a short but stiff climb to Bamwanjara Pass (4,450m) before a long descent through groundsel forest to the Kachope lakes. The route flanks Mount Savoia before climbing on to a moraine ridge to find the camp. This faces Mount Baker and overlooks the Butawu Valley which drains on to the Rift Valley floor – visible in clear conditions – in the DRC.

DAY FIVE: Hunwick's Camp (3,974m) to Margherita Hut (4,485m) (altitude gain: 511m) A great day, this one. The route passes the two lovely Kitandara lakes before ascending the great glacier-carved chasm between mounts Stanley and Baker to Scott Elliot Pass. Hopefully you'll be able to see Lake Bujuku, far below in the classic, U-shaped, vast Bujuku Valley on the eastern side of the pass, before turning up on to Mount Stanley where you'll find Margherita Hut just below RMS's Elena Hut.

DAY SIX: An early start is required to ascend Mount Stanley before cloud obscures the views. The route then descends to Hunwick Camp.

DAY SEVEN: Descend to Bugata Camp.

DAY EIGHT: From Bugata, you'll follow a different route down the mountain along the Nyamwamba Valley, spending the night at either Kiharu (3,518m) or Semulira Camp (3,170m).

DAY NINE: The trail descends through bamboo and montane forest to the hostel at Kilembe.

Getting there and away Nyakalengija is 22km northwest of Kasese. The Rwenzori Mountains National Park (RMNP) is signposted off the tarmac Fort Portal highway about 7–8km out of Kasese by an electric substation between the road bridges over the Mubuku and Sebwe rivers. Transport can be arranged through RMS or any **private taxi** driver for around Ush50,000 one-way per party. Secure parking is available at the RMS headquarters.

⌂ **Where to stay and eat** Many people overnight in Kasese immediately before and following their ascent (see page 318). There are, however, some options within the Mubuku Valley around Nyakalengija.

Moderate
⌂ **Equator Snow Lodge** (4 cottages) ✆ 0414 258273/0312 260758; e info@geolodgesafrica. com; www.geolodgesafrica.com. This new, rustic lodge in the foothills of the Rwenzori beside the Mubuku River offers accommodation in particularly solid s/c stone cottages close to the Central Circuit trailhead. *US$220/260pp/sgl/dbl FB.*

Budget
⌂ **Base Camp** (15 rooms) Ibanda Town; m 0775 784108. Decent rooms on the edge of the

village but dbl the cost of the comparable White House in Kasese – but in its favour, it's not in Kasese. (*Meals Ush10,000*) *US$25/30 s/c sgl/twin, US$20 sgl with shared bathrooms.*

⌂ **Ruboni Community Campsite** (2 cottages, 4 rooms) m 0752 503445; e info@rubonicamp. com; www.rubonicamp.org. This worthy community project is perched on the western slopes of the Mubuku River valley, 2km beyond Nyakalengija village. It has a lovely hillside location, great mountain views & is close to the RMS trailhead. Morning/afternoon walks through the Bakonjo

THE CENTRAL CIRCUIT TRAIL

For many years, the six-/seven-day circuit above Nyakalengija was the only available route into the high Rwenzori. Issues with the RMS notwithstanding (see pages 322–5 and 333), it remains an exciting and superbly scenic experience.

DAY ONE: Nyakalengija (1,615m) to Nyabitaba Hut (2,651m) (altitude gain: 1,036m) The trailhead is at Nyakalengija, 22km from Kasese off the Fort Portal Road. The RMS can arrange transport from Kasese to its main office at Nyakalengija, where you will pay park fees and finalise arrangements. There is a campsite and safe parking near the office. From Nyakalengija it's a 10km, five-hour ascent to the Nyabitaba Hut, passing first through cultivation then through forest. There is a piped water supply at the hut.

DAY TWO: Nyabitaba Hut (2,651m) to John Matte Hut (3,505m) (altitude gain: 854m) This is the longest and most strenuous day's walk; expect it to take a minimum of seven hours. From Nyabitaba Hut, the path descends through forest for a short time before it crosses the Bujuku River at the Kurt Schafer Bridge (built in 1989). Between the bridge and Nyamileju Hut, the path is good for the first couple of hours, but it becomes steeper and very rocky as you enter the moorland zone, where heather plants are prolific.

You will probably want to stop for lunch at Nyamileju, where there is a little-used and rather rundown hut, as well as a rock shelter. After leaving Nyamileju, the path passes a giant heather forest and follows the Bujuku River. John Matte Hut is about a two-hour walk from Nyamileju. The hut is in good condition and about 200m from the Bujuku River, where you can collect water.

communities cost US$15pp. *Simple meals cost Ush7,500–20,000. US$25pp B&B & US$35 FB twin s/c cottages, US$20pp twin rooms, US$5 camping.*

Shoestring

🏠 **Rwenzori Turaco Camp** (7 rooms)
m 0774 379564; e rwenzorituracoview7@

gmail.com; www.ucota.or.ug. Located in a pretty meadow 200m before Ruboni Camp, this friendly, community-run set up offers a couple of modest but clean & very cheap *bandas* using shared facilities. Simple meals prepared with plenty of notice. *US$10pp B&B.*

CLIMBING THE MOUNTAIN

Clothing and equipment If intending to climb one of the glacial peaks, you'll need to bring climbing boots and equipment such as ropes, ice-axes, harnesses, crampons and walking sticks, or hire gear from your mountain operator (RMS charges US$25 for each of these items). Make sure they are aware of your requirements and allow plenty of time so they can be sized, fitted and paid for – ideally the day before departure to avoid misunderstandings and other delays. Snow goggles, a compass and an altimeter will also be useful.

Cold and wet conditions are normal on the mountain, and it is essential that you are properly prepared. Don't make the mistake of underestimating how cold it can be on the Equator and bring plenty of warm clothing for the nights. The driest months are from late December to early March and from late June to early September, but you should be prepared for rain at all times of year. The paths are incredibly muddy after rain (knee-deep in parts), particularly around the Bigo Bogs, Lake Bujuku, and on some parts of the trail between Kitandara and Guy Yeoman huts. You'll need hiking

DAY THREE: John Matte Hut (3,505m) to Bujuku Hut (3,962m) (altitude gain: 457m) This takes up to five hours, depending on the condition of the two Bigo Bogs, which are often knee-deep in mud. On the way you will pass Lake Bujuku, which has a magnificent setting between mounts Stanley, Speke and Baker. Bujuku Hut is the base for reaching Mount Speke, and you will need to spend an extra night there in order to do this. If you want to climb to the highest point in the range, Margherita Peak on Mount Stanley (5,109m), you must do this from Elena Hut (4,541m), which is about 2km off the Central Circuit Trail and three to four hours' walk from either Bujuku or Kitandara huts.

DAY FOUR: Bujuku Hut (3,962m) to Kitandara Hut (4,023m) (altitude gain: 61m) From Bujuku Hut you will ascend to the highest point on the Central Circuit Trail, Scott Elliot Pass (4,372m), before descending to the two Kitandara lakes. The hut is next to the second lake.

DAY FIVE: Kitandara Hut (4,023m) to Guy Yeoman Hut (3,505m) (descent: 518m) A five-hour walk, starts with a steep ascent to Freshfield Pass (4,282m) then a descent to Bujongolo Cave (3,720m), the base used by the 1906 expedition. Further along the trail at Kabamba Cave (3,450m) there is an attractive waterfall and a rock shelter where you can stay overnight as an alternative to Guy Yeoman Hut.

DAY SIX/SEVEN: Guy Yeoman Hut (3,505m) to Nyakalengija (descent: 1,890m) It's a five-hour descent from Guy Yeoman Hut to Nyabitaba Hut (a descent of 851m). You can either stay overnight at the hut or else continue to the trailhead at Nyakalengija, which will take a further three hours and involve a total descent of 1,890m.

boots if scaling any peaks but above the forest and bamboo zone, you'll be happier wearing locally bought wellingtons. Pack a decent waterproof jacket and trousers and do try them before you climb; my Owino Market overtrousers shredded when I donned them for the first time during a Rwenzori downpour. Take plenty of plastic bags to keep clean clothes dry and to quarantine dirty, wet garments.

RTS rates include all meals while RMS give you the option of feeding yourself or being fed. If you opt for self-catering, you'll need to plan meals and quantities for a week or

THE BAKONJO

The guides and porters on the Rwenzori are almost exclusively Bakonjo, a group of Bantu-speaking agriculturists who inhabit the Rwenzori footslopes – some 500,000 in Uganda as compared with more than four million in the DRC – and are known for their stocky build and hardy nature. Unlike most other Bantu-speaking peoples in Uganda, the Bakonjo have no clear traditional origin. Some say that they migrated westward from Mount Elgon, not settling anywhere until they found a similar montane environment to cultivate. Other traditions claim that the Bakonjo are descended from an ancient ancestor who emerged from one of the caves in the Rwenzori – oddly echoing the prevalent creation legend among the Bagisu of Elgon. They also have no paramount leader, but are divided into a number of small clans, each of which is associated with a particular spur on the Rwenzori foothills.

Traditionally, the Bakonjo seldom ventured on to the higher slopes of the Rwenzori, which is inhabited by a number of powerful deities and spirits that place a curse on any human who glimpses them, and will sometimes strike the observer dead. Paramount among these is Kitasamba – The God Who Never Climbs – said to live on the apex of the jagged peaks, in a snowy environment associated by the Bakonjo with semen and potency. Tradition has it that Kitasamba will only remain the source of Bakonjo procreative powers so long as he is untainted by the act itself – for which reason his spirit manifests itself only in male virgins, and adult men will abstain from intercourse for a period before ascending to the Rwenzori snowline.

Kitasamba has one wife, called Mbulanene (Heavy Rain), but a more important female spirit is his sister Nyabibuya, who safeguards female fertility and protects children. The third most important spirit of the mountains is Endioka, a dark serpentine inhabitant of rivers, capable of rendering men or women infertile, as well as indulging in other acts of black sorcery. The centrality of fertility and potency in their spiritual affairs notwithstanding, sex before marriage is frowned upon in traditional Bakonjo society, monogamy is customary, divorce rare, and pregnancy outside wedlock was formerly punishable by execution.

Agriculture has always been the main food-producing activity of the Bakonjo, but hunting also plays an important role in their traditional society, partly as sport, but also for food. The spirit of hunting, and shepherd of all wild animals, is a one-eyed, one-legged, one-armed being called Kalisa, known for his addiction to pipe smoking, as well as his partiality to fresh meat. Before setting off on any hunting expedition, Bakonjo men traditionally leave an offering of *matoke* or chicken to Kalisa in a shrine consisting of a pair of small hut-like shelters (the largest about 1m high) made of bamboo and/or thatch, then place a small fence of bamboo stakes across their path to prevent evil spirits following. After a successful hunt, a further offering of meat offcuts is left for Kalisa at the site of the slaughter.

more. Vegetables and dried foods – noodles, rice, packet soups, posho, groundnut flour, etc are available in Kasese and Fort Portal. You'll also need to bring or hire a camping stove (US$50) and utensils. At altitude, eating can be a bit of a chore so do what you can to generate an appetite by varying, or at least alternating, meals. If you want RMS to feed you, you'll pay an additional US$110 per group for a cook and US$140 per person for food. Whichever you choose, you'll need to take your own snacks – chocolate and the like – and include some for the poor chap who's carrying your luggage!

The advent of colonial rule robbed the Bakonjo of Uganda of much of their former independence, since their territory was placed under the indirect rule of the Toro monarchy, to which they were forced to pay hut taxes and other tributes. Widespread dissatisfaction with this state of affairs led to the Bakonjo Uprising of 1919, which endured for two years before its leader, Chief Tibamwenda, and his two leading spiritual advisers, were captured by the authorities and executed. But the strong resentment against Toro that still existed amongst the Bakonjo and their Bwamba neighbours resurfaced 40 years later, during the build-up to independence.

In 1961, the Bakonjo and Bwamba, frustrated by Toro's unwillingness to grant them equal status within the kingdom, demanded that they be given their own federal district of Ruwenzururu (Land of the Snow), to be governed independently of Toro. This request was refused. In August 1962, two months before Uganda was to gain independence, the Bakonjo took up arms in the Ruwenzururu Rebellion, attacking several Toro officials and resulting in a number of riots and fatalities. In February 1963, the central government declared a local State of Emergency in affected parts of Toro, and the Bakonjo were invited to elect their own government agents to replace the local representatives of Toro. Instead, the Bakonjo and Bwamba unofficially but effectively ceded from Uganda, by establishing their own Ruwenzururu kingdom, ruled by King Mukirania, and placing border posts and immigration officers at all entry points.

In 1967, the researcher Kirstin Alnaes, who had made several previous study trips to the region, noted that:

The difference ... from 1960 was marked ... Earlier ... spirit possession rituals were performed surreptitiously. Now people sported houses and shrines for the spirits, and were more than willing to talk about it. It was as if the establishment of their own territory in the mountains had released a belief in themselves and their cultural identity [formerly] suppressed not only by government regulations and missionary influence, but also by their own fear of seeming 'backward', 'uncivilised', 'monkeys' and the many other epithets the Batoro had showered upon them.

The situation in Ruwenzururu deteriorated after 1967, as government troops made repeated forays into the breakaway montane kingdom to capture or kill the rebel ringleaders. Ironically, it was only under Amin, who came to power in 1971, that the right for self-determination among the Bakonjo and Bwamba was finally accorded official recognition, with the creation of Rwenzori and Semliki districts, which correspond to the modern districts of Kasese and Bundibugyo. Even so, clan elders must still today obtain a permit from the authorities before they may visit centuries-old sacrificial shrines to the various mountain spirits situated within the national park.

Health Altitude is not a major concern below the snowline. On the Central Circuit Trail, you are likely to be affected by the altitude only around Scott Elliot and Freshfield passes; this will probably be no more than a headache. Only if you climb the peaks is there a serious risk of developing full-blown altitude sickness. The guides are trained to recognise altitude-related symptoms; they will force you to turn back immediately if they feel it is unsafe for you to continue.

MOUNTAIN HEALTH

Do not attempt to climb the Rwenzori unless you are reasonably fit, or if you have heart or lung problems (asthma sufferers should be all right). Bear in mind, however, that very fit people are more prone to altitude sickness because they ascend too fast.

Above 3,000m you may not feel hungry, but you should try to eat. Carbohydrates and fruit are recommended, whereas rich or fatty foods are harder to digest. You should drink plenty of liquids, at least three litres of water daily, and will need enough water bottles to carry this. Dehydration is one of the most common reasons for failing to complete the climb. If you dress in layers, you can take off clothes before you sweat too much, thereby reducing water loss.

Few people climb above 3,500m without feeling at least minor symptoms of altitude sickness: headaches, nausea, fatigue, breathlessness, sleeplessness and swelling of the hands and feet. You can reduce these by allowing yourself time to acclimatise by taking an extra day over the ascent, eating and drinking properly, and trying not to push yourself. If you walk slowly and steadily, you will tire less quickly than if you try to rush each day's walk. Acetazolamide (Diamox) helps speed acclimatisation and many people find it useful; take 250mg twice a day for five days, starting two or three days before reaching 3,500m. However, the side effects from this drug may resemble altitude sickness and therefore it is advisable to try the medication for a couple of days about two weeks before the trip to see if it suits you.

Should symptoms become severe, and especially if they are clearly getting worse, then descend immediately. Even going down 500m is enough to start recovery. Sleeping high with significant symptoms is dangerous; if in doubt descend to sleep low.

Pulmonary and cerebral oedema are altitude-related problems that can be rapidly fatal if you do not descend. Symptoms of the former include shortness of breath when at rest, coughing up frothy spit or even blood, and undue breathlessness compared with accompanying friends. Symptoms of high-altitude cerebral oedema are headaches, poor co-ordination, staggering like a drunk, disorientation, poor judgement and even hallucinations. The danger is that the sufferer usually doesn't realise how sick he/she is and may argue against descending. The only treatment for altitude sickness is descent.

Hypothermia is a lowering of body temperature usually caused by a combination of cold and wet. Mild cases usually manifest themselves as uncontrollable shivering. Put on dry, warm clothes and get into a sleeping bag; this will normally raise your body temperature sufficiently. Severe hypothermia is potentially fatal: symptoms include disorientation, lethargy, mental confusion (including an inappropriate feeling of well-being and warmth!) and coma. In severe cases the rescue team should be summoned.

Though the Rwenzori Mountaineering Services guides are generally able to lead hikes around the Central Circuit Trail, the consensus over several years of reader feedback is that few, if any, are competent to lead climbers above the snowline. Unless you have experience in alpine climbing conditions and carry your own map, compass and GPS, it's highly questionable whether you will be safe above the snowline with this organisation. Here's an extract from a letter from a British climber which remains as relevant today as it was when it was written in 2002.

The guides vary enormously in terms of quality and experience. We had two guides, one of whom spoke no English and was utterly useless from start to finish. He had no cold-weather equipment and became a serious liability on the summit day because he had only thin cotton trousers, a light anorak and no hat. He also wore gumboots, which cannot realistically take crampons, all the way to the summit. On the glacier stages we had to continually stop in cold and windy weather while he tried in vain to get his crampons to stay on.

Our second guide at least spoke English and had a basic idea of the plants and animals of the mountains. He was a nice guy and meant well. But his technical skills were extremely rusty and on the summit day he became alarmingly confused about how to rope up and how to set up a belay. His climbing calls were all wrong, he gave no instruction to the team, and on a particularly steep and exposed rock face below the summit he was essentially hauling us up with brute strength from a non-belayed position – until we as a team made clear our climbing knowledge and insisted on better protection.

On the Stanley Plateau we got lost in thick mist and the guides became stubborn and silent when we insisted that we stop and assess our situation. As a group we had carried a map, a compass and a GPS, so knew exactly where we were and which way we should proceed. Meanwhile the guides had no such aids and were going on memory alone. It was only our team's skill that averted a disaster. Even when we located cairns and flags that marked the summit route, the guides still maintained the pretence that we were not going the right way, apparently to protect their own pride. All in all quite frightening and unprofessional.

Maps and guides Two good maps of the Rwenzori exist, though their availability is limited. The best one of the central peaks – the 1:25,000 contoured map of Central Rwenzori is obtained from the Department of Lands and Surveys in Entebbe. Andrew Wielochowski's recently revised *Rwenzori Map and Guide* must be ordered online (e *ewp@ewpnet.com; www.ewpnet.co.uk*). This shows contours and new routes and has plenty of practical and background information on the reverse side. Anyone with more than a passing interest in the mountain should obtain the definitive *Guide to the Rwenzori* (Henry Osmaston, 2006). It's available from Banana Boat outlets in Kampala or from West Col Productions, Copse House, Goring Heath, Reading, Berks RG8 7SA (\ + 44(0) 1491 681 28; *£20 + p&p*).

9

Fort Portal and Kibale Forest

Situated in the northern foothills of the Rwenzori Mountains, some 50km north of Kasese and 300km west of Kampala, Fort Portal is one of Uganda's most likeable towns. It is, however, of greatest interest to travellers for its position at the epicentre of a cluster of alluring and accessible national parks and other tourist attractions.

The primary reason for the steady stream of safari vehicles that trundle through the town is **Kibale National Park**. Located some 30km to the south, this primarily forested park is not only the best place to track chimpanzees in Uganda, but also harbours its greatest primate diversity and a thrilling variety of forest birds.

While tourists committed to an itinerary must invariably head south to Queen Elizabeth National Park after chimpanzee tracking, those with the time and inclination to dally in the area will be rewarded by a plethora of activities and attractions. Several dozen delightful crater lakes pock the landscape west of Kibale Forest, while the forested **Semliki National Park** and the grasslands of **Semliki Wildlife Reserve** extend across the Rift Valley floor at the northern base of the Rwenzori Mountain. The process of discovery is eased by a remarkable amount of new tourist development, including several worthy community projects. Sites such as the **Bigodi Wetland Sanctuary** and **Lake Nkuruba Nature Reserve** deserve the support of travellers, not least because they provide a genuine foundation to the sometimes glib assertion that independent travel is of greater benefit than package tourism at a grassroots level.

FORT PORTAL

Fort Portal is perhaps the most attractive town in Uganda, situated amid lush rolling hillsides swathed in neat tea plantations and – clouds permitting – offering excellent views across to the glacial peaks of the Rwenzori Mountains to the west. The town centre has seen a great deal of renovation since the early 1990s, including plenty of new hotels and restaurants, and is barely recognisable from the rundown 'Fort Pot-hole' of a few years back.

Fort Portal is named after a British fortress constructed between 1891 and 1893 on the site of the town's present-day golf club, with the aim of protecting the Toro kingdom (see box, pages 342–3) from guerrilla raids by King Kabalega of Bunyoro. Fort Gerry, as it was then known, was named posthumously after the British Consul General of Zanzibar Sir Gerald Portal, who arrived in Buganda in late 1892 to formalise its protectorateship and died of malaria on Zanzibar a few months later. Norma Lorimer, who travelled to Fort Portal in 1913, referred to the settlement as 'Toro', adding that it then consisted of 'about six bungalows, the bank, the Boma, the huts for a few KARs (King's African Rifles), the Indian bazaar and the native settlement'.

Fort Portal boasts few urban landmarks of note. Perched on a hill above the town is the large circular Toro Palace; built in the 1960s for Omukama Kasagama's son and successor, Rukidi III, this was destroyed and looted after the abolition of the old kingdoms under Obote and was only recently restored with Libyan money. Kasagama and Rukidi III are buried at the Karambi Tombs, 5km out of town on the Kasese Road.

GETTING THERE AND AWAY The 300km-long road from Kampala to Fort Portal is surfaced and at a comfortable 80–100km/h, the drive takes about four hours if you take a break midway in Mubende (see box below). Buses have pretty much replaced *matatus* on this route. The reliable **Post Bus** from Kampala leaves from Kampala's central post office at 08.00 daily except Sundays, arriving in Fort Portal five to six hours later. The rather faster **Link** and **Kalita** bus services shuttle between Kampala and Fort Portal several times a day (between 07.00 and 14.00) and cost Ush20,000.

Fort Portal lies only 60km north of Kasese – less than an hour's drive – along an excellent surfaced road covered by regular buses and **minibuses** throughout the day. Fort Portal can also be approached from Masindi (to the north) via Hoima, a full day's drive – or possibly two using public transport – along a route covered more fully on page 375.

TOURIST INFORMATION AND TOUR OPERATORS Kabarole Tours [344 C5] (04834 22183; m 0774 057390; e *ktours@infocom.co.ug; www.kabaroletours.com;*

08.00–18.00 Mon–Sat, 10.00–16.00 Sun) is a commendable setup of some 15 years' standing, whose positive attitude to budget travellers complements an active role in the development and support of many community ecotourism projects around Fort Portal. Their office on Moledina Street, behind Don's Plaza, plastered with flyers, maps and information sheets about regional tourist attractions, effectively functions as the local tourist information office. Although Kabarole Tours has now expanded its services to include countrywide tours, it remains very active locally and can arrange a variety of reasonably priced day or overnight driving excursions to the likes of Kibale Forest and nearby crater lakes, the Semliki Valley or Queen Elizabeth National Park.

Readers have been impressed by the authentic, grassroots experiences offered by **Fort Green Tours & Safaris** (m *0777 638415;* e *mutejo22@gmail.com*). This new company's office is located down an alley near Andrew's supermarket [344 B5].

WHERE TO STAY There's a good range of accommodation on offer, but if you are interested in shoestring options, the town's main cluster of dirt-cheapies on Balya Road [344 B6] behind the row of shops directly opposite Rwenzori Travellers and beside Frederick Lugard's jaundiced statue. The perennial **Christian Guesthouse** seems the most popular. At the other end of Balya Road, the *Top Gear* TV presenters pretended to stay in the Economic Lodge on their 2013 Africa Special before sleeping in the Mountains of the Moon hotel. For location of listings see map on page 344 unless stated otherwise.

breezy climate, fertile soil and clear springs so impressed the early colonials that in 1908 it was chosen as the site of a hill station, where weary Entebbe-based administrators could, according to a contemporary issue of the *Mengo Notes*, 'repair thither for a period of change and invigoration'. These days however, Mubende is best known as the halfway house on the Kampala–Fort Portal highway where travellers pause to enjoy a bottled soda, a bit of barbecue chicken-on-a-stick and other delights. As a result, while the main town lies 1km off the main road, much of its commercial activity has shifted out to the main road. If you need to stay the night, the **Pride Travellers Hotel** (m *0774 114547; US$16/18/28 s/c sgl+/dbl/exec*) is the conspicuous, new, six-floor and 58-room edifice visible from the snack stalls, just off the road leading into the town centre.

If you're not in a hurry to continue your journey, you could head up to the summit of **Mubende Hill**, a steep and bumpy 4km drive up from the town centre, to visit the spiritually significant Nakayima Tree; an active shrine, this is visited by people from all over Buganda and Bunyoro. It is not difficult to see why this particular tree is so revered. It really is a remarkable piece of natural engineering, towering above its park-like surrounds like an oversized surrealist sculpture – almost 40m high, many centuries old, and supported by fin-shaped buttressed roots that fan out from the base to create several cavernous hollows.

There are no further minor diversions of comparable convenience on the second half of the journey to Fort Portal until you reach Sebitoli Camp in the north of Kibale National Park (see page 356). You might, however, wish to head south from the small town of Kyegegwa to visit the **Katonga Wildlife Reserve** (40km to the south), though this would necessitate an overnight stay (see pages 371–2).

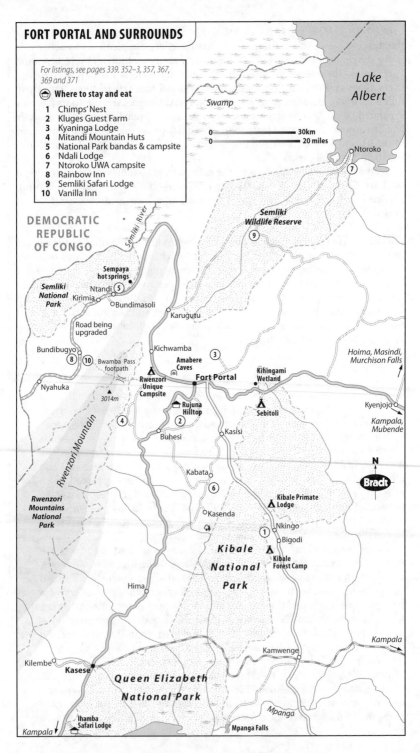

FORT PORTAL AND SURROUNDS

For listings, see pages 339, 352–3, 357, 367, 369 and 371

🏠 **Where to stay and eat**

1 Chimps' Nest
2 Kluges Guest Farm
3 Kyaninga Lodge
4 Mitandi Mountain Huts
5 National Park bandas & campsite
6 Ndali Lodge
7 Ntoroko UWA campsite
8 Rainbow Inn
9 Semliki Safari Lodge
10 Vanilla Inn

Lake Albert

Swamp

0   30km
0   20 miles

Ntoroko
⑦

DEMOCRATIC
REPUBLIC
OF CONGO

Semliki River

Semliki
Wildlife Reserve
⑨

Sempaya
hot springs
Semliki
National
Park
Ntandi ⑤
Kirimia
Bundimasoli

Karugutu

Kichwamba
Bundibugyo
⑧ ⑩ Bwamba Pass
footpath
Amabere
Caves
③
Kihingami
Wetland

Nyahuka
3014m
Rwenzori
Unique
Campsite
Fort Portal
Hoima, Masindi,
Murchison Falls

Rwenzori Mountain
④
Rujuna
Hilltop
②
Buhesi
Kasisi
Sebitoli
Kyenjojo
Kampala,
Mubende

Road being
upgraded

N

Bradt

Kabata
⑥
Kibale Primate
Lodge

Rwenzori
Mountains
National
Park
Kasenda
Nkingo
① Bigodi

Kibale
National
Park
Kibale
Forest Camp

Hima

Kilembe
Kasese
Queen Elizabeth
National Park
Kamwenge
Kampala

Kampala
Ihamba
Safari Lodge
Mpanga
Mpanga Falls

Upmarket

⌂ **Kyaninga Lodge** [map, page 338] (8 cottages) m 0794 304211/0772 999750; e info@kyaningalodge.com; www.kyaningalodge.com. Some 7 years in the making, Kyaninga Lodge finally opened in late 2010 to reveal a masterpiece of imagination, engineering & persistence. The brainchild of Steve Williams, the lodge & 8 spacious cottages are monumental structures created from massive eucalyptus logs. Connected by timber catwalks & flights of wooden steps, they perch on the rim of the stunning Kyaninga Crater Lake facing a panorama which, even by Uganda's high scenic standards, is phenomenal. Beyond the startlingly blue waters filling the cliff-lined crater, & Toro's rolling green hills beyond, the Rwenzori fills the horizon from south to north. A swimming pool overlooks the lake while the surrounding grounds have been landscaped to create a formal garden & tennis court. Kyaninga Lodge is – in a nutshell, in my book, or in anything you care to mention – one of the sights of Uganda. Head 2km out of town along the Kampala Road, then turn left up the Kijura Road by the bridge & then left again after 2km at a signposted turning & carry on for 4km. Kyaninga is about 1hr's drive from the chimp trailhead in Kibale Forest. Reservations are essential. See also advert in third colour section. *US$360/485 sgl/dbl FB, discounts for East Africa residents.*

Moderate

⌂ **Mountains of the Moon Hotel** (40 rooms) ☏ 0483 423200; e info@mountainsofthemoon.co.ug; www.mountainsofthemoon.co.ug. For years, this beautiful colonial-era hotel existed in a state of near collapse, both structurally & operationally, before withdrawing behind a corrugated tin fence for renovations in 2001. 6 years later it emerged from its metal cocoon to reveal a sumptuous makeover executed with impeccable taste. The spacious rooms were comfortably furnished with stone-tiled floors & verandas while, for the first time in 20 years, hot water arrived through taps instead of plastic buckets delivered to your door. The delightful veranda frontage has been provided with comfortable chairs & is the most attractive place in Fort Portal to enjoy a book/beer/meal, doze, watch the birdlife in the expansive garden or use the Wi-Fi. More active residents can enjoy a gym, sauna & a lovely stone-lined swimming pool. The standard of food (*meals cost Ush15,000–25,000*) & service is

variable. *US$95/125/155 sgl/dbl/twin B&B, discounts for East Africa residents.*

⌂ **Mitandi Mountain Huts (Camp Norway)** [map, page 338] (3 cottages) m 0782 500979/348475; www.mitandi.com. This small camp has a remote location in the foothills of the Rwenzori, about 26km southwest of Fort Portal, where a lovely garden, with pristine lawns & flowering shrubs, provides an unexpected contrast with the surrounding patchwork of Bakonjo farmland. A lofty site provides expansive regional views towards Kibale Forest & Lake George, as well as the looming Mount Karongora behind Mitandi on the Rwenzori. Mitandi is an Adventist setup working to improve conditions in the area. No alcohol is served. *US$120pp s/c cottages FB.*

⌂ **Kluges Guest Farm** [map, page 338] (6 rooms) m 0772/0755/0701 440099; e marketing@klugesguestfarm.com; www.klugesguestfarm.com. Pronounced *kloo-ger* rather than *kluj-es*, the guest farm occupies a pretty site above the Mahoma river valley. The entrance is a delight: a 1km avenue of gorgeous flowering plants beneath twin lines of trees. The comfortable s/c rooms are set in a formal terrace softened by a pastoral setting. A swimming pool & horseriding are available. It's signposted off the Kasese Road at Kasusu & Buhesi, 3km & 15km from Fort Portal respectively. *US$85/100 B&B, US$15pp camping.*

⌂ **Fort Motel** (18 rooms) ☏ 04834 22052; m 0772 501731; e reservations@ fortmotel.com; www.fortmotel.com. Guesthouse occupying 2 storeyed buildings & a beautifully restored colonial bungalow on the hilltop close to the site of Fort Gerry. Verandas, balconies & lawns enjoy views of the mountains beyond the town. Smart rooms with clay-tiled floors, nets, TV & fridge. A swimming pool is a recent addition. *US$90/130/135 sgl/dbl/twin deluxe rooms, US$75/95/105 sgl/dbl/twin standard rooms.*

⌂ **Dutchess** (4 rooms) m 0704 879474; www.dutchessuganda.com. 1st-floor rooms conveniently located above the Dutchess restaurant. The town centre's most varied & appetising menu is just a few steps away! *US$55/60 s/c sgl/dbl & US$25 shared bathroom B&B.*

⌂ **Ruwenzori View Guesthouse** (7 rooms) ☏ 04834 22102; m 0772 722102; e ruwview@ africaonline.co.ug. Fort Portal's outstanding hostelry is this universally praised guesthouse on the northwest edge of town. Owned &

9

managed by a friendly Dutch–English couple, the guesthouse offers comfortable accommodation in airy s/c rooms with hot water, & includes a great b/fast. The wonderful home-cooked 4-course dinners (*Ush30,000*) are a refreshing change from bland hotel fare. The pretty flowering gardens face the glacial peaks of the Rwenzori. At the price, difficult to recommend too strongly! Advance booking for accommodation or walk-in dining is essential. A selection of baskets & other local crafts are on sale. Wi-Fi is also available. 2 routes to the guesthouse are clearly signposted along the road from the post office towards the Mountains of the Moon Hotel. *US$39/52 sgl/dbl B&B, US$86 family room (sleeps 4)*.

Budget

⌂ **Rwenzori Travellers Inn** (30 rooms) Kasese Rd; ☎ 04834 22075; m 0775 299591/0712 400570; e travellersinn2000@yahoo.com. This smart 3-storey block is a popular choice with tourists & holidaying Ugandans & expats. It's also very good value. The ground floor has a bar, internet room, craft shop & a pleasant covered dining terrace where simple but tasty main dishes (*Ush10,000–16,000*) are served. The suspended orchid garden in the 1st/2nd-floor atrium is worth a look. You'll sleep most soundly in rooms as far away as possible from the lively 1st-floor bar. *US$17/25/20 for s/c sgl/dbl/twin B&B, US$33/40 for superior dbl/twin*.

⌂ **Eriba Guesthouse** (3 rooms) 22 Njara Rd; m 0777 635333/0772 451662/0712 446304. Situated on Njara Road on the northern edge of Fort Portal beyond the Mountains of the Moon Hotel (fork right at the hotel gate), this guesthouse is the family home of a charming retired Ugandan couple (so it's not really the place if you intend rolling in from Club X-tassy in the small hours). Their pristine home enjoys a lovely view towards the golf course & the Rwenzori. Advance booking is necessary. *US$30/35 sgl/dbl inc b/fast*.

⌂ **Kalya Courts** (12 rooms) 2km south of Fort Portal centre, turn left off the Kasese Road past the Toro parliament building at Mucwa; m 0705 876044; e ebooking@kalyacourts. This new & attractive-looking single-storey hotel stands in extensive green grounds (ideal for noisy w/end functions) looking towards the Toro Palace & the mountains. A lovely spot & fair prices, too. *US$25/40 sgl/dbl B&B*.

⌂ **Raja Excelsior** (30 rooms) ☎ 0483 422562; e rajaexcelsiorhotel@yahoo.com; www.ricnet.info/rajahotel.html. This new, 3-storey hotel is tucked away between the taxi park & Link bus stage. The clean, tiled rooms are spacious, while the dbls have balcony views of the mountains beyond the taxi park. The restaurant menu includes Indian dishes (*Ush15,000–20,000*). Compared with the nearby Rwenzori Travellers, the Raja scores higher for the rooms but loses marks on the public & dining spaces. *US$25/34/43 sgl+/dbl/twin B&B*.

⌂ **Rujuna Hilltop Guesthouse** [off map, 344 A7] (10 rooms) 6km down Kasese Rd; ☎ 04834 25077; m 0784 789246; e rujunaguesthouse@yahoo.com; www.rujuna-guesthouse.com. This 2-storey, family-run guesthouse enjoys a fabulous location on a high grassy slope looking towards the Rwenzori Mountains. Meals include 'full English, African traditional buffet & international cuisine'. *US$25/35/40 sgl/twin/dbl B&B*.

⌂ **Daj Guesthouse** (4 rooms) Mugurusi Rd; m 0782 775126. This smashing little hotel occupies an old Asian residence close to Stanbic bank. Since opening in 2012 it has quickly become popular so be sure to book ahead. Rooms are large. *US$17/20/24 s/c sgl/dbl/twin B&B*.

⌂ **Kenneth Inn** Rukidi III Rd; m 0772 992076. This town centre hotel has comfortable s/c rooms with tiled floors & nets. A pleasant 1st-floor veranda/bar looks across the townscape towards the mountains. The hotel bar closes at midnight when the front door is locked. *US$15/20 sgl/dbl inc b/fast*.

Shoestring

⌂ **Tabes Resthouse** (16 rooms) Malibu Rd (off Kasese Rd above Rwenzori Travellers); m 0714 775620. The town's best cheapie offers clean, tiled 1st-floor rooms above a grim courtyard. A balcony even provides Rwenzori views. No food or drink is served but there are plenty of options nearby. *US$7.50/10 s/c sgl/dbl, US$5 sgl with shared facilities*.

⌂ **Soka Hotel** [off map, 344 A7] (10 rooms) m 0772 472320. Traffic noise aside, the roadside Soka (3km out of town towards Kasese) ought to be quieter than more central shoestring offerings. Facilities include DSTV in the bar/restaurant, a gym, a wood-fired sauna (*Ush7,000*), massage (*Ush13,000*) & secure parking. *US$10 dbl s/c & US$8 sgl+ with shared bathroom B&B*.

⌂ **Youth Encouragement Services (YES) Hostel** (50 beds) e yesuganda@gmail.com;

http://www.yesugandahostel.weebly.com. A Fort Portal NGO which supports orphans, YES provides cheap dormitory accommodation which is popular with volunteers & backpackers. The fee includes the use of a self-catering kitchen equipped with a gas stove & utensils. Located near the Ruwenzori View Guesthouse, YES occupies an unprepossessing 2-storey building but one which faces a delightful pastoral setting with mountain views to the rear. *US$6pp 4- & 6-bed dorms, US$8 sgl room with shared showers, US$3 camping.*

⌂ **Visitours** ☏04834 22813. Located on the corner of Bwamba Rd, adjacent to, but better value than, the Continental. *US$5 sgl+ with shared facilities, US$10 s/c dbl.*

⌂ **Exotic Lodge** (10 rooms) Located beside the Kabarole Tours office behind Don's Plaza, the Exotic has been a favourite with the stringier end of the shoestring traveller community since the early 1990s. *US$3.20/4 sgl/dbl with shared showers.*

Camping

⚑ **Garden of Eden** ☏04834 22183; m 0774 057390; e ktours@infocom.co.ug; www.kabaroletours.com. Tucked away at the back of what passes as the town's industrial area, this new campsite occupies a lush meadow close to the Mpanga River. You'll find a bar & restaurant, a butterfly & chameleon garden, cycad nursery & a resident woodcarver. *US$4pp.*

✗ WHERE TO EAT

Patience is not so much a virtue in Fort Portal's eateries as a survival tool. The restaurants mentioned below all serve perfectly decent food but service can be slow even by the usual standards of upcountry Uganda. Order your meal with good humour and tolerance and take along a good long book or enthusiastic conversationalist. For location of listings see map, page 344, unless otherwise noted.

The most comprehensive menu in the town is offered by the new, Dutch-run **Dutchess** [334 C5] on Mugurusi Road (see page 339): burgers (*Ush10,000*), pizzas (*Ush12,000–23,000*), salads (*Ush9,000*) and sandwiches (*Ush9,000*), as well as continental dishes (*Ush20,000*). Self-caterers will appreciate the range of cheeses, breads and salamis. In the middle of town, **Rwenzori Travellers Inn** [344 B6] serves grills and stews for Ush14,000–20,000, indoors or on the pavement patio. Also in the town centre, the restaurant beside Kabarole Tours on Moledina Street does a cheap lunchtime buffet.

Just outside the town centre, the lunchtime buffet (*Ush12,000*) at **Gardens Restaurant** [344 C4] (opposite the Mpanga River bridge) is a favourite with tour groups on the go. If you've time, an extensive menu of Western and Indian dishes is reasonably priced at around Ush15,000 for a main course. The pork escalope makes a good change from the ubiquitous fish or pepper steak and there's a good craft shop to browse through, too.

On the leafier, eastern side of the Mpanga River, **Jerusalem Paradise** [344 D1] (m *0775 619557*) behind the golf course offers a bewilderingly large selection of fruit and vegetable juice cocktails with some unexpected New Age hype about their benefits. If you overdo it (and there is a conventional bar to speed the process) rooms are available (*US$30*). Easily the nicest place in Fort Portal to eat is the covered terrace facing the gardens at the **Mountains of the Moon Hotel** (see page 339). A decent choice of main courses costs Ush18,000–25,000 but the speed of service and quality of the fare can vary greatly.

If dinner arrives slowly, breakfast can be even more of a challenge. Fort Portal wakes up slowly and there's unlikely to be much activity in your hotel kitchen before 08.00. If you're intent on an early start, head straight to the **Momo Tea Room** [344 B6], right on the main Caltex roundabout which provides a cheap and fast breakfast menu.

If it's a special occasion or even if it's not, treat yourself to a meal at the dramatically located **Kyaninga Lodge**, 6km out of town (see page 339). Lunch costs Ush40,000 and dinner, Ush50,000; both 3-course set menus. A little further afield, **Ndali Lodge**

Fort Portal lies at the physical and political heart of Toro, the youngest of Uganda's traditional kingdoms, ruled – aptly – by the world's most youthful monarch, not quite four years old when he took the throne in 1995. Corresponding roughly with the present-day administrative districts of Kabarole and Kasese, Toro started life as a southern principality within the Bunyoro kingdom, from which it broke away to become an independent kingdom in the late 1820s under Prince Kaboyo, the son of the Bunyoro king, Nyakamaturu.

In the mid-1820s, Nyakamaturu, reaching the end of his 50-year reign, was evidently regarded as a weak and unpopular ruler. As a result, Kaboyo, the king's favourite son and chosen heir to the throne, had become impatient to claim his inheritance. In part, Kaboyo's haste might have been linked to a perceived threat to his future status: Nyakamaturu had already survived at least one attempted overthrow by a less-favoured son, while the elders of Banyoro openly supported his younger brother Mugenyi as the next candidate for the throne. While on a tour of Toro c1825, Kaboyo came to realise the full extent of his father's unpopularity in this southern part of Bunyoro, and he was persuaded by local chiefs to lead a rebellion that left Toro a sovereign state.

Nyakamaturu's army had the better of the rebels in the one full-scale battle that occurred between them, but the ageing king was not prepared for his favourite son to be killed, and he eventually decided to tolerate the breakaway state. It has even been suggested that Kaboyo was invited to succeed the Banyoro throne after Nyakamaturu's death in the early 1930s, but declined, leaving the way clear for Mugenyi to be crowned King of Bunyoro. By all accounts, Kaboyo's 30-year reign over Toro was marked by a high level of internal stability, as well as a reasonably amicable relationship with Bunyoro.

The death of Kaboyo c1860 sparked a long period of instability in Toro. Kaboyo's son and nominated successor Dahiga proved to be an unpopular leader, and was soon persuaded to abdicate in favour of his brother Nyaika, who was in turn overthrown, with the assistance of the Baganda army, by another brother called Kato Rukidi. Nyaika was exiled to the present-day DRC, where he rebuilt his army to eventually recapture Toro, killing Kato Rukidi and reclaiming the throne as his own. Toro enjoyed a brief period of stability after this, but Nyaika was not a popular ruler, and the long years of civil strife had left his state considerably weakened and open to attack.

The start of Nyaika's second term on the Toro throne roughly coincided with the rise of Bunyoro's King Kabalega, who avowed to expand his diminished sphere of influence by reintegrating Toro into the ancient kingdom, along with various other smaller breakaway states. In 1876, Kabalega led an attack on Toro that left its king dead. The Banyoro troops withdrew, and a new Toro king was crowned, but he too was captured by Kabalega and tortured to death, as was his immediate and short-lived successor. The remaining Toro princes fled to Ankole, where they were granted exile, and for the next decade Banyoro rule was effectively restored to Toro.

And that might have been that, had it not been for a fortuitous meeting between the prominent Toro prince Kasagama (also known as Kyebambe) and Captain Lugard in May 1891, at the small principality of Buddu in Buganda. Kasagama was eager for any assistance that might help him to restore the Toro throne, while Lugard quickly realised that the young prince might prove a useful ally in his plans to colonise Bunyoro – 'Inshallah, this may yet prove a trump card', he wrote of the meeting in his diary. Kasagama and his entourage joined Lugard on the march to Ankole, where they gathered together a small army of exiled Toro royalists. They then proceeded to march towards Toro, recapturing one of its southern outposts and most important commercial centres, the salt mine at Lake Katwe, then continuing north to the vicinity of Fort Portal, where a treaty was signed in which Kasagama signed away Toro sovereignty in exchange for British protection.

When Lugard left for Kampala in late 1891, leaving behind a young British officer named De Winton, the Kingdom of Toro had to all intents and purposes been restored, albeit under a puppet leader. De Winton oversaw the construction of a string of small forts along the northwestern boundaries of Toro, designed to protect it from any further attacks by Kabalega, and manned by 6,000 Sudanese troops who had been abandoned by the Emin Pasha on his withdrawal from Equatoria a few years earlier. In early 1862, however, De Winton succumbed to one or other tropical disease, leaving Toro at the mercy of the Sudanese troops, who plundered from communities living close to the forts, and rapidly established themselves as a more powerful force than Kasagama and his supporters. The withdrawal of the Sudanese troops to Buganda in mid-1893 proved to be a mixed blessing: in the absence of any direct colonial presence in Toro, Kasagama briefly enjoyed his first real taste of royal autonomy, but this ended abruptly when Kabalega attacked his capital in November of the same year. Kasagama retreated to the upper Rwenzoris, where several of his loyal followers died of exposure, but was able to return to his capital in early 1864 following a successful British attack on Kabalega's capital at Mparo.

Toro functioned as a semi-autonomous kingdom throughout the British colonial era. Kasagama died in 1929, to be succeeded by King George Rukidi II, a well-educated former serviceman who is regarded as having done much to advance the infrastructure of his kingdom prior to his death in 1965. In February 1966, King Patrick Kaboyo Rukidi III ascended to the Toro throne, only eight months before the traditional monarchies of Uganda were abolished by Obote. The king lived in exile until the National Resistance Movement took power in 1986, after which he enjoyed a distinguished diplomatic career serving in Tanzania and Cuba.

In July 1993, the traditional monarchies were restored by Museveni, and two years later Patrick Rukidi returned to Fort Portal for a second coronation. He died a few days before this was scheduled to take place, to be succeeded by his son Prince Oyo Nyimba Kabamba Iguru Rukidi IV who was only three years old when he came to power. The first years of the restored monarchy were marked by controversy. The sudden death of the former king just before he would have been restored to power attracted allegations of foul play from certain quarters. The plot thickened when Toro prime minister, John Kataramu (one of three regents appointed to assist the young Oyo) was convicted for ordering the murder of another prince in 1999.

Oyo is now 20 years old and is doing what he can to develop Toro. Though he recently received a useful 100 wheelchairs on behalf of his kingdom, he has yet to match the fund-raising prowess of his mother, Best Kemigisha, who hit it off rather well with Muammar Gadaffi. The dictator's munificence substantially reduced the royal family's money worries by, amongst other things, paying for the kingdom's derelict palace to be restored and funding expensive educations for Oyo and his sister Komuntale. As a result, the Great Leader's miserable end outside Sirte in October 2011 was deeply mourned in Toro, at least by those who had benefited from his philanthropy.

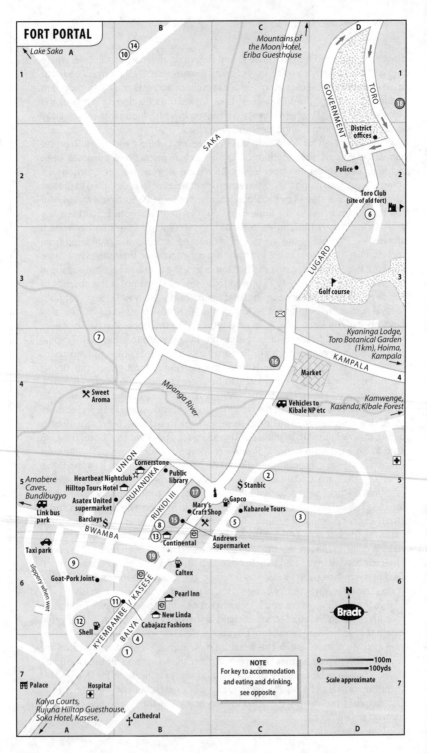

FORT PORTAL

A ← Lake Saka

B

C Mountains of the Moon Hotel, Eriba Guesthouse

D

⑭
⑩

SAKA

GOVERNMENT

TORO

⑱

District offices

Police

Toro Club (site of old fort)
⑥

LUGARD

⑦

Golf course

✉

Kyaninga Lodge, Toro Botanical Garden (1km), Hoima, Kampala

KAMPALA

⑯

Market

Mpanga River

Sweet Aroma

Vehicles to Kibale NP etc

Kamwenge, Kasenda, Kibale Forest

UNION

Cornerstone

Amabere Caves, Bundibugyo

Heartbeat Nightclub
Hilltop Tours Hotel

RUHANDIKA

Public library

⑰

$ Stanbic ②

Link bus park

Asatex United supermarket

RUKIDI III

Mary's Craft Shop

Gapco

Kabarole Tours

Barclays $

⑧

⑮

⑤

③

BWAMBA

⑬

Continental

Andrews Supermarket

Taxi park

⑨

⑲

Goat-Pork Joint

KYEMBAMBE

KASESE

Caltex

N

Bradt

Pearl Inn

⑪

New Linda

⑫ Shell

BALYA

Cabajazz Fashions

④

①

Palace

Hospital

Kalya Courts, Rujuna Hilltop Guesthouse, Soka Hotel, Kasese,

† Cathedral

NOTE
For key to accommodation and eating and drinking, see opposite

0 ――― 100m
0 ――― 100yds
Scale approximate

FORT PORTAL
For listings, see pages 337–45

(see page 357) is a similarly special destination. Bookings at both locations are essential and it is unlikely that either will accommodate you if full with overnight guests.

NIGHTLIFE There is no shortage of places to stay up late in Fort Portal. The **Mountains of the Moon Hotel** (see page 339) is the most attractive setting for a drink and indeed this may be adequate for many. If you feel otherwise, head into town, perhaps for a nod to tradition at the long-serving **Don's Plaza** [344 B5] or the **Gluepot** [344 B5] (the latter has lubricated expat throats since the 1950s, initially on Wednesdays when the settlers came into town to meet the weekly tilapia truck from a Lake George fish factory). Then onwards to **The Forest** on Rukidi III Street [344 B5], currently the liveliest spot in town for beer punctuated by tots of the hideously coloured Zappa. If things have not unravelled completely by 02.00, your party might lurch, Igor-like, across the Bwamba Road to the down-to-earth **Club Africana**, behind the Link bus park [344 A5]. If you're intent on making a fool of yourself on the dance floor, the rather smarter **Club X-tassy** also adjoins the Link park. If you're still going at 07.00, see the preceding section regarding breakfast.

SHOPPING On the main road, **Andrew's supermarket** [344 B5] stocks a good range of local and imported food and drinks, as well as fresh bread (salt as well as sweet). A couple of **craft shops** are found on the same road as well as in the Garden of Eden restaurant, Rwenzori Travellers Inn and Rwenzori View Guesthouse (see pages 339–41).

OTHER PRACTICALITIES
Foreign exchange Stanbic [344 C5] and **Barclays** [344 A5] banks provide their usual ranges of forex and ATM services (though see warning on page 107). Expect long queues, so bring sufficient funds to change money at your convenience rather than from necessity.

Internet Three **internet cafés** are found close to the Caltex roundabout [344 B6] in Rwenzori Travellers Hotel, Mugasa's stationery shop opposite on Balya Road and in the Voice of Toro building.

WHAT TO SEE Fort Portal is the normal springboard for visits to the Semliki Valley, Kibale Forest and the Ndali-Kasenda Crater Lakes, covered under separate headings later in this chapter. The following, more local sites of interest can be visited as day or overnight excursions out of Fort Portal.

Toro Botanical Gardens [off map, 344 D4] (*Informative guided walks Ush10,000*) This commendable initiative occupies the forest valley between the Mountains of the Moon Hotel and the golf course. With the objective of conserving and promoting awareness of the local flora within the Albertine Rift region, Toro Botanical Gardens contains demonstration gardens of medicinal plants, herbs and spices, fruits, flowers and trees. The gardens are signposted off Kampala Road, 1km from town.

Amabere Caves [off map, 344 A5] (*A visit to the caves costs US$3 & a tour of the lakes the same amount*) The Amabere Caves (alternatively known as the Nyakasura Caves) lie roughly 8km west of Fort Portal off the Bundibugyo Road, in a hilly area dotted with crater lakes. An attractive and peaceful **private campsite** just above the caves is one of the lesser-known gems of the Fort Portal area – in the right frame of mind you could happily spend several days here, resting up and exploring the surrounding countryside. The cycling tour offered by Kabarole Tours (see page 336) goes past the caves.

The full name of the caves is Amabere ga Nyinamwiru – Breasts of Nyinamwiru – and refers to a live stalactite formation supposedly shaped like a pair of breasts (but actually more reminiscent of deformed cow udders, certainly in numerical terms). According to local tradition, Nyinamwiru was the daughter of a local king called Bukuku, so beautiful that no man could leave her alone, and constantly plagued by marital proposals from unsuitable suitors. Bukuku cut off Nyinamwiru's breasts in the hope it would reduce her charms, but even this wasn't enough to deter his lovely daughter's many admirers, so eventually he hid her away in the caves. Whilst there, Nyinamwiru was impregnated by the Batembuzi king Isaza to give birth to Ndahura, the future founder of the Bacwezi dynasty, and – lacking breasts herself – she fed the infant with the cloudy limestone 'milk' that drips from the breast-like stalactites. Legend has it that after Ndahura surrendered the Bacwezi throne to his son, he retired to his birthplace – his footprints can still reputedly be seen in the caves' vicinity.

The main cave, though small, is very pretty, supported as it is by several pillars formed where stalactites and stalagmites have met in the middle. A powerful little waterfall lies next to the main cave – it's an exhilarating feeling to stand on the moss-covered rocks behind the waterfall, and to see a sheet of ice-cold water plunge down right in front of you, kicking spray back into your face. It's said to be OK to swim in the pool below the falls, though the water is very chilly. The riparian forest around the waterfall is rattling with birds, and it supports a few black-and-white colobus monkeys.

Getting there and away To get to the Amabere Caves, follow the Bundibugyo Road out of Fort Portal for 6km before turning right onto the signposted turn-off. After 1km, turn right just before the entrance to Nyakasura School (a Scottish-instigated institution where the boys still wear kilts). You'll soon pass a swimming pool to your right. Around 800m from the turning, turn right again to reach the campsite. No more than ten minutes' walk away from the campsite, Kigere Crater Lake is surrounded by dense stands of plantains and palms, and is reportedly safe to swim in.

Lake Saka The largest lake in the immediate vicinity of Fort Portal, Lake Saka is not strictly speaking a crater lake, but rather a flooded valley dammed by a crater. It is one of the few lakes to support fish large enough for commercial harvesting, and it is safe to swim in. It's possible to walk there from the Amabere Caves over a couple of hours or directly from Fort Portal. Head through the town's small industrial area behind

The Gardens restaurant then follow the road up a gentle slope beyond the market and bear left on to Saka Road. The lake is about 7km out of town. Walking through the church grounds isn't encouraged; better to leave the road at a col about 1km before the lake near the new Mountains of the Moon University. Climb up a steep hill to a crater rim from where you can follow the rims of two adjoining craters.

Mugusu and Rwimi markets The colourful weekly markets at Mugusu and Rwimi, which lie along the Kasese Road below the peaks of the Rwenzoris, are important social events locally, and well worth visiting if you're in town on the right day. The market at Mugusu, about 12km south of Fort Portal, takes place on Wednesdays, and is mostly concerned with secondhand clothing, attracting buyers from as far afield as Kampala. The market at Rwimi, about 45km south of Fort Portal, is a more conventional rural market, but very large and colourful, with a spectacular setting.

Rwenzori mini-hike (*Contact Kabarole Tours, for contact details, see page 336, or the Kazingo-based Abanya Rwenzori Mountaineering Association,* m *0772 621397; http://sites.google.com/site/abanyarwenzori*) This hike crosses between Fort Portal and Bundibugyo via the northern tip of the Rwenzori Mountains National Park using the 'Bwamba Pass', at one time the only access route between the Semliki Valley and Fort Portal. Despite being relatively strenuous – six to eight hours if you are driven to the trailhead, and up to 12 hours if you walk there from Fort Portal – the walk has become increasingly popular with travellers who are reluctant to pay the high fees asked for longer Rwenzori hikes based out of Kasese. From the 1,650m trailhead at Kazingo (15km from Fort Portal), a choice of routes traverse the range, ascending through farmland/grassland, forest and bamboo forest to the medial ridge before descending to Bundibugyo. It's hard going, especially if your trail takes in the 3,000m Mount Karangora. Consolation for the leg strain is provided by excellent regional views (weather permitting) and the chance to spot the four monkey species present in the forest, including the Angola colobus. If walking all the way from Fort Portal, you could stop overnight at **Rwenzori Unique Campsite** (m *0772 986235; US$7.50pp* bandas, *US$5pp camping; meals Ush5,000*), 2km from the Kazingo trailhead.

Another option, which will get you across to the Semliki Valley and save you the US$35 UWA entrance fee and some rather dull bamboo forest, is to cross the range north of the national park. Several routes traverse this lower end of the Rwenzori between Karagutu (at the junction for Semliki Wildlife Reserve) and Ntandi or Bundimasoli (on the edge of Semliki National Park, 5km from the hot springs; see page 369). Though forest cover is limited to remnant patches in steep valleys, the six-hour walk traverses a beautiful area of Bakonjo farmland hidden from the plains (and main road) on either side of the range. When I hiked between Bundimasoli trading centre and Karagutu in 2011, I found local youths disinclined to act as guides so engaged James, a Mtwa from the local Batwa Pygmy community. We paid him Ush20,000 plus funds for transport back from Karagutu. To contact him, call the Bambuti's teacher/mentor, Ezekial (m *0785 476152*). Facilities are few and transport intermittent at Ntandi, so establish a Semliki plan of campaign in advance (see pages 368–9) and do take plenty of water and snacks.

KIBALE NATIONAL PARK

(*Entrance is subject to the UWA fees for a Class A protected area; see pages 32–3*) Kibale National Park, together with the nearby Ndali-Kasenda Crater Lakes, is close to

You'll hear them before you see them: from somewhere deep in the forest, an excited hooting, just one voice at first, then several, rising in volume and tempo and pitch to a frenzied unified crescendo, before stopping abruptly or fading away. Jane Goodall called it the 'pant-hoot' call, a kind of bonding ritual that allows any chimpanzees within earshot of each other to identify exactly who is around at any given moment, through the individual's unique vocal stylisation. To the human listener, this eruptive crescendo is one of the most spine-chilling and exciting sounds of the rainforest, and a strong indicator that visual contact with man's closest genetic relative is imminent.

It is, in large part, our close evolutionary kinship with chimpanzees that makes these sociable black-coated apes of the forest so enduringly fascinating. Humans, chimpanzees and bonobos (also known as pygmy chimpanzees) share more than 98% of their genetic code, and the three species are far more closely related to each other than they are to any other living creature, even gorillas. Superficial differences notwithstanding, the similarities between humans and chimps are consistently striking, not only in the skeletal structure and skull, but also in the nervous system, the immune system, and in many behavioural aspects – bonobos, for instance, are the only animals other than humans to copulate in the missionary position.

Unlike most other primates, chimpanzees don't live in troops, but instead form extended communities of up to 100 individuals, which roam the forest in small, socially mobile subgroups that often revolve around a few close family members such as brothers or a mother and daughter. Male chimps normally spend their entire life within the community into which they were born, whereas females are likely to migrate into a neighbouring community at some point after reaching adolescence. A high-ranking male will occasionally attempt to monopolise a female in oestrus, but the more normal state of sexual affairs in chimp society is non-hierarchical promiscuity. A young female in oestrus will generally mate with any male that takes her fancy, while older females tend to form close bonds with a few specific males, sometimes allowing themselves to be monopolised by a favoured suitor for a period, but never pairing off exclusively in the long term.

Within each community, one alpha male is normally recognised – though coalitions between two males, often a dominant and a submissive sibling – have often been recorded. The role of the alpha male, not fully understood, is evidently quite benevolent – chairman of the board rather than crusty tyrant. This is probably influenced by the alpha male's relatively limited reproductive advantages over his potential rivals, most of whom he will have known for his entire life. Other males in the community are generally supportive rather than competitive towards the alpha male, except for when a rival consciously contests the alpha position, which is far from being an everyday occurrence. One male in Tanzania's Mahale Mountains maintained an alpha status within his community for more than 15 years between 1979 and 1995!

Prior to the 1960s, it was always assumed that chimps were strict vegetarians. This notion was rocked when Jane Goodall, during her pioneering chimpanzee study in Tanzania's Gombe Stream, witnessed them hunting down a red colobus monkey, something that has since been discovered to be common behaviour, particularly during the dry season when other food sources are depleted. Over subsequent years, an average of 20 kills has been recorded in Gombe annually, with red colobus being the prey on more than half of these occasions, though young bushbuck, young bushpig and even infant chimps have also been victimised and eaten. The normal *modus operandi* is for four or five adult chimps to slowly encircle a colobus troop, then for another chimp to act as a decoy, creating deliberate confusion in the hope that it will drive the monkeys into the trap, or cause a mother to drop her baby.

Although chimp communities appear by and large to be stable and peaceful entities, intensive warfare has been known to erupt within the habituated communities of Mahale and Gombe. In Mahale, one of the two communities originally habituated by researchers in 1967 had exterminated the other by 1982. A similar thing happened in Gombe Stream in the 1970s, when the Kasekela community, originally habituated by Goodall, divided into two discrete communities. The Kasekela and breakaway Kahama community coexisted alongside each other for some years. Then in 1974, Goodall returned to Gombe Stream after a break to discover that the Kasekela males were methodically persecuting their former community mates, isolating the Kahama males one by one, and tearing into them until they were dead or terminally wounded. By 1977, the Kahama community had vanished entirely.

Chimpanzees are essentially inhabitants of the western rainforest, but their range does extend into the extreme west of Tanzania, Rwanda and Uganda, which have a combined population of perhaps 7,000 individuals. These are concentrated in Tanzania's Mahale and Gombe national parks, Rwanda's Nyungwe Forest, and about 20 Ugandan national parks and other reserves, most notably Budongo, Kibale, Semliki, Maramagambo and Bwindi. Although East Africa's chimps represent less than 3% of the global population, much of what is known about wild chimpanzee society and behaviour stems from the region, in particular the ongoing research projects initiated in Gombe Stream and Mahale Mountain national parks back in the 1960s.

An interesting pattern that emerged from the parallel research projects in these two reserves, situated little more than 100km apart along the shore of Lake Tanganyika, is a variety of social and behavioural differences between their chimp populations. Of the plant species common to both national parks, for instance, as many as 40% of those utilised as a food source by chimps in the one reserve are not eaten by chimps in the other.

In Gombe Stream, chimps appear to regard the palmnut as something of a delicacy, but, while the same plants grow profusely in Mahale, the chimps there have yet to be recorded eating them. Likewise, the 'termite-fishing' behaviour first recorded by Jane Goodall at Gombe Stream in the 1960s has a parallel in Mahale, where the chimps are often seen 'fishing' for carpenter ants in the trees. But the Mahale chimps have never been recorded fishing for termites, while the Gombe chimps are not known to fish for carpenter ants. Mahale's chimps routinely groom each other with one hand while holding their other hands together above their heads – once again, behaviour that has never been noted at Gombe. More than any structural similarity, more even than any single quirk of chimpanzee behaviour, it's such striking cultural differences – the influence of nurture over nature if you like – that bring home our close genetic kinship with chimpanzees.

being an independent traveller's dream, blessed with the tantalising combination of inexpensive accommodation, easy access, wonderful scenery and a remarkable variety of activities. The park is highly alluring to nature lovers for the opportunity to view a wide range of forest birds and track chimpanzees (as well as viewing a wide range of other primates). Though the scenic appeal of the region remains undiminished, the rising cost of chimp tracking, and the conversion of the old budget Kanyanchu River Camp to an upmarket tented camp, means that the national park is no longer the mandatory backpacker destination it was a few years ago.

Gazetted in October 1993, the 766km^2 Kibale National Park extends southwards from Fort Portal to form a contiguous block with the Queen Elizabeth National Park. Interspersed with patches of grassland and swamp, the dominant vegetation type is rainforest, spanning altitudes of 1,100–1,590m and with a floral composition transitional to typical eastern Afro-montane and western lowland forest.

At least 60 mammal species are present in Kibale Forest. It is particularly rich in primates, with 13 species recorded, the highest total for any Ugandan national park. The nine diurnal primates found at Kibale are vervet, red-tailed, L'Hoest's and blue monkeys, grey-cheeked mangabey, red colobus, black-and-white colobus, olive baboon, and chimpanzee. The Kibale Forest area is the last Ugandan stronghold of the red colobus, although small numbers still survive in Semliki National Park. Visitors who do both the forest and the swamp walks can typically expect to see around five or six primate species.

Kibale Forest offers superlative primate viewing, but it is not otherwise an easy place to see large mammals – this despite an impressive checklist which includes lion, leopard, elephant, buffalo, hippo, warthog, giant forest hog, bushpig, bushbuck, sitatunga, and Peter's, red and blue duikers. The elephants found in Kibale Forest are classified as belonging to the forest race, which is smaller and hairier than the more familiar savanna elephant. Elephants frequently move into the Kanyanchu area during the wet season, but they are not often seen by tourists.

Roughly 335 bird species have been recorded in Kibale Forest, including four species not recorded in any other national park: Nahan's francolin, Cassin's spinetail, blue-headed bee-eater and masked apalis. Otherwise, the checklist for Kibale includes a similar range of forest birds to Semliki National Park, with the exclusion of the 40-odd Semliki 'specials' and the inclusion of a greater variety of water and grassland species. A recent first sighting of a green-breasted pitta caused some excitement in Ugandan ornithological circles, while the truly optimistic might want to look out for Prigogine's ground thrush, a presumably endemic species or race collected once in the 1960s and yet to be seen again! The best birdwatching spot is the Bigodi Wetland Sanctuary, where a four-hour trail has been laid out and experienced guides will be able to show you several localised species which you might otherwise overlook.

The cost of the visiting fee (see pages 32–3) is, more than any other park, a consideration when planning your itinerary, given the additional attractions just outside the park. It obviously doesn't make sense to pay for park entrance and check into park accommodation then, with the 24-hour clock ticking, head off for 'out-of-park' birdwatching in the Kihingami and Magombe swamps near Sebitoli and Kanyanchu respectively. No park fee is charged for passing through the park on the Fort Portal–Kamwenge road, for staying at the guesthouses in and around Bigodi, or for visiting the Bigodi Wetland Sanctuary.

GETTING THERE AND AWAY Kibale National Park is most normally approached from Fort Portal using the Kamwenge Road. Historically a bumpy *murram* route

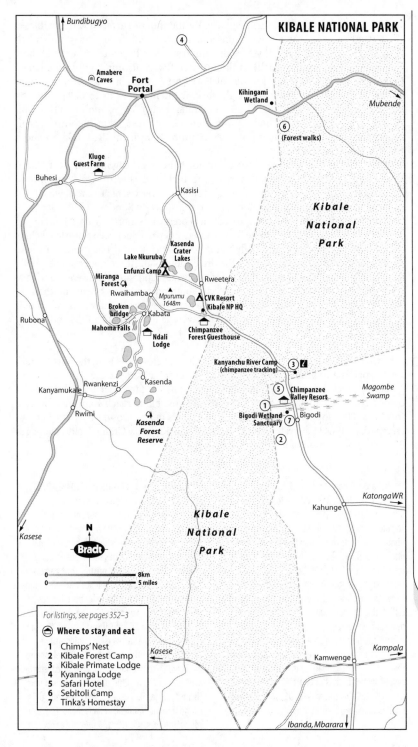

↑ *Bundibugyo*

④

Mubende

Amabere Caves
Fort Portal

Kihingami Wetland

⑥
(Forest walks)

Kluge Guest Farm

Kibale

Buhesi

Kasisi

National

Park

Kasenda Crater Lakes

Lake Nkuruba

Enfunzi Camp

Miranga Forest

Rweetera

Rwaihamba

Mpurumu 1648m

CVK Resort
Kibale NP HQ

Broken bridge

Kabata

Rubona

Mahoma Falls

Ndali Lodge

Chimpanzee Forest Guesthouse

Kanyanchu River Camp
(chimpanzee tracking)

③ ℹ

Magombe Swamp

⑤

Chimpanzee Valley Resort

Rwankenzi

Kasenda

①

Kanyamukale

Bigodi Wetland Sanctuary

⑦

Bigodi

Rwimi

Kasenda Forest Reserve

②

KatongaWR →

Kahunge

↙ *Kasese*

N

Bradt

0   8km
0   5 miles

Kibale

National

Park

Kampala

Kasese ←

Kamwenge

For listings, see pages 352–3

🏠 **Where to stay and eat**

1 Chimps' Nest
2 Kibale Forest Camp
3 Kibale Primate Lodge
4 Kyaninga Lodge
5 Safari Hotel
6 Sebitoli Camp
7 Tinka's Homestay

Ibanda, Mbarara ↓

with several steep sections, this is apparently about to be surfaced which will ease the journey no end, though with consequences for wildlife on the 10km stretch through the national park. If you're **driving** from Fort Portal town centre, follow Lugard Road downhill (north) to the Mpanga River, turning right immediately before the bridge. About 12km out of Fort Portal, you reach a major junction, where you need to fork left (the right fork, incidentally, leads to Lake Nkuruba and Ndali Lodge in the Ndali-Kasenda Crater Field). After another 11km you pass Crater Valley Resort and Chimpanzee Guesthouse, 2km before the road enters the forest, from which point it's 10km to Kanyanchu River Camp and a further 5km to Bigodi.

Regular **minibus-taxis** run back and forth between Bigodi and Fort Portal throughout the day and are far more comfortable and safer than pick-up trucks. Tourists are routinely overcharged by taxi touts, so it's advisable to check what local passengers are paying. There is normally no transport on Sunday.

A little-used alternative route to Kibale Forest runs north from Mbarara via Ibanda and Kamwenge. This route is tarmacked and passes between some lovely hills on the way to Ibanda, north of which the road is unsurfaced but mostly in pretty good condition. In a private vehicle the drive should take three hours. Using public transport, you'll probably have to change vehicles at Ibanda and Kamwenge, and may well have to overnight at one or other town – both possess a few cheap guesthouses. You can easily pick up transport from Kamwenge on to Fort Portal via Kanyanchu. If you're heading this way, you might want to investigate the Mpanga Falls and nearby cycad field between Kamwenge and Ibanda (see box opposite).

 WHERE TO STAY All of the accommodation listed below lies along the Fort Portal–Kamwenge road within 10km of the tourist centre at Kanyanchu. If you plan to go chimp tracking, your accommodation options are far wider than those listed below. With a 06.30–07.00 start it is perfectly possible to reach Kanyancu in time for the 08.00 primate walk from lodges and hotels in and around Fort Portal town (see pages 339–41) as well as those in the Ndali-Kasenda Crater Field (see pages 356–62). For location of listings see map, page 351.

Upmarket

🏠 **Kibale Primate Lodge** (*7 bandas*, 8 tents) 📞0414 267153; m 0772 426368; e info@ ugandalodges.com; www.ugandalodges.com. The old UWA-run Kanyanchu River Camp has gone upmarket with its conversion to a tented camp offering comfortable s/c safari tents & cottages. (*meals available for Ush15,000–20,000*). Set in secondary vegetation on the edge of the forest, Kanyanchu is alive with mysterious rustles & bird calls during the day &, after dark, is washed over by an almost deafening choir of cicadas & other insects. The best thing about the Primate Lodge is its location: at 07.30 on a chilly Kibale morning, the trailhead for chimpanzee tracking is just a couple of mins from your bed. *US$180/280 sgl/dbl tents, US$120/165 cottages FB, US$30 tree house, US$8 camping excl meals.*

Moderate

🏠 **Chimps' Nest** (7 cottages) 📞04834 27511; m 0774 669107; e info@chimpsnest.com. This rustic setup provides reasonably priced accommodation in a great forest setting in the Dura river valley on the edge of Kibale National Park. Compact s/c cottages set in regenerating farmland face a hillside of pristine forest across the river. The site includes a gorgeous tract of swamp forest that *drips* with palms, climbers, orchids & tree ferns (*forest walks US$10*). This is a fabulous location for a remarkable, if vertiginous, 13m-high s/c tree house & a s/c riverside family cottage. Birds, chimps & other primates, & even elephants are heard (& sometimes seen). (*3-course meals are available for US$10*) Chimp's Nest is reached from Nkingo village, 5km (& a 15min drive) from the chimp tracking trailhead at Kanyanchu. *US$75/100 sgl/dbl cottages, US$125/160 sgl/dbl tree house,*

US$140 2-bed family cottage B&B, US$8 dorm bed excl meals, US$5 camping.

🏠 **Kibale Forest Camp** (10 s/c tents) 📞0312 294894; e booking@naturelodges.biz; www. naturelodges.biz. This long-established tented camp stands in a pretty patch of forest 2km south of Bigodi. Management has been taken over by Nature Lodges who have spruced up the place & slashed the prices, which are now very good value indeed. *US$75/90 sgl/dbl B&B.*

Shoestring & camping

🏠 **Tinka's Homestay** (2 rooms) The owner of Safari Hotel (see below) also offers visitors the chance to stay with his family in his home next to the Magombe Swamp visitors' centre. Billed as a cultural experience, visitors share meals with the family & can assist with food preparation, as well as planting or harvesting crops in the garden. See *Where to eat below. US$20pp FB.*

🏠 **Safari Hotel** (6 rooms) m 0772 468113; e comm-tour@infocom.co.ug. This small family-run lodge lies about 3km past Kanyanchu on the road to Bigodi. Simple meals cost Ush4,000–6,000 including fruit salad or pineapple pie. A clean pit toilet & warm basin showers are provided. *Rooms US$12;* bandas *US$16. US$4 to pitch your own tent.*

For camping options, see **Kibale Primate Lodge** and **Safari Hotel**.

✘ **WHERE TO EAT** Tinka's Homestay (see above; *Ush15,000*) next to the Magombe Swamp visitors' centre offers visitors the chance to sample food in a traditional setting, that is to say sitting barefoot on floor mats and eating food that 'includes but is not limited to *posho*, potatoes, beans, peanuts, green bananas, rice, beef, mixed vegetables (carrots, egg plants, spinach, tomatoes, onions, cabbages, etc),

---

MPANGA FALLS

This impressive waterfall is formed by the Mpanga River as it tumbles over the rim of the 1,200m Mount Karubaguma some 15km before emptying into Lake George. Estimated to be about 50m high, the waterfall is enclosed by a steep gorge and supports a lush cover of spray forest. A remarkable feature of the gorge's vegetation is the profusion of the cycad *Encephalartos whitelockii*, a species which, so far as I can ascertain, is endemic to this single location and represents the largest cycad colony in Africa. Perhaps the closest thing among trees to living fossils, the cycads are relicts of an ancient order of coniferous plants that flourished some 300 to 200 million years ago, with the aptly prehistoric appearance of an overgrown tree fern perched on top of a palm stem up to 10m tall. Many modern species are, like *Encephalartos whitelockii*, extremely localised, and classified as endangered, partly because of their very slow life cycle.

The modern world caught up with *E. whitelockii* in 2008 when a controversial hydro-power scheme for the gorge was pushed through. Many cycads were bulldozed before a public outcry led to mitigation measures including local nurseries to grow more cycads. Whether any of these still exist I cannot say but I have seen *E. whitelockii* seedlings being tended at Fort Portal's Garden of Eden campsite. The Mpanga Falls – or what is left of them – can be reached with reasonable ease as a day trip from Kibale Forest or as a diversion from the main road between Kamwenge and Ibanda. Kamwenge is well served by public transport from both directions. From there, you'll need a special hire or boda-boda to cover the 22km from town to the gorge. Mpanga Gorge lies in the remotest corner of Queen Elizabeth National Park, so technically you'll need to clear this with the park authority in Kebuko village, 18km from Kamwenge.

cassava, yams, pumpkins, millet bread & fruits in season (jackfruit, avocado, bananas, papaya, pineapples and mangoes)'. Sounds filling! The event is a popular diversion for safari groups.

WHAT TO SEE AND DO Three primary visitor activities occupy visitors to Kibale. The main attraction is the guided **chimp-tracking** excursion out of Kanyanchu. Almost as popular is the guided **walking** trail through the Bigodi Wetland Sanctuary, which is probably better for general monkey viewing and one of the finest birding trails in the country. The third activity is the filling **lunch at Tinka's Homestay** (see above) There is also plenty of potential for unguided exploration in the area, both along the main road through the forest, and around Bigodi trading centre and Kanyanchu Camp. If time is limited, it's advisable to do the activity that most interests you in the morning – this is not only the best time to see chimpanzees, but also when birds are most active.

Guided forest walks (*The standard entry fee for a Category A protected area is charged. See pages 32–3 for current fees & those for chimpanzee tracking & the habitation experience*) The highlight of any visit to Kibale Forest will be the **chimp tracking** excursions that leave from Kanyanchu at 08.00 and 14.00 daily. Chimp sightings are not guaranteed on these walks, but the odds of encountering them have improved greatly in recent years, and now stand at around 90%. The chimpanzee community, whose territory centres on Kanyanchu, is well habituated, with the result that visitors can often approach to within a few metres of them.

Whilst in the forest you can expect to see at least two or three other types of primate, most probably grey-cheeked mangabey and red-tailed monkey. You will hear plenty of birdsong, but it's very difficult to see any birds in the heart of the forest – you're better off looking for them in the rest camp and along the road. The guides are knowledgeable and will identify various medicinal plants, bird calls and animal spoor.

Dedicated chimp enthusiasts or aspiring researchers seeking field experience can join a **chimpanzee-habituation experience**, which involves staying with the chimps all day with habituators and taking notes on their behaviour.

Another novelty is a **guided night walk** with spotlights, which runs from 19.30 to 22.00 daily, costs US$25 per person, and offers a good chance of sighting nocturnal primates such as the bushbaby and potto.

Bigodi Wetland Sanctuary This small sanctuary, which protects the Magombe Swamp, adjacent to Bigodi trading centre and immediately outside the national park boundary, is an admirable example of conservation and tourism having a direct benefit at grassroots level. Run by the Kibale Association for Rural and Environmental Development (KAFRED), all money raised from the trail is used in community projects in Bigodi – it has so far funded the creation of a small local library as well as the construction of a new secondary school in the village. The guided 4.5km circular trail through the swamp is also one of the best guided bird trails in East Africa, as well as offering a realistic opportunity to see up to six different primate species in the space of a few hours.

The trail starts at the KAFRED office on the Fort Portal side of Bigodi. Here you must pay a fee of US$20/15 per foreign tourist/resident and will be allocated a guide. Serious birdwatchers should mention their special interest, since some guides are better at identifying birds than others – and if you don't have a field guide and binoculars, then make sure your guide does. Afternoon walks technically start at 15.00 and generally take around three hours, but dedicated birders will need longer and are advised to get going an hour earlier – there are enough guides for you to start whenever you like. For morning walks, it is worth getting to the office as early as you can, or possibly even arranging a dawn start a day in advance. The trail is very muddy in parts, and if you don't have good walking shoes, then you'd do well to hire a pair of wellingtons from the KAFRED office – this costs less than US$2. For general monkey viewing, it doesn't matter greatly whether you go in the morning or afternoon, but birders should definitely aim to do the morning walk.

The sanctuary's main attraction to ornithologists is quality rather than quantity. You'd be very lucky to identify more than 40 species in one walk, but most of these will be forest-fringe and swamp specials, and a good number will be West African species at the eastern limit of their range. There are other places in Uganda where these birds can be seen, but not in the company of local guides who know the terrain intimately and can identify even the most troublesome greenbuls by sight or call. One of the birds most strongly associated with the swamp is the great blue turaco, which will be seen by most visitors. Another speciality is the papyrus gonolek, likely to be heard before it is seen, and most frequently encountered along the main road as it crosses the swamp or from the wooden walkway about halfway along the trail. Other regularly seen birds include grey-throated, yellow-billed, yellow-spotted and double-toothed barbets; speckled, yellow-rumped and yellow-throated tinker-barbets; yellowbill; brown-eared woodpecker; blue-throated roller; grey parrot; bronze sunbird; black-crowned waxbill; grey-headed Negro-finch; swamp flycatcher; red-capped and snowy-headed robin-chats; grosbeak and northern brown-throated weavers; and black-and-white casqued hornbill.

Butterflies are abundant in the swamp, and it is also home to sitatunga antelope, serval, a variety of mongoose and most of the primate species recorded in the forest. The red colobus is the most common monkey, often seen at close quarters, but you are also likely to observe red-tailed monkey, L'Hoest's monkey, black-and-white colobus and grey-cheeked mangabey. If you are extremely fortunate, you might even see chimpanzees, since they occasionally visit the swamp to forage for fruit.

Unguided walks

Tourists are forbidden to walk along forest paths or in Magombe Swamp without a guide, but they are free to walk unguided elsewhere. **Kanyanchu** itself is worth a couple of hours' exploration. A colony of Viellot's black weaver nests in the camp, while flowering trees attract a variety of forest sunbirds. You can also expect to see or hear several types of robin and greenbul, often difficult to tell apart unless you get a good look at them (little greenbul and red-capped robin appear to be most common around the camp). A speciality of the camp is the localised red-chested paradise flycatcher, a stunning bird that's very easy to find once you know its call. Other interesting birds I've seen regularly at Kanyanchu are the great blue turaco, hairy-breasted barbet, black-necked weaver and black-and-white casqued hornbill. The short, self-guided grassland trail which circles the camp is good for monkeys.

It is permitted to walk unguided along the stretch of the main road between Fort Portal and Kamwenge as it runs through the forest. The most interesting section on this road is the first few kilometres running north towards Fort Portal from Kanyanchu, where you're almost certain to see a variety of monkeys, genuine forest birds such as Sabine's spinetail, blue-breasted kingfisher and Afep pigeon, as well as butterflies in their hundreds gathered around puddles and streams. The road south from Kanyanchu to Bigodi passes through a variety of habitats – forest patches, swamp and grassland – and is also productive for birds and monkeys.

Sebitoli and the Kihingami Wetlands Sebitoli lies inside the northern part of Kibale National Park. It is little visited, which is a shame, since it is conveniently located just metres off the main Fort Portal–Kampala road and is far easier to reach than Kanyanchu. **Sebitoli** development opened in 2002 to help ease tourist pressure on the Kanyanchu sector of the park. It offers similar activities and facilities to Kanyanchu, with the exception of chimpanzee tracking, and is far more accessible for day trippers from Fort Portal. Guided forest walks cost US$15 per person (excluding UWA entrance fee) and offer a good chance of seeing red and black-and-white colobus and blue and vervet monkeys, as well as a varied selection of the (rapidly expanding) local checklist of 236 bird species – chimpanzees are present in the area but not habituated. Sebitoli is reportedly a superb site for spotlighting for nocturnal creatures such as bushbabies and pottos. Guided walks in the nearby Kihingami Wetlands outside the park offer excellent birdwatching (book through Kabarole Tours in Fort Portal; see page 336).

Getting there and away The Sebitoli Gate lies 100m off the Fort Portal–Kampala road, less than 1km west of the Mpanga Bridge and 15km from Fort Portal. It is simple to reach by either private vehicle or public transport.

Where to stay Sebitoli is convenient to reach from hotels in Fort Portal. Alternatively, the **Sebitoli Camp** (*US$14/17 sgl/dbl, US$8pp camping*) provides three cottages containing two double rooms apiece, as well as a campsite in a forest clearing and is good value. Remember though, that you will have to pay the UWA entrance fee as well. Simple meals should be available but it is better to bring your own food for preparation. Plenty of monkeys and birds can be seen in the camp.

NDALI-KASENDA CRATER LAKES

The part of western Uganda overshadowed by the Rwenzori is pockmarked with one of the world's densest concentrations of volcanic crater lakes. According to local legend, these lakes were created by Ndahura, the first Bacwezi king, when he retired to the area after abdicating in favour of his son Wamala. Less romantically, the craters are vivid relics of the immense volcanic and geological forces that have moulded the western Ugandan landscape, from the Albertine Rift to the Rwenzori and Virunga mountains. The lakes are conventionally divided into four main groups: the **Fort Portal Cluster** immediately northwest of the eponymous town, the **Kasenda Cluster** to the west of Kibale National Park, **Katwe Cluster** in part of the Rift Valley protected within Queen Elizabeth National Park (QENP), and the **Bunyaruguru Cluster** straddling the Rift Valley Escarpment southeast of QENP.

The most accessible and extensive of these crater lake fields is the Ndali or Kasenda Cluster, which formed about 10,000 years ago and consists of about 60 permanent and seasonal freshwater lakes centred on Kasenda, Rweetera, Rwaihamba and Kabata trading centres, some 20–30km south of Fort Portal. The Kasenda Lakes are all different in character and most are very beautiful, while the lush surrounding countryside, rattling with birds, monkeys and butterflies, provides limitless opportunities for casual exploration below the majestic backdrop of the glacial peaks of the Rwenzori. Despite this, the Kasenda area has only recently started to catch on with travellers, in large part as a result of the erection of a few excellent community campsites as well as the delightful Ndali Lodge. For any visitor looking to spend a few inexpensive days rambling and hiking in beautiful unspoilt surrounds, it is difficult to think of any part of Uganda as suitable as the Kasenda area.

GETTING THERE AND AWAY The Kasenda Crater Lakes are usually approached from Fort Portal, following the road to Kibale National Park for 12km to Kasisi, where there is a major fork in the road. If you're heading to the more easterly lakes, then take the left fork at Kasisi, as you would for Kibale National Park, and you'll reach CVK Resort and Chimpanzee Forest Guesthouse after 8.5km and 11km respectively. Any **minibus-taxi** or **pick-up truck** heading to Kamwenge or Bigodi can drop you at these places.

To reach the main cluster of lakes, fork right at Kasisi for Kasenda trading centre, passing Lake Nkuruba, Rwaihamba and Kabata/Ndali Lodge after 8km, 10km and 13km respectively. At least three *matatus* or pick-up trucks to Rwaihamba and Kasenda leave Fort Portal daily, from the same stand as transport to Kibale Forest Market. More transport runs on Rwaihamba market days (Mondays and Thursdays). Vehicles heading to Rwaihamba can drop you at Lake Nkuruba Nature Reserve, but stop 2km short of Kabata. **Boda-bodas** are available at Rwaihamba.

Using **private transport**, the crater lakes can also be approached from Rwimi trading centre on the main Kasese–Fort Portal road, following a dirt road branching east through Rwakenzi and Murukomba to arrive in Kabata after 16km. During the rainy season, this road may require a 4x4 vehicle.

If you're driving in a **4x4** from Ndali Lodge or Lake Nkuruba to Kibale Forest for the morning chimp tracking excursion, you can either go back through Kasisi or use one of two short cuts between the Kasenda and Kamwenge roads: an 8.5km dirt and *murram* track between Rwaihamba and CVK via Isunga, or a 5km dirt track between Lake Nkuruba and Rweetera. Both short cuts may be impassable after rain, so seek local advice.

TOUR OPERATORS **Kabarole Tours** (see page 336) run a day tour on request taking in at least four crater lakes and Mahoma Falls.

WHERE TO STAY For location of listings see maps on pages 358 and 361.

Upmarket

Ndali Lodge (8 cottages) m 0772 221309/487673; e ndalilodge@yahoo.com; www.ndalilodge.com. Situated about 1km from Kabata trading centre by road, the family-run Ndali Lodge is one of Uganda's most highly regarded lodges. It was built by the son, & is managed by the grandson, of Major Price, a British tea planter who established the Ndali Estate in the 1950s. It's a matter of opinion which outlook is finer from the fabulous site on the rim of Nyinambuga Crater; the view over the eponymous lake from the b/fast veranda or the westerly panorama from the rooms, lawn & swimming pool across rolling hills & crater lakes towards the Rwenzori & the Rift Valley plains. The spacious s/c thatch cottages offer piping-hot baths, solar bedside lights & private verandas. Colourful flowering gardens; an airy lounge decorated with etchings of flora & fauna; an excellent library (Blixen through to Wodehouse); silver cutlery & chipped teapots; & superb candlelit 5-course dinners & filling

b/fasts all contribute to create an English country-house ambience. Kibale Forest is the main draw, but guests should be sure to explore the local lakes & trot down the hill to visit the Ndali Estate farm which supplies organic Ndali Vanilla to Waitrose & Tesco supermarkets in the UK. *US$390/500 sgl/dbl cottages FB, discounts for East African residents, US$14 from room fees is used to sponsor local schoolkids.*

Moderate

Chimpanzee Forest Guesthouse (2 rooms, 4 cottages) m 0772 486415. This lovely guesthouse lies on a hillside close to the Kamwenge Rd near the Kibale National Park HQ. Set in a beautiful garden, it's essentially a low-budget, Ugandan equivalent of Ndali Lodge, insomuch as it's a homely facility owned & run by the grandchildren of a British tea planter. When Mr Switzer built the main house for himself & his Mutoro wife, he included a bright & airy lounge to enjoy the gorgeous view across rolling tea gardens

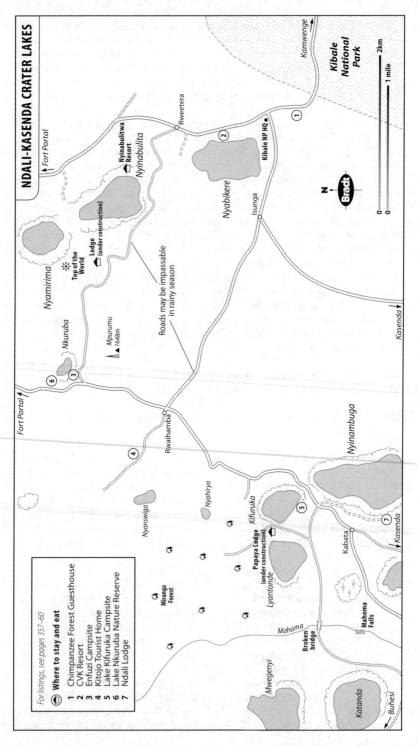

NDALI-KASENDA CRATER LAKES

Fort Portal ↑

Nyamirima

Nkuruba

⑥ ③

Fort Portal ↑

△ Mpurumu
1648m

Nyinabulitwa Resort
Nyinabulita

☀ Top of the World
Lodge (under construction)

Roads may be impassable
in rainy season

④

Rwaihamba ◉

Nyanswiga

Miranga Forest

Mwegenyi

Katanda

Buhesi

Mahoma

Broken bridge

Mahoma Falls

Lyantonde

Papaya Lodge (under construction)

Kifuruka

Nyahirya

⑤

Kabata

Nyinambuga

Kasenda ↓

⑦

Rweetera ◉

②

Nyabikere

Isunga ◉

Kibale NP HQ ●

①

Kamwenge ↓

Kibale National Park

Kasenda ↓

N

Bradt

0 ___ 1 mile
0 ___ 2km

For listings, see pages 357–60

◉ **Where to stay and eat**
1 Chimpanzee Forest Guesthouse
2 CVK Resort
3 Enfuzi Campsite
4 Kitojo Tourist Home
5 Lake Kifuruka Campsite
6 Lake Nkuruba Nature Reserve
7 Ndali Lodge

towards Kibale Forest. The view is now shared by 4 attractive thatched s/c cottages in the garden, clearly influenced by those at Ndali, & a new, open-sided lodge building. Cottages are far better value than the rooms. A range of guided walks is offered. *US$60/90 sgl/dbl cottages & US$50/70 sgl/dbl with shared bathroom B&B, US$8 camping.*

🏠 **Kitojo Tourist Home** m 0772 469333; e info@kitojotouristhome.com; www.kitojotouristhome.com. Attractively situated on a small hill 2km from Rwaihamba, this homely development enjoys good regional views. Profits support the Kitojo Integrated Development Association, a local NGO that provides medical, financial & agricultural services to HIV/AIDS-infected community members. S/c cottage accommodation available but no alcohol. *US$30pp B&B, US$40pp FB.*

Budget

🏠 **CVK Resort** m 0772 492274; e pruyoka@yahoo.co.uk; www.traveluganda.co.ug/cvk. The long-standing Crater Valley Kibale Resort – to cite its full name – has an idyllic position on the lushly vegetated rim of Lake Nyabikere. Being located beside the Fort Portal–Kamwenge road it's well placed for chimp tracking in Kibale Forest. The birdlife around the lake is excellent – more than 100 species recorded including African grey parrot, pygmy goose, fish eagle & an array of colourful sunbirds – & red-tailed monkey & black-&-white colobus are resident. Said somewhat improbably to be 400m deep, Nyabikere means 'lake of frogs' & you'll usually hear plenty of these croaking through the night. Accommodation is provided in a line of rather ordinary but affordable s/c rooms & some basic *bandas* (shared bathroom). A variety of basic meals is served. *US$14/28 sgl/dbl B&B, UDS$56 family cottage (sleeps 4), US$10pp non-s/c bandas, US$10 per tent.*

Shoestring

🏠 **Lake Nkuruba Nature Reserve** (9 cottages) m 0773 266067/0782 141880; www.traveluganda.co.ug/lake-nkuruba. Protecting a jungle-fringed crater lake close to the Kasenda Road, 2km before Rwaihamba, this well-maintained community-run reserve & rest camp (proceeds fund a local primary school) is a perfect base from which to explore the crater lakes on a budget – indeed, many travellers end up spending a week or longer enjoying its laid-back atmosphere. There is accommodation in basic bed *bandas* above the crater rim, some s/c, some not. Camping is permitted. A solitary dbl *banda* is set on the edge of Lake Nkuruba. Adrine, the friendly manageress, can rustle up decent meals for Ush10,000–13,000 & self-catering is also permitted (basic foodstuffs can be bought at nearby Rwaihamba on the market days of Mon & Thu). Beers & sodas are sold on site, boiled water is provided to campers, & paraffin lamps can be hired for a nominal fee. Other facilities include mountain-bike hire (*Ush15,000 per day*) & a short hiking trail. Guided walks to Mahoma Falls, 'Top of the World', etc, are also offered. Visitors (as opposed to guests) are charged Ush5,000 (non-resident) & Ush3,000 (resident) to visit the site. If visiting LNNR by public transport, be aware that local drivers may try to drop you at the adjacent Enfuzi Campsite instead. *US$20 s/c twin cottage, US$15 lakeside cottage, US$7pp bandas with shared bathroom, US$4pp camping.*

🏠 **Planet Rwigo Beach Resort** (5 rooms) m 0782 548326/0701 370674; e planetrwigo@yahoo.com. You might as well be in outer space: nobody will find you here! In the southern part of the crater area, beyond Kasenda village, a 1.5km track through lovely forest ends inside a crater containing a small but pretty lake. Perfect to get away from absolutely everything if you're OK with basic accommodation & basic food. *US$16/20 s/c cottage rooms, US$10 sgl room (shared facilities), US$3 camping.*

🅰 **Lake Kifuruka Campsite** (4 rooms) m 0772 562513; e lakelyantonde@yahoo.com. This basic facility overlooks Kifuruka Crater Lake close to the Kabata Road junction. The site is rather bare & exposed since the main lodge burned down in 2010, while the cottages are tucked below the crater rim. It might lack the amenities of the nearby Ndali Lodge but it does enjoy a comparable dual viewpoint & is a few hundred US dollars cheaper. Guided walks to the Mahoma Falls cost Ush15,000pp. *US$8pp cottage rooms with shared bathrooms, US$4pp camping.*

Remember thinking that Dick Dastardly might actually win the Wacky Races if he wasn't constantly stopping to implement some wicked plan? The same applies to **Enfuzi Campsite** (*www.traveluganda.co.ug/enfuzicommunitycampsite*), a basic camp adjacent to Lake Nkuruba Nature Reserve and not dissimilar in setting, standards and price. Enfuzi could enjoy an equally respectable reputation were it not for the owner's entertaining machinations and the astonishing volume of negative feedback they inspire from backpackers and local volunteers.

For camping, see also **CVK Resort**, page 359.

WHAT TO SEE AND DO There are few organised activities in the area, and many people will be quite content to spend their time idling in the blissful surrounds of their lodge or campsite. For those who want to explore, part of the joy of this area is that it's largely up to the individual traveller to take the initiative. Kabarole Tours will be able to fill you in on new developments in the area, and can give advice to walkers and hikers. Serious explorers should obtain a map to guide them. The reverse of the 'Uganda Maps' *Fort Portal and the Rwenzori* sheet (available locally) shows the crater area and a fair selection of routes and viewpoints. The 1:50,000 maps of Kuhenge (map no 66/2) and Fort Portal (map no 56/4) are more conventionally detailed but are available only from the Department of Lands and Surveys in Entebbe.

Around CVK Resort If you're based at CVK Resort, you're rather isolated from the main cluster of lakes. The trail encircling Lake Nyabikere is certainly worthwhile: you should see monkeys as well as a variety of birds – among the more interesting species found around the lake are Ross's and great blue turaco, pygmy goose, little bittern and night heron. You might also visit two more crater lakes, Nyinabulita and Nyamirima, which lie next to each other roughly 2km north of the resort on the west side of the Fort Portal Road.

Hiking between lakes Nyabikere and Nkuruba An attractive and easy walk, wherever you are based, is along the motorable track which crosses between the Kamwenge and Kasenda roads. The track leaves the Kamwenge Road at Rweetera trading centre, roughly 100m north of the derelict tea factory, and it emerges on the Kasenda Road a few hundred metres south of Lake Nkuruba. The walk takes about two hours, and on the way you'll see lakes Nyamirima, Nyinabulita and Nyabikere. There are great views over the lakes from Mpurumu Hill to the south of the track.

Lake Nkuruba and surrounds Lake Nkuruba, though small, is very beautiful, enclosed by a steep forest-lined crater in which red-tailed monkey, red colobus and black-and-white colobus are resident, together with at least 100 species of bird (a regularly updated checklist is pinned up in the office). With a bit of luck, you will also make acquaintance with the solitary hippo that divides its time between Nkuruba and a couple of nearby lakes. The water here is considered free of bilharzia so, unless the itinerant hippo is in close attendance, there's no obstacle to swimming. That said, Ndali Lodge management claim (very honestly I must say) that there is bilharzia in their own lake. If you can catch it here then this rather overturns the accepted means of transmission and usual precautions (ie: leaping into deep water off jetties rather than paddling in muddy shallows).

Based at Lake Nkuruba, you're well positioned to explore the main cluster of lakes, including those at Kabata (see below). Closer to Lake Nkuruba, the tiny Lake Nyahirya on the fringe of the Miranga Forest can be reached by walking south along the road to Kabata, passing through Rwaihamba trading centre after 2km, then about 1km further on there's a sharp westward kink in the road. The lake lies 500m west of this kink – if you're uncertain, ask in Rwaihamba for directions. The

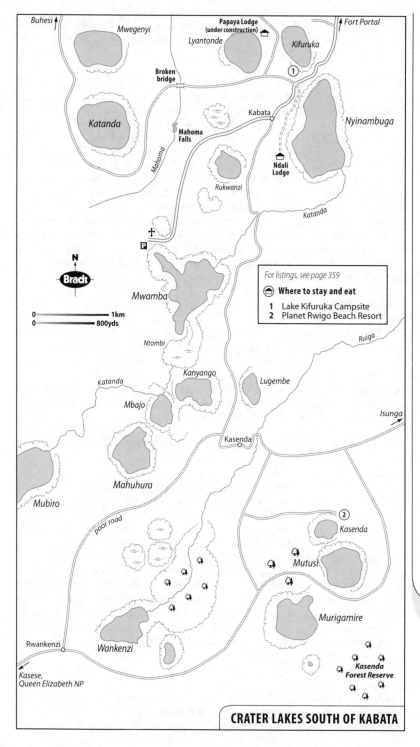

Buhesi

Mwegenyi

Papaya Lodge
(under construction)

Lyantonde

Fort Portal

Kifuruka

①

Broken
bridge

Kabata

Nyinambuga

Katanda

Mahoma
Falls

Mahoma

Ndali
Lodge

Rukwanzi

Katanda

N

Bradt

For listings, see page 359

Where to stay and eat
1   Lake Kifuruka Campsite
2   Planet Rwigo Beach Resort

0 ————————— 1km
0 ————————— 800yds

Mwamba

Ruiga

Ntombi

Kanyango

Lugembe

Katanda

Isunga

Mbajo

Kasenda

Mahuhura

②

Kasenda

Mubiro

Mutusi

poor road

Murigamire

Rwankenzi

Wankenzi

Kasenda
Forest Reserve

Kasese,
Queen Elizabeth NP

CRATER LAKES SOUTH OF KABATA

Miranga Forest could also be worth exploring, and a second crater lake, Nyanswiga, lies 1km directly to the north of Nyahirya. Rwaihamba hosts a large, colourful market on Mondays and Thursdays.

Kabata This small junction village, which lies 5km south of Lake Nkuruba by road, is the site of Ndali Lodge and the Lake Kifuruka Campsite. Coming from Nkuruba, two more crater lakes are first glimpsed about 500m before Kabata. On the left side of the road, Lake Nyinambuga – named for its mildly saline water – is one of the largest lakes in the area, enclosed by steep cliffs on which stands Ndali Lodge. This view, incidentally, appears on the Ush20,000 banknote. To the right of the road is the smaller, forest-fringed Lake Kifuruka. A troop of black-and-white colobus is evidently resident in the area, and often seen from the road, as are Ross's and great blue turaco, African grey parrot, yellow-billed duck and pygmy goose.

Turn right into the Buhesi Road at Kabata and after about 500m you'll see Lake Lyantonde to your right – a fairly small lake surrounded by a thickly vegetated crater, reminiscent in appearance of Lake Nkuruba. The road bridge over the Mahoma River washed away in 2010 so if you're intent on finding two further lakes, Katanda and Mwegenyi, you'll need to walk. Further along the Buhesi road, the Kabata Cave is large enough to hold 20 people.

Mahoma Falls (*Access to the waterfall is controlled by Lake Kifuruka Campsite which will provide you with a guide for Ush15,000pp*) From Kabata, you can also visit the Mahoma Falls, where the Mahoma River surges with more than a little conviction over a series of large boulders into a forested valley. Below the waterfall, you can swim in the river – it flows at a velocity that should negate any fears about bilharzia, and the crisp water is a welcome treat after a sweaty walk. Another point of interest – and you'll need a local guide to find it – is a small but immeasurably deep crater beyond Lake Mwanba. Named Mwitampungu (literally, the place that kills birds) it is said to suck in any bird that flies directly over it.

Towards Kasenda Three further crater lakes can easily be seen from the 6km road running south from Kabata to Murukomba. About 1.5km past the main junction in Kabata, Lake Rukwanzi lies only 100m to the right of the road, but is invisible from it. Another 1.5km further, also on the right, Lake Mwamba is one of the largest lakes in the Kasenda region, with an irregular outline suggesting that it fills two or three different collapsed calderas. Finally, another 1.5km towards Murukomba, the stunning Lake Lugembe lies at the base of a very deep and sheer-sided steep crater, no more than 25m left of the road, but also invisible from it. Directly opposite Lugembe, the larger Lake Kanyango lies within 200m of the road, also hidden by a cliff.

Everybody has their saturation point, even when it comes to crater lakes, but you could also locate a line of five lakes south of Kasenda trading centre, which lies 2km south of Murukomba. You could cover lakes Kasenda, Mutusi and Murigamire in a circular day walk of roughly 6km southeast of Kasenda trading centre. More ambitiously, you could continue west from Lake Murigamire to Lake Wankenzi and an adjoining forested crater, a circular walk of roughly 10–12km starting and ending at Kasenda.

THE SEMLIKI VALLEY

The magnificently scenic Semliki Valley lies at the base of the Albertine Rift to the west of Fort Portal, where it is hemmed in by the Rwenzori foothills to the south, Lake Albert to the north, and the Semliki River along the border with the DRC. The northern Rwenzori foothills divide the Semliki Valley into two geographically discrete and ecologically divergent sectors. Stretching northeast of the mountains through to the marshy southern shores of Lake Albert lies the moist woodland and savanna of the **Semliki Wildlife Reserve**. The northwestern footslopes, by contrast, give way to a tract of steamy lowland jungle protected within the **Semliki National Park**, whose affinities with the contiguous Congolese rainforest are reflected by the presence of dozens of bird species and other creatures found nowhere else in Uganda.

The largest town in the Semliki Valley is **Bundibugyo**, which lies about 85km from Fort Portal along a breathtaking, newly tarmacked road that rounds the northern slopes of the Rwenzori, offering spectacular views of Lake Albert and the Rift Valley plains along the way to Semliki National Park. At Karugutu trading centre, some 30km out of Fort Portal, a signposted right fork runs northeast from the Bundibugyo Road to the Semliki Wildlife Reserve and Ntoroko, a fishing village on the shores of Lake Albert.

In the mid to late 1990s, the Semliki Valley was subjected to regular attacks by the Allied Democratic Front (ADF), a small but brutally sadistic band of DRC-based guerrillas whose precise identity and agenda are both open to conjecture. The Semliki Wildlife Reserve remained operational throughout this period of instability, but the national park – situated closer to the Congolese border – was forced to close between 1997 and 1998. These days, the Semliki Valley is considered

SEMLIKI IN 1898

One of the first Europeans to enter the Semliki Valley was Dr Albert Cook, who visited it on foot in 1898, an experience he would later describe vividly in his memoir *Ugandan Memories*:

The ground descended abruptly at our feet, and we looked out over a vast plain. Beneath us the Semliki River twisted in and out across the plain like a large snake. Beyond to the west was the commencement of Stanley's Great Forest. It looked like a dark green carpet, stretching away until it was lost in the haze … After a short rest, we began to descend from the summit of the pass into the Semliki Valley. Down, down, down for seven thousand feet, we had to leap like goats from rock to rock, and it was with bleeding fingers that we reached the bottom, for there were plenty of thorns.

At the bottom … was a village of the Bwamba, hill tribes who inhabit the western slopes of the Rwenzoris. The village was composed of little beehive shaped huts, each with its own porch. The people were splendid specimens … stalking about with spears in their hands … They file their front teeth to a point, and dress their hair very carefully, frizzing it into long curls like a poodle dog. They wear brass rings on their arms and legs [and] nothing but a wisp of cloth passed between the legs and secured by a girdle.

In the afternoon we went to the celebrated hot springs … Emerging from the long grass we suddenly came on a belt of rich tropical foliage … paved with slabs of rock. From these, great sheets of steam were rising … all along the upper edge were springs of boiling water, bubbling furiously … in front were clouds of steam. In some of the holes, we boiled plantains, in other potatoes, and in a third we stuck our kettle.

safe for travel but it would still be sensible to be aware of the current situation in the Congo before heading in this direction.

FURTHER READING The Semliki Valley area is covered by Sheet 7 in the 'Uganda Maps' series, *Fort Portal & Kibale Forest*.

SEMLIKI WILDLIFE RESERVE (*The standard entrance fees for a Category B protected area apply, see pages 32–3. There is no charge to using the Karugutu–Ntoroko road through the reserves; fees are levied only if you detour off to the Semliki Safari Lodge*) This 543km² sanctuary, Uganda's oldest wildlife reserve, was originally gazetted in 1932 as the Toro Game Reserve, and is still marked as such on many maps. It lies to the northeast of the Bundibugyo Road, extending to Ntoroko on the southern shore of Lake Albert. The dominant vegetation type is open *Acacia Combretum* woodland and grassy savanna, interspersed with patches of borassus palm forest, significant belts of riparian woodland along the main watercourses, as well as some extensive swamps towards Lake Albert. The reserve itself is topographically unremarkable, set at a relatively low altitude of around 600–700m above sea level, but on a clear

THE BAMBUTI OF NTANDI

A community of roughly 40 Bambuti Pygmies live at Bundimasoli about 5km past Sempaya along the Bundibugyo Road. They are more closely affiliated to the Basua Pygmies of the Congolese Basin than to the Batwa of Kigezi and Rwanda. I first encountered them almost 20 years ago, an occasion described in previous editions of this book as follows:

One of the most depressing experiences I've had in Africa. Far from offering an insight into another lifestyle and culture, the Ntandi Pygmies are basically a bunch of shorter-than-average people who spend the day hanging around their banana-leaf huts, smoking dope, drinking and waiting for the next bunch of tourists to arrive. I've yet to meet anyone who left these people without feeling disturbed.

And many visitors who followed in my footsteps weren't merely disturbed, but also hassled, ripped off or stolen from, culminating in an incident in the mid-1990s in which an aid worker from Fort Portal was stabbed in the hand.

What I didn't realise then is that this aggression towards tourists was a manifestation of a deeper resentment against the sort of prejudice discussed in the box on Batwa Pygmies (see pages 258–9). Among their neighbours, the Bambuti are regarded to be dirty ne'er-do-wells, stigmatised by such unacceptable customs as eating snakes and monkeys, growing and smoking marijuana, and the women walking around topless. Until recently, tourist fees supposedly paid to the Ntandi community were regularly confiscated by non-Bambuti guides and the Bambuti, like the Batwa of Kigezi, were forbidden to use their traditional hunting grounds after Semliki National Park was gazetted in 1993.

Today, the Bambuti live outside the forest in a cluster of basic shacks on the edge of Bundimasoli village, ten minutes' walk from the Semliki National Park headquarters. There has been some progress and under the guidance of the self-styled 'king' of the Ugandan Bambuti, Geoffrey Nzito, and a local primary school teacher, several Bambuti have learned enough English to deal directly with tourists rather than through the medium of crooked guides. The Bambuti's relationship

day the setting is truly awesome, with the sheer Rift Valley Escarpment rising sharply from the eastern shore of Lake Albert, the 2,500m-high Congolese Blue Mountains on the western horizon, and the mighty glacial peaks of the Rwenzori visible to the southwest.

In its pre-Amin heyday, the vast geographic scale of Semliki Wildlife Reserve was complemented by some of East Africa's most prolific plains game. More than 10,000 Uganda kob were resident in the reserve, together with large herds of Jackson's hartebeest, Defassa waterbuck, elephant and buffalo. As for predators, the hunter Brian Herne wrote of Semliki: 'The area is famous for the number of massive maned lions that live there. I have never seen so many big lions in other parts of Africa ... Leopard were numerous throughout ... None of the cats in Semliki had to work very hard for their dinner; they could simply lie in the grass and throw out a paw, for some animal or another was always about.' Isolated from similar habitats by various mountain ranges, Semliki was also at one point mooted as the site of a bizarre scheme to introduce tigers to Uganda for commercial hunting purposes. Six pairs of tiger were imported to Entebbe to be released into the reserve, before the scheme was abandoned as potentially detrimental to the indigenous predators.

with the national park has also improved greatly following a concession allowing them limited rights to fish and hunt within its boundaries (the main restriction being against hunting larger mammals such as elephant, buffalo and chimps) and to barter the forest produce with other local communities. According to the king, they are also the only people in Uganda who are legally permitted to grow and smoke marijuana. The latter they do constantly and with great enthusiasm, through bubble pipes, especially – and somewhat incredibly – before they go hunting.

It's not all roses for the Bambuti by any means. Batwa women are regularly impregnated by outsiders, partially due to the belief that sleeping with one cures certain diseases, Batwa men have little hope of finding a partner outside their own community on account of their unacceptable customs. Interbreeding means that the genetic stock of Uganda's most ancient inhabitants is rapidly being diluted – the average height of its teenagers far exceeds that of the adults. Historically, their main sources of income are digging on local farms and entertaining tourists. One is hardly a key to advancement, while opportunities for the other are increasingly rare. Few visitors find their way to Bundimasoli these days, and many who do must feel that the experience veers uncomfortably close to a freak-show exhibit – look at the short people, shake their hand, snap a photograph, and off we go. It would, I think, be more edifying for all parties were the community to be facilitated to offer guided walks into the national park and to show off their consummate knowledge and mastery of the forest setting. As it stands, after haggling a fee, you'll get some semblance of a traditional dance and the opportunity to buy a selection of crafts, mostly dope pipes. It's not the most rewarding of encounters but it's also true that, existing in limbo between their hunter-gathering heritage and an uncertain future in the modern world, they do need the money more than most. Incidentally, I recently heard of a group who, after declining the offer of a performance, found their vehicle's exit blocked by logs. Nor were they allowed to leave after paying the requested fee; the roadblock was only removed after the hapless tourists had sat through a particularly long and more than usually drunken display.

Semliki's wildlife was heavily poached during the civil war, and it only really started to recover from the slaughter following the opening of Semliki Safari Lodge in 1997. As evidence of improved protection, Uganda kob, the population of which plummeted to below 1,000 in the early 1990s, today number several thousand, and are most commonly seen in areas of short grass, along with pairs of common reedbuck. Over 1,000 buffalo, up from about 50 in the early 1990s, are also resident, along with growing numbers of elephant and waterbuck, but they are not seen on an everyday basis and tend to be rather skittish when approached by a vehicle. Primates are well represented, with black-and-white colobus, olive baboon and red-tailed and vervet monkey all regularly observed in gallery forest close to the lodge and along the Wasa and the Mugiri and their tributaries. Leopards are still common and quite often spotted on night drives, while lion – at one point poached to local extinction – are gradually re-colonising the area, though they are more often heard than seen. A community of roughly 70 chimpanzees resident in the Mugiri River Forest is in the process of being habituated by volunteers from the University of Indiana, and guided forest walks offer a roughly 25% chance of chimp sightings as well as the possibility of encountering the localised forest race of elephant.

For the average tourist, Semliki is arguably more attractive for its vast scenery and wild, untrammelled atmosphere than for its game viewing, which doesn't compare to Murchison Falls or Queen Elizabeth national parks. But it is highly alluring to **birdwatchers**, with 462 species recorded. Game drives on the open plains are likely to yield Abyssinian ground hornbill and a variety of raptors, while areas of rank vegetation are good for marsh tchagra and African crake. The Mugiri River Forest is regarded to be the best site in Uganda for the elusive leaflove, and also hosts a variety of other localised forest species. Night drives are good for owls, as well as the improbable pennant-winged and standard-winged nightjars.

Boat trips on Lake Albert, offered by the lodge or by private fishermen at Ntoroko, are particularly worthwhile. For birdwatchers, this is one of the most reliable sites in Uganda for shoebill, as well as a profusion of more common waterbirds and the dazzling red-throated bee-eater, which forms large breeding colonies on sandbanks near Ntoroko between December and March. Less ornithologically minded visitors are usually boated to the base of the unexpectedly impressive Nkusi Falls, which – like a smaller replica of Murchison Falls – explode through a cleft in the Rift Valley Escarpment before tumbling noisily into the lake.

Getting there and away The turn-off to the Semliki Valley Wildlife Reserve is signposted 30km along the surfaced Bundibugyo Road at the small trading centre of Karugutu, at the end of the long, winding descent from Kichwamba. A 40km-long road connects Karugutu to Ntoroko on Lake Albert, running right through the heart of the reserve. Semliki Safari Lodge lies about 25km down this road, about 90 minutes' drive from Fort Portal – take the first right turn (signposted) after crossing the Wasa River bridge.

If you're using public transport, plenty of **trucks** and the occasional **minibus** run directly between Fort Portal and Ntoroko on most days. Alternatively, any vehicle heading to Bundibugyo can drop you at Karugutu, from where it's usually easy enough to catch a lift on one of the pick-up trucks that transport fish from Ntoroko. There's a good chance you'll see some game from the road. Once at Ntoroko, there is accommodation and camping, you can walk freely in the immediate vicinity of the village, and a boat trip on the lake – where you should encounter hippos and shoebills – will probably work out at around US$20 with local fishermen. Note that overloaded **passenger boats** do travel erratically along the lakeshore from Ntoroko all the way north to Butiaba and Wanseko, but accidents are commonplace and often result in passengers drowning.

WHERE TO STAY For location of listings see map, page 338.

Upmarket

Semliki Safari Lodge (8 tents) 0414 251182/0312 261658; m 0772 489497; e info@ wildplacesafrica.com; www.wildplacesafrica.com. Built in 1996 on the site of an older, eponymous hunting lodge that was gutted in the early 1980s, Semliki Safari Lodge is Uganda's oldest upmarket tented camp &, despite growing competition, still rates as one of the best. Accommodation is provided by large, comfortable s/c thatched tents, while the main lodge is built of stone, log & thatch & decorated in a manner that emphasises its earthy, organic, open-air feel. Facilities include a large swimming pool area overlooking a stretch of riverine forest inhabited by black-&-white colobus & vervet monkeys. Guided activities include game drives, night drives, birdwatching walks in the adjacent forest (included in the price), chimp tracking in a patch of forest 6km away, boat trips on Lake Albert & day trips to the forested Semliki National Park (charged extra). *US$360/660 sgl/dbl FB inc drinks, discounts for East African residents.*

Shoestring and camping There are several scruffy shoestring lodges in **Ntoroko** catering for local travellers heading to/from Kasenyi port across the lake in the Congo. Far more attractive is the **UWA campsite** and *bandas*, which overlook the lake about 500m from the village. UWA has recently allocated a concession to Asyanut Safaris (*www.asyanutours-safaris.com*) to upgrade and manage the site.

SEMLIKI NATIONAL PARK (*The standard entrance fee for a Category B protected area applies; see pages 32–3. No park entrance fee is charged for driving or walking along the main road to Bundibugyo, which forms the southern boundary of the park*) The 220km² Semliki National Park was gazetted in October 1993, prior to which it was more widely known as the Bwamba Forest, a name you'll come across regularly in old ornithological literature about Uganda. Situated within the Albertine Rift at an average altitude of around 700m, the national park is bounded to the northwest by the Semliki River, which runs along the Congolese border into Lake Albert, and to the east by the Fort Portal–Bundibugyo road. It protects a practically unspoilt tropical lowland forest, essentially an easterly extension of the vast Ituri Forest that stretches all the way from Uganda to the Congo River. Separated only by the Semliki River, the two forests form an ecological continuum, for which reason Semliki National Park harbours an exciting range of lowland forest species associated with the Congo Basin. At least 300 species of butterfly have been identified in the park, including 46 species of forest swallowtail (75% of the national total), together with 235 moth species.

Considering its small size, Semliki National Park protects an extraordinary faunal diversity. It is of particular interest to **birdwatchers**: 435 bird species have been recorded, including a high proportion of forest birds and roughly 45 species that occur nowhere else in Uganda (see box, page 368). For amateur ornithologists, Semliki is not only certain to throw up a clutch of 'lifers' – it also offers a faint but real possibility of a brand-new East African record. Three of the seven 'recent records' depicted in Stevenson and Fanshawe's 2002 East African field guide were discovered in Semliki during the 1990s, namely Congo serpent-eagle, grey-throated rail and black-throated coucal.

Only 53 mammal species have been recorded in Semliki, though the patchy look of the existing checklist (it includes no nocturnal primates or small carnivores, and just one species of duiker) suggests that it is far from complete. Of the listed species, 11 occur nowhere else in Uganda, including the pygmy antelope, two types of flying squirrel and six types of bat. Semliki is the only East African stronghold of the peculiar water chevrotain, a superficially duiker-like relic of an ancient ungulate family that shares several structural features with pigs and is regarded to be ancestral to all modern-day antelopes, deers, cows and giraffes. Persistent rumours that Semliki harbours an isolated population of eastern lowland gorilla probably have no factual foundation, but the national park does support a healthy chimpanzee population, not as yet habituated to humans, as well as seven other diurnal primates: red-tailed, vervet, blue and De Brazza's monkeys, grey-cheeked mangabey, olive baboon and black-and-white colobus. Other large mammals recorded in the park include elephant, bushpig, buffalo, sitatunga and white-bellied duiker. Hippos and crocodiles are common along the Semliki River.

The most popular attraction in Semliki National Park is the cluster of **hot springs** at Sempaya, which can be reached via a short walking trail. Longer guided walks, taking the best part of a day, can also be arranged at Sempaya, as can overnight hikes deep into the forest. Unless you are a keen bird- or primate-watcher, the main attraction of this national park is a visit to the hot springs, so, as it doesn't take more than a couple of hours to visit both sets of springs (see below) the park entrance fee might be considered rather steep – especially as you'll have to pay another US$15 each for a guide to escort you. To get your money's worth you'd need to be prepared to walk some of the additional trails.

Getting there and away Access to the park office, campsite and hot springs at Sempaya has been transformed by the surfacing of the slow, rocky road from Fort Portal which has reduced the 60km drive to about an hour. Sempaya is located where the forest meets the main road on the right-hand side; watch carefully for the signposts (designed for 20km/h speeds on the old dirt road) or you'll whizz right past. (For more details of driving there, or getting there by public transport, see page 371.) The area is simple enough to reach with your own vehicle, though be prepared for poor conditions on the old road. Otherwise, form a group and organise a *matatu* through Kabarole Tours (see page 336).

🏠 **Where to stay**   Aside from the basic *bandas* and campsite listed below, there is no accommodation within the national park. It can realistically be visited as a day trip from Fort Portal or Semliki Safari Lodge in the Semliki Wildlife Reserve – allow about 90 minutes each way for the drive, longer after heavy rain – but this is likely to prove frustrating to serious birdwatchers, as they'll miss out on the peak avian activity of the early morning and late afternoon. Reasonable self-contained rooms are available in Bundibugyo, only 20km past Sempaya (see page 371).

🏠 **National Park** *Bandas* **& Campsite** [map page 338] A self-catering campsite with *bandas* is located alongside the main Bundibugyo Road about halfway between Sempaya & Ntandi. Water & a kitchen building are provided & staff will cook for you but you should take your own provisions. Do also take insect repellent to discourage the annoying midges around the hours of sunrise & sunset. Long-sleeved shirts buttoned at the cuff & long trousers tucked into socks are also advisable. UWA plans to lease the site to a private operator, so check availability of the cottages before travelling. *US$9pp twin rooms, US$8pp camping.*

What to see and do

Scenic drive   Whether or not you enter Semliki National Park, it's worth making a day trip to Semliki for the scenery alone, especially now that the new and old sections of road combine to form a scenic loop around the northern end of the Rwenzori. If the weather looks clear, turn off the new tarmac highway about 10km beyond Karagutu (signposted to Itojo) and follow the old road up to the rocky Buranga Pass. The long, tightly winding descent to Sempaya enjoys fantastic views across the Rift Valley towards Congo. You can then use the tarmac to return to Fort Portal. This follows the edge of the rift valley floor as it loops around the northern tip of the mountain back towards Karagutu.

The downside is that unless you enter the national park, there is no clear-cut destination when you reach Sempaya. You could continue up to Bundibugyo; it's not much of a destination either but it's a pretty drive and you should at least find cold drinks at the **Vanilla Inn**.

Sempaya Hot Springs and eastern boundary (*The guided walks listed below cost US$15pp*) A short guided trail leads from the roadside tourist office to the Sempaya Hot Springs. Ringed by forest and palm trees, and veiled in a cloud of steam, these springs are a primeval, evocative sight and well worth the diversion. The largest spring is a geyser which spouts up to 2m high from an opening in a low salt sculpture. Take care: the emerging water has a temperature of more than 100°C and the surrounding pools are hot! The trail to the springs leads through a patch of forest where red-tailed monkey, grey-cheeked mangabey and black-and-white colobus are common. Among the more interesting birds regularly seen along this trail are eight forest hornbills, blue-breasted kingfisher, red-rumped and yellow-throated tinkerbird, Frasier's ant-thrush and honeyguide greenbul. Another spring, more of a broad steaming pool than a geyser, lies on the far side of the swampy clearing reached by a boardwalk. Rather than retracing your steps to Sempaya, you might ask whether the UWA has finally reopened an old trail that creates an attractive loop, passing through forest and a lovely tract of swamp/grassland.

A more ambitious option is the walk along the eastern margin of the park along the **Red Monkey Trail** to the Semliki River, which takes at least three hours in either direction and offers exposure to a far greater variety of localised birds than the trail to the springs. The trail can be undertaken as a day trip, or, if you carry your own tent and food, as an overnight trip camping on the bank of the river. In addition to birds, you can expect to see a variety of monkeys, hippos and crocodiles on the river, and possibly even buffalo and elephant. The guides at Semliki are exceptionally knowledgeable and enthusiastic about birds – some can even call up responsive species such as ant-thrushes and robin.

Much of the 5km stretch of road between Sempaya and Ntandi is fringed by forest and, because it lies outside the national park, you can walk there for free, without a guide (though you'll miss out on quite a bit without the local expertise). As is so often the case, you've a better chance of seeing a good variety of birds from the road than you have in the depths of the forest, and also of getting clear views of the monkeys. The patch of fig and palm forest about halfway between Sempaya and Ntandi is worth scanning carefully for the likes of swamp greenbul and various forest hornbills. Unfortunately the tract of forest near Sempaya containing the lovely Mungiro Falls has been trashed by cultivators and the waterfall now lies behind a tangle of secondary vegetation.

Kirumia River Trail (*US$100pp. Though this includes a knowledgable bird guide & park entrance, only birding enthusiasts are likely to be tempted*) Highly recommended to dedicated birdwatchers is the 15km trail that runs north from the village of Kirimia on the main Bundibugyo Road to the banks of the Semliki River, crossing the Kirimia River twice, as well as passing a succession of forest-fringed oxbow lakes. This hike offers visitors the best opportunity to see a good selection of Semliki 'specials', but realistically it can only be undertaken as a two- to four-night self-sufficient camping expedition. Among the 20–30 bird species associated with the oxbow lakes and their environs, but unlikely to be seen in the vicinity of the main road or elsewhere in Uganda, are spot-breasted ibis, Nkulengu rail, black-throated coucal, yellow-throated cuckoo, lyre-tailed honeyguide, grey ground thrush, blue-billed malimbe, Maxwell's black weaver and Grant's bluebill, while Hartlaub's duck and white-throated blue swallow are resident on the Semliki River.

The first 4km of this hike, as far as the first crossing of the Kirumia River, can be undertaken as a guided day hike from the main road. This section of the trail passes through secondary forest in which African piculet, red-sided broadbill and lemon-bellied crombec are resident, while the riverine forest harbours the likes of long-tailed hawk and black-faced rufous warbler.

The exceptionally detailed site description of Semliki National Park contained in Jonathon Rossouw and Marco Sacchi's *Where to Watch Birds in Uganda* will prove invaluable to any birdwatcher wanting to maximise the possibility of locating rare species confined to particular stretches of the trail.

BUNDIBUGYO This pretty, rather remote little town lies at the northwestern base of the Rwenzori Mountains, about 15km past Ntandi in the Semliki National Park. The town itself is nothing special – few Ugandan towns have changed so little over the course of 20 years – but it does offer wonderful views across to the mountains and the forested floor of the Albertine Rift Valley, and there is plenty of walking potential in the immediate vicinity. The **Rwenzori mini-hike** offered by Kabarole Tours terminates in Bundibugyo (see page 347), and the town is a relatively comfortable base for motorised travellers to make excursions to the Semliki National Park.

Getting there and away Bundibugyo probably lies little more than 20km west of Fort Portal as the crow flies, but the daunting obstacle provided by the Rwenzori means that the driving distance is in fact 85km. The interminable drive of over three hours has been halved by the construction of a new surfaced highway that runs mountain-wards from Fort Portal's central roundabout. Surfaced as far as Sempaya Hot Springs in January 2013, the tarmac should reach Bundibugo by the end of the same year. Public transport between Bundibugyo and Fort Portal, previously limited to a few overloaded **pick-up trucks**, has also improved. A daily Kalita **bus** (*Ush12,000*) leaves Fort Portal at 14.00 and returns from Bundibugyo at 09.00, and a few *matatus* also ply the route.

WHERE TO STAY For location of listings see map, page 338.

Vanilla Inn m 0772 669941. The town's top hotel provides tiled s/c rooms & has a pleasant central courtyard garden at the rear. A 1st-floor balcony at the front of the hotel enjoys mountain views. *US15/28 sgl/dbl.*

Rainbow Inn (15 rooms) m 0772 331593. The rooms are adequate & cheaper than the Vanilla but the courtyard is bare concrete. *US$8 sgl shared bathroom. US$14/16/16 sgl/dbl/twn s/c.*

Elsewhere, you'll save a bit more money at the long-serving **Picfare Guesthouse**, while reader, Guy Dehn, recommends the church-run **Tour Gardens** at the far end of town off the Nyahuka Road.

Where to eat The hotels listed above can provide simple evening meals. Finding lunch at lunchtime in Bundibugyo can be a challenge though, but the **Vanilla Inn** around 15.00 seems a good bet. Unless you're happy with basic local food and local meal timings, bring a picnic from Fort Portal.

What to see and do A few low-key destinations lie beyond Bundibugyo in the vicinity of Nyahuka, a little-visited trading centre with marvellous views of the Rwenzori peaks. Two beautiful Rwenzori waterfalls, **Nyahuka Falls** and **Ngite Falls** can be visited while the town's Saturday **market** is well worth a look. The ongoing roadworks in the Semliki Valley will pass through Nyahuka *en route* to the Congo border crossing over the Lamia River, and when completed Nyahuka will be no more than 20 minutes' drive from Bundibugyo. Once there, it would be a shame not to enjoy the pretty, 10km drive to the border where a large concrete bridge over the River Lamia connects the superb tarmac highway to a Congolese goat track on the opposite bank.

KATONGA WILDLIFE RESERVE

(*Entrance is subject to the prevailing UWA rates for a Class B protected area; see pages 32–3*) This little-known wildlife reserve, the closest to Kampala as the crow flies, protects 207km² of mixed savanna, papyrus swamp and rainforest along the northern edge of the Katonga river valley. The wildlife reserve was gazetted in 1964, at which time it supported large herds of zebra (now locally extinct), elephant and buffalo, as well as serving as a corridor for game migration between western Uganda, Tanzania and the Sudan. Poaching and cattle encroachment took a heavy toll on the reserve's environment and wildlife in the 1970s and 1980s, but improved protection in recent years has ensured that populations are now on the increase. The current mammal checklist stands at 40 species, including black-and-white colobus, olive baboon, Uganda kob and small numbers of elephant and buffalo. Waterbuck, reedbuck and bushbuck are common and sufficiently habituated to approach on foot. Katonga is one of perhaps three places in East Africa where the secretive sitatunga antelope is likely to be seen by a casual visitor. Katonga is also of great interest for its varied birdlife – over 338 species have been recorded. Among the more interesting species likely to be seen are green- and blue-headed coucal, Ross's and great blue turaco, crested malimbe and papyrus gonolek. The view from the campsite is of some interest and there's a certain satisfaction knowing that you're looking across one of Africa's oldest river valleys – a feature that pre-dates the Rift Valley, Lake Victoria and the Nile by many millions of years and which once flowed all the way from western Kenya to the Atlantic.

Katonga is the site of a low-key but worthwhile **ecotourism site.** The main attraction was a canoe trip through the wetland but hippos have colonised the channel used so the activity has been discontinued for safety reasons. Three guided half-day **walking trails** are available for US$10 per person. The **Sitatunga Trail** runs through a mixture of grassland and wetland habitats, offering a better than even chance of spotting the elusive antelope for which it is named. The **Kisharara Trail** passes through all the main habitats protected within the park – grassland, savanna and swamp fringes – and is also good for sitatunga, as well as monkeys and birds. The **Kyeibale Trail** loops away from the water into an area of drier scrub dotted with tall rock formations as well as forested valleys and caves. For details of further developments, ask at the UWA headquarters in Kampala (see page 168). The guides here are extremely knowledgeable about the local fauna and flora.

GETTING THERE AND AWAY The most direct route to Katonga is via Kyegegwa on the Fort Portal–Kampala road, 50km west of Mubende. At Kyegegwa, a signposted road heads south through Mparo and Kalwreni, passing the reserve's entrance gate after 40km. It's easy enough to find **public transport** to Kyegegwa and on to Katonga, possibly changing vehicles at Mparo. Kalwreni lies 7km from the entrance gate, and if you can't find transport heading along this stretch it is possible to **walk** or to hire a **boda-boda.**

It is also possible to approach Katonga from Kibale National Park via Kamwenge, Ibanda and Kabagole. Plenty of public transport services are available for all legs of this route.

 WHERE TO STAY A small campsite, **Katonga Visitors' Centre** 1km from the reserve's entrance gate has a pleasant setting overlooking the valley with a covered dining area and ablutions. You may prefer, however, to utilise the shelter at an education building 100m further uphill. Water and firewood are provided at the campsite, but you should bring everything else you require with you and camping costs US$8 per person. Contact UWA for further details and updates.

A small **guesthouse** seems to be under construction opposite the entrance to the reserve. As a last resort, you'll find the **Katonga View Tourist Lodge** in Kabagole village, on the southern edge of the valley, about 1km from the reserve entrance gate. It's very basic but affordable at Ush10,000.

10

Murchison Falls
and Lake Albert

Flanking the Victoria Nile some 300km northwest of Kampala, **Murchison Falls National Park** is the largest protected area in Uganda, and one of the most exciting. The waterfall for which the park is named is the most electrifying sight of its type in East Africa, while daily launch trips from Paraa offer the opportunity to see a profusion of hippos, crocodiles and waterbirds, including the elusive and bizarre shoebill. Wildlife throughout the conservation area is recovering from the heavy poaching of the 1980s, and a wide variety of mammals – including elephant and lion – are now routinely sighted along the road circuits north of the Nile. This recovery was in part facilitated by the displacement of local communities during the LRA war but poaching incidents are rising once more as returning villagers pick up where they left off 20 years ago. Poaching is particularly rife along the shores of the Albert Nile, which lies outside the park so poachers can legally sit just offshore in fishing canoes and later land undetected to set their odious snares. The Uganda Conservation Foundation (*www.ugandacf.org*) is currently building a marine ranger post here to help the under-resourced UWA to tackle the problem. A further concern is the long-term consequences of an ongoing oil exploration programme within Murchison's prime tourism and wildlife area (see box, pages 396–7).

The other major established attraction in the Murchison region is the **Budongo Forest**, effectively a southern extension of the national park, protected within the Budongo and Kanyiyo Pabidi forest reserves. The Budongo Forest harbours one of the most varied forest faunas in East Africa, and is a premier site for birdwatchers, as well as one of the best – and most affordable – places to track chimpanzees in this part of Africa. The primary site, which offers camping, cottage accommodation, chimp tracking and other forest walks, is found at Kanyiyo Pabidi in the northern section of Budongo along the more direct route between Masindi and Murchison Falls.

The largest town in this part of Uganda is **Masindi**, about three hours in a private vehicle from Kampala along a surfaced road, or a day's drive from Fort Portal along a wild 250km dirt road via Hoima. From Masindi, two different routes run to Murchison Falls. The shorter (85km) route heads directly north from Masindi to Paraa, cutting through the northern part of the Budongo Forest Reserve. The longer (135km) and more scenic route runs west from Masindi through western Budongo, descending the Butiaba Escarpment and running north along the Lake Albert littoral to enter the national park where it connects with the direct route, a few kilometres south of Paraa.

Although Masindi has historically been the gateway to Murchison Falls National Park, there are now alternative options. Firstly, the stable situation in northern Uganda means that Murchison is easily accessible from towns north of the Nile, notably Gulu (see pages 439–45). Secondly, though the Masindi Road is the most

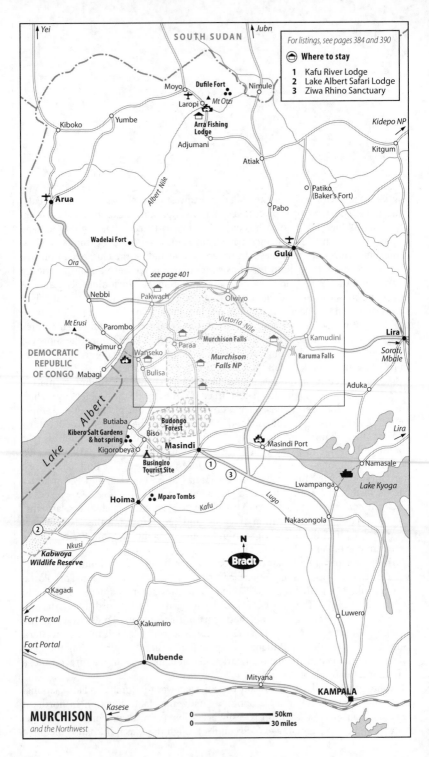

For listings, see pages 384 and 390

Where to stay

1 Kafu River Lodge
2 Lake Albert Safari Lodge
3 Ziwa Rhino Sanctuary

↑ *Yei*   SOUTH SUDAN   *Jubn* ↑

Moyo   **Dufile Fort**   Nimule

Kiboko   Yumbe   Laropi   *Mt Otzi*

Arra Fishing Lodge

Adjumani   Atiak   *Kidepo NP* ↗   Kitgum

✚ **Arua**   Patiko
                                        (Baker's Fort)

                    Pabo

Wadelai Fort •   ✈ **Gulu**

Ora   Nebbi   *see page 401*

          Pakwach   Olwiyo   **Lira**

Mt Erusi ▲   Parombo   *Victoria Nile*   *Soroti,*
                                                                Mbale

DEMOCRATIC   Panyimur   Wanseko   Paraa   **Murchison Falls**   Kamudini
REPUBLIC
OF CONGO   Mabagi   Bulisa   *Murchison*   **Karuma Falls**
                                            Falls NP
                                                            Aduka

                              Butiaba   **Budongo**   *Lira* ↗
Kibero Salt Gardens   **Forest**
& hot spring   Biso
          Kigorobeya   **Masindi**   Masindi Port

                    Busingiro   *Lake Kyoga*
                    Tourist Site   ①
                                        ③   Namasale

          Hoima   •• **Mparo Tombs**   Lwampanga

Lake   *Kafu*   *Lugo*   Nakasongola
Albert

②   Nkusi

Kabwoya
Wildlife Reserve

          Kagadi   **N**

Fort Portal ↙   Kakumiro   **Bradt**   Luwero

Fort Portal ↙

                    Mubende

                              Mityana   **KAMPALA**

MURCHISON   *Kasese*   0 ——— 50km
and the Northwest   0 ——— 30 miles

direct from Kampala, a prettier approach uses the newly tarmaced Kampala–Hoima road and a back route via Biso and Bulisa, which offers Rift Valley views and detours to Lake Albert at Kibero and Butiaba.

Other attractions have opened in the area in recent years. The more contrived and better publicised is the **Ziwa Rhino Sanctuary** on the Kampala–Masindi road. This protects reintroduced rhino and provides an interesting diversion along the otherwise unremarkable journey north towards Murchison Falls. Meanwhile, Uganda's newest conservation area, the little-known **Kabwoya Wildlife Reserve** makes for an interesting overnight detour off the long, 350km drive between Fort Portal and Murchison Falls. Situated on the shores of Lake Albert west of Hoima, Kabwoya was created in 2002 from the remnants of a denuded Controlled Hunting Area, and is enjoying a new lease of life under the committed conservation management of a private concessionaire. In order to exercise as well as amuse you, we present another, rather more obscure attraction beside Lake Albert. Though listed in this guide for the first time in 2009, the **Kibero Salt Gardens** are a far from recent development. Emin Pasha was the first foreign tourist to visit them in 1885, by which time local people had been producing 97.6% pure salt for at least 600 years. Kibero will appeal to travellers who are sound of limb and relish opportunities to descend steeply on foot off the beaten track.

HOIMA

The rather out-of-the-way town of Hoima sees little traveller traffic and is of interest primarily as a staging post between Fort Portal and Masindi. The pretty, almost park-like surrounds notwithstanding, the compact town centre feels unusually rundown and neglected, as if it has been bypassed by the restoration and development that has characterised Uganda over the past decade.

Historically, there was little reason for most visitors to Uganda to travel through or even dally in Hoima, but this has changed. Firstly, the town lies on the route to Kabwoya Wildlife Reserve (see page 383). Secondly, the surfacing of the Hoima–Kampala road means that Hoima now lies on a viable route to Masindi and Murchison Falls National Park (see page 396). Thirdly, the Kon Tiki hotel on the edge of town offers a pleasant overnight on the long and bumpy drive between Murchison Falls and Kibale Forest – this option is now used by a number of tour companies.

Eventual destinations apart, Hoima is a pleasant enough place and the local historical sites arguably add up to a good reason to hang around for a day. Mparo, 4km from the town centre, was the 19th-century capital of Omukama Kabalega; and the reigning *omukama*, Solomon Iguru Gafabusa, has his main residence in Hoima Town.

GETTING THERE AND AWAY Hoima stands at a minor route junction. It is the only major town between Fort Portal and Masindi, while additional roads run southeast to Kampala and west to Lake Albert. The Kampala road is sealed for its entire length and the 210km journey takes little more than 2½ hours. All other approach roads to Hoima are unsurfaced and prone to deteriorate after heavy rain. **Buses** run throughout the day between Hoima and Kampala's Qualicell bus terminal. This costs Ush13,000, as does the daily Post Bus. All other routes out of Hoima are served by *matatus*. These run south to Fort Portal (*Ush25,000*), north to Masindi (*Ush10,000*) and northwest to Wanseko (*Ush15,000*). The last option bypasses Masindi and takes you to the northern tip of Lake Albert, close to Murchison Falls National Park. It

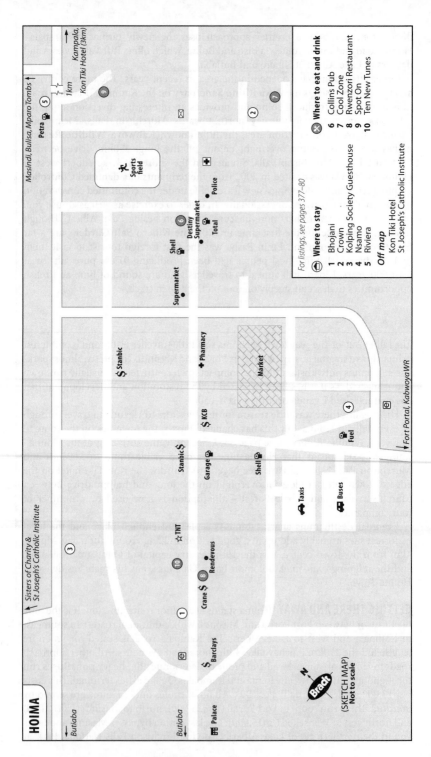

HOIMA

For listings, see pages 377–80

Masindi, Bulisa, Mparo Tombs

Sisters of Charity &
St Joseph's Catholic Institute

Butiaba

Butiaba

Kampala,
Kon Tiki Hotel (3km)

Petra

1km

Sports
field

Police

Destiny
Supermarket
Total

Shell

Supermarket

Stanbic

Pharmacy

Market

KCB

Stanbic

Garage

Shell

Fuel

Fort Portal, Kabwoya WR

TNT

Rendevous

Crane

Taxis

Buses

Barclays

Palace

N
Bradt
(SKETCH MAP)
Not to scale

seems that buses no longer connect Hoima or Masindi to Fort Portal. Other than travelling by bus via Kampala (and this would be the more comfortable and not necessarily slower choice) the only alternative appears to be a long and bumpy day cramped inside a *matatu*.

WHERE TO STAY For location of listings see map opposite.

Moderate

Kon Tiki (25 rooms) 3km down Kampala Rd; m 0772 775005/0773 304752; e info@ hoimakontiki.com; www.hoimakontiki.com. This lovely hotel is located on the edge of town & some 1,000km inland from Thor Heyerdahl's nearest possible landfall. The Kon Tiki is a perfectly good reason (& I can't think of any others) to stay overnight in Hoima instead of pushing on to Masindi or Paraa. It's also a welcome break on the long drive between Murchison Falls & Kibale Forest. Spacious thatched cottages, a stone &

thatch bar/restaurant of considerable charm & a swimming pool are set in the fast-maturing landscaped grounds. Tasty continental/Italian (including pizzas) & Indian & Chinese dishes are offered for Ush15,000–20,000. Excellent value. *US$40/48/56 sg/dbl/twin B&B.*

Budget

Kolping Society Guesthouse Butiaba Rd; m 0772 516421; e hoikolping@yahoo.com. At the rear of the town centre, this clean, Church-run guesthouse lies in pleasant grounds. Acceptable

---

TWINS

Traditionally, within what is today Uganda, the birth of twins was seen as an event of great significance, though some cultures regarded it as a great blessing while others perceived it be an omen of ill. Speke, while stuck in Bunyoro in 1862, compared some of the customs he had come across on his travels:

A Munyoro woman, who bore twins that died, now keeps two small pots in her house, as effigies of the children, into which she milks herself every evening, and will continue to do so for five months, fulfilling the time appointed by nature for suckling children, lest the spirits of the dead should persecute her. The twins were not buried, as ordinary people are buried, under ground, but placed in an earthenware pot, such as the Banyoro use for holding pombe [beer]. They were taken to the jungle and placed by a tree, with the pot turned mouth downwards. Manua, one of my men, who is a twin, said, in Nguru, one of the sister provinces to Unyanyembe, twins are ordered to be killed and thrown into water the moment they are born, lest droughts and famines or floods should oppress the land. Should any one attempt to conceal twins, the whole family would be murdered by the chief; but, though a great traveller, this is the only instance of such brutality Manua had ever witnessed in any country.

In the province of Unyanyembe, if a twin or twins die, they are thrown into water for the same reason as in Nguru; but as their numbers increase the size of the family, their birth is hailed with delight. Still there is a source of fear there in connection with twins, as I have seen myself; for when one dies, the mother ties a little gourd to her neck as a proxy, and puts into it a trifle of everything which she gives the living child, lest the jealousy of the dead spirit should torment her. Further, on the death of the child, she smears herself with butter and ashes, and runs frantically about, tearing her hair and bewailing piteously; whilst the men of the place use towards her the foulest language, apparently as if in abuse of her person, but in reality to frighten away the demons who have robbed her nest.

On 9 September 1862, Speke and Grant became the first Europeans to set foot in the capital of the Kingdom of Bunyoro, Mruli, near present-day Masindi Port. Grant described the site as 'bare and dreary'. Speke dismissed the royal palace as 'a dumpy, large hut, surrounded by a host of smaller ones … nothing could be more filthy', adding that 'it was well, perhaps, that we were never expected to go there, for without stilts and respirators it would have been impracticable'. Nor were Speke and Grant much taken with Kamurasi, the King of Bunyoro, who – understandably troubled by 'absurd stories which he had heard from the Baganda' about the cannibalistic, mountain-eating, river-drying powers of the white man – left his European visitors waiting for nine days before finally granting them an audience. When finally they met, Speke wrote:

> Kamurasi was enshrouded in his *mbugu* dress, for all the world like a pope in state – calm and actionless. One bracelet of fine-twisted brass wire adorned his left wrist, and his hair, half an inch long, was worked up into small peppercorn-like knobs by rubbing the hand circularly over the crown of the head … Kamurasi asked [Speke's translator] Bombay, 'Who governs England?' 'A woman.' 'Has she any children?' 'Yes', said Bombay, with ready impudence; 'these are two of them' (pointing to Grant and myself). That settled, Kamurasi wished to know if we had any speckled cows, or cows of any peculiar colour, and would we like to change four large cows for four small ones, as he coveted some of ours.

Speke was clearly frustrated by the mixed reception accorded to him by Kamurasi, not to mention the king's endless demands for gifts, but he also regarded him to be a more benevolent ruler than the despotic Mutesa of Buganda. 'Kamurasi conducts all business himself', Speke wrote: 'awarding punishments and seeing them carried out. The most severe instrument of chastisement is a knob-stick, sharpened at the back … for breaking a man's neck before he is thrown into the lake. But this severity is seldom resorted to, Kamurasi being of a mild disposition compared with Mutesa, whom he invariably alludes to when ordering men to be flogged, telling them that were they in Buganda, their heads would suffer instead of their backs.'

The king's attitude towards his family, Speke explained, was somewhat dictatorial: 'Kamurasi's sisters are not allowed to wed; they live and die virgins in his palace. Their only occupation in life consisted of drinking milk, of which each one consumes the produce daily of from ten to twenty cows, and hence they become so inordinately fat that they cannot walk. Should they wish to see a relative, or go outside the hut for any purpose, it requires eight men to lift any of them on a litter. The brothers, too, are not allowed to go out of his reach. This confinement of the palace family is considered a state necessity, as a preventive to civil wars, in the same way as the destruction of the Baganda princes, after a certain season, is thought necessary for the preservation of peace there.'

The only other Europeans to visit Bunyoro during Kamurasi's rule were Samuel and Florence Baker, who arrived at Mruli on 10 February 1864, remarking that it was a 'delightful change to find ourselves in comparative civilisation'. Baker waxed lyrical about 'the decency of the clothing' in the 'thickly populated and much cultivated' kingdom. 'The blacksmiths,' he noted 'were exceedingly clever and used iron hammers instead of stones … they made a fine quality of jet black earthenware, producing excellent tobacco pipes, extremely pretty bowls, and also bottles. The huts are very large … made entirely of reeds and straw, and very lofty … like huge inverted baskets, beehive shaped.'

Kamurasi, once again, made a poor impression, badgering his guests with interminable demands for gifts, culminating in the suggestion that Baker leave his wife behind at Mruli as a royal consort. But after the Bakers left Mruli for Lake Albert, they received a message from Kamurasi requesting another meeting, at which it transpired that the 'king' they had met at Mruli was an impostor, installed by Kamurasi for reasons that remain unclear. The real Kamurasi impressed Baker as 'a remarkably fine man, tall and well-proportioned … beautifully clean', but still perturbed by the earlier deceit in Mruli, he also observed in Kamurasi a 'peculiarly sinister expression'. When the king started with the customarily outrageous requests for gifts, Baker 'rose to depart, telling him I had heard that Kamurasi was a great king, but that he was a mere beggar, and was doubtless [another] impostor'.

In April 1872, the recently knighted Sir Samuel Baker returned to Bunyoro as governor of Egypt's Equatoria Province, accompanied by a detachment of Egyptian troops, and charged with stopping the Arab slave trade out of the region. Kamurasi had died three years earlier, to be succeeded by his son Kabarega. Baker was impressed by the physical attributes of the new king, describing him as 'excessively neat [and] very well clad, in a beautifully made bark-cloth striped with black … about twenty years of age … five feet ten inches in height, and of extremely light complexion'. Kabarega welcomed Baker's attempt to suppress the slave trade, but he also resented his kingdom being placed under Egyptian sovereignty, and relations between the two men swiftly deteriorated. On 8 June 1872, Kabarega led a surprise attack on Baker's fort, expecting that resistance would be minimal, since he had craftily arranged for poisoned beer to be supplied to the Egyptian troops on the previous day. But Baker repulsed the attack, and having done so burned Kabarega's capital to the ground. Kabarega retreated southward to Mparo (close to modern-day Hoima), where he established a new capital. A decade earlier, Baker had written of Bunyoro that 'the deceit of this country was incredible'. The apparently unprovoked attack on Masindi only confirmed his earlier judgement.

Britain's colonial policy towards Bunyoro was to a great extent moulded by the antipathy expressed by Sir Samuel Baker, who left Equatoria in 1873, towards its 'cowardly, treacherous, beggarly drunkard' of a ruler. Yet a very different impression is given in the writings of the first European to build a lasting relationship with Kabarega: Emin Pasha, who visited Mparo in 1877 to negotiate the peace between Equatoria and Bunyoro, and then served as Governor of Equatoria between 1878 and 1889. 'I have often visited Kabarega,' he wrote, 'and cannot say that I have ever heard him utter an improper word or make an indecent gesture, or that he was ever rude … Kabarega is cheerful, laughs readily and much, talks a great deal, and does not appear to be bound by ceremony, the exact opposite to Mutesa, the conceited ruler of Buganda. I certainly cannot charge Kabarega with begging; on the contrary he sent me daily, in the most hospitable manner, stores … which although they were intended to last one day, could easily have been made to last us a fortnight. I received a detailed account of all the events that happened during Baker's visit, a curiously different account from that given [by Baker]. I had to listen to a long account of the doings of the Danaglas [Egyptian soldiers] … the sum and substance of all being that [Kabarega] had been continually provoked and attacked by them, although he, as occupant on the throne, was entitled to rule over them.'

food is available, including a buffet of traditional foods (*Ush13,500*) at lunch & dinner. The spotless but rather dated accommodation is a little overpriced. *US$26/30/34 sgl/dbl/exec dbl B&B.*

⌂ **Crown Hotel** Off Kizungu Mandela Rd; m 0776 970150. This smart modern hotel lies just outside the town centre beyond the post office. A 1st-floor dining balcony provides regional views & you can while away those long Hoima afternoons in the sauna, steam bath & large swimming pool. *US$22/26/48 sgl/dbl/trpl B&B.*

⌂ **Riviera Hotel** (75 rooms) Kampala Rd; ℡0465 523310; e hoimarivierahotel@yahoo.com. This sprawling & rather institutional establishment is reasonably priced & has clean, tiled rooms. *US$20/28 sgl+/twin, US$20 cottage rooms, US$10 sgl+ with shared facilities.*

Shoestring

⌂ **St Joseph's Catholic Institute** (26 rooms) 3km out of town; m 0782 748984. The Cistercian Sisters of Charity provide a warm welcome at their quiet Rwenkobe convent. The rooms are spotless, though spartan (take your own nets or bring mossie spray) & set in peaceful grounds. The sisters have studied at the Vatican & the Italian-influenced food has been praised by travellers. Following the Butiaba Road out of town, take a right turn 400m past the Kolping (just before the tarmac ends), fork right after the bridge, head straight across the roundabout & continue for 2km. *US$10/16 sgl bed only/FB with shared facilities, US$12 s/c sgl bed only.*

⌂ **Nsamo Hotel** (30 rooms) Located close to the taxi park. The long-serving Nsamo Hotel is excellent value & rooms are spotless. *US$8 s/c sgl+ rooms, US$14/16 sgl/dbl larger rooms. Rates excl b/fast.*

⌂ **Bhojani Hotel** (30 rooms) m 0712 737319. This centrally located, Indian-owned hotel offers acceptable rooms & an affordable, curry-dominated menu for residents (*Ush6,000–7,500*). *US$6 small sgl with shared facilities, US$12 larger dbl rooms.*

✖ **WHERE TO EAT AND DRINK** All of the hotels listed serve food. Plenty of restaurants and bars serving cheap local fare and cold beers are scattered around the town centre. Unfortunately, the Indian-oriented menu of **Bhojani Hotel** is only offered to residents. Travellers in transit between Murchison and Kibale will appreciate the lunchtime buffets at the **Rwenzori Restaurant** and **Kolping Society Guesthouse**. The small garden outside the **Collins Pub** opposite the sports ground is the leafiest spot in the town centre for a cold drink, while a little way past the far end of the same field, the two-storey thatch 'n' timber **Spot On** bar seems a good place to enjoy drinks, snacks and televised sports events. The **Kon Tiki**, 3km down the Kampala Road, is a more refined, though costlier, setting for food and drink (see page 377).

NIGHTLIFE **Spot On** (see above) would appear to be open late while the **Ten New Tunes** nightclub (opposite Crane Bank in the middle of town) tolerates dancing. Local sources tell us that the **Cool Zone** (out of town past the Crown Hotel) is *the* place to hang out until late to drink, dance, watch big-screen football and discuss the sad condition of Bunyoro's heritage sites.

OTHER PRACTICALITIES
Foreign exchange
Forex services are provided by **Stanbic**, **Crane**, **KCB** and **Barclays** banks.

Internet
Internet facilities are available next to Kolping head office (not the guesthouse: head for the foot of the town centre's mobile phone mast beyond Nsamo Hotel).

Swimming
Pools are found at the **Crown** (*Ush10,000 for non-residents*) and **Kon Tiki** hotels.

WHAT TO SEE

Mparo Tombs Situated about 4km out of Hoima along the Masindi Road, Mparo was chosen as the capital of Omukama (King) Kabarega of Bunyoro in 1872, after Sir Samuel Baker forced his retreat out of Masindi. It was from Mparo that he led his raids into the neighbouring kingdoms of Toro and Buganda before the British drove him into hiding in 1891. After he died in exile in 1923, his body was returned to Hoima and interred at Mparo. This burial of Kabarega was in most respects traditional, but certain customs were deemed obsolete. The most grisly of these involved digging a 10m-deep hole, the floor of which would be covered in barkcloth on the morning of the burial. One of the late king's wives – usually the eldest or the favourite – would be seated in the hole, holding in her lap a parcel containing the dead man's jawbone. Onlookers were then seized randomly from the crowd, their limbs were amputated, and then they were thrown into the hole one by one until it was filled.

The tomb is protected within a large domed construction made mostly from natural materials, and not dissimilar in appearance to the more famous Kasubi Tombs in Kampala, though considerably smaller. The grave itself is surrounded by many of Kabarega's personal effects, including some spears and crowns said to be handed down from the Bacwezi dynasty. It is covered with a type of white spotted brown cowhide called *entimba*, held in place by nine traditional hoes. Kabarega's son and successor Omukama Tito Winyi is also buried at Mparo. A plaque on a small monument outside the main enclosure at Mparo marks the spot where Kabarega granted an audience to the Emin Pasha in 1877 (see box, pages 378–9).

If using a private vehicle, Kabarega's grass-roofed tomb and the whitewashed Emin Pasha monument are clearly visible on the right, about 2km down the main road towards Masindi. Otherwise, hire a boda-boda. A 'community guide' will materialise as you arrive and offer to show you around for Ush10,000 per person.

Hoima Palace The palace of Bunyoro-Kitara lies just beyond Hoima town centre on the Butiaba Road. Though the building itself is modern, a fierce sense of tradition is still evident in the Throne Room from the artefacts and the significance that's attached to them. In addition to the traditional nine-legged throne/stool swathed in leopard skins and barkcloth, an array of spears, royal headdresses and musical instruments are on display. Visits are by arrangement only: contact the Omukama's private secretary (and respected historian) Yolamu Nsamba (m *0772 471251;* e *nsambay@yahoo.com*).

Katasiha Fort Katasiha, situated only 2km from Hoima along the Butiaba Road, was the largest of the forts built by General Colville after Kabarega abandoned his capital at Mparo in late 1893. All that remains of the fort today is the 8m dry moat (now filled in) that surrounded it, and a nearby small cave that was used as a hiding place by Kabarega and later as an arsenal by the British. Still, it's a fair goal for a short walk or bicycle ride out of the town centre.

Kibero Salt Gardens and Hot Spring The small fishing village of Kibero lies on a small plain between Lake Albert and the Rift Valley Escarpment. It is distinguished from other, similarly inaccessible lakeside villages by its 'salt gardens' and an adjacent hot spring which have supplied Bunyoro with salt for centuries. The first foreign visitor to Kibero was Emin Pasha in 1885, during the period that the Pasha and his garrison were cut off from the outside world by the Mahdist rebels in Sudan.

Emin described the gardens and the salt-making process, observing helpfully that, 'When taken in large quantities, [the spring water] acts as a moderate purgative.'

To reach Kibero, head north from Hoima for 24km (or south from Biso for 16km) until Kigorobeya, where you turn west towards Lake Albert. You may see women selling heaps of salt at the junction. A decent track runs for 8km, terminating by a hut where Mr William Kato will watch your vehicle for Ush3,000. There is no vehicle access to Kibero (unless you care to risk a dry-season track from Butiaba, 20km north) and everything the village produces must be carried up the escarpment. Likewise, everything it needs must be carried down. Kato's main business is watching bicycles (*Ush500*) and motorbikes (*Ush1,000*) left in his care while their owners lug goods up and down the path. Fish, salt and empty beer/soda crates come up. Firewood and filled beer/soda crates go down. Take plenty of clean drinking water and palatable snacks as you won't find either in Kibero. It's a 45-minute walk down the escarpment. The duration of the ascent (save some water for this since it will be hot by then!) is up to you. Whatever your speed, be assured that someone carrying 30kg of salt or fish on their head will overtake you. Your legs will tell you that the path is far steeper towards the bottom of the escarpment. This fact is confirmed by the outline of more distant sections of the Rift wall that show three distinct planes corresponding to three phases of uplift. The highest section is 4.5 million years old and has eroded into a relatively gentle slope, while the lowest section was heaved above the lake within the last 1.5 million years and remains steep.

During the descent, you'll see the salt gardens laid out on the plain below you – bare patches of scraped earth in an otherwise grassy setting between the escarpment and the lake. The hot springs that you'll be shown are actually a hot stream with a rocky bed clothed with filamentous heat-loving algae. The spring itself lies hidden deep within a densely vegetated cleft in the escarpment. It's all interesting enough, but you may well discern other rewards from the visit. Kibero provides a rare opportunity to appreciate the dramatic Rift Valley scenery on foot and it is rather exciting to still be amongst the first foreigners to reach this out-

KIBERO SALT GARDENS

Text taken from the draft of Uganda Safari *by Andrew Roberts*

Like the better-known Katwe Salt Lake close to Queen Elizabeth National Park, Kibero's 'salt gardens' were an economically important asset for the Bunyoro kingdom for centuries. Glass beads found by archaeologists show that people bartered for salt here at least as far back as the 13th century, and most probably earlier.

Kibero's 'salt gardeners' use a clever technique to obtain a remarkably pure product. The 'gardens' are patches of salty ground from which grass and topsoil have been removed. These mineral-rich depressions are saturated with water diverted in earthen channels from a nearby hot spring. This already slightly salty water dissolves additional salts from the soil. Loose dry soil is then scattered across the 'garden' into which, over a week or so, the salty water is drawn up by capillary action. When the enriched earth changes colour it is scraped into jars to be repeatedly leached by a further quantity of spring water. The result is a concentrated solution of 14% salt which is boiled off to produce crystals of 97.6% pure sodium chloride. In contrast, the salt produced at Lake Katwe is just 85%.

of-the-way location. Though 125 years have passed since Emin Pasha's visit, his path to Kibero has not been trampled by tourists like those of Stanley, Speke and Baker to higher-profile locations. Perhaps the true reward from a visit to Kibero is an appreciation of the hardships which human beings will endure to survive in decidedly uncompromising locations (and to drink bottled beer).

There is currently no formal system for escorting visitors around Kibero. Etiquette suggests that the first port of call in remote places is the local chairman. I found him absent but his wife took a break from gutting outrageously undersized tilapia to request a quasi-official donation of Ush5,000, have me sign the ubiquitous visitors' book, and summon a couple of unemployed youths to take me around. At the end of the tour, they shyly asked for a guiding fee of Ush2,000 each and were overjoyed to be gratified.

KABWOYA WILDLIFE RESERVE

Text taken from the draft of Uganda Safari *by Andrew Roberts*
(*UWA Entry fees for a Category B protected area apply; see pages 32–3*) Uganda's newest protected area, the 87km² Kabwoya Wildlife Reserve, occupies an isolated but superbly scenic lake plain sandwiched between Lake Albert and the Rift's Bunyoro Escarpment. It is presently completely unknown to tourists although this situation is changing with the opening of a safari lodge by the lake. In a previous incarnation – the 227km² Kaiso-Tonya Controlled Hunting Area – Kabwoya's grasslands were famous during the 1960s for large and varied herds of game, and represented an important part of a migration route along the Rift between Semliki and Murchison Falls. This wildlife spectacle has since been lost; most animals were wiped out by poachers and the remainder dispersed when the lake plain was invaded by cattle herders. In a belated effort to protect remnant game, Kabwoya Wildlife Reserve was created in 2002 from the southern section of the Kaiso-Tonya Controlled Hunting Area when this category of protected area was deemed obsolete and discontinued. The northern part of Kaiso-Tonya was afforded the new (and some would say equally meaningless) title of 'Community Wildlife Area', Uganda's lowest category of protected area.

The Uganda Wildlife Authority has leased Kabwoya and Kaiso-Tonya to a private tourism/conservation operator who works in partnership with UWA staff and Hoima District. It has been uphill all the way for the new management team. In 2002, Land Rovers had to be winched over the escarpment to reach a reserve full of cattle but obviously not game. A further issue concerning conservationists is the discovery of oil reserves beneath the wildlife reserve and parts of Kabwoya's wilderness environment are compromised by prominent exploratory rigs There is a silver lining though, for this no-expense-spared prospecting operation has constructed an excellent access road making Lake Albert considerably easier to reach than it was for Samuel and Florence Baker when they struggled down to its shore in 1864.

Conservation progress has been impressive in Kabwoya. With the backing of local politicians and Bunyoro royalty, cattle have been relocated from the wildlife reserve to the adjacent Community Wildlife Area and game is increasing quickly in response. Buffalo now graze the airstrip near Lake Albert Safari Lodge and hippos have taken up residence in the lake below it. Uganda kob, warthog, duiker and bushbuck are now common in Kabwoya's *Combretum* savanna and even an occasional lion is seen. Hartebeest are to be reintroduced from the nearby Bugungu Wildlife Reserve near Butiaba. Primates include black-and-white

10

colobus monkey and chimpanzee, which inhabit riparian forests along the Hoywa and Wambabya rivers and tributaries, as well as the baboon troops that clamber over the lake cliff near the lodge. A full bird list has yet to be compiled, but with habitats including savanna, riverine forest and lakeshore, birders are unlikely to be disappointed.

As a game-viewing destination, Kabwoya has a long way to go, being presently in a similar situation to that of neighbouring Semliki Wildlife Reserve 15 years ago, before the lodge owners kick-started conservation activities there. The reserve does have two other, significant areas of appeal. Firstly, it is a prime location to appreciate the Albertine Rift Valley and its wide-ranging history. Secondly it allows an attractive detour and overnight stop from the interminable 350km section of the tour itinerary between Fort Portal and Paraa (Murchison Falls).

GETTING THERE AND AWAY Kabwoya Wildlife Reserve lies 76km southwest of Hoima and 215km north of Fort Portal. From Hoima, follow the Butiaba Road out of town for about 5km before turning left (ignoring a previous left turn signposted to Bugambe tea estate/ factory). Drive south through Busureka trading centre, cross the Wambabya River and go past Kabaale trading centre. After a further 9km, fork right at Kaseeta. The reserve boundary on the Rift Valley Escarpment is 8km further on, beyond Hohwa trading centre. The safari lodge and lakeshore lie another 14km across the plain. Approaching from Fort Portal, follow the tarmac Kampala Road east for 50km to the northbound (*murram*) Hoima Road at Kyenjojo. It's 101km to Kabwoya trading centre where you turn left towards Kaseeta through Bugoma Central Forest Reserve. Travellers bound for Murchison Falls from Kabwoya will head north through Kaseeta and Busereka. A left turn on reaching the Butiaba road follows the back route to Murchison Falls via Biso and Bulisa.

 WHERE TO STAY

Lake Albert Safari Lodge [map page 374] (11 cottages) m 0772 221003; e info@ lakealbertlodge.com; www.lakealbertlodge.com. This excellent lodge has been developed by the reserve concessionaire at a stunning location on top of the 60m lakeshore cliffs. It's a perfect place to watch the sun set over the Blue Mountains of the DRC across 40km of water & even to get up in the middle of the night to experience the son et lumière that accompanies the frequent storms on the lake. Accommodation is provided in attractive canvas-sided & immaculately thatched s/c cottages facing the lake & a tented camp nearby. A small swimming pool is a welcome feature in the hot trough of the Albertine Rift Valley. *US$130/200 sgl/ dbl FB, US$42pp FB own tent.*

There's also a **private guesthouse** between the Ranger Camp and Kyehoro fishing village (*US$20 B&B, dinner Ush15,000*).

WHAT TO SEE AND DO UWA entrance fees (see Category B fees on pages 32–3) are settled at the lodge where a wide variety of activities are organised, including **day and night game drives** (*US$15pp*), **fossil hunting** (*US$15pp*), **guided walks** (*US$15pp*) and **waterfall hikes** (*US$25pp*). All require a minimum of four people. A **horseback safari** costs US$25 per person and requires a maximum of two people. A limited amount of **sport hunting** is also possible, with small quotas for Uganda kob, warthog and a variety of small and medium-sized antelope being established annually by the UWA. The largest animal on offer, and the one in greatest demand, is Uganda kob; Kabwoya is the only location in the world in which this animal can be legally hunted, and the 2013 provisional quota of 20 animals (*hunting fee US$2,900 per person*) was quickly booked up.

The gateway to Murchison Falls and Budongo Forest, Masindi is a sleepy small town (population estimate 15,000), steeped in an aura of subdued commercial activity that reflects its location along a road that today leads to nowhere of great economic consequence. In the colonial era, by contrast, Masindi was a thriving hub of international trade, situated at the pivot of three key transportation routes: from Butiaba across Lake Albert to the northern DRC, north along the Nile to southern Sudan, and across Lake Kyoga to the Busoga Railway which connects to the main Uganda–Mombasa line. Commerce declined after 1962, when the rising level of Lake Albert enforced the closure of Butiaba Port, and it was further undermined by the havoc wrought on the national economy and transport infrastructure under Idi Amin. Masindi's capacity for economic recovery during the Museveni era has been restricted by several factors: the effective closure of the Congolese and (until recently) the Sudanese borders, the years of unrest in northern Uganda, and the collapse of the road–rail–steamer transport route linking lakes Albert, Kyoga and Victoria in the 1960s.

Masindi's compact town centre isn't much to look at: a tight grid of erratically surfaced roads, dusty or muddy depending on how recently it last rained, emanate from a central market, lined with the faded colonial-era shopfronts that characterise so many small Ugandan towns. Rather more appealing is the green, leafy stretch of suburbia that runs north from the town centre past the golf course. In 1924, Etta Close was charmed by Masindi and its 'European officials [who] live in trim little bungalows with little gardens full of European flowers placed in a circle around a golf course and two lawn tennis courts, the one and only hotel being not far off'. The European officials are gone, but this description otherwise feels surprisingly apposite today, right down to the now-renovated Masindi Hotel, built in 1923 and once host to the writer and hunting enthusiast Ernest Hemingway.

A group of Masindi-based VSO volunteers has produced an informative brochure that identifies a trail around the town taking in notable buildings and landmarks and providing a little of the history of the town. Visit or contact the New Court View Hotel for a copy (see page 386).

GETTING THERE AND AWAY Masindi lies 215km north of Kampala and is reached by following the excellent tarmac highway towards Gulu for 170km before turning left at a conspicuous junction just beyond Kafu Bridge. A newly surfaced road covers the final 45km to Masindi. The drive should take less than three hours in a **private vehicle**. Those coming from Kampala in a private vehicle will appreciate the new Kabalega Diner (see page 389). This much-needed rest stop is found 2km past the turning to Ziwa Rhino Sancurary and 2km before the authentic but awful roadside alternative at Kafu Bridge.

Masindi is well served by public transport and **buses** run regularly from Kampala's Qualicell bus terminal (*Ush13,000*) but the Post Bus service has been discontinued. **Minibuses** also run between Kampala and Masindi throughout the day.

The junction of the two roads to Murchison Falls lies about 1km north of the town centre opposite the Shell garage (the last opportunity to fill up at reasonable fuel prices). A right turn (signposted for Paraa via Kichumbanyobo) takes you along the direct 85km route to Paraa via Kanyiyo Pabidi and Sambiya Lodge. The road continuing straight on past the Shell garage is the Hoima Road. Regular minibuses run along this route which reverts to *murram* 3km out of town. A right turn where the tarmac ends follows a scenic, 135km-long back route to Murchison Falls via

Busingiro, Butiaba, Bulisa and Nile Safari Camp. There is no public transport to Paraa along either of the routes described, but on the latter, a daily bus connects Kampala to Wanseko via Masindi and Bulisa.

TOURIST INFORMATION Current rates and other practical information relating to Murchison Falls National Park and associated conservation areas (Budongo Forest, Bugungu Wildlife Reserve) is available at the **Murchison Falls Conservation Area tourist office** (✆ *0465 420428*), which lies on the outskirts of town, off the road towards the Masindi Hotel.

TOUR OPERATORS The Masindi-based **Yebo Tours** (✆ *0465 20029*; m *0701 637493*; e *yebotours2002@yahoo.com*; *www.traveluganda.co.ug/yebotours*) can provide vehicle hire to Murchison Falls and other local attractions at a very reasonable daily rate of US$80 per day for a 4x4 and US$100 for a minibus (inclusive of driver and unlimited kilometres, but exclusive of fuel). Yebo can also arrange all-inclusive camping tours to Murchison Falls. The office is next to Barclays bank.

New Court View Hotel (see below) also offers tours from Masindi to Murchison Falls.

WHERE TO STAY For location of listings see map opposite.

Moderate

🏠 **Masindi Hotel** (28 rooms) ✆ 0465 420023; m 0712 447676; e masindihotel@gmail.com; www.masindihotel.com. Located roughly 1km northwest of the town centre, Masindi's oldest hotel was built in 1923 by the East Africa Railways & Harbours Company as a staging point for travellers in transit between the ferry services on lakes Kyoga & Albert. For years, any lingering charm was compromised by dilapidated facilities & questionable 1960s décor (including zebra striped walls in the Zebra Bar!). Following an effective facelift, the long verandas, airy, tiled s/c rooms & revamped public areas once again exude the charm of the EAR&H years when the lake ferries ferried, the railways ran & the hotel register read like a Who's Who of celebrity safari-goers. (Hemingway, Bogart, Bacall, Hepburn ...). The Kabarega Restaurant serves decent meals (see *Where to eat*, below). *US$70/85/85 sgl/dbl/twin B&B.*

Budget

🏠 **New Court View Hotel** m 0752 446463; e courtview@utlonline.co.ug. The pick of the town's budget hotels, the New Court View is a perennial favourite with visitors & expatriates bound for Murchison Falls. Accommodation is provided in a compact cluster of small s/c *bandas* with nets & solar-heated showers. The charm lies more in the pleasant setting, the excellent menu & the fact that

fellow guests are like-minded people, also inclined to put a decent dinner & a good night's rest before a mad dash into the national park. Early (06.00) b/fasts can be served or packed for birdwatchers & other early risers. *US$25/30 sgl/dbl B&B.*

🏠 **Kolping Society Guesthouse** ✆ 0465 420458. Located less than 500m from the town centre, this is a clean & reliable Church-run hostel, with a fair restaurant attached. Some attractive new cottages are dotted around the green grounds. *US$28/20 s/c dbl/twin, US$16 twin with shared facilities. All rates B&B.*

Shoestring

🏠 **Buma Hotel** (20 rooms) Basic, centrally located hotel listed just in case you find the Alinda Guesthouse full & don't fancy the Ogwentie Inn. The cheaper rooms are fair value but the s/c options seem costly. *US$6/12 sgl/dbl shared facilities, US$16/20 s/c sgl/dbl. All rates B&B.*

🏠 **Alinda Guesthouse** (35 rooms) m 0772 550710/520382. This friendly, double-storey guesthouse, built around a large courtyard with chairs & tables, is comfortably the best value in the town centre, with clean s/c rooms with fan, net & hot water & similar rooms using common showers. The restaurant serves dishes such as chicken & chips, beef stew or spaghetti in the Ush10,000 range. *US$10 s/c twin, US$7/8/ non-s/c sgl/dbl.*

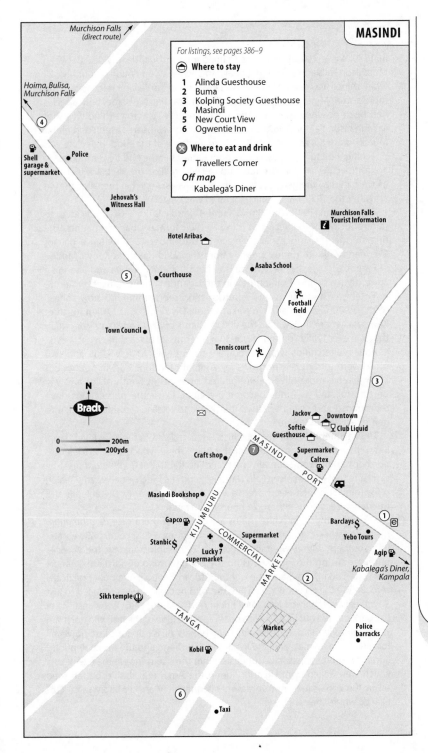

MASINDI

For listings, see pages 386–9

⌂ **Where to stay**
1 Alinda Guesthouse
2 Buma
3 Kolping Society Guesthouse
4 Masindi
5 New Court View
6 Ogwentie Inn

⊗ **Where to eat and drink**
7 Travellers Corner

Off map
Kabalega's Diner

Murchison Falls
(direct route)

Hoima, Bulisa,
Murchison Falls

Shell
garage &
supermarket

Police

Jehovah's
Witness Hall

Murchison Falls
Tourist Information

Hotel Aribas

Courthouse

Asaba School

Football
field

Town Council

Tennis court

N

Bradt

0 ———— 200m
0 ———— 200yds

Jackov
Downtown
Softie
Guesthouse
Club Liquid
Supermarket
Caltex

Craft shop

MASINDI PORT

Masindi Bookshop

KIJUMBURU

Gapco

Barclays

Yebo Tours

Stanbic

COMMERCIAL

Supermarket

MARKET

Agip

Kabalega's Diner,
Kampala

Lucky 7
supermarket

Sikh temple

TANGA

Market

Police
barracks

Kobil

6

Taxi

In 1970, some 300 black rhinos roamed wild in Uganda, divided between Murchison Falls and Kidepo national parks, while a population of roughly 120 white rhinos was resident in Ajai Wildlife Reserve, some later relocated to the more secure Murchison Falls. Within little more than a decade, both species had been poached to local extinction: Uganda's last white rhino was shot in Murchison Falls in 1982, and no black rhino has been observed in either Murchison or Kidepo since 1983. The main cause of the sudden decline was poaching – rhino horns, used as dagger handles in the Middle East and as an aphrodisiac in parts of Asia, fetch up to US$1 million on the black market – exacerbated by the general atmosphere of lawlessness that prevailed during and after the 1979 war in which Idi Amin was ousted.

Founded in 1998, the Rhino Fund Uganda is an NGO dedicated to reintroducing both species of rhino to their former Ugandan haunts. The first step in this process took place in December 2001, when a pair of 2½-year-old white rhinos, bought from the Solio Ranch in Kenya, landed at Entebbe to a festive reception. The rhinos – named Kabira and Sherino – currently reside in a holding pen in the Uganda Wildlife Education Centre in Entebbe. The focus of the reintroduction programme has now shifted to the 7,000ha Ziwa Ranch in Nakasongola District, about 170km north of Kampala, where they will be the first residents of a fenced 80km² sanctuary that will eventually contain about 30 white and 20 black rhinos.

Four white rhinos were introduced from Kenya in July 2005 and two more were introduced from Disney Animal Kingdom USA in September 2006. Twelve more have been donated by parks in South Africa and will be translocated as funds become available. Once the populations have reproduced and stabilised, the intention is to release the rhinos back into game reserves in Uganda.

Unlike Entebbe, Ziwa Ranch, which is located within the Kafu River basin, lies within the historical range of the black rhino, which was restricted to northern Uganda and contains natural rhino habitat of *Combretum* savanna similar to that in Murchison Falls National Park. The ranch is necessarily sealed off within a 2m-high electric fence and, as further security, the animals and the perimeter are monitored 24 hours by 40 rangers.

Uganda's imported white rhinos are of the southern race *Ceratotherium s. simum* rather than the indigenous northern race *C. s. cottoni*. Ziwa's first four southern whites were introduced in 2005. Unfortunately, the chances of reintroducing the indigenous northern white rhino of northern Uganda, the DRC, Sudan, Chad and the Central African Republic are now practically zero. Before the recent wars in DRC, the wild population was reduced to just 30 animals in Garamba National Park in northeastern DRC. Two censuses of the park, carried out in 2006 with possible relocation of the last wild northern white rhinos in mind, spotted only four animals. All is not quite lost, however, for nine more animals are held in zoos in San Diego and the Czech Republic. Some conservationists have suggested that the two rhinos in the Czech zoo, which were taken from Uganda during the Amin era, should be returned – but the zoo argues, not unreasonably, that they are probably safer kept exactly where they are now.

⌂ **Ogwentie Inn** (12 rooms) Recommended as the safest & cleanest of the cheapies around the taxi park. *US$4/sgl/sgl+ with shared facilities.*

✕ **WHERE TO EAT** For decent food in an attractive setting, head out of the town centre to either the **Masindi Hotel** or the **New Court View Hotel**. The former serves a variety of continental and Indian meals (*Ush25,000*) in an attractive courtyard. The **New Court View** serves a similar range, plus some tasty Chinese items (try the sizzling beef) and home-grown salads enlivened with tuna, egg, etc. Their meals are attractively priced at Ush15,000 and served with commendable promptness – a refreshing change from the upcountry norm.

The best restaurant in the centre of Masindi is **Travellers Corner**. Located on a corner plot in a colonial-era building, it has a wide balcony from which to enjoy a cold drink and watch the town go by. It's run by the New Court View Hotel and offers a condensed version of the menu above (*meals Ush12,000–15,000*). If on a tighter budget, try the **Alinda Guesthouse** or choose from the usual scattering of local eateries and bars.

If *en route* to Masindi or Murchison Falls, you could eat at the new **Kabalega's Diner** (*www.kabalegadiner.com*) on the Kampala–Gulu road, 2km before the turning to Masindi at Kafu Bridge. Main courses (*Ush16,000–20,000*), snacks and flush toilets are available. To check availability or to pre-order meals, ☏ 0414 691910. See advert in third colour section. For location of listings see map, page 387.

SHOPPING The nationwide improvement in upcountry supermarkets has yet to reach Masindi, so stock up before leaving Kampala. The best bet for provisions is still the **Lucky Seven supermarket** on Commercial Street, while your last chance for any sort of purchase before you head to Murchison is the small but relatively costly store attached to the **Shell garage** at Paraa junction. Local handicrafts are sold in **craft shops** opposite Travellers Corner and at the New Court View Hotel.

OTHER PRACTICALITIES Forex services are provided by **Stanbic** and **Barclays** banks.

WHAT TO SEE AND DO The most notable distraction *en route* to Masindi is the **Ziwa Rhino Sanctuary** (see below), which lies about two hours' drive out of Kampala, 6km south of the Kafu Bridge–Masindi junction. When you reach the town, if you've got a free afternoon, get hold of the free *Masindi Town Walking Trail* leaflet from the New Court View Hotel and follow the route described to find a selection of historic locations and buildings. However, you're most likely to be in Masindi to visit Budongo Forest and/or Murchison Falls, both of which are covered later in the chapter. If you're not in a hurry to reach these destinations, **Boomu Women's Group** makes for a worthwhile and worthy stop just before the park's entrance gate at Kichumbanyobo (see page 393).

Ziwa Rhino Sanctuary (m *0772 713410*; e *info@ziwarhino.com; www.ziwarhino. com; rhino tracking US$35/30/5 for foreign visitors/East African residents/Ugandan citizens, children between 5 & 12 pay US$17/12/3; canoe trips take about 4hrs & cost US$30/25/15; 2hr swamp walks US$15/10/7; 2hr birding walks US$10/10/5*) Ziwa Rhino Sanctuary is a 7,000ha ranch about 170km (three hours' drive) out of Kampala on the Masindi–Gulu road. It presently contains 12 rhinos (more to arrive soon) and a range of smaller game species. The rhinos can be tracked on foot

10

in the company of a ranger. The animals are habitually found in wetland areas, so be appropriately shod for the conditions. Indeed, parts of the ranch are sufficiently damp to enable canoe trips in search of shoebills.

🏠 **Where to stay**   For locations of listings see map, page 374.

🏠 **Amura Lodge**   m 0771 600812; e info@amukalodgeuganda.com; www. amukalodgeuganda.com. This new, privately run tented camp opened within the Ziwa Rhino Sanctuary in 2012. *US$220/360 sgl/dbl FB.*

🏠 **Ziwa Rhino Sanctuary**   (12 'backpacker' rooms sleeping 24 people, & 2 guesthouses) m 0775 521 035/0782 819 777; e info@ziwarhino. com; www.ziwarhino.com. Visitors to Ziwa can now stay over in a choice of accommodation set around the sanctuary's office. The setting is an attractive grassy compound cleared from the surrounding bush in which birds & mammals

abound. Meals are available. The guesthouses each typically sleep up to 8 but the number & nature of the rooms in each varies so check options. *US$40pp guesthouses B&B, US$15pp twin backpacker rooms with shared facilities, US$10pp camping. Discounts for residents.*

🏠 **Kafu River Lodge**   (3 cottages) m 0776 747333; www.neul.co.ug. This seemingly underutilised facility occupies grounds excised from ranchland beside the Kampala–Gulu road between the turnings to Ziwa Rhino Sanctuary & Masindi. Rooms in the 2-bed cottages are simple & clean. *US$20 s/c dbl.*

Masindi Port   Masindi Port, which lies 40km east of the town of Masindi, fringes the marshy area where the Victoria Nile exits Lake Kyoga. The port peaked in importance during the colonial era, but no commercial boats sail from it today. The surrounding marshes are of potential interest to birdwatchers, and there are quite a few hippos around. You'd be unlikely to have any problems organising a dugout to explore Lake Kyoga, and the Nile River is navigable to the top of Karuma Falls, 70km downstream.

Little if any formal public transport runs to Masindi Port, though on most days a pick-up truck or two heads out from Masindi Town to the port. A free ferry service crosses the Nile between Masindi Port and Maiyunge on the opposite bank. When it's not running, you can hire a dugout to take you across for a small consideration. From Maiyunge, a road heads north to Lira.

Kigoman Mixed Farm   (m *0782 793750*; e *kigomanud@hotmail.com*) On your way north (or indeed south, west or east for that matter), you'll pass numerous makeshift markets and lone ramshackle stalls groaning beneath abundant quantities of fresh fruit and veg. If you're curious to see how all this stuff is produced, take a half-day tour of the Ugandan-Dutch Kigoman Mixed Farm (17.5km north of Luwero town, turn at a signposted junction for 4km off the Gulu Road). The tour costs Ush36,000pp and includes water and fresh-fruit snacks. Advance booking essential and traditional meals by arrangement.

BUDONGO FOREST

The 790km² Budongo Forest Reserve is one of the most extensive and ecologically diverse in East Africa, with some 465 plant species recorded, most impressively perhaps a dense concentration of buttressed giant mahoganies reaching up to 60m tall. Budongo's population of 800 chimpanzees, the largest anywhere in Uganda, has been the subject of scientific research for several decades. Other common primates include red-tailed monkey, blue monkey, black-and-white colobus, potto and various forest galago species. More than 250 butterfly species have been recorded.

Budongo Forest is of great ornithological significance, with some 366 bird species recorded, including 60 west or central African birds known from fewer than five locations in East Africa. The yellow-footed flycatcher, often associated with ironwood trees, is known nowhere else in Uganda, while the Ituri batis, lemon-bellied crombec, white-thighed hornbill, black-eared ground thrush and chestnut-capped flycatcher are known from only one other East African forest. The Royal Mile, the stretch of road connecting Nyabyere Forestry College to the main research station, is regarded by some as the single best birdwatching site in Uganda. The main road past Busingiro also offers superb birdwatching.

Tourism activity dates back to 1992 when the Budongo Forest Ecotourism Project was founded with the aim of conserving Budongo and the nearby Kanyiyo Pabidi Forest through tourist projects that directly benefit local communities. Two tourist sites were created using foreign funding. The downscaled Busingiro Tourist Site is found within the Budongo Forest proper, and reached by following the Bulisa route towards Murchison Falls. The other site lies within the Kanyiyo Pabidi Forest on the direct route from Masindi to Murchison Falls and as such it is covered separately later in this chapter. Though chimpanzee tracking used to be available at Busingiro, this site now offers only general forest walks.

GETTING THERE AND AWAY The Busingiro Tourist Site lies directly alongside the Bulisa Road, 43km west of Masindi, and is clearly signposted. The 2km turn-off to Nyabyere Forestry College is about 10km closer to Masindi, and also signposted. The drive from Masindi should take about an hour in a **private vehicle**. Using public transport, any **minibus-taxi** or **bus** heading from Masindi to Butiaba or Wanseko can drop you at the camp, though you'll probably have to pay the full fare for Butiaba. A **4x4** with driver can be hired in Masindi through Yebo Tours (see page 386).

For details of continuing from Busingiro to Murchison Falls via Lake Albert, see page 393.

WHERE TO STAY There is no accommodation at Busingiro or in the vicinity.

WHAT TO SEE AND DO Though no longer used for chimp tracking, Busingiro's complex and extensive trail system remains open for **forest walks**. Some routes are of note, variously, for trees, birds or butterflies, so it is worth discussing any special interests and preferences with the guides, who will tailor your walks accordingly. A three-hour forest walk costs US$15 as does a birding walk with a specialised guide. Although you may walk unaccompanied along the main road, visitors may enter the forest on either side only when accompanied by a guide.

The best place to do a guided bird walk is along the **Royal Mile**, which runs between Nyabyere Forestry College and the research station. Unfortunately, the Royal Mile lies about 14km from Busingiro, so it's not really a viable option for a day trip unless you have private transport or stay at the forestry college. Generally regarded as being one of Uganda's best forest-birding sites, the Royal Mile supports a wide variety of localised species, with the sought-after African dwarf, blue-breasted and chocolate-backed kingfishers all very common. A long list of other local specials includes Cassin's hawk eagle, Nahan's francolin, white-thighed hornbill, yellow-billed barbet, lemon-billed crombec, black-capped apalis, forest flycatcher, yellow-footed flycatcher and Jameson's wattle-eye. Various monkeys are also likely to be seen, along with giant forest squirrels and the bizarre chequered elephant-shrew. Equally bizarre in this remote patch of forest is a **large church** built by Polish refugees who were settled in the area during World War II.

The alternative to visiting the Royal Mile is to walk along the **main road past Busingiro**. Though not on a par with the Royal Mile, the birding here is still excellent and it is generally easier to locate birds than it is in the forest proper. Among the species to look for on the road and around the campsite are brown-crowned eremomela, Ituri batis, chestnut-capped flycatcher, Cassin's and Sabine's spinetails, and grey and yellow longbills. The chocolate-backed kingfisher, common in the area, is most easily located by call. A small pool by the side of the road about 1km back towards Masindi is a reliable place to see the shining blue kingfisher and black-necked weaver. In addition to birds, you should also see at least three types of primate on this stretch of road. There's nothing to prevent you from walking along the road alone, but it's worth taking a guide from the tourism site – they are very knowledgeable, particularly with regard to bird calls, and they all carry binoculars and a field guide. With a vehicle and spotlight, the road could be worth exploring at night – we were shown a colony of gigantic hammerhead bats along the road between Busingiro to the aforementioned pool, and the nocturnal potto and tree pangolin are also resident.

KANYIYO PABIDI FOREST

The 268km² Kanyiyo Pabidi Forest, the second largest of the four forest blocks within the Budongo Forest Reserve, is essentially an eastern extension of the main Budongo Forest, to which it is linked by a forested corridor crossing the Paraa road. Kanyiyo Pabidi harbours a similar though not identical fauna and flora to Budongo, and because it has never been logged it contains a far higher proportion of large buttressed mahogany and ironwood trees. A similar range of forest primates to Budongo is present, notably black-and-white colobus and blue monkey, while large troops of olive baboon are a regular sight along the main road. Owing to the proximity of Murchison Falls, herds of elephant and buffalo regularly visit Kanyiyo Pabidi, while the occasional wandering lion supplements the resident leopard population.

The Kanyiyo Pabidi Tourist Site was established along similar lines and by the same organisation as Busingiro, but it is more convenient for people driving through to Murchison Falls, since it lies beside the main Masindi–Paraa Road. The downside for those intent on visiting Pabidi but not Murchison Falls National Park proper is that national park entrance fees are levied to visit the site. Pabidi is not only a forest reserve but also part of Karuma Wildlife Reserve and the park entrance gate is located at Kichumbanybo on the boundary of the latter. No matter that reserve fees are lower than park fees; since 1995, when an aggressively territorial German technical advisor moved the park gate 20km south to annex this Sudetenland of the Murchison Falls Conservation Area, full park entrance fees have been levied to enter Karuma and reach Pabidi.

Kanyiyo Pabidi protects a similar range of birds to Busingiro, though the denser vegetation of the pristine forest can make birding more difficult. The best place to look for birds is around the campsite, especially the gallery forest between the staff quarters and the main road, and a 600m nature trail offers good views into the canopy. Among the species we saw on a recent visit were the common shrike-flycatcher, chestnut wattle-eye, Narina trogon, little greenbul, chestnut-winged starling, grey apalis, dwarf and pygmy kingfishers, and a great many forest sunbirds and hornbills. A local speciality is Puvel's illadopsis, which, although it was recorded here for the first time only recently, and is known from no other locality in East Africa, is very common. The extremely localised and magnificently garish green-breasted pitta has also been recorded here.

GETTING THERE AND AWAY Kanyiyo Pabidi Tourist Site lies alongside the main Paraa Road, 29km from Masindi, and it is clearly signposted. In a **private vehicle**, it would be easy enough to stop here for a walk *en route* between Masindi and Paraa. The site also lies about an hour's drive from Sambiya Lodge, and can be visited as a day trip from there. There is no public transport along this road, so travellers without a vehicle are better off heading to Busingiro in the Budongo Forest.

WHERE TO STAY For location of listings see map, page 401.

Kanyiyo Pabidi Tourist Site (5 cottages & dorms) ✆0414 267153; m 0772 426368; e info@ugandalodges.com; www.ugandalodges. com. Also known as Budongo Eco Lodge, this long-running & perennially rundown NFA forest tourism site enjoyed an extremely effective makeover, courtesy of the Jane Goodall Institute & Disney, before being allocated to a private operator. Dark, clammy cement *bandas* are now very much out, & clean, light & comfortable prefabricated timber cabins are in. Spacious s/c dbl rooms (transformed into family units by fold-out sofa beds) & dormitories are supplied with hot showers & light by solar-powered systems. Evening meals are prepared in a smart modern kitchen & served in a new reception/dining/veranda building provided with informative wall-mounted exhibits. *US$66/110/128 sgl/dbl/trpl cabins & US$22 dorm beds B&B.*

Boomu Women's Group (5 *bandas*) m 0772 448950 (owing to poor reception, it's best to SMS); e boomuwomen'sgroup@yahoo. com; www.boomuwomensgroup.org. Traditional accommodation & experiences don't come any more authentic than those provided by the Boomu women. Their small tourism project is located at Kichumbanyobo, 8km from the Kayiyo Pabidi tourism site & just outside the main Murchison Falls National Park Entrance Gate in a traditional (ie: potentially muddy) homestead setting brightened by flowers & shrubs. (*Meals cost Ush10,000.*) Accommodation is provided in small, simple & spotless thatched *bandas*. The objective is to provide visitors with insights into rural Ugandan life, & an interesting variety of activities & demonstrations are provided. Boomu is a reassuring backup for backpackers trying to hitch a ride up to Paraa or Kanyiyo Pabidi: if transport is not forthcoming you can at least find a bed & learn how to weave a basket. *US$8pp beds, US$2.50pp camping.*

WHAT TO SEE AND DO (*Bookings for Kaniyo Pabidi are handled by Great Lakes Safaris; see page 76*) The 07.30 three-hour **chimp walk** currently costs US$60 for foreign non-residents and US$45 for foreign residents – though the fee excludes park entrance it remains considerably cheaper than the same activity in Kibale National Park. A more exclusive option is chimp habituation where you and a single companion can accompany the field researchers and habituators to experience a full day (minimum six hours, starting at 07.00) of chimpanzee activity. At the time of writing, rates were US$150 per person per day (maximum two people). A full day's birding walk costs US$20 per person, four-hour forest walks to Pabidi Hill viewpoint cost US$20, and 1½-hour walks cost US$15. One of the latter routes passes what is said to be the oldest (300 years old) mahogany tree found in East Africa. It's certainly the largest I've seen standing in Uganda. Note that habituators must be at least 18 years old, children over 15 years pay the adult price and children under ten are not permitted on walks exceeding two hours' duration. Low season discounts are offered for chimp tracking.

MASINDI TO MURCHISON VIA LAKE ALBERT

Although most organised tours favour the direct route between Masindi and Paraa, the longer alternative via Lake Albert is one of the most scenic roads in Uganda, with a number of possible diversions along the way. Foremost among these – and covered under a separate heading above – is the Busingiro Tourist Site in Budongo Forest (see pages 390–2), well worth visiting even if you have no intention of going on to the national park.

GETTING AROUND The 135km road between Masindi and Murchison Falls via Lake Albert is unsurfaced in its entirety and the journey takes about four hours. Follow the Hoima Road out of Masindi for about 3km until the tarmac reverts to *murram*. At this point, turn right on to the *murram* road to Bulisa. The next major landmark, 43km out of Masindi, is Busingiro Tourist Site in Budongo Forest (see pages 390–2), while another 10km past Busingiro a secondary road branches to the south at Biso, leading to Kigorobya (the turning for the Kibero Salt Gardens) and Hoima.

Beyond Biso, the road snakes down the Butiaba Escarpment on to the Rift Valley floor – baboons are usually present in this area, and the view across Lake Albert to the Blue Mountains of the DRC is stunning. At the base of the escarpment a left turn leads west to the lakeshore port of Butiaba (see box below) while the main road continues north, running roughly parallel to the Lake Albert shore through

HEMINGWAY AT BUTIABA

You'd scarcely credit it today, but back in the colonial era, the port of Butiaba – situated on the lakeshore 8km west of the Masindi–Bulisa road – was a commercial centre of some significance. In the 1920s, the colonial government earmarked the existing administrative station – contemporaneously described by Etta Close as 'a few native huts, an Indian store, and three little European houses by the edge of the water' – for a major harbour development. A regular steamer service was established out of Butiaba, effectively extending the existing import–export route between Masindi and Mombasa further west, to the Congolese port of Mahagi and to Nimule on the Sudanese border.

Butiaba's stock rose further in 1931, when it was selected as a landing site for the first seaplane flights between Cairo and East Africa. Over the subsequent decade, it also became something of a tourist focus, after a freshly dredged channel through the Victoria Nile estuary allowed boats from Butiaba to divert to a landing point a short distance downstream of Murchison Falls. During the production of the classic Bogart/Hepburn movie *The African Queen*, a boat called the *Murchison* was chartered by director John Huston to carry supplies and run errands between Butiaba and the nearby filming location.

Butiaba's celebrity connections don't end with Bogart and Hepburn. The American writer Ernest Hemingway and his fourth wife Mary Welsh arrived there on 23 January 1954, somewhat the worse for wear after a bruising 24-hour trip to Murchison Falls. The day before, their chartered Cessna had dipped to avoid hitting a flock of birds, in the process clipping a wing on an abandoned telegraph wire, and forcing a crash landing in which Hemingway dislocated his right shoulder and Mary cracked several ribs. The injured passengers and their pilot spent the night huddled on the riverbank below Murchison Falls, to be rescued the next morning by a boat headed to Butiaba.

At Butiaba, Hemingway chartered a De Haviland to fly him and his wife back to Entebbe the next morning. On take-off, however, the plane lifted, bumped back down, crashed, and burst into flames. Mary and the pilot escaped through a window. Hemingway, too bulky to fit through the window and unable to use his

the Bugungu Wildlife Reserve for 40km, to the small trading centre of Bulisa. From Bulisa, the road continues north for 6km to terminate at the lakeshore port of Wanseko. Those heading for Murchison Falls, however, must turn right at Bulisa (clearly signposted), from where it's another 20km to Bugungu Entrance Gate (passing the turn-off to Murchison River Lodge along the way). About 5km after entering the national park, the road from Bulisa connects with the direct road from Masindi, roughly 8km south of Paraa.

BUGUNGU WILDLIFE RESERVE This small reserve protects an area of savanna and seasonal swamp lying at the base of the Rift Valley Escarpment to the west of Murchison Falls National Park. It supports many of the same species as the neighbouring national park, with an estimated 1,200 head of oribi and 600 Uganda kob as well as substantial populations of leopard, buffalo, warthog, hippo, reedbuck, sitatunga, waterbuck, bushbuck, dik-dik, black-and-white colobus and baboon. Roughly 240 bird species have been recorded, including Abyssinian ground hornbill, shoebill and saddle-billed stork. There are no tourism facilities at present (a basic campsite seems to have closed down).

dislocated arm, battered open the buckled door with his head, to emerge with bleeding skull and a rash of blistering burns. The battered couple were driven to Masindi to receive medical attention and spent a few days recuperating at the Masindi Hotel. On 25 January 1954, the *Daily News* broke the news of the accident under the headline 'Hemingway Feared Dead in Nile Air Crash'. A spate of premature obituaries followed before it was discovered that the writer had survived, if only just.

Hemingway had, in addition to the dislocated arm and several first-degree burns, limped out of the burning plane with a collapsed intestine, a ruptured liver and kidney, two crushed vertebrae, temporary loss of vision in one eye, impaired hearing, and a fractured skull. In October of that year, he was awarded the Nobel Prize in Literature, but was too battered to attend the ceremony. Nor did he have the energy to work the 200,000 words he wrote on safari into publishable shape – an edited version finally appeared in 1999 under the name *True at First Light*. It is widely asserted, too, that the injuries Hemingway sustained at Butiaba sparked the gradual decline in his mental well-being that led ultimately to his suicide in 1961.

In 1962, coincidentally the same year that Uganda gained independence, unusually heavy rains caused the level of Lake Albert to rise by several metres overnight, sinking all of the ships in Butiaba harbour and leaving much of the town submerged. The port was officially abandoned in 1963, never to be redeveloped. Today it is little more than an overgrown fishing village. The airstrip where Hemingway so nearly died in 1954 still flies a windsock, but it sees little aerial activity other than ducks and herons flapping overhead. There is now little other evidence of Butiaba's former significance. Until very recently, it made an interesting detour from the Masindi–Bulisa road to walk between rusting iron derricks and other dockyard machinery on the weed-ravaged quay to the listing wreck of the SS *Coryndon* (named after Sir Robert Coryndon, Governor of Uganda 1918–22), which foundered during the floods of 1962. Sadly, indeed disgracefully, these historical artefacts have all been dismantled for scrap metal during the past year.

10

WANSEKO Situated 6km north of Bulisa, where the Nile Estuary opens into Lake Albert, Wanseko is a hot, dusty fishing village whose Wild West feel is compensated for by some impressive views across the lake to the Congolese Blue Mountains, and the estimable virtue of not being Bulisa. Definitely worth a look are the reed beds near the estuary, only a few minutes' walk from town, and home to the odd hippo or crocodile as well as a profusion of birds, notably crowned crane and, with a bit of luck, shoebill. The only reasonable place to stay is the **Wanseko Deluxe** (*Ush40,000 simple s/c sgl+*), 200m before the ferry landing. Fishing boats and a daily vehicle ferry run between Wanseko and Panyimur on the northern shore of Lake Albert – for details of this trip, see page 419.

MURCHISON FALLS NATIONAL PARK AND LAKE ALBERT

(*The standard UWA fees for a Category A protected area are levied for Murchison Falls; see pages 32–3*) Uganda's largest protected area, the 3,840km² Murchison Falls National Park lies at the core of the greater Murchison Falls Conservation Area, which also embraces the Bugungu and Karuma wildlife reserves and the Budongo Forest. Gazetted in its modern form in 1952, the national park previously formed part of the Bunyoro Game Reserve, which was proclaimed in 1910 following the evacuation of the local human population during a sleeping-sickness epidemic. During the Amin era, Murchison Falls was officially re-christened Kabarega Falls, after the former king of Bunyoro, a name that still appears on some maps of Uganda,

PETROLEUM IN UGANDA

The presence of oil beneath the Albertine Rift Valley has long been suspected: the first report on the subject, *Petroleum in Uganda,* was completed by E J Wayland in 1927. Eighty odd years later, it became official when, in 2006, test drilling programmes found significant reserves of oil in the Lake Albert–Edward basins along the Uganda–Congo border. These may contain in excess of a billion barrels of stuff suitable for diesel, paraffin and aviation fuel (but not petrol). Reaction to the news varies widely, from joy to deep concern. If effectively utilised, revenue from oil could do much for Uganda, improving the substandard services that hinder development and ushering in a new age of investment and economic activity. On the other hand, if clumsily implemented, Uganda's fistfuls of oil dollars could be gained at the expense of those generated by tourism (a useful US$800m in 2011). The catch is that the oil deposits are clustered beneath western Uganda's primary tourism destinations, most notably the Murchison Falls and Queen Elizabeth national parks. It is unfortunate, though perhaps understandable, that the Uganda government does not consider internationally recognised protected area status an insurmountable obstacle. The neatest but most drastic solution mooted involves excising the oil-rich sectors from the protected areas. This possibility has given rise to tremendous concern from the tourism industry as well as environmentalists – though interestingly it has failed to ignite public passion in the fashion of the Mabira Forest debacle of 2007 (see page 27). The supposed sanctity of protected areas apart, apprehension is founded on the fact that (within a conservation area exceeding 5,000km²!) Murchison's oilfields are found in the Paraa and Buligi areas where the park's wildlife, tourism activity and investment are also concentrated, while those in Queen Elizabeth National Park lie below the fabulous wilderness of Ishasha. UWA, fortunately, does not seem prepared to

even though it fell into official and vernacular disuse soon after Amin departed the country. But, whatever you elect to call it, Murchison Falls – the wide, languid Nile being transformed into an explosive froth of thunderous white water as it funnels through a narrow cleft in the Rift Valley Escarpment – is easily the most impressive sight of its type in East Africa.

Spanning altitudes of 619m to 1,292m, Murchison Falls National Park is low lying by Ugandan standards, and of those parts of the country that are regularly visited by tourists, it is the only one that regularly becomes stiflingly hot. The average annual rainfall of 1,085mm, though significantly lower than in the forests of the southwest, compares favourably with most other East African savanna ecosystems. The Victoria Nile, flowing in a westerly direction between Lake Kyoga and Lake Albert, divides the park into two roughly equal parts. North of the river, the vegetation broadly consists of tall, green grassland interspersed with isolated stands of borassus palms, acacia trees and riverine woodland. South of the river, the park is characterised by denser woodland, giving way in the southeast to closed canopy forest around Rabongo Hill, the highest peak in the park.

In the 1960s, Murchison Falls – with its spectacular waterfall, prolific game and clutch of outstanding lodges – was universally regarded as one of East Africa's most compelling national parks. It was particularly renowned for its prolific elephant population: herds of 500 or greater were a common sight, and the total count of 14,500 was probably the densest on the continent. According to the 1969 census, the park also supported around 26,500 buffalo, 14,000 hippo, 16,000 Jackson's hartebeest,

allow an emergent oil industry to make free with, or within, its estate, and Moses Mapesa, UWA's executive director, assures me that 'degazettement' is not an option. Nevertheless, exploration will go ahead, with up to ten wells being sunk by Heritage Oil at the western end of Murchison Falls and six in and around Ishasha. UWA is insisting on stringent measures to limit impacts on the environment, wildlife and tourism. Environmental Impact Assessments stipulate that drilling in each location will be phased, a single vehicle-mounted rig (one-third the height of the usual 50m structure) being moved between sites and timed to limit activity during high tourist seasons. My own view has been that Murchison is quite large enough to absorb any adverse visual effects from the exploration programme (it is 30km from Paraa to the peninsula's extremity at Delta Point) and this was borne out on my most recent visit.

Of far greater concern than these short-lived drilling sites is what will happen in the long term. As yet, it's pointless to speculate on how oil will be extracted, transported and refined until the results of the exploration are known. In the meantime, there is fervent hope that future operations are also carried out by a company from North America or Europe, rather than a part of the world not renowned for environmental sensitivity or accountability.

There are also international issues to consider. The Rift Valley drains directly into the Nile, a river subject to international treaties and which Sudan and Egypt would not wish diluted with spilled oil. Secondly, since the Uganda–Congo border runs along the Rift Valley, some reservoirs beneath Murchison, Ishasha and also Lake Albert will certainly be shared between these two countries. Exploration in Uganda is keenly monitored by Congo which will certainly wish to share in the rewards from extraction along the common border.

30,000 Uganda kob and 11,000 warthog, as well as substantial populations of Rothschild's giraffe and both black and white rhinoceros, the last introduced from the West Nile in the early 1960s. Ironically, in hindsight, the main conservation issue associated with Murchison Falls in the 1960s was overpopulation, particularly of elephant, and associated environmental destruction – indeed the authorities opted to cull some 3,500 elephants and 4,000 hippos during the last years of the decade.

SECURITY IN MURCHISON FALLS AND NORTHERN UGANDA

Murchison Falls borders the historically volatile north of Uganda, the area plagued by the Lord's Resistance Army rebellion for 20-odd years, and both the national park and the roads approaching it were subject to sporadic security problems throughout this time. The original Paraa, Chobe and Pakuba lodges and the park headquarters at North Paraa were all destroyed by bandits/rebels in the late 1980s. The national park north of the Nile was declared unsafe, as park management relocated their offices to South Paraa and tourism facilities were scaled down from the three grand lodges to a cluster of mud huts on the site of the present Red Chilli Rest Camp. As security improved during the 1990s, Paraa Lodge and the Buligi game tracks were reopened and a basic tourist rest camp (now Red Chilli Rest Camp) was built at South Paraa. There have, however, been sporadic incidents since then. In 1996, the park closed briefly when clashes between Joseph Kony's Lord's Resistance Army and the military spread across its boundaries. Then, in March 2001, a student party was ambushed by rebels a few kilometres north of Paraa. Jimmy Sekasi, the college principal, ten of his students and a ranger were killed. Though security was beefed up to make the Buligi area safe (there is a military detachment near Paraa) the vast northeastern sector remained off-limits. The danger in this area proved very real in November 2005 when Steve Willis, the owner of the Red Chilli Rest Camp, was shot dead by rebels – or bandits – in northeastern Murchison whilst evacuating a rafting expedition that had got into trouble on the river above Murchison Falls.

Today, there is every reason to think that the north of Murchison Falls National Park is permanently safe. The US Embassy and the British High Commission have both removed the park and northern Uganda (with the exception of Karamoja in the northeast) from their travel advisories. Visitors can now drive directly to the park from Gulu – a ridiculously risky action a few years ago – while a restored Chobe Lodge, located in the historically dangerous eastern sector, opened its doors in 2010, and a budget backpacker camp – Murchison Falls Safari Lodge – has appeared near Purongo on the Karuma–Pakwach road. In the fifth edition of this book, we hoped that 'peace talks between the government and the rebels of northern Uganda [would] make the need for such a text box redundant'. Indeed, there is a strong case for removing it from this seventh edition as for several years now, travel in Murchison Falls National Park and northern Uganda has been no more dangerous than anywhere in Africa, and considerably safer than many places. You need only take the same sensible precautions that you would if travelling independently anywhere in Africa. Avoid travelling at night and keep aware of the security situation by talking to people and enquiring at police posts if uncertain. Yet this history still appears, in greatly condensed form, with a new purpose: no longer to warn but rather to remember.

Murchison Falls remained a popular tourist draw in the early days of the Amin regime, but the gates closed in September 1972 when foreign visitors were banned from Uganda. Within a couple of years, conservation activities within the national park had practically ceased, making its wildlife easy prey for commercial and subsistence poachers. In 1980, a year after Amin was ousted, aerial surveys indicated that the number of elephants and hippos had been reduced to around 1,400 and 1,200 respectively, while buffalo and other large-mammal populations stood at half of what they had a decade earlier. During the turbulent 1980s, the slaughter continued unabated, as a succession of military factions occupied the park and treated it as a moving larder. By 1990, fewer than 250 elephant and 1,000 buffalo survived; the hartebeest and kob herds had plummeted to around 3,000 and 6,000 respectively; rhinos and African hunting dogs had been hunted to local extinction; and the dwindling populations of giraffe and lion threatened to go the same way. Meanwhile, the combination of declining tourist arrivals and ongoing guerrilla activity had rendered all three of the park's lodges inoperative.

This downward trend was reversed in the early 1990s, and although wildlife populations have yet to re-approach their pre-Amin highs, nobody who has visited the park regularly over the past decade will be in doubt as to the steady and significant growth in animal numbers. A 2010 survey suggested that buffaloes numbered over 9,000 and elephants over 900. The latter figure is in fact a cause for concern being a couple of hundred fewer than recorded ten years ago. Though the park contains plenty of forests and dense bush to frustrate elephant surveys, Murchison, like many other African wildlife reserves, has suffered a recent resurgence in poaching. Nevertheless, Murchison also contains obviously healthy populations of kob, hartebeest, oribi and giraffe, the numbers of which have doubled or even trebled in the last twenty years. Particularly pleasing has been a sudden explosion in the lion population: scarce and skittish into the late 1990s, lions are now readily located on the plains north of the Nile, and it has been credibly estimated that the park supports a healthy population of 150–200 lions across some 15–20 prides.

In total, 76 mammal species have been recorded in Murchison Falls. Aside from those species already mentioned, bushbuck, Defassa waterbuck, Bohor reedbuck, oribi, warthog and side-striped jackal are frequently observed on game drives, as are vervet monkey and olive baboon. Also present on the plains, but less frequently observed, are leopard, spotted hyena and the localised patas monkey. The Rabongo Forest harbours black-and-white colobus, chimpanzees and other forest primates. The bird checklist of 460 confirmed and 19 unconfirmed species is headed in desirability by the shoebill, most common along the stretch of river between Nile Safari Camp and the estuary into Lake Albert. Many other water-associated birds are prolific along the river, while raptors make a strong showing on the checklist with 53 species recorded.

Paraa, situated alongside the Nile a few kilometres downriver of Murchison Falls, is the focal point of tourist activities in the national park. All access roads leading into the park converge at Paraa, where a regular motor ferry provides the only means of crossing between the northern and southern banks of the Nile within the park. The popular launch trip to the base of the falls departs from Paraa, as does the main game-viewing circuit north of the river. Paraa is also the site of Paraa Safari Lodge, on the north bank of the river, while the budget Red Chilli Rest Camp faces it on the south bank. Sambiya Lodge lies 30 minutes south of Paraa while Murchison River Lodge and Nile Safari Camp lie just outside the park boundary, 20 minutes distant. An old lodge at Chobe, which was trashed in the pre-Museveni era, has been resorted and it reopened in 2011.

All visitors who stay at Paraa Safari Lodge or do a game drive north of the Nile will need to make use of the motor ferry at Paraa, which takes about five minutes to cross the river. The UWA state that the ferry makes the return trip between South and North Paraa once an hour on the hour between 07.00 and 19.00, except at 09.00, 13.00, 15.00, 17.00 and 18.00. The 19.00 crossing is for visitors resident in the park and not for transit vehicles. This timetable is subject to change so check in Masindi or at the entrance gates before heading for a specific crossing. Anybody who plans on taking the last ferry of the day, at 19.00, or who urgently needs to cross at a specific time, should be ready and waiting at the jetty about ten minutes ahead of schedule. Paraa Lodge has a small boat which can ferry late-arriving guests across the river (minus vehicle) from South Paraa. Don't race to get a particular ferry; the road surface in the park is loose and gravelly and it is easy to lose control of a vehicle. A daily fee of Ush20,000 per vehicle and Ush2,000 per passenger, driver, or pedestrian is charged to use the ferry, good for as many scheduled crossings as are made on that day. No fee is charged for taking motorbikes or bicycles on the ferry. Unscheduled crossings can be arranged, but at a cost of Ush100,000.

FURTHER READING Shaun Mann's 36-page *Guide to Murchison Falls National Park and the Surrounding Game Reserves* (1995, revised in 2004) is an exemplary booklet with good ecological and historical coverage of the national park. It also includes a pull-out checklist of birds and mammals. The booklet costs Ush10,000 and can be purchased at the UWA office in Kampala, occasionally in the national park office in Masindi, and sometimes even in the national park itself. Sheet 8 in the 'Uganda Maps' series contains maps of the national park and Buligi game tracks plus a wildlife checklist and general information.

GETTING THERE AND AWAY
Self-drive
Southern approaches Most travellers heading to Murchison Falls from Kampala will first drive to Masindi, which usually takes about three hours (see pages 385–6). From Masindi there is a choice of two different routes to Paraa. The direct route is 85km long and can be covered in two to three hours, depending on road conditions. The more scenic 135km route via Lake Albert (see pages 393–4) can take up to five hours. Both routes are generally in fair condition, but sections become muddy after heavy rain. If you are heading to Paraa or Sambiya Lodge, the direct route is definitely the best choice from a practical point of view. Heading to the cluster of accommodation outside the Mubako Gate, it doesn't make a great deal of difference which route you take, though unless you intend to visit locations within the park on the same day, you will avoid paying park fees for that day by using the Bulisa route. Though there is a fuel station at Bulisa, it would not be prudent to rely on it so fill up at Masindi. Petrol and diesel are available from the garage at Paraa Safari Lodge, though at a higher price than in Masindi.

Northern approaches Murchison Falls can be approached from three locations north of the Nile. The closest to Kampala and Gulu is the Chobe Track which turns off the Gulu road, 2km north of Karuma Bridge and immediately

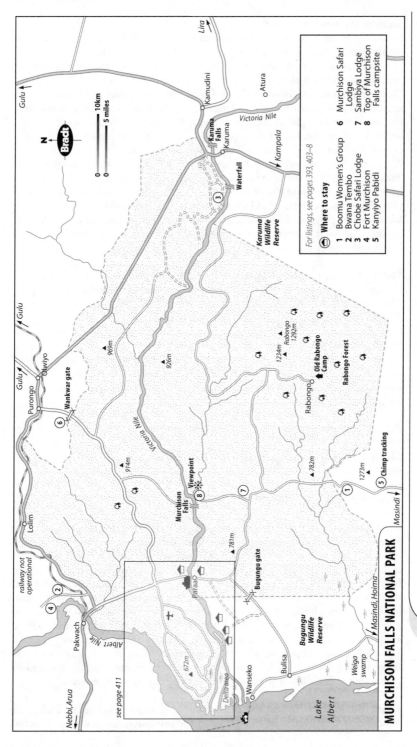

MURCHISON FALLS NATIONAL PARK

For listings, see pages 393, 403–8

ⓘ **Where to stay**

1 Boomu Women's Group
2 Bwana Tembo
3 Chobe Safari Lodge
4 Fort Murchison
5 Kanyiyo Pabidi
6 Murchison Safari Lodge
7 Sambiya Lodge
8 Top of Murchison Falls campsite

south of the junction with the surfaced road. Chobe Gate lies 18km along this track, immediately before the refurbished Chobe Safari Lodge. It is possible to continue along the Chobe Track to Paraa (95km) but the first 40km of the route are heavily wooded. In addition to being monotonous and poor for game viewing, it is tricky country in which to bypass the trees commonly pushed over by elephants. Most drivers travelling between Chobe Lodge and Paraa prefer to backtrack to the tarmac and follow the Pakwach road to either Wankwar or Tangi gates. Wankwar is the best option for sighting game on the way; this gate lies 10km south of Purongo which is 58km along the Pakwach road. If speed is of the essence, follow the tarmac for a further 53km to the Tangi Gate turning, just before Pakwach Bridge. At present, the optimum route to the park from Gulu follows the Kampala and Pakwach roads. This roundabout approach will be simplified when a bumpy 60km back road between Gulu and Olwiyo (2km from Purongo) is widened and surfaced (10km have been completed as I write). This development will bring the game-rich Wankwar-Purongo section of Murchison Falls National Park within an hour's drive of Gulu – an exciting prospect, not least for the management of Murchison Safari Lodge just outside Wankwar Gate!

Tours Organised tours to Murchison Falls can be organised from any tour agent in Kampala (see pages 75–6). The Kampala-based **Red Chilli Hideaway** (see page 156) runs budget excursions for backpackers to the Red Chilli Rest Camp at Paraa. A typical trip includes return transport, park entrance, game drive, launch trip on the Nile and visit to the Top of the Falls viewpoint and costs US$280 per person. This has the added bonus of departing the park through the game-rich Wankwar sector on the north side of the Nile (rather than returning back down the bushy road to Masindi), and a visit to Karuma Falls. The noticeboards at Red Chilli and Kampala Backpackers may advertise other options or carry notices from travellers seeking to form a group for a trip.

Public transport Travellers without private transport can reach Murchison Falls by a number of means. Inevitably, their goal will be Red Chilli Rest Camp at Paraa where the nearby river launch trip more than compensates for the lack of a game-viewing vehicle.

From Masindi via Kanyiyo Pabidi Forest
The standard procedure to reach Paraa from Masindi is to take a **special hire** from Masindi (*Ush140,000 upwards*). Alternatively contact Yebo Tours (see page 386) or New Court View Hotel (see page 386) in Masindi regarding **vehicle hire**. These options would give you the chance to detour to the Top of the Falls viewpoint. You could also ask about lifts at the national park's office in Masindi – a **national park vehicle** usually heads up from Masindi to Paraa a few times a week, most often leaving at around 14.00, and the driver will normally give travellers a lift, space permitting. More of a long shot, but by no means impossible, would be to try to **hitch** to Paraa from the junction opposite the Shell garage in Masindi – though do make sure that the vehicle will be going as far as Paraa to drop you at the rest camp. Incidentally, the managers of the Red Chilli Camp at Paraa, who have seen people arrive on moped and even bicycle boda-bodas from Masindi 85km away, suggest that this is *not* a sensible thing to do on account of buffalo and other potentially stroppy animals on the road.

From Masindi or Hoima via Bulisa
Public transport to Butiaba, Bulisa and Wanseko is straightforward enough using the **minibus-taxis** that leave Masindi

and Hoima throughout the day. All transport between Masindi and Butiaba or Wanseko will pass the Busingiro Tourist Site in Budongo Forest, but transport headed to Butiaba turns off the main road before passing through the Bugungu Wildlife Reserve and reaching Bulisa.

From Bulisa, you'll need to find other means of covering the last 20km to Murchison Falls National Park. The obvious strategy of hitching along the main road to the Bugungu gate is an uncertain one since most Paraa-bound traffic uses the direct route from Masindi while any tourist vehicles you see on the Bulisa route are most likely headed for the cluster of accommodation outside the park's Mubako Gate (which is essentially a back route into the UWA staff village). If you can get a lift this far, you can use nearby shoestring accommodation (see page 408) or trek to the gate to see if a **UWA vehicle** is heading from the village to Red Chilli at Paraa, 6km distant. Alternatively, don't leave your *matatu* at Bulisa but continue to Wanseko (see page 396) where you can take a boda-boda along a much shorter back route to Mubako. Be sure to distinguish between Mubako village outside the park and Mubako Gate/UWA village; the difference is a 4km walk.

Via Pakwach Entering Murchison from the north is also feasible. The Nile-side town of Pakwach lies on the Kampala–Arua **bus** route, has basic but acceptable accommodation (see page 420) and **special hire taxis** to take you into the park. I was quoted Ush240,000 (including vehicle entrance fee) for the return trip to Paraa for the launch trip – not too bad if shared between a group. Global Village Guesthouse in Pakwach (see page 420) has a proper, open-sided safari vehicle which costs Ush450,000/day including fuel and vehicle entrance into the park. If you set off early, the 24km drive through the park should provide a decent game drive on the way to connect with the morning **launch trip** at Paraa. You could also consider hopping off the **bus** 50km east of Pakwach at Purongo, 8km from the cheap Murchison Safari Lodge and 10km from the Wankwar Gate. Beyond lie some of the park's densest concentrations of game though you'd have to enquire at the lodge about how to reach them. In either case, assuming you manage to reach the Red Chilli Rest Camp at Paraa, you should be able to get a lift out to Masindi, or at the very least, to Mubako Gate.

By air Two airstrips are found close to Paraa: Bugungu on the south side of the river and Pakuba on the north. Another airstrip lies adjacent to Chobe Lodge in the northeast of the park. **Fly Uganda** (*www.flyuganda.com*) and **Aerolink** (*www. aerolinkuganda.com*) run scheduled flights to Murchison. As well as dodging the dull drive from Kampala, the flight also provides the thrilling prospect of viewing Murchison Falls from the air.

 WHERE TO STAY For location of listings see maps, pages 401 and 411.

Upmarket

🏠 **Nile Safari Lodge** (12 cottages/tents) 📞 0414 258273/0312 260758; e info@ geolodgesafrica.com; www.geolodgesafrica.com. Nile Safari Lodge is situated a short distance west of the park boundary on the southern bank of the Nile. The s/c standing tents, wooden cottages, & timber lodge buildings blend unobtrusively into the surrounding bush. All enjoy a great river view, as does a discreetly located swimming pool. Hippos, crocodiles & a variety of waterbirds can be seen on the river while the facing northern bank & mid-channel island is regularly visited by waterbuck & elephants. Nile Safari Lodge is particularly recommended to birders. Shoebills inhabit a mid-river island opposite the lodge, while a 1km guided walk through the adjacent riverine forest is likely to yield 30–40 bird species

10

in the space of an hour, & is perhaps the best place in East Africa for sightings of the localised white-crested turaco, red-headed lovebird & red-winged grey warbler. Nile Safari Lodge is 500m east of Murchison River Lodge, see directions for Murchison River Lodge on page 406. If using the shorter route from Masindi, turn left from the main road at the MRL signpost (1km before Paraa) & exit the park through Mubako Gate. A boat transfer can run you upriver to connect to the Paraa launches. *US$200/320 sgl/dbl FB, camping is also possible (see Shoebill Camp, page 408).*

🏠 **Chobe Safari Lodge** (63 rooms) ➘0312 260260/1; e mweyaparaa@africaonline.co.ug; www.chobelodge.co.ug. On my 1st visit to Chobe Lodge during a lull in rebel activity in 1999, the

IN SEARCH OF KING WHALE-HEAD

Perhaps the most eagerly sought of all African birds, the shoebill is also one of the few that is likely to make an impression on those travellers who regard pursuing rare birds to be about as diverting as hanging about in windswept railway stations scribbling down train numbers. Three factors combine to give the shoebill its bizarre and somewhat prehistoric appearance. The first is its enormous proportions: an adult might stand more than 150cm (5ft) tall and typically weighs around 6kg. The second is its unique uniform slate-grey colouration. Last but emphatically not least is its clog-shaped, hook-tipped bill – at 20cm long, and almost as wide, the largest among all living bird species. The bill is fixed in a permanent Cheshire-cat smirk that contrives to look at once sinister and somewhat inane, and when agitated the bird loudly claps together its upper and lower bill, rather like outsized castanets.

The first known allusions to the shoebill came from early European explorers to the Sudan, who wrote of a camel-sized flying creature known by the local Arabs as Abu Markub – Father of the Shoe. These reports were dismissed as pure fancy by Western biologists until 1851, when Gould came across a bizarre specimen amongst an avian collection shot on the Upper White Nile. Describing it as 'the most extraordinary bird I have seen', Gould placed his discovery in a monotypic family and named it *Balaeniceps Rex* – King Whale-Head! Gould believed the strange bird to be most closely allied to pelicans, but it also shares some anatomic and behavioural characteristics with herons, and until recently it was widely held to be an evolutionary offshoot of the stork family. Recent DNA studies support Gould's original theory, however, and the shoebill is now placed in a monotypic subfamily of Pelecanidae.

The life cycle of the shoebill is no less remarkable than its appearance. One of the few birds with an age span of up to 50 years, it is generally monogamous, with pairs coming together during the breeding season (April to June) to construct a grassy nest up to 3m wide on a mound of floating vegetation or a small island. Two eggs are laid, and the parents rotate incubation duties, in hot weather filling their bills with water to spray over the eggs to keep them cool. The chicks hatch after about a month, and will need to be fed by the parents for at least another two months until their beaks are fully developed. Usually only one nestling survives, probably as a result of sibling rivalry.

The shoebill is a true swamp specialist, but it avoids dense stands of papyrus and tall grass, which obstruct its take-off, preferring instead to forage from patches of low floating vegetation or along the edge of channels. It consumes up to half its weight in food daily, preying on whatever moderately sized aquatic creature might come its way, ranging from toads to baby crocodiles, though lungfish are especially favoured. Its method of hunting is exceptionally sedentary: the bird might stand semi-frozen for several hours before it lunges down with remarkable

3-storey, 50-room place was nothing more than a shell: doors, light switches, sinks ... *everything* ... had been looted or destroyed. In 2010, Chobe reopened its doors (or opened new ones, rather) to reveal a sumptuous, multi-million dollar restoration by Marasa, the owners of Paraa & Mweya lodges. The site was initially developed as a base for sport fishing but most visitors will consider the magnificent view sufficient incentive. The pools, dining veranda, rooms & tents all overlook the 500m-wide Nile as it rushes audibly between dozens of forested islands & over minor obstacles. Like its sister lodges, Chobe fits firmly into the 'hotel in the bush' category – its centrepiece is a superb tier of 4 swimming pools. Inevitably, many will feel that a hotel room,

speed and power, heavy wings stretched backward, to grab an item of prey in its large, inescapable bill. Although it is generally a solitary hunter, the shoebill has occasionally been observed hunting co-operatively in small flocks, which splash about flapping their wings to drive a school of fish into a confined area.

Although the shoebill is an elusive bird, this – as with the sitatunga antelope – is less a function of its inherent scarcity than of the inaccessibility of its swampy haunts. Nevertheless, BirdLife International has recently classified it as near-globally threatened, and it is classed as CITES Appendix 2, which means that trade in shoebills, or their capture for any harmful activity, is forbidden by international law. Estimates of the global population vary wildly. In the 1970s, only 1,500 shoebills were thought to exist in the wild, but this estimate has subsequently been revised to 10,000–15,000 individuals concentrated in five countries – Sudan, Uganda, Tanzania, DRC and Zambia. Small breeding populations might also survive in Rwanda and Ethiopia, and vagrants have been recorded in Malawi and Kenya.

The most important shoebill stronghold is the Sudd floodplain on the Sudanese Nile, where 6,400 individuals were counted during an aerial survey undertaken over 1979–82, followed by the inaccessible Moyowosi–Kigosi Swamp in western Tanzania, whose population was thought to amount to a few hundred prior to a 1990 survey that estimated the population to be greater than 2,000. Ironically, although Uganda is the easiest place to see the shoebill in the wild, the national population probably amounts to fewer than 1,000 birds, of which perhaps half are concentrated in the Kyoga–Bisina–Opeta complex of wetlands. For tourists, however, the most reliable locations for shoebill sightings are Murchison Falls National Park, Semliki Wildlife Reserve and the Mabamba Swamp near Entebbe – none of which is thought to hold more than a dozen pairs. Visitors to Uganda who fail to locate a shoebill in the wild might take consolation from the Wildlife Orphanage in Entebbe, where a few orphaned individuals are kept in a large aviary.

The major threat to the survival of the shoebill is habitat destruction. The construction of several dams along the lower Nile means that the water levels of the Sudd are open to artificial manipulation. Elsewhere, swamp clearance and rice farming pose a localised threat to suitable wetland habitats. Lake Opeta, an important shoebill stronghold in eastern Uganda, has been earmarked as a source of irrigation for a new agricultural scheme. A lesser concern is that shoebills are hunted for food or illegal trade in parts of Uganda. In the Lake Kyoga region, local fishermen often kill shoebill for cultural reasons – they believe that seeing a shoebill before a fishing expedition is a bad omen. As is so often the case, tourism can play a major role in preserving the shoebill and its habitat, particularly in areas such as the Mabamba Swamp, where the local community has already seen financial benefits from ornithological visits.

however beautifully restored & appointed, is not a conducive setting for communing with nature in a national park. Worry not! The main hotel is flanked by 2 luxurious tented camps in which you can commune to your heart's content. While both enjoy Nile views, 1 is right down by the river in the thick of the nocturnal hippo-grazing action. A golf cart will shuttle you safely between your tent & the main lodge. Chobe is accessed by a 18km track which leaves the Karuma–Gulu road about 2km north of Karuma Bridge. See advert in third colour section. *US$180/325 sgl/dbl rooms, US$220/350 sgl/dbl standard tents & US$300/390 sgl/dbl deluxe tents FB.*

🏠 **Paraa Safari Lodge** (54 rooms) ☎ 0312 260260/1; e mweyaparaa@africaonline.co.ug; www.paraalodge.com. Sister to Chobe Safari Lodge in the northeast of Murchison Falls National Park, Paraa Lodge is situated on the north bank of the Nile opposite the launch jetty. It was reconstructed in 1997 using the shell of an original lodge built in 1959 & gutted by bandits during the civil war. Architecturally, it is a double-storey monolith that in most respects wouldn't look out of place on a beach or in a city, although it sits more easily in its wilderness setting thanks to the extensive use of (now well-weathered) gumpole cladding. The grounds are dominated by a large & curvaceous swimming pool (free for guests, while passing bathers are discouraged by a US$25 fee) overlooking the Nile & the low hills beyond. The panorama is somewhat flat during the day, but low light & haze add depth at dawn & dusk. The 'hotel in the bush' genre has its critics, but the internalised hotel layout (& the superb pool) makes Paraa a reassuring choice for families with young children. The large, luxurious s/c rooms have AC & walk-in nets. All rooms have a private balcony facing the river; those upstairs enjoy the view while those downstairs are metres from the pool (try not to be booked into a rather isolated western block). There are 2 rooms for those with limited mobility, & one of the suites was occupied by the Queen Mother during a visit in 1959. Logistically, Paraa Lodge is the most convenient accommodation to combine game drives in the north with a launch trip to the base of Murchison Falls. See advert in third colour section. *US$151/232 sgl/dbl B&B, US$175/280 sgl/dbl FB, US$352 suite FB, Royal Cottage US$720 FB.*

Moderate

🏠 **Murchison River Lodge** (5 cottages, 3 tents) m 0714 000085/0782 007552; e bookings@murchisonriverlodge.com; www.murchisonriverlodge.com. This excellent new riverside lodge opened in late 2010 to fill the gap between the basic Red Chilli Rest Camp at Paraa & the neighbouring Nile Safari Camp. If anything, it exceeds this brief. The moderately priced s/c cottages are every bit as good as those in many supposedly 'upmarket' Ugandan lodges, while simpler accommodation caters for tighter budgets. The cool, thatched lodge building is a perfect spot to relax while enjoying the view of the Nile & whatever might be hanging about on the mid-river island. The spacious s/c thatched cottages each have a ground floor dbl bed & a mezzanine dbl above to cater for families – the appeal for families is enhanced by a swimming pool. A line of classic twin bed s/c safari tents face the river, while simpler furnished tents at the rear of the site use facilities in a palatial bathroom block. MRL is located just outside the park on the south bank of the Nile. To reach the lodge, drive 10km east from Bulisa before leaving the main road at Ngwedo village & following signposts for 12km. No park entry fees apply to this route. If using the shorter route from Masindi, turn left from the main road at the MRL signpost (1km before Paraa) & exit the park through Mubako Gate. See advert in fourth colour section. *US$140/200 sgl/dbl or twin share Family Cottages (additional adults US$75 each), US$250 family package (2 adults & up to 4 children), US$90/140 sgl/twin safari tents, US$45pp 'lazy camping'. All rates FB.*

🏠 **Fort Murchison** (12 rooms, 10 tents) ☎ 0312 294894; e booking@naturelodges.biz; www.naturelodges.biz. This new lodge on the east bank of the Nile, across from Pakwach, offers reasonably priced s/c rooms & standing tents with shared facilities. Architecturally, the place is inspired by the chain of riverside forts established by imperialists & traders along the Nile corridor. Looking out from a 1st-floor rooftop lounge, it doesn't take much imagination to picture General Gordon's exploratory flotillas of canoes & steamships coming into sight around the broad sweep of the Nile. A bold break from the usual safari style, the imposing storied gatehouse is a good take on a period etching of Emin Pasha's

The most spectacular lodge in the country...

Beautiful Crafts
African Style

Supporting craftsmen and women
throughout Uganda

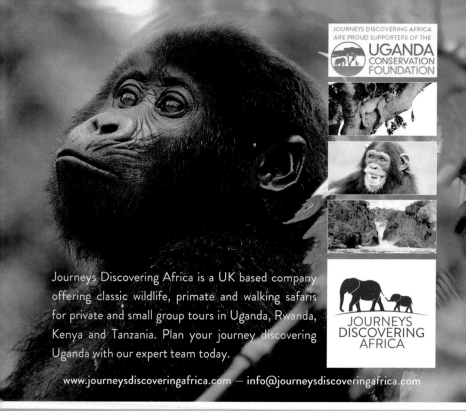

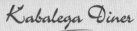

Dufile Fort while the s/c rooms are what you imagine the Pasha might have aspired to. I doubt very much whether his cook managed dinners of such excellence or indeed, in such generous quantities. To reach the lodge, turn north for 3km from the Karuma–Pakwach road, about 2km east of Pakwach bridge & 1km east of MFNP's Tangi Gate. Very good value. *US$90/110 s/c sgl/dbl, US$25/40 tents, US$15 camping.*

🏠 **Bwana Tembo** (10 units) m 0791 217028/0772 957850; e davide_francescotours@yahoo.com; www.davidefrancescotours.com, www.davidefrancesocotours@yahoo.com. New, Italian-run camp in the same area as Fort Murchison (see above), but just 1km from the main road so very convenient for Tangi Gate. The round, s/c cottages are clean & comfortable, while some furnished s/c tents offer the safari touch. The Italian menu (with freshly made pasta) is reportedly quite excellent. *US$90/180 sgl/dbl cottages, US$80/160 sgl/dbl safari tents. For high season rates, add US$20.*

🏠 **Sambiya Lodge** (20 cottages) ✆ 0414 233596; e afritour@africaonline.co.ug; www.afritourstravel.com. This facility occupies a pleasant if low-key location in woodland off the Masindi–Paraa road, a few hundred metres from the turning to Murchison Falls. Accommodation is provided in cottages, some s/c & others with shared facilities. Sambiya is just 20mins' drive from the Top of the Falls (great for the sunset) & about 40mins from Paraa. A small swimming pool is provided. *US$155/220 sgl/dbl FB. Prices increase at Christmas/New Year & Easter.*

Budget (See also page 408.)

🏠 **Red Chilli Rest Camp** ✆ 0312 202903 (reservations); m 0772 709150 (camp), 0772 509150 (reservations); e reservations@redchillihideaway.com; www.redchillihideaway.com. A scion of Kampala's popular Red Chilli Hideaway, Red Chilli Rest Camp celebrated its 10th birthday with a memorable bash on 29 Sep 2012. Following this brief lapse in normal service, RCRC

THE BAKERS AT MURCHISON FALLS

Murchison Falls is first alluded to in the writings of Speke, who upon visiting Karuma Falls to the east in 1862 was told that a few other waterfalls lay downriver, mostly 'of minor importance' but 'one within ear-sound … said to be very grand'. Speke does not record the name by which this waterfall was known locally, but his guide did inform him that a few years earlier 'at the Grand Falls … the king had the heads of one hundred men, prisoners taken in war against Rionga, cut off and thrown into the river'. Two years later, partially to fulfil a promise they had made to Speke, Samuel and Florence Baker became the first Europeans to explore the stretch of river between Lake Albert and Karuma Falls. As they were paddling about 30km east of the estuary, Samuel Baker wrote:

We could distinctly hear the roar of water [and] upon rounding the corner a magnificent site burst upon us. On either side of the river were beautifully wooded cliffs rising abruptly to a height of about 300 feet [100m]; rocks were jutting out from the intensely green foliage; and rushing through a gap that cleft exactly before us, the river, contracted from a grand stream, was pent up in a passage of scarcely 50 yards [46m] in width; roaring furiously through the rock-bound pass, it plunged in one leap of about 120 feet [36m] perpendicular into a large abyss below. The fall of water was snow white, which had a superb effect as it contrasted with the dark cliffs that walled the water, while the graceful palms of the tropics and wild plantains perfected the beauty of the view. This was the greatest waterfall of the Nile, and in honour of the distinguished president of the Royal Geographic Society, I named it the Murchison Falls, the most important object through the entire course of the river.

continues to provide pocket-friendly bed & board in the heart of the park. Chilled drinks & meals (*Ush12,000*) are served in the welcome shade of a thatch restaurant, while accommodation is provided by a variety of *bandas* & tents boasting electricity, fans & mosquito nets. Though river views are rather distant, Red Chilli is just 700m from the South Paraa jetty, thus backpackers are 10mins' walk from the launch while motorised tourists are ideally placed for the early morning ferry across the Nile to the Buligi game tracks. Not that you need to go that far to find wildlife as the camp itself is frequented by warthog, bushbuck & a wide variety of birds. Chilli is frequently booked solid so try to reserve accommodation well in advance. *US$40 s/c twin banda, US$70 s/c family banda sleeps 5, US$25 twin banda with shared facilities, US$20 twin safari tents with shared facilities, US$5pp camping, US$2.50 tent hire. Rates excl food.*

⌂ **Murchison Safari Lodge** (6 units) www. murchisonsafarilodge.com. Allied to the Kampala Backpackers' Hostel, this basic facility stands just outside the northerly Wankwar Gate, close to the park's greatest concentrations of herbivores & the route to the northern side of Murchison Falls. The lodge is located 10km from Purongo, midway along the 110km tarmac highway between Karuma & Pakwach – that's a long way from any alternative accommodation, so be sure to book before travelling. *US$32 dbl bandas & US$16pp dorm tents B&B with shared facilities.*

Shoestring & camping
⌂ **Waterview Camp** (4 rooms) m 0777 605510/0775 484514. This no-frills (& no water

view either) option is located 1km outside Mubako Gate near Murchison River Lodge. The utilitarian accommodation is considerably costlier than the comparable twin *bandas* at Red Chilli – until you factor in the saving on the park entrance fee. *US$35/50 sgl/dbl B&B.*

⌂ **Yebo Tours Safari Camp** (4 rooms) Run by the Masindi-based Yebo Tours (see page 386); m 0701 637493; e yebotours2002@yahoo.com. Set back from the river, a couple of kilometres outside Mubako Gate & 8km from Paraa, this basic but pleasant set-up is conveniently located to minimise expenditure on park fees. Accommodation is provided in traditional thatched *bandas*, while a dining shelter provides much needed shade. Book in advance so they can turn the fridge on to cool the drinks. (*Meals cost Ush15,000.*) *US$30pp FB, US$10 camping.*

Å **Shoebill Camp** An extension of the upmarket Nile Safari Lodge, see page 403. This campsite stands on a plateau overlooking the Nile, 10mins' walk from the main lodge. The camping fee allows access to the lodge's bar, restaurant & swimming pool. Self-catering is permitted & camping costs are very reasonable. (*Meals cost Ush25,000 b/fast, Ush30,000 lunch & Ush38,000 dinner.*) *US$10pp.*

Å **Top of Murchison Falls** Visitors with a private 4x4 vehicle can pitch a tent at this secluded & little-used campsite a couple of hundred metres upstream from the waterfall. The site has a beautiful location above a natural pool that's apparently safe for swimming, & there's great birding – look out for the localised bat hawk towards dusk. *US$10pp.*

WHAT TO SEE AND DO For information on game viewing, see pages 412–13.

Activities
Nile launch trip The superb boat trip from Paraa to the base of the Murchison Falls is the park's most popular and longest-running attraction – the Queen Mother made an inaugural voyage in a spanking-new launch back in 1959. In addition to the stalwart UWA launches, two private companies, G&C Tours and Marasa (owners of Paraa Lodge), now also run a variety of craft on the river. Consequently, it is now easy to arrange voyages to meet your schedule and requirements. Keen photographers, for example, would certainly wish to leave slightly earlier in the morning and later in the afternoon than the UWA boats to capture the best light. On the way to the falls, the boats follow a stretch of the Nile with a compelling African atmosphere, fringed by borassus palms, acacia woodland and stands of mahogany. Game viewing is excellent – hippos in their hundreds, some of the largest crocodiles left in Africa, small herds of buffalo, waterbuck and kob, and as often as not giraffe,

bushbuck and black-and-white colobus. Elephant are frequently observed playing in the water, often within a few metres of the launch, and fortunate visitors might even see a lion or leopard.

The birdlife on the papyrus-lined banks is stunning, with the top prize being the shoebill, seen here less often than it is on the trip to the delta, but nevertheless a distinct possibility in the dry season. More certain to be seen are African fish eagle, Goliath heron, saddle-billed stork, African jacana, pied and malachite kingfishers, African skimmer, piacpiac, rock pratincole, black-headed gonolek, black-winged red bishop, yellow-mantled widowbird, yellow-backed weaver and, at the right time of year, a variety of migrant waders. The dazzlingly colourful red-throated bee-eater nests in sandbanks between Paraa and the falls, and is more likely to be seen here than anywhere in East Africa.

The **UWA's double-decker boats** have chugged up and down the river for decades and the long-serving guides and pilots are especially knowledgeable. The boats, which can carry 40 passengers, leave at 08.00 and 14.00 and take around three hours. See pages 32–3 for updated rates. At least ten paying passengers are required. **G&C Tours** (m *0773 897275/0702 152928;* e *murchisonboats@gmail.com; www.wildfrontiers.co.ug*) operate a small armada (comprising a 35-seater boat, two 14-seater craft (also with upper viewing platform) and two five-seater boats) from Paraa's south jetty that provides plenty of scope for flexibility. G&C boats depart for the falls daily at 09.00 and 14.30 subject to demand (*US$30pp*). Other options include fishing trips, scheduled (*US$50pp*) and private boat trips to the delta as well as sunset (*US$15*), sundowner (*US$25 with drinks*), breakfast (*US$25*) and wine and cheese (*US$60 per couple*) cruises. Minimum numbers apply. **Paraa Lodge** (m *0772 788880/0752 788880*) also runs a similar variety of trips using identical boats from the jetty on the north bank. Boats to the falls run at 08.30 and 14.30 and cost US$24 per person (subject to a minimum of seven people). The lodge also has a five-person speedboat for fishing trips.

Though the UWA guides are perhaps more experienced, the new craft are far more comfortable. Also, after a leisurely game-cruise upriver to the falls, they return more swiftly downriver to Paraa (a useful consideration if travelling with kids). All boats are provided with lifejackets and river guides.

Top of Murchison Falls Murchison Falls is an impressive sight from the boat, but for sheer sensory overload be sure to visit the viewpoint at the top of the falls. Though these exist on opposite banks of the river, the viewpoint on the south side is the only one worth visiting.

South bank viewpoint The viewpoint on the south side of the river is reached along a 15km road (with some steep sections that should be negotiated carefully) that branches north from the main Masindi–Paraa road, a few hundred metres from Sambiya Lodge. From a picnic site/parking area, a short footpath leads downhill to a fenced viewpoint at the waterfall's head. Only here can you truly appreciate the staggering power with which the Nile crashes through the narrow gap in the escarpment, not to mention the deafening roar and voluminous spray generated by the phenomenon.

From this main viewpoint, a longer footpath, perhaps 20 minutes' walking time, leads to the so-called **Baker's View** on a ridge looking directly towards Murchison Falls and the far broader Uhuru Falls a hundred or so metres to the north. Historical records suggest that this latter falls was an impermanent (possibly seasonal) feature until the great floods of 1962, since when it has been more or less constant, though still subject to dramatic variations in volume. The face-on view of the two cataracts – separated by a lushly forested hillock – is truly inspiring, but surpassed perhaps by following another footpath down to the base of the short gorge below the two waterfalls. If you want to check out all the viewpoints, allow at least two hours – ideally in the afternoon, when temperatures are lower and the sun is better positioned for photography. Another option, which requires a bit of planning, is to ascend from the Paraa launch a few hundred metres downstream and climb to the viewpoints. Alternatively, you could be driven to the top of the falls and walk down to be collected by the boat. In both cases, you'll pay for a ranger to escort you through the riverine forest between Baker's View and the landing point.

Though a ranger escort is advisable in the latter situation, there is not much wildlife in the vicinity of the falls and it is considered safe to walk unaccompanied between the various viewpoints. You may encounter troops of baboons and black-and-white colobus while the so-called 'bat cliff', immediately south of the main waterfall (visible from Baker's View), is worth scanning with binoculars for raptors and swallows. Wait around until dusk and you should also see some impressive flocks of bats emerging from the caves in this cliff, as well as a few bat hawks soaring around in search of a quick dinner. After dusk, the drive from the top of the falls back to the main road is particularly good for nocturnal birds. The spotted eagle owl is likely to be encountered on the road throughout the year, as – in season – are Africa's three most spectacular and distinctive species of nightjar: long-tailed (March–August), pennant-winged (March–September) and standard-winged (September–April).

North bank viewpoint In 2010, as part of mitigation measures relating to the oil exploration programme in the national park, Tullow Oil funded the reopening of a long dormant track to the northern side of Murchison Falls. Unfortunately, the reality of this northern viewpoint falls way short of expectations. In fairness, any northerly sighting of Murchison Falls is destined to compare poorly with the phenomenal view into the chasm from the south bank and indeed it does; the main waterfall is identifiable only by a distant plume of spray beyond the mid-river island. The main attraction for this new access route attaches to the prospect of visiting the comparably voluminous Uhuru Falls. But sadly, this secondary ambition is also thwarted as the flight of concrete steps that descends from the parking area terminates at a nondescript riverside spot in sight of neither waterfall. Though there is something to be said for the broadside-on sight of this huge, heaving torrent, this minor appreciation is tempered by the feeling that the folk waving cheerfully from the fabulous south bank viewpoint are laughing at you.

Don't write off this excursion entirely, however. Trails may eventually be opened to access Uhuru and the possibility of rebuilding the bridge across the gorge has also been raised. If this happens, the northern approach, with its magnificent variety of wildlife along the way, will become the preferred route. Until that time, though, it's a poor incentive for a three-hour round trip from Paraa. For what it's worth, it takes an hour to drive the 34km from Paraa, using the Wankwar track, to the turning to the Falls. It takes another 30 minutes to follow the 20km track to the 'viewpoint.'

Walking safaris (*US$15pp*) UWA has allocated a concession to run extended walking safaris within the park to **The Far Horizons** (*www.thefarhorizons.com*) but full details are yet to be confirmed. In the meantime, you can enjoy a short two-

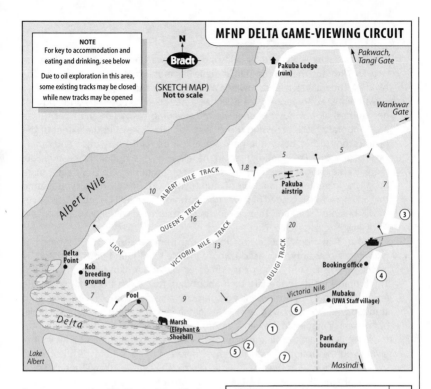

NOTE
For key to accommodation and eating and drinking, see below

Due to oil exploration in this area, some existing tracks may be closed while new tracks may be opened

N

(SKETCH MAP)
Not to scale

Pakwach, Tangi Gate

Pakuba Lodge (ruin)

Wankwar Gate

Albert Nile

ALBERT NILE TRACK   10   1.8

Pakuba airstrip

5   5

7   3

QUEEN'S TRACK   16

LION

VICTORIA NILE TRACK   13

BULIGI TRACK   20

Delta Point

Kob breeding ground

Booking office   4

Pool   7

9

Victoria Nile

Mubaku (UWA Staff village)

Delta

Marsh (Elephant & Shoebill)

6

1

Park boundary

5   2

7

Lake Albert

Masindi

hour taster with a UWA guide at Chobe in the northeastern corner of the park. The route explores riverine forest beside the Nile (a habitat you may share with hippo and buffalo) before entering open acacia grassland where giraffe are often found.

Forest walks (*Guided nature walks US$10pp*) **Rabongo Forest**, in the far southeast of the park, is reached

via a signposted and tsetse-infested road that branches from the main Paraa–Masindi road a few kilometres south of Sambiya Lodge. General forest walks at Rabongo are of interest mostly to birdwatchers, though black-and-white colobus and red-tailed monkeys are also likely to be seen, and the number and variety of butterflies is impressive. Frankly, there is better forest birding and a greater chance of seeing chimps at the more accessible Kanyiyo Pabidi (see page 392) on the Paraa–Masindi road.

Fishing There is good fishing along the Murchison Nile, with large Nile perch and tiger fish offering the main challenge. The record for rod and line in Murchison was established by Tim Smith in 2009. His mammoth catch weighed 113kg, eclipsing the previous official record of 73kg, set by C D Mardach in 1959 (though a fish landed in 2001, being too large for the available scales, was estimated at 106kg). Local fishermen have netted specimens weighing up to 160kg. You can fish from

10

The Delta Circuit is reached by following the Pakwach Road northwest from the jetty for 7km, and then turning left at the Te Bito crossroads (signposted to Pakuba Airstrip). The right turn leads towards Wankwar Gate and Chobe.

As I write, exploration of the Buligi area has been confused by a plethora of new routes, all obviously opened recently, leading off to left and right. These are temporary roads accessing the exploration sites assessing the extent of the hydrocarbon riches below the park. Since new oil routes may open and others close at any time, I'm ignoring them in the following description. To reassure you, there is little danger of getting lost since uncompromising 'No Entry' signs mark the oil tracks. As an additional rule of thumb, you won't go far wrong if you assume that any broad, well-graded highway not shown on the map ('Uganda Maps' Sheet 8) will be an oil road and that any narrow, rutted route will be an official game track (see box, pages 396–7).

About 3km from Te Bito crossroads, the road passes through a patch of whistling thorns, a type of acacia whose marble-sized round pods – aerated by insects – whistle softly when a wind comes up. About 3km further, the **Buligi Track** branches off to the left, then about 3km further on the road passes the fenced airstrip. The above roads pass through a scenic area of rolling grassland studded with tall borassus palms, where game concentrations are unpredictable, but generally highest in the rainy season.

About 2km past the airstrip, the road forks twice in the space of a kilometre, giving you the option of following three different tracks, all of which lead west towards the delta. For those with limited time, the central 10km **Queen's Track** is not only the shortest route, but also the smoothest, and generally the most productive for game viewing. The 12km **Albert Nile Track** to its north is in relatively poor condition, passing through patches of dense acacia woodland that will be as attractive to birdwatchers as they are, unfortunately, to tsetse flies. The 25km **Victoria Nile Track** to the south is far longer and game concentrations are generally low, except as it approaches the delta.

The three tracks converge on a grassy peninsula, flanked by the delta to the south and the Albert Nile to the north, and crossed by a network of interconnecting tracks that run through several kob breeding grounds. Large concentrations of Uganda kob are a certainty, as are family parties of Defassa waterbuck and the rather doleful-looking Jackson's hartebeest, as well as small groups of the dainty oribi. A striking feature of the area is its giraffe herds, which often number 50 or more, something I've seen nowhere else in Africa on a regular basis. Substantial

the banks below Murchison Falls or hire a boat from G&C Tours (see page 409). Paul Goldring, a keen fisherman and co-owner of G&C Tours is the best person to contact in this respect.

Paraa Museum The Jinja-based NGO Soft Power Education informs us that it is working with the UWA in Murchison Falls National Park to put together an 'international standard' museum at Paraa. Income from entrance fees, a coffee shop and craft sales will enable Soft Power to replicate its successful Jinja District education programme (see box, page 514) in parishes adjoining the national park. The museum, will occupy a restored building near the student education centre 500m past Paraa Lodge.

buffalo herds are also common around the delta, usually containing a few individuals whose colouration indicates some genetic input from the smaller, redder forest buffalo of West Africa. About 3km south of the main kob breeding grounds, the Victoria Nile Track runs adjacent to the delta for a few hundred metres – plenty of hippos around, and elephants are present practically from late morning until late afternoon.

The limitless supply of kob has attracted several prides of lion to the delta area. One of the best places to look for these languid predators is along an anonymous 2.5km track (marked **'lion track'** on the map) connecting the Albert Nile and Queen's tracks. At least one pride maintains an almost permanent presence in this area, often lying out in the open in the early morning and late afternoon, but generally retreating deep into the thicket during the heat of the day. The most reliable way to locate the lions is by observing the behaviour of the male kobs that always stand sentry on the edge of a herd. If one or two kobs persistently emit their characteristic high wheezing alarm whistle, they are almost certainly conscious that lions are around, so follow their gaze towards the nearest thicket. Conversely, should you hang around a kob herd for a few minutes and not hear any alarm calls, you can be reasonably sure that no lions are to be found in the immediate vicinity. The 'lion track', incidentally, is also a good place to look for the endearingly puppyish side-striped jackal, and troops of the localised and rather skittish patas monkey.

The delta area offers some great birdwatching. Noteworthy ground birds include the preposterous eye-fluttering Abyssinian ground hornbill, the majestic grey-crowned crane and saddle-billed stork, the localised Denham's bustard, the handsome black-headed and spur-winged lapwings, and the Senegal thick-knee. The tall acacia stands that line the Albert Nile Track, immediately north of the junction with Queen's Track, harbour a host of good woodland birds, including the rare black-billed barbet and delightfully colourful swallow-tailed, northern Carmine, blue-breasted and red-throated bee-eaters. Herds of grazers – in particular buffalo – are often attended by flocks of insectivorous cattle egret, piacpiac and red-billed and yellow-billed oxpeckers. An abundance of aquatic habitats – not only the rivers and lake, but also numerous small pools – attracts a wide variety of waterfowl, waders, herons and egrets, while the mighty African fish eagle and both species of marsh harrier are often seen soaring above the water. We've seen shoebill in flight at the part of the delta fringed by the Victoria Nile Track (referred to above), while the hippo pool about 1km further along the track evidently hosts a resident osprey.

Game viewing
Delta boat trip Though the boat trip is the highlight of most visits to Murchison Falls, the voyage downriver from Paraa towards the Lake Albert Delta is favoured by **birdwatchers**, since it offers one of the best opportunities to see shoebills anywhere in Africa, particularly during the rainy season. The two occasions on which I've done this trip yielded a total of eight sightings, but not everybody is so fortunate – one of the guides told me that he once took a visitor along this stretch of river on three successive days without luck. Without the shoebill as a motivating factor, the trip towards the delta is not as worthwhile as the one to the falls, since there is less wildlife to be seen and the general birding more or less duplicates what you would see from the launch.

Game drives (*The services of a ranger cost US$20*)

Buligi area The bulk of Murchison Falls' wildlife is concentrated to the north of the Nile, and the established area for game drives is a circuit of tracks within the Buligi area, an extensive promontory of grassland west of the Paraa–Pakwach road (see box, pages 412–13). Routes through this 40km² triangular area converge in the vicinity of Delta Point, a somewhat contrived destination at the spot (more or less) where the Victoria Nile flows into and out of Lake Albert as the Albert Nile. Though you may have wondered during the southern approach from Masindi whether the park contains any animals other than baboons, such suspicions will be well and truly laid to rest by the impressive concentrations of wildlife found around the delta. In the northern part of the game-viewing area, you'll find the derelict Pakuba Lodge on a low ridge enjoying a long view south down the Nile towards Lake Albert and the DRC mountains. This facility has had a yo-yo history: raised in the 1970s, it was razed by rebels in the 1980s. Another ascendant phase is imminent following the allocation of a concession for a 68-room hotel.

To reach the Buligi area from Paraa, turn left at Te Bito crossroads, 7km north of the ferry crossing. If arriving from Pakwach, you can turn right onto the Pakuba track, about 7km south of Tangi Gate.

North of Murchison Falls The established assumption that the Buligi area will throw up the best game viewing is actually being challenged by the area to the east of the Te Bito crossroads (coming from Paraa turn right at this junction). Off-limits for years due to the insecurity, interest in this area has recently been revived by access to the north side of Murchison Falls. Though the new viewpoint is sadly underwhelming, the drive is worthwhile for the fabulous amount of game along the way. Without looking particularly carefully, we passed groups of giraffe, elephant, buffalo, hartebeest, waterbuck, Uganda kob, oribi, duiker, warthog and a crocodile, the last in one of a series of newly created roadside waterholes, a full 15km from the river. A recommended stop on this road, just a few kilometres east of Te Bito crossroads, is the **Nyamsika Cliffs viewpoint**. Lions and buffaloes often come to drink at the river below, while the cliffs host seasonal colonies of several types of bee-eater, and the shallows are one of the few places in East Africa where the dashing Egyptian plover is frequently recorded.

Shortly before reaching Wankwar Gate, a right turn leads to Chobe Lodge, 53km away. Much of this route passes through woodland and, other than in scattered patches of open acacia woodland, little wildlife is seen. The same applies to the hinterland of the riverside Chobe Lodge. As a result, Chobe Lodge advises guests intent on a game drive to head back out to the tarmac and whizz along the Pakwach highway to re-enter the park through Wankwar Gate.

South of the river The combination of dense vegetation and low concentrations of wildlife mean that game viewing is generally poor south of the river. Nevertheless, there is a lovely open area along the Sambiya–Karuma road beyond the Rabongo turning where Uganda kob, Jackson's hartebeest, waterbuck, baboon and oribi may be encountered as – more occasionally – are elephant and lion. This road was renovated in 2012 and it is possible to drive all the way to the Gulu Road. If you do so, be aware that the drive takes at least two hours and the eastern section is monotonously bushy.

Practicalities It is permitted to drive in the main tourist areas of the park without an armed ranger, but there are several advantages in hiring one. They will generally know where the wildlife is concentrated at any given time, and are also adept at spotting well-camouflaged animals such as lion and leopard. Most of them are also very knowledgeable about animal behaviour. You won't get lost with a ranger either – a useful point since the clear network of tracks shown on park maps is sometimes confused by unmarked routes created to bypass seasonally boggy areas, and access kob breeding areas. Other new routes have been opened by oil exploration teams. Visitors should specify an ornithological bent in advance, since some of the rangers are extraordinarily knowledgeable about the local birdlife, others somewhat less so.

Travellers without their own transport can arrange game drives through **Red Chilli Rest Camp** (see page 407) or – more expensively – through **Paraa Safari Lodge** (m *0775 593123*, see page 406).

Experience the Elements of Nature

Rwenzori Mountains
National Park

Mabira Forest

Queen Elizabeth
National Park

Murchison Falls
National Park

GeoSafaris

We'll organize your tailor-made Safari in Uganda.

For Reservations:
reservations@geolodgesafrica.com
+(256) 414 258 273
www.geolodgesafrica.com

11

West Nile

On the map of Uganda, West Nile is the northwestern bulge beyond the Albert Nile. The only sizeable town is Arua (population 46,000), which lies close to Uganda's northwestern border with the DRC. In the south, the main towns are Pakwach, Panyimur and Nebbi, and in the north, Kiboko and Moyo.

Historically, this isolated chunk of territory beyond the Nile has always been somewhat separate from the rest of Uganda. In early colonial times, West Nile, though nominally part of Uganda, was administered by the Belgian Congo as the Lado Enclave. Though this situation ended in 1910, West Nile retains strong connections with the DRC, while only one bridge (at Pakwach) spans the Nile to connect the region with the rest of Uganda. Alternative river crossings are vehicle ferries at Panyimur on the northern tip of Lake Albert (see page 419), and Laropi in the far north (see pages 424–6). This sense of West Nile as a land apart is underscored by the region's best-known legend. This describes a feud between two sons of a Luo chief, which caused one to lead his people in an exodus into the lands beyond the river to found the Alur tribe of present-day Nebbi District (see page 419) – a Nilotic enclave in a region inhabited by Sudanese tribes.

West Nile's isolation is further compounded by bad press. In the United States, the province has become a household name thanks to a chance discovery by an arbo virologist, Dr Kenneth Smithburn, in 1937. After examining blood taken from a female patient he wrote: 'I have uncovered a new virus and called it West Nile Virus.' This was both unfortunate and unfair since the patient had emerged from the Wamba forests across the border in Congo. The fact remains that West Nile – and Uganda – is now forever associated with a nasty, mosquito-borne condition that causes inflammation of the brain and potentially, death. Initially, this association was no more than a curiosity when cases of West Nile Fever were rare. However, in recent decades the disease has spread far beyond equatorial Africa, with outbreaks occurring in Egypt in the 1950s, southern Russia in the 1960s and Israel in 1997. In 2012, West Nile virus was felling senior citizens across the southern states of the US.

Closer to home, Ugandans also associate the West Nile with death and suffering. As far as most citizens are concerned, it was responsible for giving the world Idi Amin Dada, Uganda's most famous son. Though it is not certain whether Amin was actually born in West Nile, he was certainly 100% West Niler, his mother hailing from Arua and his father from Kiboko. Though the people of West Nile enjoyed preferential treatment during the dictator's regime, his brutal excesses elsewhere exacerbated the region's isolation after his downfall. After the statutory reprisals from the 'liberating' army in 1979, West Nile was largely ignored and for many years, as far as most Ugandans were concerned, the region might as well still have been part of the Congo. For some 30 years after Amin's exit, few bothered to make the long, difficult and often dangerous journey to West Nile. Though the region was not directly involved in the Lord's Resistance Army (LRA) war, which is described in the following chapter, the route to West Nile passed through the conflict zone, discouraging casual and commercial visits and increasing the area's detachment. Rebel ambushes caused the closure of the Mbale–Pakwach railway and forced vehicle traffic along the notorious Karuma–Pakwach road to move in convoys with armed escorts. Others resorted to boats travelling between Wanseko in Bunyoro to Panyimur in West Nile – though for many the voyage in overcrowded fishing boats across the stormy tip of Lake Albert was no less terrifying. While the narrow track through Murchison Falls National Park latterly offered safe passage, it was unsuited for buses and large trucks. Trading with West Nile was simply too complicated and production of tobacco and cotton slumped, there being no point producing the stuff if nobody came to buy it. By 1996, revenue from cotton in Nebbi was half what it had been in the mid-1970s.

Happily, access has improved dramatically in recent years. Thanks to a continuous, 450km ribbon of tarmac, the journey between Kampala and Arua can now be made in a single day and the trip is even quicker on one of Eagle Air's scheduled daily flights from Entebbe. Most importantly, the route is safe to travel. Another cause for optimism is stability in Southern Sudan: West Nile is no longer a cul-de-sac but lies on the highway leading across the border to the regional capital of Yei. These developments represent opportunities but not, as yet, results and, compared with most other parts of Uganda, the northwest corner still remains extremely poor. Certainly in no other part of the country can you speed along a fine tarmac road lined by homes still predominately roofed with thatch instead of iron sheets; an unmistakable indicator of poverty and lack of economic opportunity.

As is the case throughout northern Uganda, tourism is unlikely to be the key to prosperity. Attractions are few. Though pretty enough, the regional town of Arua hardly justifies the long trip from Kampala, while the landscapes of the northwest cannot hold the proverbial candle to those in southwestern Uganda. The highlands west of Panyimur merit some exploration, but the only real drama lies in the **Moyo–Laropi hills** near the Sudanese border. Rather fortuitously, this area also contains West Nile's only cluster of tourist attractions, providing opportunities to visit the site of **Emin Pasha's fort** at Dufile, **sport fish** on the Nile, search for shoebills and other wildlife along the riverbanks, climb **Mount Otzi**, and hike and birdwatch in **Otzi Forest Reserve**. This apart, West Nile has the appeal of being a remote region distanced from any established tourism circuit. Moreover, what most struck the few people who visited this area in past times was the extreme friendliness of the people (and this in a country long renowned among travellers in Africa for its friendly people) and I can confirm that this is still the case.

GETTING TO WEST NILE/ARUA

Most travellers will enter West Nile by crossing the bridge at Pakwach. It is also possible to cross the river using **vehicle ferries** at Laropi (see pages 424–6), and between Wanseko and Panyimur (see opposite). If driving north from Kampala towards West Nile, ensure you have sufficient fuel to reach Pakwach. Beyond Byetale on the Kafu Bridge–Karuma road, your only option on the 150km drive to Pakwach is costly fuel in dirty jerrycans at Karuma Falls – and don't bank on detouring to Kamudini to find cleaner fuel either.

KARUMA FALLS TO ARUA VIA PAKWACH The simplest means of reaching Arua from Kampala is by following the excellent 450km tarmac road from Kampala, passing the Masindi/Murchison Falls junction at Kafu Bridge before crossing the Nile twice on the bridges at Karuma Falls and Pakwach.

From Gulu, head south towards Kampala and Karuma for 75km before turning left on to the 110km Pakwach road. Soon a 60km short cut will be possible between Gulu and Olwiyo which is halfway between Karuma junction and Pakwach; this rotten old goat track is currently being upgraded into a tarmac highway. Pakwach can also be reached from Murchison Falls National Park: the bridge is visible from the park's northeastern gate at Tangi, 24km north of Paraa.

The drive beyond Pakwach through Nebbi to Arua is interesting rather than scenic, and perhaps most notable for the immensity of the open spaces. Rocky, scrubby plains extend south and west towards distant mountains in the DRC, while to the east they merge into a distant, perfectly level horizon somewhere beyond the Nile Valley.

BUNYORO TO WEST NILE VIA LAKE ALBERT The southern route to West Nile uses a **vehicle ferry** across the northern tip of Lake Albert from Wanseko (page 396) to Panyimur. Ignore the large timetable sign suggesting that the ferry shuttles back and forth twice a day. It only does so on Saturdays since there is no service on Sunday. On other days, it leaves Wanseko at 07.00 and starts the return from Panyimur between 11.00 and noon. The Wanskeo landing is at the end of the road while the jetty at Panyimur is off a side turning, 500m south of the town. The crossing takes about two hours and is free.

If you're not constrained by a vehicle, **fishing boats** also travel throughout the day between Wanseko and Panyimur. Be warned: they are frequently crowded and overloaded and can sink during the tempests to which Lake Albert is particularly prone. Oil exploration workers at Kaiso-Tonya tell me that a few dozen people drown on the lake each month so you're strongly advised to stay put if there's any hint of an oncoming storm. The crossing between Panyimur and Wanseko costs US$3 and takes about one hour.

If you want to explore the Mount Erusi area or take the morning ferry to Wanseko you may want to spend the night in Panyimur. The best option appears to be the **Quality Guesthouse** (*US$5/7.50 basic sgl/twin rooms with shared facilities*) towards the southern end of the main street.

The simplest route from Panyimur to Arua heads north along a 30km *murram* road to join the tarmac Kampala highway just west of Pakwach. A more adventurous option is to follow a *murram* road west out of Panyimur up the northernmost remnant of the Rift Valley Escarpment. This steep climb provides good views of the higher Rift Valley wall as it follows Lake Albert's Congo shore south towards the 2,500m Mount Hoyo. The road then passes through a pretty, hilly and distinctly rural hinterland, reaching the small town of Parombo about an hour from Panyimur. The quicker route to Nebbi then heads north, reaching the main highway at Nyaravur 18km before Nebbi. Attractive pottery is sold by the roadside. The longer but considerably more scenic route passes around the 1,618m Mount Erusi before heading north towards the main road. Aside from being achievable in a private vehicle, my feeling is that this would be a great trip on a motorcycle, hot work on a bicycle and a real adventure/right chore using public transport, which consists mostly of pick-up trucks.

GULU TO WEST NILE An alternative route enters the extreme north of West Nile using the free **vehicle ferry** at Laropi (see pages 424–6), 20km north of Adjumani, to reach Moyo. From Karuma Bridge, it's a three- to four-hour drive, passing through Gulu, bearing left at Atiak and passing through Adjumani to reach the Laropi ferry.

The gateway to West Nile is perched on the west bank of the Albert Nile. Little more than a broad main street, Pakwach is primarily of interest to travellers as an economical staging point for a visit to Murchison Falls National Park (see pages 396–415). As yet, however, this potential is little exploited and Pakwach's meagre wealth is generated from the sale of snacks to bus passengers, cheap rooms to truck drivers, and crude wooden carvings of local fauna to anyone. Do consider buying a wooden tortoise: as well as providing a lightweight and affordable souvenir, it will also excuse you from purchasing a more expensive piece of wood shaped to resemble a giraffe.

Other than admiring your purchase or congratulating yourself on avoiding one, the only other thing to do in Pakwach is walk down to the river. Not that the area is lacking in historical interest. A local legend holds that Pakwach is where the Alur and Luo peoples split into separate tribes, the result of an argument that arose over the loss of a hunting spear (or, in another version, the daughter of one swallowing a bead belonging to the other), between Gipir and Labongo, the sons of the Luo chief on the east bank of the river. The matter escalated and resulted in the death of Labongo's son (or the girl being cut open to remove the bead). The brothers went their separate ways, Labongo remaining in Acholiland while Gipir crossed the river with his people to establish the Alur tribe of West Nile. It is said that the troublesome spear (or bead?) can sometimes be seen floating in the river at certain places.

Easier to corroborate are events in the 19th century when Europeans began travelling up and down the Nile between Khartoum and Lake Albert, the first being General Gordon's lieutenant, Romolo Gessi, in 1876. Nobody with a sense of African history could fail to be conscious of the fact that Emin Pasha's camp at Wadelai once stood on the west bank of the Nile, roughly 40km north of Pakwach. However, the site is difficult to reach without private transport, and the only evidence of its significance is the inevitable plaque.

GETTING THERE AND AWAY Several buses pass through Pakwach *en route* to/ from Arua and Kampala/Gulu. Gaga and KKT are the West Nile **buses** that run from Kampala's Arua Stage on Johnston Street at 07.30 and 10.00; the journey costs Ush23,000. Kampala-bound Gaga buses leave Arua at 07.30 and KKT at 08.30, and pass through Pakwach around 90 minutes later. If you book in advance, the staff at the KK or Gaga offices in Pakwach will call Arua to reserve a seat for you.

Transport options for visiting Murchison Falls National Park via the nearby Tangi Gate are described on page 403.

 WHERE TO STAY AND EAT The mid-range safari lodges, **Fort Murchison** and **Bwana Tembo** are located on the eastern side of the river, across from Pakwach. More details can be found on pages 406–7.

Budget

🏠 **Global Village Guesthouse** (10 rooms)
☎ 0392 848729. This modern guesthouse is located 3km north of the town on the Wadelei Road. The smart s/c rooms are tiled & provided with much-needed fans. The rates reflect the fact that this is the only hotel of this standard in Pakwach. *US$30/36 sgl/dbl, US$60 sgl/dbl/trpl B&B.*

Shoestring

🏠 **Sunrise Guesthouse** (12 rooms) m 0777 260750. Located at the eastern end of town beside the main road, the Sunrise offers basic stews with *posho*/rice for Ush7,000. *US$9 sgl+ rooms.*

Heritage Courts (7 rooms) 500m further along Weatherhead Park Lane; m 0782 080194. This annexe to Heritage Park is in a small terraced garden opposite the golf course. *US$18/25 s/c sgl+/dbl B&B.*

Hotel Pacific (28 rooms) At the northern end of Arua Av near the **Eagle Air** office; m 0772 667314. Long-serving budget hotel close to the town centre. A bar & basic restaurant on the ground floor. *US$13/16 sgl/dbl.*

✗ WHERE TO EAT AND DRINK
You didn't come to Arua for the food, but here are a few survival options anyway. For location of listings see map opposite.

Eripak Beach Resort Nebbi Rd, beyond White Castle. The beach in question is actually a riverbank beside a lovely garden. Though still a work in progress it's a pleasant place for drinks & snacks.

✗ **Ethiopian Restaurant** Avenue Rd. Authentic, warts, *njeera* 'n'all Ethiopian cuisine, tucked into an alley next to Arua supermarket. *Meals around Ush12,000.*

✗ **Heritage Park & Heritage Courts** Weatherhead Park Lane. The HP kitchens are capable of mouth-watering roasted meats & salads but, as with the Oasis (see below), it's a matter of luck. *Meals Ush10,000–15,000.*

✗ **Indian Restaurant** Rhino Camp Rd. This accurately named establishment is easily the best

eatery in the town centre with excellent curries, etc. *Main course with rice Ush20,000.*

✗ **Oasis** Weatherhead Park Lane. A popular place for a meal & a drink. Arua's most ambitious & wide-ranging menu lists main courses & pizzas. What's actually available is another matter entirely: pot luck according to local volunteers. *Main courses Ush10,000–20,000.*

♀ **West Nile Golf Club** When the heat of the day is past, the clubhouse terrace overlooking the course is a fine place for a sundowner.

✗ **White Castle Hotel** 2km on Nebbi Rd; see page 421. The hotel restaurant is considered Arua's safest bet for visitors & they usually have most items on the menu. *Continental, Indian & Italian dishes cost Ush15,000.*

NIGHTLIFE
☆ **Arua Paradise** [422 C2] Transport Rd. The creation of the charming former Ugandan Ambassador to the DRC, Arua Paradise is as down & dirty as it gets. Food & drink is served 24hrs, during some of which (22.00–04.00) a disco booms. Should you need to lie down (or something), a score of dreadful bedrooms named after the owner's 12 children lead directly off the

main hall (*US$5 with shared facilities, US$8 with a shower*).

☆ **Club Matonge** [422 C2] Hospital Rd. I didn't have the pleasure of being treated to a morning beer & a guided tour by the owner of this rival establishment, but I imagine it is slightly upmarket from the Arua Paradise. Difficult not to be! Popular with local Peace Corps & other volunteers.

SHOPPING There are a few **supermarkets** [422 C2] on Arua Avenue. If you missed out on a carved tortoise in Pakwach, there's a good little **craft shop** [422 C2] between Arua Avenue and Transport Road offering handmade sandals and vibrantly patterned waxed cotton from DRC.

OTHER PRACTICALITIES
Foreign exchange Both **Stanbic** [422 B2] and **Barclays** [422 C2] offer forex services at Kampala rates.

Golf The West Nile Golf Course [422 D3–4] still boasts a playable nine holes – a commendable achievement up on the northwestern frontier. The green fees are Ush5,000. Willing caddies and ball spotters can be recruited for Ush1,500. Club hire is also available.

Internet Internet facilities can be found at OB Plaza internet [422 B2], in the storeyed building on the main street, opposite the junction with Rhino Camp Road.

Swimming The **White Castle hotel** on the Nebbi Road (see page 421) has a swimming pool. A dip costs Ush5,000 during the week, rising to Ush10,000 at weekends.

FURTHER INFORMATION Readers with a particular interest in Arua and West Nile will enjoy *Oh Uganda, may God uphold thee*, a new memoir by John Haden and John Odoma. The two men were teachers in West Nile when Idi Amin took power. As the story unfolds, and Uganda starts to unravel, you appreciate how the book's title, borrowed from the first line of the national anthem, must have assumed equal significance as a prayer. (*The book costs £12.99 + p&p from www.barnybooks.biz while the Kindle e-book costs £6.55 from Amazon.*)

KIBOKO

For many Ugandans, this small town in their country's northwestern corner close to the borders with Sudan and the DRC is the epitome of remoteness. It's little more than a disproportionately wide main street with a roundabout at the northern end. Branch left for Yei in Southern Sudan (via the border crossing at Oraba) or right to Moyo.

GETTING THERE AND AWAY **Buses** and **taxis** pass through Kiboko on their way between Arua and the Sudan border. Traffic headed east to Moyo is lighter but you should find a bus before resorting to a perch in the back of a truck.

 WHERE TO STAY AND EAT

🏠 **L'Ambiance** (7 rooms) Lurojo (Moyo) Rd. Smart, tiled s/c rooms are contained within a terraced line. Dinner is served under a simple but shady thatch shelter. Luxury! *US$12/16 sgl/dbl.*

🏠 **Hotel Pacific** (24 rooms) Arua Rd; m 0777 466611. Only if L'Ambiance is full! Cheap & simple rooms have nets & use shared facilities. Cottages are provided with bucket showers.

SHOPPING A Bata shoe shop can be found in town.

OTHER PRACTICALITIES

Foreign exchange There is a branch of **Stanbic** Bank in the main street.

Fuel Kiboko has perhaps the most expensive fuel in Uganda, 33% higher than Kampala, and significantly more than in Arua. If driving in this direction from Kampala, fill your tank before you cross the Nile and top up in Gulu or Arua (see pages 439–45 and 421).

MOYO AND LAROPI FERRY

Though it hardly leaps off the map, Laropi is a place of considerable significance due to the vehicle ferry that plies between this small town on the west bank of the Nile and Umi landing on the east. The nearest alternative to this crossing is the bridge at Pakwach, some 130km to the south. Downtown Laropi, 1km from the ferry landing, is a small and sleepy place: commercial activity seems to have gravitated to the ferry landing where vendors provide travellers with drinks and snacks (including grisly-looking dried fish) from inside some ramshackle structures. There is nothing more to Umi, on the opposite bank, than a row of similar shacks, though it is surrounded by some spectacular rock outcrops. Though most traffic here is simply intent on crossing the river, the area has plenty to offer an interested visitor and, if you've taken the trouble to travel all the way up there, it's well worth taking a few days to explore. Most obviously, the area is notable for some superb scenery, dominated by the 1,562m **Mount Otzi**, towering above the west bank of the Nile. This comes as welcome relief after some expansive but uninspiring landscapes on the routes north from both Arua and Gulu. Indeed the Nile Valley, around Laropi, is the nearest thing in northern Uganda to a tourism hub, albeit a low-key one troubled only intermittently by tourists, most of whom are are guests of the excellent Arra Fishing Lodge near Umi (see page 426).

Moyo, on the west side of the Nile, and 23km from Laropi, is a small and rather pretty town on the edge of an elevated plateau. Approaching from the west (from Kiboko or Arua) there is little sign that it stands at some altitude, until the road east of the town starts to drop sharply downhill towards the Nile. Moyo is a convenient base for most of the activities listed below. Also, if you're running late for the last ferry, Moyo's relatively high altitude is preferable to a hot room in Laropi.

GETTING THERE AND AWAY The Laropi **ferry** lies about 20km north of Adjumani and around 140km from Gulu via Atiak. Moyo is some 24km away on the west side of the Nile. Ferry crossings start daily at 06.30 and run throughout the day whenever full until 17.30. There is no charge. **Buses** run throughout the day to Moyo from Arua (*Ush15,000*) and Adjumani (*Ush8,000*). The Zawadi bus

---

OTZI FOREST RESERVE

Information based on reports supplied by Dr Tim Davenport

Otzi Forest Reserve is found 18km northeast of Moyo Town and covers an area of 188km^2 with an altitudinal range of 760–1,667m. The forest is located on an escarpment overlooking the White Nile as it flows northward, and is bounded to the northeast by the international border with Sudan. The vegetation is broadly classified as *Butyrospermum-Hyparrhenia* and *Combretum* savanna with some undifferentiated semi-deciduous thicket and riverine forest. Surveys have recorded 261 tree species and show that the reserve comprises 8% bushland (>4m), 40% grassland and 52% forest/woodland. Otzi has been identified as one of Uganda's Important Bird Areas with 168 bird species recorded. Of particular interest is the fox kestrel (recorded elsewhere in Uganda only in Kidepo Valley National Park), one of 14 of the 22 Sudan–Guinea savanna biome species found in Uganda. The others are the white-crested turaco, red-throated bee-eater, Uganda spotted woodpecker, Emin's shrike, the red pate and foxy cisticolas, chestnut-crowned sparrow weaver, black-bellied firefinch, brown-rumped bunting, black-rumped waxbill, bronze-tailed glossy starling, purple glossy starling and the piacpiac. This total is matched in a Uganda protected area by the far larger Murchison Falls National Park and exceeded only in Kidepo (16) and Mount Kei Forest Reserve (15) north of Kiboko. A population of chimpanzees was recorded in the reserve during the 1995 Forest Department survey but their present status is unclear.

company runs to Moyo (*Ush35,000*) via Adjumani from its Kampala office on William Street. A **special hire** between Moyo and Arra Fishing Lodge costs Ush120,000.

WHERE TO STAY AND EAT

Arra Fishing Lodge (7 rooms) Umi; m 0752 212260/0772 374560/975468; e arra_fishinglodge@live.com; www.uganda-fishing.com. This delightful riverside lodge stands on the east bank of the Nile, 1km along the Adjumani Road from the Umi ferry landing. It's a small tented camp, supplemented by a couple of cottages (all s/c) that look out across the river, past a fringe of acacia trees & papyrus towards the hills of Moyo District. In the early morning, birdlife abounds, while a couple of hippo grunt in the reeds. Temperatures can be high so guests are grateful for the small swimming pool & the cool thatched lodge with its covered veranda, both overlooking the river. Good meals are served (*around Ush20,000*), including (not surprisingly) a tasty selection of fish dishes. A wide variety of activities around the lodge is possible; indeed there's something for everyone, be they fishermen, hikers, history buffs, birdwatchers, swimmers, or pool-couch potatoes (for more details, see *Activities*, below). The prices are extremely fair. *US$60/80 sgl/dbl B&B.*

Penthouse Inn Moyo; m 0772 962601; e penthouseinn@gmail.com. Since this smart-looking hotel opened after my last visit, I can only paraphrase from the superbly composed brochure. Penthouse presents gracious splendour & majestic elegance & exudes aesthetic excellence & grandeur through a combination of Madi Cultural Mystique & Ugandan Vintage Heritage décor. It has a trendy lobby, cottages & health studio. Thrilling & romantic botanical preservation gardens offer spectacular sunset views, unique architecture & unparalleled decorations for amusement & optical nutrition & ... the perfect Nicodemus hideout in case you fancy for indulgence a little privy Casanova debut. Fantastic! *US$16–26 sgl, US$26 dbl B&B.*

Multipurpose Centre Moyo. This Church-run facility has basic rooms. *US$6.*

If Arra Fishing Lodge represents a truly serendipitous discovery at Umi, don't bank on the same good fortune on the west bank at **Laropi**. However, if you choose not to head up to Moyo, you'll have no difficulty in finding a shoestring lodge.

WHAT TO SEE AND DO The range of activities described below have been identified and operated by Arra Fishing Lodge and the prices are those charged by the lodge.

It is possible to find local guides and boatmen to assist you at reduced cost, though you are unlikely to enjoy the same level of expertise.

Birdwatching boat cruises (*US$40 for up to 4 passengers*) A variety of waterbirds can be sighted in wetland habitats along the banks of the Nile, of which the prize is undoubtedly the shoebill. To name but a few others: open-billed and yellow-billed storks, African spoonbill, knob-billed duck, Pygmy and Egyptian geese, giant kingfisher, and green-backed, giant, purple, night and grey herons. The birding cruise takes three hours. For those lacking in ornithological intent, an early evening cruise to enjoy a cool beer and the terrific scenery is highly recommended.

Fishing (*US$15/hr for 2 fishermen; additional charges apply for hire of equipment & lost lures*) The Nile at Arra provides a good opportunity to catch sizeable Nile perch (the local record with rod and line is 75kg), catfish, and to battle with the aggressive tigerfish. Excursions use a motorised canoe with captain and guide.

Mount Otzi (*US$100 for 4–5 people inc transport to the trailhead*) This day-long trip visits the most distinctive peak in northwest Uganda, the 1,562m Mount Otzi

Dufile Fort was established by Emin Pasha in 1879 as a station of the Egyptian colonial province of Equatoria which extended across southern Sudan and northwestern Uganda to Lake Albert. At its busiest, Dufile was inhabited by some 4,000 people – soldiers and officials along with their families, workers and camp followers. However, by 1885, Emin had relocated most of these people south – along with the population of his main station at Lado in southern Sudan – to Wadelei in order to increase the distance between them and the Mahdist insurgents who had expelled the Anglo-Egyptian colonialists from Sudan, and killed General Gordon. A reduced garrison remained in Dufile to guard the new, northern limit of Emin's shrinking domain. In 1888, Henry Stanley's Emin Pasha Relief Expedition arrived to assist Emin's withdrawal from Equatoria. The Pasha returned to Dufile for the last time with Stanley's lieutenant, A J Mounteney-Jephson, to evacuate his men. Rather than following their leader, however, the soldiers mutinied and imprisoned the Europeans in the fort. They were soon released and returned to Stanley's camp on Lake Albert. Shortly afterwards, Dufile was attacked by the Mahdi's army in November 1888. Though Emin's men won the battle, they were clearly bound to lose the war, and Dufile – and indeed the whole province of Equatoria – was finally abandoned in January 1889, when its erstwhile defenders hotfooted south to Lake Albert only to find that Emin and Stanley had already left. These men remained near Lake Albert where, two years later, they were sought out and headhunted by Frederick Lugard in 1890 to add some backbone to his understaffed garrison in Old Kampala fort. Dufile was later reoccupied and reconstructed by Belgian forces between 1902 and 1907 when West Nile was known as the Lado Enclave and temporarily formed part of the Belgian Congo.

which rises some 960m above the Nile. If you're driving yourself, a track – mostly good but with some extremely steep and rocky 4x4 sections – leaves the mountain road midway between Moyo and Laropi. I followed it for 5km as far as a couple of mobile-phone masts but it clearly goes a good distance further.

Pakele Hot Springs A drive to these hot, sulphurous pools, 20km from Arra Lodge, can be arranged on request.

Dufile Emin Pasha's fort at Dufile lies on the northern (West Nile) bank of the Albert Nile about 20km upstream from Arra and Laropi, and can be reached by either boat or vehicle. The return boat trip from Arra Fishing Lodge takes seven hours and costs US$130 for up to four people. Though the fort provides a definite purpose for the outing, the real pleasure lies in the river journey. The only obvious evidence of the site's fortification is part of the perimeter ditch that surrounded the 5ha site. Though archaeological excavations during 2006–07 ascertained the positions of a number of buildings, their age and significance is uncertain as the original layout was overlaid by Belgian structures during 1902–07. Dufile lies close to a site where General Gordon established a base to reassemble river steamers that had been dismantled for portage around the rapids at nearby Nimule. However, this older site lies in a border area disputed by Uganda and Southern Sudan and cannot currently be visited.

12

Gulu and the North

Culturally, economically and geographically, the far north of Uganda has always been somewhat dislocated from the rest of the country. Looking at the map, the broad, swamp-fringed fingers of Lake Kyoga, sitting squarely in the centre of the country, form an obvious natural barrier. Progress around the lake to the east is constrained by the vast wetlands of the Apedura river system, traversed by only one major highway. To the west, only one bridge (at Karuma Falls) spans the Nile on its 160km course between Lake Kyoga and Lake Albert.

Lake Kyoga also represents a massive cultural divide, separating northerly Nilotic and Sudanese tribes from those of Bantu origin in the south. The most populous of the northern tribes is the Acholi (technically a relatively recent confederation of chiefdoms created by the British) in the Gulu area, while the Langi are concentrated around Lira. The largest ethnic groups in West Nile are the Alur (Nebbi District), Lugbara (Arua), Kaka (Kiboko) and Madi (Moyo). Northern languages are quite distinct from the Bantu dialects spoken in the south, having as much in common as English has with, say, Chinese. The languages of northern Uganda are guttural sounding (not dissimilar to Arabic which is spoken in neighbouring Sudan) and you'll quickly notice that the English spoken in northern Uganda sounds very different from the regional accents of the varied Bantu dialects used in the south.

The north's isolation was intensified during Joseph Kony's – leader of the Lord's Resistance Army (LRA) – war against the NRM (National Resistance Movement) government during the late 1980s onwards and it became virtually absolute. As far as most Ugandans, expatriates and tourists were concerned for at least 20 years, most of northern Uganda was a no-go area. I've lived in Uganda, and travelled more widely than most, since 1993, yet my first visit to Gulu was to research this chapter in 2009 – for the very good reason stated in several previous editions, 'Travel in the vicinity of Gulu, Lira and other areas north of the Nile is highly risky, if not downright suicidal.'

Ongoing problems notwithstanding (see below), it is now safe to travel throughout Uganda north of Lake Kyoga (with the exception of Karamoja in the northeast where caution is still advised). Unfortunately, as the Acholi and Langi look to ease their economic woes, tourism is an unlikely panacea. True, **Purongo** and **Pakwach** have some potential as new staging points for entering Murchison Falls National Park from the north, while **Gulu** and **Kitgum** towns can service the trickle of travellers headed for the remote Kidepo Valley National Park (see pages 452–9) but the fact is that new attractions up north are disappointingly thin on the ground, certainly compared with the myriad number and variety found in the southwest. Other than the remains of Samuel Baker's fort at **Patiko** near Gulu (see pages 439–45), scope for conventional tourism is limited to the Nile corridor at Laropi close to the Sudanese border, where the management of **Arra Fishing**

Lodge has identified a worthwhile range of activities to occupy the few travellers who make it up there (see pages 444–5).

Most visits by foreigners continue to be related to the conflict, and there is much to be done. In previous years, NGO activity concentrated on sustaining IDPs (Internally Displaced People); the focus has now shifted towards helping a disordered society return towards a functional and self-sufficient existence. But though the information in this chapter may prove most useful to NGO workers headed for Gulu and Kitgum, and travellers headed for Kidepo, wider exploration in the region should not be discouraged. Northern Uganda genuinely lies off any beaten tourist track and it is arguably worth visiting for that reason alone.

HISTORY

Historically, it was northern cotton and tobacco rather than southern produce that first enabled the fledgling Uganda protectorate to turn a profit. Northerners earned a reputation as tough and hard-working that persists today. In 1959, activity in Gulu made it Uganda's second-largest town with 30,000 residents – at a time when Kampala's population numbered only 46,000. Lira, incredibly, was placed third with just 14,000. Northerners formed the backbone of the protectorate army, and many, used to hard graft on plantations in their homeland, migrated south to work on sugar estates in Buganda. But if the north provided the raw materials and the manpower for Uganda's development, it was the south that tended to enjoy the rewards.

In the years that followed independence in 1962, the historic economic divide developed into tribal persecution and bloodshed. Obote's Acholi- and Langi-dominated armies terrorised southerners during his two terms as president, while Amin and his West Nile cronies (known as 'Sudanese') terrorised everyone; though curiously the people targeted on account of their ethnicity were fellow northerners, the Acholi and Langi. Come 1986, when Museveni seized power, the north had good cause to fear, their menfolk having brutalised the Ugandan population over the best part of 20 years. They were right to be worried, for Museveni's southern-dominated army mounted a decidedly heavy-handed campaign to stamp their authority on northern Uganda. Amidst an atmosphere of fear, resentment and hatred of the NRM regime, the stage was set for Alice Lakwena's short-lived but almost successful rebellion, and the subsequent 20-year campaign waged by Joseph Kony against the NRM government. These interconnected episodes are described in the boxes on pages 432–3 and 436–7.

Thankfully, the conflict has now ended despite the failure to secure a formal peace deal, and the affected areas of Gulu, Lira and Kitgum have enjoyed peace for eight years.

However, the legacy of the war is now apparent as a displaced and brutalised populace adapts to the peace. While the rest of the country has enjoyed the benefits of stability and economic growth, the north has lagged far behind. It will take years to achieve some sort of normality and the challenges are both numerous and daunting. Many of the abducted combatants have returned home where they must reintegrate into the society they were forced to terrorise. Collectively, this society also faces its own problems. For the best part of 18 years, most of the rural populace was forced to live in squalid and insanitary IDP (Internally Displaced People) camps guarded by the army, or migrate into local towns. Fed by aid agencies, few were able to do any useful work for years (it is ironic that while northern industry and agriculture stalled, influxes of IDPs caused Gulu and Lira to once more rise towards the top of the population table, leapfrogging southerly towns growing, more conventionally, through economic activity). The best part of two million people, though grateful not to have been maimed, murdered or abducted, nonetheless wasted 20 years of their lives. As they sat in the protected camps, their original homes crumbled, furniture was converted to dust by termites, fields vanished into bush, and boundary lines were lost. For many, it's not simply a matter of just getting back to work – a massive psychological hurdle in anyone's book – but a case of struggling back to a starting line from which they can move forward (a major problem is re-establishing land ownership boundaries on farms that were poorly demarcated to start with). Nor has everyone left the camps. Many people have nowhere else to go and with no other source of support many old people, alcoholics, infirm, sick and various other disadvantaged people remain dependent on charity.

KARUMA

The small town of Karuma stands beside the Kampala–Gulu road on the southern bank of the Nile, where it survives by meeting the needs of truck drivers. Though unremarkable in most respects, Karuma is the primary gateway to northern Uganda owing to the bridge that spans the river at this location. The significance of this Nile crossing is not merely symbolic. **Karuma Bridge** is the spot where, a few years ago, fearful tension gripped northbound travellers, while the mood on vehicles headed south lightened immeasurably. Today, it's a beautiful location: beneath the bridge, the river races down rapids between high, forested banks. On the north side these lie within Murchison Falls National Park, and on the southern, downstream side, in the Karuma Wildlife Reserve. Unfortunately, the soldiers posted to guard the bridge view photography as an Eighth Deadly Sin. Simply pausing on the bridge is sufficient to stir them into activity. Whether this outdated prohibition remains official policy or simply a rare chance for soldiers to extort some beer money hardly matters. It's not worth it.

WHERE TO STAY If you're stuck for the night in Karuma, the **Golden Guesthouse** at the southern end of town looks the best of some grim lodges. If funds permit and you have transport, the new, upmarket **Chobe Safari Lodge** (see pages 404–6) lies 18km inside Murchison Falls National Park on the north side of the river. Otherwise, if headed north across the bridge, it would be prudent to leave time to reach Gulu or Pakwach.

WHERE TO EAT There's an abundance of cheap restaurants and roadside grills. If you are heading to Gulu, **Kamudini Corner**, 15km away, is a far more popular stopping point.

WHAT TO SEE

Karuma Falls Few grotty truck stops lie so close to such a fine but little-visited panorama. Though the bridge crosses a lovely section of rapids, this is not the best place to view the river. The falls lie upriver (while photography is prohibited on the bridge). To find them, you need to walk or drive about 2km behind the town to an elevated promontory overlooking a broad gorge, forested on the northern side. The waterfall is the first of an 80km-long stretch of low falls and rapids, and represents the point where an enlarged Lake Kyoga burst its banks to scour a new course for the Nile to the Rift Valley. It's a worthwhile diversion although, curiously, Speke was sufficiently underwhelmed in 1864 to record it by its local name rather than allocating it to a contemporary royal or sponsor.

The present-day civil war in the Acholi districts of Kitgum and Gulu has deep roots. They stretch to the beginning of the colonial era, when the culturally divergent northern territories were arbitrarily annexed to the Uganda protectorate and effectively placed under joint British–Baganda rule. And they reach back through 60 years of colonial underdevelopment: education in the northwest, and associated prospects of employment were deliberately stifled by the British, in order that the region might remain a ready source of military recruits and manual labourers. The roots of the present-day conflict are also embedded in the complex Jok system of spiritual belief, possession and sorcery that informs Acholi culture past and present. And they cannot easily be disentangled from the teachings of the early Christian missionaries who appropriated traditional Acholi spiritual concepts and icons into their biblical translations, in order that they might better hawk their exotic religious product to the locals.

As good a place to start as any, however, is June 1985 when Alice Auma, or Alice Lakwena as she had recently started calling herself, was introduced to General Tito Okello at the Acholi Inn in Gulu. Auma was then a 29-year-old Acholi woman whose largely undistinguished life – divorced, childless and eking out a living as a fish-seller in Pakwach – had been transformed three months earlier when she was possessed by the spirit of an Italian soldier called Lakwena. Okello, by contrast, was the chief of the defence force (UPDF), slowly coming to the realisation that his troops would be unable to hold out indefinitely against the rebel National Resistance Army (NRA), and frustrated at President Obote's refusal to negotiate with NRA leader Yoweri Museveni. Lakwena was made aware of Okello's plans to oust Obote, and offered her services as his spiritual advisor, to be passed over in favour of an established peer. Whether the general and the medium ever met again goes unrecorded, but both would play a leading role in national events over the next two years.

On 27 June 1985, the Obote regime was toppled by Okello and his Acholi supporters within the military. In the aftermath of this coup, the NRA captured Fort Portal, to eventually assume control over western Uganda as close to the capital as Masaka. Okello, who had no great personal ambition to power, formed a broad-based Military Council (MC) that included representatives of all political factions except the NRA. Museveni was invited to the party, and in December 1985, following protracted negotiations in Nairobi, a peace accord was signed leaving Okello as chairman of the MC and installing Museveni as vice-chairman. On 25 January 1986, less than two months after the accord had been signed, the NRA marched into Kampala to topple Okello.

Museveni's given reason for breaking the peace accord was the ineffectiveness of Okello's MC and in particular its inability to curb atrocities against civilians being perpetrated by its defence force. To the Acholi, the coup against Uganda's first Acholi head of state was betrayal pure and simple. And, whatever the rights and wrongs of the matter, Museveni's coup undeniably did represent a loss of power and prestige to the Acholi. It also prompted thousands of Acholi soldiers to flee north for fear of reprisal, while the subsequent NRA occupation of Acholi territory was allegedly accompanied by a spate of unprovoked civilian killings. Put simply, in 1986, when most Ugandans perceived or willed Museveni to be a national saviour, the Acholi viewed him as a liar and an oppressor – indeed, a full ten years later, Museveni would poll a mere 20% of the Acholi vote in the 1996 presidential election, as compared with 75% countrywide.

After being rebuffed by Okello, Alice Lakwena continued using her powers as a medium and healer to tend wounded Acholi soldiers. On 6 August 1986, however, the spirit Lakwena ordered his medium to abandon her healing to form the Holy Spirit Mobile Forces (HSMF) and lead a war against the forces of evil in Uganda. Alice assembled an initial force of 150 Acholi men, all of whom had served in the UPDF prior to the NRA coup, and made them undertake an elaborate purification ritual, laced with elements of both Christian and traditional Acholi ritual, as laid out to her by the spirit Lakwena. The newly inducted soldiers were also issued with a list of 20 commandments – the Holy Spirit Safety Precautions – ranging from the predictable 'Thou shalt not commit adultery' to the decidedly left-field 'Thou shalt have two testicles, neither more nor less'.

A compelling book could be – and indeed has been – written about the outwardly contradictory aims and beliefs of the HSMF (see page 538). One central aim of the movement was the elimination of witchcraft (allegations of which were rife in the early days of the HIV pandemic) in favour of Christian values. Yet it could be argued that the movement's obsession with sorcery itself stood in contravention of biblical teachings, as certainly did some of its more obtuse beliefs, for instance that smearing a soldier's body with *shea* butter would make him immune to bullets. And even if Alice herself was sincere in her beliefs, it is difficult to say whether her mostly ex-UPDF followers – at least 3,000 at the movement's peak – were motivated primarily by spiritual considerations or simply by the prospect of exacting revenge on the hated NRA.

Whatever their motives, this improbable army came closer to ousting Museveni than anybody has before or since. Led by the spirit Lakwena and his earthly vessel Alice, the HSMF marched through Kitgum, Lira, Soroti, Kumi, Mbale and Tororo, inflicting significant defeats on the NRA and replacing the dead and wounded with new recruits along the way. Defeat came finally in November 1987, on the outskirts of Jinja, where the HSMF enjoyed little public support and its movements were relayed to the government forces by local villagers. After the defeat, the spirit of Lakwena abandoned Alice in favour of her father Severino, who resuscitated the HSMF with some success, at least until March 1988, when 450 of his followers were killed in an attack on Kitgum. Six months later, Severino was captured and beaten up by the UPDA (a rival anti-NRA army) and informed by a leading officer – an HSMF deserter – that there would be no more talk of spirits.

Following the defeat at Jinja, Alice fled into exile in Kenya, where she died in 2005, despite being pardoned in January 2003 under an act granting amnesty to combatants who surrender voluntarily. Alice's father escaped from the UPDA in May 1989, was arrested by the NRA six months later, and released in 1992. The spirit of Lakwena eventually abandoned Severino, who has renounced violence in favour of prayer and fasting. The UPDA officer who so violently exhorted Severino against spiritual talk back in 1988 has subsequently stated that he is possessed by Lakwena, a claim publicly refuted by Severino, who describes his former tormentor as a 'devil'. And that former UPDA officer, whether spirit medium or devil, has exerted a murderously destabilising influence over the whole of northern Uganda for almost two full decades. His name is Joseph Kony, and the chilling story of his subsequent career continues on pages 436–7.

It is just possible at Kamudini Corner that, instead of continuing north to Gulu, you might be seized by a sudden urge to turn right and drive 60km east to visit Lira. If you do, you'll observe that this is a town for which the term 'backwater' might have been specially coined. Lake Kyoga provides the water and Lira lies at the back of it. Routes from Kampala to West Nile, Sudan and Gulu are diverted around the lake's western side, and to Soroti and Karamoja to the east. In consequence, from Kampala anyway, Lira is not on the road to anywhere, though it has been suggested to me that the town is an important transport centre for people following cross-country routes between, say, Mbale and Arua. Point taken!

Nevertheless, Lira is a pleasant and particularly bustling little place. This derives in part from the fact that its central streets seem narrower than is usual in Ugandan towns – rather curiously since space north of Lake Kyoga is hardly lacking. Or perhaps they seem so because they are more crowded, though few of these people thronging the town are doing so for the economic opportunities or the nightlife, or indeed to change buses between Mbale and Arua. Most are villagers forced to take refuge from the LRA war. Although Kony's activities concentrated on Acholiland to the north, Lira District was not spared: indeed the conflict's most famously heart-rending episode, namely the abduction of 159 schoolgirls from St Mary's School at Aboke, occurred just 28km from Lira Town. By 2004, 39% of the district's total population had been displaced. Though lower than the 95% recorded in Gulu District, a similarly comprehensive figure would have applied to the northern part of Lira most affected by the conflict. As a result, between 1991 and 2002, an annual growth of 10.1% (a rate second only to the 10.3% in similarly affected Kitgum) saw the population of Lira Town rise from 27,568 to 89,781 and shoot up from 12th place to fourth in the national ranking. Though many people have now returned to their rural homes, it is obvious that many have also opted to remain in town.

GETTING THERE AND AWAY Lira lies 60km from the Kampala–Gulu road junction at Kamudini Corner using a recently repaired tarmac road. Soroti lies 120km further east on a newly surfaced road. If driving to Lira from Kampala, ensure you have sufficient fuel to reach your destination as there are no conventional opportunities to refuel on the 40km section before Karuma Falls and very few along the 70km drive beyond the bridge to Lira. There is no reliable station in Kamdini though Karuma trading centre can provide dirty jerrycans of expensive fuel.

Lira is well served by **buses** running to/from Kampala's Qualicell bus terminal (5–6hrs; Ush25,000), Soroti (2½hrs; Ush15,000), Gulu (2hrs; Ush12,000) and Arua (4hrs; Ush20,000). Buses between Soroti and Gulu stop in Lira only to pick up and set down passengers. This avoids the usual early start and the customary wait for the vehicle to fill. If driving to Gulu, a shorter route on *murram* leaves the tarmac at Aboke (28km from Lira) and joins the Gulu road at Paranga (28km before Gulu). I doubt whether this makes the journey any quicker but it is 25km shorter and does provide an interesting cross section through rural life off the main highways.

All conventional public transport to Kitgum passes via Gulu. If intent on travelling direct, head to Kitgum stage on Oyam Road and be prepared for a bumpy ride on the back of a laden truck.

WHERE TO STAY Lira is about the only major town in Uganda which lacks at least one decent moderate hotel. However, the five hotels listed below come closest. For location of listings see map, page 438.

Moderate

⌂ **Lillian Towers** (25 rooms) Inomo Rd; ☎0473 420955; m 0774192310; e lillian_towers_hotel@ hotmail. Last time around, this orangey-pink storied construction was Lira's newest & smartest offering but it now seems a little bit tired. The landline is off, the bespoke email has downgraded to a hotmail address & the swimming pool is broken, none of which suggest an establishment ahead of the game. Anyway, the tiled rooms are still spacious & s/c with nets, fan & TV. A restaurant is provided. *US$37/45/49/53 sgl/dbl/twin/exec B&B.*

⌂ **Gracious Palace** (32 rooms) A couple of streets back on the quieter & less crowded side of Main St/Obote Rd; m 0775 329338; e gracepathotelltf@yahoo.co.uk. If you're not put off by the strange lines, blue glass & soft pink façade of Lira's latest smart but slightly odd offering in this category, you'll find the interior cool & pleasant. 'We don't deny you comfort' is the hotel's motto & nor do they, the s/c rooms are spacious & well appointed. The sgl beds are huge! *US$34/42/48/ sgl+/dbl/twin B&B.*

⌂ **Kanberra Hotel** Oyam Rd. Recommended by a reader for decent food, Wi-Fi & s/c rooms. *US$24/32 sgl/dbl B&B.*

⌂ **Lira Hotel** (20 rooms) m 0772 594184. This stalwart, former government hotel is located on the exclusive (for which read 'less crowded') side of town near the open space formerly known as the golf course. The dining & bar areas open on to a central courtyard beneath a few shady trees, while commendable efforts have been made to patch up the rooms. Though Lira has hotels that are newer & smarter, these attributes are poor compensation for age, character & a good design. (*Meals cost around Ush15,000.*) *US$29/41 s/c sgl+/dbl with nets B&B.*

⌂ **Grand Pacific Hotel** (24 rooms) m 0784 350325. This smart hotel lies at the top end of the high street off the road to Soroti. The grounds & communal areas lack for character but the reasonably priced s/c tiled rooms are provided with nets, fans & TV. Dbl rooms have king-sized beds. (*Meals cost around Ush12,000.*) *US$20/25/25 sgl+/ dbl/twin B&B.*

Budget

⌂ **Day's Inn Hotel** (31 rooms) m 0753 316159. This new hotel near the taxi park is distinguished by a vivid salmon pink exterior. The colour theme continues inside, salmon pink corridors & staircases lead to the rooms (carpeted, with nets & fans). *US$19/25/29 sgl/dbl/twin.*

⌂ **White House** (29 rooms) ☎0372 271112. Named for its white, tiled exterior, the centrally located White House provides clean s/c rooms with nets & fan close to the taxi park. Secure compound parking. *US$16/20/25 sgl+/dbl/twin, US$14 small s/c sgl.*

Shoestring

⌂ **Fortress Guesthouse** (12 rooms) Oyam Rd. Check out the Olilim Guesthouse next door & you'll think this classic shoestring dive is luxurious. *US$10 s/c room, US$6/8 sgl+/dbl with shared bathroom.*

⌂ **Caravan Guesthouse** (14 rooms) Distinguished by an orange-pink façade, Lira's best cheapie is found a couple of blocks up from the taxi park. The 1st-floor s/c rooms with nets are excellent value. Though there's a bar/restaurant of local flavour downstairs, the log-themed bar next door looks more fun (though the rooms behind are grim). *US$8 s/c sgl+, US$6+ basic sgl/sgl+ with shared facilities.*

⌂ **Olilim Guesthouse** Oyam Rd. To reach the rooms you pass though Lira's equivalent of the bar scene in Star Wars. Rooms are cell-like. Classic shoestring! *US$4/6 sgl+/dbl with shared bathroom.*

✗ **WHERE TO EAT AND DRINK** All of the hotels listed have restaurants attached. Of these, the **Lira Hotel** is easily the most attractive place to dine, though I can't vouch for the quality of the food. Main courses cost around Ush15,000. What really makes the difference for Lira's expatriate NGO community is the new **Sankofa Café** (m *0772/0704 712198*) opposite the Mayor's Gardens on Kamudini Road. Like its Gulu counterpart, it offers juices, smoothies, coffees, snacks, burgers, pizza, chicken gizzards ('when available') and salads.

In addition, reader Ian Baird-Smith suggests that his two-year stint in Lira was enlivened by the tasty and reasonably priced menu of Indian, Chinese and African dishes at the Prince Restaurant on Bala Road.

For most of the quarter century since Museveni assumed power in January 1986, the districts of Gulu and Kitgum in northern Uganda have rarely, and only intermittently, been at peace. After the demise of the HSMF (see box, pages 432–3) in November 1987, the government sought to defuse the surviving UPDA, an army of ex-soldiers who'd served under Obote and Okello, and in 1988 a peace deal was signed. But although some 20,000 rebels accepted the offered amnesty, others remained dubious – Museveni had, after all, reneged on a similar accord with Okello in 1985 – and were persuaded to throw their lot in with a newly formed Ugandan People's Democratic Christian Army (now known as the Lord's Resistance Army, or LRA) and their charismatic leader, Joseph Kony.

Kony's sketchy biography varies with the teller. He has claimed to be related to Alice Lakwena, and to be possessed by her spirit (and by others), and he almost certainly served briefly with the HSMF. Sometime in 1987, when Kony first became possessed, he was instructed to start a new movement to 'liberate humans from disease and suffering'. Initially, Kony's doctrines were based primarily on the Christian HSMF's 20 'safety precautions', but many Muslim rituals were added in the 1990s. And Kony's ferment of possessive spirits often guided him along paths less ascetic than those cut by Lakwena – the precaution 'Thou shalt not fornicate', for instance, would eventually be discarded in favour of something along the lines of 'Thou shalt abduct, rape and sexually enslave schoolgirls at whim'.

The LRA's political objective has eluded most observers. Attempts to topple the government ended long ago and since 1989, when Kony attacked several villages he perceived as disloyal to his cause, the LRA has targeted the people it is ostensibly trying to liberate: the rural Acholi. In 1991, a government campaign called Operation North significantly reduced rebel activity, but violence flared up again in 1993. An attempt at peace talks failed and the next three years saw suffering like never before in the form of mass abduction of children and the callous massacre of villagers.

Perhaps the single most important reason why the LRA survived all attempts by the Ugandan government to defeat it was the support it received from the National Islamic Front (NIF) government of Sudan. In a tit for tat scenario, the NIF aided Kony in retaliation for Ugandan support for the rebel Sudanese People's Liberation Army (SPLA) in southern Sudan. Between 1993 and early 2002, Kony and the LRA were based in Sudan, able to flee across the border whenever things heated up in Uganda.

This changed in March 2002, when Sudan signed a protocol allowing the UPDF (Uganda People's Defence Force) to follow LRA rebels into southern Sudan. However, despite some victories, the ensuing Operation Iron Fist failed to destroy the rebels, and sparked off the LRA's most vicious civilian attacks yet. On 24 July, Kony's rebels killed 48 people in a village near Kitgum – the adults hacked apart with machetes and knives, the young children beaten against a tree until their skulls smashed open – before abducting an estimated 100 teenagers. On 24 October, the New Vision printed a chilling picture of a singularly callous attack: the LRA executed 28 villagers, chopped off their heads and limbs, boiled them in a pot, and had been about to force the surviving villagers to eat the human stew when the government army arrived on the scene.

The LRA became more vulnerable following the signing of a peace accord between the Sudanese government and the SPLA in January 2005. The LRA moved outside Uganda and Sudan into the forests of Garamba in northeastern DRC. In

October of that year, the outside world finally took a firm stance on the LRA when the International Criminal Court (ICC) in The Hague issued warrants against Kony and his deputies for crimes against humanity. In June 2006, Interpol issued wanted persons' notices to 184 countries. The rebels let it be known that they were prepared to talk peace with the Ugandan government and in July 2006, negotiations began in the southern Sudanese town of Juba mediated by Riek Machar, Vice President of the Government of Southern Sudan. Once again, a definite end to the conflict proved elusive. Though an estimated 3,000 rebels massed in southern Sudan to be demobbed and returned to the Acholi society from which most of them had been abducted, Kony failed to turn up to to sign a peace agreement. Though many rebels did return home, others melted back into the bush. This period of uncertainty saw new divisions in the LRA's ranks. Kony's 59-year-old deputy, Vincent Otti, supposedly in favour of a peace deal, was executed in November 2007, casting doubt on Kony's own commitment to the peace process. The stumbling block remained – and, it would seem, still remains – the warrants issued by the ICC. Though Acholi people seemed content for returning rebels to be reabsorbed into society through traditional ceremonies of cleaning and forgiveness, and the Ugandan government was prepared to give amnesty, the ICC insisted that the warrants cannot be revoked.

By the end of 2008, the peace process was going nowhere. On 14 December, the forces of Uganda, the DRC and southern Sudan reacted to reports from the DRC that the LRA was rearming and abducting fresh recruits by attacking the rebel stronghold in Garamba. Operation Lightning Thunder was aptly named, with plenty of flashes and bangs, but no Kony, dead or alive. The rebels fled towards the Central African Republic, murdering hundreds of Congolese peasants living in their path.

Though efforts to formally end the war have failed, the fact remains that the LRA has not operated in Uganda since 2005. As long as Kony remains at liberty, however, the big question remains: why did the war drag on for so long? The standard answer cites a lack of motivation in Kampala to end it. A more telling reason was a general feeling in northern Uganda that although Kony might be bad, Museveni is worse. Were Kony to return from his five-year absence he would find a change of mood in Acholiland; popular support for the LRA and antipathy towards the government have been overtaken by a desire to live in peace.

The legacy of the war is a brutal one. The civilian death toll in Gulu and Kitgum districts exceeded 10,000 while a similar number of schoolchildren were abducted and thousands more people maimed or disabled. However, some two million people – 90% of the rural population in the affected areas – were forced to take refuge in towns or protected IDP camps offering limited food and facilities, and appalling sanitation – for up to 18 years. Dozens of schools were destroyed, while lamentable medical facilities were highlighted by a 30% mortality rate among children under the age of five. Average annual per-capita household income (US$30) was just 10% of the national average, while the number of cattle in the region fell to only 2% of 1986 figures (compared with an increase of 100% countrywide). Since 2005, though, most people have left the camps and returned home to start rebuilding a normal existence. Inevitably, the process of achieving this will take time.

Joseph's Kony's story is well told in Matthew Greens's Wizard of the Nile *(see page 538).*

12

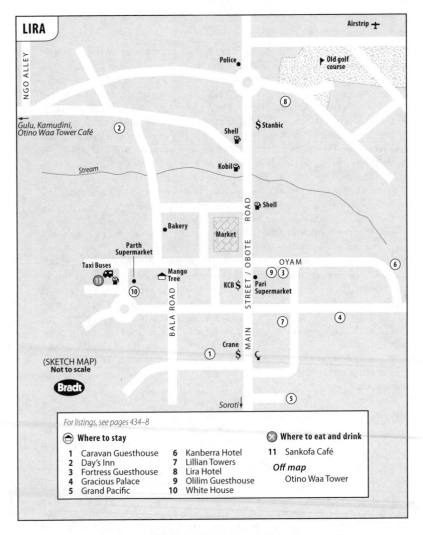

LIRA

NGO ALLEY

Airstrip ✈

Police

Old golf course

⑧

Gulu, Kamudini,
Otino Waa Tower Café ← ②

$ Stanbic

Shell ☕

Stream

Kobil 🏪

🏪 Shell

●Bakery

Market

MAIN STREET / OBOTE ROAD

OYAM ⑥

Parth
Supermarket

Mango
Tree 🌳

⑨③

⑥

Taxi Buses 🚌

⑪

⑩ ●

KCB $

Pari
Supermarket

BALA ROAD

⑦

④

Crane
① $ ⚡

(SKETCH MAP)
Not to scale

Bradt

Soroti ↓

⑤

For listings, see pages 434–8

🏠 Where to stay

1 Caravan Guesthouse
2 Day's Inn
3 Fortress Guesthouse
4 Gracious Palace
5 Grand Pacific

6 Kanberra Hotel
7 Lillian Towers
8 Lira Hotel
9 Olilim Guesthouse
10 White House

❌ Where to eat and drink

11 Sankofa Café

Off map
Otino Waa Tower

Further afield is the **Otino Waa Tower**. This roadside café is a wholly unexpected treat with a small, landscaped garden and craft-shop facility 7km down the Kamudini Road. Offerings include proper coffee, juices, muffins, pizzas, tortilla chips and ice cream. Buffet meals are available by arrangement. Otino Waa has been developed by American faith-based NGO workers (ie: missionaries) as an appendage to an adjacent school, orphanage and apiary. It's fabulously unsustainable but equally fabulous while it lasts.

SHOPPING The town's best supermarkets are reportedly **Pari** supermarket on Main Street, opposite KCB, and New Lira on Olwol Road.

OTHER PRACTICALITIES **Forex** services are provided by Stanbic, Crane and Barclays banks. **Internet** is available at **Lillian Towers** and **Gracious Palace** (see page 435).

The name of Gulu Town will be well known to anyone who has taken the slightest interest in Uganda's history over the last 20 years. For all but a few, however, familiarity is borne of unhappy repute rather than first-hand experience. Vaguely redolent of a mysterious, modern-day Timbuktu, or a sinister, perennially besieged Mafeking, for most Ugandans, and their visitors from abroad, Gulu was simply 'up there'. Now that northern Uganda is safe for travel, the secrets of Gulu are no longer a mystery. And there are surprises in store, the first being how close Gulu is to the rest of Uganda: after crossing Karuma Bridge, for so many years considered the safe limit of northerly travel in Uganda, Gulu's mobile-phone masts hove into view after little more than an hour's drive.

No less surprising is how familiar and ordinary the place is. Rather than a beleaguered, bullet-pocked fortress, Gulu seems a perfectly normal-looking town. Just like Mbale, or Fort Portal, or Arua, or anywhere you care to mention, it is a town of two halves. On one side of a gentle valley are the usual quiet streets lined with government offices, the better hotels and smarter housing. On the other is the standard grid of commercial streets that surround the market and taxi park. These are busy and prosperous-looking; the roads choked with bicycle traffic, the shops filled with goods and the central market with produce, while a rash of banks and other corporate concerns occupy freshly painted premises with smartly tiled verandas. It seems inconceivable that only a few years ago, the smart frontages of Warid, MTN, Bata, Kenya Commercial Bank, etc, were the sleeping quarters for up to 25,000 children who filed into town each evening to escape the clutches of the LRA.

On the face of it, Gulu and the surrounding area may look familiar and ordinary, but there are pointers that normality is still some way off. In the wake of the conflict, homes and schools need rebuilding and hundreds of thousands of lives and livelihoods restoring. One clue is the forest of signposts at road junctions that direct visitors towards the offices of international NGOs. These, if nothing else, indicate that Gulu has more unresolved issues than most districts in Uganda. Other, more sinister, signs warn of the danger of handling unexploded ordnances. From this pointer, you'll notice that a high proportion of farmland still stands fallow. Landmines are, however, only one disincentive to cultivation: it is also boring. Urban life is far more entertaining, a fact evidenced by the extreme busyness of Gulu Town. Though many of the 113,000 population recorded by the 2002 census were displaced villagers who have since returned home, a significant number have clearly opted to hang around town in preference to returning to life in the sticks.

GETTING THERE AND AWAY

By road Getting to Gulu from Kampala could not be more straightforward, a good tarmac road running all the way, crossing the Nile at Karuma Falls (see page 431). The drive takes about four hours. North of Karuma Bridge, a pot-holed tarmac road runs north for 80km to Gulu, passing the left turn to Pakwach after 3km, and the turning for Lira at Kamudini Corner, 13km from the river. In northern Uganda you take your pleasures as and when you can, and this small, nondescript junction town enjoys almost legendary status as *the* place where travellers stop for roasted roadside chicken. If **driving** yourself from Kampala, note that reliable opportunities to top up along the way are few and far between, especially on the 60km sections north and south of Karuma.

Regular **buses** and **taxis** run between Gulu and Kampala's Qualicell bus terminal (*Gulu Coach costs Ush25,000*), and other regional urban centres. The Zawadi bus (also Ush25,000) leaves at 06.00 from its William Street office behind Equatoria Mall. In the event that you're trying to reach Gulu from Masindi, you'll need to find some rustic form of public transport to cut across country to Kigumba on the Kampala–Gulu road where you'll board a more conventional taxi. If you want to travel between Gulu and southeastern Uganda, a daily bus leaves Gulu at 07.00 and passes through Lira, Soroti and Mbale on its way to the Kenyan border crossing at Busia (and vice versa).

By air Eagle Air (*www.flyeagleuganda.com*) flies from Entebbe to Gulu on Mondays (departing 12.30, arriving 14.20), Wednesdays and Fridays (departing 12.30, arriving 13.30). The timetable is subject to change.

WHERE TO STAY The ongoing proliferation of NGOs means that Gulu is well provided with hotels for all budgets. At the same time, growing competition means that the town's previously inflated accommodation rates have been reduced,

DRIVING IN NORTHERN UGANDA

The myriad cultural differences between northern and southern Ugandans extend to the use of vehicles. Anyone who has travelled any distance in Uganda will soon raise an eyebrow at one particular idiosyncrasy. The women ride bicycles! Indeed, some of the cheeky madams even ride motorbikes! This sort of thing is simply not done south of Lake Kyoga. And that is not all! In Arua a significant number of cyclists actually use lights at night, a precaution that would seem to remove much of the happy uncertainly of nocturnal bicycling. However, this cautious approach does not extend to other aspects of vehicle use. In the south, large vehicles such as buses and trucks enforce the maxim of 'might is right'. Beyond the Nile, passage belongs to whoever is prepared to push hardest for it, and that includes bicycles and boda-bodas. Southern drivers work on the assumption that cyclists will get out of their way: rather than waiting for a gap in a stream of urban bicycle traffic, they are apt to create one with their vehicle. This is not acceptable up north. If inconvenienced, a rider will quickly inform you; and in the event of a knock, a vocal civil society, in the form of the town's considerable community of cyclists and bystanders, will flock to his (or indeed her) cause. This uncompromising approach is disconcerting enough in towns, but terrifying on rural roads where larger vehicles approach each other head on in the manner of medieval jousters, doubtless a legacy of the northern warrior tradition. That any vehicles remain on the roads means that one of a pair of drivers must give way, although the goodly amount of shattered glass on the roads suggests that this is not always so. In my own experience, the driver giving way was always me.

The need for a prudent approach to driving is underlined by the nature of the dirt roads in northern Uganda. Geology dictates that, instead of the compactable red laterite used down south, engineers must often work with more gravelly material that though less slippery in wet weather, is all too easy to lose grip on in dry weather. It is also particularly prone to erosion, and deep gullies can develop parallel to or indeed across the road. Since you'll want to negotiate these additional hazards at your leisure, rather than driving into them to avoid a fellow road user, my advice is to slow down on sighting any approaching vehicle.

in effect making Gulu cheaper to visit now than in 2009. Apart from a couple of new hotels on Market Street, the town's smartest offerings are located in the select northern suburb beyond the river. The central cheapies are clustered around Olya Road in the east and Coronation Road in the west. Gulu sees regular influxes of NGO staff, partners and stakeholders for workshops, meetings, conferences, participatory planning processes, quarterly and annual reviews, etc, meaning that your first choice of hotel may be full so do book ahead if possible. For location of listings see map, page 443.

Moderate

⌂ **Churchill Courts** (23 rooms) Churchill Drive; ☏0471 432245; m 0777 764409; e gcchotel@ gmail.com; www.churchillcourtshotel.com. The friendly staff are clearly proud of their smart, secluded and comfortable hotel on the northern edge of town. It *is* very smart (apart from the health club which has burned down) & the generously sized, carpeted rooms are provided with nets, fans & TV. An ideal location in which to insulate visiting NGO country directors from the challenges of the north, Churchill Courts is often full. *US$36/45/55/65sgl/dbl/twin/exec dbl B&B & (eventual) use of health club.*

⌂ **Acholi Inn** (65 rooms) ☏04714 32880. Rather than a place to escape the issues of northern Uganda, Gulu's largest & oldest hotel is *the* place to pursue them, being a popular hangout & conference venue for government & military. I've met tourists eager to visit the shabby bar in which MPs, army officers & retired rebels mingle in the *Wizard of the Nile*. It's also notable for Gulu's only swimming pool. In such situations, I'd usually write something about age & character, albeit somewhat tarnished, being preferable to blue-glass modernism. But not in this case, though the best rooms *are* in the older part of the hotel (spacious, s/c, tiled, nets, AC) rather than in the newer extension. Rates include free internet & use of the health club. *US$40/49/49 sgl/dbl/suite B&B.*

⌂ **Bomah Hotel** (60 rooms) Eden Rd; ☏0471 432479; m 0779 945063; e bomahhotelltd@ yahoo.com. This small, long-serving guesthouse in the northern part of town has been transformed into Gulu's top hotel with the completion of a very smart 4-storey block. Everything the visiting aid worker could wish for is on site: fresh airy rooms (s/c, nets, TV, ACc), a conference hall (the Ush350,000 daily rate includes a flip-chart stand, paper & pens) & a popular garden restaurant in which members of the NGO community congregate to drink, dine & talk shop (see below). Rates

include b/fast, business centre, internet & steam/ sauna. *Old wing US$25/40/46 sgl/dbl/twin, new wing US$33/49/73 sgl/dbl/exec dbl.*

⌂ **New Kakanyero** (33 rooms) Bank Lane; m 0775 554554. The entrance into this smart new hotel serves as a portal between the hot, dusty & distinctly ordinary (but central) setting of Bank Lane & a proximate dimension provided with comfortable bedrooms with Wi-Fi & AC. If you can't cope with the contrast or the room rates, pop next door to the original Kakanyero (see budget listings, below).*US$30/36/56 sgl+/larger sgl+/ dbl B&B.*

⌂ **Hotel Free Zone** (50 room) Market St; m 0790 913342; e freezonehotel@yahoo.com. New hotel along the same lines as the nearby New Kakanyero. In their favour, the HFZ is slightly cheaper, the rates are for HB & you have to applaud management's ambitious if unrealistic goal: 'To exceed customers' expectations'. Architecturally, however, it attaches firmly to the 'Friday-afternoon-after-a-pub-lunch' school of design. The bedroom & bathroom doors tangle in the cramped AC rooms while the executive rooms are in a sort of basement. *US$26/30/49 s/c sgl/dbl/exec HB.*

Budget

⌂ **Dove's Nest** (16 rooms) Lower Churchill Drive; m 0774 591206. This smart, family-run guesthouse in the quiet 'Senior Quarters' suburb is clearly targeting the NGO market. It's billed (& justifiably so) as an 'oasis of peace & quietude where one can relax & get rejuvenated after a long day of struggle to improve the livelihood of the disadvantaged communities in the region'. Attractively furnished s/c rooms with nets, TV & fans are tremendous value. *US$36 spacious 'executive' rooms & US$26/30 sgl/db B&B.*

⌂ **Pearl Afrique** (36 rooms) Off Acholi Rd; ☏04714 32055; m 0772 435032; e hotpearlafriq@yahoo.com. This smart, storeyed hotel is the preferred choice of many visiting NGO workers. There's no garden, but the tiled terrace is a pleasant enough setting for a drink & a meal from the limited continental menu (*Ush15,000*). Internet is available. Rooms are s/c with fans, generously sized nets & piping-hot showers. The standard rooms are small but larger rooms are available. Good value for Gulu! *US$18/23/35 sgl/dbl/exec dbl.*

🏠 **Hotel Florida** (16 rooms) Olya Rd; m 0782 085803. The street frontage of this spruced-up courtyard lodge is the most distinctive of the several offerings in Olya Road. The small, tiled s/c sgl rooms are named after obscure saints (St Esther, anyone?) & are provided with nets & fans. The upstairs rooms get more in the way of air & views. *US$16 sgl+.*

🏠 **Hotel Kakanyero (Old wing)** (39 rooms) Bank Lane; ✆04714 32153. Though supplemented by a smart new middle-market extension block (see above), the original Kakanyero Hotel remains an economically priced favourite & a good fallback if your hotel of choice is full. No garden or communal areas, other than a 1st-floor restaurant with street-facing balcony. Courtyard parking. *US$16/24/24 s/c sgl/dbl/twin, US$6/8 sgl/dbl with shared facilities.*

Shoestring

🏠 **Hotel Abolo-Lapok** (12 rooms) Olya Rd; m 0774 505098. A small restaurant is attached,

but the excellent Kope Café is just metres away. Clean tiled rooms with AC, nets & fan. *US$13/15/17/17 sgl+/sgl+/dbl/twin.*

🏠 **Payero Rest House** (8 rooms) Coronation Rd; m 0772 410927. An attractive street-front veranda/bar with comfortable seating (volume reduced at a sensible hour) lends the Payero more character than other Coronation Road hotels. Rooms are small with nets & fans. Good value. *US$13/17 s/c sgl/dbl.*

🏠 **Franklin Guesthouse** (13 rooms) Nehru Rd/Main St; m 0782 331531. This pocket-friendly, centrally located lodge with street-front veranda was good enough for the chap who wrote the *Wizard of the Nile* while he pieced together the story of Moses, the LRA escapee (see page 538). *US$13 s/c sgl+, US$9/10 sgl/dbl with shared facilities.*

🏠 **Sunset Hotel** (50 rooms) Coronation Rd; m 0775 978671. This 3-building establishment centring on a cavernous central courtyard is reminiscent of Cell Block Number Nine, but good enough value for a short stretch. A basic restaurant is attached. *US$10/15 s/c sgl+/twin, US$7/9 sgl/dbl with shared facilities.*

🏠 **Binen Inn** Coronation Rd. For those on a *real* budget, here's the Binen Inn! Classic courtyard shoestring lodge with shared facilities. *US$5 sgl+.*

✘ WHERE TO EAT AND DRINK For location of listings see map opposite.

✘ **Abyssinia** Lagara Rd. Gulu's best Ethiopian food apparently – though that could mean anything since the town's other Ethiopian diner on Coronation Road closed down. *Meals Ush12,000–25,000.*

✘ **Bomah** ower Churchill Drive. The open-sided thatched shelter in the gardens of the Bomah Hotel (see above) is Gulu's most popular dining arena for the NGO crowd. A decent selection of grills & curries are served promptly & are reasonably priced. *Ush15,000–20,000.*

🍴 **The Coffee Hut** Awich Rd. Next to the Country Bakery, the juices, smoothies, toasted sandwiches (*Ush10,000*), wraps (*Ush10,000*) & free Wi-Fi make this new café a popular hangout for iThing & laptop users. Rather cleaner than the Kope, too.

🍷 **Corner Café** Busy drinking joint with BBQ chicken available on the street.

✘ **Country Bakery** Awich Rd. A lifeline for resident NGO workers & volunteers, this bakery serves Uganda's best upcountry selection of bread, pies & pasties.

✘ **Kakanyero Hotel** Bank Lane. The 1st-floor restaurant has a balcony overlooking the town (see above). *Meals around Ush9,000.*

✘ **Kope Café** Olya Rd. Comfortably furnished, if slightly down-at-heel eatery popular with volunteers & backpackers. Offerings include full English b/fast (*Ush10,000*), yoghurt-muesli, smoothies, sandwiches, curries (*Ush8,000*) & burgers (*Ush8,500*). Service is slow but it's all in a good cause: profits (which for the prices charged must be minimal) support activities by the HEAL (Health Education Literacy Sports) programme.

✘ **KSP** Queen's Rd. Diners are attracted by the menu rather than the setting & décor of this Indian restaurant at the back of the Post Bank building. At least a coat of paint has more or less obscured some dreadful murals. *Main courses Ush10,000 plus rice/naan.*

🍷 **Payero Guesthouse** Coronation Rd. The terrace with log tables & gumpole furniture is a good spot for drinks & snacks. See also *Where to stay*, above.

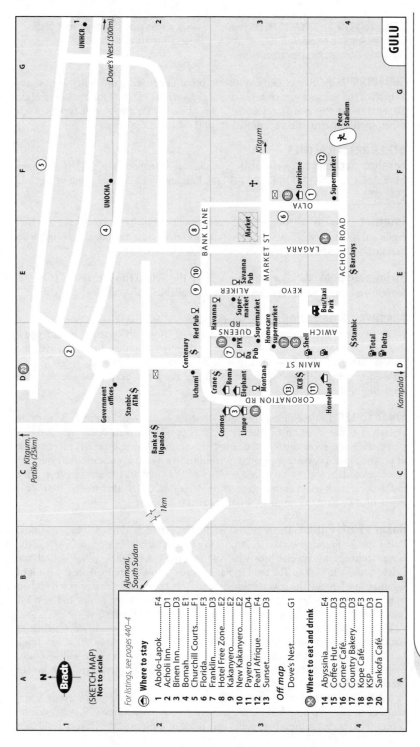

GULU

(SKETCH MAP)
Not to scale

Kitgum,
Patiko (25km)

Ajumani,
South Sudan

Dove's Nest (500m)

Kitgum

Kampala

For listings, see pages 440–4

UNHCR

UNOCHA

Red Pub

Havanna

Super-
market

Savanna
Pub

ALIKER

BANK LANE

Market

Davitime

Supermarket

OLYA

LAGARA

ACHOLI ROAD

Bardays

MARKET ST

KEYO

Homecare
supermarket

Supermarket

PYK

Da
Pub

QUEENS
RD

Centenary

Uchumi

Crane

Roma

Elephant

Montana

Cosmos

Limpe

CORONATION RD

KCB

Homeland

MAIN ST

AWICH

Shell

Bus/taxi
Park

Stanbic

Total

Delta

Government
office

Stanbic
ATM

Bank of
Uganda

Pece
Stadium

N

Bradt

1km

Sankofa Café m 0776/0701 712198. Located behind the Acholi Inn beyond the TAKS Centre, this new garden café offers juices, smoothies, coffees, snacks, burgers, pizza, chicken gizzards & salads. There's a sister branch in Lira, too.

SHOPPING Indicative of Gulu's growing prominence is Uganda's first upcountry branch of the Kenyan supermarket chain, **Uchumi** [443 D2], at the bottom of Main Street. Though this two-storey outlet is your best bet for one-stop shopping, a few other, small supermarkets are dotted around the town centre.

OTHER PRACTICALITIES
Foreign exchange Represented in Gulu are **Stanbic** [443 D2], **Centenary** [443 D2], **Crane** [443 D3], **KCB** [443 D3], **Barclays** [443 E4] and **Bank of Uganda** [443 C2].

Internet Most of the budget and moderate hotels listed above have internet facilities. In the town centre, there are a cluster of internet cafés – though with extremely slow systems – towards the bottom of Queen's Road.

Swimming pool The only pool in town is at the **Acholi Inn** (see above; *Ush7,000 for non-residents*). Sauna and steam are also available (*Ush7,000*).

FURTHER INFORMATION As intimated above, Gulu has a large population of NGO workers, both Ugandan and expatriate. If there's any possibility that you'll need to communicate with such people, I strongly recommend that you visit the website http://mysite.verison.net/grantspeak for a little preparatory work. With a little effort you'll be capable of understanding the introductory paragraph in the following section.

WHAT TO SEE In developing countries, tourism is commonly seen as a keystone activity for the creation of alternative livelihoods through implementation of sustainable and economically viable social ventures. Though there is no shortage of potential local partners prepared to commit to impactful and culturally relevant revenue models, the reality is that tourism in the Gulu area is unlikely to replace indigenous grass-root revenue-generating strategies. Or in other words, all there is to see near Gulu at the moment is Baker's Fort (see below).

Baker's Fort, Patiko The remnants of the fort established in 1872 by Sir Samuel Baker can be found at Patiko, 25km north of Gulu (about 45 minutes' drive). The return journey by special hire will cost around Ush120,000, while boda-boda riders quote Ush15,000. The road to Patiko leads out of town opposite the Bank of Uganda, just beyond the government offices. Bear right after 800m or you'll end up in Kitgum. On reaching Patiko, pass through the small trading centre and turn left immediately in front of a shiny row of police uniports to the fort.

Understandably, there is currently little in the way of organised tourism at Patiko. A visitors' book is kept in a caretaker's hut on the right of the access track but I've always found it locked. Somebody purporting to be a guide will no doubt materialise; a tour of the site is more interesting with local interpretation, however skewed, so sign them up to show you around.

Patiko Fort centres on a large kopje consisting of several rock outcrops and a number of massive boulders. Three mortared stone structures still stand on the central plateau but rather disappointingly none of these was the Bakers' residence but rather stores for grain. Mud houses stood below the kopje on an area of levelled ground and though these buildings have long gone an encircling defensive ditch remains, 100m in diameter, curved into opposite ends of the kopje like the ring through a bull's nose. This ditch was reinforced with a wooden palisade with access through a small surviving gatehouse with a narrow doorway and rifle ports. Your guide, if you find one, will show you fissures between the rocks, the holding cells in which men and women were separately confined prior to 'sorting' on an adjacent rock plateau; and the passage between two boulders through which rejected wretches were led to be speared to death and tossed off the kopje for the hyenas. On a lighter note, the tour includes two massive boulders – separated by a gap and a drop slightly too wide for carefree leaping – between which Baker is said to have regularly jumped 'for exercise'; a feat which you'll be invited to emulate (for the record, I declined, and I bet you do too!).

ATIAK

This small town lies 72km north of Gulu on the main route to Sudan (heavy truck traffic is apt to churn the Gulu–Atiak road into a quagmire during rainy seasons). A junction in the town centre forks left to Adjumani, Laropi and West Nile and right to Nimule and the Sudanese border. At the southern end of town, a reasonable road leads east to Kitgum (110km), passing a turning to Patiko after about 25km. This Kitgum route is recommended at Arra Fishing Lodge as a viable route from Laropi/Arra to Kidepo Valley National Park.

Atiak is remembered for one of the LRA's most notorious atrocities, which took place in April 1995. After repulsing an enthusiastic but ill-advised attack by a newly trained home guard, the rebels drove the vigilantes back into the town and killed 200 people. A memorial erected by the surviving townsfolk 'remembers our sons and daughters massacred on 20th April'. It is a sorry monument: the words are inscribed into a cement plaque mounted on a pillar with cracking plaster, brushed brown by the flanks of goats whose droppings litter the steps. Yet somehow the grubbiness seems more appropriate than a shiny cenotaph. The Atiak murders were utterly inglorious, as were the lives of the survivors barricaded nightly into their IDP camp for a full ten years after the massacre.

ADJUMANI AND AROUND

This small town is best known as the site of some massive refugee camps that sustained tens of thousands of Sudanese refugees for many years, most of whom have now returned home following the peace agreement. There's no particular reason to stay in Adjumani, though accommodation is cheaper than in Gulu.

The area of north-central Uganda with greatest appeal for tourists is the Nile corridor around the **Laropi ferry**. Though only 20km from Adjumani, the areas of most interest lie beyond the river and are covered in pages 424–7.

GETTING THERE AND AWAY Adjumani lies 117km north of Gulu on the *murram* road that branches off the main Sudan route at Atiak, 72km from Gulu. Of more interest to travellers is an alternative and more-or-less equidistant road to Atiak via Baker's Fort at Patiko, 25km north of Gulu. Beyond Baker's Fort (see opposite), the road heads north for another 25km to a T-junction where a left turn leads to Atiak (25km) and a right turn leads to Kitgum and Kidepo. The road beyond Patiko is a particularly remote one so ensure you leave Gulu supplied with ample fuel, water, etc.

12

Adjumani is well served by public transport. The Zawadi **bus** company's Moyo-bound buses run though Adjumani (*Ush30,000*) from Kampala's William Street.

Other services run to Gulu and Arua. If attempting a full circuit of the north between Arua, Kitgum and Kidepo, note that all public transport to Kitgum passes via Gulu. There are no services along the direct route branching at Atiak.

 WHERE TO STAY
Budget
⌂ **Zawadi Hotel** (27 rooms) m 0755 899041. This unexpectedly smart hotel in the tiny town centre has a Mediterranean feel with clay-tiled roof & white walls softened with climbing plants surrounding a courtyard. Pristine, tiled & s/c rooms are provided with walk-in nets, fans & TV. A pleasant restaurant serves main courses for

Ush15,000. Very attractively priced. *US$20/25/30 sgl/dbl/twin.*

Shoestring
⌂ **Grand Hope Lodge** (8 rooms) Behind the Grand Hope Bookshop. Centrally located shoestring option with limited parking in the courtyard. *US$7/9 sgl+/twin with shared facilities.*

KITGUM

The most northerly of Uganda's major towns, Kitgum is located two hours' drive northeast of Gulu. The 108km drive on a long dirt road, through landscapes only a sweet potato farmer could love, is an unpromising approach and quite reasonably, you wonder what sort of place to expect at the 120 minute mark. To my pleasant surprise, I found the answer to be quite a decent little town. Kitgum's compact

THE BAKERS AT PATIKO

Samuel and Florence Baker made repeated visits to Patiko (which they recorded as Fatiko). On the first occasion in 1864 they were explorers in search of geographical prizes of which Speke had heard mention but failed to nail to the map. Headed south from Gondokoro on the Nile in Sudan, they passed Patiko, before locating Lake Albert and the Murchison Falls and returning by the same route. At the time, Patiko was the southernmost outpost of a vast territory from which Egypt's Turkish rulers and their mercenaries plundered slaves, cattle and ivory.

The Bakers returned to Patiko in 1872 on a crusade to stamp out slavery in the region. On this occasion they marched under a different flag; ironically, that of Egypt. The wind had changed in Cairo with the opening of the Suez Canal in 1869. Egypt's ruler, the Khedive Ismail, was aware that while this ultra-modern development had gained him recognition from the great powers, Egypt's international standing remained tempered by the ongoing medieval barbarism in Sudan and northern Uganda. Slavery, banned a full half century earlier by Britain and France, needed to be stopped or at any rate, a high-profile attempt to do so needed to be seen to be made. Samuel Baker, whose 1865 travelogue *The Albert N'yanza* had exposed the practice to the world, was the ideal candidate and in due course (after accepting the fabulous salary of £10,000 per year) Baker returned to central Africa with his wife and nephew to formalise Egypt's presence in southern Sudan and northern Uganda by officially annexing it as a province, to be named Equatoria. Specifically, he was to establish a chain of forts to pacify the region, and end the slave trade. He found the territory around Patiko so ravaged by the Egyptian Turks that they struggled to capture sufficient people or cattle to transport their vast hauls of ivory north to Khartoum. Baker headed south to Masindi in his vain attempt to include Bunyoro

centre contains a Stanbic bank, reliable fuel stations, a couple of excellent little supermarkets and the usual corporate telecom offices. There's also a four-bar 3G internet signal to keep in touch with global trends in the sweet potato market.

Radiating outwards into the suburbs, you'll find a selection of perfectly acceptable hotels (the Bomah has a decent sized swimming pool) and an abundance of decent food and cold drinks, notably at the NGO hangout, Fugly's. Further out, however, there's a feeling that Kitgum really is rather larger than you would expect. The reason is that Kitgum, like Gulu, expanded hugely during the LRA war when the regional population was forced into IDP camps and the environs of Kitgum town. During these years, the urban population grew almost fourfold from 12,000 in 1991 to 43,000 in 2002.

As a result of the war, Kitgum has a substantial NGO presence and it is relief and rehabilitation work that brings most outsiders to the town. As far as tourism is concerned, however, Kitgum is of interest solely as a staging point to rest, refuel and stock up before the final section of the journey to Kidepo Valley National Park, another 137km to the northeast.

GETTING THERE AND AWAY Kitgum is readily accessible on the Homeland **bus** from Kampala. The eight hour journey passes via Gulu where the smooth tarmac ends and the dirt road starts. There are no scheduled flights to Kitgum. If you want to let the plane take part of the strain, the only options are **Eagle Air**'s thrice-weekly flights to Gulu and Pader. These still leave you with the challenge of covering a bumpy 108km and 70km of *murram* road respectively.

into the Egyptian Empire (see box, pages 378–9), before returning to Patiko where he established his headquarters around the kopje, from which he was able to banish the slavers and pacify local tribes made belligerent by their activities, at least in Gulu region. A long-running wrangle with a notorious slaver, Abu Saood, culminated in the slavers being routed in a battle at Patiko. When Baker finally returned to Britain, he felt able to write: 'The White Nile, for a distance of 1600 miles from Khartoum to Central Africa was cleansed of an abomination of a traffic which had hitherto sullied its waters'. In truth, Baker had merely inconvenienced the slavers of Equatoria; he had lopped off their tentacles around Gulu – an area too despoiled to be of further interest – but more soon grew elsewhere. It was, for the time being, a hopeless cause anyway, for little real success could be achieved without the support of the Egyptian administration in Khartoum. By way of example, the defeated Abou Saood fled north to Gondokoro where, to Baker's outrage, Egyptian officials did not detain him but allowed him to return to Khartoum to regroup.

Baker's legacy in Uganda is an interesting one. Speke and Stanley are remembered simply as explorers who passed through and their achievements are cited as historical fact. Baker, however, was the first to spend any significant time in the region, in the process making both friends and enemies. Around Masindi, he is remembered with little warmth as the colonial aggressor who sought to conquer Bunyoro (and kick-started a history of poor relations between Britain and Bunyoro) and you will find no Sir Samuel Baker Senior Secondary School in town. It's a different story in Gulu though, where Baker is still remembered to this day with genuine warmth as the man who drove the Arabs from Patiko.

12

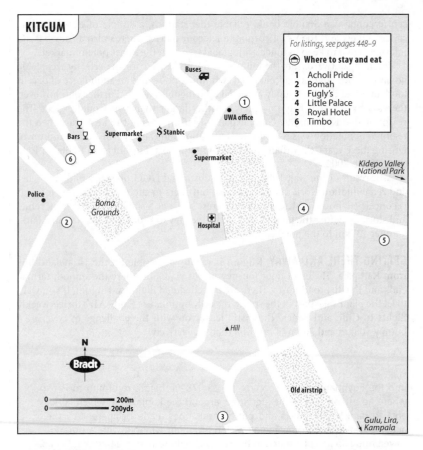

For listings, see pages 448–9

KITGUM

Where to stay and eat
1 Acholi Pride
2 Bomah
3 Fugly's
4 Little Palace
5 Royal Hotel
6 Timbo

Buses

UWA office

Bars **Supermarket** **$ Stanbic**

Supermarket

Kidepo Valley National Park

Police

Boma Grounds

Hospital

Hill

N

0 ——— 200m
0 ——— 200yds

Old airstrip

Gulu, Lira, Kampala

TOURIST INFORMATION The **UWA** office in the town centre is a useful source of information, especially if looking for transport to Kidepo Valley National Park. Alternatively, the owners of **Fugly's** (see below) are a fount of local knowedge, especially since they also operate Nga Moru Wilderness Camp at Kidepo.

WHERE TO STAY For location of listings see map above.

Moderate

Fugly's (14 rooms) m 0785 551911/072 448844; e afrimax.holdings@gmail.com. Located in a converted residential building near the airfield & the AVSI compound, Fugly's contains a bar, restaurant, small swimming pool & a variety of accommodation. The rooms range from a pair of spacious, s/c clay-tiled garden suites to a selection of basic non-s/c units. The appeal of the latter derives largely from their position at the core of the local aid community: Fugly's bar is *the* place to (a) chill out with a beer & (b) tell everyone about your day working with partners & stakeholders

to develop capacity for secure & sustainable livelihoods in Kitgum District. S/c garden suites (2) & s/c rooms in main house (2) US$60/80 sgl/dbl. US$30pp sgl/twin rooms with shared facilities.

Bomah (20 rooms) Uhuru Drive; 0471 439388; m 0775 593123; e bomahhotelktgm@ yahoo.com. Set in small but pleasant grounds just outside the town centre, the privately run Bomah was originally the Kitgum link in the government-owned (& long defunct) Uganda Hotels chain. It's not nearly as smart as the related Bomah Hotel in Gulu, but delivers the goods nonetheless. Elements of bygone charm remain while the affordable, refurbished, s/c rooms, secure parking, decent menu & Uganda's most northerly swimming pool make it an ideal overnight stop for Kidepo-bound safari-goers. Steam/sauna & free Wi-Fi. *US$20/40/37/50 sgl/dbl/twin/exec B&B.*

Budget
🏠 **Little Palace** (10 rooms) ✆0471 440201. Located just east of the Lira–Gulu road, down the last turning before the town centre/Kidepo roundabout. Tiled s/c rooms with nets & fans. Secure parking. Popular with NGO drivers. *US$20 sgl+ B&B.*

🏠 **Royal Hotel** (11 rooms) 300m beyond the Little Palace (see above); ✆0414 580305; m 0701 189911. Behind the smart, stone-clad façade, the courtyard is softened by pot plants & a fountain.

The s/c rooms are tiled with nets & fans, & Wi-Fi is available. There's a restaurant inside & an evening pork roast outside. Good opportunity to save money without resorting to the shoestring options below. *US$17/20 sgl+/dbl B&B.*

Shoestring
🏠 **Timbo Hotel** (17 rooms) On the western edge of the town centre. This spruced-up courtyard hotel offers tiled rooms & a clean communal bathroom. *US$9/12 s/c sgl/dbl, US$9 dbl with shared facilities.*

🏠 **Acholi Pride** (12 rooms) Basic, centrally located lodge & restaurant next to the UWA office. *US$11 s/c dbl, US$5 sgl with shared facilities.*

✕ WHERE TO EAT AND DRINK The compound at **Fugly's** (see opposite) is an oasis for local NGO workers. The three-course dinners (*Ush30,000*) and lunches (*Ush15,000*) enjoy a legendary status in the region – one admittedly enhanced by the absence of comparable fare within a 100km radius. One step down, the **Bomah hotel** offers a selection of decent, if predictable, upcountry continental/Indian staples (*Ush18,000*). For less sophisticated fare, a popular local restaurant is attached to the **Acholi Pride** guesthouse in the town centre. There's also the usual line of bars/shops with street barbecues serving roast goat and chicken pieces.

SHOPPING Kitgum has a couple of surprisingly good supermarkets. **A-One** and **Women's Initiative** are both located close to the Stanbic bank. Kitgum scores poorly for fresh produce so if self-catering on a Kidepo safari, stock up on fruit and veg well in advance.

OTHER PRACTICALITIES
Foreign exchange The nationwide forex and ATM services of **Stanbic** bank extend as far north as Kitgum.

13

Eastern Uganda: Kidepo to Mount Elgon

If you're a resident or returning visitor to Uganda, if you've done the gorillas, glimpsed the Rwenzori snow peaks, had your photo taken at the Equator and you're wondering what to do next, this reworked chapter is for you. The fact is (subject to the qualifications in the box on page 452), all of eastern Uganda is finally open for exploration. Follow the itinerary outlined in the box on page 453 for an unforgettable safari (one, moreover, with not a gorilla or chimpanzee in sight). Before we get down to details though, I should explain why this is such a welcome development. As far as tourism goes, the Uganda–Kenya border region has long been considered the poor relation of the southwest. While the latter boasts plenty of worthwhile attractions, the east has but two: **Mount Elgon** and **Kidepo Valley National Park**. Up in Uganda's remote northeastern corner, Kidepo Valley, arguably Uganda's finest wildlife preserve, contains rolling savannas extending towards mountain ranges in three countries, Uganda, Kenya and South Sudan. This arid and seemingly almost uninhabited region could hardly be more different from the 4,321m Mount Elgon, an extinct volcano straddling the Uganda–Kenya border. Fertile and well watered, its lush slopes support the country's highest human population density. Resorts and campsites beside delightful waterfalls provide alluring retreats while, above the *shambas*, the forests and moorlands of **Mount Elgon National Park** offer terrific hiking opportunities.

The stumbling block is that these two destinations, though quite superb in very different ways, are 425km apart. Though Elgon is easily reached by tarmac roads, most tourists, whether arriving overland from Kenya or jetting into Entebbe, head straight for the far denser cluster of attractions in Uganda's southwest. Kidepo's problem is not only that it lies a distance up the road from Mount Elgon, but that access (other than by an expensive charter flight) was long considered dangerous. The shortest route from Kampala (590km) via Gulu and Kitgum was closed for the best part of 20 years by the LRA war, while the road north from Mount Elgon (645km from Kampala) crossed the equally iffy region of Karamoja. The risk in this area was possible entanglement in armed inter-tribal cattle rustling (see box, page 457) and while the threat to foreign travellers was probably not that great – assuming they resisted the temptation to take along a herd of prime cattle – the prevalence of unsupervised AK47s in the region has etched Karamoja on to the embassies' travel advisories and placed it effectively off-limits to tourists.

Happily, the complications along both routes have now been removed and the expanses of eastern Uganda have been thrown open to modern-day explorers. The LRA war has ended, enabling travellers to reach Kidepo via Gulu and Kitgum and travel in Karamoja is also widely considered safe and practical for the first time in many years (see box, page 452 for details). The government has disarmed the Karamojong warriors and made significant improvements to regional roads, while mobile phone networks now cover the region. Karamoja might still separate Mount Elgon and Kidepo but the 400km distance is now an adventure rather than a hazard; a marvellous journey through a land of wild, rugged and often breathtaking beauty inhabited by a people who have clung to their traditional way of life with admirable persistence. The remainder of this chapter describes locations as encountered during a clockwise tour of eastern Uganda starting with Kidepo Valley National Park (see box opposite). Kitgum and Gulu, both potential stopovers on the way to Kidepo, are covered in Chapter 12.

KIDEPO VALLEY NATIONAL PARK

(The standard UWA entrance fees of US$30/20 day for foreign visitors & foreign residents apply) This remote national park lies in the far northeast of Uganda, isolated from the rest of the country by the sparsely populated, arid badlands of Karamoja region. Seldom visited by tourists due to the expense and difficulty of getting there, Kidepo is nevertheless one of the most alluring destinations in the country, boasting a strong wilderness atmosphere, rugged mountain scenery and exceptional game viewing and birdwatching.

The park covers an area of 1,442km², and it has an altitude range of between 914m and 2,750m above sea level. The highest point in the park is Mount Morungole (2,750m) on the southeastern border, and the slightly higher Mount Lutoke (2,797m), which lies just within the Sudanese border, is visible from several points. The mountainous terrain is broken by the Narus Valley in the southwest and the Kidepo Valley in the northeast. The dominant habitat is open or lightly wooded savanna, interspersed with patches of montane forest, riparian woodland, thick miombo woodland, borassus palms and rocky kopjes. Kidepo protects one of the most exciting faunas of any Ugandan national park, although its total of 86 mammal species has been reduced to 77 after a rash of local extinctions in recent years. The bird checklist of 463 confirmed and 26 unconfirmed species is second only to Queen Elizabeth National Park, and more than 60 of the birds listed have been recorded in no other Ugandan national park. That said, the variety of butterflies and other smaller creatures is far less than in the forested national parks of western Uganda.

SECURITY IN EASTERN UGANDA

To qualify my statement that Karamoja is safe for travel, I'm referring to the main roads between Mbale and Kidepo via Moroto and Kotido. Everyone we spoke to – UWA officials, hoteliers and local expatriates – affirmed that this route is safe. The only reservations were that travel after dark should be avoided, as should exploration off the main route in the direction of the Kenyan border. I should point out, however, that the ultimate sanctioning of travel in Karamoja, the lifting of long-standing travel advisories by the UK and USA diplomatic missions in Kampala, has yet to happen. If your movements are subject to such restrictions, then you should avoid Karamoja. Though both advisories permit flying to Kidepo, they are more vague on the Kitgum route. It would in any case be prudent to ask around before heading overland to Kidepo. UWA, which has staff on the ground in Kitgum, Mbale, Moroto and Kotido, as well as Pian Upe, Matheniko and Bokora wildlife reserves and Kidepo National Park, would be a good source of advice.

The establishment of stability in areas until recently off-limits due to the LRA war and Karamojong cattle raiding enables a fabulous loop through the eastern half of Uganda to explore Kidepo Valley National Park, Karamoja and Mount Elgon. From Kampala, a practical itinerary is as follows (the driving times assume reasonable road conditions): Kampala–Kitgum (six hours' drive excluding stops); Kitgum–Kidepo (three hours); Kidepo–Moroto (six hours); Moroto–Sipi Falls (five to six hours); Sipi Falls–Kampala (five hours). To fully appreciate this 1,500km circuit, plan to spend at least three nights in Kidepo and ideally a couple of nights resting up at Sipi or Mbale. If time is not an issue, there are plenty of potential diversions along the way. While you're heading north from Kampala, you may care to pop into Murchison Falls National Park (see pages 396–415) and on the way south from Kidepo, photographers will be particularly keen to capture the superb landscapes of northern Karamoja in the right light, which could mean spending a night in Kaabong. You might also delay in Moroto to visit a traditional Karamojong *manyatta* (homestead) or hike the eponymous mountain behind the town. Further south, you could also climb the even more dramatic Mount Kadam from the town of Nakapirpirit before exploring the little-visited Pian Upe Wildlife Reserve.

WILDLIFE Five primate species have been recorded in Kidepo, including the localised patas monkey. Predators are particularly well represented, with 20 resident species. Of these, the black-backed jackal, bat-eared fox, aardwolf, cheetah and caracal are found in no other Ugandan national park. Other predators recorded in Kidepo are the side-striped jackal, spotted hyena, leopard, lion, and a variety of mustelids, genets, mongooses and small cats. Twelve antelope species occur in Kidepo of which the greater kudu, lesser kudu, Guenther's dik-dik and mountain reedbuck occur nowhere else in Uganda, and other antelope species found in Kidepo are Jackson's hartebeest, eland, bushbuck, common duiker, klipspringer, oribi, Defassa waterbuck and bohor reedbuck. Kidepo also supports populations of elephant, Burchell's zebra, warthog, bushpig and buffalo. The black rhinoceros recently became extinct in Kidepo, but giraffes have been saved from local extinction by the translocation of several animals from Kenya. Kidepo's long bird checklist is made even more impressive by the relatively small size of the park and the fact that as many as 100 of the birds listed are either dry-country species, which within Uganda are practically confined to Kidepo, or else northern or eastern species, which have been noted elsewhere only in the north of Murchison Falls National Park or in the Mount Elgon area. Raptors are particularly well represented: there are 56 species in total, of which the most commonly observed are the dark chanting goshawk, pygmy falcon, tawny eagle, bateleur, secretary bird and several types of vulture. Other birds which must be regarded as Kidepo specials, at least within Uganda, include the ostrich, kori bustard, fox and white-eyed kestrels, white-bellied go-away bird, carmine, little green and red-throated bee-eaters, Abyssinian roller, Abyssinian scimitarbill, d'Arnauds, red-and-yellow and black-breasted barbets, red-billed, yellow-billed and Jackson's hornbills, Karamoja apalis, rufous chatterer, northern brownbul, golden pipit, chestnut weaver, red-billed and white-headed buffalo weavers, and purple grenadier – to name only a few of the more colourful and/or visible species.

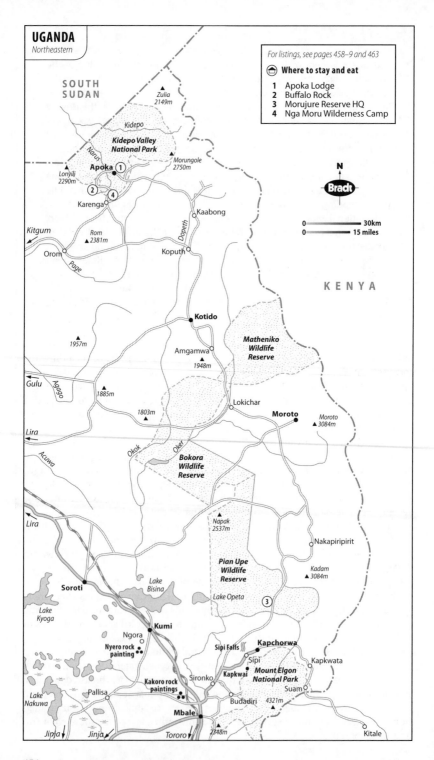

SOUTH
SUDAN

For listings, see pages 458–9 and 463

Where to stay and eat

1 Apoka Lodge
2 Buffalo Rock
3 Morujure Reserve HQ
4 Nga Moru Wilderness Camp

Zulia
2149m

Kidepo

**Kidepo Valley
National Park**

Narus

Morungole
2750m

Apoka ①

Lonyili
2290m

②

④

Karenga

Kaabong

Kitgum

Rom
▲ *2381m*

Dopeth

Orom

Page

Koputh

N

Brdt

0 ————————— 30km
0 ————————— 15 miles

KENYA

Kotido

▲ *1957m*

Amgamwa
▲
1948m

**Matheniko
Wildlife
Reserve**

Gulu

Agago

▲ *1885m*

▲ *1803m*

Lokichar

Moroto

Moroto
▲ *3084m*

Lira

Okok

Oker

**Bokora
Wildlife
Reserve**

Acuwa

Lira

▲
Napak
2537m

Nakapiripirit

**Pian Upe
Wildlife
Reserve**

Kadam
▲ *3084m*

Soroti

*Lake
Bisina*

Lake Opeta

③

*Lake
Kyoga*

Kumi

Ngora

**Nyero rock
painting**

Sipi Falls

Kapchorwa

Sipi

Kapkwai

Kapkwata

**Mount Elgon
National Park**

Sironko

**Kakoro rock
paintings**

Suam

*Lake
Nakuwa*

Pallisa

Budadiri

4321m
▲

Mbale

Jinja

Jinja

Tororo

2348m
▲

Kitale

AROUND THE PARK Kidepo Valley National Park is ringed by mountains, but its area is dominated by the broad valleys of the Kidepo River to the north, and the Narus River to the south. Apoka – the site of the park's headquarters, lodge and hostel – overlooks the Narus Valley, which is the prime game-viewing area. The park enjoys just one wet season each year, and during the long, hot, dry season game migrates south from the semi-arid Kidepo Valley to find what moisture it can in swamps and remnant pools along the seasonal channel of the Narus. The Narus Valley is explored by two game loops: the Kakine and Katurum circuits. Game is scarce in the Kidepo Valley, a result of poaching by Sudanese visitors and dry conditions. Worth a visit is the Kidepo River itself, which is beautiful in its unorthodox fashion. Lined by lovely borassus palm forest, it is for 95% of the year completely dry and its 50m-wide course is a swathe of white sand. Hot springs are found at Kanatarok on the Sudanese border, though these are a low-key event that don't compare to those in Semliki National Park in western Uganda.

En route to the Kidepo Valley, the Kanatarok Road passes through a rather incongruous 10km^2 gated enclosure contained within a 2m-high electrified fence. This was created in 2001 as a secure location for the introduction of locally extinct or endangered species, including giraffe, eland, Grant's gazelle and roan antelope. The intention is to import breeding pairs of each species and, as their numbers increase, release animals into the wild. A number of eland were brought up from Lake Mburo National Park in 2003 but unfortunately, less than rigorous firebreak maintenance enabled fire to sweep through the compound in 2005, whereupon the eland crashed through the fence and dispersed. The compound awaits new residents.

FURTHER READING Sheet 11 in the 'Uganda Maps' series covers Kidepo Valley National Park (*Ush12,500*) and contains lists of bird and mammal highlights.

GETTING THERE AND AWAY

By air For many years insecurity in northern Uganda meant that most visitors flew to Kidepo from Kampala. Even now, the distance still means that the two-hour flight to the Apoka Airstrip remains the quickest and most convenient means of reaching Kidepo. Flights to Kidepo with **Fly Uganda** (m *0776 236 699;* e *www.flyuganda. com*) cost from US$550 per person each way. **Aerolink** (e *info@aerolinkuganda. com*) fly to Kidepo on Mondays and Fridays and charge US$422/690 single/return per person. Both companies require a minimum of four passengers to make the journey.

By road Now that peace has broken out across northern Uganda, **driving** to Kidepo is feasible, either via Mbale and Moroto, or Gulu and Kitgum (see box on page 453). The road north from Kampala is tarmac, some of it pretty pot-holed beyond Karuma Falls, as far as Gulu. If you're following the loop described in the box above (see page 446), you'll be on dirt roads for some 600km until you reach Mount Elgon. Coming from Kitgum (see page 446), the 140km drive takes about three hours in good conditions. At Orom, approximately 60km out of Kitgum, a signposted left turn follows a scenic route through mountains to Kidepo's Katurum Gate via Karenga. Beyond the mountainous pass on the approach to Karenga, take care on a steep downhill section where vehicles can slide into the bushes. A **4x4** is essential. This route should be in reasonable condition, with the exception of parts of the Orom–Karenga stretch during the rains. Conditions vary on the drive south from Kidepo through Karamoja, the most notorious section being on the plain between

THE KARAMOJONG

Adapted from the draft of Uganda Safari *by Andrew Roberts*

The northeast is home to Uganda's most distinctive ethnic group, the Karamojong; nomadic agro-pastoralists known primarily for their love of cattle and cattle rustling and their resistance to the trappings of modern civilisation. The idea of 'the Karamojong people' is in fact an administrative invention, a convenient lumping together of several tribes. These do admittedly have plenty in common. The various Karamojong factions are all 16th- or 17th-century migrants from Ethiopia, all speak dialects of a common language, Akarimojong, and, most significantly, most are obsessively keen cattle keepers. This latter point is a dividing rather than a uniting factor, thanks to the fact that 'keeping thy neighbours' cattle', ideally after obtaining them by force, is equally central to Karamojong ideology. Without a patchwork of distinct tribes and clans to enable feuds, grudges, reprisals, alliances and understandings, cattle rustling would lose much of its appeal.

The so-called Karamojong people arose from a southerly migration by the Jie, an Abyssinian pastoralist tribe, 300–400 years ago. On reaching the Kenya–Uganda–Sudan border region, the Jie split to create the Toposa of Southern Sudan, the Turkana of Kenya and the Dodoth of northern Karamoja. Some of the Turkana Jie then crossed the mountains that line the present-day Kenyan border on to the plains of northeastern Uganda. Some groups remained around Kotido as the Uganda Jie. Others continued further until they were, quite literally, fed up with walking; the gist of the word 'Karamojong' means 'the old men sat down'. Some Jie groups reached southern Karamoja where they gave rise to the Matheniko (around Mount Moroto), the Bokora (on the plain to the west) and the Pian (on the plains below Mount Kadam) while others continued southwest to become the Iteso people around Soroti. The 'old men …' line is in fact attributed to a hardcore group of walkers who continued even further west before finally 'sitting down' as the Langi of Lira District.

The language of the Karamojong people is an interesting and apparently ancient curiosity. Scotsman John Wilson, who lived in and around Karamoja for 30 years, has identified numerous words and phrases of similar meaning in Akarimojong and Gaelic. Subsequent investigation has identified further similarities with other widely spaced languages including Hebrew, Spanish, Sumerian, Akkadian and Tibetan among others. To give just a few examples, we have *bot* (a house in Gaelic) and *eboot* (a temporary dwelling in Akarimojong); *cainnean* (live embers in Gaelic) and *ekeno* (a fireplace in Akarimojong); *oibirich* (ferment in Gaelic) and *aki-pirichiar* (to overflow as beer foam in Akarimojong); *cuidh* (an enclosure in Gaelic) and *aki-ud* (to drive cattle into an enclosure in Akarimojong).

Elsewhere, the Spanish word *corral*, for a circular stock enclosure, is uncannily close to the Akarimojong synomym *ekorr*, and the Spanish *ajorar* for 'theft of cattle' is not dissimilar to the Akarimojong *ajore* meaning 'cattle raid'. The thinking is that these various, far-flung modern languages are legacies of a common tongue spoken by an ancient human population, presumably before the Tower of Babel incident and perhaps as far back as the late Pleistocene. If corroborated, this would be of more than just a passing interest, for such linguistic evidence helps us to identify practices that fail to show up on the archaeological radar.

From the commonalities identified we might infer that, before they went their separate ways, the speakers of this mother tongue were (for example) cultivating land, harvesting ears of grain, creating simple reservoirs, getting drunk, plastering houses and pinching each other's cows. (Source: http://treasuresofafricamuseum. blogspot.com/)

More recently, the Karamojong have been something of an embarrassment to more Westernised Ugandans. The common view was that they were a backward lot who ran around naked and, half a century ago, the latter point was certainly true. Male attire consisted solely of an elaborately styled hairdo, a feathered headdress, a small, T-shaped stool and a spear, while female dress was represented by a heavy roll of neck beads and a bit of a skirt. These minimalist styles were driven underground in the 1970s when Idi Amin sent soldiers to force Western dress on the Karamojong at gunpoint. Men took to wearing, at the very least, a light blanket/cloak, usually of a striped or – interestingly given the suggestion of a Gaelic connection – tartan pattern. During the 1990s, this was frequently worn as a sole item of clothing but these days, some additional layers now seem mandatory, most obviously in the undercarriage department. Flashers – at least along the routes you're likely to explore – are now rare in Karamoja.

Despite expanding wardrobes and pressure from Kampala to join the modern world, most rural Karamojong remain true to their traditional way of life. Communities still commonly inhabit *manyattas*: traditional homesteads in which concentric, defensive rings of thorny brushwood surround a central compound containing huts, granaries and cattle pens. Unlike the rest of Uganda, some semblance of cultural dress remains part of everyday attire. For men this is epitomised by the cloak and some form of Western hat with ostrich feathers added to indicate status. Though the great beaded ruffs of yesteryear are less common, neck beads remain very much in vogue with the ladies.

The recent history of the region owes much to another, more sinister addition to the well-dressed warrior's kit. In 1979, when Amin's army fled north, leaving a well-stocked arsenal in Soroti barracks unattended, the Karamojong, who had suffered terribly at the hands of the dictator's soldiers, took the opportunity to arm themselves against future depredations. Thereafter, a warrior's personal effects consisted of an AK47 as well as a spear. This development transformed the nature of regional cattle raiding. Outgunned, the Pokot and Turkana sourced their own armaments from the perennial conflict in Southern Sudan. Traditional cattle rustling escalated from a violent form of football hooliganism (with perhaps more spear wounds than usually recorded on the terraces) to intentionally murderous assaults. The possibility of being caught up in such events meant that few risked visiting the region and Karamoja's isolation deepened. Between 2006–11 however, the Ugandan army managed to effectively disarm the Karamojong warriors, a process sometimes nastier than the violence it sought to suppress, but which does bring the long-term chance of regional security. That being said, the immediate border region remains subject to armed cattle raids since the Kenyan government has not disarmed its own pastoralists; now reduced to their traditional spears, the Karamojong in this area are at a distinct disadvantage.

Nakipiripirit town and Mount Elgon. We found this section so degraded that buses no longer use this route between Moroto and Mbale. However, we were told that the Chinese are preparing to surface the road as far as Moroto.

Unlike the comparably tame routes through southwestern Uganda, eastern routes pass through wild country with some challenging conditions. The following suggestions are all based on experience. Firstly, don't head north without contacting UWA or recent visitors to the region to ask about road conditions; it's pointless heading up there if the game tracks are too wet to use. Though it's better to travel during the official dry season months (October through to April), don't assume that the tracks will be totally dry either. If driving yourself, you'll need a 4x4, recently serviced and checked over by a mechanic, and with good clearance. Pack something for digging yourself out and take a tow rope if you can. Keep plenty of drinking water and snacks in the car as a matter of routine. If you know where you are going within the park, tell someone at your lodge or hostel and get a phone number. As regards your own phone, MTN and Airtel both work in the park; Orange doesn't work anywhere in Karamoja. Fill your fuel tank when you can and don't bank on finding further supplies between Kitgum and Moroto. If the pump's working, you can top up at the UWA workshop at Apoka. You'll also find a mechanic there if your vehicle is making strange noises.

By public transport It is possible to reach Kidepo without your own vehicle. The Homeland **bus** travels daily to Kitgum from Kampala, departing the Kasenyi bus park near Nakivubo Stadium daily at 07.00 and 09.00 (*Ush30,000*) and the journey takes eight hours. In Kitgum, enquire at the town's UWA office whether a **park vehicle** is headed up to Kidepo. If there's nothing doing, the UWA clerk can help you arrange a **special hire** for about Ush600,000, which includes return transport, one night in the park and a game drive. Unless you manage to **hitch a lift** with a tourist vehicle, your only other option is to board a Karenga-bound **truck** at the Little Village park opposite the Stanbic bank (*Ush20,000*). These leave around 09.00 and 10.00. Once in Karenga, 6km from the Katurum gate and about 25km from Apoka, you can call a **UWA vehicle** to collect you at Ush4,000/km. You could save a bit of money by taking a **boda-boda** to the gate but I'd hesitate to take a boda into the park itself. If you're stuck in Karenga for the night, **Number 7** is suggested as the best of a few shoestring lodgings.

To get away from Kidepo, the conservative option is to retrace your steps to Kitgum with a UWA vehicle, a truck from Karenga or by hitching a lift with other visitors. Theoretically, it should be possible to get a truck down to Kotido to find a bus to Kampala via Soroti or Mbale but I haven't heard of anyone doing this.

 WHERE TO STAY   For location of listings see map, page 454.

Upmarket

Apoka Lodge (20 beds) `0414 251182; m 0772 489497; e info@wildplacesafrica.com; www.wildplacesafrica.com. The Apoka Lodge occupies a superb location looking across the rolling plains of the prime game-viewing Narus Valley towards the Napore–Nyungea mountains beyond the national park. The main lodge building comprises a large timber deck covered by a massive thatched roof & set into the side of a kopje. Part of this outcrop has been used to create a magnificent swimming pool with a natural rock floor & a typically panoramic Kidepo view. Accommodation is provided in spacious s/c canvas-walled cottages facing the plains. *US$630/900 sgl/twin (inc drinks, game drives & walking safaris but excl park entrance) FB.*

Moderate

Nga Moru Wilderness Camp (6 cottages, 4 tents) m 0785 551911;

@ ngamoruwildernesscamp@gmail.com; www.ngamoru.com. Owned & run by a hospitable South African couple who know the importance of home cooking & cold beer, Nga Moru is an ideal base for exploring Kidepo. You'll find it overlooking the Narus Valley on a low hillside just outside the park's southern boundary & 2km east of Katurum Gate. The spacious s/c cottage accommodation is provided with large mesh windows that bring the expansive panorama right inside. Basic s/c furnished tents are also available. Though fully functioning, some final touches remain, primarily the completion of a new lodge building, superbly sited on a rock outcrop from which the view is nothing less than you would expect. See advert on page 449. *US$160/240 FB. Discounts for East African residents.*

⌂ **Buffalo Rock** (8 units) @ info@ buffalorockskidepo.com; www.buffalorockskidepo. com. This new camp, scheduled to open by the end of 2013, will offer a selection of tented accommodation (s/c & with shared facilities). The road to Buffalo Rock goes round the outside of the park to the west of Katurum Gate to find the camp on a ridge above the minor Kalukudo Gate. I hardly need tell you that the view across the Narus Valley towards Apoka is quite superb. Vehicle collection from Orom (*US$15pp*) or Kitgum (*US$30pp*),

min 3 people. *US$70/120pp sgl/dbl basic tents & US$180/280 s/c sgl/dbl tents FB. Discounts for residents.*

Budget

⌂ **Apoka Rest Camp** (24 rondavels) ☏0414 355000 (UWA Kampala HQ). Only 500m from the lodge, this UWA camp uses renovated rondavels formerly occupied by park rangers. The rest camp doesn't have a great outlook – it's about the only spot in the park that doesn't – but it is just mins from the prime Narus Valley game tracks. Bottled water, sodas & beers & simple meals are usually available, but if you require more than the basics bring it with you. A gas cooker & cook can be hired for Ush20,000. Don't expect to treat yourself at the nearby Apoka Lodge, which caters only for pre-paid overnight guests. An excellent, no-frills option. *US$25/29 s/c sgl/dbl, US$16/21 with shared facilities.*

Camping

⋏ **Kakine & Nagusokopire Campsites** UWA provides 2 campsites in the Narus Valley a few kilometres from Apoka, which have basic shower/latrine blocks & shelters. You may need to fill water jerrycans at Apoka before heading out to pitch a tent. *US$10pp.*

WHAT TO DO If you have your own vehicle, you'll have no problem exploring the park, though it would be wise to enquire about road conditions. All is not lost if you don't have a vehicle, as the UWA can provide **game drives** on a park truck at a cost of Ush5,000 per kilometre. It is also possible to arrange **guided walks** around the Apoka area in the hope of seeing more common species such as elephant, buffalo, zebra, waterbuck and hartebeest.

SOUTH FROM KIDEPO TO MOROTO

Heading south from Kidepo, the route passes through Kaabong Town and the rather larger settlement of Kotido before reaching Karamoja's largest urban centre, Moroto. We covered this 260km journey in a single day and also managed a visit to Nakaperumoro *manyatta*, 10km outside Kotido. In hindsight though, we regretted not dallying in the fabulously scenic environs of Kaabong; a mistake that became all too apparent about 30km further south when the striking montane landscape faded into a nondescript. Another decision which caused us no regrets was deciding to push on south from Kotido to Moroto where the food, setting and accommodation are infinitely superior.

KAABONG The small town of Kaabong lies some 80km south of Kidepo, surrounded by Karamoja's most spectacular scenery, a bleak and somewhat surreal landscape of mountain ranges and scattered volcanic plugs. The town is divided in two by a large seasonal river channel and the more developed section is found on the south side. There you'll find a Stanbic bank providing the usual ATM and forex services and, if you want to stay over (perhaps in the hope of a superb sunset or sunrise), the **Memama Lodge** (*US$8/11 sgl/dbl*). Located towards the southern edge of town, this offers basic rooms with shared bathrooms. A roadside sign just outside the town advertises self-contained rooms at the Sachavarian Hotel.

Getting there and away If using public transport, resign yourself to uncomfortable rides in trucks and pick-ups running north to Karenga (for Kidepo) and south to Kotido.

KOTIDO There's not much to the dusty town of Kotido, Karamoja's second-largest urban centre, and compared with Kaabong, its setting is not particularly interesting. The Stanbic bank and ATM may be useful if you need to withdraw additional funds for fuel. Kotido's fuel supply is notoriously erratic so what little is available can approach twice the normal price.

Getting there and away Kotido is 67km south from Kaabong, a drive that takes about 90 minutes on a reasonable dirt road. Though your map may suggest that the main road between Kotido–Kaabong runs north out of central Kotido, an alternative, parallel route (shown on few maps) is now used. To reach this, follow the Pader/Soroti road west out of Kotido for 3km before taking an obvious right turn to the north. Moroto is 112km south from Kotido, a slow drive on a dirt road with some bad sections which can take three hours. If arriving from Kaabong, head straight across the central roundabout for Moroto. If you don't have a vehicle, Kotido is connected to Soroti, Moroto and Kampala by a daily Gateway bus. If headed for Kidepo or Moroto, ask at the UWA office (just off the central roundabout) in case a UWA pick-up is going your way.

 Where to stay and eat When construction of the **Kotido Resort** is completed, this will be the best place in town to stay. In the meantime, **La Maison** and **Giggles Nest** are budget options signposted off the road in from Kaabong. In the middle of town, the **Discovery** (on the edge of town behind the market area; *US$10/12 s/c sgl/ dbl*) is the best of a few central shoestring lodges. Menus are limited to local dishes.

What to see The main point of interest in the Kotido area is **Nakaperumoro** *manyatta*, 8km out of town. With a population of 10,000, this is said to be the largest such settlement in East Africa. Though visits by foreign NGO workers, missionaries and other concerned parties are commonplace, bona fide tourists are rare. With, as yet, no understanding of expectations of either visitors or hosts, our visit was a strange and somewhat uncomfortable event. With a cluster of filthy children in tow, we followed our guide, a Kotido basketball hero and small-town cool dude, as he had us crawl through tiny apertures in thorn-bush pallisades to peer into peoples' huts before dragooning a posse of young warriors into a photo opportunity.

The carton of glucose biscuits we had been instructed to bring from Kotido was then distributed to children causing a small but intense riot. We were somewhat relieved when we had to return our guide to Kotido in time to take to the court for a local grudge match against Moroto. Even so, everyone we met was perfectly friendly and if structured, a visit to Nakaperumoro could be an extremely interesting experience for visitors and a useful money-spinner for the local community. To arrange a visit, the clerk at the Kotido UWA office (just off the main roundabout) will locate a guide for you. For the record, our visit cost us Ush10,000 per person plus a carton of biscuits. Expect to pay more when they get organised!

MOROTO AND AROUND

Moroto Town nestles at the base of an eponymous 3,084m volcanic massif that dominates the regional landscape for miles around. Though this remote outpost of civilisation is by far the largest urban centre in Karamoja, there isn't much to it. The central business district consists of a 100m length of tarmac lined (admittedly on both sides) by shabby, single-storey trading premises enlivened only by the renovated and freshly painted whitewashed façades of Stanbic and Centenary banks. Where local folk get the money to deposit in these institutions is also unclear as the only economic activities I heard mentioned were gold panning and cattle keeping – and the latter hardly counts as such for, traditionally, the Karamojong sell their cattle with great reluctance. Though there's not much to see or much choice regarding where to stay you'll almost certainly need to spend a night in Moroto if traversing Karamoja. In which case, thank heavens for the Moroto Hotel!

GETTING THERE AND AWAY As described in the Kotido section above, Moroto and Kotido are 112km and about three hours apart. About 100km out of Kotido, the road ends at a T-junction. Turn left towards the conspicuous bulk of Mount Moroto town to cover the last few kilometres to Moroto Town.

To travel south from Moroto to Mbale and Mount Elgon, follow the main road out of town for 9km before turning left. After 40km, this road forks, the left-hand route passing through Nakapiripirit and the right turn through Nabilutuk. Each route covers a similar distance before converging about 15km beyond Nakapiripirit at the base of Mount Kadam. Beyond Nakapiripirit, a further 110km of dirt road remains before reaching the tarmac Kapchorwa–Mbale highway at the base of Mount Elgon. This final section of *murram*, which traverses the plain separating mounts Elgon and Kadam, and which contains the Pian Upe Wildlife Reserve (see below), can be in appalling condition. It is however due to be surfaced. In the meantime, alternative routes run out of (or into) Karamoja via Soroti. One route runs from Moroto via Katakwi. You could also bypass Moroto and head straight to Soroti from Kotido via Amuria and Abim. This latter route, which passes the impressive Mount Rwot, takes about four hours in reasonable conditions.

If heading north towards Moroto from Mbale, head north up the Soroti road for 6km before turning right onto the Kapchorwa/Moroto road. You'll cruise along the base of **Mount Elgon** on a fine surfaced road for about 20km before it veers right to climb towards Sipi Falls. You're left to continue across the Pian Upe plains towards Mount Kadam on the seasonally notorious road described above. Beyond Kadam, the next volcanic landmark to aim for is **Mount Moroto**, 90km further north. This can be reached, as described above, via Nakapiripit or Nabilituk. These routes may be bumpy but passable. On joining the Soroti–Moroto road; turn right for Moroto Town (9km).

If using public transport, the Gateway **bus** runs daily from Kampala via Mbale and Soroti to Moroto (*over 8hrs*) and Kotido (*over 10hrs*). Gateway is nobody's favourite bus company so you may want to travel as far as Mbale or Soroti with a more reputable outfit.

WHERE TO STAY

🏠 **Moroto Hotel** (40 rooms) m 0787 540966/0772 320172; e morotohotel@gmail.

com. The pick of the town's accommodation is this old Uganda Hotels facility, now privately run.

Though slightly faded, the old-world charm is still apparent. Whichever direction you approach from, you'll have had a long day & you'll be more than happy to roll up here to wash off the dust & enjoy a cold drink. Located 3km beyond the town centre, this hotel has a superb setting, nestled in a great, grassy bowl in the foothills of the mountain. Acceptable meals are available but allow plenty of time for preparation. The tiled s/c rooms are fairly priced. *US$26/26/36 sgl/dbl/ twin B&B.*

🏠 **Hotel Leslona** (20 rooms) \0392 943977/0454 470137; e online@hoteleslona.com; www.hoteleslona.com. Modern hotel at the top end of the 100m section of tarmac that constitutes the town centre. To my mind, it lacks the charm of the Moroto Hotel but some regular visitors prefer it. *US$20/28/36 sgl/twin/exec.*

🏠 **Exclusive Royale** (8 rooms) Don't let the name get your hopes up, this is a basic shoestring lodge located in the town centre next to Stanbic bank. *US$7/12 with shared facilities.*

WHAT TO SEE AND DO Given that the most obvious, indeed sole, landscape feature within a 100km radius is **Mount Moroto**, it follows that the most obvious, indeed sole activity to undertake from Moroto Town is to climb the thing. Rambling over the mountain is a popular Sunday afternoon activity for the local expats, and visitors are welcome to join in. Options range from the ten-hour round trip to one of several summits, to a ten-minute potter to a lesser viewpoint behind the Moroto Hotel. I'm told that this grass- and scrub-covered mountain is home to the Tepeth people whose dwellings are concealed among jumbles of rocks. There's a waterfall up there as well as cave paintings and a plethora of bird species, including the recently sighted Boran's cisticola and blue-capped cordon bleu, previously unrecorded in Uganda. At the base of the mountain, between the town and the Moroto Hotel, a 1km track leads to a **Karamoja Museum & Cultural Centre**. If it's not locked, you can view an exhibition of regional paleontological discoveries by French scientists.

Further out of town, it should be possible to visit a traditional **Karamojong** *manyatta* and both the Moroto and Leslona hotels can arrange this. Alternatively, visit the Moroto UWA office to see what they can suggest.

Nakapiripirit Some 80km south of Moroto, this small town lies at the base of the stunning form of Mount Kadam, an isolated range of spectacularly tortured turrets and bleak volcanic plugs that rises above the plains to an altitude of 3,068m. If you have provisions and tents, it's possible to climb this 40km-long range and you can obtain guides in the town. Kadam veteran Cam McLeay suggests you try to find one who actually knows the way and plan for at least one night on the mountain. A couple of acceptable hotels in town will enable you to make an early start. If you're just passing through, there's a decent lunchtime restaurant on the west side of the main road.

PIAN UPE WILDLIFE RESERVE

(*The standard UWA fees for a Class B protected area are levied; see pages 32–3. No fee is charged for using the public road through the reserve*) Continuing our route south from Kidepo and Moroto, next up is the Pian Upe Wildlife Reserve. Though little known, this 2,788km² area is actually the second-largest protected area in Uganda after Murchison Falls. It lies in semi-arid country, which usually receives some rain in April and more substantial showers from June to early September, but there are years when the rains fail completely. The predominant cover of mixed *Acacia Commiphora* savanna is essentially the Ugandan extension of an eastern savanna belt encompassing much of northern Kenya and the Amboseli–Tsavo–Mkomazi complex of reserves on the border between Kenya and Tanzania.

Pian Upe is home to the two pastoralist tribes for which it is named: the Pian are a sub-group of the Karamojong, and the Upe a Kalenjin-speaking people more widely referred to as the Pokot within Kenya. These two tribes have a history of armed conflict, most of it related to cattle rustling. At times, the Pian and Upe have teamed up together to take on neighbouring tribes in Kenya or Uganda; at other times they have directed their violence towards each other. This insecurity is the main reason why the reserve has seen little development for tourism to date.

No reliable wildlife population estimates exist for Pian Upe, and poaching has undoubtedly taken a heavy toll since the 1970s, but anecdotal information suggests that Pian Upe still harbours a wide variety of large mammals, furthermore that populations have stabilised or even increased in recent years. Leopard, cheetah and spotted hyena are all seen quite regularly by ranger patrols, and a small population of lion is present. Among the ungulate species are Burchell's zebra, buffalo, eland, hartebeest, greater kudu, topi, oribi, dik-dik and Uganda's last population of roan antelope. In addition to the widespread vervet monkey and olive baboon, the far more localised patas monkey is quite common on the savanna. Wildlife concentrations are highest in the vicinity of the Loporokocho Swamps, which lie near the eastern border and are inhabited by Upe pastoralists who (unlike the Pian) have no tradition of killing wild animals for food. Pian Upe is of some ornithological interest, since the dry plains harbour several dry-country species with a restricted distribution in Uganda, for instance ostrich, yellow-necked spurfowl, Hartlaub's bustard, Jackson's hornbill and white-headed buffalo weaver.

If we assume (and I hope that we can) that security is no longer an issue, the main problem concerning tourism in Pia Upe is now the restricted internal road network. Other than the main road between Mbale and Moroto, this is limited to a recently reopened track leading towards Loporokocho Swamp. **Guided game walks** can be arranged, accompanied by an armed ranger, as can informal visits to one of the **Pian/Karamojong villages** within the reserve. The UWA now runs the reserve in partnership with a private operator (Karamojong Overland Safaris), and improved facilities and an expanded game track network is planned. Current information can be obtained from the UWA offices in Kampala and Mbale.

GETTING THERE AND AWAY The headquarters at Morujore are situated right alongside the direct Mbale–Moroto road, roughly 50km south of Nakapiripirit, 90km north from Mbale and 11km north of the reserve's southern boundary. For the first 30km (as far as the junction to Sipi) this road is surfaced and in a good state of repair. However, the condition of the subsequent dirt road can be pretty dire, especially after rain. You'll know you've entered the reserve when, shortly after passing through the trading centre of Chepsikunya, the road crosses a bridge over the forest-fringed Kerim River. In theory, a couple of daily **buses** run right past the reserve headquarters on their way between Mbale and Moroto but in practice, because of the condition of the road between Pian Upe and Muyembe, public transport has ceased on this route.

 WHERE TO STAY AND EAT Four *bandas* exist at the Morujure reserve headquarters [map page 454] (*US$12 each*), and a canteen serves a limited selection of drinks. Expect to bring anything else you need with you, unless advised to the contrary.

MOUNT ELGON NATIONAL PARK

Straddling the Kenyan border east of Mbale, Mount Elgon is the eighth-highest mountain in Africa, and it rises from the broadest base of any free-standing

13

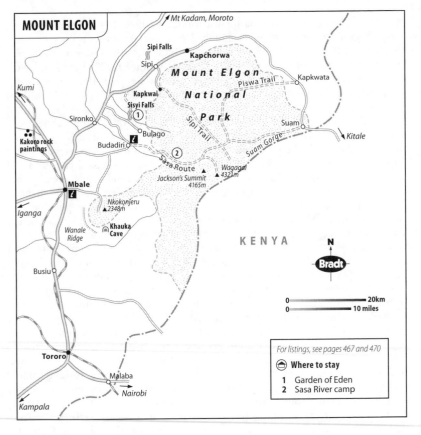

For listings, see pages 467 and 470

Where to stay
1   Garden of Eden
2   Sasa River camp

mountain in the world. Like most other major East African massifs, Elgon is the relic of an extinct volcano, whose formation was associated with the tectonic activity that created the Rift Valley several million years ago. This volcano probably first erupted at least 20 million years ago and it is thought to have remained active for another 14 million years, when it would have stood far higher than Kilimanjaro does today. Elgon's tallest peaks form a jagged circle around the more-or-less-intact caldera, which has a diameter of about 8km (making it one of the largest in the world) and is dotted with small crater lakes and hot springs created by Pleistocene glacial activity. The tallest peak, set on the Uganda side of the border, is **Wagagai** (4,321m), which lies on the southwest caldera rim. Other major peaks are **Kiongo** (4,303m) in the south, **Mubiyi** (4,210m) in the north and **Jackson's Summit** (4,165m) in the east. Elgon is an important watershed, the main source of fresh water for more than two million people in Uganda alone.

Stanley obtained a distant view of Elgon in 1875, but the first European to reach the mountain's lower slopes was Joseph Thomson, who approached it from the direction of Maasailand in 1883. Thomson called the mountain Elgon, an anglicisation of El Kony, the name given to both the massif and its inhabitants by the Maasai, who frequently visited the area on cattle raids. The local Bagisu call the mountain Masaba, the name of their founding ancestor, who is said to have emerged from a cave on the slopes several centuries ago. Masaba's spirit is believed to be personified by Jackson's Summit, which appears to be the tallest peak from many vantage points, while Wagagai is named after and associated with Masaba's wife. In February 1890, Jackson and Gedge ascended Elgon from a base camp at modern-day Kapchorwa, crossing the caldera and climbing one of the peaks (long assumed to have been Jackson's Summit, but more probably the taller Kiongo Peak). The Kenyan portion of Mount Elgon has been a national park for several decades, whereas the Ugandan part of the mountain above the 2,000m contour was gazetted as a 1,145km² national park only in October 1993.

Elgon's vegetation zones are similar to those of other large East African mountains. Below the 3,000m contour, the mountain supports a contiguous belt of evergreen forest extending over roughly 750km² within Uganda. This forest belt can be divided into two broad strata: tall Afro-montane forest below 2,500m, and low canopy montane forest and bamboo between 2,500m and 3,000m. The slopes below the 2,000m contour, which lie outside the national park, also supported significant forest cover a century ago, but much of this forest has since been cleared for cultivation. Above 3,000m lies the heather belt, giving way at around 3,500m to other-worldly Afro-alpine vegetation studded with stands of giant lobelia and groundsel, including the endemic *Senecio barbatipes* and *Senecio elgonensis*.

Hikers on Elgon are unlikely to encounter many large mammals aside from blue monkey and black-and-white colobus. A small number of elephant are, however, resident on the mountain, as is a population of the localised and striking De Brazza's monkey, as well as leopard, bushpig, buffalo, sitatunga and common duiker. The official checklist of 24 mammal species will surely expand when an intensive survey is done, especially as an increasing number of animals are crossing back to Uganda from Kenya.

The bird checklist of 305 species, of which more than 20% are unconfirmed, further indicates that more studies are required before knowledge of the park's fauna can be considered anywhere near complete. The mountain supports a rich variety of forest birds, as well as several which are endemic to East Africa's montane moorlands. Twelve of the species listed for Elgon occur in no other Ugandan national park, in many instances because Elgon lies at the most westerly extent of its range. Of particular interest are Jackson's francolin (recorded only once), moorland francolin (elsewhere common only in Ethiopia's Bale Mountains), moustached green tinkerbird, red-throated wryneck, black-collared apalis, Hunter's cisticola, alpine chat, marsh widowbird and Weyn's weaver. The endangered bearded vulture or lammergeyer is regularly observed soaring at higher altitudes.

Despite its enormous hiking potential, Mount Elgon has never really caught on with hikers. In large part, this has been due to intermittent security problems,

ELGON WARNINGS

Elgon lies below the snowline, but it can be very cold at night or in windy weather. You must be sure to bring enough warm clothing. It is not high enough for altitude sickness to be a major cause of concern, but you may experience headaches and other altitude-related symptoms near the peaks. Water on the mountain should be purified or boiled before drinking. The ascent of the escarpment via a tricky path known as the Wall of Death on the Sasa Route is not recommended if you are afraid of heights. It is mandatory for trekkers visiting the hot springs area between Mude and Hunters caves to be escorted by an armed ranger.

13

particularly on the Kenyan slopes, but it's probably also that Elgon lacks the popular mystique of Kilimanjaro, Mount Kenya or the Rwenzori. The ascent of Elgon is, however, far less financially draining than that of any other major massif in East Africa, while offering similar exposure to the weird and wonderful world of the Afro-alpine zone. In past decades, Elgon was most often climbed from Kenya, but this has changed with the creation of better facilities and guides in Uganda. Logistically, the trailheads of the Ugandan national park are far easier to reach on public transport than their Kenyan counterparts. It is also worth noting that Wagagai, the tallest peak, stands on the Ugandan side of the border. Note that it is now possible to traverse the mountain, ascending the Ugandan side and descending through the contiguous national park in Kenya. Ask at the Mbale UWA office for further details (see page 477). For more on hiking, see below.

For less serious hikers, the area around Mount Elgon also offers plenty of alluring prospects which are detailed later in this chapter, on pages 467–76.

GETTING THERE AND AWAY The national park can be explored only on foot, but most of the trailheads can be reached on **public transport**. The most established route up Elgon is the **Sasa Route**, the trailhead for which is at Budadiri on the western slopes. Two more recently established trails to the peaks lead from the northern footslopes: the **Piswa Route** (trailhead at Kapkwata) and the **Sipi Route** (trailhead at Kapkwai). Information on accessing the trailheads can be found under the heading *Around Mount Elgon* later in this chapter. Transport from Mbale to any of the trailheads can also be arranged through the national park information office in Mbale (see page 477).

WHERE TO STAY Accommodation exists at all three trailheads (see *Around Mount Elgon* for details). There's only one hut for hikers on the mountain so you'll need a tent and sleeping bag. Porters will cut grass to make you a 'mattress' to put under your sleeping bag and this is useful for comfort and warmth at higher altitudes.

HIKING A daily hiking fee of US$90 per person includes the park entrance fee and a guide. Additional fees are charged at US$8 per night for camping and US$6 per day for each porter.

Elgon is not a difficult mountain to climb. Aspirant hikers need to be reasonably fit, but no specialised equipment or skill are required to reach the peaks, and there's no serious risk of the altitude-related illnesses that regularly afflict hikers on the upper slopes of mounts Kilimanjaro or Kenya. Elgon can be climbed at any time of year, though the dry seasons (June to August and November to March) are best, in particular November and December when the highland flowers are in bloom. Another attraction is the cost: compared with other large mountains in East Africa, the price of ascending Mount Elgon is very reasonable. Allowing a generous US$28 for food, you'll spend just US$130 a day.

All hikes must be arranged directly through the national park staff. This can be done at the Mount Elgon tourist office in Mbale, which lies about 100m from the Mount Elgon Hotel, or the equivalent office at the trailheads of Budadiri, Kapkwata or Kapkwai. It doesn't really matter where you make arrangements, but it probably does make sense to drop into the central office in Mbale to talk through route options before you decide on a trailhead. Porters (carrying a maximum of 18kg each) must also be arranged through the national park offices. Most hikers cater for themselves, but this can be talked through with the park staff.

Several hiking routes are available. Traditionally, the most popular has been a four-day round trip from Budadiri to Wagagai following the Sasa Route in both directions. Other possibilities include a five-day round hike from Budadiri, taking in Wagagai and the hot springs, and a six-day hike between Budadiri and Kapkwata via Wagagai and the hot springs. These days, however, it's probably best to ascend via the newer Piswa or Sipi routes, which start at much higher altitudes than Budadiri, making for a more gradual and far less strenuous ascent, then to return using the Sasa Route. The experienced national park staff can give more detailed advice on the various options.

On the first day out of Budadiri (1,250m), the Sasa Trail involves a stiff six- to eight-hour walk via the village of Bumasifwa to Sasa River Camp (2,900m). This is followed on the second day by a four- to five-hour walk to the 16-berth hut at Mude Cave (3,500m). Many people use the spare afternoon at Mude Cave to ascend Jackson's Summit (4,165m), which is a round trip of around five hours. On the third day, you will ascend from Mude Cave to Wagagai (4,321m) and back, a long hike of eight to nine hours. Hikers doing the standard four-day route will descend from Mude Cave to Budadiri the following day.

Alternatively, day four will see hikers doing the full trek to Kapkwata proceed from Mude Cave to Hunters Cave Camp (3,870m) via the hot springs, a trek of at least ten hours. On the fifth day, they will descend to Piswa Camp, a five-hour trek, and on the sixth day to Kapkwata, a further four hours. It is possible to combine the last two days into one, thereby cutting the duration of the trek to five days. As already noted, hikers who want to do the full route should consider starting at higher elevation at Kapkwata or Kapkwai rather than Budadiri.

The construction of a 16-bunk hut at Mude Cave means that a tent is no longer absolutely necessary. In theory, trekkers can hike up from Budadiri to Mude Cave Hut on the first day, make a round trip between Mude and the peak on the second, and descend to Budadiri on the third. These are long days though and you'll need to be a strong climber to appreciate them.

AROUND MOUNT ELGON

The sites discussed below, starting in a clockwise direction from Budadiri, all lie on the footslopes of Mount Elgon, and in most cases they stand as worthwhile travel destinations in their own right, as well as being trailheads for hiking routes into the national park. Traditionally, the most popular destination in the Elgon area is **Sipi Falls**, which is not only readily accessible on public transport, but also offers a good range of accommodation for all budgets as well as several day-walking possibilities outside the national park. The **Mount Elgon Exploration Centre** at Kapkwai is, however, a more worthwhile goal for those with a strong interest in natural history, but also more costly as park visitation fees must be paid.

BUDADIRI Budadiri, a small trading centre situated a few kilometres outside the western park boundary, is the established starting point for hikes on Mount Elgon. Although non-hikers seldom visit Budadiri, one interesting local attraction is the **Numagabwe Cave**, which lies about 3km away and is decorated with ancient rock paintings. Either of the hotels in Budadiri can organise a day trip to the caves, as well as longer caving expeditions for those with the necessary equipment.

Getting there and away Budadiri lies about 35km from Mbale by road. The best route entails following the surfaced road towards Sipi and Kapchorwa out of town for 24km to Sironko, then after another 2–3km turning into the signposted dirt road to the right. Several **minibus-taxis** and **pick-ups** run daily to Budadiri from Mbale, leaving from a stand along the Kumi Road about 300m north of the clock tower, and taking roughly 45 minutes in either direction.

BAGISU CIRCUMCISION CEREMONIES

The western slopes of Mount Elgon are home to the Bagisu, a Bantu-speaking group with few cultural or historical links to the linguistically affiliated kingdoms of western Uganda. The origin of the Bagisu is uncertain; their oral traditions assert simply that the founding ancestor Masaba emerged from a cave in the synonymous mountain perhaps 500 years ago. Masaba – also the local name for the mountain – is said to still inhabit Elgon's upper slopes, where he holds meetings with lesser deities at a place where stones have been laid out to form chairs and tables. Bagisu society recognises no central leadership and each autonomous clan is presided over by its own non-hereditary chief, appointed by a committee of elders. Traditionally, the judicial powers of the chief were in many respects subservient to those of sorcerers and witch-finders, who used to exert a steel grip on the social affairs and perceptions of the Bagisu.

The Bagisu, together with their Sabiny neighbours, are the only Ugandans to practise male circumcision (unlike the Sabiny, however, the Bagisu do not circumcise females – see box, pages 474–5). The origin of this custom is obscure, and several contradictory traditions have been recorded. One somewhat improbable legend has it that the first Bagisu man to be circumcised had a reputation for seducing the wives of his neighbours, and was taken before the committee of elders, who decreed that he should be semi-castrated as both punishment and deterrent. This plan backfired when, having recovered, the offender went back to his seductive ways, and – it was whispered – had become an even more proficient lover following the operation. After that, his rivals decided that they too would have to be circumcised in order to compete for sexual favours! Nice story, but all things considered it's more likely that the custom arose through contact with a neighbouring people who had an existing tradition of circumcision, for instance the Kalenjin of western Kenya.

Whatever its origin, the circumcision ceremony or *imbalu*, held on even-numbered years, is the pivotal occasion in Bagisu society, an individual rite of passage to manhood that involves the entire local community. Unusually among those African societies that practise circumcision, the year in which an individual will undergo the ritual is dictated not by strict convention nor by the council of elders, but by his own personal choice – any age between 16 and 26 is considered acceptable. Those who elect to be circumcised in any given year announce their intention in May or June, and spend the next few months preparing for the main ceremony. The most visible facet of the preparations involves the initiate, adorned in plantain fronds or animal skins and ash-plastered face, and accompanied by a band of cheering friends, parading and dancing through the streets to visit all his close relatives and seek their approval.

The climactic ceremony, according to certain historical sources, is traditionally held in August by the Bagisu and in December by the Sabiny, but these days it appears that both groups hold ceremonies during both of these months, though mainly in December. It normally takes place in the morning, well before 10.00, and involves all the initiates from a given clan – anything from one to several dozen young men – being marched by a whistling, cheering crowd to the circumcision ground. The initiates have their faces plastered in ash, and they are stripped below the waist on the way to the circumcision ground, where they must line up in front of a crowd of family and friends of both sexes and all ages. Elsewhere in Africa, the circumcisions are normally performed indoors, with only a handful of associates in attendance. This was previously the case with the Bagisu, as only the initiates and the circumcisor were allowed into the special initiation enclosure. Today, however, the circumcision is a public event that anybody – including tourists – may attend.

The operation lasts for about one minute. The initiate holds both his arms rigid in front of him, clasping a stick in his hands, and staring forward expressionlessly. The circumcisor then makes three bold cuts around the foreskin to remove it from the penis. When the operation is complete, a whistle is blown and the initiate raises his hands triumphantly in the air, then starts dancing, proudly displaying his bloodied member to an ululating crowd. Any initiate who cries out during the painful procedure is branded a coward (as is any Bagisu man who is circumcised by a doctor under local anaesthetic). Once the crowd is satisfied of his bravery, the initiate is led away to a quiet place by a few friends, and seated on a stool and wrapped in cloth while he waits for the bleeding to cease. He is then taken to his father's house, where he will be hand fed by his relatives for three days. Finally, the initiate's hands are ritually washed, after which he is permitted to eat with his own hands, and his rite to manhood is completed.

While it is wholly acceptable for a Bagisu man to delay circumcision into his late 20s, he will not be considered a true man until he has undergone the rite, and will be forbidden from marrying or attending important clan meetings. A man who refuses to be circumcised past the accepted age parameters will be hunted down by his peers, and cut by force. It is not unknown for octogenarian men to be denounced as uncircumcised by a younger wife, and dragged off by a mob for a forced operation. And in one famous incident a few years ago, a Bagisu man who had lived overseas for decades, and had thus far escaped the knife, was abducted by his peers when he arrived at Entebbe International Airport, and taken away to be circumcised. When I first visited Mbale in 1992, a local councillor made the front page of the national papers when, accused by his drinking pals of being uncircumcised, he dropped his trousers in a bar. When later he was accused of having faked a circumcised appearance using an elastic band, he responded by exposing himself at a public gathering, where doubters could ascertain his adulthood for themselves.

Travellers who visit Mbale, Sipi or Kapchorwa during the circumcision season are welcome to attend any local ceremonies that take place – they occur on practically a daily basis during December and to a lesser extent August, of all even-numbered years. The easiest way to find out about upcoming ceremonies is to ask local hotel staff. A small fee will usually be asked – particularly if you're thinking of taking pictures – but the Bagisu and Sabiny seem genuinely keen to have outsiders attend their most important ceremony. There is no taboo on women being present. Male visitors can expect a few (joking?) invitations to join the initiates as they line up to be cut!

⌂ Wagagai Hotel (28 rooms) m 0776 613664 Appropriately, the number of rooms in this hotel equates to the number of years that elapsed between the start of construction in 1980 & eventual opening in 2008. The long-awaited product is clean, smart but otherwise unremarkable – save for a 1st-floor balcony with a stupendous view up the valley from Budadiri towards a montane amphitheatre crowded by Elgon's high peaks. A new campsite & dorm block make this the town's most attractive

option for climbing groups. *US$10/18 s/c sgl/dbl, US$8 dorm bed, US$4 camping.*

⌂ Rose's Last Chance m 0772 623206; e lastchance.hotel@yahoo.com. This long-serving & hopefully-priced guesthouse is split between a decidedly scruffy old guesthouse opposite the UWA office & newer but similarly rustic premises just up the road. *US$18/26/14/10 sgl/dbl/dorm/camping HB.*

BULAGO An attractive detour on the way up to the Sipi area leads to the scenic village of Bulago. Approaching from Mbale, turn off the new, tarmac Sipi Road (see below) on to the *old* Sipi Road at Kaserem about halfway up the mountainside. The turning is signposted to Kamu, an important local market centre. After 2–3km turn left up the mountain. The road winds beneath some superb cliffs and passes through a small but pretty rock gorge before reaching Bulago. The village stands on a cliff top above a lovely waterfall dropping into a pretty, grassy meadow. A rocky plateau beyond the village overlooks the Simu Valley to Butandiga Ridge, and a path climbs to the cliffs bordering the national park, over which a couple of streams fall. There is no official accommodation in Bulago (we were kindly allowed to sleep on the floor of a nearly completed clinic and departed with feet full of jiggers). Also bear in mind that the road to Bulago is steep and deteriorates quickly after rain so be aware of the weather and retreat if necessary.

SISYI FALLS This pretty waterfall is visible for miles around as it plunges over a lofty cliff from the direction of Bulago village (see above). The base of the falls is occupied by a basic resort named, not at all presumptuously, the **Garden of Eden** (m *0703 588284; US$32 s/c dbl cottage room B&B, US$20pp lazy camping, US$10pp own tent, all rates B&B; day visitors Ush5,000 entrance*). Dotted with house-sized basalt boulders softened by lichen and surrounded by lush, tropical vegetation (tamed sufficiently to be garden-esque) the result is a delightful 'Lost World' feel. The falls are a couple of minutes' walk uphill but their constant sound permeates the gardens. In the middle of all this are a couple of cottages, each containing two self-contained rooms. Whilst crying out for a Sipi River Lodge-style facelift (see Sipi Falls below) they are very fair value. The real jewel is a camping ground set among the boulders which is one of the loveliest in the whole country. Sisyi Falls lies 5km off the main tarmac road at Buyaga, about 7km north of Sironko town.

SIPI FALLS The Sipi River rises on the upper slopes of Mount Elgon before cascading down the foothills over 7km to form a series of four pretty waterfalls culminating in a 99m drop at an altitude of 1,775m outside the small trading centre of Sipi, 60km from Mbale by road. Overlooking the main waterfall is a choice of resorts and campsites that cater to all budgets and make an agreeable base for gentle day walks in the surrounding hills, with their spectacular views over the Kyoga Basin and glimpses of the nearby Elgon peaks.

The most popular walking trail, only 20 minutes in each direction, leads from behind the post office in Sipi trading centre to the base of the main waterfall, where a small entrance fee is levied. If you choose, you can continue along this trail for another 20 to 30 minutes to reach a cluster of caves on the cliff above the river. The largest of these caves extends for about 125m into the rock face, and contains rich mineral salt deposits that have clearly been worked extensively at sometime in the past, as well as traces of petrified wood. Walking back to the trading centre from the caves along the main road, you'll pass the top of the main waterfall, as well as an important local shrine set within a small forest-fringed cavern.

More ambitiously, it is possible to undertake a day hike from the main waterfall to the three smaller falls that lie upstream, one of which has a tempting swimming pool at its base.

If you do intend to visit the waterfalls, you'll need a guide. This is not only necessary to help you locate some of the sites, but also because the guiding fees include a contribution to local landowners for access to each of the falls. It's far simpler to pay a flat fee for guiding and entrance than worry about access fees for up to five sites. If you're staying at Sipi, your lodge will arrange a guide. If you're a day visitor or a new arrival, you'll quickly find that Sipi is one of those travel hotspots – the only one in Uganda – where it's difficult to walk more than five paces without an annoying youth latching on and asking to guide you (or running out in front of your vehicle as you enter the village). Don't hire a guide off the street; instead drop in at one of the lodges and have them find one for you. Though a guide is more-or-less mandatory to visit the waterfalls, casual exploration of the area remains possible. If you follow the right turn up the motorable *murram* track about 500m beyond the village, several left turns make for pleasant walks, one of them climbing to the hillside above the highest waterfall for great views.

Getting there and away
Sipi trading centre lies about 60km from Mbale on the Kapchorwa–Suam road. From Mbale, follow the Kumi Road out of town for 5km, and then turn right on to the Moroto Road. The turning to Kapchorwa lies 33km further on and the tarmac also turns right here, rather than heading to Moroto! The waterfall is clearly signposted just after you pass through Sipi trading centre. Formerly notoriously bad (the villagers immediately below Sipi did good business putting up bogged travellers), the road to Sipi has now been surfaced in its entirety, and it is currently one of the best roads anywhere in Uganda.

Without private transport, the best way to get to Sipi is with one of the **minibus-taxis** that head to Kapchorwa from Mbale at least once every hour. These leave Mbale from the small taxi park on the Kumi Road about 300m past the clock tower. Expect the trip to take between 60 and 90 minutes and cost Ush7,000.

Tour operators
A local company called **Rob's Rolling Rock** (m *0752 963078*) arranges abseiling on the cliffs around the waterfall for US$50.

🏠 Where to stay
Upmarket
🏠 **Sipi River Lodge** (4 cottages) m 0751 796109; e info@sipiriverlodge.com; www. sipiriverlodge.com. This terrific little lodge is not only the best on Mount Elgon, it's the best beyond Jinja. Indeed, if we factor in affordability, it tops my list for anywhere east of Kampala. Set in lovely, lightly wooded grounds at the foot of the middle waterfall & with a distinctly homely atmosphere, it's a great place to rest up for a couple of days after the long haul down from Kidepo. The pick of the accommodation is a pair of new cottages, s/c with sitting area, dbl bed, 2 sgl beds & large picture window facing the waterfall. If your budget objects, simpler s/c & non-s/c accommodation is also available. The main lodge occupies a transformed bungalow with a homely lounge, bar & an excellent library with internet. Activities include Sipi walks, coffee tours, mountain biking, archery ascents of Mount Elgon & fly fishing in the river above the waterfall. *US$150/200 s/c with waterfall view Kapsurur & Aniet cottages,*

US$105/170/275 s/c sgl/dbl/family *Chepkui Cottage*. US$85/105 sgl/dbl banda *with shared facilities*, US$50pp dorm banda. *All rates FB.*

Moderate

⌂ **Lacam Lodge** (6 rooms) m 0752 292554; e info@lacamlodge.co.uk; www.lacamlodge.co.uk. Lacam occupies a steep hillside provided with plenty of steps immediately beside the main Sipi Falls – so close that the waterfall is mostly heard rather than seen. Though the steep cliff below the site will give parents with young kids the willies, the sudden drop makes the view down the Sipi Valley to the vast plain containing lakes Bisina & Kyoga particularly dramatic. Cottages fashioned from log offcuts are topped with roofs thatched in the local style. These are s/c with hot showers & compost toilets. US$32/48/72 sgl/dbl/trpl s/c cottages & US$24pp dorm bed B&B.

⌂ **Sipi Falls Resort** (5 cottages) m 0752 529040/0753 153000. Sipi's oldest resort was initially a quaint retreat for the Governor of the Uganda protectorate in the 1950s. His small resthouse served as a backpacker hostel during the 1990s before the site was expanded as the Sipi Falls Resort with the addition of 5 simple, s/c bamboo-&-thatch *bandas*. As you'd expect, it occupies a great site overlooking the main waterfall. The food is surprisingly good too. US$70/96 sgl/dbl cottages FB, negotiable.

Budget & shoestring

⌂ **Noah's Ark Sipi** (5 rooms) m 0779 060104. This small & unremarkable guesthouse is nonetheless useful due to its location directly across the main road from the Sipi River Lodge. It's ideally placed if you'd like to enjoy the hospitality of the latter for lunch or dinner (see below) but funds don't stretch to an overnight stay. US$24/32 sgl+/dbl B&B.

⌂ **The Crow's Nest** (8 rooms) m 0772 687924/0752 515389; e thecrownets@yahoo.com (note 'nets', not 'nest'); www.sipifalls.isrepresenting.com. Built in the 1990s with the assistance of 2 former Peace Corps volunteers, the Crow's Nest has a wonderful situation on a small hill about 500m before Sipi trading centre, offering a grandstand view of all 4 waterfalls along the Sipi River as well as the peaks of Mount Elgon. Accommodation is in simple log cabins. The equally rustic restaurant has a great view, see below. A short nature trail encircles the hill above the camp, while longer guided walks can be arranged to the various waterfalls. US$28 twin cabin, US$14pp (decker bed) or US$14pp (dbl bed) log cabins, US$3pp camping, inc tea/coffee & bananas at b/fast time.

⌂ **Moses's Campsite** m 0752 208302/0788 060401. Though this is by far the simplest of Sipi's offerings, I've never failed to find at least 1 happy camper in residence at this long-serving, family-run set-up. Camping & basic *bandas* (non-s/c) are provided on a cliff-top site with a terrific view (again, not one for parents with young kids) & friendly & helpful hosts. Meals can be provided with plenty of notice. US$6 bandas, US$3pp camping.

✗ **Where to eat and drink** All the resorts and lodges listed above serve food. Though the pick of the bunch is **Sipi River Lodge**, lunch Ush20,000 and four-course dinners Ush30,000, the dinners at **Sipi Falls Resort** are also very good. Non-residents are welcomed for meals at all of the lodges, provided that they give a few hours' advance notice and some advance payment. **Crow's Nest** serves a selection of stir-fry, spaghetti & local dishes for around Ush10,000.

KAPKWAI (MOUNT ELGON FOREST EXPLORATION CENTRE) (*The UWA entrance fees for a Category B protected area apply to stay in the Exploration Centre & to walk the forest trails. The standard guided walk fees apply to the latter, see pages 32–3*) The Forest Exploration Centre at Kapkwai, situated at an altitude of around 2,050m immediately within the national park boundary, was originally designed as an educational facility for schoolchildren living around Mbale. Over the past few years, it has also been developed for tourism, with the opening of a network of day trails, a hiking trail to the Elgon peaks, and a comfortable rest camp consisting of four log cottages, a similar number of standing tents and a good canteen. Only

1–1½ hours from Sipi village on foot, Kapkwai is an excellent destination for travellers who don't want to do an extended hike on Mount Elgon.

Three connecting, circular day trails run through the exploration centre. The 7km, four-hour **Mountain Bamboo Loop** leads past a cave before climbing to the main viewpoint (from where, on a clear day, the peaks of Mount Elgon can be seen), and then follows a ridge northwards through montane forest to a large bamboo forest. The popular 5km, three-hour **Chebonet Falls Loop** passes the eponymous waterfalls as well as involving a climb up a rock chimney and passing through areas of montane and bamboo forest leading to the main viewpoint. The 3km, two-hour **Ridge View Loop** involves a relatively easy ascent of the ridge, where it connects with the other trails at the main viewpoint.

In addition to passing through areas of regenerating forest, fields of colourful wild flowers and extensive stands of bamboo, the day trails offer a good chance of sighting black-and-white colobus and blue monkeys. The centre is highly rewarding to birders, with a high proportion of the 305 species recorded in the national park present. The lovely cinnamon-chested bee-eater, Doherty's bush-shrike and golden-winged sunbird head a long list of highland species resident in the riverine scrub close to the rest camp. Among the more conspicuous birds of true forest – the Mountain Bamboo Loop is probably the most productive trail – are black-and-white casqued hornbill, Hartlaub's turaco, bar-tailed trogon, grey-throated barbet, montane oriole, mountain greenbul and black-collared apalis.

Getting there and away The exploration centre lies roughly 12km from Sipi by road. To **drive** there, follow the surfaced Kapchorwa Road out of Sipi for 6km, where a prominent signpost to the right indicates the 6km dirt road to the entrance gate and rest camp. Except after heavy rain, the road should be passable in any vehicle. For those without private transport, there are two options. Most straightforward is to catch any vehicle running between Mbale and Kapchorwa via Sipi and ask to be dropped at the junction to Kapkwai, from where the 6km **walk** to the rest camp shouldn't take longer than 90 minutes. Alternatively, the guides in Sipi can lead you along a more direct 90-minute **walking trail** for about Ush15,000 per person. It should also be possible to arrange a **special hire** out of Sipi or Mbale.

Where to stay and eat

Kapkwai Cottages & Rest Camp [map page 464] \0414 355000 (UWA Kampala HQ), 04544 33170 (Mbale office); e uwaface@imul. com. The rest camp at Kapkwai sprawls attractively across the slopes near the source of the Sipi River. There are 3 simple s/c timber cabins with twin beds & hot water, & camping is also permitted.

The attractive Bamboo Grove Canteen serves basic but decent meals for around Ush10,000, as well as air-cooled beers & sodas. The reasonable rates are less so when the UWA park entrance fee is added. *US$20 for a solitary 'exec' dbl banda, US$16 cottage, US$8pp camping, rates excl park entrance.*

KAPCHORWA The administrative headquarters of the synonymous district, Kapchorwa lies at the heartland of Uganda's main Arabica coffee-production area, and the major development within the town is a vast and recently rehabilitated coffee-processing plant. Kapchorwa is an odd little place: a vast but unfocused semi-urban sprawl of only 10,000 inhabitants that somehow manages to straddle the Suam Road for perhaps 2km. An attractive and breezy montane setting goes some way to compensating for the town's rather scruffy appearance, but you could argue – convincingly – that the best thing about Kapchorwa is the scintillating ascent road from Sipi, which offers some wonderful views to Lake Kyoga and the

The Sabiny people of Kapchorwa District are the only ethnic group in Uganda to practise female genital mutilation (FGM) – often and somewhat euphemistically referred to as female circumcision. Traditionally, Sabiny girls are expected to succumb to the knife shortly after reaching puberty, but before they marry, in the belief that having the clitoris removed reduces the temptation to indulge in promiscuity. Should a female Sabiny refuse to be cut, she will forever be accorded the social status of a girl – forbidden from marrying, or from speaking publicly to circumcised women, or from undertaking women's tasks such as milking cows, collecting dung to plaster walls and drawing grain from the communal granary.

FGM is traditionally performed during the December of every even-numbered year. Several girls generally participate in one communal ceremony, and the festivities last for several days before and after the actual operation, which takes only a few minutes to perform. One by one, the girls are instructed to lie down with their arms held aloft and their legs spread open. Cold water is poured on the vagina, and the clitoris is pulled and extended to its fullest possible length before it is sliced off, together with part of the labia minora. Should a girl cry out during the procedure, she will be branded a coward and bring shame and misfortune to her family. When all the participants have endured the operation, they are herded to a collective enclosure. Here, according to J P Barber, who witnessed a ceremony in the 1950s: 'they bend and kneel, they moan and whistle, in an attempt to lessen their extreme agony. Their faces … are drawn and contracted. They are too conscious of pain to notice or care about anything or anybody.'

No anaesthetic or disinfectant is used, and the operation is often performed on several girls in short succession using a non-sterilised knife or razor, or even a scrap of sharp metal or glass. Short-term complications that frequently follow on from the procedure include haemorrhaging, urinary retention and temporary lameness. In the years that follow, mutilated women often experience extreme pain during sexual intercourse, and bear an increased risk of complications related to childbirth. For some, circumcision will prove fatal. A small proportion of girls will die immediately or shortly after the operation from uncontrolled bleeding, shock or infection. Others face a lingering death sentence: the HIV virus is occasionally transmitted during mass operations, and mutilated women are often prone to vaginal tearing during intercourse, which makes them especially vulnerable to sexually transmitted diseases.

Public debate around the subject of FGM is traditionally taboo. The first local woman to come out strongly against the custom was Jane Kuka, head of a local teacher-training college in the 1970s. Herself defiantly uncircumcised, Kuka educated her students about the dangers of FGM, hoping they would act as ambassadors to the wider community. In 1986, encouraged by Museveni's strong commitment to women's rights, and assisted by the local representative of the WHO, Kuka launched a more open campaign, one that met strong opposition from community leaders who felt that outsiders were criticising and interfering with their culture. In response to this provocation, a district by-law was passed in 1988 requiring all Sabiny women to undergo FGM – any woman who did not submit to the knife voluntarily would do so by force. Kuka visited the cabinet minister for women in Kampala, and together they flew a helicopter to

Kapchorwa to rescue as many victims as they could. At the minister's insistence, the by-law was revoked shortly after it came into being, but still too late for the hundreds of women that had been seized, bound and forcibly circumcised by the district authorities.

Kuka's major breakthrough came in 1992, with the formation of the Sabiny Elders Association, which aimed to protect the Sabiny culture by preserving songs, dances and other positive customs, but also wanted to eliminate more harmful traditions, notably FGM. At the same time, Kuka consolidated her network of local women's groups to launch the UN-funded REACH programme, which adopted a culturally sensitive strategy, endorsing most Sabiny traditional values but highlighting the health risks associated with FGM. In 1996, coinciding with the start of the initiation season, the two organisations staged the first Sabiny Culture Day, which highlighted the positive aspects of local traditions while doubling as a substitute for the traditional female initiation ceremony. In place of a rusty knife, female initiates were given a symbolic gift, and counselled on subjects such as HIV prevention, family planning and economic empowerment. The number of girls who underwent FGM in 1996 was 36% lower than it had been in 1994.

In 1996, Kuka swept to a landslide victory in local elections for a parliamentary representative, to be appointed Minister of State for Gender and Cultural Affairs, giving her a more prominent forum for her campaign. Her new appointment also ensured that she had the ear of President Museveni, who made a personal appearance at the 1998 Culture Day to deliver a speech about the dangers of FGM. The efforts of Kuka and Museveni were undermined that year by those of a short-lived organisation called the Promote Sabiny Culture Project, which outspokenly advocated FGM and offered a payment of US$100 and gifts of cloth and animals to families who agreed to cut their daughters. In reaction, an American non-profit anti-circumcision organisation called the Godparents started offering cattle, goats and money for scholarships to parents of girls who pledged not to undergo FGM.

Many Sabiny traditionalists regard female circumcision as integral to their cultural identity: the rite of passage that transforms a girl into a woman. In more remote parts of the district, uncircumcised women still experience social discrimination, and their families stand to gain materially from the substantial gifts they customarily receive from friends and relatives on the day of initiation. One strongly reactionary element is the female elders who are paid to perform the operations – finance aside, these women are not eager to relinquish their elevated status as community advisors and custodians of tradition and magic. But FGM is now illegal in Uganda, and while clandestine ceremonies are still held in certain remote areas, the number of women who undergo it today is a mere fraction of those who would have been cut a decade ago.

The remarkable progress made towards eradicating FGM locally within the space of one generation can be attributed partially to the Sabiny being culturally anomalous in Uganda – the rest of the population has never subscribed to the practice. It is sobering to realise that, according to WHO estimates, some 100 million women across 26 countries elsewhere in Africa have suffered some form of genital mutilation, and there are several countries in which more than 90% of females have undergone the procedure.

13

isolated Mount Kadam. If you're up for some exploration, the surrounding slopes must also offer plenty of good walking, with one possible goal being a little-known series of caves on a cliff outside town.

Getting there and away Kapchorwa lies 14km past Sipi along the road to Suam (the road is surfaced 1km beyond the town but no further). Regular **minibus-taxis** run between Mbale and Kapchorwa, leaving Mbale from the taxi park about 300m north of the clock tower on Kumi Road, and stopping at Sipi on request.

Where to stay and eat For location of listings see map, page 464.

Pacific Hotel (25 rooms) m 0775 981069. The views from this new storied hotel aren't as splendid as might be expected, something to do with having the bathrooms rather than the balconies looking towards Mount Kadam. It's still the smartest place in town though. A restaurant is attached. *US$16/18 s/c sgl+/twin B&B.*

Noah's Ark Hotel (30 rooms) m 0779 060104. This rambling lodge uphill from the main road is painted orange inside & out, & offers s/c rooms, & rooms using common showers. The rooms look somewhat timeworn & there is no running hot water (a bucket will be supplied on request), but all things considered it's reasonable value. The large restaurant & bar serves a limited menu of local dishes & cold beer. Don't confuse this hotel with the related but overpriced Noah's Ark Resort up the road ('For VIPs only'). *US$10/16 s/c sgl/dbl & US$8/12 non-s/c sgl/dbl B&B.*

Mosop Guesthouse (12 rooms) Situated on the main road, this simple, salmon pink-fronted lodge offers basic s/c, lino-floored rooms. *US$8 sgl+.*

KAPKWATA The small trading centre of Kapkwata, which lies about 30km from Kapchorwa along the *murram* road to the Kenyan border crossing at Suam, is of interest mainly as the trailhead for the **Piswa Trail** up Mount Elgon. In addition to being a trailhead, Kapkwata offers travellers heading to Suam a good excuse to break up the journey, in the form of an obscure **forestry resthouse**, situated at the rangers' post roughly 500m past the trading centre. The resthouse has three rooms – one single (*US$8*), one double (*US$14*) and one six-bed dormitory – and camping is also permitted. No park entrance fees are charged. Staff can cook meals to order, or you can eat in one of the small restaurants in the trading centre. There are several good **day walks** from the resthouse to local viewpoints.

SUAM Suam lies at an altitude of 2,070m on the Kenyan border, and it is only likely to be passed through by travellers crossing between Kitale and Mbale north of Mount Elgon. A few trucks run between Kapchorwa and Suam daily, taking roughly four hours when the road is dry and a great deal longer in wet conditions. This is likely to be a pretty hairy trip, so it would be worth trying to secure a seat in the front. There are a couple of basic lodgings in Suam as well as a **UWA guesthouse** nearby (*US$8/14 sgl/dbl*). Alternatively, you can continue directly across the border, which is connected to Kitale by a reasonable surfaced road and regular minibuses.

MBALE

Mbale was, until the recent population booms in Gulu and Lira, the third-largest town in Uganda, with a population estimated at 75,000 (in 2002). Set at an altitude of around 1,200m at the foot of Mount Elgon, it has considerably more going for it than any other Ugandan town east of the Nile. While the likes of Iganga, Pallisa, Soroti and Lira, etc, seem to float in the featureless plains of eastern Uganda, Mbale enjoys a welcome sense of place being firmly moored, as it were, to the foot of

Mount Elgon's dramatic Wanale cliffs, the westernmost limit of the massif. On a clear day, the volcanic peaks of the 4,321m Mount Elgon are also visible from the town centre.

Relatively few travellers pass through Mbale, and those who do are generally *en route* to Mount Elgon or the Sipi Falls. There is no overwhelming reason to stop over in town for longer than is required to change public transport, but if you do, you'll find the range of tourist facilities is among the best in Uganda. That Mbale was less scarred by the events of 1971–86 than most other Ugandan towns is reflected in the healthily bustling atmosphere of the modern town centre, and several well-preserved examples of colonial-era Asian and European architecture. The leafy suburbs around the Mount Elgon Hotel make for a pleasant afternoon stroll.

GETTING THERE AND AWAY Mbale lies about 235km from Kampala along an excellent surfaced road through Jinja and Iganga. Traffic congestion on the outskirts of Kampala plus slow trailers and tankers on the Jinja Road mean that the trip can take up to four hours. Turn left about 3km east of Iganga to avoid Tororo and follow the zippy and almost traffic-free Turini Road (100km) straight to Mbale. There is plenty of public transport from Kampala to Mbale. The **Post Bus**, which leaves Kampala from the main post office on Kampala Road at 08.00 daily except Sundays takes about six hours. The **Elgon Flyer bus** also runs between Kampala and Mbale, and departs from opposite La Bonita theatre in the city centre. Regular **minibus-taxis** are a lot quicker, but are driven with less care. Regular taxis connect Mbale to Jinja and Tororo, as well as Kumi, Soroti and Moroto in the north. Most local places of interest can be reached by minibus-taxi and details are given under the individual sites later in this chapter.

TOURIST INFORMATION The **Mount Elgon National Park tourist information office** [480 F4] (☎ *04544 33170;* e *uwaface@imul.com*) lies about 15 minutes' walk from the town centre, on Masaba Road just before the Mount Elgon Hotel. The helpful staff can arrange all aspects of hikes on Mount Elgon, including equipment hire, and will also do their best to provide current information about other sites associated with the mountain, such as Sipi Falls and the Pian Upe Wildlife Reserve. A useful information board is posted with flyers from various hotels and restaurants within the Elgon region.

 WHERE TO STAY For location of listings see map, page 480.

Upmarket

🏠 **Mbale Protea** (74 rooms) ☎ 0454 433920; e res@phmbale.co.ug; www.proteaotels.com/mbale. The plush annex attached to the adjacent Mbale Resort Hotel has been signed over to the South African Protea hotel chain, along with the popular swimming pool. As you'd expect, the Mbale Protea provides everything the business traveller might expect: a smart 1st-floor restaurant (see page 482), a pool & carpeted s/c rooms with AC, DSTV, tea-/coffee-making facilities & Wi-Fi. If you can't quite believe you're in a Protea in Mbale, branded bottles of bathroom unguents add verisimilitude. *US$220/240 exec sgl/dbl, US$120/140 sgl/dbl.*

Moderate

🏠 **Mount Elgon Hotel & Spa** (50+ rooms) ☎ 04544 33454; e info@mountelgonhotel.com; www.mountelgonhotel.com. If the bland indulgence of the Protea is not your cup of tea, you'll appreciate this stalwart former government hotel on Masaba Road, 2km from the town centre. Refurbished by Italian investors, this listed, 1950s building is set in spacious grounds. Beyond the swimming pool terrace & a luxurious spa (steam, sauna, jacuzzi, massage), the Wanale cliffs provide a lovely backdrop when lit by the early evening light. There's also a crazy golf course, a feature which (free to residents & Ush2,000 to visitors) is as fun as it is

In 1900, the narrow belt of no-man's-land that divided the cultivated footslopes of Nkokonjeru and its Bagisu inhabitants from the pastoralist people of the Kyoga Basin made a less than favourable impression on visitors. C J Phillips described the area as 'a long wilderness of scrub', William Grant deemed it 'a dreary waste', while one early Muganda visitor called it 'a small and fearsome place, swarming with wild animals'. Back then, certainly, it would have taken a bold soul to suggest this area would become the site of the third-largest town in Uganda! But then Mbale is possibly unique among comparably sized East African towns in that it isn't rooted in a pre-colonial settlement, nor is it truly a colonial creation, but was instead founded by the controversial Muganda administrator and soldier Semei Kakunguru.

Between 1889 and 1901, Kakunguru had single-handedly – or rather with the assistance of a private army of 5,000 Baganda soldiers – subjugated and administered the region of eastern Uganda known as Bukedi (a disparaging Luganda term meaning 'Land of Naked People') as an agent of the British Crown. By 1901, however, Kakunguru was perceived by his colonial paymasters to have developed into a tyrannical force – the self-appointed 'King of Bukedi' – that they could neither stem nor control. In the words of A L Hitching, Kakunguru had indeed 'first reduced [Bukedi] to order, cut the roads, and began to direct the local chiefs', but it was 'rather after the method of making desolation and calling it peace'. And bad enough, that Kakunguru and his army evidently regarded Bukedi 'as a sort of El Dorado', raiding the local cattle and crops at whim. Worse still, the authorities at Entebbe had every reason to believe that their employee was less than scrupulous when it came to declaring and returning the tax he had collected in his official capacity for the Crown.

The Entebbe administration decided that this untenable situation could be resolved only by retiring the self-styled King of Bukedi from the colonial service. But how to achieve this when any hint of force might prompt Kakunguru's army to stage a rebellion the authorities would find difficult to contain? A series of tense communications resulted in a mutually agreeable compromise: Kakunguru would resign his post and hand over his fort at Budoka (30km west of present-day Mbale). In exchange, he would be given 20 square miles (52km^2) of land at a site of his own choosing. Kakunguru selected the plains below Nkokonjeru, which, although practically unoccupied, were run through by several perennial streams and lay close to a reliable supply of the favoured Baganda diet of *matoke*.

Kakunguru and his Baganda followers relocated to Mbale in March 1902, and immediately set about building a new township, one that by several accounts bore strong similarities to the Buganda royal enclosure on Kampala's Mengo Hill. The first European visitors to trickle through Mbale in early 1903 were astonished at the transformation wrought by Kakunguru in one brief year. Bishop Tucker reported that 'on what was little better than a wilderness … we found ourselves surrounded by gardens, well cultivated and well kept; houses, too, had sprung up on every hand, most of them well built'. An equally gushing William Grant described Mbale as 'flourishing with gardens, teeming with life' and added that 'good wide roads have been cut, rivers have been bridged and embankments made through marshy ground, all at [Kakunguru's] expense and for public use'. A map of Mbale dating to 1904 indicates that the central market was situated roughly where the clock tower stands today. Running southwest from the market, a wide road lined with shops and houses approximated the equivalent stretch of present-day Kumi Road. This road continued southwest for about 300m to Kakunguru's fortified compound, which consisted of a large rectangular stone building and seven smaller huts protected within a tall reed fence.

This rapid growth of Mbale was not solely due to its founder's estimable ambition and drive. One contemporary visitor, the missionary J J Willis, described the town's location as 'a natural centre' for trade, elaborating that: 'An excellent road connects Mbale with Jinja to the southwest. A caravan route, very far from excellent, connects it with Mumias to the south. Caravans [from Karamoja] pass through Mbale laden with ivory. And to the northwest a caravan route passes through Serere and Bululu to the Nile Province.' Mbale usurped nearby Mumias as the most important regional trading centre; indeed its market soon became the largest anywhere in the protectorate after Kampala and Entebbe. The permanent population of the nascent metropolis – estimated by Willis to stand at around 3,000 – comprised not only Kakunguru's Buganda followers, but also a substantial number of Greek, Arab, Indian and Swahili traders.

In hindsight, it might be said that when Kakunguru handed over Budoka Fort to Britain, he did not so much abandon his 'El Dorado' as relocate it (and expand it) at his personal estate of Mbale. That much was recognised by the new commissioner, James Sadler, when he made a tour of Bukedi in January 1904. Sadler characterised the established administrative centre at Budoka as consisting of 'two wattle and daub houses and some dilapidated police lines' on a 'bad' site that was 'neither liked by Europeans nor natives'. Mbale, by contrast, impressed him as 'the natural trade centre of the district [and] centre of a Baganda civilisation [of] flourishing plantations [and] substantially built grass-roofed houses'. Sadler decided that Mbale should forthwith replace Budoka as the administrative centre of Bukedi, and attempted to rein in Kakunguru by reappointing him to the regional administration. In 1906, the authorities realised that they would gain full control over Bukedi only in the physical absence of Kakunguru, which they achieved not by retiring him, but by tantalising him away to Jinja to serve as the official head of state of Busoga, a position he held until 1913.

Mbale's rise to prominence had its setbacks. In 1909, Cook described it as a 'thriving little place entered along a broad well-kept road, nearly a mile in length, bordered by thousands of *emsambya* trees and numerous native houses … crowded with the once-turbulent Bagisu engaged in the peaceful activity of bartering their native produce'. A year later, the colonial administration – for a variety of opaque reasons – banned the ivory trade from Karamoja, causing foreign traders to desert Mbale and the district commissioner to bemoan that 'a legacy of debts is about all that remains of what used to be a profitable and flourishing business'. A few years later, tentative plans to relocate the regional administration to Bugondo, a newly developed ferry port on Lake Kyoga and the site of two large ginneries, were shelved following the outbreak of World War I. As it transpired, Bugondo's brief heyday would be curtailed by a post-war drought that left it high and dry, while the strategic location chosen by Kakunguru took on fresh significance with the rise of the motor vehicle as the natural hub of the road network east of Lake Kyoga.

13

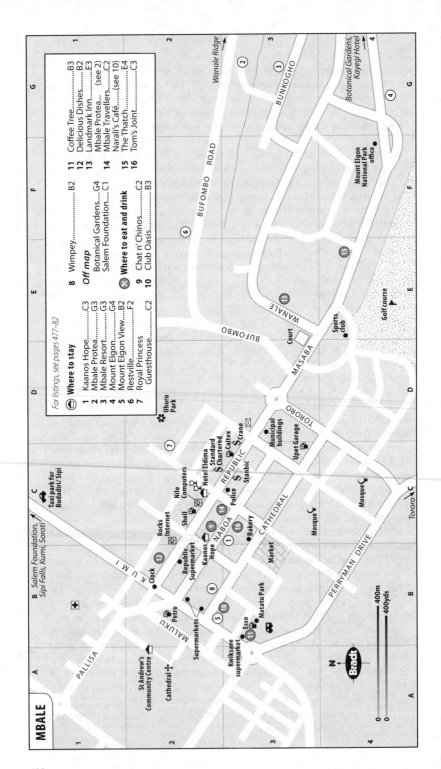

MBALE

Wanale Ridge

WANALE

BUNKOGHO

BUFOMBO ROAD

Botanical Gardens,
Kayegi Hotel

Mount Elgon
National Park
office

Golf course

Sports
club

BUFOMBO

MASABA

Court

Municipal
buildings

Upet Garage

TORORO

Uhuru
Park

Standard
Chartered

Hotel Eldima

Crane
Caltex
REPUBLIC

Stanbic

Nile
Computers

Police

Rocks
Internet

Shell

NABOA

Kaanos
Hope

Bakery

Mosque

Mosque

Mosque

CATHEDRAL

Taxi park for
Budadiri/Sipi

Clock

KUMI

Republic
Supermarket

Market

Matatu Park

Esso

Kwiksave
supermarket

Supermarkets

Petro

MALUKU

PALLISA

St Andrew's
Community Centre

Cathedral ✝

B *Salem Foundation,*
Sipi Falls, Kumi, Soroti

PERRYMAN DRIVE

Tororo C

N

Brädt

400m
400yds

0

unexpected. A restaurant serves acceptable meals for around Ush20,000. The rates for the spacious, s/c rooms include use of the pool, crazy golf & the spa. There are also some great-value basic s/c rooms in a guesthouse annex just across the road. *US$130/150 exec sgl/dbl, US$100/130 superior sgl/dbl, US$80/100 sgl/dbl, US$17/25 sgl/dbl in guesthouse annex. All rates B&B.*

⌂ **Mbale Resort Hotel** (19 rooms) 2km east of the town centre; ✆04544 33920/34485; e sales@ mbaleresorthotel.com; www.mbaleresorthotel. com. Once the automatic choice for visitors to Mbale, the Mbale Resort is reduced to a shadow of its former self, having leased its smart annex & popular swimming pool to the Protea hotel chain (see above). The rates for the remaining rooms may be more affordable than those of its illustrious neighbour but for what's on offer, they seem foolishly optimistic. Guests intent on swinging a cat should insist on 1 of the 4 larger units above the health club; those in the main block have insufficient room. The gym/sauna is free to guests who now pay Ush10,000 to use the pool. *US$39 small s/c sgl, US$64/72s/c sgl/dbl B&B.*

⌂ **Kayegi Hotel** (25 rooms) ✆04544 432118. This storeyed hotel is located beyond the Mount Elgon Hotel at the eastern end of town. It ignores the view of the nearby Wanale cliffs, but the s/c rooms are smart & the room rates are extremely fair. Nets, fan & DSTV provided. *US$30/34/34/40 sgl/dbl/twin/exec B&B.*

⌂ **Hotel Restville** (10 rooms) Bufombo Rd; m 0703 880000; e info@hotelrestville.com; www. hotelrestville.com. This hotel has a quiet location (except when it hosts a function) on the road to Wanale cliffs. The pick of the current choice (s/c & smartly tiled with nets, fans, & attractive soft furnishings) is a couple of sumptuous executive rooms. Wi-Fi is available. *US$25/29 exec dbl, US$17/21 dbl/twin B&B.*

Budget

⌂ **Wimpey Hotel** (29 rooms) Cathedral Rd. This hotel has smart, tiled rooms with fans & nets. Front rooms enjoy small street-facing balconies. Basic meals are available in the revamped Wimpey Restaurant on the ground floor, while roasted meats are served in an open-air bar in the courtyard behind. *US$20/26/28 s/c sgl+///dbl/twin B&B.*

⌂ **Mount Elgon View Hotel** (21 rooms) Cathedral Rd; m 0772 445562. The long-serving

Mount Elgon View is conveniently located for the taxi park, restaurants, bars & internet. Offers clean & spacious s/c dbls with netting, fan & a table & chair, as well as similar-quality rooms with use of clean common showers. Bus horns will wake you before dawn but it's worth it to be able to wander on to the rooftop balcony to enjoy the sunrise over Mbale's roofscape & the Wanale cliffs beyond. An annex, just across Kumi Road, offers large, s/c dbl rooms with secure parking. *US$8/12 sgl/dbl with shared facilities. US$15/18 sgl/dbl s/c in annex.*

⌂ **Salem Foundation** (16 cottages) 10km from Mbale along the Soroti Rd, 15mins' walk from the turn-off at Nakaroke; ✆04544 36030; m 0772 505595. The hostel run by the Salem Brotherhood lies in a rustic setting, & beer & good vegetarian meals are available. Proceeds support the foundation's work which includes healthcare & the support of orphans. The large, clean, simple *bandas* with dbl beds are good value. *US$15/24 sgl/dbl B&B.*

⌂ **Botanical Gardens** Follow the road past either the Sunrise or Mbale Resort hotels; ✆04544 36076. This Church-oriented guesthouse is set in a pleasant, palm-shaded garden. The quiet, suburban location at the eastern end of town is appealing, as are the rates. Rooms are basic but clean. *US$13/22 s/c sgl/dbl B&B.*

Shoestring

⌂ **Kaanos Hope** ✆04544 36341. Cheaper than the annex (100m away) but with tiny s/c rooms. *US$8.*

⌂ **Landmark Inn** (3 rooms) East of town centre; ✆04544 33880. Set in a colonial homestead – complete with red-tiled roof & pillared veranda – the Landmark stands in large grounds a short distance from the town centre. Any temptation to modernise the building has been resisted, resulting in a dated & acceptably rundown interior – & a slide into the shoestring category. Plentiful birdlife includes nesting pelicans. Excellent Indian food is served (see page 482). With only 3 rooms, booking is advisable. Good value. *US$14 s/c dbl.*

⌂ **Kaanos Hope Annex** (12 rooms) Naboa Rd; m 0772 511954. This spruced-up courtyard hotel is centrally located & offers s/c rooms with TV, fans & net. A restaurant/bar provides drinks & a snack menu with a pleasant pavement terrace. Seems good value. *US$10/14 sgl+/twin.*

13

🏠 **Royal Princess Guesthouse** (6 rooms) m 0714 321993/0752 321882. Tucked away down the hill behind the Eldima Hotel, this small hotel is a favourite with volunteers in the area. A restaurant & additional rooms are being constructed. Terrific value. *US$10/12 s/c sgl/dbl.*

✗ **WHERE TO EAT AND DRINK** In addition to the options listed below, **Mount Elgon Hotel** and **Mbale Resort** (see page 481) all serve good Western dishes. Meals cost around Ush12,000–25,000. An emergent line of **pavement bars** and attendant **street barbecues** can also be found on the side road off Republic Avenue next to the Eldima Hotel. For location of listings see map, page 480.

🍴**Chat 'n' Chinos** Naboa Rd. A bold excursion into alien territory, this one! This new venture serves coffees, lattes, smoothies, milkshakes, hummus, tacos, & provides internet facilities. *Meals Ush6,000–15,000.*

✗ **Coffee Tree Bar & Restaurant** The menu is rather limited & none too exciting – meat, rice & not much else – but it's a good place for a drink, & (with several DSTV screens) it tends to be packed on Sat & Sun afternoons during the English football season. *Meals Ush8,000–15,000.*

✗ **Delicious Dishes** Republic Av, Clock Tower end. Ignoring the daft name & ordinary interior, this new restaurant serves huge portions of terrific Indian food. *Main courses costs Ush16,000 exc rice/naan.*

✗ **Landmark Inn** East of town centre; ☎04544 33880. Recommended for the food & the garden setting, the Landmark Inn (see *Where to stay*, page 481) serves top-notch Indian cuisine. *Main course inc rice, chips or naan bread around Ush20,000.*

✗ **Mbale Protea** ☎0454 433920; www. proteaotels.com/mbale. The smartest venue in town, the Protea's 1st-floor restaurant is worth digging out your clean set of clothes for. *Mains Ush16,000–30,000, desserts & starters from Ush10,000 upwards.*

✗ **Mbale Travellers Inn Café** We were too bloated from lunch at Delicious Dishes (see above) to spot this new café opposite the police station but it's apparently very good indeed. Local & basic continental dishes.

✗ **Narali's Café** Centrally located (below the Mount Elgon View Hotel), this excellent Indian restaurant serves a wide selection of meat & vegetarian dishes. A selection of non-Indian dishes is available, too. The bar is a good place to hang out at any time. *Meals Ush10,000–20,000.*

🍷**Tom's Joint** Naboa Rd. Mainly a drinking hole, this cosy bar serves grilled chicken or beef in the evening.

NIGHTLIFE

☆**Club Oasis** Next to Narali's Café; m 0772 552150. Mbale's nightclub is Club Oasis, where there's a disco most nights & live music on occasion.

🍷**The Thatch** Masaba Rd. New garden complex dominated by a large thatched building. Pleasant place for music, drinks & roasted snacks.

SHOPPING Good, centrally located **supermarkets** are found on the road to Tororo between the clock tower and the Mount Elgon View Hotel, and on Republic Road. The central **market** [480 B3 and C3] on Cathedral Road is usually overflowing with fresh produce from the surrounding agricultural lands.

OTHER PRACTICALITIES

Foreign exchange The **Stanbic** [480 C3], **Crane** [480 D3] and **Standard Chartered** [480 C2] banks on Republic Road will change foreign currency at their Kampala rates.

Internet Try **Chat 'n' Chinos** café on Naboa Road [480 C2], otherwise a couple of internet cafés are found near the Caltex on Republic Road. Internet facilities are also available at the **Mbale Resort** and **Mount Elgon hotels**.

WHAT TO SEE The main tourist attractions in the Mbale area are Mount Elgon National Park and the Sipi Falls, both covered earlier in this chapter. The following site also makes for an interesting and straightforward day excursion out of Mbale.

Wanale cliffs The waterfall-streaked cliffs of Wanale Ridge dominate Mbale's eastern skyline, marking the end of the 2,348m Nkokonjeru 'Arm', a 20km ridge of lava extruded through a parasitic vent on the western flank of Mount Elgon. A 20km road from Mbale climbs up on to the ridge through a cleft in the cliffs, meandering through superb mountain scenery before terminating at a cluster of radio masts which provide a map-like view of Mbale and vast panoramas towards distant horizons. The ridge is also accessible from Mbale using a steep footpath (find a guide in Mbale or at the UWA office) or on one of the few daily minibus-taxis. Mount Elgon National Park extends along Nkokonjeru to Wanale, and the UWA offers two guided walking trails of 3km and 6km in length through regenerating forest. An interesting geological feature along the trail is **Khauka Cave**, which contains logs of petrified wood. The cost of US$25 plus US$15 guide fee per person is rather off-putting, since walking along the road or public lands is equally attractive. A considerably more exciting means of viewing the ridge is by **tandem paragliding** (*www.flymamiafrica.com*). Excursions from Jinja to Mbale, including transport, two nights' half-board accommodation and flights with a qualified instructor cost US$225–200 for one or two people.

KUMI AND AROUND

Kumi, founded in 1904 by Semei Kakunguru as an administrative substation of Mbale, is named after the jackal-berry tree *Diospyros mespiliformis* (known locally as *ekum*) that proliferates in the vicinity. Kumi is today the headquarters of Kumi District, a full 35% of which comprises wetland habitats associated with Lake Kyoga and its drainage basin, while the remainder is covered in dry savanna studded with spectacular volcanic outcrops. A rather sleepy and nondescript small town (population 12,000), Kumi is of interest to travellers primarily as a springboard for visits to the nearby Nyero Rock Paintings and Lake Bisina.

GETTING THERE AND AWAY Kumi straddles the surfaced Mbale–Soroti road roughly 55km north of Mbale and 45km south of Soroti. The drive from either of these towns should take less than an hour in a private vehicle. Plenty of **minibus-taxis** run along this road, stopping at Kumi.

 WHERE TO STAY AND EAT Though the Nyero rock paintings are conveniently visited as a day trip from either Mbale or Soroti, there is good range of budget and shoestring accommodation in Kumi Town; useful perhaps for an early start to visit Lake Bisina (see page 487). The first choice with NGO workers is the smart, 22-room **Kumi Hotel** (m *0772 434380/490659*; e *kumihotel1@yahoo.com; www. kumihotellimited.co.ug; US$21/27 sgl/dbl B&B*) on the outskirts of town, while their drivers seem to favour the **Home Again** (*US$8 sgl+*), a centrally located shoestring guesthouse on Nyero Road. On the main Soroti Road, the **Green Top Hotel** (m *0772 542340; US$10/16/20 s/c sgl/dbl/twin B&B*) is distinguished by a pleasant open-sided bar-dining area and a bit of a garden.

WHAT TO SEE
Nyero Rock Paintings (*Admission Ush10,000 non-residents, Ush5,000 residents*)
The finest of several rock-art sites scattered around this part of Uganda (see box

Situated on the outskirts of Mbale, Nabugoye Hill is the site of the Moses Synagogue, spiritual home to a small, isolated community of Ugandan Jews known as Abayudaya. The Abayudaya are not officially accepted as Jews, nor will they be until they undergo an official conversion recognised by a court of rabbis. Nevertheless, they are devout in their observance of Jewish customs and rituals, recognising the same holidays as other Jews, holding their Sabbath services on Friday evening and Saturday morning, and keeping kosher according to Talmudic law. They do not participate in local Basigu circumcision rituals, but instead circumcise males eight days after birth. And those who marry outside the community are no longer considered Abayudaya unless their spouses agree to convert.

Abayudaya is simply the Luganda word for Jews, coined in the late 19th century when missionaries attempted to dissociate their exotic religion from British colonialism by explaining to locals that the Bible was written not by Europeans but by Jews – the People of Judea or Ba-Judea. This ploy backfired somewhat when the first Luganda translation of the Bible appeared and literate Muganda started to question why, for instance, their local tradition of polygamy was condemned by the missionaries when many of the Abayudaya in the Old Testament unashamedly possessed more than one wife.

The most prominent of these religious dissidents was Malaki Musajakawa, whose Africanist Christian sect called the Malakites managed to attract up to 100,000 Ugandans away from more conventional denominations during its short-lived heyday. The Malakite doctrine was based on a fairly random selection of Old Testament verses: it was vehemently against the consumption of pork and the use of any medicine whatsoever, and – of course – it came out in strong support of polygamy. Not surprisingly, the British colonists were less than enamoured with this development and tensions between the authorities and the sect came to a head in 1926, when the plague swept through Uganda and the Malakites launched a violent protest against the use of inoculations to combat the disease. In the aftermath, Malaki Musajakawa was imprisoned and exiled to northern Uganda, where he died after a protracted hunger strike, and the sect gradually disbanded.

The main proponent of the spread of Malakitism in eastern Uganda was Semei Kakungulu, who – embittered with the colonial authorities after his retirement from the 'presidency' of Busoga in 1913 – heartily embraced the anti-establishmentarianism of the breakaway faith. Kakungulu withdrew from politics to focus his attention on spiritual matters, dedicating his life to reading the Bible and other Christian tracts. And, somewhat inevitably, he soon started to develop his own variations on the established Malakite doctrines, leading to a dispute that would eventually split the Mbale Malakites into two opposing factions. The key issue was male circumcision, which Kakungulu and his followers believed to be in line with Old Testament teachings, but which most other Malakites regarded as sacrilege. The true reason behind the widespread Malakite objection to circumcision was rooted in Kiganda tradition, which forbade bodily mutilation of any sort. But this was rationalised away by claiming that circumcision was the way of the Abayudaya, people who don't believe in Jesus Christ.

The present-day Abayudaya community was founded in 1920, when Kakungulu, fed up with the quarrelling, announced to the Malakites that 'because of your insults ... I have separated completely from you and stay with those who want to be circumcised: and we will be known as the Jews.' Kakungulu – at the age of 50 – was circumcised along with his first-born son. He circumcised all his subsequently born sons eight days after their birth, and gave all his children Old Testament names. In 1922, he published an idiosyncratic Luganda religious text steeped in the Jewish religion, demanding complete faith in the Old Testament and all its commandments from himself and his followers.

In reality, Kakungulu's version of Judaism was a confused hotchpotch of Jewish and Christian customs. Neither he nor any of his followers had actually ever met a genuine Jew, and they knew little of real Jewish customs. As a result, the Abayudaya referred to their temple not as a synagogue but as a 'Jewish Church', and they placed as much emphasis on the Christian baptism of children as on the severing of their foreskins! That would change after 1926, however, when Kakungulu spent six months under the instruction of one Yusufu, the Jewish settler who effected the community's final conversion to Judaism. Under Yusufu's guidance, Kakungulu deleted all the Christian prayers from his book, and he instructed his followers to cease baptising their children, to observe the Saturday Sabbath, and to eat meat only if it had been slaughtered within the community according to Jewish custom. Ever the iconoclast, however, Kakungulu did remain vehement when it came to at least one pivotal Malakite doctrine that has no place in modern Judaism: the rejection of medicine. On 24 November 1928, Semei Kakungulu died of pneumonia, refusing to the last to touch the medication that might have saved his life.

By this time, a community of 2,000 Jewish converts lived on Kakungulu's estate at Nabugoye Hill, also known as Galiraya, a Luganda rendition of Galilee. After their founder's death, the Abayudaya had little contact with their neighbours and eschewed materialistic values: it is said that they could be recognised in a crowd by their 'backward' attire of animal hides and barkcloth. The Abayudaya suffered mild persecution during these early years, especially from neighbouring Christian communities who regarded Jews to be Christ killers. But essentially the community thrived until 1971, when Idi Amin banned Judaism, closed 32 synagogues and ordered the Abayudaya to convert to Christianity or Islam. During the Amin years, some 3,000 Abayudaya abandoned their faith rather than risk being beaten or tortured by the military. And some of the more stubborn among them – one group, for instance, who were beaten to death by Amin's thugs for collecting remnants of a synagogue roof that had blown away in a storm – did not survive. Today, the national community of Abayudaya amounts to roughly 500 individuals, most of them living around Nabugoye Hill, the site of Kakungulu's original 'Jewish Church' and his engraved tomb. A smaller community and synagogue exist at nearby Namanyoyi, and two others lie further afield in the town of Pallisa and in a village called Namatumba.

Under Kakungulu, the Abayudaya developed a distinct style of spiritual music, setting the text of recognised Jewish prayers to African melodies and rhythms. Several of these songs, sung in Hebrew or Luganda over a simple guitar backing, are collected on a CD called *Shalom Everybody Everywhere*, available online (*www. ubalt.edu/kulanu*). The community generally welcomes visitors with a genuine interest in its faith. There is no charge for spending time with them, but a donation should be left behind. To reach the synagogue, catch a minibus-taxi from central Mbale to Makadui, from where it's a short walk to the Semei Kakungulu High School on Nabugoye Hill. For more information contact the Abayudaya Community (*PO Box 225, Mbale, Uganda;* e steno@ swiftuganda.com *(mark emails for the attention of the Abayudaya); www.kulanu.org*).

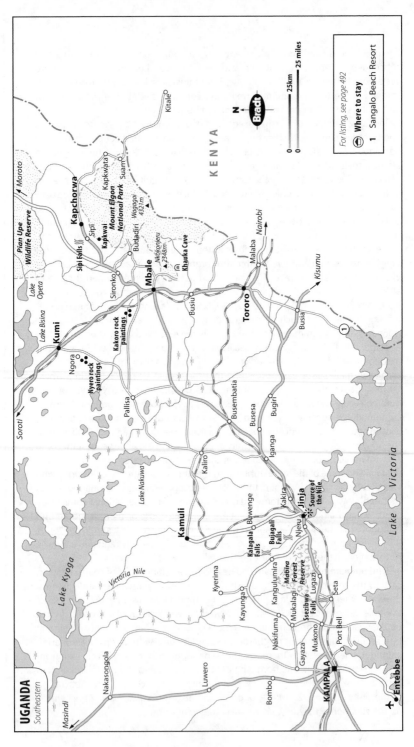

UGANDA
Southeastern

For listing, see page 492
(●) **Where to stay**
1 Sangalo Beach Resort

N
Bradt

0 ___ 25km
0 ___ 25 miles

KENYA

Kitale

Kapkwata
Suam
Mount Elgon
National Park
Wagagai
4321m
Kapchorwa
Sipi
Kapkwai
Sipi Falls
Budadiri
Wokonjeru
2348m
Khauka Cave
Pian Upe
Wildlife Reserve
Moroto
Sironko
Mbale
Lake Opeta
Busiu
Malaba
Nairobi
Tororo
Busia
Kisumu
Busia
1
Lake Bisina
Kumi
Kakoro rock
paintings
Ngora
Nyero rock
paintings
Soroti
Pallisa
Busembatia
Busesa
Bugiri
Iganga
Kaliro
Lake Nakuwa
Kakira
Source of
the Nile
Jinja
Njeru
Bulwenge
Kalagala
Falls
Bujagali
Falls
Kamuli
Kyerima
Mabira
Forest
Reserve
Kangulumira
Mukalagi
Seezibwa
Falls
Lugazi
Seta
Kayunga
Nakifuma
Gayaza
Mukono
Port Bell
Victoria Nile
Lake Kyoga
Nakasongola
Masindi
Luwero
Bombo
KAMPALA
Entebbe
Lake Victoria

486

page 488), Nyero is also perhaps the most accessible. Set on a prominent granite outcrop called Moru Ikara near Nyero trading centre, the site consists of three discrete panels, all of which lie within a few hundred metres of each other. The most impressive is **Panel Two**, which covers a 6m-high rock face reached via a narrow cleft between two immense boulders. At least 40 sets of red concentric circles are partially or wholly visible on the face, as is one 'acacia pod' figure. At the top right are the (very faded) remains of a painting of three zebras. The most striking naturalistic figures on the panel are two large canoes, of which one is about 1.5m long and evidently carrying people. **Panel One** is somewhat less elaborate: six sets of white concentric circles, as well as a few 'acacia pod' figures. **Panel Three** consists of just one white set of concentric circles on the roof of a low rock shelter.

To reach the rock-art site from either Mbale or Soroti, head about halfway down the tarmac road that connects the two towns to Kumi. Here you turn west along the Ngora Road for 8km to the tiny trading centre at Nyero – somewhat incongruously the site of a large new private university. A kilometre beyond Nyero, you'll see the 100m side road to the rock-art site clearly signposted on the right side of the Ngora Road. Any public transport heading between Kumi and Ngora can drop you at the site.

SOROTI

Soroti, with a population of 42,000, is the headquarters of a district of the same name which, like Kumi to the south, is mainly populated by Iteso people. It is most relevant to tourist traffic as a potential stopover on the route north through Karamoja to Kidepo Valley National Park. Though this route was long discouraged by insecurity, it is likely to grow in popularity following the disarmament of the Karamojong warriors. The town, however, offers little in the way of mandatory sightseeing. The most prominent local attraction is **Soroti Rock**, a striking granite formation that towers above the shady town centre, offering good views across to Lake Kyoga from the pinnacle.

GETTING THERE AND AWAY Soroti lies 100km northwest of Mbale along a currently appalling tarmac road, passing through Kumi and the marshy fringes of Lake Bisina on the way. There is plenty of **public transport** heading up to Soroti from Mbale – a few buses daily as well as the occasional minibus – and the trip shouldn't take longer than two hours. Direct buses from Kampala cost Ush25,000.

A good surfaced road runs between Soroti and Lira to the west. Several buses and minibuses cover this route each day. Transport north to Moroto is less regular, but at least one bus does the run daily, leaving Soroti at around noon and taking five hours.

WHERE TO STAY The usual renovated legacy from the defunct Uganda Hotels chain is present in the form of the **Soroti Hotel** (m *0414 561269*), which lies in pleasant grounds facing a small rock outcrop, about 1km out of town along Serere Road. Otherwise, the town's smartest hotel seems to be the **Landmark**. The **Golden Ark** and **Paradise** have been recommended for decent self-contained rooms, while the **Savanna Hotel** and **Company Inn** have single and double rooms with shared showers.

TOUR OPERATOR Soroti and Kumi are staging points for the range of rather low-key attractions described below. Though it's possible to locate them by yourself

A dozen discrete panels of prehistoric rock art are known from five different localities in Kumi and Soroti districts, namely Nyero, Kakoro, Obwin Rock, Ngora and Lolui Island (Lake Kyoga). The paintings are in most cases monochromatic – typically either red or white – and the predominant figures are sets of four or five concentric circles, and strange compartmentalised sausage-shaped figures reminiscent of acacia pods. It would be misleading to compare the impact of these geometric rock paintings, many of which are very faded, to their more naturalistic and better-preserved counterparts in central Tanzania or southern Africa. Nevertheless, a visit to one of the more accessible sites, in particular Nyero, is recommended to anybody with a passing interest in archaeology or human prehistory.

The limited palate drawn on by the artists of Kumi and Soroti was sourced from whatever natural materials were available to them. Red pigments were created by scraping the surface of a ferruginous rock, while white paint was derived from a combination of clay, dung and sap, and black from oxidised organic matter such as charcoal and burned fat. The raw ingredients would be ground finely then mixed into a thick liquid such as albumin to form an adhesive paste that was applied to the rock surface using a rudimentary brush of animal hair. Unless you assume that the artists had one eye focused on posterity, it is reasonable to think that the surviving paintings constitute a minute proportion of their work, much of which would have been painted on to exposed rocks or more ephemeral surfaces such as animal hide.

The age of the rock art is a matter for conjecture, as is the identity of the artists. The Iteso people who have inhabited the region for the last 300 years reckon that the art has always been there. Iteso tradition does relate that the region's rock shelters were formerly occupied by a short, light-skinned race of people, and excavations at Nyero have unearthed several microlithic tools of a type not used by the Iteso. Most likely, then, that the artists were hunter-gatherers with ethnic and cultural affiliations to the so-called Bushmen who were responsible for much of the rock art in southern Africa. The paintings must be at least 300 years old, and are possibly much older.

As for the intent of the artists, the field is wide open. The circle is a universal theme in prehistoric art and its use could be mythological, symbolic (for instance, a representation of the cycle of the seasons) or more literal (the sun or moon). A possible clue to interpreting the rock art of eastern Uganda comes from a style of house painting practised in northeast DRC in association with rainmaking ceremonies. Here, concentric circles represent the sun, while wavy lines symbolise the moon's feet, which – it is said – follow the rain (a reference to the link between the new moon and stormy weather). Could a similar purpose reasonably be attributed to the rock art of eastern Uganda? Quite possibly, since Nyero is known to have been the site of Iteso rainmaking ceremonies in historic times. But it is a considerable part of these ancient paintings' mystique that they pose more questions than there are answers forthcoming – the simple truth is that we'll never know.

you'll get considerably more out from your exploration of Teso with a little local knowledge. Margaret Stevens of Loughborough, UK, suggests that the grassroots tour operator listed below provides the necessary spark.

Homestead Tours `\`0784 685856; e homesteadtours@gmail.com. A community tourism project based on the main road at Kapir halfway between Soroti & Kumi. Activities offered include guided walks, cycle rides & boat trips; fishing; rock paintings on Kapir Hill; processing & eating traditional foods including peanut butter; ox ploughing; birdwatching (inc wetland rarities); traditional musical instruments, singing, dancing & storytelling; visiting local markets ...

WHAT TO SEE The Nyero rock art site near Kumi (see page 483) can be visited as a day trip from Soroti, while a couple of minor sites of interest lie closer to the town. About 7km down the tarmac road to Mbale stands a tall granite outcrop known as **Obwin Rock**, which means 'place of hyenas' in Ateso. You'd be fortunate to see any hyenas at Obwin today, but the formation is riddled with small caves and shelters, one of which is the site of an ancient red rock painting. There's just one pattern on the panel, a set of six concentric circles, but – unusually – the outer circle is decorated with eight rectangles, while what might be a pair of legs dangles from the circle's base. Another possibility is to catch a minibus-taxi to **Serere**, 30km southwest of Soroti near Lake Kyoga, and arrange to take a dugout canoe on to the lake with one of the local fishermen.

Birders will be keen to visit a couple of minor lakes, Bisina and Opeta, to the east of Soroti. These are two of numerous patches of open water set in an extensive tract of permanent and seasonal wetland that forms the eastern part of the swampy Kyoga Basin. Both lakes and their soggy catchments have been designated as Ramsar Sites in recognition of their scientific importance. In addition to supporting a rich and rare birdlife, both sites contain endemic cichlid fish species considered extinct in the more accessible lakes Kyoga and Victoria. **Lake Bisina** is a long, narrow and shallow freshwater body extending over roughly 190km² along an eastern arm of the Kyoga drainage system. It's an attractive lake, fringed by extensive swamps and towered over by the (normally obscured) peaks of Elgon to the south and the jagged outline of Mount Kadam to the east, but tourist development along the shores is non-existent. Lake Bisina and its enclosing swamps support a number of localised species, including the legendary shoebill and localised papyrus gonolek, white-winged warbler, pygmy goose and lesser jacana. More significantly, it is also one of a handful of localities known to harbour Fox's weaver, a swamp fringe-associated bird endemic to this one small part of eastern Uganda. It is most conveniently reached from the village of Kipiri on the tarmac road, midway (22km) between Soroti and Kumi. A 2km side road leads east to the western tip of Bisina. Once at the lakeshore, you'll need to negotiate for a local dugout to ferry you towards the reedy northwestern shore, where up to 50 pairs of Fox's weaver have been recorded breeding.

The smaller **Lake Opeta** lies 50km east of Soroti and is home to one of the most prolific shoebill populations in Africa, as well as the marsh-dwelling sitatunga antelope, breeding colonies of the endemic Fox's weaver, and several other localised species including rufous-bellied heron and papyrus gonolek. Lake Opeta cannot be reached on public transport. To get there in a private vehicle, follow the Moroto Road out of Soroti for 55km, turning right a few hundred metres past the village of Katakwi. From here, it's another 50km or so to the lakeshore village of Peta, passing *en route* through the villages of Toroma and Magoro. A trip to Lake Opeta could be combined with a diversion to the northern shore of Lake Bisina, which lies about 10km south of Toroma.

13

This medium-sized town (population estimate 45,000) is situated a few minutes' drive from the Malaba border post with Kenya, just off the road to Jinja and Kampala. These days, few travellers pass through Tororo unless they make a specific effort to do so. This is because the Busia rather than Malaba border crossing is normally used by traffic between Nairobi and Kampala, while public transport between Kampala and Mbale now uses the more direct Turini Road from Iganga.

Supporting roughly 1,000 Asian and European settlers, well located for cross-border trade and the site of Uganda's main cement factory, Tororo ranked among the ten most populous and prosperous towns in Uganda in the 1950s. Today, the exaggeratedly wide pavements, lined with a straggle of flowering trees and colonial-era façades, pay testament to Tororo's former prosperity, as does a pair of impressive Hindu temples (one of which long ceased functioning), but the overall impression is one of a sleepy backwater that long ago saw its heyday. Altogether more diverting than the town centre is **Tororo Rock**, a steep volcanic plug that protrudes several hundred metres above the southern skyline. Visible from miles around, this distinctive isolated outcrop takes about an hour to climb – guides can be found at the Rock Classic Hotel in town – and offers panoramic views towards Mount Elgon and, reputedly, to Lake Victoria in very clear weather.

GETTING THERE AND AWAY A poor surfaced road connects Tororo to Mbale (40km to the north) while an excellent road runs to Jinja (130km to the east). Regular **minibus-taxis** connect Tororo to both of the above towns. Note that public transport running directly between Kampala or Jinja and Mbale bypasses Tororo in favour of the new, shorter, surfaced Turini Road which branches off near Iganga. Regular minibus-taxis run between Tororo and the Malaba border post.

 WHERE TO STAY For location of listings see map opposite.

Moderate

🏠 **Rock Classic Hotel** (91 rooms) 3km out of town, Malakasi Rd; ☎ 04544 45069; m 0704 539638; e rockclassichotel@yahoo.com. This former government hotel presents an imposing stone-clad frontage to travellers on the main Jinja–Malaba road. Inside, however, the echoing common areas lack character. The s/c rooms are contained in old & new wings. The latter, which occupies previously wooded grounds, is finished to the standards expected of modern Ugandan craftsmen (that's irony in case you missed it). A more useful addition to the site is a swimming pool with bar & sauna. The dbl rooms have fans & DSTV. More strikingly, they also have maroon carpets & round beds with shiny red covers; the indelicate term, 'tart's boudoir' comes to mind. Reasonably priced, though. *US$40/72/60 sgl/ dbl/twin.*

🏠 **Prime Hotel** (26 rooms) Off Malakasi Rd; ☎ 0392 791862; m 0772 591862; e primehoteltororo@gmail.com; www.prime-hotel-tororo.com. This modern hotel, set in a green, garden compound in the leafy Malakasi suburb, seems to be the popular choice for visitors to Tororo. Staff members are friendly, articulate & seem efficient, & there's a restaurant (see opposite). The rates for spacious tiled rooms with nets, fan & TV are extremely friendly, too. *US$23/25/29/29 sgl/dbl/twin/exec.*

Budget

🏠 **Town Lodge Tororo (TLT)** (11 rooms) Bazaar Rd; m 0454 445243. Smart hotel in a central location & with a good restaurant. Tiled rooms with TV, nets, fan & beds offered. *US$22/26 sgl/ dbl B&B.*

🏠 **Motel Dot Com** (14 rooms) Bazaar Rd; m 0776 434722. A cheaper & only slightly inferior alternative to the neighbouring TLT. Nets, fans, TV & king-sized dbl beds. Popular bar downstairs with pool table & DSTV. *US$16/20/25 sgl/dbl/twin B&B.*

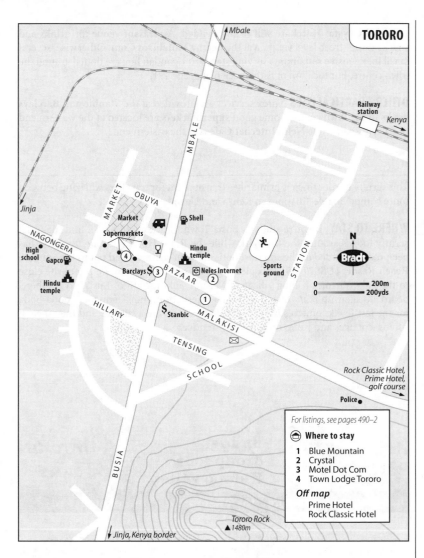

For listings, see pages 490–2

⊖ Where to stay

1 Blue Mountain
2 Crystal
3 Motel Dot Com
4 Town Lodge Tororo

Off map
   Prime Hotel
   Rock Classic Hotel

🏠 **Crystal Hotel** (20 rooms) Bazaar Rd;
m 0772 555174. For many years, this storied
building was central Tororo's standout hotel & with
recent renovations, the tiled s/c rooms (fan &
a private balcony facing Tororo Rock) are still a fair
deal. The ground-floor restaurant remains a good
option. *US$16 sgl/dbl B&B.*

Shoestring

🏠 **Blue Mountain Guesthouse** (6 rooms)
Bazaar Rd; m 0774 695976. The pick of Tororo's
cheapies, this small guesthouse is found at the
quieter end of Bazaar Road opposite Crystal Hotel.
Tiled s/c rooms. *US$9/11 s/c dbl/twin B&B.*

✗ **WHERE TO EAT AND DRINK** The pool terrace at the **Rock Classic Hotel** is a
pleasant spot for a meal and a drink, while the continental and Indian menu at the
Prime Hotel looks good. In the town centre, the top spot for a meal is undoubtedly
the **Town Lodge Tororo** – known as TLT – where a wide range of continental meals
cost Ush15,000–30,000. Dropping down a peg, the local dishes and snacks at the

good old **Crystal Hotel** are still recommended. A pleasant venue for drinks and snacks is the street-level veranda at the nearby **Motel Dot Com**. Otherwise, several small inexpensive restaurants serving standard Ugandan fare are dotted around the town centre. For location of listings see map, page 491.

OTHER PRACTICALITIES Forex services are provided at the **Stanbic** and **Barclays** banks in the town centre. Some good **supermarkets** are located at the western end of Bazaar Road while **Neles Internet Café** is at the eastern end.

BUSIA

This scruffy border town is primarily a transit point for travellers whizzing between more compelling destinations in Kenya and Uganda.

WHERE TO STAY If you're stuck in Busia Town for the night, you'll find the usual scruffy lodges around the taxi park while the **Rand Hotel** (*US$30/40 sgl/dbl*) has been recommended as the smartest option. If you've time, head out to the **Sangalo Beach Resort** (*US$20–50*) This pleasant, low-key set-up enjoys a pretty site close to the Lake Victoria fishing village of Majanji, 30km south of Busia. To get there, board a beaten-up *matatu* by the Busia police station, transferring to a boda-boda for the last few kilometres if necessary. Basic meals are available, and the range of rooms, cottages and suites on offer vary in price.

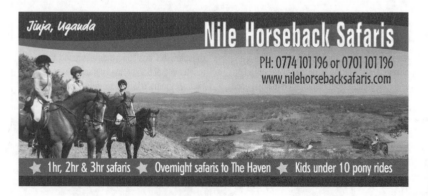

14

Jinja

Uganda's second-largest town (assuming that you treat the satellite settlement of Njeru on the opposite bank of the Nile as a suburb), Jinja lies about 80km east of Kampala, overlooking the point where the Nile flows out of Lake Victoria. And it is the mighty river rather than the moderately interesting town that attracts visitors to Jinja. There is a certain poignancy attached to standing on the slopes from where Speke first identified that geographical holy grail which, less than a decade earlier, had lured an obsessed (and hopelessly misdirected) Livingstone to a feverish death near Lake Bangweulu in Zambia. No less impressive is the knowledge that the water flowing past these green slopes will eventually drain into the Mediterranean, following a 6,500km journey through the desert wastes of Sudan and Egypt. But what really pulls the crowds these days is the thrilling series of rapids along the Nile north of the town. Rafted by three different companies, these now represent Uganda's most popular tourist activity, surpassing even the mountain gorillas of the southwest. The appeal of the rafting epicentre at Bujagali Falls was further enhanced by additional developments such as kayaking, quad biking and even a bungee jump. However, the last two years have been a testing time for Jinja's adventure tourism industry as three major rapids, including the talismanic Bujagali Falls, disappeared beneath the reservoir created by a new hydro-power dam. But life goes on. While the embarkation points for rafting have shifted across to the western bank of the river and Bujagali Falls has been replaced by the so-called Lake Bujagali, the east-side cluster of tourism developments and activities at 'The Location Previously Known As' Bujagali Falls seems as busy as ever.

JINJA

Jinja has an attractively lush location on the northern shore of Lake Victoria above the Ripon Falls, identified by Speke in 1862 as the source of the Nile, but submerged following the construction of the Owen Falls Dam in the 1950s. Jinja was formerly the industrial heartland of Uganda, and according to the most recent census in 2002 its population is (or rather was then) 86,500, while that of Njeru directly across the river somehow exceeded 50,000. The combined 136,500 population of the Jinja–Njeru conurbation makes this Uganda's second-largest urban centre. Yet this is far from being a great metropolis straddling the source of the Nile and first-time visitors wandering around Jinja's compact, low-rise town centre might reasonably wonder what they can expect of Uganda's lesser provincial cities.

Jinja suffered badly during the Amin years and subsequent period of economic and political turmoil, but a more recent economic upswing (see box, pages 498–9) has been mirrored by the emergence of the river corridor as a major tourism centre in the region, with the emphasis strongly on adrenalin-oriented activities. The town centre admittedly boasts little of genuine historical note, though some fine

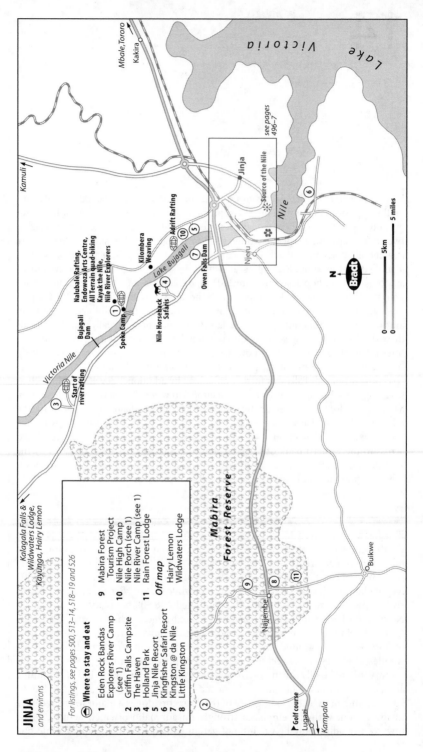

JINJA
and environs

For listings, see pages 500, 513–14, 518–19 and 526

Where to stay and eat
1. Eden Rock Bandas
   Explorers River Camp
   (see 1)
2. Griffin Falls Campsite
3. The Haven
4. Holland Park
5. Jinja Nile Resort
6. Kingfisher Safari Resort
7. Kingston @ da Nile
8. Little Kingston
9. Mabira Forest
   Tourism Project
10. Nile High Camp
   Nile Porch (see 1)
   Nile River Camp (see 1)
11. Rain Forest Lodge

Off map
Hairy Lemon
Wildwaters Lodge

Kalagala Falls &
Wildwaters Lodge,
Kayunga, Hairy Lemon

Kamuli

Mbale, Tororo

Kakira

Nalubale Rafting,
Endowoza Arts Centre,
All Terrain quad-biking
Kayak the Nile,
Nile River Explorers

Kilombera
Weaving

Adrift Rafting

Victoria Nile

Bujagali Dam

Speke Camp

Nile Horseback
Safaris

Start of
river rafting

Lake Bujagali

Owen Falls Dam

Njeru

Jinja

Source of the Nile

*see pages
496–7*

Nile

Lake Victoria

Mabira
Forest Reserve

Najjembe

Buikwe

Golf course

Lugazi

Kampala

N

Bradt

0   5km
0   5 miles

494

colonial-era Asian architecture – epitomised by the restored 1919 Madhvani House on Main Street – complemented by a spread of thickly vegetated residential suburbs carved from the surrounding jungle, does give Jinja a compelling sense of place.

GETTING THERE AND AWAY Jinja lies along the surfaced Nairobi–Kampala road, 82km east of Kampala and 131km west of Tororo. Owing to heavy traffic in Kampala and slow trucks along the way, the journey in a **private vehicle** now takes almost two hours. On the outskirts of Jinja, the road from Kampala crosses the Owen Falls Dam, shortly after which it reaches a roundabout where a right turn leads to the town centre and a left turn to Bujagali.

Regular **minibus-taxis** (*Ush8,000*) run between Jinja taxi park and Kampala's old taxi park throughout the day. The larger and safer **coaster buses** (*Ush5,000*) run to Jinja bus park. Buses to Mbale leave the bus park between 06.00 and 08.00. Later travellers must head out to the police barracks roundabout on the Jinja bypass to catch buses travelling between Kampala and locations east. All of the rafting companies offer a **free transfer** between Kampala and Jinja as part of their rafting package.

Many regular commuters between Kampala and Jinja now prefer a northerly route via Gayaza and Kayunga to the slow and congested main Jinja highway. This alternative is 30km longer, but the drive it allows is quieter, safer and more enjoyable. The journey is only a little slower, if at all. To reach Gayaza, head north out of Kampala through either Wandegere junction or Mulago hospital roundabout. These roads meet after 1km at a roundabout where you bear right (turn left and you'll head to northern Uganda). Alternatively, head north to Gayaza from Ntinda past the Ndere Troupe Centre. Though the initial section leaving Kampala is pretty hectic, beyond Gayaza a quiet road runs all the way to Jinja (the road emerges on to the Kampala–Jinja highway opposite Nile Breweries at Owen Falls Dam). This road is recommended to travellers headed to Kalagala Falls and other tourist sites on the west bank of the Nile (see page 517).

GETTING AROUND

Vehicle hire Land Rovers with a driver, for use around Jinja or for longer safaris countrywide, can be rented from **Walter Egger** (0434 121314; m 0772 221113; e *wemtec@source.co.ug*) and **The Tourist Centre** and **Advanced Tours** (see tour operators below).

Cycle hire Jinja Town's level terrain is ideal for exploration by bike. **Fabio** [504 C6] (*9 Main St, post office end;* 0434 121255; m 0773138289; *www.fabio.or.ug*), an NGO, hire single-speed bikes for Ush10,000 an hour or Ush15,000 for the full day. For information on hiring mountain bikes to explore further afield, see page 517.

TOURIST INFORMATION The most useful sources of current travel information for Jinja and the surrounding area are the **Nalubale Tea House** [496 D3] and **Explorers Backpackers** [496 C3] (see page 501), and the **backpacker camps** at Bujagali. In the town centre, visit **The Tourist Centre** [494 C6] (see below).

TOUR OPERATORS

Advanced Tours [504 C5] Plot 28/30, Clive Rd West; 0434 120457; e www.advancedtours.ug
Safari Wildz www.safariwildz.com. Large & small group tours customised with various activities to client's requirements.

The Tourist Centre [504 C6] Post office building; www.jinjatouristcentre.co.ug. Offer a ½-day day tour of Jinja Town & a full-day tour of the town & the surrounding area on foot or by car. Also vehicle hire & safaris.

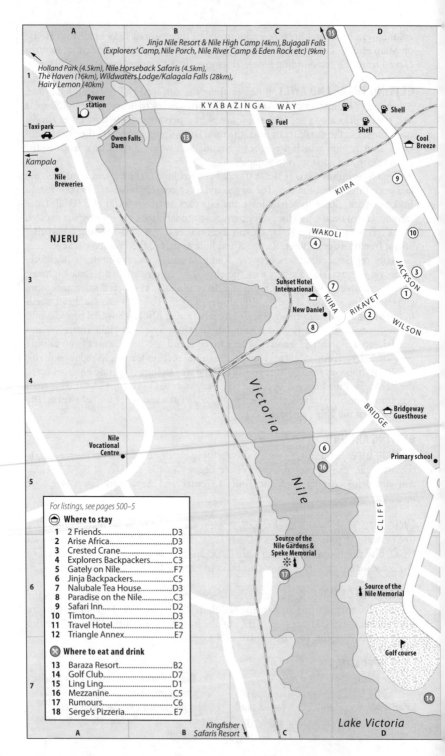

Jinja Nile Resort & Nile High Camp (4km), Bujagali Falls
(Explorers' Camp, Nile Porch, Nile River Camp & Eden Rock etc) (9km)

Holland Park (4.5km), Nile Horseback Safaris (4.5km),
The Haven (16km), Wildwaters Lodge/Kalagala Falls (28km),
Hairy Lemon (40km)

Power station

Taxi park

Owen Falls Dam

KYABAZINGA WAY

Fuel

Shell

Shell

Cool Breeze

Kampala

Nile Breweries

NJERU

KIIRA

WAKOLI

Sunset Hotel International

New Daniel

KIIRA

RIKAVET

JACKSON

WILSON

Victoria

Nile

Nile Vocational Centre

BRIDGE

Bridgeway Guesthouse

Primary school

CLIFF

Source of the Nile Gardens & Speke Memorial

Source of the Nile Memorial

Golf course

Lake Victoria

Kingfisher Safaris Resort

For listings, see pages 500–5

⌂ **Where to stay**
1	2 Friends	D3
2	Arise Africa	D3
3	Crested Crane	D3
4	Explorers Backpackers	C3
5	Gately on Nile	F7
6	Jinja Backpackers	C5
7	Nalubale Tea House	D3
8	Paradise on the Nile	C3
9	Safari Inn	D2
10	Timton	D3
11	Travel Hotel	E2
12	Triangle Annex	E7

✕ **Where to eat and drink**
13	Baraza Resort	B2
14	Golf Club	D7
15	Ling Ling	D1
16	Mezzanine	C5
17	Rumours	C6
18	Serge's Pizzeria	E7

496

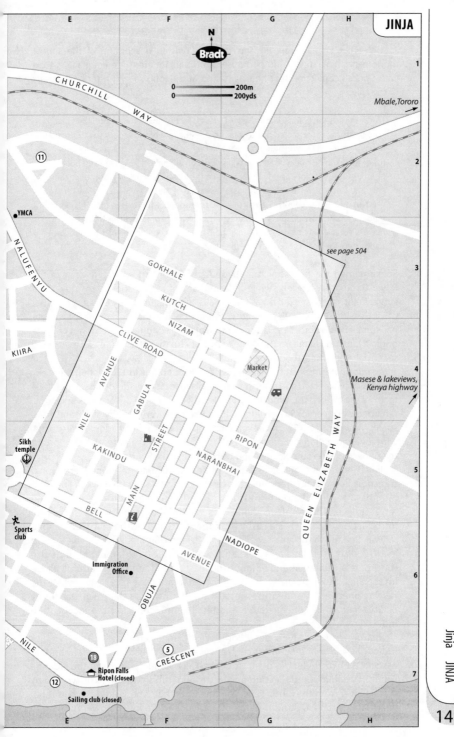

E   F   G   H

1

N

Bradt

0 ————————— 200m
0 ————————— 200yds

Mbale, Tororo →

CHURCHILL WAY

2

⑪

• YMCA

NALUFENYU

see page 504

3

GOKHALE

KUTCH

NIZAM

KIIRA

CLIVE ROAD

4

AVENUE

GABULA

NILE

Market

Masese & lakeviews,
Kenya highway →

Sikh
temple
🔯

RIPON

KAKINDU

STREET

NARANBHAI

QUEEN ELIZABETH WAY

5

✦
Sports
club

MAIN

BELL

𝑖

Immigration
Office •

NADIOPE

AVENUE

6

OBUJA

NILE

⑱

Ripon Falls
Hotel (closed)

⑤

CRESCENT

⑫

• Sailing club (closed)

7

E   F   G   H

A somewhat elegiac tone informs the first written description of the site of modern-day Jinja, less to do perhaps with the its inherent scenic qualities than with Speke's conviction that he was staring at the long sought-after headwaters of the Nile:

> The 'stones', as the Waganda call the falls, was by far the most interesting sight I had seen in Africa … It attracted one to it for hours – the roar of the waters, the thousands of passenger-fish leaping at the falls with all their might; the Wasoga and Waganda fishermen coming out in boats and taking post on all the rocks with rod and hook, hippopotami and crocodiles lying sleepily on the water, the ferry at work above the falls, and cattle driven down to drink at the margin of the lake – made, in all, with the pretty nature of the country – small hills, grassy-topped, with trees in the folds, and gardens on the lower slopes – as interesting a picture as one could wish to see … I felt as if I only wanted a wife and family, garden and yacht, rifle and rod, to make me happy here for life, so charming was the place.

Speke named the falls after the Marquess of Ripon, a former president of the Royal Geographic Society, while a second set of rapids about 1km downriver subsequently became known as Owen Falls, after Major Roddy Owen, a member of Sir Gerald Portal's 1893 expedition to Uganda. But the local name for the site has survived, too, since Jinja is a corruption of Ejjinja (Stones), which is not only the original Luganda name for the Ripon Falls, but also that of a village and associated sacrificial stone that stood close by.

An informal European settlement was founded at Jinja in 1900, when the rocky waterfall was selected as the most suitable place for the telegraph line to Kampala to cross the Nile. At this time, the administrative centre for Busoga was at Iganga, regarded by Governor Sir Harry Johnston to be 'not a very healthy place, and, so to speak, "nowhere"'. In 1901, however, Johnston relocated the headquarters to Jinja, with its 'aggregation of European settlers' at the head of a potentially important riverine transport route north along the Nile and Lake Kyoga.

Jinja's rapid emergence as a pivotal commercial centre and international transport hub was further cemented by the completion of the railway line from Mombasa to the lake port of Kisumu, and the introduction of a connecting ferry service. The local economy was further boosted by the successful introduction of cotton as a cash crop for export, and by the construction of a railway line north to Namasagali in 1912. Even so, Sir Frederick Treves, writing in 1913, dismissed Jinja as 'a little tin town … a rough settlement of some size [but] purely utilitarian and without the least ambition to be beautiful'. Jinja's importance as a port undoubtedly diminished after the late 1920s, when the railway line was extended to Kampala, but by this time the town was firmly established as an administrative and retail centre servicing the local cotton industry.

Instrumental in Jinja's post-World War II emergence as Uganda's major industrial and manufacturing centre was the construction of a dam and an associated hydro-electric plant at Owen Falls. As early as 1904, the Uganda Company had mooted erecting 'an electric generating station to be worked by waterpower from the Ripon Falls'. Winston Churchill, who visited the falls three years later, supported this notion enthusiastically: 'So much power running to waste, such a coign of vantage unoccupied, such a lever to control the natural forces of Africa ungripped, cannot but vex and stimulate imagination. And what fun to make the immemorial Nile begin its journey by driving through a turbine!'

Only in 1946, however, did the colonial administration look seriously at damming the lower Nile, initially as part of a proposed Equatorial Nile Project that involved Egypt, Sudan, Uganda and other indirectly affected nations. The broad idea behind this scheme was that Egypt would fund the construction of a large dam at the outlet of each of the two largest lakes along the Nile's course: Victoria and Albert. The advantage to Uganda was that the dams could be harnessed as a reliable source of hydro-electric power, not only for domestic use, but also to sell to neighbouring Kenya. At the same time, the dams would transform the lakes into vast semi-artificial reservoirs from where the flow of the Nile downriver to Sudan and Egypt could be regulated to prevent the sporadic flooding and droughts that had long been associated with annual fluctuations in the river's water level.

Protracted and often acrimonious negotiations between the various governments over the next two years eventually broke down as both Uganda and to a lesser extent Kenya objected to the significant loss of land that would result from the construction of the proposed dams. In 1949, Egypt reluctantly signed a treaty allowing Uganda to build a hydro-electric plant at Owen Falls, provided that it did not significantly disrupt the natural flow of the river and that an Egyptian engineer would regulate the water flow through the dam. The Owen Falls Dam cost seven million pounds sterling to construct, and was formally opened in 1954.

Jinja's proximity to this reliable source of cheap electricity proved attractive to industry, and several textile and other manufacturing plants, including the country's major cigarette factory and brewery, were established. For two decades, the local economy boomed. The modern town centre – one of the few in East Africa to display clear indications of considered urban planning – essentially dates to the early 1950s, when the population increased from 8,500 to more than 20,000 in the space of three years. A settler community of 800 Europeans and 5,000 Asians is reflected today in the ornate Indian façades of the town centre, as well as the sprawling double-storey mansions that languish in the suburbs. Other relics of this period are the impressive town hall and administrative buildings at the southern end of the town centre.

Jinja's fortunes slumped again following the expulsion of Asians from Uganda in 1972. Most of the town's leading industries had been under Asian management, and the cohorts of Amin who were installed in their place generally lacked any appropriate business experience or managerial skill, resulting in a total breakdown in the local economy. In the early 1990s, the town centre's boarded-up shops and deeply pot-holed roads epitomised a more general aura of lethargy and economic torpor. Today, however, while Jinja remains somewhat sleepy in comparison with Kampala, it no longer feels unhealthily so. Many of the industries have returned, and the freshly painted shopfronts that line the neatly tarred roads of the town centre seem emblematic of a broader sense of urban rejuvenation, as are the once-rundown suburban mansions that have been restored as private houses or hotels.

WHERE TO STAY There's no shortage of accommodation in Jinja with options ranging from the two boutique, mid-range guesthouses listed immediately below, to the hardcore, shoestring dives near the taxi park. The largest category is represented by budget options and here you'll find teetotal accommodation favoured by visiting Church groups, popular conference venues (likely to either be very quiet or fully occupied on any given night), and hotels favoured by NGO and business travellers. Possibly most relevant to budget tourists are the town's three backpacker hostels, Explorers' Backpackers, Jinja Backpackers and Nalubale Tea House. These are run by rafting companies which offer a free dorm bed or equivalent discount on other rooms to rafting clients. And with rafting trips now starting on the west bank of the Nile, these (and indeed other Jinja hotels) are as relevant to rafters as the camps at Bujagali. They are also where travellers will encounter like-minded souls and find useful sources of information. All three hostels offer shoestring options in the form of camping and US$10 dorm beds. At Jinja Backpackers and the Nalubale Tea House, however, the main concession to the traditional backpacker-shoestring association is not the prices but the communal facilities used by all accommodation. The same might be said of the Explorers and Nalubale camps at Bujagali.

Moderate

🏠 **Gately on Nile** [497 F7] (21 rooms) Nile Crescent; ☎ 0434 122400; m 0772 469638; e stay@gatelyonnile.com; www.gately-on-nile. com. This Australian-owned retreat is a short distance south of the town centre, close to the old port. The main guesthouse occupies a restored bungalow in a lush, tropical garden. Across the road, 3 distinctive storied suites each boast a s/c lounge, kitchenette & sofa bed below & a s/c wood-floored bedroom & balcony upstairs, the latter overlooking the lake & old port. Facilities include office & broadband/Wi-Fi email services, & local travel advice & bookings. See also advert in fourth colour section. *US$120/160 lake view suites & US$100/140 sgl/dbl in main house B&B.*

🏠 **2 Friends** [496 D3] (19 rooms) Jackson Crescent; ☎ 0434 122999; m 0783 160804; e post@2friends.info; www.2friends.info. Perhaps Jinja's most attractive guesthouse, 2 Friends is located in a leafy suburb just behind the Crested Crane (see opposite). The prime rooms face a swimming pool & terrace, a setting softened by tropical plants which separate the informal pool zone from the more serious business of wining & dining in the open-sided, thatch roof & timber-floored restaurant. The s/c rooms (nets & fan) are elevated from the crowd by just the right amount of 'safari-style'. Relax in the exclusive atmosphere of the guesthouse grounds or pop next door to the popular 2 Friends bar/restaurant (see page 503). *US$115/130 poolside sgl/dbl & US$90/115 sgl/dbl in main house B&B.*

Budget

🏠 **Kingfisher Safari Resort** [Map page 494] (40 rooms) m 0772 510197/632063; e kingfishersafaris@gmx.net; www. kingfishersafaris.net. Across the bay from Jinja, Kingfisher's 3 interconnected swimming pools attract missionaries & others blessed with large families. *US$150 2-room family unit s/c cottage, US$135 small family unit, US$75/105/120 sgl/ small dbl/larger dbl B&B. Approx 45% discount for residents.*

🏠 **Hotel Paradise on the Nile** [496 C3] (69 rooms) ☎ 0434 121912/162; e hotel@ paradiseonthenile.com. Originally an annex to the moribund Sunset Hotel up the road, this smart modern hotel has been greatly expanded by a new accommodation block. The implied river view is not provided from the rooms, but from a pleasant private garden 50m from the main hotel, complete with gym, swimming pool & bar/ terrace. Comfortable s/c rooms. *US$64 'deluxe' dbl & US$34/44/44 standard sgl/dbl/twin B&B.*

🏠 **Jinja Backpackers** [496 C5] Bridge Close, off Bridge St; m 0784 591 252; www. jinjabackpackers.com. This new facility occupies a pretty site that extends right down to the river, a short distance north of the Source of the Nile. There's plenty of scope for eating, for as well as the Backpackers canteen, the site contains the popular Mezzanine Restaurant (see page 505). If you're peckish between meals, chips, chocolates & freshly baked muffins, cakes, biscuits & slices are available throughout the day. Non-s/c rooms are a little pricey for shared bathrooms. Family rooms have 4 beds. *US$50 s/c dbl, US$40/40/60/ dbl/twin/family with shared facilities, US$10 dorm bed (linen & nets). Rates excl food.*

🏠 **Travel Hotel** [496 E2] ☎0434 120837; 📱 0772 758081; www.travelhotel.co.ug. Initially the Hotel Triangle, more recently the Hotel Zamo, & now Travel Hotel, this multi-storey business/NGO hotel is bland & distanced from any points of interest, but the s/c rooms with hot baths are good value. The garden restaurant is good & reasonably priced. *US$29/33/41 sgl/dbl/twin B&B.*

🏠 **Hotel Triangle Annex** [496 E7] (132 rooms) ☎0434 122098/9; e hoteltriangle@source.co.ug. How this concrete monstrosity was permitted to blight the fabled headwaters of the Nile is a mystery! Aesthetic niceties apart, this large hotel enjoys a superb shoreline location between the sailing club & golf course, with comfortable & affordable rooms with carpet, hot water, fan, DSTV & private lake-facing balcony. The rooms are fair value for Jinja. There's a swimming pool on site & a restaurant that serves unexciting but reasonably priced meals. *US$25/37/53/41 s/c sgl/dbl/large dbl/twin B&B.*

🏠 **Crested Crane Hotel** [496 D3] (110 rooms) Hannington Sq; ☎0434 121954; 📱 0703 241315. Though this large, suburban government hotel seems to undergo constant facelifts, it never seems to change. The s/c rooms still have hot water, nets, fan & DSTV, & are still fair value. The large grounds also contain the Uganda Hotel & Tourism Training Institute, which provides trainee staff, eager to please but still uncomfortable with the complexities of cutlery & matching numbered door keys to numbered doors (I kid you not!). Plenty of scope for Fawlty Towers-style entertainment. *US$24/33 sgl/dbl B&B.*

🏠 **Safari Inn** [496 D2] (17 rooms) ☎0434 122955; 📱 0704 629992; e innsafari@yahoo.com. The 1st hotel on the right as you head into town from Bujagali roundabout on the bypass. The long-serving Safari Inn stands in green grounds with a new swimming pool, & the nicely furnished 1st-floor rooms seem a bargain. *US$20/24/26/36 sgl/dbl/twin/family B&B.*

🏠 **Arise Africa Guest House** [496 D3] Wilson Rd; 📱 0782 364292; www.ariseafricainternational.org. Clean, spacious, old-fashioned & friendly, this Christian guesthouse is found on a quiet suburban road (behind 2 Friends).

Popular with Christian groups visiting from abroad. No alcohol is served. B/fast is plentiful. *US$18/26 B&B.*

🏠 **Timton Hotel** [496 D3] Jackson Crescent; 📱 0711 564814. Situated behind the Crested Crane Hotel, this long-serving suburban budget hotel has a pleasant setting. Though long-promised internal renovations are now well overdue, it's acceptable value. *US$18/26 s/c sgl/dbl B&B. Prices negotiable.*

🏠 **Nalubale Tea House** [496 D3] 38 Kira Rd; 📱 0782 638938; e bookings@nalubalerafting.com; www.nalubalerafting.com/rooms. The home of Nalubale Rafting, the freshly spruced-up premises give an idea of how lovely Jinja's suburbs must have been in their heyday. This 1950s town house is quite the happening place for both tourists & the extended Jinja rafting community. Opening directly on to the large garden, the light & airy lounge area is a pleasant place to hang out, check emails & watch TV, while a diary of regular events include a weekly movie night, w/end BBQs & a Sun market. The restaurant offers a varied menu of meals & snacks. *US$25 dbl, US$10 dorm beds, US$5 camping, all with shared facilities. Rates excl food.*

🏠 **Mayfair** [504 C2] Clive Rd; ☎0434 120859. The pick of the town centre's hotels, Mayfair provides clean & comfortable s/c rooms. A lunchtime buffet (*Ush8,000*) is available while the terrace facing the street is a good place to watch the world go by. *US$15/19/21/22 s/c sgl/dbl/twin/exec.*

Shoestring

🏠 **Explorers Backpackers** [496 C3] (45 beds) Wakoli Pl; ☎0434 120236; 📱 0772 422373; e rafting@raftafrica.com; www.raftafrica.com. The base for the rafting company Nile River Explorers (NRE), Jinja's oldest travellers' refuge maintains the increasingly tenuous relationship between the terms 'backpacker' & 'shoestring accommodation.' Cheap dorm beds & camping are offered & there's a lively bar for residents, with a pool table & DSTV, free Wi-Fi & laptop connections. Inexpensive meals can be ordered & free tea & coffee is served until 10.00. The management can book gorilla permits for Uganda. Travellers who raft with NRE are given 1 free night's dorm bed. Entering Jinja from Kampala take the 1st right after the railway bridge & then 2nd left. *US$25 dbl (1 room only), US$10pp dorm bed, US$5pp camping. All using shared facilities.*

⌂ Bellevue Hotel [504 B1] (20 rooms) Kutch Rd; ☎ 0434 120328; m 0712 889900/986608; e bellevuehotel@yahoo.com. This long-standing favourite on the budget–shoestring borderline lies on the smarter side of the Main Street. It's a 5min walk downmarket to the bus & taxi parks. Rooms are clean. *US$13/18 s/c sgl/dbl, US$8.50 sgl with common showers.*

⌂ Khalinie Hotel [504 D3] (27 rooms) m 0772 456904. The standard of accommodation in this town centre dive varies wildly. The upstairs rooms are OK (& even enjoy a distant lake view beyond unfinished concrete structures), while the downstairs rooms are just grotty. Notable primarily for the attached Indian restaurant; see page 505. *US$8/10 s/c sgl/dbl.*

You'll find three classic shoestring lodges on Kutch Road close to the taxi park. The grotty entrance alone at the **Fairway** [504 D1] (*US$8/10 s/c sgl/dbl*) should be enough to send you scurrying to the **Crystal Palace Inn** [504 D1] (*US$8/10/12 s/c sgl/dbl/twin*), or the marginally cheaper **Victoria View** [504 D1] (*US$6/9/11 sgl/dbl/twin*) where the implied outlook is found on the rooftop laundry area.

Camping The most popular camping options in the Jinja area are at Bujagali & Mabira Forest (both covered later in this chapter), but there are a few options in the town, primarily the **Jinja Backpackers**, **Nalubale Teahouse** and the **Explorers Backpackers**. Though camping is offered at the rundown Source of the Nile Gardens across the river from Jinja, I'm told it is not safe.

✗ WHERE TO EAT AND DRINK The hotels listed under the upmarket, moderate and budget headings all have decent restaurants serving Western-style food. The bars at

---

THE DEATH OF BISHOP HANNINGTON

The Rev James Hannington first set foot in East Africa in June 1882 as the leader of a reinforcement party for the Victoria Nyanza Mission in Kampala, but he was forced to return to England before reaching Uganda owing to a debilitating case of dysentery. In June 1884, he was consecrated in London as the first bishop of Eastern Equatorial Africa. In November of the same year, he left England to assume his post, inspired by Joseph Thomson, who months earlier had become the first European to travel to Lake Victoria through Maasailand, rather than the longer but less perilous route pioneered by Speke around the south of the lake.

Thomson advised future travellers against attempting to reach Buganda through the territory occupied by the militant Maasai, but Bishop Hannington – attracted by its directness and better climatic conditions – paid him no heed. And, as it transpired, Hannington and his party of 200 porters negotiated the route without encountering any significant resistance from the Kikuyu or Maasai, to arrive at Mumias (in present-day western Kenya) on 8 October 1885. A few days later, accompanied by a reduced party of 50 porters, Hannington continued the march westward, obtaining his first view of Lake Victoria on 14 October.

Hannington had been fully aware of the risks involved in crossing Maasailand, but he had no way of knowing about the momentous change in mood that had marked Buganda since the death of King Mutesa a year earlier. Mutesa was succeeded by his son Mwanga, who became increasingly hostile towards outsiders in general and the Anglican Church in particular during the first year of his reign. Worse still, Mwanga was deeply affected by a vision that foretold the destruction of Buganda at the hands of strangers who entered the kingdom through the 'back door' – the east – as opposed to the more normal approach from the southwest.

Explorers Backpackers [496 C3] and **Nalubale Tea House** [496 D3] are often good places to meet travellers and volunteers, particularly when major sports events are screened on DSTV. Numerous small bars and local eateries, not listed individually below, are scattered along Main Street and around the market area. If you've got transport, you might drive the 9km out to Bujagali to try the steaks (*Ush25,000*) at the excellent **Black Lantern** (see also page 514; m *0782 321541*).

✗ **2 Friends** [496 D3] Jackson Crescent. This outdoor bar/restaurant, set in a large suburban garden, is one of the more chilled-out drinking & eating spots in town. Grills, pizzas & Indian & African dishes served. *Meals Ush15,000–30,000*.

♀ **Babez** [504 C5] Main St. Pronounced 'babes', this is the liveliest, loudest & latest bar on Main Street. A full-on drinking joint where the bad girls go when they've been banned from everywhere else (see the Golf Club listing below).

✗ **Baraza Resort** [496 B2] Situated on the northern edge of town, & a bit of a hassle to get to since it's only accessible off the Kampala Road, this resort is set in a riverside garden facing the upstream wall of the dam. It's right in the path of the proposed new bridge over the Nile but in the meantime, it serves good Indian food & pizzas. *Main courses Ush17,000*.

🍴 **Flavours** [504 C5] Main St. This smart café on Main Street serves coffee, juices, smoothies & salads, as well as steaks & other fortifying dishes. Internet facilities available. Broot, a Kampala-based Dutch bakery, delivers bread & croissants on Tue. *Meals Ush18,000–28,000*.

♀ **Golf Club** [496 D7] Habitually a pleasant location for a quiet drink watching reputations being made & broken on the 18th green, the golf club is occasionally prone to some real entertainment. A letter pasted to the door decries 'The February 15th Fight', an obviously lively event distinguished by 'obscene language & dog behaviours', & bans 12 offending females from the premises.

On 21 October 1885, Hannington and his party entered the fort of Luba, an important Basoga chief with strong loyalties to the King of Buganda. Hours later, the bishop was attacked and imprisoned, and Luba sent a party of messengers to Mwanga to seek instructions. The messengers returned on 28 October accompanied by three Baganda soldiers. The next morning, Hannington wrote in his diary: 'I can hear no news. A hyena howled near me last night, smelling a sick man, but I hope it is not to have me yet.' On the afternoon of 29 October, Hannington was informed that he would be escorted to Buganda immediately. Instead, he was led to a nearby execution rock, stripped of his clothes and possessions, and speared to death. That night, Luba's soldiers massacred the bishop's entire party of 50 porters, with the exception of three men who managed to escape and one boy who was spared on account of his youth.

It is said locally that the murder of Bishop Hannington displeased the spirits and resulted in a long famine in Busoga. King Mwanga, not entirely plausibly, would subsequently claim that he had never ordered Hannington's death; instead, his instructions to release the bishop had been misinterpreted or disregarded by overzealous underlings. In 1890, the bishop's skull – identifiable by his gold fillings – and some of his clothes were brought to Sir Frederick Jackson in Mumias by the one member of Hannington's party who had been spared by Luba's soldiers. The mortal remains of Bishop Hannington were interred at Namirembe Cathedral on 31 December 1892 in a lavish ceremony attended by Mwanga. On 29 October 1939, the 54th anniversary of his death, a bronze memorial dedicated to Bishop Hannington was erected on a boulder near the small port of Buluba (Place of Luba), some 60km east of Jinja.

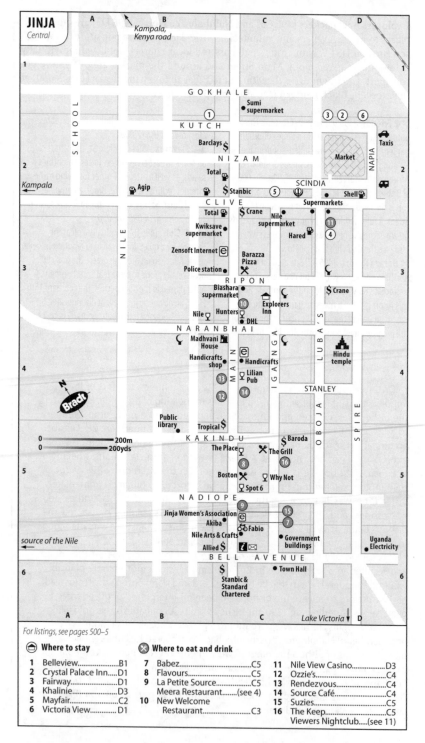

JINJA
Central

A   B   C   D

Kampala,
Kenya road

GOKHALE

Sumi
supermarket

KUTCH

Barclays

NIZAM

Total

SCINDIA

Agip

Stanbic

CLIVE

Market

Taxis

NAPIA

Shell

Supermarkets

Total

Crane

Nile
supermarket

SCHOOL

Kwiksave
supermarket

Zensoft Internet

Police station

NILE

Hared

RIPON

Barazza
Pizza

Kampala

Biashara
supermarket

Explorers
Inn

Crane

Nile

Hunters

DHL

NARANBHAI

Madhvani
House

Handicrafts
shop

Handicrafts

Lilian
Pub

MAIN

IGANGA

LUBA'S

Hindu
temple

STANLEY

Public
library

Tropical

KAKINDU

Baroda

OBOJA

SPIRE

0 —————— 200m
0 —————— 200yds

The Place

Boston

The Grill

Why Not

Spot 6

NADIOPE

Jinja Women's Association

Akiba

Nile Arts & Crafts

Fabio

Allied

Government
buildings

Uganda
Electricity

source of the Nile

BELL   AVENUE

Stanbic &
Standard
Chartered

Town Hall

Lake Victoria

For listings, see pages 500–5

🛏 **Where to stay**

1   Belleview......................B1
2   Crystal Palace Inn.....D1
3   Fairway.........................D1
4   Khalinie.........................D3
5   Mayfair.........................C2
6   Victoria View...............D1

✖ **Where to eat and drink**

7   Babez............................C5
8   Flavours........................C5
9   La Petite Source.........C5
   Meera Restaurant........(see 4)
10 New Welcome
    Restaurant...................C3

11 Nile View Casino................D3
12 Ozzie's.................................C4
13 Rendezvous.......................C4
14 Source Café........................C4
15 Suzies...................................C5
16 The Keep.............................C5
   Viewers Nightclub.....(see 11)

🖳 **The Keep** [504 C5] Iganga Rd. This popular new café owes its existence to a particularly devout & determined Christian couple from the USA, with more than a little help from their maker, as the menu-biography relates. Within a mock castle-walled setting, tasty salads, pizzas, coffees & sandwiches are served. Even the most committed of Jinja's atheists concede that the milkshakes are influenced by divine intervention. Profits to community projects. Wi-Fi available. *Meals Ush6,000–20,000.*

✗ **La Petite Source** [504 C5] Main Street near the post office. Recommended for good Ugandan food. Nearby, the rather smarter **Suzie's** does a good lunchtime buffet for Ush10,000.

✗ **Ling Ling** [496 D1] This long-serving Chinese restaurant occupied the obviously Chinese building on Bujagali roundabout for 20 years before shifting to a new building in 2012, 1km down Bujagali Road. *Main courses around Ush16,000.*

✗ **Meera Restaurant** [504 D3] Not much to look at from the outside, Meera – situated on the ground floor of the rather grim Khalinie Hotel – serves good, authentic & inexpensive Indian food. *Chicken tikka masala Ush12,000 excl rice/naan.*

✗ **Mezzanine** [496 D5] Bridge Close, off Bridge St; m 0774 730 659; www.mezzanine-jinja.com. Located in the Jinja Backpackers compound, this new bar/restaurant is the best spot in town for a riverside drink &/or a meal. Mezzanine serves snacks, tapas, pizzas & an à la carte menu that includes seafood dishes. *Prices range from Ush6,000 for snacks to Ush30,000 for the Surf & Turf (fillet steak topped with garlic prawns).*

✗ **New Welcome Restaurant** [504 C4] Main St. This site was originally – & is still recognisably so – a filling station. It's now a popular Indian restaurant dedicated to filling its customers with curries, kormas, masalas, etc. *Chicken tikka masala 11,000, rice Ush6,000, naan Ush2,000.*

✗ **Ozzie's Café** [504 C4] Main St. This great little Australian-run restaurant, situated directly opposite the Source Café, has become a 'home from home' for scores of local volunteers & gap-year students over the years. It serves toasted sandwiches, steaks, salads, burgers & vegetarian dishes. Closes at around 19.00. *Meals Ush10,000–14,000.*

✗ **Moti Mahal** [504 C4] 46 Iganga Rd. Jinja expats rave about the northern Indian menu, the pocket-friendly prices, the huge thalis, the tasty & tender goat curries, & the speed of the service. *Meals + rice + naan Ush22,000.*

♀ **Rendezvous Bar** [504 C4] Jinja sees plenty of bars opening, thriving for a while, & then fading away, but the brick-fronted Rendezvous has been quietly dishing out beer & snacks for over 2 decades.

✗ **Rumours** [496 C6] This pleasant riverside bar/restaurant has had some poor reviews from readers over the years but it seems to have got its act together recently.However, as it lies within the Source of the Nile site you'll pay a Ush10,000 entrance fee just to look at the menu. *Continental meals Ush18,000.*

✗ **Serge's Guesthouse/Pizzeria** [497 E7] Just off Obuja Rd. Behind the defunct Ripon Falls Hotel, in a rambling colonial town house with a pretty garden, Serge's serves good pizzas. *Ush20,000–24,000.*

✗ **Source Café** [504 C4] Main St; ⏰ 09.00–18.00 Mon–Sat. Set in a restored 1920s warehouse, this excellent café looks & smells like an old-time coffee house. The menu offers freshly brewed coffee, including cappuccino & mochas, & juices, plus a variety of cakes & light meals. It's a pleasant place to hang out, with an attached internet café (*Ush2,000/hr*), craft shop & several tables on the pavement. Source Café is a non-profit initiative helping schools in the area. *Meals up to Ush10,000.*

NIGHTLIFE Jinja's first casino **Nile View** [504 D3], is found on Luba's Road in the same building as the **Viewers Nightclub** [504 D3].

SHOPPING Though none of the main Kenyan or South African chains are represented, Jinja is exceptionally well supplied with supermarkets. The highest concentration lies along Clive Road, while **Biashara supermarket** [504 C3] on Main Street is closer to the main cluster of craft shops and cafés frequented by tourists. This includes a number of good craft shops on this street between Ozzie's and the Rendezvous Bar. If you're looking for fresh fruit and vegetables, visit the

The Victoria Nile, running past Jinja, forms the boundary between the kingdoms of Buganda and Busoga, the latter being the home of the Basoga, Uganda's second most populous linguistic group. The Basoga speak a Bantu language very similar to Luganda – particularly close to the dialect of the Ssese Islands – but they claim a different origin from the Baganda, and traditionally adhere to a far less centralised political structure. It is also the case that many traditional Basoga customs – for instance, the largely abandoned practice of extracting six teeth from the lower jaw of a boy as an initiation to adulthood – are clearly influenced by the Nilotic-speaking Luo.

Basoga has been subject to numerous migrations and a great deal of cultural intermingling over the past few centuries, for which reason its traditions are more diverse and contradictory than those of Uganda's other kingdoms. It is generally agreed, however, that the Basoga originate from the eastern side of Mount Elgon. A popular tradition has it that Busoga was founded by a hunter called Makuma, who crossed the western slopes of the mountain accompanied by his wives, dogs and other followers about 600 years ago to settle in the vicinity of present-day Iganga. Makuma had eight sons, each of whom was appointed ruler of a specific area of Busoga. Makuma was buried at Iganga, where it is said his tomb magically transformed into a rock that is known today as Buswikara and forms the site of an important ancestral shrine.

Uniquely, Busoga's modern status as a kingdom is not rooted in any pre-colonial political or social structure, but is instead a result of 20th-century developments. Pre-colonial Busoga was divided into about 70 autonomous principalities ruled by hereditary chiefs who originally paid tribute to the King of Bunyoro, but had mostly transferred allegiance to the King of Buganda by the end of the 19th century. This traditional system of decentralised government was undermined in 1900 when Britain divided Busoga into 14 larger principalities for administrative and tax purposes. It was shattered entirely six years later, when Busoga was amalgamated into one cohesive political entity, modelled on Buganda, and administered by a Muganda 'president', Semei Kakunguru. The office occupied by Kakunguru was abandoned after his retirement in 1913, but the traditional leaders of Basoga put pressure on the British authorities for it to be reinstated – and awarded to a prominent Musoga.

In 1919, Britain created the title of *kyabazinga*, transforming Busoga into a centralised monarchy that enjoyed a similar status within the Uganda protectorate to the ancient kingdoms of Bunyoro or Buganda. Ezekieri Wako Zibondo was crowned as the first kyabazinga, to be succeeded by Sir Wilberforce Nadiope Kadhumbula, whose active rule was terminated when Obote abolished the traditional kingdoms of Uganda in 1967. In 1996, when the kingdoms were reinstated, Henry Wako Muloki – the son of the first kyabazinga – was installed on the throne. Today, the kyabazinga is regarded as the overall leader of Basoga, but he is supported by a parliament of 11 semi-autonomous hereditary Saza chiefs. Five of these chiefs claim accession from Makuma, the founder of Busoga, and the kyabazinga is picked from one of these élite families using a system of rotating accession, to be succeeded only upon death, abdication or serious illness. Muloki ruled until his death in 2008. Perhaps not surprisingly, given the vague process set out for succession, the clans of Busoga have not yet managed to identify an heir acceptable to all.

main market [504 D2] near the taxi park. It's worth a browse too, if you're short of a dried fish, door handles, traditional cloth, secondhand T-shirts, cow's stomachs, spanner sets ...

Books An excellent Jinja-based book exchange has outlets at **Gately on Nile Guesthouse** and **Explorers Camp** at Bujagali Falls (see page 501). Swap an old book and pay Ush1,000. The proceeds go to Soft Power (see box, page 514–15).

OTHER PRACTICALITIES

Foreign exchange Foreign exchange is possible at **Barclays** [504 C2], **Stanbic** [504 C6], **Standard Chartered** [504 C6] and **Crane** [504 D3] banks, either over the counter or using your credit cards in the ATMs.

Immigration If your three-month tourist visa is stamped for only one month on arrival in Uganda, you can get it extended with no hassle (and no charge) at the immigration office behind the town hall (opposite Stanbic bank) [504 C6].

Internet There are plenty of internet cafés in the middle of Jinja: **Flavours** [504 C5], **Source Café** [504 C4] and the **Jinja Women's Association** [504 C5], to name but three at the post office end of Main Street. Most of the better hotels offer some sort of internet facility.

Maps Apart from Kampala, Jinja is the only Ugandan town for which a number of maps are available – fortunately, since it is easy to become disoriented (rather than actually *lost*) in the central grid of streets and surrounding suburban crescents. The fine old Lands and Surveys map is still available from the Entebbe map office (see page 198). More useful in navigating between modern landmarks is the freebie ad-map by 'MAD' and the *Jinja and the Nile* title in the 'Uganda Maps' series. The reverse of the latter contains a map of the Nile Valley north of the town.

WHAT TO SEE AND DO It is possible to take a tour of Jinja Town and the surrounding area; see the tourist centre on page 495 for details.

Jinja Golf Club [496 D7] This lovely course, overlooking the Nile and at one time famous for games being interrupted by a stray hippo, is open to non-members at Ush20,000 per round. Golf clubs are available. A fee of Ush5,000 is charged to visitors who want to use the 25m swimming pool or squash or tennis courts. Keen golfers may also wish to stop at the **Mehta Golf Club** (m *0772 748211*) in Lugazi, midway between Kampala and Jinja, where the Asian owners of the town's sugar factory have created an utterly surreal golfing paradise in a lush valley hidden from the vulgar gaze of the masses toiling in the factory and in the surrounding cane plantations. Has to be seen to be believed! Good curry lunches can be arranged.

Source of the Nile (*Admission Ush10,000pp, plus Ush5,000/10,000 for a car/minibus*) The Ripon Falls, the natural landmark associated with the source of the Nile, was submerged in the early 1950s following the construction of the Owen Falls Dam a short distance upriver. The site is still of interest, however, with a landscaped park and commemorative plaques on both banks of the Nile as it exits Lake Victoria.

The **Source of the Nile** site on the **eastern bank** is the more accessible from central Jinja. From Jinja town centre, it can be reached by boda-boda or a 30-minute walk. From the **post office** [504 C6] on Main Street, follow Bell Street west to the roundabout with Nile Crescent, cross the roundabout and continue for 200m along Bridge Street, then turn left to find the entrance gate at the end of Cliff Road. It's a pleasant spot and deserving of a once-in-a-lifetime visit, though its significance is less obvious than in Speke's day. While the prominent plaque provides a useful clue ('This spot marks the place where the Nile starts its long journey to the Mediterranean'), an alley of craft shops block the river views from this location. You'll need to negotiate these to reach the water's edge where (perhaps sporting a newly purchased 'I visited the Source of the Nile' safari hat), you'll find a small rocky island bearing a few straggly, guano-coated trees – all that remains of the emblematic Ripon Falls since they vanished beneath the reservoir created by the Owen's Falls Dam. What you're actually looking at today is an extension of Lake Victoria since the dam now regulates the flow out of the lake. An additional plaque with a sculpted bust close to the river commemorates Mahatma Gandhi, some of whose ashes were scattered into the river here following his death in 1948. Refreshments are available in a concrete terrace beside the remnants of Ripon Falls but greater choice and a nicer setting are provided by the riverside **Rumours** (see page 505) bar/restaurant, 100m distant in a patch of riverine woodland. If you can agree an acceptable price with the riverside boat operators, you can enjoy a 30-minute round trip. The destination is a supposed underwater spring that is locally considered to be the true source of the Nile. I'm told that you can obtain better deals from boat operators at the fish landing by the Old Sailing Club (insist on a life jacket).

The **original plaque** at this site commemorated Speke's discovery of the Source of the Nile, but this was removed some years back on the basis that local people knew the place long before any European arrived there. Frankly, this particular concession to political correctness strikes me as somewhat delusional. Of course, Speke did not really 'discover' Lake Victoria or the Ripon Falls: people had been living there for millennia before any European arrived. But Speke was the first person to make the connection between the effluent from Lake Victoria and a sacred river that flows into the Mediterranean 6,500km further north.

Ironically, the **new plaque** referred to above is itself somewhat contentious. The Ripon Falls is *a* source of the Nile, but its semi-official status as *the* source of the Nile is arbitrary and sentimental – posthumous recognition of Speke's momentous but contemporarily controversial discovery – rather than being based on any geographical logic. The most remote headwater of the Nile is in fact the most distant spring of the Kagera River, and the location of this is another cause for debate. German explorer Oscar Baumann placed it in Burundi's Kabera Forest in 1892, and his countryman, Richard Kandt, located a spring in Rwanda's Nyungwe Forest in 1903. However, in March 2006, modern GPS equipment led a modern-day expedition up the Nile from Alexandria to a 'new' source in Rwanda, 15km from the location identified by Kandt in 1903. If corroborated, the full length of the river will become 6,718km – 107km longer than previously accepted. Though Rwanda might host the most distant headwater, there are still other alternative sources to consider. The Victoria Nile is not the only river to flow into Lake Albert, from which the true Nile emerges. This lake is also fed by the Semliki which in turn receives streams from the river's highest and certainly most fabulous source on the Rwenzori Mountains. Nyungwe, Rwenzori or the effluent of Lake Albert – any of these would be an equally logical candidate for the spot where the Nile starts its journey to the Mediterranean.

To appreciate the historical context of the Victorian source, you might cross to the western bank of the river to the lower-key **Source of the Nile Gardens** [496 C6] and the spot (more or less) from which Speke viewed Ripon Falls in 1862. Unlike the outlook from the Jinja gardens, the view from the western bank puts the whole thing into context. As you behold the sight seen by Speke – of the river being funnelled towards you out of a broad bay of Lake Victoria – you'll appreciate his conviction that he had solved the age-old mystery. Speke's visit is remembered by an inscribed **pillar** which, erected in 1954, has thus far survived any attempt to replace it with something more politically correct. There are, however, no facilities or services in these rather neglected gardens and unless you feel a specific need to view the memorial, the general vicinity is equally rewarding. If you do enter, a caretaker will materialise to ask you for Ush5,000. The gardens can be reached by canoe from the east bank or by following the Kampala Road across Owen Falls Dam to Njeru where you turn left (just before Nile Breweries). Follow the signs for Kingfisher Safaris Resort for about 3.5km, then cross the railway line on your left and bear to the left. You can also walk. Follow the track at the end of Bridge Street (beyond the old showground), cross the railway bridge (there's an underpass below the track for pedestrians), then follow the line for a couple of kilometres until you find an acceptable view towards the lake.

Kilombera Weaving [map page 494] (m *0782 306602/0772 824206;* ⏰ *09.00–17.00 Mon–Fri, 09.00–13.00 Sat, after hrs by appointment*) This venture, located midway between Bujagali Falls and Jinja Nile Resort, sells attractive handwoven cotton fabrics and can provide a demonstration of the weaving process by arrangement.

Jinja Sailing Club [497 E7] The sailing club was, for many years, a pleasant lakeshore garden and restaurant rather than a centre for waterborne activity. It has been closed for several years now, awaiting renovation. Hopefully it will soon reopen as a pleasant and peaceful place to enjoy a drink or meal whilst pondering the ambiguities of the 'Crocodiles Do Not Swim Here' sign. You can walk to the sailing club by heading directly south from the town centre past the town hall, but a more scenic route along Nile Crescent leads you past the very attractive golf course, an avenue of palm trees laden with fruit bats, and some fine old colonial houses. Many of these have been beautifully renovated, though sadly no attempt has been made to restore and reopen the historic **Ripon Falls Hotel** [497 E7].

BUJAGALI FALLS AND THE NILE

Fifteen years ago, tourism activity on the Nile north of Jinja was limited to a peaceful and rather obscure picnic site at Bujagali Falls – one of a series of impressive rapids below the source of the Nile – visited by a handful of travellers annually. Goodness, how this has changed! Today, the eastern bank of the Nile between Jinja and Bujagali has developed into East Africa's premier adventure-tourism centre, serviced by several bustling backpacker facilities, and an upmarket tented camp and hotel. This is because the 50km stretch of the Nile north of Jinja is now a legendary white-water rafting and kayaking route, widely regarded to be as exhilarating as the more famous Zambezi Gorge below Victoria Falls. Additional activities include bungee jumping, horseriding and quad biking (more details below). Although most visitors to Bujagali are primarily there to undergo their trial by white water, it's also a relaxed and scenic place to spend a few days, with the wide Nile fringed by lush riparian woodland rattling with birds and the odd monkey. Tourism facilities are also appearing along the equally scenic western bank of the river, relaxed set-ups that complement rather than compete with the high-adrenalin activities centred on Bujagali.

As a tourism destination, Bujagali Falls has recently undergone significant changes. Historically, rafting voyages launched just above Bujagali Falls and

The first European to see Lake Victoria was John Hanning Speke, who marched from Tabora to the site of present-day Mwanza in 1858 following his joint 'discovery' of Lake Tanganyika with Richard Burton the previous year. Speke named the lake for Queen Victoria but, prior to that, Arab slave traders called it Ukerewe (still the name of its largest island). It is unclear what name was in local use, since the only one used by Speke is Nyanza, which simply means 'lake'.

A major goal of the Burton–Speke expedition had been to solve the great geographical enigma of the age, the source of the White Nile. Speke, based on his brief glimpse of the southeast corner of Lake Victoria, somewhat whimsically proclaimed his 'discovery' to be the answer to that riddle. Burton, with a comparable lack of compelling evidence, was convinced that the great river flowed out of Lake Tanganyika. The dispute between the former travelling companions erupted bitterly on their return to Britain, where Burton – the more persuasive writer and respected traveller – gained the backing of the scientific establishment.

In 1862–63, Speke and Captain James Grant returned to Lake Victoria, hoping to prove Speke's theory correct. They looped inland around the western shore of the lake, arriving at the court of King Mutesa of Buganda, then continued east to the site of present-day Jinja, where a substantial river flowed out of the lake after tumbling over a cataract that Speke named Ripon Falls. From here, the two explorers headed north, sporadically crossing paths with the river until they reached Lake Albert, then following the Nile to Khartoum and Cairo.

Speke's declaration that 'The Nile is settled' met with mixed support back home. Burton and other sceptics pointed out that Speke had bypassed the entire western shore of his purported great lake, had visited only a couple of points on the northern shore, and had not attempted to explore the east. Nor, for that matter, had he followed the course of the Nile in its entirety. Speke, claimed his detractors, had seen several different lakes and different stretches of river, connected only in Speke's deluded mind. The sceptics had a point, but Speke had nevertheless gathered sufficient geographical evidence to render his claim highly plausible. His notion of one great lake, far from being mere whimsy, was backed by anecdotal information gathered from local sources along the way.

Matters were scheduled to reach a head on 16 September 1864, when an eagerly awaited debate between Burton and Speke – in the words of the former, 'what silly tongues called the "Nile Duel"' – was due to take place at the Royal Geographic Society (RGS). And reach a head they did, but in circumstances more tragic than anybody could have anticipated. On the afternoon of the debate, Speke went out shooting with a cousin, only to stumble while crossing a wall, in the process discharging a barrel of his shotgun into his heart. The subsequent inquest recorded a verdict of accidental death, but it has often been suggested – purely on the basis of the curious timing – that Speke deliberately took his life rather than face up to Burton in public. Burton, who had seen Speke less than three hours earlier, was by all accounts deeply troubled by Speke's death, and years later he was quoted as stating 'the uncharitable [say] that I shot him' – an accusation that seems to have been aired only in Burton's imagination.

Speke was dead, but the 'Nile debate' would keep kicking for several years. In 1864, Sir Samuel and Lady Baker became the first Europeans to reach Lake Albert and nearby Murchison Falls in present-day Uganda. The Bakers, much to the delight of the anti-Speke lobby, were convinced that this newly named lake was a source of the Nile, though they openly admitted it might not be the only one. Following the Bakers' announcement, Burton put forward a revised theory, namely that the most remote source of the Nile was the Rusizi River, which he believed flowed out of the northern head of Lake Tanganyika and emptied into Lake Albert.

In 1865, the RGS followed up on Burton's theory by sending Dr David Livingstone to Lake Tanganyika. Livingstone, however, was of the opinion that the Nile's source lay further south than Burton supposed, and so he struck out towards the lake along a previously unexplored route. Leaving from Mikindani in the far south of present-day Tanzania, Livingstone followed the Rovuma River inland, continuing westward to the southern tip of Lake Tanganyika. From there, he ranged southward into present-day Zambia, where he came across a new candidate for the source of the Nile, the swampy Lake Bangweulu and its major outlet, the Lualaba River. It was only after his famous meeting with Henry Stanley at Ujiji, in November 1871, that Livingstone (in the company of Stanley) visited the north of Lake Tanganyika and Burton's cherished Rusizi River, which, it transpired, flowed into the lake. Burton, nevertheless, still regarded Lake Tanganyika as the most likely source of the Nile, while Livingstone was convinced that the answer lay with the Lualaba River. In August 1872, Livingstone headed back to the Lake Bangweulu region, where he fell ill and died six months later, the great question still unanswered.

In August 1874, ten years after Speke's death, Stanley embarked on a three-year expedition every bit as remarkable and arduous as those undertaken by his predecessors, yet one whose significance is often overlooked. Partly, this is because most histories have painted such an unsympathetic picture of Stanley: a grim caricature of the murderous, pre-colonial White Man blasting and blustering his way through territories where Burton, Speke and Livingstone had relied largely on diplomacy. It is also the case, however, that Stanley set out with no intention of seeking headline-making fresh discoveries. Instead, he determined to test methodically the theories advocated by Speke, Burton and Livingstone about the Nile's source. First, Stanley sailed around the circumference of Lake Victoria, establishing that it was indeed as vast as Speke had claimed. Stanley's next step was to circumnavigate Lake Tanganyika, which, contrary to Burton's long-held theories, clearly boasted no outlet sufficiently large to be the source of the Nile. Finally, and most remarkably, Stanley took a boat along Livingstone's Lualaba River to its confluence with an even larger river, which he followed for months with no idea as to where he might end up.

When, exactly 999 days after he left Zanzibar, Stanley emerged at the Congo mouth, the shortlist of plausible theories relating to the source of the Nile had been reduced to one. Clearly, the Nile did flow out of Lake Victoria at Ripon Falls, before entering and exiting Lake Albert at its northern tip to start its long course through the sands of the Sahara. Stanley's achievement in putting to rest decades of speculation about how the main rivers and lakes of East Africa linked together is estimable indeed. He was nevertheless generous enough to concede that: 'Speke now has the full glory of having discovered the largest inland sea on the continent of Africa, also its principal affluent as well as its outlet. I must also give him credit for having understood the geography of the countries we travelled through far better than any of us who so persistently opposed his hypothesis'.

14

Based on information supplied by Speke Camp

The waterfall at Bujagali, held sacred by the local community, is named after a powerful river spirit that has manifested itself in more than 30 successive human reincarnations over the centuries. Anyone who claims to be the new reincarnation of the spirit is required to prove it by sitting on a magical piece of barkcloth and drifting across the rapids. Only if he succeeds in this risky venture will local villagers accept him as their new spiritual leader.

The last uncontested Bujagali died without nominating an heir in the 1970s, and the identity of his successor has been the subject of a heated dispute. Most villagers believe the spirit resides in a local called Ja-Ja, who is said to have crossed the rapids on the magical piece of barkcloth while evading military arrest during the Amin era. Ja-Ja's rival for the title is an outsider called Jackson, who dreamed that he was the reincarnation of Bujagali more than 20 years ago. Jackson arrived at the village to stake his claim and, assisted by a companion, he ran off with the magic barkcloth in order to float over the rapids. Before he could attempt the crossing, however, the villagers caught him and killed his companion. Jackson was banished from the village to live out his days on what is now known as Jackson's Island, opposite Speke Camp. However, this was flooded by the new reservoir and Jackson's current whereabouts is unknown.

concluded below Itanda Falls, 20km north. This long-standing arrangement has been forced to change following the construction of a new hydro-power dam across the river channel, 3km below Bujagali at Dumbbell Island. Three major rapids, the emblematic Bujagali Falls and the Grade 5 Total Gunga and Silverback/Big Brother have disappeared beneath the reservoir impounded by the dam. As a result (and since the powers-that-be have forbidden rafters to lug their craft over or around their US$500 million dam) the rafting companies have moved their embarkation points 8km below the dam to new sites on the opposite, western bank of the river and rafting now continues a commensurate distance further downriver. So where does this leave Bujagali as a tourism destination? Stripped of its status as the rafting launch point, and with the eponymous rapid underwater, Buj' (as it is known to the rafting fraternity) would seem to be left high and dry. In fact, life goes on, apparently as busy as ever albeit with some adaptations. Thanks to the supplementary activities (quad biking, mountain biking, bungee jumping, etc), Bujagali has its own momentum while the calm waters of the newly created 'Lake Bujagali' offer new recreational opportunities such as birding, fishing, sit-on-top kayaking, stand-up paddle boarding, wine-and-nibbles sunset voyages and down-yer-neck booze cruises. The serene expanse of the new lake has its own visual charm too, especially given a half-decent sunset and a suitable sundowner.

GETTING THERE AND AWAY There are two tourism hubs on the east bank of the river north of Jinja. The first of these, the Nile High Camp and Jinja Nile Resort Hotel complex is about 4km along a poor tarmac road leading off from the main roundabout on the Kampala–Kenya road (notable for a very obvious Chinese restaurant) which skirts the northern edge of Jinja. The second and larger centre is at Bujagali, 5km further along the same road, the latter section being *murram*. Both sites are signposted off the roundabout. Occasional **minibus-taxis** run between Jinja and a junction about 500m from the tourism sites. A **boda-boda** from Jinja direct to the falls costs Ush5,000. In practice, most visitors will not be dependent on public transport, since the rafting companies either operate regular shuttles from their bases in Jinja or provide transport from Kampala, including pick-ups from the main hotels.

WHERE TO STAY Note that listings for accommodation across the river from Bujagali Falls are given in a separate section entitled *Kalagala Falls and the west bank* (see pages 517–23). For location of listings see map, page 494.

Upmarket

Jinja Nile Resort (70 rooms) \0434 122190–2/0414 233593; e nileresort@source. co.ug;www.madahotels.com. The sumptuous Jinja Nile Resort – part of a Kenyan hotel chain – borders a stretch of the Nile studded with forested islands about 1km downriver of the Owen Falls Dam along the road towards Bujagali Falls. The atmosphere of bland internationalism may not be to everybody's taste, but taken on its own terms the resort is difficult to fault – especially the fabulous swimming pool & outdoor bar area. The plush, spacious mini-suites all have 2 beds (1 dbl, 1 sgl), a small sitting area with DSTV, & fan, netting & private balcony. Facilities include a gym, massage parlour, business centre, & squash & tennis courts. The resort caters mainly to business travellers & conferences during the week. Ask about w/end deals. *US$180/220/250 sgl/dbl/trpl suites B&B, river view costs US$20 extra.*

Moderate

The Nile Porch (8 tents, 2 family cottages) m 0782 321541/0772 900451; e relax@nileporch. com; www.nileporch.com. Superbly located on an elevated plateau fringed by acacia trees, the Nile Porch tented camp overlooks the serene expanse of Lake Bujagali. The tents are spacious enough yet marvellously cosy, romantic even, with inner, walk-in mosquito netting & verandas facing the river. It's worth waking early to watch day break over the misty valley. There's a swimming pool to cool off in, while meals are provided in the adjacent Black Lantern Restaurant (see page 514). The room rates, which include a filling b/fast, are excellent value, especially compared with tented camps in & around the national parks, which cost-wise lie firmly in the 'upmarket' category. 2-bedroom cottages for families are also available. Highly recommended. *US$95/115/140 sgl/dbl/trpl. US$180 cottage (sleeps 6) B&B.*

Budget & camping

Adrift Riverbase/Nile High Camp (6 cottages, & tents & dorms) m 0772 454206; www.adrift.ug. The activity centre for the rafting company Adrift, the camp is actually located several kilometres before Bujagali, behind the upmarket Jinja Nile Resort Hotel, 3km along the Bujagali Road from Jinja's Shell/Ling Ling roundabout. The site boasts a timber bar-restaurant deck & wooden cottages, all perched on poles above the lofty river cliff & enjoying views across the Nile Valley. The communal (hot) shower & toilet block is artfully constructed using natural slates & cobblestones. Dinners cost Ush12,000–25,000 & include good pizzas. *US$40/60 sgl/dbl cottages, US$40/50 sgl/dbl furnished tents, US$10 dorm bed, US$5 camping. All using shared facilities.*

Eden Rock Bandas (20 rooms) m 0754 997149; www.edenrockresorts.com. Eden Rock centres on a large & spacious thatched restaurant/ lounge building set in an expansive lawn. The lack of a river view is redeemed by the recent addition of a good-sized swimming pool & it's the only option at Bujagali to offer budget s/c rooms. Spacious s/c family *bandas* sleep up to 5 in 1–2 rooms. Cheaper accommodation is provided by an adjacent row of s/c cottages (recently rebuilt but still rather closely spaced), a dormitory & camping. *US$45 (sleeps 4) & US$65 (sleeps 6) family bandas, US$35 dbl small bandas B&B, US$5pp camping.*

Nile River Camp m 0776 900450/0772 900451; e chill@camponthenile.com; www. camponthenile.com. This new, budget friendly, family-oriented camp is adjacent to (& owned by) the Nile Porch & enjoys the same great lake view. Accommodation is provided in dorms & lake-view furnished tents. A burgers & fish 'n' chips style menu (*Ush10,000–15,000*) is available in the large, open-sided lodge/bar. For more choice, head next door to the Black Lantern restaurant (see page 514). NRC offers a variety of activities, including cycling, kayaking & birding cruises. If the small swimming pool doesn't appeal, swing off the river cliff rope swing into the lake. *US$45 tent, US$10 dorm beds, US$pp camping. All using shared facilities. Rates excl food.*

⌂ **Explorers River Camp aka NRE Camp** (22 standing tents, 4 rooms, 7 dorms) ☎ 0434 120236; m 0772 422373/0782 320552 (campsite bar); e rafting@raftafrica.com; www.raftafrica. com. Superbly located on a high bluff above Lake Bujagali, Explorers Camp is a popular base for rafters, particularly overland truckers & independent travellers with their own vehicles. The potent cocktail of post-rafting high & alcohol can lead to lively evenings in the well-stocked bar (closes at 01.00). A particularly raucous highlight is the screening of the day's rafting highlights on DVD (yours to take home for US$35). Good meals are served; try the Everything Burger (*Ush15,000*). Like its namesake hostel in Jinja, Explorers Camp is operated by Nile River Explorers (NRE) & a free night's dorm accommodation is offered to anybody who rafts with them. Other activities include sunset booze cruises, jet boating & kayaking (see page 516). *US$30 for tents with lake view, US$25 dbl rooms & 'standard' furnished twin tents, US$10pp dorm beds, US$5pp camping. All using shared facilities. Rates excl food.*

✖ **WHERE TO EAT** Diners really are spoilt for choice these days along the Jinja Nile. Decent hotel food is dispensed at the **Jinja Nile Resort** and **Nile High Camp**, meals at the latter being served on a superbly positioned covered deck above the river and costing between Ush8,000 and Ush22,000. At 5km north, the **Black Lantern Restaurant** at the **Nile Porch** serves great steaks (*Ush25,000*) salads, and huge plates

SOFT POWER

Bujagali Falls is something of a phenomenon, not only because of its role as the adrenalin capital of East Africa, but also because of numerous initiatives through which the backpacker-driven tourism industry along the Nile corridor is actually giving something back to the locality that supports it. This is as it should be. For while the Nile rafting industry and spin-offs generate an estimated US$1 million annually, local schoolchildren sit on hard benches catching jiggers in their feet through the earth floors of mud-and-thatch classrooms. Or rather they did. Thanks to Hannah Bayne, an English overland truck driver, conditions for many kids have improved in various ways. Dilapidated classrooms have been replaced by new brick structures with concrete floors, rainwater-collection tanks have been fitted, and safe latrines built. These date from 2000 when Hannah returned to Africa with the intention of doing something for some of the communities through which she had travelled over the years. Gravitating back, quite understandably, to the lovely Bujagali Falls, her chance came when the Bwenda village community provided her with a plot of land, hoping that she would be able to provide them with a pre-school facility. And with the assistance of like-minded travellers willing to provide labour and financial assistance, Hannah was indeed able to do so. Today, 120 AIDS orphans and other deserving infants attend a brightly painted brick-built school at Bwenda, with a grassy compound and an adventure playground. A school for another 120 kids followed at nearby Kyabirwa. These initial activities have been formalised as 'Soft Power Education', an English-registered charity and a name that few visitors to Buji will miss these days. Soft Power gained momentum in 2002 when Hannah married Bingo Small, co-director of Nalubale Rafting, and since that time local schoolkids have benefited immensely from logistical backup, marketing and a ceaseless flow of donations and volunteers from NRE's Explorers River Camp. Soft Power Education is now co-ordinated by full-time volunteers and has to-date worked in seven sub-counties and at over 40 primary schools, predominantly in Jinja District

of spare ribs in an atmospheric thatched building high above the river. A filling English breakfast here costs Ush16,000. Note that last orders for evening meals are taken at 21.15. All of the **budget camps** at Bujagali Falls serve reasonable meals at affordable prices or you can order a pizza (*Ush16,000–24,000*) from **Flags Pizzeria** nearby. The cheapest food is served in a scattering of wooden shacks that have sprung up opposite the entrance to Explorers Camp. Offerings range from *chapatis* and *rolexes* (see box, page 159), to simple rice and beans (*Ush3,500*), and daily specials such as spicy fish and roast potatoes (*Ush6,000*). For location of listings see map, page 494.

WHAT TO DO

Rafting Rafting trips on the Nile are offered by three companies: **Adrift** (m *0772 454206; www.adrift.ug; see also advert in third colour section*), **Nile River Explorers (NRE)** (*0434 120236; www.raftafrica.com*) and **Nalubale Rafting** (m *0782 638938; www.nalubalerafting.com*). Rafting excursions can be booked directly with the rafting company, or through the Kampala Backpackers' and Red Chilli hostels (see pages 152 and 156), or any tour operator.

All three companies offer similar one-day itineraries starting on the west bank of the river above Overtime rapid and finishing near Hairy Lemon Island, about 20km downriver. The route includes eight Grade 3–5 rapids (two are Grade 5: Overtime and The Bad Place/Itanda Falls). While on the river, you'll get to see a

but also including several around the Murchison Falls National Park. They have built new classrooms, refurbished dilapidated classrooms and painted all the buildings – at last count they had worked on over 400 classrooms. Developmental cynics will be pleased to note that rather than relieving the local education authority of its responsibility for developing infrastructure, it liaises with the authorities in order to work where funding is apparently not available. In 2008, Soft Power Education raised over £250,000 through the support of visiting overland passengers, independent long-term volunteers, groups of university students, standing orders, one-off donations (of up to £5,000) and fundraising by ex-volunteers in their home countries. An impressive education centre sits in the heart of Kyabirwa village, where Ugandan tutors instruct daily groups of visiting schoolchildren in topics either poorly represented in the local curriculum or lacking for materials, such as drama, arts and crafts, library, and computer use, as well as science and agriculture. Soft Power Education welcomes volunteers from one day through to 12 months. For more details, enquire at NRE's Explorers Camp at Bujagali Falls, contact e info@softpowereducation.com or check out www.softpowereducation.com.

Local support from the tourism industry is not limited to Soft Power Education. An independent sister project, Soft Power Health, provides improved healthcare to villagers at affordable prices. All Terrain Adventures makes payments to the local parishes through which their quad bikes pass. NRE is helping to train interested local people in kayaking, a process that has, for the most talented, led to opportunities exceeding their wildest dreams. The best among them have become professional river guides and some have acquitted themselves extremely well in international competitions in Switzerland and Australia. In 2003, a team of Ugandan villagers, Paulo Babi, Juma Kalakwani and Geoffrey Kabirya, reached the quarter-finals of the World Championships in Australia, while Babi was placed eighth in the 2004 European Championships in Switzerland.

14

lot of different birds, and you can swim in the calm stretches of water between the rapids. All companies charge US$125 for a full-day excursion. The deal includes rafting equipment, return transportation from Kampala or Jinja, buffet lunch, and beers and sodas. Stiff competition ensures that rafting operators offer an ever-growing list of additional inducements such as free dorm accommodation (or an equivalent discount on other rooms), a post-rafting barbecue, discounts for a second trip, and optional extras such as souvenir clothing and DVDs (*US$35*) and photo CDs (*US$25*) of the day's action. Look out too for combo-deals that combine rafting with additional activities, for example jet boating, paddle-boarding, tandem kayaking and bungee jumping.

Two-day rafting trips (*NRE: US$199 or US$250 depending on accommodation; Nalubale: US$240; Adrift US$250*) are also available through the same companies. Spread over two days, the effect of the dam becomes rather clearer. While the first day provides plenty of thrills, day two offers fewer rapids but plenty of opportunity for paddle-boarding.

In addition to the above prices, an additional US$15 per person may apply for portage around the un-raftable Itanda Falls through the Nile Bank Forest Reserve. This will be shared between the rafting company Adrift (which has been awarded a tourism concession within the reserve) and the local community. This will certainly be contested by other rafting and kayaking companies who will cite laws concerning public access along the Nile corridor. We'll keep you updated in the Bradt Uganda blog!

Kayaking Bujagali is also a top spot for kayaking, attracting experienced proponents from across the world. More testing than rafting, kayaking offers (in the words of an appreciative reader) 'the opportunity to develop your own skills, rather than just bouncing along in a raft controlled by the professionals'. Courses and expeditions are offered by **Kayak the Nile** (m *0772 880322*; e *info@kayakthenile.com*; *www. kayakthenile.com*), based at NRE's Explorers River Camp at Bujagali Falls.

Instructors are trained to the UK's BCU standard. Options start with a half- or one-day introductory course (*US$85/115*) and progress to longer and more testing two-, three- or five-day courses. Full-on Grade 5 tandem kayaking (*US$140*) tackles the river's wildest water, while open-top kayaks explore the placid Lake Bujagali (*US$20/hr or US$30 with a guide; sunset option includes a complementary G&T*). **Nile River Camp** at Bujagali offer similar 'sit on top' kayaks (*US$20/30 for 1/2 people for 2hrs*). A guide costs US$20 extra.

Lake cruises Both **Nalubale** and **NRE** now offer additional excuses for messing about in boats, notably a variety of river cruises on Lake Bujagali in new, two-storied aluminium craft. Both offer sunset cruises. Nalubale's version is a genteel excursion from Nile River Camp and provides snacks, sodas and two beers per person (*US$25pp*). The crepuscular competition from NRE runs out of Explorers Camp, usually carrying a younger and more boisterous clientele, and US$45 per person gets you a boat trip, all the lager you can drink in two hours and, if you're paying attention, a sunset. Mind how you go as you disembark!

Considerably cheaper trips on wooden boats are available from the remnants of Speke Camp, the original viewpoint and backpacker camp beside Bujagali Falls. Eight people typically pay about Ush120,000 for a full hour's cruise (contact Geoffrey m 0755 643070) so don't expect comfortable seats. Despite the disappearance of the camp and the waterfall beneath the reservoir, a Jinja Council official still collects Ush3,000 from each foreign visitor and Ush1,000 for each vehicle entering the site.

Birding and fishing Lake Bujagali offers excellent opportunities for birding (the white-backed night heron being a particular draw) and fishing (yellow fish, Nile perch and catfish). **Fin and Feather Pursuits** (m *0776 900450; www.ffp.ug*), which runs out of Bujagali's Nile River Camp, offers a range of tailor-made birding and fishing trips.

Quad biking The company **All Terrain Adventures** (m *0772 377185;* e *info@ atadventures.com; www.atadventures.com*) run quad-biking trips out of Bujagali between some stunning Nile viewpoints using local footpaths and tracks. Day rates range from US$45 per person for an hour-long ride to US$185 per person for an eight-hour day with lunch. A two-day trip along the Nile Valley, overnighting at Hairy Lemon Island, costs US$275.

Horseriding and mountain biking As an alternative to quad biking on the east bank (see above) you might try horseriding at **Nile Horseback Safaris** on the west bank (see page 522). The area can also be explored by **mountain bike**. These can be hired from Eden Rock, Nile River Camp, Nalubale Tea House and NRE's Explorers Campsite and Jinja hostel (see page 501). Guided local routes explore Jinja and Bujagali Falls, and Bugembe viewpoint, while vehicle transfers are required to explore the depths of Mabira Forest. Self-guided cycle hire is also available. NRE and Nalubale rates include transport from Kampala on the rafting shuttle buses.

Bungee jumping While most activities along the Jinja Nile explore water and terra firma, at Adrift's Nile High Camp (between Jinja and Bujagali) you can investigate (fleetingly) a 44m column of thin air – an experience enabled by a 12m cantilevered steel bungee tower atop a 32m riverside cliff. The cost is US$95, a second jump US$60 and the third is free. If rafting with Adrift, a jump costs US$70. In fact, the jump is free of charge; the fee actually applies only to the climb up to the bungee platform; you'll discover this technicality if you get this far, look at the 44m drop towards the Nile, and ask for a refund. Note that, following complaints from local people (presumably those equipped with telescopes), clothing is now mandatory for daytime jumps. Naked bungee jumping is now permitted only at night and at the discretion of the management.

Other activities It seems that no activity is too desperate or extreme to maintain Bujagali's position as East Africa's adventure tourism capital – check out the new **Big Game Crazy Golf Course** (concrete hippos, tigers, buffalo, etc) at All Terrain Adventures's quad-biking compound. Alternatively, try wood-print carving, pottery, tie dyeing, weaving, etc, at Soft Power's **Endowoza Arts Centre** (*Ush15,000–20,000 for 2hr activities*) at Bujagali. Other new initiatives include **paintballing** at Nile River Camp (*US$20pp with 50 balls*), and **Stand-up Paddle-boarding** (SUP) in the river (m *0775 837478;* e *rockslide83@gmail.com*). **Tandem paragliding** excursions run from Jinja to Mount Elgon's Wanale Ridge above Mbale town and are arranged by **Fly Mami Africa** (*www.flymamiafrica.com; see also page 483*).

KALAGALA FALLS AND THE WEST BANK

Though Bujagali-minus-the-Falls remains the primary tourism hub on the Jinja Nile, additional tourism developments on the western side of the river are emerging. The undoubted jewel in this area is the section of river between the west-bank Kalagala

Falls Forest Reserve (KFFR) and the east-side Nile Bank Forest Reserve (NBFR), 28km north of Jinja. Though tree cover within the KFFR is unremarkable and the NBFR is a conifer plantation, three stunning rapids (Kalagala Falls, Hypoxia and Itanda Falls/The Bad Place) thunder between the rocky channels created between the two reserves and two naturally forested mid-river islands.

Tourism activity in the vicinity of Kalagala Falls is being driven by the rafting company, Adrift. A fabulous upmarket lodge has been built on Kalagala Island and a jet boat brought up from Bujagali, a mid-range tented camp is under construction on a KFFR promontory overlooking all three rapids, an inter-island zip line is being erected, a bungee tower is planned and one of the craft used in the 1954 *African Queen* movie is being restored for river cruises. Visit www.adrift. ug for updates.

The KFFR is also a prominent Baganda cultural site: a massive tree beneath which visiting *kabakas* sat stands on the aforementioned promontory, while a shrine, still of considerable importance to traditionalists, is found with a jumble of massive riverside boulders. Other relaxed tourism sites on this side of the river are the mid-range Haven and the self-catering Holland Park, the budget Hairy Lemon Island to the north and the self-explanatory Nile Horseback Safaris.

GETTING THERE AND AWAY Kalagala Falls and the west-bank lodges are accessed from the quiet tarmac road that loops around Mabira Forest between Jinja's Owen Falls Dam and Kampala, via Gayaza and Kayunga. If driving yourself from Kampala, use the Gayaza–Kayunga–Jinja route described in *Getting there and away* for Jinja (see page 495). If starting from Jinja, Holland Park and Nile Horseback Safaris are 3km along this road towards Kayunga, the turning to The Haven river lodge is 15km and Kangulumira (for Kalagala Falls) is 26km. Nazigo trading centre (for the Hairy Lemon) is another 10km further on. **Public transport** on this road runs from Kampala's old taxi park and Njeru taxi park opposite Nile Breweries.

WHERE TO STAY
Upmarket

Wildwaters Lodge (10 cottages) 9277 6669; m 0772 237400; www.wild-uganda.com. This magnificent addition to Uganda's tourism portfolio opened in 2010 to deserved acclaim. Everyone, Joanna Lumley among them, agrees that the setting – a forested island between 2 raging channels of white water – is simply fabulous. J-Lu's appreciation concerned her night in a sleeping bag on the wooden floor of a half-built cottage above Hypoxia rapid, *sans* loo, *sans* roof, during her 2009 TV show *Joanna Lumley's Nile*, but you'll get the finished product: a huge, beautifully appointed, thatch-roofed, canvas-sided s/c cottage suite with a private balcony provided with a bathtub & full complement of lotions & smelly salts. Wildwaters fits its island setting perfectly & each cottage is individually shaped to the terrain & the forest setting (no trees exceeding 10cm girth were harmed to make this lodge). 6 cottages look directly into the terrible Hypoxia & one of the things you'll miss most on leaving Wildwaters is this rapid's omnipresent roar. The remaining suites enjoy peaceful outlooks across the placid river as it approaches the island & the rapids. The main lodge building is also equally accommodating to trees (which grow upwards through the thatch) & guests. A well-stocked library corner is provided with cosy armchairs, while the bar/b/fast counter & dining areas overlook the swimming pool (a natural rock pool artfully isolated from the river) & some baby rapids approaching Hypoxia. The 5-course dinners are superb, though the naturally greedy might complain that quality is prioritised over quantity. Day visitors pay US$15 entrance fee & another US$10 to swim. (*Lunches cost Ush20,000–40,000.*) Pending a bridge over the Kalagala Falls, access to Wildwaters is by boat from a landing upstream of the rapids. The only conceivable drawback is the price. See also advert in fourth colour section. *US$250pp FB inc 5-course dinner. Discounts for residents.*

Moderate

⌂ **The Haven** (8 cottages) m 0702 905959/0782 905959; e thehavenuganda@ yahoo.com; www.thehaven-uganda.com. This riverside lodge, 10km south of Kalagala Falls, enjoys a great location overlooking the Grade 5 Overtime rapid. 6 spacious, s/c, solar-powered, river-view cottage suites are constructed using natural materials & with earthy tones. There are also a couple of s/c cottages, while pitch-your-own & lazy camping are popular options. The Haven has also gained a reputation as a romantic retreat, thanks in part to the 'Honeymoon Cottage' with its floor-level bathtub in front of a picture window overlooking Overtime rapid. You can swim in the new swimming pool or in the river (bathing areas of low risk & high risk for bilharzia are thoughtfully signed!) or go fishing, boating or mountain biking. Shoreline wildlife includes fish eagles & other birds, red-tailed monkeys, otters & monitor lizards. The Haven lies 17km up the Kagunga Road. Advance booking required. See also advert in fourth colour section. *US$230 Honeymoon Cottage, US$190 dbl Family House (extra adult beds US$60pp, under 12s US$30), US$125/190 sgl/dbl s/c river-view suites, US$100/170 smaller s/c sgl/dbl cottages, US$60/110 sgl/dbl laxy camping, US$40pp camping. All rates FB.*

⌂ **Holland Park** (3 cottages, 1 safari tent) m 0782 507788; e info@hollandpark.com; www. hollandparkuganda.com. Spread across a lovely, 4ha garden on the lofty plateau above Lake Bujagali, this strictly self-catering set-up is deservedly popular with Kampala residents. With thatched roofs, mezzanine bedrooms, beautiful Indonesian wooden furniture & fitted kitchens (solar fridge, gas stove & all utensils) the s/c cottages are quite delightful, as indeed is a more modest safari tent (also s/c with kitchen). Though relaxing in these exquisite surroundings – a pool with Wi-Fi lounge is provided – would seem sufficiently time-consuming, some guests manage to squeeze in a lake cruise or a boat trip across to the east-bank Black Lantern restaurant for a slap-up lunch (see page 514). Holland Park is signposted 4.5km down the Kayunga Road. *US$80/120 sgl/dbl self-catering cottages (ages 2–12 US$25), US$75/100 sgl/dbl safari tent.*

Budget

⌂ **The Hairy Lemon** (6 rooms) m 0752 828338 (SMS due to poor network); e hairylemonuganda@gmail.com; www. hairylemonuganda.com. This great little camp, accessed from the west bank of the river, stands on 1 of a cluster of islands close to the rafting takeout point about 15km northwest of Kalagala Falls. There is an abundance of birdlife on the island, & red-tailed monkeys & a family of otters are resident. Guests typically fall into 1 of 2 categories: Kampala families attracted by the island's pretty setting & relaxed atmosphere, or (& with noticeably flatter stomachs than the expat dads) international kayakers, drawn by the nearby Nile Special rapid. This being 1 of the best 'play-holes' anywhere, it is not unusual for its devotees to spend a month or more on the island following a laid-back daily progression between the tent/dorm, the dining area, the amply cushioned chill-out shelters, the 'frisbee golf' course & of course the river. There's a supposedly bilharzia-free swimming area with a white-sand bottom but I'd be wary. The rates include filling communal fare thrice daily (& tea/coffee at any time) with both meat & vegetarian food. You can pitch your own tent, sleep in a dorm, or stay in a non-s/c *banda* overlooking its own stretch of burbling backwater. If the rates for the last seem steep, consider them in the context of 'the whole Hairy Lemon thing'. What price paradise? Advance booking is essential & day visitors are not catered for. The island is 10km from Nazigo trading centre on the Jinja–Kayunga road (a boda-boda is Ush5,000), where you bang on a tyre rim to alert a boatman to collect you for the 2min boat crossing. Secure parking for vehicles is provided. *US$60/120/150 sgl/dbl/family of family banda with private shower & river view, US$60/102 sgl/ dbl twin bandas with river view, US$48/84 sgl/dbl twin bandas, US$26 dorm bed, US$22 camping. All FB & all using shared facilities.*

Shoestring

⌂ **Kingston@da Nile** (3 *bandas* & 8 dorm beds) m 0712 563133; e flandersrazaka@yahoo. com. Look out for this new backacker-oriented place overlooking the river, a short distance up the Kayunga Road from Njeru. Under construction as I write, it will offer camping, dorm beds, a couple of s/c *bandas* & a river-view bar. With river access for boating & Jinja a short boat ride across the dam, it's bound to be popular.

WHAT TO DO

Jet boating The latest feather in Adrift's sweaty, adrenalin-soaked cap is the jet boat, an 11-seater beast powered by a 7.5l Chevrolet engine and capable of speeds of over 90km/h. The 30-minute blast on the river between the Kalagala Falls and Overtime rapid won't reduce your carbon footprint, but it is an amazing white-knuckle ride, racing up and down remnant rapids, throwing 360° spins and playing chicken with riverine rocks. Reassuringly, the drivers are New Zealand-trained, with a minimum of 500 hours' experience. Trips depart daily at 10.00 and 14.00 (subject to a minimum of four passengers) and cost US$75 per person (*under 12s US$50*).

THE NILE RIVER

Based partially on text kindly supplied by Laura Sserunjogi, of the Source of the Nile Gardens in Jinja

The Nile is the world's longest river, flowing for 6,650km (4,130 miles) from its most remote headwater to the delta formed as it enters the Mediterranean in Egypt. Its vast drainage basin occupies more than 10% of the African mainland and includes portions of nine countries: Tanzania, Burundi, Rwanda, the DRC, Kenya, Uganda, Ethiopia, Sudan and Egypt. While passing through southern Sudan, the Nile also feeds the 5.5-million-hectare Sudd or Bar-el-Jebel, the world's most expansive wetland system.

A feature of the Nile Basin is a marked decrease in precipitation as it runs further northward. In the East African lakes region and Ethiopian Highlands, mean annual rainfall figures are typically in excess of 1,000mm. Rainfall in south and central Sudan varies from 250mm to 500mm annually, except in the Sudd (900mm), while in the deserts north of Khartoum the annual rainfall is little more than 100mm, dropping to 25mm in the south of Egypt, then increasing to around 200mm closer to the Mediterranean.

The Nile has served as the lifeblood of Egyptian agriculture for millennia, carrying not only water, but also silt, from the fertile tropics into the sandy expanses of the Sahara. Indeed, it is widely believed that the very first agricultural societies arose on the floodplain of the Egyptian Nile, and so, certainly, did the earliest and most enduring of all human civilisations. The antiquity of the name Nile, which simply means 'river valley', is reflected in the ancient Greek (Nelios), Semetic (Nahal) and Latin (Nilus).

Over the past 50 years, several hydro-electric dams have been built along the Nile, notably the Aswan Dam in Egypt and the Owen Falls Dam in Uganda. The Aswan Dam doesn't merely provide hydro-electric power; it also supplies water for various irrigation schemes, and protects crops downriver from destruction by heavy flooding. Built in 1963, the dam wall rises 110m above the river and is almost 4km long, producing up to 2,100MW and forming the 450km-long Lake Nasser. The construction of the Aswan Dam enforced the resettlement of 90,000 Nubians, whilst the Temple of Abu Simbel, built 3,200 years ago for the Pharaoh Ramesses II, had to be relocated 65m higher.

The waterway plays a major role in transportation, especially in parts of the Sudan between May and November, when transportation of goods and people is not possible by road owing to the floods. Like other rivers and lakes, the Nile provides a variety of fish as food. And its importance for conservation is difficult to overstate. The Sudd alone supports more than half the global populations of Nile lechwe and shoebill (more than 6,000), together with astonishing numbers of

Adrift also offer packages combining a whirl on the jet boat and lunch at Wildwaters Lodge for US$135 (*under 12s US$105*), including return transport from Kampala.

African Queen **river tours** One of two craft used to film the Lake Albert/Murchison Falls sequences of the classic 1951 movie, this steel-hulled boat was rescued from a reed bed at Paraa (Murchison Falls National Park) by engineer Yank Evans in the 1990s. It has now found its way to Kalagala Falls where, with a newly refurbished steam boiler, it takes guests on birding/sundowner cruises (*US$85pp*).

other water-associated birds – aerial surveys undertaken between 1979 and 1982 counted an estimated 1.7 million glossy ibis, 370,000 marabou stork, 350,000 open-billed stork, 175,000 cattle egret and 150,000 spur-winged goose.

The Nile has two major sources, often referred to as the White and Blue Nile, which flow respectively from Lake Victoria near Jinja and from Lake Tana in Ethiopia. The stretch of the White Nile that flows through southern Uganda is today known as the Victoria Nile (it was formerly called Kiira locally). From Jinja, it runs northward through the swampy Lake Kyoga, before veering west to descend into the Rift Valley over Murchison Falls and empty into Lake Albert. The Albert Nile flows from the northern tip of Lake Albert to enter the Sudan at Nimule, passing through the Sudd before it merges with the Blue Nile at the Sudanese capital of Khartoum, more than 3,000km from Lake Victoria.

The discovery of the source of the Blue Nile on Lake Tana is often accredited to the 18th-century Scots explorer James Bruce. In fact, its approximate (if not exact) location was almost certainly known to the ancients. The Old Testament mentions that the Ghion (Nile) 'compasseth the whole land of Ethiopia', evidently in reference to the arcing course followed by the river along the approximate southern boundary of Ethiopia's ancient Axumite Empire. There are, too, strong similarities in the design of the papyrus *tankwa* used on Lake Tana to this day and the papyrus boats depicted in ancient Egyptian paintings. Furthermore, the main river feeding Lake Tana rises at a spring known locally as Abay Minch (literally 'Nile Fountain'), a site held sacred by Ethiopian Christians, whose links with the Egyptian Coptic Church date to the 4th century AD. Bruce's claim is further undermined by the Portuguese stone bridge, built c1620, which crosses the Nile a few hundred metres downstream of the Blue Nile Falls and only 30km from the Lake Tana outlet.

By contrast, the source of the White Nile was for centuries one of the world's great, unsolved mysteries. The Roman emperor Nero once sent an expedition south from Khartoum to search for it, but it was forced to turn back at the edge of the Sudd. In 1862, Speke correctly identified Ripon Falls as the source of the Nile, a theory that would be confirmed by Stanley in 1875. Only as recently as 1937, however, did the German explorer Burkhart Waldecker locate what has since been recognised as the most remote of the Nile's headwaters, the source of the Kagera River, a hillside spring known as Kasumo (Gusher) and situated some 4° south of the Equator in Burundi. In 2006, however, the Ascend the Nile rafting expedition located what it claims to be an even more remote headwater of the Kagera in Rwanda's Nyungwe National Park, a source that will add almost 100km to the documented length of the world's longest river if formally accepted by geographers.

14

To illustrate its historical significance, the sister craft is in Florida where it is registered as a national historic site.

Mountain biking Mountain-bike hire is available at **The Haven** for US$10 a day. A map is provided to guide you around the locality.

Horseriding (*Nile Horseback Safaris (NHS);* m *0701 101196/0774 101196;* e *info@nilehorsebacksafaris.com; www.nilehorsebacksafaris.com*) Explore the Nile

---

BARKCLOTH

When Speke prepared for his first audience with King Mutesa of Baganda, he put on his finest clothes, but admitted that he 'cut a poor figure in comparison with the dressy Baganda [who] wore neat bark cloaks resembling the best yellow corduroy cloth, crimp and well set, as if stiffened with starch'.

The stiff, neat barkcloth cloak or *mbugu*, as described by Speke, was the conventional form of attire throughout Baganda for at least 100 years prior to the coronation of Mutesa. Exactly how and when the craft arose is unknown. One legend has it that Kintu, the founder of Baganda, brought the craft with him from the heavens, which would imply that it was introduced to the kingdom, possibly from Bunyoro. Another story is that the Bacwezi leader Wamala discovered barkcloth by accident on a hunting expedition, when he hammered a piece of bark to break it up, and instead found that it expanded laterally to form a durable material.

Whatever its origin, barkcloth has been worn in Baganda for several centuries, though oral tradition maintains that the cloth was originally worn only by the king and members of his court, while commoners draped themselves more skimpily in animal skins. In the late 18th century, however, King Semakokiro decreed that all his subjects should grow and wear barkcloth – men draped it over their shoulders, women tied it around their waist – or they would be fined or sentenced to death. At around the same time, barkcloth exported from Baganda grew in popularity in most neighbouring kingdoms, where it was generally reserved for the use of royalty and nobles.

Ironically, the historical association between barkcloth cloaks and social prestige was reversed in Baganda towards the end of the 19th century, when barkcloth remained the customary attire of the peasantry, but the king permitted his more favoured subjects to wear cotton fabrics imported by Arab traders. During the early decades of colonial rule, the trend away from barkcloth spread through all social strata. W E Hoyle, who arrived in Kampala in 1903, noted that barkcloth clothing was then 'so very common'. By 1930, when Hoyle departed from Uganda, it had been 'discarded in favour of "amerikani" (cotton sheeting); and later *kanzus* (of finer cotton material known as "bafta"), with a jacket of the cheaper imported cloth and a white round cap, the ideal "Sunday best"'. Hoyle also noted that while 'women kept to barkcloth much longer than men ... by the 1920s many were attired in the finest cotton materials and silks'. In the early 1930s, Lucy Mair recorded that 'European [cloths] are popular and barkcloth is made for sale by not more than three or four men in each village'. By the time of independence, barkcloth had practically disappeared from everyday use.

Barkcloth – *olubugo* in Luganda – can be made from the inner bark lining of at least 20 tree species. The best-quality cloth derives from certain species in the genus *Ficus*, which were extensively cultivated in pre-colonial Baganda and regarded as the most valuable of trees after the plantain. Different species of tree yielded different

valley in the company of Nile Horseback Safari's calm, well-cared-for horses. Short safaris leave daily at 10.00 and 14.00, and sunset safaris leave at 16.30 on Fridays and Saturdays *(US$40pp/1hr, US$50pp/1½hrs, US$60pp/2hrs, US$75pp/3hrs)*. Overnight, multi-day safaris and kids' pony rides are also available on request. The stables are located 4.5km along the Jinja–Kayunga road and cater for all ages and abilities. Easy transport is also now available via water taxi from Bujagali, Nile River Explorer and Adrift campsites. See also advert on page 492.

textures and colours, from yellow to sandy brown to dark red-brown. The finest-quality rusty brown cloth, called *kimote*, is generally worn on special occasions only. A specific type of tree that yielded a white cloth was reserved for the use of the king, who generally wore it only at his coronation ceremony.

The common barkcloth tree can be propagated simply by cutting a branch from a grown one and planting it in the ground – after about five years the new tree will be large enough to be used for making barkcloth. The bark will be stripped from any one given tree only once a year, when it is in full leaf. After the bark has been removed, the trunk is wrapped in green banana leaves for several days, and then plastered with wet cow dung and dry banana leaves, to help it heal. If a tree is looked after this way, it might survive 30 years of annual use.

The bark is removed from the tree in one long strip. A circular incision is made near the ground, another one below the lowest branches, and then a long line is cut from base to top, before finally a knife is worked underneath the bark to ease it carefully away from the trunk. The peeled bark is left out overnight before the hard outer layer is scraped off, and then it is soaked. It is then folded into two halves and laid out on a log to be beaten with a wooden mallet on alternating sides to become thinner. When it has spread sufficiently, the cloth is folded in four and the beating continues. The cloth is then unfolded before being left to dry in the sun.

There are several local variations in the preparation process, but the finest cloth reputedly results when the freshly stripped bark, instead of being soaked, is steamed for about an hour above a pot of boiling water, then beaten for an hour or so daily over the course of a week. The steaming and extended process of beating is said to improve the texture of the cloth and to enrich the natural red-brown or yellow colour of the bark.

Although it is used mostly for clothing, barkcloth can also serve as a blanket or a shroud, and is rare but valued as bookbinding. At one time, barkcloth strips patterned with the natural black Muzukizi dye became a popular house decoration in Kampala. Sadly, however, barkcloth production appears to be a dying craft, and today it would be remarkable to see anybody wandering around Kampala wrapped in a bark cloak. It is still customary to wear it in the presence of the king, and at funerals, when barkcloth is also often wrapped around the body of the deceased.

One place where you can be certain of seeing some impressive strips of red barkcloth is at the Kasubi Tombs in Kampala. If you're interested in looking for barkcloth at source, the forests around Sango Bay in Buddu County, south of Masaka, are traditionally regarded as producing the highest-quality material in Baganda. The Ugandan artist Mugalula Mukiibi is dedicated to reviving the dying craft through his work, and a number of his abstracts painted on traditional barkcloth can be viewed online (*www.mugalulaarts.com*).

14

MABIRA FOREST RESERVE

(*The official tariff states that foreign visitors pay US$15/25/35 & foreign residents pay US$10/20/30 entrance fees to the reserve for 1/2/3 days. A guided walk costs US$15/10 foreigner visitor/resident. In practice, foreign visitors still pay Ush10,000 (US$4) for entrance, & the same again for a guided walk*) Extending over more than 300km², the Mabira Forest Reserve, which straddles the Kampala–Jinja road about 20km west of Jinja, is primarily composed of moist semi-deciduous forest, in which more than 200 tree species have been identified. The forest is interspersed with patches of open grassland, while several of the valleys support extensive papyrus swamps. In the colonial era, Mabira was heavily exploited for timber and rubber (half-a-million wild rubber trees, *Funtuma elastica*, grow there), while its proximity to Kampala and Jinja led to an estimated 1,500 tons of charcoal being extracted annually in the

THE NAKALAGA OF MABIRA

'Mabira' is a Luganda word literally meaning 'large forests', and the first European survey of the area referred to it as Mabira Nakalanga: the large forests of Nakalanga, the latter being the name of the mischievous spirit said to inhabit them. According to folklore, Nakalanga is associated with one specific stream that runs through Mabira, the source of which was until recent times the site of an important sacrificial shrine consisting of several huts.

Several early colonial writers reported that Mabira harboured a Pygmy tribe called the Banakalanga (people of Nakalanga) and assumed that it was related to the Batwa Pygmies of the Congolese border area. Local Luganda legend, however, doesn't regard the Banakalanga as a tribe, but rather as sports of nature. The belief is that the forest spirit punishes families that have fallen out of favour by cursing one of its children to be a puny and often mildly deformed dwarf.

In the 1950s, Rapper and Ladkin of the Uganda Medical Service investigated the Nakalanga and determined that they did indeed appear to be born randomly to physiologically normal parents with other healthy offspring. They concluded that the Banakalanga were affected by a form of infantilism linked to a pituitary defect, one that generally first showed itself when the afflicted person was about three years of age. The disease, Rapper and Ladkin believed, was pathological rather than genetic in origin, but its precise cause was indeterminate, as was its apparent restriction to one small area around Mabira Forest. Subsequent studies confirmed that Nakalanga dwarfism is a complication of a pituitary malfunction caused by onchocerciasis (a disease spread by the *Simulium* blackfly) and note that the condition also occurs in the Kabarole District of western Uganda.

Interestingly, the first written references to the Banakalanga interchangeably calls them the Bateemba (people of the nets), evidently in reference to a hunting method used by pygmoid peoples elsewhere in Africa. Furthermore, Rapper and Ladkin record that a local Saza chief in the early 20th century had stated that a race of true Pygmies did once live in the forest, but sometime before Europeans arrived in the area. It seems probable, then, that both Nakalanga and the medical condition attributed to the spirit's mischief-making derive their name from that of a pygmoid tribe which once inhabited Mabira Forest.

1960s. During the civil war of the early 1980s, roughly 25% of the forest was cleared or degraded by subsistence farmers, who were evicted in 1988. Since then, much of the degraded forest has recovered through the replanting of indigenous trees, and illegal felling has practically ceased. A more recent, and equally serious, threat to the integrity of the reserve was the 2007 proposal to allocate a third of the forest to the Lugazi-based Sugar Corporation of Uganda for conversion to sugarcane cultivation (see page 27).

Public outrage suppressed this controversial scheme, for the time being anyway, and Mabira remains by far the largest remaining stand of indigenous forest in central Uganda. Thus it is not only of immense ecological value, but also – situated so close to the country's two largest cities – offers great potential for recreation and tourist development. Certainly, the combination of accessibility, affordable accommodation, good monkey viewing and lovely walking trails makes it a highly recommended stopover for any traveller with an interest in natural history. Large mammals are relatively scarce today, though a small population of elephants was present as recently as the 1950s. The red-tailed monkey is regularly seen in the vicinity of the camp, however, and grey-cheeked mangabey and blue duiker are quite common. Leopards are reputedly present but unlikely to be seen. More than 200 species of butterfly have been identified from Mabira.

Mabira also ranks as one of the most important **ornithological** sites in Uganda, with more than 300 (mostly forest-associated) species recorded, including several rarities. The excellent network of forest trails that emanates from the visitors' centre can be explored unaccompanied, but you'll benefit greatly from taking a guide, whose knowledge of bird calls will assist in locating more elusive forest species. Conspicuous larger birds include the stunning great blue turaco and more familiar African grey parrot, while three forest hornbill species and a variety of colourful sunbirds are often seen around the camp. Mabira is one of only two places in East Africa where the pretty tit hylia has been recorded, and this rare bird is seen here with surprising regularity. It is also one of the few places in Uganda where the localised forest wood-hoopoe, African pitta, purple-throated cuckoo-shrike, leaflove, Weyn's weaver and Nahan's francolin are regular. Note, however, that the forest's reputation as a good place to see the rare blue swallow is based on one vagrant sighting many years ago. One of the best individual birding sites at Mabira is a forest-fringed pond that can be reached by following the Jinja Road east for 5km past Najjembe, then turning left and following a small dirt road for a few hundred metres.

For more details, you could always try to contact the National Forest Authority (NFA) in Kampala (☏ 0414 230365). However, for more reliable sources of information, call the lodges and camps listed below. Keen birders can phone to arrange a walk with Ibrahim Senfuma (m 0752 920515), a highly rated Mabira-based bird guide of 16 years' experience. Ibra also escorts countrywide birding tours by arrangement.

A separate community forest tourism project has recently opened close to Waswa village, 10km north of Lugazi Town in the western part of central Mabira (see below for details of how to get there). The main attraction is the forest walk to the pretty **Griffin Falls**. Be prepared for the water to have a whiff of molasses, thanks to the Sugar Corporation of Uganda, which dumps effluent from its Lugazi factory into the Musamya River. The entrance fees above apply.

GETTING THERE AND AWAY The Mabira Forest Reserve is easily accessible by private vehicle and public transport since the surfaced Kampala–Jinja highway runs right through the forest. The main tourism site lies 500m north of this highway at the forest-enclave village of **Najjembe**. The 55km drive from Kampala should take about an hour in a **private vehicle**. To reach the new tourism site near **Waswa village**, follow the dirt road beyond Najjembe for 6km until the route crosses a linear clearing created for the main Owen's Falls–Kampala pylon line. Turn left and follow the track below the pylons to Waswa village. If using public transport, disembark in Lugazi and take a **boda-boda** through the sugar plantations to Waswa (*Ush5,000*). If you're driving this route, it's also a good idea to hire a boda to guide you through the maze of plantation tracks.

🏠 WHERE TO STAY AND EAT   For location of listings see map, page 494.

Upmarket
🏠 **Rain Forest Lodge** (12 cottages) ☎0414 258273/0312 260758; e info@geolodgesafrica. com; www.geolodgesafrica.com. This upmarket lodge consists of several beautifully furnished timber cottages scattered across the side of the forested Gangu Hill, each set into a small clearing looking into forest downslope. Hornbills, turacos & red-tailed monkeys abound. An elevated restaurant building & swimming pool-sauna area enjoy similar views. The lodge lies 2km south of Najjembe village on the main road. *US$220/360 sgl/dbl FB, discounts available for Ugandan residents.*

Shoestring
🏠 **Mabira Forest Tourism Project** (3 *bandas*) ☎0414 230365 (National Forest Authority HQ). In 1995, a community tourism project at Mabira by the Forest Department resulted in a beautiful rest camp consisting of 2 dbl *bandas* & a 4-bed family unit, all with private balcony, garden & washing area (a bucket of hot water is provided on request). Unfortunately, the volume of road haulage traffic has increased hugely since the camp was established & noise from trucks on the main road is audible day & night. This is perhaps the reason why the facilities are looking slightly tired these days. Your best bet is to pitch your own tent in the lovely but under-utilised campground. There is no need to bring food with you. The staff will prepare reasonable meals for around Ush10,000 by

advance order & beers & sodas are also available. Alternatively, head back to the market on the main road which is renowned by motorists for its cheap & succulent grilled chicken. You can also buy fruits & vegetables as well as refrigerated beers & sodas. Otherwise, try the menu at the Little Kingston (see below). *US$20 dbl bandas, US$5pp camping. Rates excl reserve entrance fees.*

🏠 **Little Kingston da Global Village** (4 rooms) m 0712 536133; e flandersrazaka@ yahoo.com Located in Najjembe village, this small Belgian–Ugandan lodge offers a bar/restaurant with pool table, with shoestring accommodation & camping behind. This is the answer if the dank NFA *bandas* don't appeal & you're short of the necessary funds for the Rain Forest Lodge. Though the bar specialises in reggae music, other genres are available 'on request'. Activities include mountain biking & village/forest walks. Secure parking is available in the compound. *US$6pp twin or US$8pp dbl with shower, US$4pp dorm bed, US$3pp, US$5 tent rental.*

🏠 **Mabira Forest Camp aka Griffin Falls Campsite** (2 *bandas*) m 0751 949368; e info@ mabiraforestcamp.com; www.mabiraforestcamp. com. This community-run site at Wasswa village near Griffin Falls in western Mabira is located 10km from the main road at Lugazi – far from any possibility of traffic noise! Forest/village walks & mountain biking are possible. *A simple* banda *costs US$12 while an improved version costs US$20. Camping US$2pp. A Ush10,000 entrance fee applies.*

Appendix 1

LANGUAGE

Although 33 local languages are spoken in Uganda, the official language is English, spoken widely by most urban Ugandans, and certainly by anybody with more than a moderate education level and/or who works in the tourist industry. It is not uncommon to come across Ugandans from different parts of the country using English to communicate, and most English-speaking visitors to the country will have no problem getting around.

Of several indigenous languages, the most widely spoken is Luganda, which to some extent serves as a lingua franca for the uneducated. So, too, does Swahili (more correctly KiSwahili), a Bantu language that is no more indigenous to Uganda than is English. Swahili developed on the East African coast about 1,000 years ago and has since adopted several words from Arabic, Portuguese, Indian, German and English. It spread into the East African interior along the 19th-century slave caravan routes and is today now the uncontested lingua franca in Tanzania and Kenya, as well as being spoken widely in parts of Uganda, Malawi, Rwanda, Burundi, DRC, Zambia and Mozambique.

There is a certain stigma attached to the use of Swahili in Uganda, particularly among the educated. This is perhaps rooted partially in the perception that it is a peasant language, but most of all because it gathered negative associations during the Amin and Obote eras, when it was the language of the military. Basically, it would not be the done thing to try out Swahili as a first choice of language in Uganda. Nevertheless, and contrary to what people might tell you, my experience is that in rural areas where English is not understood, Swahili generally will be. On the whole, it strikes me as more pragmatic to fall back on this widely spoken regional tongue in such circumstances, than it would be to attempt to learn a smattering of each of the dozen or more languages that are indigenous to the various parts of Uganda that might be passed through in the course of a standard trip.

Numerous Swahili–English dictionaries have been published, as have various phrasebooks and grammars. The most useful dictionary is D V Perrot's *Concise Swahili and English Dictionary* (Hodder and Stoughton, 1965) as it has two sections – one translating each way – as well as a basic grammar. Peter Wilson's *Simplified Swahili* (Longman, 1985) is regarded as the best book for teaching yourself Swahili. Of the phrasebooks, Lonely Planet's is probably the best. If you want a Swahili book, buy it before you arrive in Uganda, as it will be difficult once there.

For short-stay visitors, all these books have practical limitations. Wading through a phrasebook to find the expression you want can take ages, while trying to piece together a sentence from a dictionary is virtually impossible. What follows is no substitute for a proper dictionary or phrasebook; it is not really an introduction to Swahili, but more an introduction to communicating with Swahili speakers.

SWAHILI
Pronunciation Vowel sounds are pronounced as follows:

a   like the a in *father*
e   like the e in *wet*
i   like the ee in *free*, but less drawn-out
o   somewhere between the o in *no* and the word *awe*
u   similar to the oo in *food*

The double vowel in words like *choo* or *saa* is pronounced like the single vowel, but drawn out. Consonants are in general pronounced as they are in English. L and r are often interchangeable, so that Kalema is just as often spelled or pronounced Karema. The same is true of b and v.

You will be better understood if you speak slowly and thus avoid the common English-speaking habit of clipping vowel sounds – listen to how Swahili-speakers pronounce their vowels. In most Swahili words there is a slight emphasis on the second-last syllable.

Basic grammar Swahili is a simple language insofar as most words are built from a root word using prefixes. To go into all of the prefixes here would probably confuse people new to Swahili – and it would certainly stretch my knowledge of the language. They are covered in depth in most Swahili grammars and dictionaries. The following are some of the most important:

Pronouns

ni	I/me	*wa*	they/them
u	you	*a*	he or she
tu	us		

Tenses

na	present	*li*	past
ta	future	*ku*	infinitive

Tenses (negative)

si	present	*siku*	past
sita	future	*haku*	negative infinitive

From a root word such as *taka* (want) you might build the following phrases:

Ninataka soda	I want a soda	*Tutataka soda*	We will want a soda
Unataka soda	You want a soda	*Alitaka soda*	He/she wanted a soda

In practice, ni and tu are often dropped from simple statements. It would be more normal to say *nataka soda* than *ninataka soda*.

In many situations there is no interrogative mode in Swahili; the difference between a question and a statement lies in the intonation.

Vocabulary
Greetings There are several common greetings in Swahili. Although allowances are made for tourists, it is rude to start talking to someone without first using one or other formal greeting.

The first greeting you will hear is *Jambo*. This is reserved for tourists, and a perfectly adequate greeting, but it is never used between Africans (the more correct *Hujambo*, to which the reply is *Sijambo*, is used in some areas).

The most widely used greeting is *Habari?*, which more-or-less means What news? The polite reply is *Mzuri* (good). *Habari* is rarely used on its own; you might well be asked *Habari ya safari?*, *Habari ako?* or *Habari gani?* (very loosely, How is your journey?, How are you? and How are things? respectively). *Mzuri* is the polite reply to any such enquiry.

It is respectful to address an old man as *Mzee*. *Bwana*, which means Mister, might be used as a polite form of address to a male who is equal or senior to you in age or rank, but who is not a Mzee. Older women can be addressed as Mama.

The following phrases will come in handy for small talk:

Where have you just come from?	*(U)natoka wapi?*
I have come from Kampala	*(Ni)natoka Kampala*
Where are you going?	*(U)nakwenda wapi?*
We are going to Mbale	*(Tu)nakwende Mbale*
What is your name?	*Jina lako nani?*
My name is Philip	*Jina langu ni Philip*
Do you speak English?	*Unasema KiEngereze?*
I speak a little Swahili	*Ninasema KiSwahili kidigo*
Sleep peacefully	*Lala salama*
Bye for now	*Kwaheri sasa*
Have a safe journey	*Safari njema*
Come again (welcome again)	*Karibu tena*
I don't understand	*Sielewi*
Say that again	*Sema tena*

Counting

1	*moja*		40	*arobaini*
2	*mbili*		50	*hamsini*
3	*tatu*		60	*sitini*
4	*nne*		70	*sabani*
5	*tano*		80	*themanini*
6	*sita*		90	*tisini*
7	*saba*		100	*mia (moja)*
8	*nane*		150	*mia moja hamsini*
9	*tisa*		155	*mia moja hamsini na tano*
10	*kumi*		200	*mia mbili*
11	*kumi na moja*		1,000	*elfu* or, more commonly
20	*ishirini*			in Uganda, *mia kumi*
30	*thelathini*			

Swahili time Most Ugandans use Western time, but you may come across Swahili time at some point. The Swahili clock starts at the equivalent of 06.00, so that *saa moja asubuhi* (hour one in the morning) is 07.00, *saa mbili jioni* (hour two in the evening) is 16.00, etc. To ask the time in Swahili, say *Saa ngape?*

Day-to-day queries The following covers such activities as shopping, finding a room, etc. It's worth remembering that most Swahili words for modern objects, or things for which there would not have been a pre-colonial word, are often similar to the English. Examples are *resiti* (receipt), *gari* (car), *polisi* (police), *posta* (post office) and – my favourite – *stesheni masta* (station master). In desperation, it's always worth trying the English word with an ee sound on the end.

Shopping The normal way of asking for something is *Iko?*, which roughly means Is there?, so if you want a cold drink you would ask *Iko soda baridi?* The response will normally be *Iko* or *Kuna* (there is) or *Hamna* or *Hakuna* (there isn't). Once you've established the shop has what you want, you might say *Nataka koka mbili* (I want two Cokes). To check the price, ask *Shillingi ngape?* If your Swahili is limited, it is often simpler to ask for a brand name: Omo (washing powder) or Blue Band (margarine), for instance.

Accommodation The Swahili for guesthouse is *nyumba ya wageni*. In my experience *gesti* or lodgings works as well, if not better. If you are looking for something a bit more upmarket, bear in mind *hoteli* means restaurant. We found self-contained (*self-contendi*) to be a good keyword in communicating this need. To find out whether there is a vacant room, ask *Iko chumba?*

Getting around The following expressions are useful for getting around:

Where is there a guesthouse?	*Iko wapi gesti?*
Is there a bus to Moshi?	*Iko basi kwenda Moshi?*
When does the bus depart?	*Basi ondoka saa ngapi?*
When will the vehicle arrive?	*Gari tafika saa ngapi?*
How far is it?	*Bale gani?*
I want to pay now	*Ninataka kulipa sasa*

Foodstuffs

avocado	*parachichi*	onions	*vitungu*
bananas	*ndizi*	orange(s)	*(ma)chungwa*
(cooked)	*matoke/batoke*	pawpaw	*papai*
beef	*nyama ya ngombe*	pineapple	*nanasi*
bread (loaf)	*mkate*	potatoes	*viazi*
bread (slice)	*tosti*	rice	
chicken	*kuku*	(cooked plain)	*wali*
coconuts	*nazi*	rice (cooked	
coffee	*kahawa*	with spices)	*pilau*
egg(s)	*(ma)yai*	rice	
fish	*samaki*	(uncooked)	*mchele*
food	*chakula*	salt	*chumvi*
fruit(s)	*(ma)tunda*	sauce	*mchuzi/supu*
goat	*(nyama ya) mbuzi*	sugar	*sukari*
maize porridge	*ugali*	tea	*chai (ya*
mango(es)	*(ma)embe*	(black/milky)	*rangi/maziwa)*
meat	*nyama*	vegetables	*mboga*
milk	*maziwa*	water	*maji*

Days of the week

Monday	*Jumatatu*	Friday	*Ijumaa*
Tuesday	*Jumanne*	Saturday	*Jumamosi*
Wednesday	*Jumatano*	Sunday	*Jumapili*
Thursday	*Alhamisi*		

Other useful words and phrases

afternoon	*alasiri*	no	*hapana*
again	*tena*	no problem	*hakuna matata*
and	*na*	now	*sasa*
ask (I am asking for ...)	*Omba (ninaomba ...)*	OK or fine	*sawa*
		only	*tu*
big	*kubwa*	passenger	*abiria*
boat	*meli*	pay	*kulipa*
brother	*kaka*	person (people)	*mtu (watu)*
bus	*basi*	please	*tafadhali*
car (or any vehicle)	*gari*	road/street	*barabara/mtaa*
		shop	*duka*
child (children)	*mtoto (watoto)*	sister	*dada*
cold	*baridi*	sleep	*kulala*
come here	*njoo*	slowly	*pole pole*
excuse me	*samahani*	small	*kidogo*
European(s)	*smzungu (wazungu)*	soon	*bado kidogo*
evening	*jioni*	sorry	*polepole*
far away	*mbali sana*	station	*stesheni*
friend	*rafiki*	stop	*simama*
good (very good)	*mzuri (mzuri sana)*	straight or direct	*moja kwa moja*
goodbye	*kwaheri*	thank you (very much)	*asante (sana)*
here	*hapa*	there is	*iko/kuna*
hot	*moto*	there is not	*hamna/hakuna*
later	*bado*	thief (thieves)	*mwizi (wawizi)*
like (I would like ...)	*penda (ninapenda ...)*	time	*saa*
		today	*leo*
many	*sana*	toilet	*choo*
me	*mimi*	tomorrow	*kesho*
money	*pesa/shillingi*	want (I want ...)	*taka (ninataka ...)*
more	*ingine/tena*	where	*(iko) wapi*
morning	*asubuhi*	yes	*ndiyo*
nearby	*karibumbali kidogo*	yesterday	*jana*
night	*usiku*	you	*wewe*

Useful conjunctions include *ya* (of) and *kwa* (to or by). Many expressions are created using these; for instance *stesheni ya basi* is a bus station and *barabara kwa* Mbale is the road to Mbale.

LUGANDA Luganda is the first language of Buganda and most widely spoken of the languages indigenous to Uganda. Pronunciation is very similar to Swahili. Some words and phrases follow. A detailed phrasebook and dictionary can be viewed online at www. buganda.com.

Greetings

Hello (informal)	*Ki kati*	Goodnight	*Sula bulungi*
How are you?	*Oli otya?*	Farewell	*Weraba*
I am OK	*Gyendi*	See you later	*Tunalabagana*
Have a nice day	*Siba bulungi*	Please	*Mwattu*

Thank you (very much)	Webale (Nyo)	Come here	Jangu wano
Excuse me	Owange	Madam	Nnyabo
Sorry	Nsonyiwa	Mr	Mwami
Sir	Ssebo	Mrs	Mukyala

Useful phrases

Where are you from?	Ova mukitundu ki?
I am from England	Nva mu England
Where have you come from?	Ovude wa?
I have come from Kampala	Nvude Kampala
Where are you going?	Ogenda wa?
I am going to Mbale	Ngenda Mbale
How can I get to Mbale?	Ngenda ntya okutuka e Mbale?
Does this bus go to Kampala?	Eno baasi egenda e Kampala?
Which bus goes to Kampala?	Baasi ki egenda e Kampala?
What time does the bus leave?	Baasi egenda sawa meka?
Where can I buy a bus ticket?	Tikiti ya baasi nyinza kugigula wa?
What time does the bus arrive?	Baasi etuka ku sawa meka?
Where is the road to Kampala?	Olugudo lwe Kampala luliwa?
Where is this taxi going?	Eno taxi eraga wa?
Where is it?	Kiriwa?
How far is it?	Kiri wala wa?
Is it far?	Kiri wala?
Is it near?	Kiri kumpi?
How much does it cost?	Sente meka?
Do you speak English?	Oyogera oluzungu?
Do you have any …?	Olinayo ko …?
I would like …	Njagalayo …
I want a room	Njagala kisenge
There is	Waliwo
There is not	Tewali
What is this called?	Kino kiyitibwa kitya?
What is your name?	Amanya go gw'ani?
My name is Philip	Nze Philip

Words

big	kinene	OK	ye
come (here)	jangu (wano)	please	bambi
good	kirungi	possible	kisoboka
here	wano	slow down	genda mpola
hurry up	yanguwa	small	katono
later	edda	today	lero
many	bingi	toilet	toileti
me	nze	tomorrow	enkya
morning	kumakya	water	mazi
no	neda	yes	ye
not possible	tekisoboka	yesterday	jjo
now	kati	you	gwe

Foodstuffs

avocado	*kedo*	melon	*wuju*
banana (green)	*matooke*	onion	*katungulu*
banana (sweet)	*menvu*	orange	*mucungwa*
beans	*bijanjalo*	pawpaw	*paapaali*
beef	*nte*	peanuts	*binyebwa*
cabbage	*mboga*	pepper	*kaamulali*
carrot	*kalati*	pineapple	*naanansi*
cassava	*muwogo*	pork	*mbizi*
chicken	*nkoko*	potato	*lumonde*
corn	*kasooli*	rice	*muceere*
fish	*kyenyanja*	salt	*munnyo*
goat meat	*mbuzi*	sugar	*sukali*
lamb/mutton	*ndiga*	sugarcane	*kikajo*
mango	*muyembe*	sweet potato	*lumonde*
meat	*nyama*	tomato	*nyanya*

AFRICAN ENGLISH Although a high proportion of Ugandans do speak English as a second language, not all get the opportunity to use it regularly, and as a result they will not be as fluent as they could be. Furthermore, as is often the case in Africa and elsewhere, an individual's pronunciation of a second language often tends to retain the vocal inflections of their first language, or it falls somewhere between that and a more standard pronunciation. It is also the case that many people tend to structure sentences in a second language similar to how they would in their home tongue. As a result, most Ugandans, to a greater or lesser extent, speak English with Bantu inflections and grammar.

The above considerations aside, I would venture that African English – like American or Australian English – is overdue recognition as a distinct linguistic entity, possessed of a unique rhythm and pronunciation, as well as an idiomatic quality quite distinct from any form of English spoken elsewhere. And learning to communicate in this idiom is perhaps the most important linguistic skill that the visitor to Uganda (or any other anglophone country in Africa) can acquire. If this sounds patronising, so be it. There are regional accents in the UK and US that I find far more difficult to follow than the English spoken in Africa, simply because I am more familiar with the latter. And precisely the same adjustment might be required were, for instance, an Australian to travel in the American south, a Geordie to wash up in my home town of Johannesburg, or vice versa.

The following points should prove useful when you speak English to Africans:

- Greet simply, using phrases likely to be understood locally: the ubiquitous sing-song 'How-are-you! – I am fine', or if that draws a blank try the pidgin Swahili *Jambo*! It is important always to greet a stranger before you plough ahead and ask directions or any other question. Firstly, it is rude to do otherwise; secondly, most Westerners feel uncomfortable asking a stranger a straight question. If you have already greeted the person, you'll feel less need to preface a question with phrases like 'I'm terribly sorry' or 'Would you mind telling me' which will confuse someone who speaks limited English.
- Speak slowly and clearly. There is no need, as some travellers do, to take this too far, as if you are talking to a three year old. Speak naturally, but try not to rush or clip phrases.
- Phrase questions simply, with an ear towards Bantu inflections. 'This bus goes to Mbale?' might be more easily understood than 'Could you tell me whether this bus is going to Mbale?' and 'You have a room?' is better than 'Is there a vacant room?' If you are not understood, don't keep repeating the same question more loudly. Try a different and ideally simpler phrasing, giving consideration to whether any specific

word(s) – in the last case, most likely 'vacant' – might particularly obstruct easy understanding.

- Listen to how people talk to you, and learn from it. Vowel sounds are often pronounced as in the local language (see Swahili pronunciation above), so that 'bin', for instance, might sound more like 'been'. Many words, too, will be pronounced with the customary Bantu stress on the second-last syllable.
- African languages generally contain few words with compound consonant sounds or ending in consonants. This can result in the clipping of soft consonant sounds such as 'r' (important as eem-POT-ant) or the insertion of a random vowel sound between running consonants (so that pen-pal becomes pen-i-pal and sounds almost indistinguishable from pineapple). It is commonplace, as well, to append a random vowel to the end of a word, in the process shifting the stress to what would ordinarily be the last syllable (eg: pen-i-PAL-i).
- The 'l' and 'r' sounds are sometimes used interchangeably, less often in Uganda perhaps than in Tanzania or Malawi, but it does happen – Rubaga Hill in Kampala, for instance, is sometimes spelt Lubaga. This transference can cause considerable confusion, in particular when your guide points out a lilac-breasted roller! The same is to a lesser extent true of 'b' and 'v' (Virunga versus Birunga), 'k' and 'ch' (the Rwandan capital, spelt Kigali, is more often pronounced 'Chigari') and, very occasionally, 'f' and 'p'.
- Some English words are in wide use. Other similar words are not. Some examples: a request for a 'lodging' or 'guesthouse', is more likely to be understood than one for 'accommodation', as is a request for a 'taxi' (or better 'special hire') over a 'taxi-cab' or 'cab', or for 'the balance' rather than 'change'.
- Avoid the use of dialect-specific expressions, slang and jargon! Few Africans will be familiar with terms such as 'feeling crook', 'pear-shaped' or 'user-friendly'.
- Avoid meaningless interjections. If somebody is struggling to follow you, appending a word such as 'mate' to every other phrase is only likely to further confuse them.
- We've all embarrassed ourselves at some point by mutilating the pronunciation of a word we've read but not heard. Likewise, guides working in national parks and other reserves often come up with innovative pronunciations for bird and mammal names they come across in field guides, and any word with an idiosyncratic spelling (eg: yacht, lamb, knot).
- Make sure the person you are talking to understands you. Try to avoid asking questions that can be answered with a yes or no. People may well agree with you simply to be polite or to avoid embarrassment.
- Keep calm. No-one is at their best when they arrive at a crowded bus station after an all-day bus ride. It is easy to be short-tempered when someone cannot understand you. Be patient and polite; it's you who doesn't speak the language.
- It can be useful to know that the Ugandan phrase for urinating is 'short call'. Useful, because often you will be caught short somewhere with no toilet, and if you ask for a toilet will simply be told there is none. By contrast, if you tell somebody you need a 'short call', you'll be pointed to wherever locals take theirs!
- Last but not least, do gauge the extent to which the above rules might apply to any given individual. It would be patently ridiculous to address a university lecturer or an experienced tour guide in broken English, equally inappropriate to babble away without making any allowances when talking to a villager who clearly has a limited English vocabulary. Generally, I start off talking normally to anybody I meet, and only start to refine my usage as and when it becomes clear it will aid communication.

Appendix 2

GLOSSARY

acacia woodland	any woodland dominated by thorn trees of the acacia family
Albertine Rift	western Rift Valley between Lake Albert and northern Lake Tanganyika
Amin, Idi	dictatorial President of Uganda 1971–79
Ankole	extant medieval kingdom centred on modern-day Mbarara
askari	security guard
Bacwezi	legendary medieval kingdom, centred on present-day Mubende
Baker, Lady Florence	wife and travel companion to Sir Samuel
Baker, Sir Samuel	first European to Lake Albert, Murchison Falls 1864, Governor of Equatoria 1872–73
balance	change (for a payment)
banda	any detached accommodation such as a hut or chalet
barkcloth	traditional material made from the bark of the fig tree
Batembuzi	legendary medieval kingdom, possibly centred on present-day Ntusi
Bell, Sir Henry Hesketh	Commissioner to Uganda 1905–09 after whom Port Bell (and thus Bell Beer) is named
boda-boda	bicycle or motorcycle taxi
boma	colonial administrative office
Buganda	extant kingdom for which Uganda is named, centred on modern-day Kampala
Bunyoro	extant kingdom centred on modern-day Hoima
Bwana	Mister (polite Swahili term of address, sometimes used in Uganda)
chai	tea
Colville, Colonel	led the attack on Mparo that drove Kabalega into hiding, 1894
cowrie	small white shell used as currency in pre-colonial times
Daudi Chwa, Kabaka	crowned King of Buganda at age one in 1897, ruled until death in 1939
DSTV	South African multi-channel satellite television service
duka	stall or kiosk
endemic	unique to a specific area
exotic	not indigenous, for instance pine plantations
forest	wooded area with closed canopy
forex bureau	bureau de change
fundi	expert (especially mechanic)
Grant, Captain James	accompanied Speke on journey to Source of the Nile, 1862

guesthouse	cheap local hotel
Hannington, Bishop James	missionary killed on Mwanga's instructions *en route* to Buganda in 1885
hoteli	local restaurant
indigenous	occurring in a place naturally
Interlacustrine Region	area between Lake Victoria and Albertine Rift Lakes: Rwanda, Burundi, south Uganda, northwest Tanzania
Isuza	legendary Batembuzi ruler
Kabaka	King of Buganda
Kabalega, Omakuma	King of Bunyoro from 1870, exiled to Seychelles by the British 1897, died there 1923
Kaggwa, Sir Apollo	Katikiro of Buganda 1889–1926, and copious chronicler of Kiganda folklore and history
Kakunguru, Semei	Muganda leader who conquered east Uganda for the British in the 1890s and founded Kumi and Mbale
Kamurasi, Omakuma	powerful Bunyoro King, ruled c1852–69, met by Speke and Baker
Katikiro	'Prime Minister' of Buganda
Kiganda	relating to the culture or religions of Buganda
Kiira	Luganda name for the Victoria Nile
Kintu	legendary founder of Buganda
Kony, Joseph	leader of the LRA
kopje/koppie	small, often rocky hill (from Afrikaans meaning 'little head')
Kyebambe III, Omakuma	King of Bunyoro c1786–1835
LRA	Lord's Resistance Army
Lubaale (plural Balubaale)	important Kiganda spirit
Luganda	language of Buganda
Lugard, Captain Frederick	Representative of the Imperial British East Africa Company who signed a provisional treaty with Mwanga in 1890
mandazi	fried doughnut-like pastry
matatu	see *minibus-taxi*
matoke	staple made from cooking plantains (bananas)
mbugo	barkcloth (traditional dress of Buganda)
minibus-taxi	minibus used as a shared taxi typically carrying ten to 13 passengers
mishkaki	meat (usually beef) kebab
mobile	mobile satellite phone
MTN	main satellite-phone provider in Uganda
Muganda	citizen of Buganda kingdom (plural: Baganda)
Museveni, Yoweri	President of Uganda 1986–present
Mutesa I, Kabaka	King of Buganda 1857–84, hosted Speke 1862
Mutesa II, Edward Kabaka	King of Buganda 1939–66, President of Uganda 1962–66, died in exile 1969
muzungu	white person
Mwanga, Kabaka	King of Buganda 1884–93, exiled to Seychelles 1897, died there 1903
Namasole	'Queen mother' or more accurately mother of the Kabaka of Buganda
Ndahura	legendary founder of Bacwezi dynasty, son of Isuza
netting	mosquito net
NRM	National Resistance Movement (governing part of Uganda)

Nyerere, Julius	President of Tanzania who initiated the war that ousted Amin in 1979
Obote, Milton	dictatorial President of Uganda, 1962–71 and 1981–85
Okello, Tito	military President of Uganda, July 1985–January 1986
Omakuma	King of Bunyoro/Toro
Omugabe	King of Ankole
Owen, Roderick	companion of Portal in 1893 for whom Owen Falls at the source of the Nile is named
panga	local equivalent of a machete
Pasha, Emin	Governor of Equatoria 1878 until 'rescued' by Stanley 1889
pesa	money
pombe	local beer
Portal, Sir Gerald	Governor of Zanzibar, visited Uganda 1893, Fort Portal named in his honour
QENP	Queen Elizabeth National Park (often called QE or QENP)
riparian/riverine	strip of forest or lush woodland following a watercourse, often woodland rich in fig trees
Ruhanga	legendary king of the underworld and founder of the Batembuzi dynasty
Runyoro	language of Bunyoro
safari	Swahili word for journey, now widely used to refer to game-viewing trip
savanna	grassland with some trees
Saza chief	ruler of a County (Saza) of Buganda, answerable to the kabaka
self-contained (s/c)	room with private toilet and shower attached en suite
shamba	small subsistence farm
short call	urinate
soda	fizzy drink such as Fanta or Coca-Cola
special hire	taxi
Speke, John Hanning	first European to visit Buganda, Bunyoro and the source of the Nile, 1862
Ssemogorere, Paul	one-time prime minister under Museveni, stood in the 1996 presidential election
Stanley, Henry Morton	explorer to Uganda in 1875–76 and 1889, discovering Rwenzoris on latter trip
surfaced (road)	road sealed with asphalt or similar
tented camp	rustic but generally upmarket small camp offering canvassed accommodation
Thomson, Joseph	in 1883, became the first European to enter present-day Uganda from the east
Toro	extant 19th-century kingdom centred on modern-day Fort Portal
tot packet	sachet of whisky or waragi
track	motorable minor road or path
trading centre	small town or village where local villagers would go to shop
ugali	staple porridge made from maize (corn) meal
UPDF	Uganda People's Defence Force
UWA	Uganda Wildlife Authority
Wamala	legendary Bacwezi ruler, son of Ndahura
Waragi	local brand of gin
wazungu	plural of Mazungu
woodland	wooded area lacking closed canopy

Appendix 3

FURTHER INFORMATION
BOOKS
History and background

Apuuli, K *A Thousand Years of Bunyoro-Kitara* Fountain, 1994. Inexpensive and compact locally published book that ranks close to being essential reading on pre-colonial events, despite being riddled with internal contradictions.

Behrend, Heike *Alice Lakwena & The Holy Spirits* James Currey, 1999. The bizarre and disturbing story of the emergence of the spirit medium in northern Uganda in 1986, which laid the foundation for the present-day Lord's Resistance Army and its brutal leader Joseph Kony. By no means easy reading, but worth the effort!

Bierman, J *Dark Safari* Albert Knopf, 1990. As the name suggests, a no-holds-barred biography of Henry Morton Stanley, who twice travelled through what would later become Uganda in the late 19th century. Its repugnant central figure might have been designed to give Victorian explorers a bad name – mercenary, avaricious, callous, unsympathetic to local customs, and utterly fascinating.

Blixen, Karen *Out of Africa* Penguin, 1937. Though based in Kenya, this famous autobiography offers fascinating glimpses into the colonial era, and just about everybody who sets foot in East Africa ends up reading it.

Bussman, Jane *The Worst Date Ever* Macmillan, 2009. Readable investigation into the LRA war by a British comedienne/journalist and first-time visitor to Africa. Against a subplot of a supposed romantic agenda, Bussman combines a sharp wit and purported naivety whilst stumbling through murkier issues to raise some reasonable questions concerning the failure of government and the international community to end the conflict.

Carruthers, John *Mrs Carruthers is Black* 2004. An autobiographical account by a Scottish insurance chairman of his marriage to a Ugandan during the days when mixed-race marriages were something of an eyebrow raiser. It covers some lively years prior to the family's flight from Uganda during the Amin regime and their return to live in Kampala some 20 years later. An entertaining read, liberally seasoned with salacious tales in which names have been changed to protect the guilty. Available from Aristoc bookshop in Kampala.

Green, Matthew *The Wizard of the Nile* Portobello, 2008. This investigative travelogue tackles the war in northern Uganda and does much to explain the complex, internecine baggage behind this apparently futile conflict. Highly recommended.

Hall, Richard *Empires of the Monsoon: A History of the Indian Ocean and its Invaders* HarperCollins, 1996. Highly focused and reasonably concise book conveying a strong international perspective on the last 1,000 years of East and southern Africa to the general reader, with a good storytelling touch. Highly recommended, though centred on Kenya and Tanzania more than Uganda.

Herne, Brian *African Safaris* Winchester Press, 1979. Chatty, anecdotal and sometimes revealing accounts of hunting and other safaris in Uganda before the Amin coup.

Jeal, Tim *Stanley: The Impossible Life of Africa's Greatest Explorer* Faber and Faber, 2007. This new and readable biography draws on new archival material to delve beneath the standard image of Stanley as the classic, imperialist bully and paint a new and more reasoned portrait of Africa's greatest explorer. *The Times* reviewer is convinced, challenging readers to suggest that, if faced with the same dangers, they would behave any better than Stanley.

Karugire, S *A Political History of Uganda* Heinemann, 1980. The most concise introduction to Ugandan history on the market, highly readable, with a useful chapter covering pre-colonial events and razor-sharp commentary on the colonial period.

Leggett, Ian *Uganda: An Oxfam Country Profile* Oxfam, 2001. Solid and not overwhelmingly academic overview of Uganda today, with special reference to social and economic issues such as HIV/AIDS.

Miller, Charles *The Lunatic Express* 1971, reprinted Penguin Classics, 2001. Eminently readable account of the building of the Uganda Railway with an excellent history of the events in Uganda that brought about the project.

Moorehead, Alan *The White Nile* Hamilton, 1960. Classic example of the history-as-adventure-yarn genre, detailing the race to discover the source of the Nile and its leading characters. A more recently published illustrated edition has plenty of good paintings and photos, too.

Museveni, Yoweri *Sowing the Mustard Seed* Macmillan, 1997. The acclaimed autobiography of Uganda's president, mostly devoted to his wilderness years fighting the Amin and Obote regimes but with good coverage of post-1986 reconstruction. Inevitable bias notwithstanding, a frank and insightful read.

Mutibwa, Phares *Uganda since Independence* Fountain, 1992. Subtitled 'a story of unfulfilled hopes', no better overview exists on post-colonial Ugandan politics prior to the 1990s.

Nzita, Richard *Peoples and Cultures of Uganda* Fountain, 1993, 3rd edition 1997. Useful introduction to the various ethnic groupings of Uganda, and the monochrome photos make for an interesting browse.

O' Connor, Kevin *Uganda Society Observed* Fountain, 2006. A collection of light-hearted (sometimes exploring serious themes) articles written for *The Monitor* newspaper by an expat columnist.

Oliver, R and Fage, J D *A Short History of Africa* Penguin, 6th edition, 1988. Standard introduction to African history, though too compact to be satisfying on any specific region or period.

Osmaston Henry, *Guide to the Rwenzori: Mountains of the Moon* Rwenzori Trust, 2006. This beautifully compact pocket-sized book represents the eagerly awaited revision of the long-out-of-print 1971 Osmaston and Pasteur Rwenzori guide, published to coincide with the 2006 celebrations of the mountain's first ascent by the Italian duke of Abruzzi. It contains pretty much everything the aspiring Rwenzori visitor needs to know. It is also a fitting memorial to Henry Osmaston (84), the long-time sage of the Rwenzori, who died only a week after completing the exhausting task of overhauling his work of 35 years earlier. It's distributed in the UK by West Col Productions (℡ *01491 681284*).

Packenham, Thomas *The Scramble for Africa* Weidenfeld & Nicolson, 1991. Gripping and erudite 600-page account of the decade that turned Africa on its head – a 'must read', aptly described by one reviewer as 'Heart of Darkness with the lights switched on'.

Reader, John *Africa: A Biography of the Continent* Penguin, 1997. Bulky, and working the broadest canvas, this excellent introduction to Africa past and present has met with universal praise as perhaps the most readable and accurate book to capture the sweep of African history for the general reader.

A3

Reid, Richard *Political Power in Pre-colonial Buganda* James Currey, 2002. Accessible and clearly written introduction to the kingdom that lies at the heart of Uganda.

Seftel, Adam *The Rise and Fall of Idi Amin* Bailey's African Photo Archives, 1993. This is a compelling as-it-happened document of Ugandan politics from 1955 to 1986 focusing mainly on events between the joyous coup that brought Amin to power in 1971 and the Tanzanian invasion that forced him into exile eight years later. Essentially a series of articles reprinted from the archives of the seminal *Drum* magazine, the book peaks with a chapter entitled 'The Truth About Amin' brilliantly capturing the uneasy realisation circa late 1972 that Uganda's new president was anything but the grinning saviour he had seemed initially. Superb and in some cases deeply moving (even gruesome) monochrome photographs, and chuckle-inducing reprints of original covers on which pouting dolly birds do their utmost to undermine the more serious content of 'Africa's Leading Magazine' – a wonderful period package!

Speke, John *Journal of the Discovery of the Source of the Nile*, 1863, reprinted Dover Press, 1996. In this classic account of Victorian exploration, John Hanning Speke comes across as the most courteous and respectful of travellers, of his time for sure, and occasionally rather petty, yet with a wonderful ability to capture without judgement the flavour of local cultures he encountered, nowhere more so than in the series of chapters about the Buganda court under Mutesa contained in this unique document. An enjoyable, instructive and occasionally mind-boggling read!

Twaddle, Michael *Kakungulu and the Creation of Uganda* James Currey, 1993. Excellent and readable biography of the enigmatic and controversial Semei Kakunguru, a Muganda who started his career as a British expansionist and ended it as the founder of a bizarre Judaic sect that still thrives in the Mbale area to this day. Essential stuff!

Nature and wildlife If you have difficulty finding African natural history books at your local bookshop and you're not flying directly to South Africa (where you can pick them up easily) get hold of the Natural History Book Service (*2 Wills Rd, Totnes, Devon TQ9 SXN;* 01803 865913), or Russel Friedman Books in South Africa (011 702 2300/1).

Mammals

Dorst, J and Dandelot, P *Field Guide to the Larger Mammals of Africa* Collins, 1983. Once the standard mammal field guide to Africa, this has been rendered close to obsolete by several newer and better books listed here.

Erickson Wilson, Sandra *Bird and Mammal Checklists for Ten National Parks in Uganda* European Commission, 1995. Increasingly difficult-to-locate 88-page booklet containing a complete checklist of all mammals and birds known in Uganda, and in which national parks, if any, each species has been recorded.

Estes, Richard *The Safari Companion* Green Books UK, Chelsea Green USA, Russell Friedman Books South Africa, 1992. Not a field guide in the conventional sense so much as a guide to mammalian behaviour, this superb book is very well organised and highly informative, but rather bulky perhaps for casual safari-goers.

Fossey, Dian *Gorillas in the Mist* Hodder and Stoughton, 1983. Thirty years after its original publication, this seminal work remains the best introduction to gorilla behaviour in print. Read it!

Goodall, Jane *In the Shadow of Man* Collins, 1971. Classic on chimp behaviour based on Goodall's acclaimed research in Tanzania's Gombe Stream National Park.

Haltennorth, T *Field Guide to the Mammals of Africa* (including Madagascar) Collins, 1980. See comments for Dorst and Dandelot.

Kingdon, Jonathan *Field Guide to African Mammals* Academic Press, 1997. The definitive field guide of its type, with immense detail on all large mammals, as well as a gold mine of information about the evolutionary relationships of modern species, and good coverage of bats, rodents and other small mammals. Excellent illustrations, too. Arguably too pricey and heavy for casual safari-goers, but an essential – and in my case much-thumbed – reference for anybody with a strong interest in Africa's mammals.

Schaller, George *The Year of the Gorilla* Chicago University Press, 1963. Subsequently overshadowed, at least in popular perception, by *Gorillas in the Mist*, this formative behavioural study of gorillas in the Virungas did much to dispel their violent image on publication in 1963, and it remains a genuine classic (with the somewhat parochial advantage over later gorilla books in that most of the action takes place in Uganda rather than Rwanda).

Stuart, Chris and Tilde *Field Guide to the Larger Mammals of Africa* Struik Publishers, 1997. Solid and well-organised field guide covering large mammals only, better suited than Kingdon's to space- and/or price-conscious travellers who are nevertheless serious about putting a name to any large mammals they encounter.

Stuart, Chris and Tilde *Southern, Eastern and Central African Mammals: A Photographic Guide* Struik Publishers, 1993. Commendably lightweight and inexpensive pocketbook that manages to squeeze in detailed accounts and pictures of 152 mammal species – ideal for backpackers!

Weber, Bill and Veder, Amy *In the Kingdom of Gorillas* Aurum Press, 2002. Written by the Americans who initiated gorilla tourism in Rwanda, this excellent new book includes detailed information about all aspects of the mountain gorillas of the Virungas. There's also good coverage of the monkeys of Nyungwe Forest, and an admirably unsentimental account of working alongside the notoriously strong-willed Dian Fossey. In 2003, *BBC Wildlife* listed it – along with the Goodall, Fossey and Schaller titles mentioned above – as one of 40 classic wildlife books of the past 40 years.

Birds

Russouw, Jonathan and Sacchi, Marco *Where to Watch Birds in Uganda* Uganda Tourist Board, 1998. This excellent little book is out of print and hard to find these days so if you see a copy snap it up! It contains detailed descriptions and advice for all key birding sites in Uganda, with special reference to local rarities and specials, as well as an up-to-date national checklist referencing all the bird species recorded at each of 15 locations in Uganda. The ideal companion to a good field guide.

Stevenson, Terry and Fanshawe, John *Field Guide to the Birds of East Africa* T & A D Poyser, 2002. The best bird field guide, with useful field descriptions and accurate plates and distribution maps covering every species recorded in Uganda as well as Kenya, Tanzania, Rwanda and Burundi. No other book will suffice for serious birdwatchers, but it is much bulkier and pricier than Van Perlo's competing title.

Van Perlo, Ber *Illustrated Checklist to the Birds of Eastern Africa* Collins, 1995. Useful, relatively inexpensive and admirably compact identification manual describing and illustrating all 1,488 bird species recorded in Eritrea, Ethiopia, Kenya, Uganda and Tanzania. Unfortunately, however, the distribution maps and colour plates are often misleading, and the descriptions too terse, to allow for identification of more difficult genera.

Williams, John *Field Guide to the Birds of East Africa* Collins, 1971. Pioneering but obsolete field guide lacking plates for half the species found in Uganda and omitting a few hundred from the text. Still referred to in many travel guides and brochures, a sure sign that whoever compiled the information is desperately out of touch when it comes to East African birdwatching.

Zimmerman, Turner, Pearson, Willet and Pratt *Birds of Kenya and Northern Tanzania* Russell Friedman Books, 1996. A contender for the best single-volume field guide available to any

African country or region, but lacking coverage for the 150 or so Ugandan species not recorded in Kenya. The exemplary text is, however, far more thorough than its counterpart in any field guide covering Uganda, and the plates are brilliant. Highly recommended to any serious birder as a supplement to Stevenson and Fanshawe.

Butterflies

Carter, Nanny and Tindimubona, Laura *Butterflies of Uganda* Uganda Society, 2002. Very useful albeit non-comprehensive field guide illustrating and describing roughly 200 of the more common butterfly species in Uganda.

Health Self-prescribing has its hazards so if you are going anywhere very remote consider taking a health book. For adults there is *Bugs, Bites & Bowels* by Dr Jane Wilson-Howarth, published by Cadogan (2006); if travelling with the family look at *Your Child: A Travel Health Guide* by Dr Jane Wilson-Howarth and Dr Matthew Ellis, published by Bradt Travel Guides (2005).

Coffee-table books

Gonget, Barbara, et al *Imagine Uganda* Excellent and reasonably priced pocket-sized compilation of images by four Ugandan and expatriate photographers: an eclectic representation of landscapes, activities, people, wildlife, etc. Available locally.

Guadalupi, Gianni *Discovery of the Source of the Nile* Stewart, Tabori and Chang, 1997. This hefty and expensive-looking volume contains superb and lavish illustrated spreads of maps and coloured engravings from the age of exploration. The text (translated from the Italian) includes explorers usually omitted from the standard Anglophonic accounts of the search for the Nile's origins. The original hefty price tag notwithstanding, copies can be found for a few pounds on Amazon.

Kampala Attractively produced photo book with a difference. Instead of notable buildings and standard panoramas, *Kampala* depicts the reality of Uganda's hectic capital. Ugandans have complained that that reality does not present their city in a very complimentary light!

Michel, Kiguli, Pluth and Didek *Eye of the Storm: A Photographer's Journey across Uganda* Camerapix, 2002. Sumptuous book, which boldly contrasts evocative scenic and wildlife photography with more gritty urban and rural images reflecting the realities of day-to-day life in Uganda.

Pluth, David *Uganda Rwenzori: A Range of Images* Little Wolf, 1996. Absorbing photographic and verbal portrait of the legendary Mountains of the Moon, with contemporary photographs supplemented by old monochromes taken by the first Italian expedition to conquer it almost 100 years ago. An excellent post-trek souvenir.

Fiction Surprisingly few novels have been written by Ugandans or set in Uganda. My favourite, and one of the best books I've read for some time, is *The Ghosts of Eden* (Picnic 2009) by Dr Andrew Sharp, the grandson of Dr Leonard Sharp of Lake Bunyonyi fame. I'm thrilled to see that Amazon.co.uk notes as 'Frequently Bought Together', *Ghosts of Eden* and this guidebook, together with perhaps Uganda's best known work of contemporary fiction, *The Abyssinian Chronicles* (Picador) by Ugandan author, Moses Isegawa. Of less literary merit, but nonetheless worthwhile, is *The Invisible Weevil* (FemRite, 1999) by Mary Karooro Okorot, a Ugandan MP. As well as being a good read, it provides an insight into the many problems (notably Ugandan men) that Ugandan women must endure. FemRite is an organisation that encourages Ugandan female writers. Its catalogue also includes a good anthology, *Gifts of Harvest*. All these titles should be available in Kampala's Aristoc bookshop. More widely available is the Whitbread Prize-winning novel *The Last King of Scotland* by Giles Foden (Faber and Faber, 1998), a fictional account of a young Scots doctor working in the service of Idi Amin. Also recommended is Paul Theroux's *Fong and the Indians*, set in post-colonial, pre-Amin Kampala, originally published in 1968 and reprinted in the three-book Penguin compedium *On the Edge of the Rift Valley* in 1996. Set in the Belgian Congo rather than Uganda, but still one of the most astonishing and insightful novels I've read about Africa in some time, is Barbara Kingsolver's *The Poisonwood Bible* (HarperCollins, 2000).

MAPS It's perfectly possible to travel around Uganda with only the maps in this book but there are situations where your enjoyment will be enhanced by additional maps. Detailed 1:50,000 contour maps, useful for hiking in areas such as the Fort Portal crater field and the high Rwenzori, are available from the Maps and Surveys Office in Entebbe (see page 198) for Ush15,000. Most of these were revised in the 1960s.

A decent countrywide map is also a great asset. The 1:800,000 map of Uganda published by International Travel Maps (ITMB) of Vancouver is the smallest-scale map available for the whole country, and more accurate than most (one major error being a displacement of latitudinal lines, causing the Equator, for instance, to be marked as 1°N, etc). The most accurate Uganda map readily available in the country (Ush24,000 from Banana Boat or Aristoc) is Nelles's 1:700,000 map. Also excellent, but available only in Europe, is the German-produced 1:600,000 Uganda sheet (*www.reise-know-how.de*). The 1:1,350,000 *Uganda Traveller's Map* published by Macmillan is cheaper (*Ush10,000*) but inferior to both, and contains several errors. Those interested in detailed and up-to-date coverage of specific areas can order bespoke prints of GIS land cover maps from the National Forest Authority (*Ush50,000*).

More illustrative maps are available in the popular 'Uganda Maps' series (*Ush12,500*). The current range covers Uganda, Jinja and the Nile, Kampala, Fort Portal and the Rwenzori, and Murchison Falls, Kidepo Valley, Mount Elgon, Lake Mburo, Queen Elizabeth and Bwindi national parks (e *ugandamaps@gmail.com; www.uganda-maps.com*).

TRAVEL MAGAZINES For readers with a broad interest in Africa, an excellent magazine dedicated to tourism throughout Africa is *Travel Africa*, which can be visited online at www.travelafricamag.com. Recommended for their broad-ranging editorial content and the coffee-table-standard photography and reproduction, the award-winning magazines *Africa Geographic* (formerly *Africa Environment and Wildlife*) and *Africa Birds and Birding* can be checked out at the website www.africa-geographic.co.za. Another South African magazine devoted to African travel is *Getaway*, though this tends to devote the bulk of its coverage to southern Africa.

UGANDA ONLINE The internet is an increasingly valuable tool when it comes to researching most aspects of a trip to Uganda or elsewhere in Africa, though it is advisable to be somewhat circumspect when it comes to heeding advice on personal websites. Do also be aware that the internet is clogged up with sites constructed but never maintained and thus prone to be rather out of date. Websites for individual hotels, lodges, tour operators and other institutions are included alongside the relevant entries elsewhere in this guide. What follows is a list of more generic websites that might prove useful to travellers planning a trip in Uganda.

Uganda-specific sites
www.africatravelresource.com/africa/uganda Superb website operated by a high-end safari company containing reviews and hundreds of excellent pictures of Uganda's best tourist accommodation.
www.buganda.com Detailed historical and cultural essays about the Buganda kingdom past and present.

www.monitor.co.ug Similar to below, though generally takes a more independent stance than the government-backed *New Vision*, but has inferior archiving and search facilities.

www.newafrica.com/profiles/uganda/htm Good Uganda section in site covering all Africa, but beware of out-of-date information.

www.newvision.co.ug News, travel features, etc, posted by the country's most established English-language newspaper; also has thorough archive dating back several years and good search facilities.

www.traveluganda.co.ug This address leads to the Uganda Travel Planner, the most useful site for the independent traveller in Uganda. In addition to detailed travel information, there are numerous links for tour companies and many smaller private and community-based tourism sites.

www.ugandawildlife.org The recently revamped website of the Uganda Wildlife Authority contains some terrific photography. Worth checking for the latest on gorilla-tracking permits and other fees and facilities in the national parks and wildlife reserves.

www.visituganda.com The official website of Tourism Uganda (aka Uganda Tourist Board) has some stunning photographs as section headers and a few useful links.

General sites

www.africa-geographic.com Site for the South Africa publications *Africa Geographic* and *Africa Birds and Birding* – useful news and archives, subscriptions, special offers and tours.

www.auswaertiges-amt.de/5_laende/index3.htm#fgypten German equivalent of FCO (below).

www.brookes.ac.uk/worldwise/directory.html General practical information about visas, costs, transport, etc.

www.fco.gov.uk/travel British Foreign & Commonwealth Office site, containing up-to-date, generally rather conservative information on trouble spots and places to avoid.

www.kampala-entebbe-hotels.travel and **www.ugandasafarilodges.travel**. A couple of useful sites for information and online bookings.

www.odci.gov.cia/publications/factbook/country.html Another site focusing on security and safety matters, based on CIA files; judgements once again tend to be on the conservative side.

http://philipbriggs.wordpress.com A blog by Philip Briggs that provides an interactive update service for Bradt readers and other travellers, volunteers and service providers in Uganda.

www.travelafricamag.com Site for the quarterly magazine *Travel Africa* – good news section, travel archives and subscriptions.

travel.state.gov/uganda.html US State Department equivalent to FCO.

www.uk.multimap.com/world/places.cgi Free online maps of countries and major towns.

www.usatoday.com/weather/forecast/wglode.htm Weather forecasts and archives covering many remote parts of Africa; try also www.worldclimate.com or weather.yahoo.com/regional/Africa/Uganda.html.

Art

www.theartroom-sf.com Fine Arts Centre for East Africa, San Francisco.

www.cwdl.com/Iwasakak Website for artist Patrick Iwasampijja.

www.kibuuka.com Website for artist David Kibuuka.

www.nnyanziart.com Website for artist Nuwa Nnyanzi.

www.sekanwagi.com Website for artist Dan Sekanwagi.

www.y-art.net Canadian representative for Ugandan artists.

Index

Page numbers in **bold** indicate main entries; those in *italics* indicate maps.

INDEX OF ADVERTISERS

PHOTOGRAPHS AND ILLUSTRATIONS

Photographs Greenshoots Communications/Alamy (GC/A); IMAGEBROKER, ROLF SCHULTEN/Imagebroker/FLPA (FLPA); Christopher Kidd Photography (CK); Matoke Tours (MT); Nalubale Rafting (NR); Shutterstock: Daniel Barquero (S/DB), Kubica Boleslaw (S/KB), Mohamed El Hebeishy (S/MEH), Anton Ivanov (S/AI), Pecold (S/P), M Rutherford (S/MR), Sergey Uryadnikov (S/SU); SuperStock (SS); Ariadne Van Zandbergen (AVZ)
Front cover Mountain Gorilla (AVZ)
Back cover A lion at Murchison Falls National Park (AVZ); Rafting near Jinja (NR)
Title page Going to market on Lake Bunyonyi (AVZ); Grey-crowned crane (S/DB); Misty morning in Bwindi Impenetrable National Park (S/KB)

Illustrations Annabel Milne, Mike Unwin